NATIONS OF THE MODERN WORLD

ARGENTINA   H. S. Ferns
*Professor of Political Science,
University of Birmingham*

AUSTRALIA   O. H. K. Spate
*Director, Research School of Pacific Studies,
Australian National University, Canberra*

AUSTRIA   Karl R. Stadler
*Professor of Modern and Contemporary History,
University of Linz*

BELGIUM   Vernon Mallinson
*Professor of Comparative Education,
University of Reading*

BURMA   F. S. V. Donnison
*Formerly Chief Secretary to the Government of Burma
Historian, Cabinet Office, Historical Section 1949–66*

CEYLON   S. A. Pakeman
*Formerly Professor of Modern History, Ceylon
University College*

CYPRUS   H. D. Purcell
*Professor of English,
University of Libya, Benghazi*

DENMARK   W. Glyn Jones
Reader in Danish, University College London

MODERN EGYPT   Tom Little
*Managing Director and General Manager of
Regional News Services (Middle East), Ltd, London*

ENGLAND
A Portrait   John Bowle
*Professor of Political Theory, Collège d'Europe,
Bruges*

FINLAND   W. R. Mead
Professor of Geography, University College London

EAST GERMANY	David Childs *Lecturer in Politics, University of Nottingham*
WEST GERMANY	Michael Balfour *Reader in European History, University of East Anglia*
MODERN GREECE	John Campbell *Fellow of St Antony's College, Oxford* Philip Sherrard *Lecturer in the History of the Orthodox Church, King's College, London*
MODERN INDIA	Sir Percival Griffiths *President India, Pakistan and Burma Association*
MODERN IRAN	Peter Avery *Lecturer in Persian and Fellow of King's College, Cambridge*
ITALY	Muriel Grindrod *Formerly Editor of* International Affairs *and* The World Today *Assistant Editor* The Annual Register
KENYA	A. Marshall MacPhee *Formerly Managing Editor with the* East African Standard *Group*
LIBYA	John Wright *Formerly of the* Sunday Ghibli, *Tripoli*
MALAYSIA	J. M. Gullick *Formerly of the Malayan Civil Service*
MOROCCO	Mark I. Cohen *Director of Taxation, American Express* Lorna Hahn *Professor of African Studies, American University*
NEW ZEALAND	James W. Rowe *Director of New Zealand Institute of Economic Research* Margaret A. Rowe *Tutor in English at Victoria University, Wellington*

NIGERIA	Sir Rex Niven *Administrative Service of Nigeria, 1921–54 Member, President and Speaker of Northern House of Assembly, 1947–59*
PAKISTAN	Ian Stephens *Formerly Editor of* The Statesman, *Calcutta and Delhi, 1942–51 Fellow, King's College, Cambridge, 1952–58*
PERU	Sir Robert Marett *H.M. Ambassador in Lima, 1963–67*
POLAND	Václav L. Beneš *Professor of Political Science, Indiana University* Norman J. G. Pounds *Professor of History and Geography, Indiana University*
SOUTH AFRICA	John Cope *Formerly Editor-in-Chief of* The Forum *and South Africa Correspondent of* The Guardian
THE SOVIET UNION	Elisabeth Koutaissoff *Professor of Russian, Victoria University, Wellington*
SPAIN	George Hills *Formerly Correspondent and Spanish Programme Organiser, British Broadcasting Corporation*
TURKEY	Geoffrey Lewis *Senior Lecturer in Islamic Studies, Oxford*
YUGOSLAVIA	Stevan K. Pavlowitch *Lecturer in Balkan History, University of Southampton*

NATIONS OF THE MODERN WORLD

YUGOSLAVIA

YUGOSLAVIA

By
STEVAN K. PAVLOWITCH

PRAEGER PUBLISHERS
New York · Washington

BOOKS THAT MATTER

Published in the United States of America in 1971
by Praeger Publishers, Inc.
111 Fourth Avenue, New York, N.Y. 10003

© 1971 by Stevan K. Pavlowitch

All rights reserved

No part of this publication may be reproduced, stored in a retrieval system or transmitted in any form or by any means, electronic, mechanical, photocopying, recording or otherwise, without the prior permission of the Copyright owner.

Library of Congress Catalog Card Number: 77-148138

Printed in Great Britain

Contents

List of Illustrations   11
Maps   13
Preface   17

PART ONE
BEFORE UNIFICATION, UNIFICATION, AND BEYOND

Chapter 1: THE YUGOSLAV LANDS UNTIL THEIR UNIFICATION: TO 1918
- From the coming of the Slavs to the Turkish conquest   25
- The Turkish period   32
- From nationalism to unification   39

Chapter 2: THE YUGOSLAV KINGDOM: 1919–41
- The formation of the new state   53
- The parliamentary régime   65
- King Alexander's personal rule   77
- Prince Paul's regency   87
- The last days   103

PART TWO
THE CHAOTIC GAP

Chapter 3: THE CHAOTIC GAP: 1941–45
- Defeat, occupation, and revolt   107
- A complex pattern emerges   123
- The turn of the war   138
- From Drvar to Belgrade, via Bari and Moscow   155

PART THREE
REUNIFICATION, REVOLUTION, AND BEYOND

Chapter 4: STALINISM–TITOISM: 1945–50

The setting-up of the Communist régime	175
Economic reconstruction and transformation	187
Foreign policy	195
Excommunication	204
Stalinism without Stalin	211

Chapter 5: TITOISM: 1950–60

Rapprochement with the West	223
Decollectivization, decentralization, relaxation	229
Reconciliation with the Soviet Union	245
A reconciliation difficult to consummate	256
An uneasy period of stricter controls	267

PART FOUR
MONOCRATISM AND POLYETHNISM

Chapter 6: REFORMISTS AND CONSERVATIVES: 1961–67

The reforms of 1961	283
Party trends and regional trends	289
The reforms of 1965	303
The fall of Rankovich and its effects	308

Chapter 7: CRISIS AND BEYOND: 1968–70

The crisis of 1968	331
Holding the system together	344
Religions and nations	353
Diplomacy and sales promotion	360

CONCLUSION

Drawn together yet drawn apart	372
The polarization of Party and society	378
'What is thy name? And he said, Legion'	388
Suggestions for further reading	399
Index	405

List of Illustrations

(*All are inserted between pages* 192 *and* 193)

1 The Romanesque portal of Trogir cathedral
2 The Turkish mosque of Mustafa-Pasha, Skopye
3 The monastery church at Visoki Dechani, near Pech
4 Dushan of Serbia, with his wife and son – a fresco at Visoki Dechani
5 The Baroque altar screen in the church of St Nicholas, Zemun
6 The Baroque façade of the Ursuline church, Ljubljana
7 The Byzantine church of Staro Nagorichino, near Skopye
8 *The Migration of the Serbs* (P. Yovanovich, 1896)
9 *Eclipse of the Sun* (M. Kovachich, 1964)
10 *Mother at Prayer* (I. Meshtrovich, 1928)
11 A Moslem noble of Bosnia (early twentieth century)
12 A merchant in a provincial town of Serbia (late nineteenth century)
13 Croatian 'Frontiersmen' (early nineteenth century)
14 The proclamation of the Kingdom of the Serbs, Croats and Slovenes – 1 December 1918.
15 Serbian war graves, 1915
16 Stjepan Radich addressing a political meeting
17 The infant Crown Prince Peter being taken to his christening
18 Members of the Serbian government and of the Yugoslav Committee, Corfu, 1917
19 Members of the Communist leadership in their mountain headquarters, 1943
20 The German ransom in gold for Tito and Mihailovich, 21 July 1943
21 King Alexander
22 Marshal Tito
23 Cardinal Sheper and Patriarch Gherman, spring 1968
24 Belgrade University students, spring 1970
25 The young heroine of Makaveyev's film, *Switchboard Operator*
26 An elderly peasant tasting plum brandy

Maps

1 The Yugoslav lands on the eve of the First World War 49
2 The territory of Yugoslavia during the Second World War 116
3 The federated units of Yugoslavia since the Second World War 228

   Yugoslavia: general map *facing page* 398

Acknowledgements

ACKNOWLEDGEMENT for kind permission to reproduce illustrations is made to the following, to whom the copyright of the illustrations belongs:

Agence Belga, Brussels: 22
Art Gallery of Toronto (gift of Mrs Timothy Eaton): 10
Eastern Churches Review: 23
Hunter Films Ltd: 25
Mr I. S. Ivanović: 9
Mr Douglas Pike: 24
Radio Times Hulton Picture Library: 15, 26
Yugoslav National Tourist Office: 1

Preface

THIS HAS BEEN a difficult book to write. Its method of geometrical progression through history has, at one end, involved compressing centuries into paragraphs: selecting what was essential for the understanding of contemporary Yugoslavia, and omitting all the rest, however important. At the other end, it has meant writing 'instant history': trying to interpret events which were still taking place and assessing situations which inevitably underwent changes before anything could appear in print. Thus it will satisfy few people, least of all the author. Even so, in so far as it wedges itself between ignorance and modishness, it may not be entirely without value.

In Yugoslavia, as in Spain,[1] few foreign tourists either know or care that the attractive Mediterranean scenery they flock to every summer for cheap sun and spirits, covers an ossuary. Except when revealed to the occasional naïve British plane-spotter arrested for espionage, there are few outward signs of the tension behind the scenery.

[1] An interesting parallel could be drawn between Spain and Yugoslavia, isolated at opposite ends of the Mediterranean world, respectively in western and eastern Europe, each anxious to establish better relations with both East and West. In both countries, the régime is the outcome of a tragic civil war, involving ideological, ethnic, religious, and foreign rivalries. In each, the political framework has been modified outwardly, and even in content, though its foundations have remained unchanged, whereas the social and economic structure has undergone very significant changes since the victory of the Crusade in the case of the one, of the People's Liberation Movement in the case of the other. Continuous references are made to 1936 and 1943 respectively, references which still have a meaning to those who make them, but hardly any to those who hear them. Generalissimo Franco and Marshal Tito are contemporaries: elderly survivors from another age, their succession uncertain (in spite of a series of shrewd moves to prepare for it), their ruling movement disunited, and yet with those who oppose them ever more disunited still. Increasingly, vocal dissatisfaction among certain groups of the population, mixed with sectional nationalism, non-conforming religious attitudes, and wildcat industrial action, is counterbalanced by the gratitude of other groups of the community for improved standards of living and a stable political order, and by the apathy of the average citizen and the common knowledge that the authorities can crack down on any individual or group whose activities they really want to stop.

It is not simply tourists who know next to nothing of the realities of Yugoslavia: precious little is apparent even to many of those who elect to write about Yugoslavia. The country has been in the limelight almost continually since that day at the end of March 1941 when a British prime minister suggested that 'Yugoslavia has found her soul'. More books on Yugoslavia have appeared in the West in the past twenty years than in the previous century. From time to time a scholarly monograph appears which illuminates a specialist topic for the benefit of Western – and even Yugoslav – scholars, without reaching a wider public. On the whole, the presses churn out a frightening amount of hurriedly prepared, superficial, repetitive, and even erroneous information, some of it adding insult to injury by tricking itself out in the trappings of scholarship and appearing under eminently reputable imprints. It could be an amusing relaxation to compile a kind of *anti*-bibliography on Yugoslavia.

Because – or in spite – of such a spate of publications, the general ignorance of Yugoslav history is almost unbelievable.[2] Thus, con-

[2] For one whose *métier* is the study of Yugoslav history, it is no longer amusing to read the endlessly repeated statements about the 'religious and racial hatred' among Yugoslavs which is alleged to have been the cause of centuries of conflict – statements which project the events of 1941–42 back into an unknown past, and see race (a fashionable word) where there is none. One would like to ask these budding anthropologists how they distinguish a Moslem Turk from a Balkan Christian, or a Greek from a South Slav, yet alone a Serb from a Croat!

When it comes to the twentieth century, it is strange how the prejudices of individuals and groups are readily taken as objective data, and how easily certain authors can draw their conclusions from their own premisses. With Yugoslavia, historical analysis is more often than not still at the stage of the Protocols of Zion and Masonic explanations. One recent American scholarly gathering was informed by an expert of the 'well-known influence' on the Karageorgevich dynasty of the Orthodox Church, and the 'strong and direct influence' which the Catholic Church has always exercised on Croatian political leaders. Another American 'Yugoslavist' has written, not long ago, of '1805, when the first Peter Karageorgević led a revolt which overthrew the Turkish rule of Serbia' (*sic*).

Some words sound good: *ustasha*, for instance. From May to September 1970, I noted the following, written admittedly by people who did not claim any expert knowledge of Yugoslavia, but who nevertheless should have known better. The Berlin correspondent of a distinguished London daily, explaining the word in a report of a court case, wrote that '*Ustasha* was a resistance movement during the Second World War.' A sensitive French film critic and director, writing about the Yugoslav super-production *The Battle of the Neretva*, talked about the 'Slovak Ustashi separatists of Anton Pavlevitch'. An intelligent French author-journalist, reporting on an Asiatic country, described his taxi-driver as having 'un beau visage d'oustachi farouche et moustachu' – and no one will ever know what he meant by it! (Could it have been simply the alliteration of *oustachi moustachu*?)

cerning the period since 1941, there seems to be an improbable cross between Manichaeism and the Hollywood western, with Good confronting Evil, and the world divided up into the good guys and the bad guys. Of the writings on the Civil War itself, let it suffice to quote a continental historian:

> History is rarely tender-hearted towards the losers. With the advantage of hindsight, it takes pleasure in stressing their errors and their lack of judgment. Since they have not been able to bear out their claims to the end, the losers should have abstained, and accepted without a fight what has finally been imposed on them. The blood which they have shed appears to have been shed in vain, and the most guilty do not appear to be those who have vanquished them.

As for the writings on the post-war period, they have, over the years, projected an image of Yugoslavia as a country which – except for a short interval between 1946 and 1948 – has gradually and systematically liberalized in every respect the régime that emerged from the war, even to the point where it can no longer simply be called either Communist or totalitarian. This view derives partly from generalizing on the basis of particular experiences with the country since the end of the Cold War, partly from wishful thinking.

Many observers have tried to see Titoist Yugoslavia as the great success of independent – and hence liberal – national communism, and in effect have usually discovered what they wanted to discover. Some of them wanted to justify the attraction that communism had for them when they were young, and to ensure that at least one Communist revolution had not degenerated into tyranny. Others reacted against the excesses of Cold War attitudes. Others yet again were so anti-Soviet, or at least anti-Russian, that any force which actually stood up to Soviet Russia was of necessity bound to be good; and if, furthermore, it was Communist, it proved their point even more forcibly and gave them a good conscience.

Some of the myths about Yugoslavia were generated in Yugoslavia itself, for the propaganda apparatus of the Yugoslav government had capacity enough to make a tremendous impact. But if the Yugoslav system 'sold' so well, it was not just due to its 'sales promotion'. Some of the self-engendered myths about Yugoslavia have persisted in the West in their original form, even though they have thinned out or even melted away in Yugoslavia itself. Other myths were manufactured wholly in the West.

If history is rarely tender-hearted towards the losers, it is often more than kind to the winners. Tito's was a successful venture, and the prosperous, modern, industrial societies of the West tend to judge enterprises mainly in terms of success. The Yugoslav Communists under Marshal Tito not only won the Civil War, they have remained in power and kept order in Yugoslavia ever since. And if a successful enterprise is popular, so is a romantic one. A naïve romanticism characterizes the dreams of the industrial West, as if to camouflage the importance that in reality it attaches to success for its own sake. Not only was Tito a successful leader, he was also a romantic hero: by the way in which he and his Balkan guerrillas resisted both Hitler and Stalin, harsh reality was transformed into idealized heroics. In so far as Yugoslavia was in fact not always able to generate new, exciting things to polarize popular sentiment, such things had to be created artificially – or even simply wished into existence.[3]

Lastly, to myth-making, oversimplification, and wishful thinking we must add a tendency to overemphasize certain formal phenomena at the expense of basic issues which only a knowledge of history enables the observer to sense. Such an overemphasis comes all too often from an abuse of the more modish kind of system-construction employed by social scientists, made even worse by a complete neglect of the historian's traditional tools.

The horrible truth about Yugoslavia is that it is so complex that it cannot be simplified or conceptualized without also being distorted out of all recognition. This is what I have tried to show. This book makes no attempt to be a history of the Yugoslav lands from the arrival of the Slavs up to the last constitutional and economic reform measures of Tito's era. In order to write such a work, one would have to be a great historian with a wealth of experience: in fact, a political, a constitutional, an economic, and a social historian; a historian of art, of ideas, of religion, and of literature; a military and a diplomatic historian; and something of an economist, a sociologist, an ethnologist, and a psychoanalyst as well. As a second best, one would need to read through a library of individual scholarly works covering every period and aspect, while enjoying a sabbatical decade in which to do so. The best I could do in three years was to try and make a clearing here and there where the jungle was particularly dense, to summarize sound scholarship where it existed, to contribute some of my own research where I happened to have looked personally into a particular question, and generally to collate

[3] Cf. Professor Hugh Seton-Watson's interesting remarks on 'Decline and Durability' in a recent symposium on 'Myths, Perceptions, Policy' regarding communism: 'Situations which remain the same are boring . . . new and exciting things must be discovered, and if there are none to discover, then they must be wished into existence. This passion for novelty is also connected with another pathological feature of the mass democratic mind, or at least of the minds of its mass-media prophets: the determination to see world politics as a struggle between vice and virtue' (*Problems of Communism*, XXX/1, Washington, 1970, p. 11).

and compare, to suggest trends, to question accepted views, and to show what could be done on the basis of the very unsystematic and haphazard material available – in short, the sort of endeavour one normally undertakes with one's students.

I have pointed to the facts, and at times I have not stopped myself from attempting judgements on the basis of facts which to me seemed unassailable on the basis of the evidence available, and which I consider to have been distorted. If I have betrayed any emotion, it was out of irritation with the fashionable vulgarizers, ignorant myth-makers, pontificating would-be experts, pompous parrots, and all those who dash off a new book simply to exploit the market, after a visit here, an interview there, and with only a shaky knowledge of the language involved.

The reader is entitled to a few preliminary explanations. This is a general work of reference, not a work of ambitious scholarship. References to other works are made only in the case of direct quotations and similar explicit indebtedness, as well as in the case of figures. (In the last part, when figures are quoted without such references, they are taken from official Yugoslav statistical year-books or from the Yugoslav press.) The reader is then usually referred to books that are reasonably accessible. Only in the case of statements that conflict with commonly held views or rely on little-known documentary evidence do I refer back to original sources.

Like all authors writing about a region where the Roman alphabet is not the only one in use, I have been faced with problems of transliteration. In a book aimed at the general reader who is not a Slavonic linguist, I have been reluctant to follow the practice laid down by Slavists and contemporary Yugoslav officialdom, because the diacritically marked consonants of the 'Croatian' (or 'Slovenian') Roman alphabet are hardly less difficult to decipher than their 'Serbian' (or 'Macedonian') Cyrillic counterparts. Too often have I heard that the prime minister of Serbia during the First World War – Nikola Pashich, or Pašić – was someone called 'Passick', or that an important present-day Yugoslav official well known in international circles – Antun Vratuša, or Vratusha – masqueraded as 'Vratooza'. So I have written Yugoslav names and words as phonetically as possible, though with apologies to all those Roman-writing Yugoslavs, the usual spelling of whose names I have taken the liberty of altering. In the index, however, I have also given the modern official transliteration or spelling. In footnotes, wherever the reader might want to look up an author or a title in a library catalogue, I have always used the official transliteration, or the author's own. 'In short,' as one American writer once put it when faced with a similar problem, 'I have been inconsistent in an effort to be helpful.' For place-names I have used accepted English usages where they existed – e.g. Belgrade, Bosnia, Croatia, Dalmatia, Danube, Herzegovina, Macedonia, Montenegro, Serbia, Slovenia, Yugoslavia.[4]

I owe much to many people – relatives, friends, colleagues, and students – who have borne with me while my mind was running along a single track, and especially to those few precious friends who read and discussed what I wrote, and were kind enough to point out mistakes, offer suggestions, and express their disagreement or even their agreement. They know how grateful I am to them. In order, however, to be able to assume full responsibility for every single line, I shall refrain from singling out anyone by name, even – departing from what is rapidly becoming accepted practice – the women without whom this book would either never have been written, or would have been written sooner.

Audruicq (Pas-de-Calais), ST. K. PAVLOWITCH
October 1970

---

[4] The 'z' of Herzegovina is admittedly Germanic, but then so is the entire first half of the name, and to write 'Bosnia-Hercegovina', as some fashionable writers do, is a blatant inconsistency. As for 'Jugoslavia', apart from turning the Slav word for 'south' into a 'deep vessel for holding liquids, with handle and often with spout', it is a linguistic hybrid, neither English nor Yugoslav.

PART ONE

Before Unification, Unification and Beyond

Chapter 1

The Yugoslav Lands until their Unification: to 1918

From the coming of the Slavs to the Turkish conquest

Geographically, as in all other respects, Yugoslavia is a land of transition, from the southern uplands of hard rock and the young calcareous mountains of the coast, to the northern plains. The south is an old land mass broken up into many sections and continued northwards to the Danube by the levelled plateau of Shumadiya, once covered with forests. The narrow Dalmatian coast of the Adriatic Sea is isolated from its hinterland by the Dinaric chain of bare limestone which slopes down by karst plateaux to the fertile Pannonian plains.

There is no natural centre to the Yugoslav lands although they provide one of the two stretches of Danubian plains by which one penetrates from the north into the Balkan peninsula, and one of its two Mediterranean coastal fronts. In spite of its relatively modest elevation, the Dinaric chain is an obstacle to penetration, so that the main way in is not by the coast, but rather from the north where the Danube and its tributaries converge towards Belgrade. Most traffic, persons or goods, is forced into a gap between the western coastal mountains and the central land mass of the Balkans, from the plains of Central Europe to the Aegean Sea. This is a complex route, but one which anchors the Yugoslav lands to the Balkans, in spite of their maritime face looking towards the West, and in spite of their opening to Central Europe. From the Danube to the Gulf of Salonika, the valleys of the Morava and of the Vardar, end to end, form a continuous line through the plateaux and basins of Serbia and Macedonia.

We know little or nothing of the autochthonous inhabitants of present-day Yugoslavia, and not much more of the Slav settlers who came in the early Middle Ages, during the last phase of the struggle of the Barbarian peoples against the Roman order. Originating from an area behind the Carpathians, between the Baltic Sea and the region of Kiev, the Slavs – more precisely the South Slavs or Yugoslavs – began to move in compact masses to the left bank of the Danube at the beginning of the sixth century A.D. They came in search of new land, in the wake of the hordes of nomadic marauders who swept over the Balkans from the steppes of Asia. They went as far as Istria and the eastern Alps (in present-day Austria) where they met Germanic populations who had settled there not long before. They poured across the Danube and down its tributaries, over the plains and to the sea, into the Morava-Vardar corridor, and as far south as the Peloponnese. In the course of the seventh century the newcomers gradually turned into settlers, and they were to modify completely the ethnic structure of the whole peninsula. The Romanized earlier inhabitants were partly exterminated, partly assimilated, partly pushed into the mountains, the coastal cities, and the offshore islands. Only the extreme southern tip of the Slav wave was itself assimilated and Hellenized. In the process, the general name 'Slavs' stuck in the frontier regions, where there was distinct contrast between compact Slav and non-Slav populations, e.g. Slovenes. The very old names of Serbs and Croats, inherited from leading tribes in tribal alliances, ultimately spread, the latter to those Slavs who settled in the west, from the plains to the sea, and the former to those in the east, along the southern tributaries of the Danube and in the depressions of the ancient land mass.

The border between the eastern and the western Roman Empire had run across the territories to which the South Slavs had come, and their process of settling into the Balkans coincided with the forming of two new powers in Europe whose influences once again touched in these very same lands: the Byzantine, successor to the Eastern Empire, and the Frankish, claiming to be the heir to Rome in the West. The tribes in the east were converted to Christianity in the course of the ninth century by Byzantine missionaries. For a while these held their ground among the Croatian tribes as well, but there, the combined influence of the Franks and of the old Roman cities of Dalmatia prevailed, and Byzantine influence petered out in the western Balkans. Christianity generally helped to develop a new sense of kinship among the scattered tribes, but especially so among the converts to its Eastern form, for while the Franks imposed the Christian faith in its Western form and with a Latin liturgy which could not become a vehicle for an autonomous development on a Slav basis, the adaptation of the Byzantine liturgy to native ecclesiastical needs by Cyril and Methodius, the 'Apostles of the Slavs', was an important asset for their later autonomous cultural and political development.

Towards the middle of the ninth century the Byzantine-Frankish dualism began to break up. The Bulgars broke into the eastern Balkans and the Magyars into the Pannonian plains, while Venice, the last remaining Byzantine province in Italy, was developing into a new power on the Adriatic. This period of fluidity lasted until the turn of the tenth century, when the German state, heir to the Frankish power and the imperial crown in Central Europe, with the help of the Latin Church stopped the onslaught of the Magyars, who began to settle, and when Byzantium once again, but for the last time, found itself in control of the whole peninsula. It was an important period, when all the South Slavs (including for a while the Slovenes on the northern Germanic border and the Slav population of Macedonia on the southern Hellenic fringe) tended to free themselves from foreign rule, and when their social structure began to be feudalized. In the Slovenian lands, feudalization was carried out under Germanic rule, while in Macedonia, it meant the Hellenization of the local nobility. Among the Croats and Serbs, however, feudalism was a native development which emerged out of tribal and communal structures. The Croats benefited most from these developments. They emerged as an independent power, centred in northern Dalmatia and dominating the roads from the sea to the plains. In 925, their ruler, Tomislav, received the royal title from Rome, the first Balkan ruler to assume the title of king.

The twelfth century marked the great turning-point of the Middle Ages for the Yugoslavs. The Serbs' embryonic states of Zeta and Rashka – the former around Scutari (the present-day Shkodër in Albania) and towards the southern Adriatic coast, the latter inland in the Dinaric uplands around Ras (the present-day Novi Pazar) – had been extending their domain towards the sea and the plains. At the end of the century, when the Byzantine Empire started on its long and final decline, began the process which was to lead them to the most complete political development attained by the South Slavs in the Middle Ages.

Earlier in the century, increasing feudalization and the constant contest with Venice over the Dalmatian towns led the Croats to accept a personal union with Hungary. The proclamation of the union of the two crowns in 1102 marks the beginning of Croatia's eight-century association with Hungary. Paradoxically, Croatia was now stronger against the spread of German influence, for it was only under its first Hungarian king that the realm extended over its full historic range, though never obliterating its basic triunity – that of Slavonia, inner Croatia, and Dalmatia. The northern plains of Slavonia had been subjected to Hungarian influence earlier and more intensively, while the coastal towns of Dalmatia continued under Hungarian-Croatian control the struggle to uphold their autonomies. Croatia's links with and control by the Hungarian monarchy tightened or loosened according to circumstances, but it was always to retain its separate identity.

Hungary also extended a loose suzerainty over Bosnia in 1138. Situated between Croatia and Serbia, this land too had developed its own feudal class, though it was only in the twelfth century, and always more or less linked to Hungary, that it initiated an autonomous development. Sinking roots in this feudal class, at the junction between Eastern and Western Christianity, the Bogumil heresy, similar to that of the Cathars in western Europe, impressed on the region the characteristic division into three faiths it has had ever since.

With the break-up of the German Empire into its feudal units in the latter half of the thirteenth century, begins the expansion of the Habsburg family. Originating from Switzerland, they acquired Styria in 1278, the first of their Slovene-inhabited provinces and the stepping-stone to territorial power in the Austrian provinces. During that time the struggle continued for supremacy over the rich Dalmatian trading cities. The richest, Ragusa – better known nowadays by its Slavonic name of Dubrovnik – had managed to remain its own master by manoeuvring between the powers of the day. In 1205 it recognized the largely nominal overlordship of Venice, until 1358 when it switched to that of Hungary, an even more nominal one for what had in fact become an independent aristocratic republic owing its thriving existence to diplomacy and trade. Its economy was based on exchanges between the South Slav hinterland and Italy, and Ragusa developed as an important intermediary, in more ways than one, between East and West.

After the twelfth century, while in the north and west of the Yugoslav lands foreign pressure, Hungarian or Venetian, intensified, and, in the case of the Alpine fringe, the ethnic advance of the Germanic element followed closely on political dominion, in the south the decline of Byzantium gave the South Slavs their chance. Under the leadership of the rulers of Rashka, the two small Serbian units had merged, though Zeta was always to be kept as a separate entity in the mediaeval Serbian monarchy.

The Serbian realm had begun to take shape in regions which, though nominally Byzantine, were not directly dominated by the Empire, and its Nemanjich dynasty fully exploited the fall of Constantinople to the crusaders in 1204. Playing off the Latin pope against the Greek patriarch, it obtained recognition from the one of its political independence, with a royal crown in 1217, and from the other of its ecclesiastical independence, with a native archbishop in 1219. Thus with King Stephen the First-Crowned (1196–1228) Serbia was launched on the way to nationhood, a task in which the monarch was helped by his brother, the monk Sava. The Church in the Serbian lands had hitherto been ruled from

Constantinople or from Ohrid (a Byzantine creation of the eleventh century) with little understanding, so that Bogumilism had made much headway, while rulers hesitated between the Eastern and the Western Churches. The status of autocephaly, obtained according to Eastern practice, reflected Sava's own prestige as well as that of his brother's realm. First archbishop of Serbia (later its patron saint), Sava took up again the essential spirit of Cyrillism by making Christianity more real to the Serbs.

Favoured by its economic wealth, based on mining and trade, and its alliance with the Church, at once popular, dynastic, and in touch with the higher culture of Byzantium, the Serbian monarchy continued its rise. It extended down the Adriatic coast and into Bosnia, but especially down the vital Morava-Vardar corridor into Macedonia, thus interrupting there the process of Hellenization. After the defeat of the Bulgars in 1330, and with the accession of King Dushan the following year, Serbia, the strongest state in the Balkans, aimed at replacing the worn-out Byzantine Empire with a powerful Serbo-Hellenic state. Dushan's conquests stretched his dominions out from the Sava and the Danube to the Adriatic and the Gulf of Corinth. In 1345 he raised himself from king to emperor, and the Serbian archiepiscopal see of Pech correspondingly to patriarchate. At that moment, however, the Ottoman Turks too emerged as a new power to the east, and this threat gave a new dimension to Serbia's links with the West. The Serbian monarch was negotiating with the pope to be appointed 'Captain against the Infidels', and at the same time preparing his final takeover of the Empire by an expedition against Constantinople, when he died suddenly in 1335. Dushan had lacked both the time and a cultural tradition to weld together the disparate elements of his empire, which did not survive him. Nevertheless, under his reign, the increased political and economic links with the Italian West had combined with native Serbian elements to modify the predominant Byzantine influence in culture and government and give interesting original blends.

The end of Serbian power created a vacuum in the Balkans. This was to be filled by the Turks, advancing up the Macedonian ways of penetration and gradually pushing the Serbian state back, while the Habsburgs were basing themselves solidly in the Slovenian lands (the provinces of Carinthia, Carniola, Istria, and Trieste were added to Styria in the course of the fourteenth century), Venice was increasing its pressure on the Adriatic coast, and Hungary on Bosnia and northern Serbia. The power of the great feudal lords in the Serbian monarchy had developed on a par with its territorial expansion, and after Dushan's death the magnates of Macedonia accepted one by one the suzerainty of the Ottoman sultan. In 1389, the Serbian ruler Lazar, allied to the ruler of Bosnia, was defeated on the field of Kosovo – a battle which, because it was a great massacre, impressed contemporaries as a portentous event. The remains of the Serbian state nevertheless survived well into the fifteenth century; wedged between Turks and Hungarians, it acknowledged the suzerainty alternatively of each.

It was during this period that Bosnia, freed from the overbearing shadow of Serbia, and one stage removed from the Turkish advance, reached its zenith under Tvrtko I (1353–91). Expanding into Serbian lands where he wanted to appear as heir to the Nemanjich dynasty (to which he was related through his mother), Tvrtko also extended his rule into Croatia, and assumed the titles of king of Serbia, Bosnia, Croatia, and Dalmatia. The Bosnian monarchy, however, remained poised between its Catholic Hungarian suzerain and its Bogumil vassals. The heresy was a source of both weakness and strength. It was the backbone of the feudal structure, for the dynasty did not, as in Serbia, have the support of the spiritual power. It was also the backbone of its independence, for it was through the Hungarian overlordship that the papacy tried to streamline the local ecclesiastical organization. Thus after Tvrtko's death, Bosnia in turn slid down the path of feudal anarchy, caught between Turks and Hungarians.

By 1459 the Turks had taken over directly in Serbia, though Zeta, soon to be known as Montenegro, kept up the struggle until the end of the century. Likewise, neighbouring Herzegovina survived for a while when, in 1463, Bosnia fell to the Turks. Serbian feudal society gradually dissolved, partly eliminated in wars and repressions, partly included for a time in the new Ottoman order, partly taking refuge in the mountains of Zeta, in the towns of Dalmatia, or across the rivers in the devastated frontier zone of Hungary, whose power was in full decline. With royal power practically in abeyance and feudal anarchy rampant, the position of Croatia too was weakened at the very moment when the Turkish threat grew near.

Ragusa hastened to readjust its position. In 1442 it changed its nominal allegiance once again, and in return for a tribute to the sultan, was left in peace by the Turks. The republic became a great banking centre as well as a haven for refugees. Indeed it could be described as a fifteenth-century Switzerland, where Balkan potentates kept their money and took refuge, trading with everyone and left in peace.

After Serbia and Bosnia came the turn of Croatia. In 1493, a big Turkish offensive went across Slavonia, right up to Styria, and back through the heart of Croatia. The Croatian nobility overcame its rivalries on the field of Krbava, only to be defeated in a great massacre not unlike that of the Serbian nobility a century earlier at Kosovo. This had been only a plundering expedition, yet the danger caused most of the surviving nobles from the exposed southern regions to leave for Venetian or Habsburg territory, unless they chose to come to terms with the Turks. With Venice again in control of the littoral, and southern Croatia abandoned to its own resources, the centre of the Croatian kingdom, and its very name, moved north, a geopolitical shift of a historic name not unlike that previously undergone by Serbia.

By the beginning of the sixteenth century, when the Turkish danger was at the gates, the Hungarian-Croatian realm was breaking up. The Slovenian lands had already been unified in the family domains of the Habsburgs (a process which had also reduced the ethnic territory of the Slovenes), whose influence had also been expanding into the lands of the Hungarian crown until the great Turkish offensive which followed the fall of Belgrade in 1521. When in 1526, the Hungarians were routed at Mohacs, where their heirless King Louis II met his death, the Habsburg takeover of what remained of his state was given legal sanction with the election of Ferdinand of Habsburg as king of Hungary. The following year, the Croatian diet elected him king of Croatia, thus reminding him of Croatia's special position. War raged on, and it was not until 1537 that the Habsburg king was able to organize the defence of his Croatian dominions, by which time the Turks had conquered half of them. The remains of the Hungarian-Croatian kingdom were henceforth linked to a new power – that of the Habsburgs, later to develop into the Austrian Monarchy.

The mediaeval period ends for the Yugoslav lands with their falling to Turks and Habsburgs, which added yet another dividing-line between western and eastern South Slavs. Because so many divides had run through their territory which was also devoid of a geopolitical centre, their historical development in the Middle Ages did not allow their ethnical affinities to come to full expression in a political community. Separate Croatian and Serbian monarchies developed, the former soon to be linked to Hungary. Interferences, links, and common developments were numerous, however, in the later period, and more particularly on the eve of the Turkish conquest.[1] Like all the other frontiers which divided the Yugoslavs,

[1] At a time when both Croatian and Serbian feudalism was in decline and when the two 'orthodox' branches of the Church were hardening their positions, Bosnia had united 'Serbs' and 'Croats' in a state which, in matters of religion, looked to neither Rome nor Constantinople.

the one between Austrian and Ottoman powers was to be not an 'iron curtain', but one across which there would be many sorties.

The Turkish period

Directly or indirectly, the Turkish advance into Europe was to affect the whole Yugoslav territory, for even what remained outside their pale after the middle of the sixteenth century was to serve as a buffer zone into which the Turks directed their raids, and from which Habsburgs and Venetians defended their dominions. Simultaneously, massive migrations altered the pattern of population.

It was the wealth of the Balkan states crumbling into feudal fragments, and not the wish to extend Islam, that had attracted the Turks to Europe. Koranic law provided the Christians with a status. The Eastern Orthodox Church, to which the great majority of the conquered populations belonged, tended to be suspicious of the West, and so it was not only kept in being, but the jurisdiction of the senior patriarchate of Constantinople was strengthened by the conquerors to prevent their Christian subjects from being tempted to unite with the Catholic Church, associated as it was with the struggle against the Ottomans. Furthermore, the Ottoman system of landholding, connected with service to the sultan, and limited by precise obligations, was less oppressive for the South Slav peasantry than the Western-type feudalization which the Turkish conquest interrupted.

Though the Turks themselves hardly settled, the Ottoman period witnessed migrations on a scale unprecedented since the arrival of the South Slavs. The Turkish wars were accompanied by extensive devastations, with the result that newly conquered territories were always underpopulated and ready to take the overspill from the mountainous south. It was in Macedonia – last to be added to the Serbian monarchy and first to fall to the Turks – that it all began. Part of the population went north with the remnants of the Serbian state, and the process of amalgamation of the Macedonian Slavs with the Serbs was stopped. Then as Shumadiya fell, the Hungarians started on a policy, later to be perfected by the Habsburgs, of welcoming refugees to till and defend the border area. The Turks, too, had to restore the economy and man the defences of their more recently conquered territories, and so attracted settlers as free peasants from the more mobile, but poorer, pastoral populations of their earlier conquests.

Geographic and economic conditions had favoured a semi-nomadic and patriarchal way of life in the uplands of Montenegro and Herzegovina, the main sources of migration. This way of life had hardly been touched by feudalism, nor was it going to be much affected by any other outside influences for a long time to come, which enabled it to preserve its own traditions intact. Each successive wave of migrants served to freshen historical memories and carry a step further the process of mixing together ethnic groups and dialects, until the majority of Serbs and Croats came to share the same speech and the same way of life. This unification, however, could not be fully achieved because of the division between dominating powers and religions. While those converted to Islam became tied to the Ottoman order, Orthodox and Catholics were to become practically identified with Serbs and Croats.

With almost all Orthodox South Slavs included in one political unit and the Serbs migrating from their historical centre, the development of a national Serbian consciousness, started by the Nemanjich monarchy in the Middle Ages, was continued and progressively extended by its one surviving institution – the Church, which thus made the transition from mediaeval antecedents to modern nationalism. The archbishopric of Ohrid was the first Christian ecclesiastical organization to be included in the Ottoman system, and the Turks extended its jurisdiction as they advanced to the north. After the conquest of Hungary, however, in order to give some measure of satisfaction to the Serbs, who had taken a large part in the war on both sides, and to ensure that they should remain under a spiritual authority which he could control, the sultan restored the patriarchate of Pech in 1557, with its largest jurisdiction ever, from northern Macedonia and eastern Bulgaria, across Serbia, Montenegro, Bosnia, and Herzegovina, to the Serbian settlements in Habsburg and Venetian territory. In Bosnia alone did a native Moslem class develop, as Bogumil lords accepted Islam; many Catholics fled, identified with the West, while the Turks resettled Orthodox colonists, as they did in Serbia and in Hungary.

The South Slavs of Dalmatia and Slovenia were the most affected by European developments of the sixteenth century. In the course of the fifteenth, Venice had again gained control of the coast, with the exception of Dubrovnik, but this did not curb the increasingly Slav character of Dalmatia, because of the inflow of refugees due to endemic warfare thereafter between Turkish hinterland and Venetian shore. The Ragusan republic remained both independent and neutral. At a time when Venice was past its prime, and the West had not yet begun seriously to enter the Levant trade, Dubrovnik was better placed than ever to act as intermediary between the developing manufacturers of Europe and their sources and markets in the Ottoman East. Its wealth enriched the city-state culturally too, and it fully participated in the Renaissance. Its unique position between Italy and the Balkans gave its inhabitants the feeling of a distinct identity, while their contacts with all the South Slavs made them aware of the similarities – an awareness shared by the Catholic clergy in Dalmatia in their dealings with the populations across the border.

Among the Slovenes, foreign rule meant not only Germanic domination, but Germanic feudal landlords and townsfolk.[2] It also meant that they were directly touched by events in Central Europe, and far ahead of the other South Slavs in cultural, technical, and economic progress. The Reformation spread to their lands through the nobles, whose position was affected by the progress of capitalism and centralization, who resisted the Catholic-backed centralism of the Habsburgs, and who wanted the lands of the Church. The peasants, on their side, took to other aspects of Protestantism which suited their spirit of revolt against the increased demands of the nobility. One important feature of the Reformation in Slovenia was the written use of the vernacular.

In Habsburg Croatia, peasants and nobles had the same kind of grievances, but the Reformation affected Croatia much less, for the nobles appreciated the protection afforded by their Catholic Habsburg rulers against the Turkish danger. Croatia, or rather 'the relic of relics' of the Croatian realm, was, like Serbia, moving northwards where a renewed feeling of its separate historical identity emerged, carried by the nobility, many of whose members had escaped from the Turkish conquest and taken with them the tradition of the mediaeval state. Like the Church in Serbia, but in different circumstances, the nobility in Croatia carried on the process of nurturing a national consciousness. Throughout the sixteenth century, the Turkish danger was indeed outstanding, for not until 1593 did the defeat of the Turks at Sisak put an end to their incursions. The problem of defending the border was partly one of resettlement, and it was solved by attracting over to the other side the frontiersmen whom the Turks had settled on their side, but whose privileges they had not respected for long. From the 1530s on, the Habsburg frontier was organized as a separate military territory where refugees and 'transfugees' were resettled as free peasants in return for military service.

After the conquests in Hungary, the relatively favourable situation in which the population of Serbia had been kept came to an end. Although the Ottoman domination had settled down in Serbia, armies still went through and hibernated there, and the sultan's new professional infantry, the janissaries, were under no obligation to the local population. The demands of Europe's growing urban

[2] Except in Istria where they were Romance.

population stimulated the production of new crops in the Balkans, thus providing a further incentive to break away from Ottoman 'feudalism'. Military service was becoming professional and landholding commercial, which meant a breakdown of the traditional system according to which the obligations of the peasants had largely been lighter than in Christian Europe. The remains of Serbia's upper class, who were gradually being pushed out, resisted, and out of the oppressed peasantry grew a tradition of unrest. However much under increased pressure, it was the Church that enabled the Serbs to remain a political factor throughout the seventeenth century, for this resistance was co-ordinated by the Serbian Church which soon found itself in open conflict with the Turks.

For Bosnia, too, the seventeenth century was a disturbed period. Warfare and the tolerated growth of practical serfdom worsened the lot of the peasants, many of whom – Catholics particularly – continued to leave for Habsburg or Venetian territory, while others accepted Islam, which spread from the holders to the tillers of the land and contributed to impressing Turkish influence more deeply than in other Yugoslav lands.

During the Austro-Turkish war of 1593–1606, which was linked to a serious revolt in Serbia, the Habsburgs stimulated a mass transfer of population to bolster up their defences, and immigration of this kind went on, at a reduced rate, throughout the following century. The majority of the settlers were Orthodox, who brought with them their ecclesiastical organization dependent on the see of Pech, but the solidarity between Catholics and Orthodox became a characteristic of the farmer-soldier society of the so-called Military Frontier. The Frontier, however, also reduced the hold of the Croatian diet and nobility over their already meagre remains, for under the emperor's German generals, it was both a bulwark against further Turkish encroachments and an instrument of Habsburg ascendancy. The Counter-Reformation which, by the middle of the century, had brought Croats and Slovenes back to the fold of the Catholic Church, was also accompanied by a reduction in the power of the provincial estates. This was easily accomplished in the Slovenian lands, but less so in Croatia, where the native nobility defended the special position of the Croatian realm as well as its own position. With Turkish danger in abeyance, the nobles felt less dependent on the Habsburgs. Their resistance was particularly directed against encroachments in the Military Frontier, but it was inconsistent in so far as many, especially of the lesser nobility, appreciated the relative economic recovery which they owed to the safety of the border defences. It was thus that a conspiracy led by Zrinski and Frankopan, the two most powerful magnates in

Croatia, failed, and their execution in 1661, followed by the confiscation of their estates, further strengthened the hold of the imperial court.

If there was relative peace on the Habsburg frontier between 1606 and 1683, it was warfare as usual on the Venetian border, with its accompanying drift of population which made Dalmatians increasingly aware of the similarities between all those who spoke a common 'Illyrian' tongue. While Dubrovnik regressed, as a result of the combined effects of the wars, the new far-away trade routes, Venetian pressure in the Adriatic, and the competition of local traders in the Ottoman Empire, Montenegro profited from its border position with Venetian territory. This, added to the topography, prevented the Turks from being able to control these mountain clans, leaving the Church as the only remaining binding institution.

The failure of the last Turkish thrust into Central Europe in 1683 turned the tide. More than ever, Yugoslavs participated in the war as Austria and Venice repulsed the sultan's armies. Having reconquered most of Hungary, the Austrians – with many Serbian soldiers – marched deep into Serbia in 1689, and the population rose in support. The war, however, ground to a halt and the Austrians withdrew, along with tens of thousands of Serbs – the richer élite, most of the urban population, and all those who had collaborated with the Austrians – led by their patriarch, Arseniye III. The peace concluded at Karlovtsi on the Danube (treaty of Karlowitz, 1699) nevertheless returned to the emperor most of Hungary with Croatia. The war of 1714–18 and the peace of Passarowitz (Pozharevats in Serbia) completed the Habsburg conquest of Hungary, supplemented with Shumadiya – the Ottoman province of Belgrade. In 1736, the Austrians marched south again, and again the Christians moved, spurred on by both Patriarch Arseniye IV and the archbishop of Ohrid. When the Austrians withdrew, the patriarch with several thousand refugees accompanied them and in 1739, the peace of Belgrade returned Belgrade and Serbia to the sultan.

Leopold I found southern Hungary practically depopulated, and in order to keep the intractable Hungarian nobility out of this strategic region, he resettled it with foreigners. In 1690, he invited the immigration of the mass of Serbian refugees gathered around Belgrade by issuing a charter which granted them recognition as an Orthodox 'nation', with the right to elect an archbishop who would head their Church in Hungary. Earlier on, when he had appealed to the Serbs to rise, he had promised various other privileges, including the right to elect their own leader or *voyvoda*. This the Hungarian diet, sensing a new encroachment on its prerogatives, would not have, but the name of Voyvodina stuck to the territory, and military reasons helped the Serbs to implement what they had been granted, for the Austrian generals needed them. Thus the Serbian metropolitanate of Karlovtsi was organized, as an offshoot of the patriarchate of Pech, and the Church took up the leadership of the Serbs in Hungary as well.

Croats had played an important part in the liberation of Croatian lands,[3] but most of the estates in the recovered territory were granted to foreign nobles by the Habsburgs, who also further extended the Military Frontier. Any chance, however, of the Croatian nobles leaguing up with their Hungarian counterparts against the centralism of Vienna was foiled by the Magyars themselves who, feeling stronger since they had got rid of the Turks, wanted to hold Croatia down at the same time as they resisted the emperor. The attempt to liberate the South Slavs from the Turks had made the Croats even more sensitive to their past at the same time as they were also becoming aware of the links of speech and way of life. There was an echo of the ideas of Pavle Vitezovitch who, writing at the turn of the seventeenth century, had stressed the identity of language, way of life, and common origin of the South Slavs, whom he wanted to tie up with the existing political identity of Croatia. In such a mood, the Croatian nobility was not likely to give in to Hungarian claims, and this enabled the court to manoeuvre between the two.

It was to the Croatian diet that Charles VI first put the Pragmatic Sanction in 1712 before submitting the delicate question of succession through females to the reluctant Hungarian estates, and the Croats voted for it because they were discontented with Hungary, yet stressing once again their country's special status through the person of the common monarch. The centralization of the Austrian monarchy made rapid headway in the eighteenth century, more particularly under Joseph II (1765–90), whose enlightened despotism improved the position of the Slav peasants and extended the benefits of education. The number of literate Slovenes, Croats, and Serbs increased, and there grew up among the South Slavs of the Monarchy a class of rationalist and nationally conscious intellectuals

[3] The emperor's South Slav subjects played an important part in the wars of the eighteenth century, and not only in the Balkans. The Frontier regiments were gradually turned into regular troops, increasingly used on all fronts, and Croatia as a whole provided the greatest number of soldiers of all the Austrian Monarchy. They fought in Italy, Silesia, Bohemia, the Netherlands, and northern France. Brave and undisciplined, they were often left to pillage in order to frighten people with their 'Turkish' aspect. Thus Croat (which incidentally represented as many Serbs as Croats) became a household word all over Europe.

writing in their own language and interested in the culture of their own people. Both Hungary and Croatia lost their special status. New economic and administrative developments generally weakened the influence of the Croatian nobility, while Dimitriye Obradovich (1740–1811) attracted the attention of his contemporaries as the first Serbian writer who identified the nation not by the faith it adhered to but by the language it spoke.

Dalmatia had continued to decline in neutrality (for Venice too kept out of the wars after 1718), and Montenegro had embarked on its long war of liberation, with the metropolitan of Tsetinje asserting himself as the leader of his flock. After 1697, the see was in fact becoming hereditary from uncle to nephew in the Petrovich family. Leaning on foreign powers, the Montenegrins developed in their struggle against the Turks both a feeling of unity and the legend that theirs was the only Serbian land which had not lost its freedom after the battle of Kosovo.

In the south, emigration and warfare had left Macedonia largely abandoned and devastated, and the Church in decline. The Hellenized hierarchy of Ohrid had not only been, like that of Pech, agitating against the Turks: it was also looking to Rome for support. This led the sultan to abolish the archbishopric in 1767, six months after he had abolished the patriarchate of Pech, both jurisdictions being turned over to the patriarch of Constantinople. Uncertain of the loyalty of their Christian subjects, the Turks, in the eighteenth century, encouraged Islamization in particularly sensitive regions. They favoured the expansion of Moslem Albanians into the lands vacated by the Serbs in the plains of Kosovo and Metohiya, at the foot of their mountains, and into the Morava-Vardar corridor. In Bosnia, the local Moslem element was strengthened by Turks returning from Hungary, Croatia, and Dalmatia.

Shumadiya or northern Serbia after 1699 once again found itself a border province and, from 1718 to 1739, under the authority of Austria. During that twenty-year period, the territory was officially called Serbia for the first time since 1459, and the emperor assumed the title of 'king of Serbia'. A native militia was organized, and a system of local autonomy. The economy was developed and intercourse established between both sides of the Danube. When the Austrians left, many Serbs left too rather than face Turkish reprisals. During the last Austro-Turkish war, that of 1788–91, the population of northern Serbia rose again, but this time, when the Turks returned, there were no reprisals. As part of Sultan Selim III's general attempt to face the challenge of defeat and anarchy, the local autonomy of the province of Belgrade was confirmed. In these circumstances immigration from the south continued, giving new vigour to the patriarchal structure of the territory, while links with the Serbs over the border were kept up.

At the end of the eighteenth century, the Yugoslav lands were in a phase of transition. The Serbian migrations had brought South Slavs of various traditions together in the western and northern regions, where intellectuals influenced by the Enlightenment and latent Romanticism were discovering their own nations according to new criteria. In this changing world, the French Revolution was to sow the seeds of modern nationalism. The historical forces which had carried the historic inheritance of Serbia and Croatia to this point, and continued, throughout the period, the process of forming two separate national identities, were weaker at the end of the eighteenth century. The Serbian Church was no longer a united spiritual force extending across the frontier of empires, and the Turks had suppressed it altogether in their territory. At the same time the position of the Croatian nobility had deteriorated as a result of economic and political developments in Austria. Joseph II's attempt at extreme centralization had died with him, but it had opened a new era in the history of the Hungarian-Croatian union, for the Hungarians, by developing modern nationalism as a novel line of defence, were in turn to cause a nationalist reaction among the Croats. It was, however, the Serbian division between the advanced and strong Austrian Monarchy and the backward and weak Ottoman Empire that was destined to start the process of emancipation. The contact between the new ideas north of the Danube and the flight of peasants driven to desperation south of the river, was eventually to spark off revolution.

From nationalism to unification

In 1797, French troops came to Slovene-inhabited regions, and the Venetian republic was extinguished and handed over to Austria, until 1805 when its domain was ceded to Napoleon, who in 1809 also obtained a large part of Slovenia and Croatia. These Yugoslav provinces of the French Empire were known as the Illyrian Provinces and included the Ragusan republic, which had managed to survive Venice by just over a decade. The provinces reverted to Austria after Napoleon's fall, but French rule – although only an interlude – had a disturbing effect. Particularly important was its intellectual stimulus and, seen in retrospect as an experiment in associating for the first time the majority of Slovenes, many Croats, and some Serbs in one unit outside the framework of the existing Austrian and Ottoman Empires, it was to act as a powerful posthumous inspiration.

The impact of the French Revolution and of Napoleon was manifest too in the peasant revolt which laid the basis of the modern state of Serbia. With the failure of Selim III's policy, by 1804 the province of Belgrade had fallen into the hands of the rebellious janissaries. Under Karageorge's leadership, the frightened peasantry of Shumadiya rose against them. By the time they had rid the province of the janissaries they had also, however, carried out a real revolution which destroyed the foundations of Turkish power in Serbia. This significant event attracted little attention in Europe where the powers were busy getting rid of Napoleon, and Turkey was able to crush the Serbs in 1813. They rose again in 1815 under Milosh Obrenovich and this time, by exploiting the prolonged crisis of the Ottoman state, they achieved more lasting success. By 1830, the liberated territory had been recognized by the sultan as an autonomous principality, covering 38,000 square kilometres with a population of just over 700,000.[4]

Unfettered, the self-contained and static economic structure of the past immediately began to break apart. The free peasant soon became an indebted peasant, in spite of measures taken by Prince Milosh's paternalistic government to protect him. But the liberator-prince himself belonged to the past and, with Russian help, in 1839 a constitution was forced upon him which also consecrated Russia's tutelage. Milosh abdicated; modern Serbia had freed itself from the Turks and from its liberator, but it found itself unable to stand alone against Ottoman power without looking either to Austria or to Russia for support.

Until the nineteenth century, except for the mountaineers of Montenegro and the merchants, mariners, intellectuals, and aristocrats of Ragusa, Europe had forgotten the South Slavs. The Romantic Movement, however, enabled it to discover the Balkans, and the peoples of the Balkans to discover both Europe and themselves. Kopitar (1780–1844), the polyglot Slovenian scholar in Vienna, urged South Slav scholars to study the folk literature of their peoples, caused their collections to be translated, and passed the result of their work to the writers of western Europe. Indeed, one could say that the autonomy of the nascent Serbian state was obtained, as much as by Karageorge and Milosh Obrenovich, by Kopitar and his Serbian friend Vuk Karadjich (1787–1864). By his research into and publication of Serbian folk ballads Karadjich had his nation accepted by the writers of Europe before it was accepted by its statesmen, and at the same time he moulded the unvitiated dialect of Herzegovina into an acceptable common Serbo-Croatian literary language.

[4] S. Pavlowitch, *Anglo-Russian Rivalry in Serbia, 1837–1839*, Paris and The Hague, 1961, p. 27.

It was a movement of intellectuals which simultaneously carried the 'Illyrian' idea[5] from the Napoleonic interlude to 1848 among the South Slavs of the Austrian Monarchy, caught between the repressive measures of the post-1815 Austrian reaction and the rising pressure of Hungarian nationalism. Although all Croats were under Habsburg rule, they remained divided, for Dalmatia – with Dubrovnik – became an Austrian province, while the connexion of the Croatian realm – still limited to inner Croatia and Slavonia – with Hungary was renewed. Against the threat of Magyarization, the Illyrian ideal of a wide South Slav cultural community, based on the similarities of speech, spread among the young urban intelligentsia of Croatia, fostered by the writer Ljudevit Gay (1809–1872). Translated into political terms by the National Party in the 1840s, the movement realistically narrowed its immediate aims to demanding the unification of the Croatian ethnic territory, but kept in touch with Belgrade.

In Serbia, since 1839, the government had been in the hands of the Constitutionalist oligarchy which had ruled with Milosh's son Michael until 1842, and then with Karageorge's more pliant son, Alexander Karageorgevich. The Constitutionalists needed more educated people to run their new institutions and did much to step up education. Through the scholars they sent to France, French influence entered Serbia as a rival to Central European, and the new intelligentsia turned into a liberal opposition advocating a Western-style parliamentary system to replace the existing Central European bureaucratic system. This was the trend which, in association with the popular demand for the return of Prince Milosh, was to lead to a change of régime in 1858. In the meantime, the Constitutionalist government formulated, as the ultimate aim of Serbia's foreign policy, unity with all the other South Slavs. Unity with Montenegro and an outlet on the Adriatic, in case of a break-up of the Ottoman dominions, was seen as a first aim to strengthen Serbia and enable it to go on working for a unified Yugoslav state.[6] Both the Serbian Constitutionalists and the Croatian Nationalists, in touch with each other, kept the mystique of South Slav unity as an ultimate aim and

---

[5] The term 'Illyrian', resurrected by Napoleon for its memories of Rome, coincided with that used by earlier Croatian writers.

[6] An important figure was Garashanin, Serbia's foreign minister and a link, not only between the older Constitutionalists and the younger French-orientated Liberals, but also with the other South Slav nationalists. He affirmed the need for real independence, political and economic, not only from Turkey, but also from Russia and Austria, which could be achieved by leaning on the Western powers (notably France). Ultimately, only a unified Yugoslavia could stop Russia and Austria expanding into the ruins of the Ottoman Empire.

used it as an auxiliary to further the realization of a nearer aim – the unification of Serbian and Croatian lands respectively.

It was, however, through diplomacy that the Constitutionalists planned to carry out their programme, and the revolutionary fire that spread through the Habsburg lands in 1848 did not fit into their policy. Hungary revolted against Vienna and the South Slavs tried to take advantage of the upheaval, but whereas Croatian Nationalists hoped to unite Croatia with Dalmatia, and even Voyvodina, into one Illyrian kingdom under the constitutional rule of the Habsburgs, Hungarian nationalists wanted to incorporate Croatia into the Magyar state. Public opinion in Croatia was outraged, and the Serbs of southern Hungary declared Voyvodina autonomous; proposals were made for Serbo-Croatian unity, and Vienna was able to rally the South Slavs against Budapest, thus saving the Habsburg monarchy. Thus 1848 had for the first time evoked a popular Yugoslav movement, but Austria and Russia, added to its natural reluctance, prevented any intervention by the Serbian government, in spite of popular pressure, while the intransigent nationalism of the Hungarian nobility prevented united action against Vienna. Croats and Serbs obtained little reward, for if Croatia and Voyvodina were separated from Hungary in 1849, from then on the centralizing absolutism of the imperial government pressed as heavily on the South Slavs as on the Magyars.[7]

The young had been deeply affected by 1848, which helps to explain the developments of the 1860s and the close links established between Belgrade and Zagreb. In Serbia, the Obrenovich restoration soon brought Milosh's son Michael to the throne again, after the old hero's death in 1860. Prince Michael shared the aspirations of those South Slavs who, aroused by the events in Italy, dreamt of freeing themselves from foreign rule and of uniting. His ambition was to make Serbia fit to play the part of a Yugoslav Piedmont, and to unite Balkan governments and nationalist movements against the Turks. He started by altering the constitution so as to strengthen the ruler's position. This was not what the Liberals had hoped for, so that their opposition to his domestic policies increased as years went by; but Michael's foreign policy had their full support. The European diplomatic situation in the 1860s was favourable.[8] The

---

[7] The abolition of serfdom was little more than the legal acknowledgement of an accomplished fact. Peasants became owners of the plots they had formerly tilled, but the gentry received compensation and kept the remaining lands, which enabled large estates and the power of the (largely alien) landed aristocracy to survive until the First World War.

[8] Napoleon III was sympathetic to the aspirations of the emerging nationalities, and Russia seconded him in the hope of regaining influence in the Balkans. Austria was weakened by its defeats in Italy (1859) and in Germany

Serbian government established contacts with Croatian Nationalists with a view to working for a future united independent state, and in 1867 obtained the evacuation of the Ottoman garrisons, after which the principality was a vassal in name only. Prince Michael could put the finishing touches to his Balkan League and step up the great propaganda effort in Ottoman and Habsburg lands.

Croatia's Nationalists, while they kept in touch with Belgrade, hesitated between Vienna and Budapest; outside their ranks Starchevich's new extreme nationalistic Party of the Right (i.e. the 'right' of the Croatian state) uncompromisingly advocated the restoration of Croatia's individuality as a separate state under the Habsburgs. The outstanding personality in Croatia in these years was the Catholic Bishop Strossmayer (1815–1905), a truly nationalist Croat as well as a genuine Yugoslav.[9] Dalmatian nationalists, Croats, and Serbs asked for union with Croatia on the basis of the Illyrian idea, while Prince Nicholas of Montenegro served as an auxiliary to Prince Michael, whose state appeared as the champion of the Slavs still under Ottoman domination. For both poles of the South Slavs – Belgrade and Zagreb – the denouement which seemed imminent turned out to be an anticlimax, for by the time the Balkan countries were ready for war, the opportunity had passed. In 1867, the Habsburg monarchy was reorganized on the basis of a compromise which satisfied the Hungarians at the expense of the other nationalities, and the following year Prince Michael's assassination (a private vendetta) signalled the disintegration of his Balkan League.

Croatia and Voyvodina reverted to Hungary, while Dalmatia and the Slovenian provinces remained Austrian, thus keeping the South Slavs more divided than ever in the reorganized Dual Monarchy. The Austro-Hungarian arrangements were, however, complemented by a Hungarian-Croatian compromise (1868) which recognized Croatia as a separate unit[10] linked to the Hungarian crown, with a legislature and an executive competent for local affairs under a Hungarian-appointed governor. The Nationalist Party, in (1866), and its constitutional experiments (1860–61), while Turkey was preoccupied by the Cretan revolt (1866–68).

[9] Strossmayer was so much ahead of his time that his views, at once realistic and idealistic, have since been given a variety of interpretations. He believed that only a deepening of true nationalism – Croatian or Serbian – and true Christianity – Catholic or Orthodox – could lead to a better understanding between Yugoslavs, and that this could best be achieved through culture and education. It was increasingly in these fields that he worked towards overcoming the differences between Catholic Croats and Orthodox Serbs, and founded the Yugoslav Academy in Zagreb (1867). He is also known as having been opposed to the definition as a dogma of papal infallibility at the Vatican Council of 1870.

[10] Soon to include the Military Frontier, abolished in 1881.

order to become the governing party, accepted the limited reforms which appeased the moderates. From then on, South Slav pressure mounted in Austria-Hungary, but the various groups and territories, carefully kept apart, fought unco-ordinated struggles which varied with local conditions. In Voyvodina, the Serbs were left again only with their Church, and steadily lost ground to the Hungarian and German element. In Croatia, people like Strossmayer withdrew from political life into cultural action, while Starchevich's party gained strength. In Dalmatia, the Nationalists gained a majority in the provincial diet in 1870 and continued to agitate for union with Croatia. The Slovenes concentrated on obtaining concessions on the use of their language.

The Yugoslav idea, though still fluid, was nevertheless a reality. It was at the root of Austria-Hungary's distrust of Serbia, and of its relief at developments there after Prince Michael's death. The regents for his successor, Milan, came to an agreement with the Liberals and the new constitution of 1869 gave that party a majority in parliament. At the same time, the permissive political atmosphere, the appearance of a new generation of the intelligentsia, and the dissatisfaction of the peasants who were paying the price of economic progress that seemed to benefit mainly the towns, combined to give birth to a new radical movement whose call was to be for more realism in politics, and a state run for and by the peasants. Yet in spite of Liberals and Radicals, Milan, when he came of age in 1872, tried to govern with the Conservatives – the successors to the Constitutionalists and a party of the past. In 1875, when the revolt of the Christian peasantry of Herzegovina and Bosnia started the Eastern Crisis, Serbia was in no position to give a lead to the South Slavs who had been aroused by the plans of the 1860s. Nevertheless, Serbia and Montenegro went to war against the Turks, and Russia followed them in 1877. At the Congress of Berlin which, in 1878, put an end to the crisis, Serbia and Montenegro were formally recognized as independent states and allowed to keep much of the territories which they had liberated to the south, but Bosnia and Herzegovina were entrusted to Austro-Hungarian administration.

The international settlement had left Serbia, along with all the western Balkans, in the Habsburg sphere of influence, and Austria in 1881 was able to impose on Prince Milan and his government commercial and political agreements by which the newly independent state ceased to be, in form, a tributary of the Ottoman Empire, only to become, in fact, a vassal of the Austrian. The younger intelligentsia turned away from the Liberals, whose party had nothing more to offer, and so did the peasantry which had had to pay for the war. The Radicals organized themselves as the first mass party, with a programme aimed at limiting the power of the crown and of the bureaucracy, and opposition increased to Milan's subservience to Austria-Hungary. In order to divert attention from it, Serbia was proclaimed a kingdom in 1882, and in 1885 went to war with Bulgaria which, an autonomous principality since 1878, had incorporated the province of Eastern Roumelia. Unpopular, the war turned to humiliating defeat, from which Milan was only rescued by Austrian intervention. His position was untenable and he began to prepare for his withdrawal. He accepted a freely elected Radical parliament and had a new constitution drawn up by an all-party commission, which, ratified by parliament and promulgated in 1889, finally introduced parliamentary government; then, at the age of thirty-five, he abdicated in favour of his thirteen-year-old son Alexander.

With the new constitution and Milan's abdication, the Radicals acceded to power, but very soon the young king showed the same authoritarianism as his father. By a series of coups, beginning when he was not yet seventeen, he first dismissed his regents, then turned constitutional government into a farce by abolishing, restoring, granting, and suspending constitutions, and married his mistress – an older, intriguing widow, whose past was not above reproach. The opposition grew to revolutionary proportions and in 1903, a group of army officers murdered the twenty-seven year-old monarch and his queen who had turned Serbia into a figure of international fun. A provisional government was formed of representatives of political parties, and summoned the last regularly elected parliament. This assembly immediately restored the constitution of 1889 and elected king, in succession to the extinct Obrenovich line, the sixty-year-old Peter Karageorgevich, grandson of Karageorge and son of Prince Alexander Karageorgevich.

Independent Serbia in the last quarter of the nineteenth century was clearly not an attractive proposition even for the Serbs outside its frontiers, not to mention the other Yugoslavs. Montenegro, it is true, had affirmed itself under a succession of able rulers from the Petrovich-Njegosh dynasty and retained its prestige,[11] but it could not make up for the decline of the larger Serbian state, and neither was able to play a decisive role in the movements of the South Slavs

---

[11] Peter II, the last of the prince-bishops (1830–51), is generally recognized as one of the greatest Yugoslav poets and a precursor of the Yugoslav idea. Prince Danilo, his successor, secularized his position and reigned until 1860, when he was in turn succeeded by Nicholas, 'the father-in-law of Europe', who was to assume the title of king in 1910 on the fiftieth anniversary of his accession.

within the Dual Monarchy. In Bosnia-Herzegovina, the Moslem element was gradually reconciled by the fact that the social structure of the countryside was left untouched by the new Austro-Hungarian administration which, however much it improved material conditions, did not much affect agriculture, in which the majority of the population – mainly Orthodox – was engaged.[12] The Austro-Hungarian authorities generally resorted to a policy of fostering antagonism between Croats and Serbs. In Croatia, they granted various facilities to the Serbs[13] and otherwise pursued a policy of repression and Magyarization, which did succeed in breaking up Croatian forces, though at the price of increasing anti-Magyar resentment. While the Strossmayerist trend seceded from the National Party, the Rightists also split, with Frank's 'Pure Right' launching a pro-Habsburg, Catholic-orientated brand of Croatism deeply suspicious of the Orthodox Serbian element. Even in Dalmatia, where South Slav nationalism had united both Croats and Serbs, the Austrians managed to divide them for a while.[14] The Slovenes were a smaller group, scattered through six Austrian provinces,[15] whose economic conditions were relatively favourable and where the government, after 1878, had made considerable cultural concessions. Thus Slovenian agitation, mainly represented by the Catholic Slovenian People's Party, though ideally pro-Yugoslav, aimed rather at getting the best of existing circumstances.

[12] According to the Austro-Hungarian census of 1910, the population of Bosnia-Herzegovina was 1·9 million, 43% Orthodox, 32% Moslem, and 23% Catholic. In 1878, 6,000–7,000 Moslems owned large estates on which 85,000 serf families worked, 74% of whom were Orthodox (H. Darby, 'Bosnia', in S. Clissold (ed.): *A Short History of Yugoslavia*, Cambridge, 1966, p. 71 n., and L. Stavrianos, *The Balkans since 1453*, New York, 1963, p. 462).
[13] In the Croatian kingdom in 1910, out of a total population of 2·6 million, the Serbs amounted to almost 25% (0·6 million compared to 1·6 million Croats). In Voyvodina, out of just over 1·3 million, there were 382,000 Serbs, 69,000 other Yugoslavs, 422,000 Magyars, and 301,000 Germans. Altogether, the Yugoslavs formed 13% (6·8 million) of the total population of Austria-Hungary (Austro-Hungarian census, 1910).
[14] In Dalmatia, the Serbian minority tended to unite with the Croatian majority in one same brand of South Slav nationalism because the history of the province within the Venetian context had weakened the separate traditions of the Croatian and of the Serbian states, because both Croats and Serbs had to assert in common their Slavism against the continued economic predominance of the Italian urban element, and because ethnic divisions did not entirely coincide with religious divisions. Dalmatia was the only region with a substantial number of Catholic Serbs. In 1910, out of a total population of 635,000 there were 18,000 Italians. Croats numbered 80% of the 610,000 Yugoslavs.
[15] In 1910 there were 1·2 million Slovenes in Austria, 0·5 million of them in Carniola (where they formed 93% of the population). There were also slightly over 67,000 in Hungary (Austro-Hungarian census, 1910).

By blocking Serbia's possibilities of action to the west, Austria had diverted them to the south and Macedonia – a zone where several ethnic groups met and overlapped, and where the majority of the inhabitants, speaking a range of Slavonic dialects imperceptibly passing from Serbian to Bulgarian, felt no strong national identity, as a result of having been kept under Turkish rule longest and most intensely. Michael's Serbia had been a source of hope there, but it had concentrated its attention mainly on Bosnia, and Bulgarian nationalism had been the first to challenge the position of Hellenism. Later in the century, fearing that Bulgaria might go on to incorporate Macedonia as it had done Eastern Roumelia, the Serbian government began in turn to indulge in a considerable propaganda and educational effort there, and the Serbian cause made rapid progress. Pro-Bulgarian Macedonians retorted by organizing armed bands, followed in turn by Serbian and Greek bands, and the anarchy that ensued made mockery of what had been Prince Michael's plans for a combination of Balkan forces to drive the Turks out of Europe.

A new phase opened in 1903, for the dynastic change in Serbia coincided with a new internal crisis of the Dual Monarchy, and both facilitated the development of the Yugoslav movement. In Croatia, faced with the intransigent attitude of the authorities, a new generation was beginning to break with legalism, while the Serbs there were turning against concessions designed to promote Hungarian rather than Serbian interests, and the young in both communities were joining to demand social reforms and the democratization of political life. The Strossmayerists united with the remnants of the Rightists in a new opposition Croatian Party of the Right, and a new Croatian Peasant Party was formed which aimed at bringing the peasant masses to politics. In 1905, the Croatian opposition deputies attempted a bargain with the Hungarians, offering support against Vienna in return for reforms and the union of Dalmatia and Croatia, a step which was endorsed by the political leaders of the Serbs in Croatia, both groups merging into a Croato-Serbian Coalition which won the 1906 elections to the Croatian diet. The Hungarians, however, came to terms with Vienna and ignored the Croats.

Serbia thus once again came to focus the hopes of most Yugoslavs on account of both its political and its cultural development. The 1903 elections had given the Radicals an overwhelming majority, and King Peter tactfully limited himself to his constitutional role. Pressed between Austria-Hungary and the Ottoman Empire, Serbia began to draw nearer the other Balkan states in order to try and undermine Turkish rule to the south, and to stand up to Austria-

Hungary's pressure by supporting the Yugoslav movement. There was an intensification of cultural co-operation between South Slavs and, particularly in Serbia, there were widespread South Slav manifestations. In order to intimidate Serbia, the Austrian government closed the borders to its livestock exports. Ignoring the blockade, Serbia found new outlets for its agricultural products,[16] and its success in breaking away from Austria-Hungary both increased its prestige and deepened the Yugoslav movement.

By formally annexing Bosnia-Herzegovina in 1908, Austria-Hungary wanted to strengthen its position in the Balkans and on the Adriatic, and alter the course of the South Slav movement taking shape around Belgrade. The annexation of this Slav region, kept as a 'colonial' condominium of Austria and Hungary, ensured, however, that Croatian discontent with Budapest would turn to solidarity with the Serbs. Unable to govern with the diet, the Hungarian authorities resorted to governing without it in Croatia from 1908 to 1910, stepping up persecutions, which merely increased unrest, to the point where they had to come to terms with the Croato-Serbian Coalition. In exchange for an extension of the franchise, the coalition agreed to collaborate with Budapest, but the younger generation did not. Rejecting legal action for piecemeal reforms and fractional unification within the Monarchy, it turned to violent action for a united, complete, and independent Yugoslav state.

Serbia's practical hopes turned yet again to the sea and to Macedonia. Terrorism and anarchy there had culminated in the uprising of 1903 which, if it was not able to stand up to Turkish repression, did nevertheless drive the powers to initiate a policy of reforms. This was interrupted by the Young Turks' revolution of 1908 which promised effective equality, but along with Ottomanization. Threatened first with the intervention of non-Balkan powers in Macedonia, then with Ottomanization, the Balkan states and the Christians of Macedonia combined for self-protection. By 1911-12, they had managed to triumph over distrust and combine into a league, much stronger than that of the 1860s.[17]

When the Balkan states attacked Turkey, that country was already at war with Italy in Libya, and the great powers, divided, did not intervene, though Austria-Hungary managed to block Serbia's access

[16] Serbia gained economically as well as politically, for the need to process its agricultural exports for more distant markets helped to develop industry; yet the country remained predominantly agricultural. In 1910, industry still occupied only 7% of the population, which had increased to 2·9 million from 1·7 million in 1878 (L. Stavrianos, op. cit., p. 457).

[17] The annexation of Bosnia-Herzegovina had put an end to Austro-Russian co-operation, and Russia favoured the formation of a Balkan alliance as an obstacle to Austro-German advance in the region.

THE YUGOSLAV LANDS UNTIL THEIR UNIFICATION 49

to the Adriatic. The Turks were practically ousted from Macedonia, but the division of the spoils led to dissension among the allies and to a second war, in 1913, against Bulgaria. Serbia gained northern and central Macedonia, and a common frontier with Montenegro, but it had to face the task of assimilating, in its new acquisitions, a heterogeneous and neglected population which included an important proportion of Moslem Albanians as well as many Orthodox Slavs with no clear national consciousness, many of whom looked to Bulgaria.

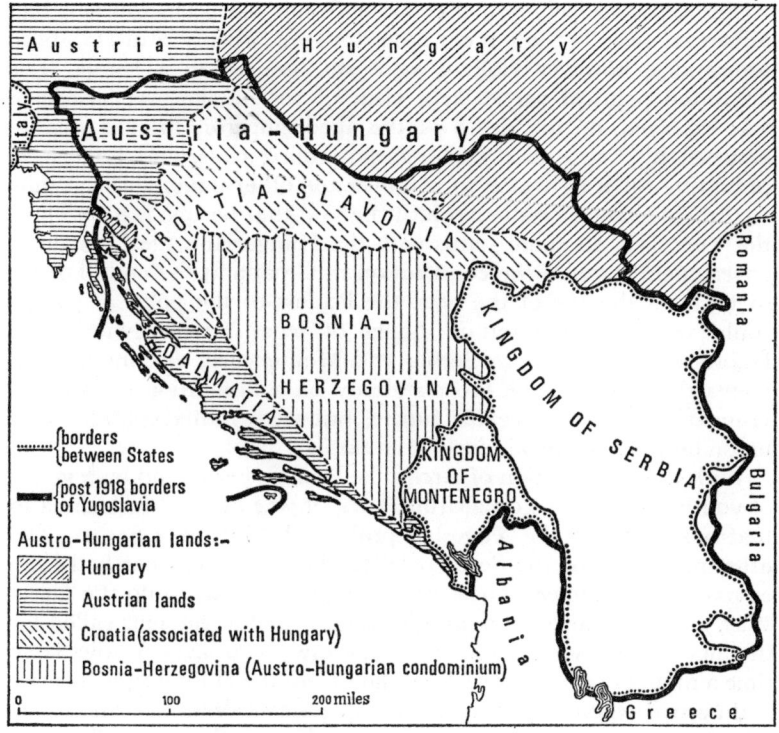

1 The Yugoslav lands on the eve of the First World War

From 1912 onwards, the situation deteriorated rapidly throughout the South Slav provinces of the Dual Monarchy. In Croatia, pro-Serbian demonstrations and strikes led to a renewed suspension of constitutional arrangements. In Dalmatia, the young were entirely won over to the ideal of a united Yugoslavia, and even the students of Slovenia turned to revolutionary activity. South Slav solidarity was particularly reflected in Bosnia-Herzegovina where agricultural unrest and the neighbourhood of Serbia made the revolutionary movement exceptionally strong. That generation of Croatian, Serbian, and Slovenian students in Austria-Hungary was the first to think in terms of a violent break-up of the centuries-old dynastic state. The Sarayevo conspiracy was not born in isolation. It was linked with this revolutionary ferment spreading throughout the Yugoslav territories of the Habsburg Empire – the students' and workers' strikes, the demonstrations and repressive measures, the dozen or so previous plots against state dignitaries, the links with the students, political parties, and secret societies of Serbia.

The growing feeling of a common South Slav consciousness had advanced fast, yet, on the whole, in 1914, openly anti-Habsburg aspirations, however violent, were still limited to a fringe. The organized political parties kept clear of such action. A showdown was expected, on the death of the aged emperor, Francis Joseph, between his heir and the Hungarian ruling class, and both were preparing for it by trying to win over the other nationalities. While Archduke Francis Ferdinand let it be said that he was ready to give the Yugoslavs an equal status with the Hungarians, the Hungarian government restored the constitution in Croatia at the end of 1913, so that, on the eve of the war, the leaders of the political parties could once again entertain hopes of legal reforms within the Habsburg framework. In Serbia and Montenegro, too, the governments did not envisage the possibility of a dissolution of Austria-Hungary in any foreseeable future, but were rather considering a union between the two independent states.

With the assassination of Archduke Francis Ferdinand by a group of youths in Sarayevo on 28 June 1914, it was decided in Vienna to find a solution to the Yugoslav problem by invading Serbia. The attempt failed, for the Serbs repelled the invasion; what had been envisaged as an operation of domestic policy turned into the Great War, and both the Serbian and Montenegrin governments called for the liberation and unification of all the Yugoslavs. At the same time a number of influential Yugoslavs from the Habsburg monarchy fled abroad where they formed the Yugoslav Committee and made it their task to advocate the union of all Croats, Serbs, and Slovenes of Austria-Hungary with Serbia and Montenegro. Nevertheless, the world at large was oblivious of the Yugoslav question, and the Allies were more interested in winning over Italy, which had aspirations to take over the mostly Slav-inhabited former Venetian lands of Austria-Hungary. In 1915 they succeeded, by promising these territories to Italy if they won the war, but Austria and Germany won over Bulgaria, with promises of Serbian Macedonia, and their combined forces overran Serbia, whose king, government, parliament, and army, along with countless civilian refugees, retreated in winter through the mountains of Albania to the Adriatic coast – and Allied shipping.

So far, the war had not brought the realization of the Yugoslav idea much nearer. The Serbian government, in Corfu, was more concerned with the restoration of its country after the war than with the pursuance of an ideal which might prove impossible to attain, especially since the promises to Italy had become known, and the death, at the end of 1916, of Emperor Francis Joseph raised hopes of peace with Austria-Hungary. Thus, the freely elected Croato-Serbian Coalition in Zagreb continued to profess loyalty to the Hungarian crown, and no revolution had broken out in Croatia, while Yugoslav soldiers put up a good fight against Italy whom they had no wish to see take the place of the Habsburgs in Yugoslav lands.

The year 1917 was a confused one. Russia dropped out of the war, and the U.S.A. joined the Allies. At the same time as Russia's new leaders and President Wilson talked of the self-determination of nationalities, the Allies, whose position was shaky, were examining the possibility of detaching Austria-Hungary from Germany. Neither the Serbian government nor the leaders of the Habsburg South Slavs knew what was going to be the outcome of the war, or what was going to happen to Austria-Hungary; hence both played on two fronts. On the one hand, each aimed at ensuring what could be obtained, from the Allies and the Habsburgs – leaving to the future the complete unification of the South Slavs. On the other, both sides kept up their contacts with the Yugoslav Committee which advocated the necessity of establishing a common Yugoslav front towards the Allies. While, in Corfu, Serbian government and Yugoslav Committee discussed the basic principles of a future state of the Serbs, Croats, and Slovenes, in Zagreb and in Vienna, Yugoslav political leaders bargained over their loyalty.

At the beginning of 1918, the Allies were still in two minds about Austria-Hungary, and it was the latter's refusal to face the facts and make any concessions which precipitated events. Yugoslav feelings in Croatia were by then widespread and by the summer, anti-Habsburg manifestations and military mutinies were increasing. When, in September, the Allied offensive – with a restored Serbian army – broke through from Salonika into Macedonia, put Bulgaria out of action, and started liberating Serbia, the authority of Vienna and Budapest rapidly crumbled in the South Slav provinces. Deputies of the Slovenes, Croats, and Serbs of all the Habsburg lands formed in Zagreb a National Council which virtually became a provisional government for the South Slav territories of the Monarchy, and demanded the unification of the Yugoslavs into one independent state. When the Austrian government asked for an armistice, it handed over the local authority to the Zagreb Council. On 29 October, the Croatian diet broke off all links with Austria and Hungary, proclaimed the union of Croatia, Slavonia, and Dalmatia with all other South Slav provinces, and handed over its authority to the National Council. The equivocal attitude of the Allies, and Italy's insistence on redeeming the territorial promises which had brought it into the war, quickened the pace of the unification process which had been started in Geneva between the Serbian government and the National Council. The National Council voted to send a delegation to Belgrade, inviting Prince Alexander, who was regent for his aged father, to proclaim the act of union and assume the regency of the new state. On 1 December 1918, Alexander duly proclaimed the Kingdom of the Serbs, Croats, and Slovenes, in the presence of the Zagreb delegation and of members of the Serbian government.

What four years earlier still seemed a distant ideal had been achieved by the end of 1918, owing to the combination of Serbia's prestige and military contribution to the Allied cause, the political realism of the leaders of the Habsburg Slovenes, Croats, and Serbs within the Monarchy, and the idealism of those who had gone abroad to propagate the cause of unity and independence. The precipitation of events, however, also meant that the leaders of the various sections of the Yugoslavs had not had time to work out beforehand clear ideas about how the union was to be implemented in practice.[18]

[18] H. Darby and R. Seton-Watson, 'The Formation of Yugoslavia', in Clissold (ed.): *A Short History of Yugoslavia*, pp. 159–60.

Chapter 2

The Yugoslav Kingdom: 1919–41

The formation of the new state

The new state was made up of very different components: two independent kingdoms – Serbia and Montenegro, both of which included territories that had been Turkish until 1912; parts of Austria – most of the Slovenian lands – and Dalmatia; a realm under the Hungarian crown with its own home rule – Croatia-Slavonia; parts of Hungary – Voyvodina and the north-eastern tip of Slovenia; an Austro-Hungarian condominium – Bosnia-Herzegovina. The national territory was in a chaotic state, and much of it had been depopulated by warfare which, for Serbia and Montenegro, had been almost incessant since 1912. Serbia and Montenegro were just out of occupation, their economy was at a standstill, the consequences of their losses inestimable. The combined loss of population suffered by all the regions forming Yugoslavia, as a result of the wars from 1912 to 1918, is estimated at slightly under 2 million.[1] In the Austro-Hungarian provinces, the losses, though relatively smaller, were still heavy. Separated from the old Monarchy, their economic life was disorganized. Peasants were in a revolutionary frame of mind, overrunning the large estates. In the towns generally, conditions were characterized by war damage, unemployment, inflation, acute food and housing shortages. To make things worse, Italian troops were in occupation of parts of the territory.

Generally speaking, the Kingdom of the Serbs, Croats, and Slovenes still had no frontiers, and its recognition had not been immediate. The first power to recognize it had been the U.S.A., on 2 February 1919. The other Allies gradually followed, with the exception of Italy. Faced with a new nation in birth pangs across the Adriatic, the Italians were not only intent on obtaining all that

[1] The toll for Serbia and Montenegro amounted to about 0·75 million. (Serbia's military losses alone were relatively 2·5 higher than those of France.) About 150,000 Yugoslavs of the Dual Monarchy died in the war. Epidemics account for the rest. These estimates are all according to neutral sources (I. Lederer, *Yugoslavia at the Paris Peace Conference – A Study in Frontiermaking*, New Haven and London, 1963, pp. 221–5).

they had been promised in 1915, but also aimed at getting the port of Fiume (Riyeka for the Yugoslavs) which their armistice agreement with Austria-Hungary had given them the right to occupy on behalf of the Allies. Italian troops had moved into territories claimed by both Italy and Yugoslavia, and occupied Fiume. When, however, the Peace Conference decided that other Allied troops should join the Italians there, the writer Gabriele D'Annunzio seized Fiume as an exercise in private enterprise, and against the will of the Italian government which nevertheless continued to insist that the Yugoslavs of the former Monarchy were enemies to be excluded from the Conference. Italians and Yugoslavs were directed to settle the territorial issue on their own, and the Peace Conference ended without solving that particular problem.

Eventually, common fear of a Habsburg restoration, with pressure from the Allied governments, and the need felt by both countries to devote their energies to domestic problems, brought Italy and Yugoslavia to agree. On 12 November 1920, at Rapallo, Italy obtained Istria, some islands, and the enclave of Zara (Zadar for the Yugoslavs). Fiume was to be a free city, and D'Annunzio had to evacuate it. The treaty of Rapallo saved Dalmatia and most of the offshore islands for Yugoslavia, but deprived it of its only possible economic outlet on the Adriatic, and left half a million Yugoslavs in Italy.[2]

Just as Istria separated Yugoslavia from Italy, so Carinthia separated it from Austria. The peace treaty had decided on an Allied-controlled plebiscite there, which went against the Yugoslavs. The Slovenes of that province were dominated economically and culturally: they felt that the partition of Carinthia would have created material difficulties, and this, as well as the lack of compulsory military service in the new Austrian state, made a sufficient number of them vote Austrian for the scales to be tilted against Yugoslavia in October 1920.

There were yet other territorial issues. To Serbia's acquisitions in Macedonia as a result of the Balkan wars, the peace settlement made Bulgaria cede a little more territory with another 70,000 inhabitants of uncertain loyalties. The acquisition of Voyvodina from Hungary brought most of the Serbs of Hungary into the confines

[2] In Istria, generally, the towns were Italian in a Slav countryside, and the Rapallo settlement also left some 10,000 Italians in Yugoslavia. Trieste and Fiume had been developed as the trade outlets for Austria and Hungary respectively. In both ports the population, irrespective of ethnic origins or feelings, spoke Italian, which was the maritime language of the Habsburg Monarchy. In both, deprived of their natural hinterland, and faced with the competition of the Yugoslav Adriatic and the German North Sea ports, traffic was destined to decline sharply thereafter.

of the Yugoslav state, but many Magyars and Germans as well. The debate over the border with northern Albania had dragged on ever since the powers, after the Balkan wars, had undertaken to organize an Albanian state, and not until 1926 was a settlement achieved. It left nearly half a million Albanians on the Yugoslav side, in the Kosovo region, to which the Serbs were attached by deep historical roots, but in which the Turks had steadily encouraged Albanian settlement. Only the division of the former Hungarian Banat between Yugoslavia and Romania, although leaving many Serbs and Romanians on the wrong side, effectively put an end to contestation. When all was said and done, the Kingdom of the Serbs, Croats, and Slovenes extended over 247,500 square kilometres with some 12 million inhabitants (5·6 million Orthodox, 4·7 million Catholics, 1·3 million Moslems), of whom about 2 million were non-Yugoslav minorities (500,000 Germans, 470,000 Magyars, 440,000 Albanians, 230,000 Romanians, and others).

The new Yugoslav state was based on two revolutionary principles: 'The self-determination of peoples'; 'the land to those who till it'.[3] In some of the former Habsburg lands – the rich northern regions of Slovenia, Croatia-Slavonia, and Voyvodina – there were large private estates, owned to a large extent by German-Austrians and Magyars, while in Bosnia-Herzegovina and Dalmatia there were even remains of feudal relationships. Announced by the prince regent soon after unification, the general lines of an agrarian reform were set out in a preliminary decree of February 1919. Since the problem varied according to regions, the same measures could not be applied to the whole territory, but while specific legislation was being prepared to deal with each area, the principle was established that feudal rights and obligations were abolished, and large estates expropriated and divided. To administer the entire operation, a special ministry for the agrarian reform was set up. The delay gave landlords time to organize themselves and to bargain over compensation, and in certain regions the full legal settlement was not achieved until the early 1930s, but a tremendous amount of land changed hands throughout the former Austro-Hungarian territories as a result of the agrarian laws enacted during the following years.

In the northern provinces all agricultural estates above one hundred hectares were subject to redistribution to landless peasants, or peasants whose holdings were too small to support them. Landowners were compensated in state bonds, and all who obtained land were to repay the state over a period of thirty years – except for war veterans who had served with the Allies. Politically unavoidable,

[3] Stavrianos, op. cit., p. 593.

socially desirable, the reform in these regions turned out to be economically doubtful. The new holdings were too small, the new owners lacked both capital and experience of modern techniques. Many large estates had been economic units with processing industries, and their break-up caused a drop in labour demand in the very areas where labour supply was excessive because there was not enough expropriated land to go round.

In Bosnia-Herzegovina, the problem was rather one of transferring legal ownership of the land to peasants who already lived on it, by releasing them from feudal obligations, and the reform there had an immediate positive effect on agricultural production. In Dalmatia too, the basic principle was followed that the peasant should become the owner of the land he had tilled as a quasi-serf, and compensation was mostly paid by the state.

Because of the losses in population, much of the better lands of south Serbia and Macedonia were thinly inhabited, and only in these parts was the available land – expropriated from Moslem estate-owners, Turkish or Albanian – more than sufficient locally. Legislation provided for colonization, along with an extensive programme of reclamation, and land-hungry peasants from the barren mountainous regions of Montenegro and Herzegovina began to pour in, thus initiating a timid reversal of the old Ottoman policy which had favoured the expansion of Moslem Albanians into the plains of Kosovo and Metohiya and into the Morava-Vardar corridor. Up to 1936, almost 2·5 million hectares had been redistributed to more than 630,000 peasant families[4] – over a quarter of all the arable land, to more than a quarter of the total number of peasant families in Yugoslavia.[5] The chief difficulty, after the reform, was to lie in the relative overpopulation and the extreme fragmentation of rural property; but an end had been put to the contrast between the small peasant holdings of Serbia and Montenegro,[6] and the large estates of the former Habsburg provinces.

The task facing the new state did not consist solely in trying to leave outside its borders as few Yugoslavs as possible and to carry out an agrarian reform, so as to make the land of the Serbs, Croats, and Slovenes theirs both to live in and to own. It was also one of fusing the various sections into a single political and economic unit. There were not only several land systems, but also several fiscal

[4] *La Yougoslavie par les chiffres, 1937*, Bureau central de presse, Belgrade, p. 44.

[5] Stavrianos, op. cit., p. 620.

[6] In both, small holdings were already the rule. In Serbia, half the holdings were under 5 hectares, and more than 96% under 60. The few larger holdings belonged to co-operatives (B. McCown, 'Agriculture', in R. Kerner (ed.): *Yugoslavia*, Berkeley, 1949, p. 151).

systems, several legal systems, several transport networks. The government was beset with the double task of reconstruction and integration, of coping with the man-made differences which had, over the centuries, been added to the natural barriers, without always coinciding with them. For if the old kingdom of Serbia was more advanced socially, and the richer of the former Austro-Hungarian provinces were further ahead economically, some of the poorest regions were also in the Habsburg Monarchy. And these tasks were to be carried out with a national illiteracy rate which amounted to 51 per cent at the beginning,[7] and had gone down to only 40 per cent at the end, of the inter-war period.

The current towards unification, though an overwhelming one, was full of contradictions. At the very moment of revolution, when historical legalism was losing all significance, the representatives of an increasing number of Yugoslavs from the Dual Monarchy appeared to be torn between reliance on the principle of self-determination and insistence on the continued existence of their historical units. This was because they were torn between their faith in some form of Yugoslav unity, and their increased distrust of the tremendous moral capital and psychological strength of Serbia with its state institutions, its prestige as partner of the Allies in victory, and its standing as exclusive protector against the threat of Italian expansion. A conflict at once arose on the conception around which to build the united Yugoslav state, and two historical experiences were confronted: that of the Serbian and that of the Croatian political traditions. The Serbian leaders viewed the state through the vision of their people's liberation struggle against the Turks, to which they assimilated the liberation from Habsburg rule. At each successive stage in this struggle, more territory with kindred population had been liberated and integrated into the existing unifying, centralized state structure which had given strength to Serbia. According to this vision, the Yugoslav state was just the final stage in the process of liberation and unification.

The Croatian leaders, on the other hand, viewed it through the experience of the autonomous Croatian realm and its historical rights, the struggle for which, however legalistic, had managed to keep it in existence as a frame for development through centuries of Habsburg rule and right up to the final unification with the other Yugoslav lands. For half a century, since 1868, they had practised the cunning of bargaining, and they now came to desire a Yugoslav structure which, in order to balance an enlarged and strengthened Serbia, would allow for an enlarged and strengthened Croatia. If

[7] With huge variations, from 8·8% in Slovenia, to 80·5% in Bosnia-Herzegovina and 83·8% in Macedonia (Yugoslav census, 1921).

the Serbian vision focused strictly on centralism, the Croatian knew only of dualism, and envisaged the new state as a better dualistic system which would improve Croatia's old position. To accommodate the Yugoslav diversity and smooth the process of integration, federalism might have been the best answer, and the magic of federalism was indeed invoked by many. Federalism, however, was alien to the political traditions of the Yugoslavs, and the basic contest for the organization of the unified state, whatever the words used, was not so much one between unitarism and federalism, as one between unitarism and dualism.[8]

The continued territorial crisis with Italy postponed general elections for a Constituent Assembly, and, for a while, a confused constitutional situation prevailed. A central combined authority was nevertheless gradually established. After the assumption of authority by the regent, and lengthy discussions as to its composition, a common cabinet was formed on 20 December 1918, representing all major political groups and all provinces. The National Council in Zagreb, however, did not dissolve until a week later, and the Serbian National Assembly met once again to acclaim the act of union, while temporary provincial executives continued to function for a while, until a provisional pre-parliament was summoned for March 1919, to give the government representational backing and prepare for the Constituent Assembly. This Provisional National Representation was made up of delegates chosen by the Serbian parliament, the National Council, and other regional representative bodies in proportion to the population and the strength of the parties. No attempt was made by the transitional régime to settle litigious questions, yet the assumption of authority by the regent, the formation of a common cabinet, and the gathering of a provisional parliament did begin a process of tightening up the institutional framework. Further, the Constituent Assembly was not elected until the frontiers of the new state, along with its unitary character from an international standpoint, had been established by the peace treaties, and thus accepted as part of the public law of Europe.

On the eve of the first general elections, some forty political groups were in activity, most of them regional. Some were representative of individuals rather than of well defined social, religious, or ethnic groups. Others tended to represent such groups, but limited themselves to the defence of their interests. Others, finally, aimed at reorientating society around a new ideology, and often, to confuse later analysts, political groups belonged to more than one such category.

[8] M. Graham, 'Constitutional Development, 1914–1941', in Kerner (ed.): op cit., p. 119.

In Croatia, those who had helped to create the new state belonged to the traditional parties which, because of the limited pre-war electorate, represented the middle classes and the intelligentsia. The main parts had been played by men who believed in the intrinsic ethnic unity of Croats and Serbs. They were interested less in the actual state of facts, and more in moulding these to fit their model. They had little contact with the masses, and had come to accept the centralizing trend. The movement for unification was too strong for anyone to stand up against, but outside the traditional political spectrum stood the Frankists, who rejected the principle of a unitarist monarchy proclaimed without reference to electorates or parliaments, and the Peasant Party, which wanted Croatia to retain its identity as a 'peasant republic' within the Yugoslav community. Whereas the once pro-Habsburg Frankists were a reactionary force, the Croatian Peasant Party, which had stood little chance before the war, was to come into its own as soon as the Croatian peasant masses were enfranchised in Yugoslavia.

This was a party which voiced the aspirations of the Croatian peasantry, sick of fighting for and being administered by a ruler and a government in a distant capital. Its leader, Stjepan Radich, a believer in South Slav brotherhood, was suspicious of the Serbian state machinery and, although no separatist, he intended to insist on Croatia keeping its separate identity in order to carry out within it the social aims of his party. For this reason, he had protested against the proclamation of unification by the prince regent of Serbia rather than by a constituent assembly, and refused the two seats his party had been assigned in the provisional parliament. To face this rising tide, the old Croatian political groups formerly in the Croato-Serbian Coalition gathered together in a new Croatian Union.

In Slovenia, the clerical People's Party still represented the majority. Fearful of bolshevism, though socially quite progressive, it dominated the countryside, while smaller anti-clerical Liberal and Social Democratic groups represented respectively the intelligentsia and the workers in the towns. In the former Habsburg territories, Social Democrats were generally reformist. They had co-operated with other parties at the time of unification, and were represented both in the common government and in the provisional parliament. More radical, the Serbian Social Democrats had refused to take part in the work of the pre-parliament and generally opposed co-operation with the 'bourgeois' parties. It was they who had taken the initiative in unifying Marxist forces, and by June 1919, centre and left-wing socialists were united in a 'Socialist Workers' Party of Yugoslavia (Communist)' which joined the Communist International.

Soon after, the Comintern called a general strike throughout Europe in protest against Allied intervention in Russia and Hungary. This had a remarkable echo in Yugoslav industries in July, and there was another wave of strikes in the summer of 1920. The government, however, did not lose control of the situation, and the Serbian Marxist centrists began having second thoughts about the wisdom of the new party's line of action. They argued that, in spite of the post-war difficulties, a revolutionary situation did not exist in Yugoslavia, and that it would be better to concentrate on reforms to improve the lot of workers and peasants. The Communist Left genuinely believed the Soviet model was the answer to Yugoslavia's problems, and in June 1920 a party congress adopted a programme calling for a social revolution, the dictatorship of the proletariat, and the establishment of a Soviet republic. Soon after the elections the centrists were expelled, and in 1921 they combined with most of the Social Democrats to form the Socialist Party of Yugoslavia. By the time of the general elections, a Communist network of party and trade union organizations was already established throughout the country. Local elections held in 1920, before the general elections, clearly showed the appeal of the new party. The Communists obtained a majority in many towns, including Zagreb and Belgrade. In the regions where there were no specifically peasant parties and in the towns, the absence of a major opposition party enabled the Communists to focus all forms of discontent and exploit the chaotic state of the economy.

In Bosnia and Herzegovina, the Yugoslav Moslem Organization was formed to defend both the religious and cultural interests of the Moslems generally, and the economic interests of the Moslem landlords in particular, while a new Serbian Agrarian Party made appreciable progress especially among the poorer Serbian peasantry of these provinces.

The most interesting of the new political formations was undoubtedly the Democratic Party. Early in 1919, the small Serbian opposition groups of the urban intelligentsia combined with the dissident younger Radicals and, together with the main party of the Habsburg Serbs, other elements of the Croato-Serbian Coalition, and Slovenian Liberals, merged into the first party to represent Yugoslavs of all parts of the state. Its programme rejected religious, provincial, and sectional interests as the basis for either political action or administrative divisions. Unitarists and centralists, advocates of strict parliamentary liberalism and social progress, the Democrats called for a centralized state and an immediate land reform, to level out political and social differences.

The old Serbian Radical Party remained a major force. Ever since

1903 it had gradually become less radical and more conservative, a process accelerated after 1918. In spite of this, and in spite of the secession of its more progressive wing, not only did the prestige of its leader, Nikola Pashich, and the efficiency of its party machine enable it to retain its hold over the peasantry of Serbia, but also it attracted a large proportion of the Serbs of the former Habsburg provinces. Radicals and Democrats were the two largest parties in the country and in the provisional parliament, but neither could command an absolute majority. In the end, their common centralism got the better of their rivalry, and they coalesced to enact an electoral law based on proportional representation and universal male suffrage, and to hold the first general elections – after almost two years, and six cabinets, had elapsed since the day of unification.

In the elections for the Constituent Assembly, held on 28 November 1919, 65 per cent of the electorate went to the polls to elect 419 deputies. Democrats and Radicals were confirmed as the major parties, polling respectively 19·9 per cent and 17 per cent of the votes cast, and winning 92 and 91 seats. The two major newcomers to the parliamentary stage were the Croatian Peasants and the Communists. The Croatian Peasant Party won 50 seats with 14·3 per cent of the votes. Expressing itself for the first time, the majority of the Croatian peasantry voted for Radich's party, and the old Croatian groups were down to 6 seats. The Communist and the Democratic were the only parties with deputies from every province. With 58 seats and 12·4 per cent of the votes, the Communists had polled more than three times as many votes as they had party members, while the Social Democrats were down to ten deputies.

Generally speaking the Communist votes had been protest votes. Weakest in the more industrialized provinces of Slovenia, they had scored their greatest successes in Montenegro and Macedonia, the two least industrialized provinces, than in urban centres and frontier regions. In the countryside, the agrarian reform had satisfied the peasants to a certain extent, and they had mostly voted for parties which appealed to their democratic instincts, their own class interests, their religious or ethnic background. But in the towns, the disorganization of economic life provided an audience for the Communists. They also attracted the votes of the minority groups opposed to the newly created state and its tendencies, such as aliens who, especially on the borders, had lost their privileged positions, Macedonians who were dissatisfied at being Serbianized, or Montenegrins who were nostalgic at the loss of their independence and dynasty.

There was enough discontent in Yugoslavia to provide any opposition party with a certain amount of support, and both the

Croatian Peasant Party and the Communist Party were essentially parties – the one homogeneous, the other heterogeneous – opposed to the shape the new state seemed to be taking. Behind them numerically, Serbian Agrarians, Moslems, and clericals formed three middling groups of 25 to 40 seats.

Two series of events were to affect the opposition parties before the newly elected Constituent Assembly settled down to its task. The government having decided that the constitution would be passed by a majority of half the total number of deputies plus one, and not by a majority within each ethnic group, the Croatian Peasant Party resolved to boycott the Assembly. As for the Communists, about to add the strength of their parliamentary representation to their extra-parliamentary industrial action, they threatened to turn an existing coal-miners' strike into a general strike. Fearing their subversive potential generally, and more particularly the threat of a total disruption of fuel supplies on the threshold of winter, the government, on 30 November, took a series of temporary measures aimed at curbing subversive Communist activities. It ordered, pending the enactment of a constitution, the dissolution of Communist organizations, and forbade any form of propaganda calling for dictatorship, revolution, violence, or general strike. Communist deputies and local councillors, however, were not interfered with in the exercise of their functions. Although the provisional parliament had empowered the government to adopt legislative measures to deal with problems which could not be postponed until the Constituent Assembly met, doubts were expressed over the legality of these measures. They were thus put to and approved by the Constituent Assembly once it had met. Communist trade unions were soon allowed again.

The Constituent Assembly met for the first time on 12 December, with only 342 out of its 419 elected members present. By that date, the division was no longer one between the two major parties of the old Radicals and the new Democrats, but one between the centralists and the anti-centralists. The Radical-Democratic coalition continued in office, the Serbian Radical leader Pashich returning to head the new cabinet.

Several constitutional drafts were tabled for the Assembly to consider. The government's proposal adapted the Serbian constitution, and brought it up to date by proclaiming the equality of all religions, and by incorporating progressive economic and social principles. Otherwise, the form of government was to be the Serbian monarchical one, with a parliament elected by adult male franchise through secret ballot. The crown was to have the right of dissolution and choose the prime minister who, in turn, was to have the confidence of parliament. The country was to be divided into French-style departments with delegated powers.

There was no unity between the other drafts. The tiny Republican Party put forward a republican one which gave the state less social duties than the government draft. The Socialists too submitted a republican draft, which gave the state a greater social role, and encouraged social ownership of the means of production. The Agrarians would have had a semi-presidential, semi-parliamentary system in monarchical dress, with regional autonomies. The drafts of the ethnic parties, Croatian or Slovenian, aimed at preventing the administration from being controlled by the largest group, the Serbian. Thus the clericals proposed a limited amount of regional autonomy to balance three regions with a Catholic majority against three with an Orthodox majority. The Croatian Union, disappointed with its electoral failure and the narrow centralism of the two major parties, now veered to a division of power between a federal government and regional governments. Finally, the absentee Croatian Peasant Party published a draft, not presented to the Assembly, which was little more than the rationalization of the pre-war status of the Yugoslav lands within a loose confederation.

The issue at stake between the Radical-Democratic bloc and the rest was not one of republicanism versus monarchism. The Radicals and Democrats were criticized rather for thinking that there could be no unity without centralism. Against this they argued that it was wrong to institutionalize the existing historical differences, and that in a democratic state, the play of parliamentary and local government would prevent the tyranny of any one group. The whole political development of the modern Serbian state had taken place in a centralistic mould, and Serbian politicians of the old kingdom mistrusted the very notion of federation, of which they had no experience, but they were not automatically averse to any measure whatever of regional autonomy. It was the Serbs of Austria-Hungary who, more than all the other Habsburg Slavs, had looked to Serbia as a unifying force with its successful state structure, and it was they, and their leader Stoyan Pribichevich, who insisted on rigid centralism, the more so since Radich's boycott and his toying with republicanism were interpreted as separatism.

By not taking part in the constituent work, Radich indeed made his movement appear as separatist, and weakened the case of the Croats in the Assembly. As for Pashich, the prime minister, he underestimated the nature of the Croatian opposition. He did not realize he was witnessing the beginning of a popular movement not unlike his own in the 1890s, and believed this was just another opposition group to be out-voted. Between the government side and the Croatian side, two men – one from each side – tried to bridge the gap. The Radical leader Stoyan Protich, who had been prime minister of the first common Yugoslav government, tabled a personal draft with limited regional decentralization, which took into account the existence of historic regions. The Croat Ante Trumbich, who had been president of the Yugoslav Committee, fearful of Radich's negative influence on the Croatian masses, tried to obtain a large measure of home rule with which he hoped later to defeat Radich in Croatia. Neither Protich nor Trumbich had the necessary following, and they failed.

It was Pribichevich who insisted on so much centralism being enshrined in the constitutional act itself. A believer in Yugoslav unity, he considered that constitutional instruments and legislation could do away with historic individualism. For Pashich, the main thing was to obtain a working constitution as quickly as possible. Since the Democrats were the Radicals' only possible allies, the prime minister could not have a constitution without Pribichevich, and Pashich played a larger part in getting the constitution through than in actually shaping it. Added to the Croatian Peasant deputies who had never come, all the Croatian Union, the clericals, and the Communists withdrew before the final vote, while Agrarians, Socialists, and Republicans let it be known that they would vote against the government draft. In order to make sure of the votes of the Moslem group, the government had to agree to concessions on the land reform: in Bosnia it would be implemented only gradually, and the principle of compensation would be extended to feudal rights as well.

In the final voting on the full and amended text, on 28 June 1921, 258 deputies out of 419 took part, and 223 voted in favour – Radicals and Democrats, with the Moslems and a handful of other Slovenes and Croats. The necessary majority, as fixed by the government, was 210, and the constitution was passed by a majority of twenty-seven, on the full strength of the Constituent Assembly, including the absentees. Viewed in retrospect, the constitution of 1921 of symbolized the triumph of the unitary, centralist, Serbian tradition over the Austro-Hungarian tradition of ethnic and constitutional complexity. It made few modifications to the constitutional structure inherited from Serbia, and established for the common state a democratic, parliamentary, centralized, monarchical form of government, while retaining the triple name of Kingdom of the Serbs, Croats, and Slovenes as a concession to Croatian feeling.

The parliamentary régime

The day after it had been accepted, the regent took the oath to the constitution. As he was returning from the ceremony, a bomb was thrown at his carriage, and missed him. Disappointed by the parliamentary opposition of their party leadership which had failed to stop the new state from consolidating itself, or the police from restricting Communist activities, some of the younger Communists turned to individual acts of terrorism during the summer of 1921. They aimed at the top. Less than a month after attempting the life of Prince Alexander, they turned on the 'father' of the anti-Communist regulations, the minister of home affairs, Drashkovich, and succeeded in fatally wounding him.

With these acts of terrorism, the public mood changed, and the government was able to pass legislation to curb the subversive activities of the Communist Party. In August it enacted a law for the protection of public security and order. Heavy penalties were imposed for inciting to terrorism and disturbance of public order, for advocating changes by violence, and for being linked with persons or organizations abroad in order to obtain support for such activities. The Assembly annulled the mandates of Communist deputies and local councillors. By 1922, according to Comintern estimates, the Communist Party of Yugoslavia had almost ceased to exist, and that mainly because of its intrinsic shortcomings. Its internal development had not followed its external growth, nor indeed had the party consciousness of its members, and it was unable to resist persecution or fragmentation. Outlawed and no longer able to serve as a channel for non-party discontent, communism lost much of its popular support, as well as many of its adherents. Driven underground or abroad, the Communist Party of Yugoslavia entered an esoteric phase of factional disputes.

It was under such not altogether favourable auguries that the post-war parliamentary system began to function. The multiplicity and the diversity of parties represented spelt government by unstable coalition, with a fair amount of royal moderative power, especially as this was exercised by a man of the standing of Prince Alexander, the regent, who formally succeeded his ailing father to the throne on King Peter's death, 16 July 1921.

The Communists had overreached themselves in their opposition to the foundations of the Yugoslav state, yet the constitution of 1921, though voted into being by a majority, was unacceptable to or disapproved of by many others. That same summer, in August, the smaller Croatian groups joined the Croatian Peasant Party in a common Croatian Bloc to strengthen what had now become the

Croatian case for a federal union of Croatia with the other Yugoslav lands. The fact that Pashich's Radical-Democratic-Moslem government ignored this question, pretending that it had been solved by the constitution, and went on to implement a centralistic structure even down to administrative territorial divisions, caused great disappointment among the Croats. They felt particularly bitter against Pribichevich, Drashkovich's successor at the home ministry and the driving force behind the policy.

On the one hand, there was the government, under the Serbian Radical leader Pashich – an old-time politician and past master in parliamentary manoeuvre, seconded by Pribichevich – considering that the constitution had settled once and for all for centralism, and insisting on implementing it administratively in order to iron out whatever differences remained within the framework. On the other there was the Croatian Bloc, under the Croatian Peasant leader Radich – a brilliant organizer and generous demagogue, endowed with a deep social conscience and given to unpredictable behaviour – feeling increasingly frustrated. Part of the Democratic leadership began to see the need to find a third way between boycott and intransigence, and initiated the two congresses of intellectuals held, one in June 1922 at Sarayevo, the other at Zagreb in October. These meetings discussed the political situation openly and without prejudice, apportioned the blame to both government and Croatian opposition, and called on the state to use a policy of cultural unification and decentralized administration to overcome existing differences. The congresses led to feelers being put out between certain elements in both the Croatian Peasant and the Democratic Parties, to the disgust of many others in their respective parties and coalitions.

The net result was that Democrats and Radicals parted company in December 1922, and that Pashich formed a Radical-Moslem government and obtained a dissolution. The proportional principle, according to which the constituent elections had been held, had since been altered in an effort to reduce the number of parties represented in parliament, and the general elections of March 1923 were held on the issue: for or against a revision of the constitution. Broadly speaking, the Serbian masses wanted to keep it as it was, the Croatian masses wanted to revise it, and the electorate voted for the sectional parties – the Serbs for the Radicals and the Croats for the Peasants. Whereas proportional representation had favoured the Democrats, whose voters were more scattered, they were now down to fifty-one deputies out of 312, with roughly the same number of votes as before. The Radical and the Croatian Peasant emerged as the major parties, the former with 108 seats (25·8 per cent of the votes), the latter with seventy (21·8 per cent).⁹ Far from solving anything, the elections had hardened the existing differences.

After the elections, the Croatian Peasant Party tried to rally Slovenes and Moslems against centralism, and serious strains began to appear in the Democratic Party. While the majority under Davidovich now definitely wanted to meet the Croats halfway, the minority under Pribichevich were opposed to any tampering with the centralist constitutional set-up. Both the Croatian Peasant and the Radical leaderships looked round for allies, and, in order to prevent a coalition from rallying around Radich, Pashich, as leader of the Serbian majority party, tried to come to an agreement with the Croatian majority party. In April, Radicals and Croatian Peasants concluded what amounted to an armistice: the government would not go ahead with the administrative division of the territory, while talks would continue; at the same time, the Croatian Peasant Party would stay away from parliament. This made it easier for Pashich to obtain a majority, and he formed a purely Radical government in May. Once again, he had used his skill to keep the government in office rather than to attempt to find an answer to the problems at stake. Disappointed by this approach, Radich decided to go abroad and attempt to rouse foreign support. In July, after publicly denouncing the dynasty, the constitution, and the government, he went into voluntary exile in Vienna. He then visited London and Paris, where he was advised to fight his battle in parliament in Belgrade. Consequently he instructed his party to try and come to an agreement with the opposition in parliament, while he waited in Vienna.

Gradually, the deputies of Radich's party began to arrive in Belgrade, submit their mandates for verification by parliament, and establish contacts with the opposition. If the opposition united, it could outvote the Radicals. In March 1924, Pashich resigned but the king refused to grant him a dissolution. He was able to reconstruct a cabinet because Pribichevich and a group of Democratic deputies seceded from the party and passed to the government. Unwilling to consider any compromise solution with the Croatian Peasant Party, they founded the Independent Democratic Party. Pribichevich and three of his friends joined the cabinet. This reinforcement did not offer a long respite, for by the end of May all the deputies of the

⁹ The Moslem Organization and the Slovenian Populists kept their forces. The other Croatian parties had vanished. The Serbian Agrarians were down to 2 seats, and so were the Socialists. The Communists had formed a legal Independent Workers' Party, which obtained 24,000 votes but won no seat. There was a 73% poll. (All election results are given according to the official statistical analyses published by parliament after every general election.)

Croatian Peasant Party – except for Radich and one of his assistants, who were still abroad – had duly taken their seats. The king persisted in refusing to dissolve, and Pashich was reduced to adjourning parliament until the autumn. In order to put pressure on Belgrade political circles, Radich tried another manoeuvre. If going to London and Paris had not impressed them, perhaps going to Moscow would: so this he did in the summer. Meanwhile, in Belgrade, Democrats, Moslems, Slovenes, and Agrarians, united around Davidovich, and supported by the Croatian Peasant Party, clamoured for parliament to be recalled. Failing yet again to obtain a dissolution, Pashich resigned in July.

King Alexander called for Davidovich[10] who formed a cabinet of Democrats, Moslems, and Slovenes, and asked the Croatian Peasant Party to give him its support, pending an agreement on the administrative organization of the state which could bring it into the government. Radich returned to Zagreb, and his party decided to take Davidovich's outstretched hand. Neither the Croatian leader nor the king, however, was enthusiastic about Davidovich. Radich soon disturbed the precarious equilibrium being established around the new prime minister by explosive speeches. In one of these, he sharply attacked the army and the army minister who, by tradition, was a general. The incumbent handed in his resignation, and the king asked Davidovich to step aside so that an all-party cabinet could deal with the situation. Davidovich resigned after a hundred days in office and, as Radich thundered against the sovereign and the dynasty, King Alexander turned to Pashich again, granting a dissolution with new elections for February 1925.

Radich's stay in Moscow coincided with the fifth congress of the Comintern, which had come out in favour of a break-up of the Yugoslav state and was thus, at that particular moment, out to woo both the Croatian opposition and the revolutionaries of I.M.R.O., the Internal Macedonian Revolutionary Organization. The Croatian Peasant leader had been given a good reception by a government not yet recognized by Yugoslavia; moreover, he had been talked into affiliating his party to the Comintern-controlled Peasant International. This operation of political blackmail went wrong, however, for it created the impression not only that Radich was some sort of an agrarian bolshevik, but also that he was conspiring with the enemies of the Yugoslav state. Back home after the emergence of a new governing team had seemed to indicate that things had finally begun to move in the right direction, he contributed, by his

[10] Ljubomir Davidovich, who had brought the secessionist Radicals of Serbia into the Democratic Party, had been prime minister once before, in the transitional period, from August 1919 to February 1920.

exaggerated motions, to bringing Davidovich down and had to face Pashich and Pribichevich again.

Pribichevich believed that Croatian obstructionism could and should be broken by determined action, and Pashich thought it sound electoral tactics to discredit Radich and his party by branding them as crypto-Communists. The new Pashich-Pribichevich cabinet decided to apply the law for the protection of security and order to the Croatian Peasant Party as linked to the Comintern. In December 1924, the Croatian Peasant leaders were arrested, and judicial proceedings were initiated against them.[11] Davidovich's Opposition Bloc and the Croatian Peasant Party concerted for common action, the latter, under the threat of dissolution, being careful to withhold fire against the constitution and the dynasty.

For the first time, the government parties attempted to use their control of the state machinery to try and improve their chances with the electorate, but it was difficult in a democratic system to press hard on universal suffrage, the more so since public interest in these elections was great. The Croatian Peasant Party, with sixty-seven deputies returned, had lost only three seats, but the Democrats were down to thirty-six. The total number of votes cast for the government parties was only 300,000 above that of all the other parties together, but the Radicals, with 142 deputies out of 313, and their twenty-two Independent Democratic allies, commanded an absolute majority even if the Croatian Peasants came and coalesced with all the other parties in the new parliament.[12] By going to Moscow, Radich had weakened his potential allies and strengthened the government parties, although his opponents had not been able to weaken his own party.

All the same, the Croatian Peasant Party and the other opposition parties agreed in March 1925 to form a common opposition alliance based on the programme of Davidovich's government. Radich's spokesman in parliament went so far as to state that his party acknowledged the constitution and the dynasty as facts, that their desire for regional autonomies was not incompatible with the unity of the state or the ideal ethnic unity of its inhabitants, and that they rejected any links with Moscow. Radich, though in custody, freely received visitors, and the biggest surprise was yet to come. Parallel

[11] Machek claims in his memoirs (Maček, *In the Struggle for Freedom*, New York, 1957, p. 102) that the king had unsuccessfully urged the Davidovich administration to have Radich arrested.

[12] Moslems and Slovenian clericals, once again, roughly kept their numbers. Agrarians doubled their representation to four. The Socialists, with 23,000, and the Independent Workers' Party (Communist), with 16,000 votes, obtained no seats. Of the registered voters, 76·9% had gone to the polls. The courts had accepted the validity of the Croatian Peasant Party lists.

negotiations had been going on between him and Pashich, and their bargain, announced in July, had the effect of a high-explosive detonation: the Croatian Peasant Party gave up its opposition and joined forces with the Radicals, apparently dropping all the political side of its programme. On 18 July, Pashich formed a new administration which included four Croatian Peasant ministers. Proceedings against the party and its leadership were dropped. Radich was freed and received in audience by the king. In November, he personally joined the government as minister of education. The Independent Democrats were furious and turned against the Radicals, but in the country at large, and abroad as well, the alliance of the largest Serbian and of the largest Croatian parties, commanding a majority of more than fifty in parliament, was welcomed with relief. Tension dropped, and when King Alexander went to Zagreb in August for the millennium celebrations of the Croatian realm, he was received with enthusiasm.

Team-work between the two parties in government was not easy. Prime minister for the first time in 1889, and then for the best part of the twenty-three years since 1903, in Serbia and later in Yugoslavia, Nikola Pashich, the Radical leader, was fast approaching the end of his career. The Yugoslav historian Slobodan Yovanovich has remarked[13] that the united state in the twenties needed at its helm either a Yugoslav prophet who could have transmitted his faith to both Serbs and Croats, or a constructive statesman who could have reduced the differences between the two in a compromise geared to the interests of the common state. Pashich was neither. In his youth he had been a true Balkan revolutionary; in his prime, a great party leader, an able diplomatist, and a skilled parliamentarian. After half a century in politics, he remained a legendary figure in whom the Serbian peasantry saw the main architect of unification. To most other people, however, he appeared to have become little more than an opportunist whose only aim was to remain in power. His policy of bargaining with individual groups for the continued existence of a government based on shifting coalitions seemed to further neither the consciousness of national unity nor the higher interests of the state.

The biggest capitalist in Yugoslavia was the state and, as is often the case in underdeveloped countries, private capitalism was naturally closely associated with the state. Around the ageing leader there were people who wanted to use his authority to grow rich at the expense of the state. In March 1926, a corruption scandal broke out in which Pashich's son was implicated, and the eighty-year-old prime minister had to resign. He was to die before the year was out.

[13] S. Jovanović, *Moji savremenici*, Windsor, Ont., 1962, p. 190.

Radich's co-operation with Pashich had been somewhat erratic. As a minister, he had joined in the accusations levelled by the opposition against Pashich's son.

Uzunovich, another Radical, took over as prime minister. But the party too was growing old and increasingly divided. Many Radicals were bitter towards the Croatian Peasant Party for the humiliation imposed on their old leader, especially since Croatian deputies participated in the opposition campaign against Pashich and his party, even to the extent of voting against the government which included their leaders. This forced Uzunovich to deal with several crises and reconstruct his cabinet more than once. Local elections, held over the winter of 1926–27, showed that the divided Radicals had lost some popular support. There were complaints in parliament of irregularities at the polls, and the Croatian Peasant Party decided to break with the Radicals. In February, Uzunovich formed another administration with the Slovenian Populists, in exchange for the clericals becoming virtually the governing party in their own region, but their support could not make up for the opposition of Radich's party, and as the old problems of finding a government majority loomed up again, Uzunovich gave up in April 1927.

The king turned to Vukichevich, yet another Radical, and granted him a dissolution in the hope that a general election, to be held in September 1927, would clarify the political situation, which was confused. The new prime minister did not satisfy all of his own party, and the Democrats were divided, for and against his government. Out of the 315 seats, the Radicals lost thirty. They were down to 112, and they were not united. The Croatian Peasant Party, too, lost 6 seats, and was down to sixty-one, but the Democrats gained from the failure of the Radical-Croatian Peasant alliance, and with fifty-nine deputies, had almost caught up with the Radichists.[14] As the new parliament was opened, Radich performed his last somersault. In the summer of 1925, everyone had been surprised by Radich's acceptance of the centralistic constitution and by his alliance with the Radicals. Now came the shock of an even more sensational alliance. The arch-centralist Pribichevich suddenly turned federalist, and the Independent Democratic Party joined the Croatian Peasant Party in a Peasant-Democratic Coalition.

[14] Voting was down from 73% to 68%. The Independent Democratic group kept its number. The Agrarians made another leap to nine. The Socialist Party was back in parliament with one member, and another legal Communist group, the Workers' and Peasants' Republican Alliance, polled 43,000 votes.

Parliament met in an atmosphere heavy with strife and reproach. There were strong complaints of electoral irregularities, and they arose from many sides, including even the Radical. Vukichevich offered Radich a resumption of the Radical-Croatian alliance, but the Croatian leader would accept only if his new friends were brought in as well, which the Radical Party could not accept, and so it was with Moslems, Slovenes, and some Democrats that Vukichevich reorganized his government in February 1928. The Peasant-Democratic Coalition announced that it would fight the government mercilessly, and it did. Accusations of irregularities, corruption, and police brutality flared up. That year, parliament turned into an arena for verbal and gymnastic displays. Obstructionist tactics altered with fisticuffs. Insults, threats, and blows were exchanged in an alarming *crescendo* between Radicals, on the one hand, and deputies of the Peasant-Democratic bloc, on the other. More and more sittings were suspended because of disorders. While tension increased in parliament to breaking-point, extremist Frankists in Croatia talked openly of the need to break away, and Radich invited the king to step in, as arbiter, to appoint an extra-parliamentary government under a general, to make a clean sweep, and start afresh from scratch.

On 20 June, a debate in parliament turned into pandemonium, and a Radical member answered insults with revolver shots, killing two Croatian deputies on the spot and wounding three others, including Radich. King Alexander hurried to the Croatian leader's bedside. 'Now only the king and the people are left,' Radich is said to have stated, indicating that the parliamentary system had collapsed, and that the Croats desired a direct deal with the sovereign. He urged his deputy, Machek, to avert violence. Machek declared: 'There is no longer a constitution.' Public opinion was appalled. The eighty-three deputies of the Peasant-Democratic Coalition left Belgrade for Zagreb, refusing to attend parliament any longer, and demanding a dissolution. The Croatian Peasant Party rejected a state funeral for the deputies who had been killed, and even the condolences of the government. The funeral in Zagreb turned into a mass demonstration. Vukichevich resigned, and the king consulted party leaders for the formation of an all-party government. The opposition demanded immediate dissolution and constitutional revision, but Radicals and Democrats objected that it would aggravate the situation. So King Alexander attempted a compromise to satisfy both sides. General Hadjich, who had been minister of the army, tried to form an all-party government, without dissolution, and failed. In the end, the king decided to turn to the Slovenian Populist leader, Mgr Koroshets, a non-Serb and a

THE YUGOSLAV KINGDOM: 1919–41

Catholic, whose party was not controversial. He rallied Radicals and Democrats, Slovenes and Moslems, but the Peasant-Democratic Coalition stayed away in Zagreb and went on clamouring for new elections followed by a revision of the constitution.

On 8 August, Radich died from the consequences of his wound. A legend who had become the symbol of the Croats, his funeral was a national demonstration, and separatist feelings rose in Croatia. Radich's assassination was a tragedy. Backed as he had been by the Croatian masses, he had managed for a while to rally Slovenes and Moslems as well until it seemed as though he and the Democrats could have provided an alternative to the series of unstable Radical-led coalitions, and started a new chapter. By going to Moscow, he put his party in an impasse, destroyed the chances of a wide opposition coalition under Davidovich, and had to give in to the Radicals in order to extricate himself. The alliance with the Radicals, unnatural and shaky, did not, in spite of appearances, provide the solid basis the government needed, and its collapse made parliamentary rule virtually impossible. Radich's last opposition alliance with Pribichevich was even more unnatural. His death removed an influential leader who, however erratic, had been neither a fanatic nor a separatist. After the shots of June 1928, parliament no longer seemed a safe forum for the expression of sectional and political feelings. For five months, Koroshets tried to carry on in government, with the sensation that the parliamentary system was breaking down. In December, feeling that his government was leading nowhere, the Democrats withdrew their support in order to break the deadlock with the opposition in Zagreb, and Koroshets resigned.

The situation appeared desperate. The king again consulted the party leaders. What did the Croats want? he asked Machek, Radich's successor at the head of the Croatian Peasant Party. They had no desire to break away from Yugoslavia, Machek said, but they wanted a federal Yugoslavia. Both Machek and Pribichevich told the sovereign that the only way out was to change the structure of the state. The new Croatian leader advised that the whole procedure of new elections and constitutional revision should be carried out under the auspices of an extra-parliamentary government appointed by the king – perhaps with a general as prime minister. He also outlined his idea of a new federal organization in which common affairs would be limited to foreign policy, defence, customs, and currency. Democratic and Radical leaders would not accept this, arguing that it was tantamount to the old Austro-Hungarian dualism, although they were willing to discuss. To the king, Machek's demand that the army be divided according to the federated units, and not used outside them without the approval of the respective local legislatures, was particularly unacceptable.[15] Alexander was a soldier who did not really like politicians. After a decade of playing the political game, it seemed to him that political parties were threatening to destroy the work for which he and so many other people had fought. Genuinely patriotic, and assured of the support of the army, equally impatient of Serbian and Croatian particularism, dismayed by the sectional interests of parties, he had been thinking for some time of an extra-parliamentary solution. For months there had been talk of a government under a general. Authoritarian régimes had already appeared in the twenties in half a dozen countries of southern and eastern Europe. On 6 January 1929 King Alexander issued a proclamation: 'My sacred duty is to preserve by every means within my power the unity of the nation and of the state.' Party passions being such that no parliamentary solution to the crisis could guarantee this unity any longer, he was taking it upon himself to organize, in the shortest possible time, those institutions which would best correspond to the needs of the nation and of the state.

The first confused decade of unified Yugoslavia was over, and its political system had failed. In foreign policy, however, in the economy, and, last but not least, in culture,[16] the results had been more gratifying. For the first time in history, frontiers in that part of the world had been drawn up more or less according to the wishes of the population. This had been possible because of the power vacuum which had resulted from the collapse of the old imperial structures, and Yugoslavia's foreign policy was to secure the frontiers it had thus obtained. The Greek port of Salonika, as the natural outlet of the Morava-Vardar corridor, was of fundamental importance to Yugoslav trade, and in 1925 Yugoslavia obtained from Greece the lease of a free zone there. This was an arrangement between friendly neighbours, but other neighbours were less friendly. Hungary wanted to revise the frontier settlement, and so did Bulgaria, as the only Balkan country to have found itself on the

[15] Machek's version of his discussions with King Alexander is contained in his memoirs, op. cit., pp. 121 seqq.; the king's, in an article by Hamilton Fish Armstrong, 'After the Assassination of King Alexander', in *Foreign Affairs*. XIII/2, New York, January 1935, pp. 204 seqq. (more particularly 213–14).

[16] It is frustrating not to have the space to give some idea of the quality and variety of development in the arts and literature. For the sake of sampling some particularly interesting instances, mention should nevertheless be made of Ivan Meshtrovich (1882–1962), the Croatian shepherd who became one of the great sculptors of the century, and of the surrealist school of writers in Belgrade. Both incidentally also serve to illustrate the interaction between nationalism, politics, and arts. The bard of nationalism, Serbian, Yugoslav, and Croatian, Meshtrovich was the confidant of rulers and party leaders, while most of the surrealists were involved with communism, and a few of them were to become ambassadors, ministers, and generals.

losing side during the war. Italy intrigued in Albania, which further intensified Yugoslavia's already uneasy neighbourhood with the former in the northern Adriatic.

As early as November 1919 negotiations had begun that were to lead to the Little Entente between the three succession states of Austria-Hungary – Yugoslavia, Czechoslovakia, and Romania. Based on three separate bilateral alliances concluded in 1920 and 1921, the *entente* was intended to prevent Hungary from attempting forcibly to break up the peace settlement, and the Habsburgs from attempting a restoration, the two being considered as closely linked. In 1921 the former emperor-king, Charles, twice attempted a return to the Hungarian throne. The determined attitude of the succession states was the main reason for his failure, and the attempts were not repeated. At the same time, both Yugoslavia and its partners tried to make for themselves a place in the new European order and generally ensure peace in south-east Europe. France was the one power that stood firm on the territorial settlement of the peace treaties. To offset Italy's friendship with the revisionist states, and its steadily increasing stake in Albania, France had linked itself to the Little Entente partners. A Franco-Yugoslav treaty of friendship was concluded in November 1927, and Yugoslavia generally acted, in the field of international relations, with and through the League of Nations and its agencies.

In spite of the Rapallo settlement of November 1920, Italy remained the major danger, especially since Mussolini's rise to power in the autumn of 1922. Italy had done much to make life difficult for its new Adriatic neighbour. It had encouraged anti-Serbian feelings in Zagreb as well as anti-Croatian feelings in Belgrade, and was slowly building up a Balkan bridgehead in Albania. There was constant friction over the Free State of Fiume, until local Italian Fascists carried out a coup there in March 1922, and Italian troops were sent in again in September 1923. Yet Mussolini was careful not to push things too far, for he would not have wanted a war at that time with Yugoslavia, and France encouraged conciliation between the two Adriatic states, both of which it considered as possible allies against Germany. A new *modus vivendi* was reached in January 1924, when the Rome agreement gave Fiume to Italy. The following July, all pending economic and juridical questions were settled by the conventions of Nettuno.[17]

---

[17] The conventions of Nettuno were concluded by the Pashich administration, just before the Davidovich interlude. Later, Radich's opposition to the conventions which, he alleged, had yielded too much to Italy, long prevented their ratification. They were ratified only in November 1928, by the Koroshets government, after Radich's death.

Yugoslavia quickly put its economic house in order after the initial post-war chaos. The aim of the government's economic policy was to reinforce the country's political independence and its integration by strengthening its economy. Agriculture made a rapid recovery, but it had to provide a living for too many people.[18] Since the overwhelming majority of holdings were primarily still subsistence units worked with primitive methods, it was difficult to increase agricultural productivity. Net emigration overseas absorbed no more than 13 per cent of the total increase in population in that first decade,[19] and so the government sought to stimulate the development of industry. War reparations, of which Yugoslavia had secured its share of 5 per cent, were extremely useful, since they were mostly paid in capital goods, and were received in the years of greatest need. The state owned and operated telecommunications and railways, as well as many forests, mines, lumber-mills, spas, and sugar refineries, quite apart from the tobacco and salt monopolies. As such, it was the biggest capitalist, and could direct trends in the private sector. The government invested heavily in transport, in order to integrate the railway network, and in the state-owned industries. Since domestic capital was limited, it attracted foreign capital from friendly countries with favourable concessions. Its cautious financial policy enabled it to repay the war debts by the end of 1926, and the stabilization of the dinar in 1927 opened the door to an influx of foreign capital. Foreign investments did not solve the problem of rural overpopulation, but they did contribute to reducing its pressure. Last but not least, the government also aided industry with a high protective tariff, introduced in June 1925. From 1924 to 1926, Yugoslavia's trade balance was favourable, while the development of its mercantile marine and of its tourist industry were an appreciable aid to its balance of payments.

Improving economic conditions and the government's social legislation are additional reasons which help to explain why workers were disinclined to rally round any Communist-controlled movement.[20] And yet, in spite of this progress, miserable poverty – e.g.

---

[18] According to the census of 1931, 86% of the population was rural, and it is estimated that over 60% of the rural population was 'surplus', i.e. not really needed for the performance of agricultural work (Stavrianos, op. cit., p. 634).

[19] J. Tomasevich, 'Foreign Economic Relations, 1918–1941', in Kerner (ed.): op. cit., p. 181.

[20] Police persecution and the squabbles between Communists have already been mentioned. Although the Communist Party had been outlawed, the Communists did take part in both general and local elections throughout the twenties, and the returns of their legal organizations were disappointing. The Communist-controlled independent trade unions likewise attracted only

in the poorly endowed karst regions – co-existed with relatively favourable peasant incomes – in the northern plain regions or in Shumadiya.[21]

King Alexander's personal rule

On 6 January 1929, on the same day as he dispensed with parliament and the constitution, King Alexander appointed a new government and enacted two laws which established the foundations of the new régime. Thus an extra-parliamentary administration, presided over by a general, at last came into being, after having been talked of for so long. The general, however, was no national figure. Petar Zhivkovich, the new prime minister, had been commander of the King's Guard, and was known as the monarch's confidant. At the head of the government, he was simply the king's representative. Otherwise the composition of the cabinet reflected Alexander's desire for widely based support and advice. The ministers were all parliamentarians, many of them well-known party figures with experience of ministerial office. The king had wanted to gather representatives of all parties around him, and the members of General Zhivkovich's administration did truly come from all the major political groups represented in the last parliament, but only Mgr Koroshets, the outgoing premier, could claim to have joined the new government with his party's backing. All the others had joined as individuals and appointees of the king – not as party representatives, some of them in fact against their parties' wishes, others as outright dissidents.

Of the two enactments, one, the law on the royal power and the supreme administration of the state, was a short working statute for the royal dictatorship. It transferred legislative power to the crown, fusing it with the executive, the judiciary remaining nevertheless intact. The other law, that on the defence of the state, strengthened the anti-Communist legislation of 1921 and extended it to all activities directed against the new régime. Existing political parties were dissolved. Henceforth, parties based on regional, ethnic, or religious sectionalism were forbidden, as well as all parties advocating a change of the new set-up. The formation of new parties,

a small percentage of the workers and never had more than 30,000 members (I. Avakumović, *History of the Communist Party of Yugoslavia*, I, Aberdeen, 1964, p. 187).

[21] The estimated income per head of working population, in international units (an 'international unit' represents the amount of goods and service that could be purchased for $1 in the United States) over the period of 1925–30, was 330 in Yugoslavia (Stavrianos, op. cit., p. 601). This was well above some Balkan neighbours (Romania 243, Bulgaria 284), but far behind the industrialized countries of Europe (Czechoslovakia 455, Great Britain 1,069).

or the renewal of old ones, would have to be authorized. All existing elected local authorities were dissolved and replaced by new appointed ones.

The royal coup provoked no real protest. Machek issued a statement welcoming the repeal of the constitution, and the majority of the Croats probably subscribed to this as a first step towards meeting their wishes. The majority of Serbs also accepted the king's assumption of responsibility because they cherished the unity of the state. Thus, at first, the takeover was generally well received. The prestige of politicians had fallen rather low in the past year, and people were not sorry to have a respite from politics.[22]

No one considered the arrangements as permanent. They were announced as a temporary expedient to mark time until passions had subsided, and to create a sense of national unity, that being the only ideology behind them. By directing the minds of people away from party, religious, or regional differences towards a common patriotism, by stepping up at the same time the task of administrative and legal integration, the king proposed to provide more favourable conditions for true democracy. The statement issued by the government soon after its formation confirmed this. Its programme was to maintain order, to unify legislation, to strengthen finances, and to solve the country's economic problems.

No time was lost in implementing this programme. For the sake of security and order, what remained of legal Communist activity in the press and trade unions was suppressed. To prepare legislation, a Supreme Legislative Council of experts was instituted and got down to work rapidly. Thus within two months, a unified penal code was promulgated, as well as a code of penal procedure. School curricula were streamlined and public holidays made uniform throughout the country. All other flags were made to give way to the Yugoslav national colours, and the old Serbian regimental flags were laid up as historical exhibits in exchange for new Yugoslav flags. The Croatian and Slovenian *Sokol* societies (Slav patriotic gymnastic societies dating back to Austro-Hungarian days) were fused into a single national, government-backed Yugoslav *Sokol* organization. In October 1929, the administrative territorial division of the country was reorganized into nine geographical regions, thus recognizing the need for larger units, but at the same time breaking with the historical pattern.

In its effort to strengthen the Yugoslav economy, the government

---

[22] Abroad too, the coup was generally accepted by friends of Yugoslavia under the assumption that the only other possible course was dissolution. 'The maintenance of Yugoslav unity is a European interest,' wrote *The Times*, London, of 8 January 1929.

was initially helped by conditions of relative prosperity. The lack of capital had already, in pre-war Serbia, given impetus to the establishment of co-operative associations, and similar developments had occurred among Yugoslav smallholders in the different Habsburg lands. Since unification, co-operatives had multiplied, performing a variety of economic functions which their members were unable to perform individually, the most numerous being credit co-operatives. The state had encouraged this trend, and the new government now adopted measures to give it more efficient backing and to co-ordinate the co-operative movement. Other measures were taken in favour of the peasantry, notably the institution of a Chartered Agricultural Bank to provide credit on favourable terms. Successful efforts were made to educate farmers in the use of more modern techniques, better-quality seeds, and improved breeds of livestock. Diversification was encouraged, along with the production of intensive and speciality crops. The government was active in protecting and stimulating export outlets for agricultural commodities, and an Office of Foreign Trade was set up to develop and rationalize exports.

Such conditions, however, were very short-lived, for by 1927 the fall in world farm prices began to affect Yugoslavia, even before it was hit by the full effect of world depression. The fall in agricultural prices undermined the whole of its economy, since their level determined the purchasing power of the great majority of the population. Generally speaking the prices of Yugoslavia's exported goods (agricultural produce and raw materials) dropped more quickly than those of the manufactured goods imported, thus upsetting the trade balance. The steady profitable export of speciality crops depended in any case upon the tariff policies of the more industrial countries of Europe, and these in the 1930s began to turn to protectionism, reducing their imports of both agricultural produce and raw materials. The depression was also destined to bring emigration virtually to a halt, at a time when Yugoslavia's high rate of population increase had more than enabled it to make up for its war losses. The essential inflow of foreign capital continued as long as multilateral trade was based on free exchange, but by 1930, the withdrawal of short-term credits from Yugoslavia had started. In 1931, economic conditions generally began to deteriorate.

The régime claimed that it had saved the state. It had certainly dealt severely with expressions of particularism. The accelerated integration of administration and law, along with the efforts made to merge both Croatian and Serbian feelings into a common Yugoslav nationalism through the schools, the army, and the youth organizations, no doubt offered the possibility of long-range action on the coming generations. But separate historical traditions could not be eradicated overnight. Public opinion, because of a general feeling of wariness, had been at least tacitly willing to give King Alexander a chance, different sections expecting different things from a temporary suspension of parliamentary government.

The Croats had expected that it would usher in the solution to the 'Croatian question'. They had not expected a crash programme of Yugoslav nationalism artificially imposed from above. King Alexander's Yugoslavism appeared to them to be just a more efficient way of getting them to accept the Serbian style of centralism, or even Serbian hegemony over the common state. Far from strengthening the idea of the common state among the Croats, the royal dictatorship tended to have an opposite effect and to increase the emotional separation from Belgrade which Radich's death had caused.

In October 1928 the former Frankist member of parliament Ante Pavelich had published a manifesto in Zagreb calling for an independent Croatia. At the time of the royal coup, he had left the country, and soon after, he had been sentenced *in absentia* under the provisions of the law for the defence of the state. He soon became the symbol of a dissatisfied, desperate, and radical fringe of Croatian opinion. From abroad he began to organize the secret and revolutionary *Ustasha* (insurrectionary) movement, whose aim was to fight by all means for Croatian independence.

The Croatian separatists turned for support to Italy and Hungary – revisionist states that aspired to change the territorial settlement in the Balkans. Born as an outgrowth of the Frankist 'pure' Croatian trend, Ustashism developed as an extremist nationalist movement, increasingly totalitarian-inspired, and operated from abroad. Italy and Hungary gave shelter to Ustashas, and offered facilities for the training of specially picked terrorists. To Mussolini, Pavelich's movement was a weapon with which he could threaten Yugoslavia.

Although such extremism attracted but few supporters in Yugoslavia, the dissatisfaction on which it fed was widespread. The Croatian Peasant Party had also dispatched abroad one of Machek's deputies to make propaganda for Croatian autonomy. Cut off from parliamentary activity, it began to change its character from that of a party voicing the aspirations of the Croatian peasant masses through political democracy and social reforms within a South Slav federation, to one gradually more sensitive to the new mood of the urban classes in Croatia, interested more in the rights of the Croatian nation than in democracy and social progress. Many Serbs were alarmed by what appeared to them to be the negative attitude of the Croats towards the state, and in December 1929 Machek himself was arrested. At the trial, in which a very mixed bag was arraigned, Machek was accused of encouraging those who were advocating secession through terrorism, and acquitted.

Although 1930 passed off quietly, the revocation of the constitution of 1921 had not solved the Croatian question. Apart from the Croats, the Serbs too were disappointed. For the sake of what, to many Croats, appeared as a régime of Serbian hegemony, the Serbs had been made to give up much, and more particularly the political liberties gained after a struggle which had lasted three-quarters of a century, and which they had come to appreciate in the old kingdom during the decade preceding the First World War. The first political leader to turn publicly against the royal assumption of power had been Pribichevich, and he had been interned as early as May 1929.[23] To this political resentment among both Croats and Serbs was added in 1931 the economic crisis which made life difficult for all Yugoslavs.

Dictators who step in to save the situation with extra-parliamentary remedies rarely intend their intervention to be more than temporary, and they are always surprised to find that the problems do not vanish overnight with a wave of the wand of extraordinary powers. King Alexander was no exception. In the summer of 1931, he felt that his temporary exercise of non-constitutional rule had lasted too long, and yet he could not simply revert to the old order since he had not accomplished his aims. He really needed to keep most of his special powers, but under a legalized form, and with parliamentary endorsement. On 3 September 1931 he accordingly granted a new constitution. This was a far shorter document than that of 1921. It made no pretence to ideological motivations, included no new social creed,[24] and curtailed individual liberties. It instituted a bicameral parliament, made up of a Senate, partly elected by provincial colleges on the French model (comprising parliamentary deputies, provincial councillors, and mayors), partly appointed by the crown; and a National Assembly elected directly by universal male suffrage. The government, however, was responsible to the king alone, who appointed and dismissed ministers. The king was described as 'the guardian of the unity of the nation and

[23] In August 1931, because of ill-health and the intervention of friends in the Czechoslovak government, he was allowed to go abroad. He died in Prague in 1936.

[24] This could, in a way, be justified by the fact that much of the social programme of the 1921 statute had been carried out, and that there was no more need for constitutional commitments to measures which were being achieved by concerted treaty action, through Yugoslavia's participation in the International Labour Office and other League of Nations agencies.

of the integrity of the state'; his consent was needed to amend the constitution, and he was even authorized, under article 116, in exceptional cases, to enact provisional measures under emergency powers. All existing laws were upheld unless and until repealed or altered under the new legislative arrangements. A particularly sad deviation from what had become accepted as constitutional practice was the suspension, for five years, of the irremovability of judges – a precious heritage of the constitutional struggle in Serbia which even the royal dictatorship had not tampered with.

Once again, no one considered these arrangements final, but merely a first step towards further change. A week after the constitution, a new electoral law was enacted, and a general election announced for November. Designed to break down the former regional stratification of political life and to reduce the number of political groups, the electoral law of 1931 allowed only countrywide lists with at least sixty supporters registered in each electoral division. Voting was public, and the list heading the poll was to be entitled to two-thirds of the seats, the rest being divided in proportion among all the lists obtaining more than 50,000 votes – including the majority list.[25]

In such conditions, only one list was presented, the government's, headed by General Zhivkovich. The election was widely boycotted, with one-third of the registered voters not turning up at the polls. When the new parliament met, it gave the government blanket approval for all its work since 6 January 1929. A constitutional façade had been erected, and the king's government could continue with its task. In order to give it popular backing, to propagate its ideas, and to organize its supporters, a government party was formed in December 1931, with right-wing Radicals and dissidents, genuine or opportunist, from practically every section of the former political spectrum. The strong-general image was now out of place, and in April 1932 Zhivkovich was replaced at the head of the government by Marinkovich, a distinguished Democratic parliamentarian who had been in charge of foreign affairs in Davidovich's short-lived administration, and later under Vukichevich and Koroshets, before joining Zhivkovich's government in the same capacity in January 1929.

This was generally taken as an indication of King Alexander's intention to return to some sort of parliamentary practice. There was a relaxation of the political climate. The old party leaderships began to emerge again, to meet, and to talk. Two Croatian members of the government, former Croatian Peasant dissidents, even

[25] The provisions were inspired by, and actually improved on, Mussolini's electoral reform of 1923.

resigned because Croatian demands had not yet been satisfied. Marinkovich's aim was to introduce a milder course, gradually return to a more regular political life, bring in a more liberal electoral law, and, eventually, revise the constitution. He even considered federation. This was going too far for some cabinet ministers, for while the prime minister publicly aired the possibility of a referendum on the question of federation, perhaps in order to test public reactions, his home minister, the Radical Srshkich, had the Slovenian leader Koroshets interned as a warning to the former party leaders against going too far in their political comeback. Marinkovich resigned in July, after less than a hundred days in office, to be replaced by none other than Srshkich. The king, manifestly, was on the side of those who did not want to liberalize too quickly, and not too happy about mentioning federation at this stage. A few weeks after Marinkovich's resignation, the government party held its first congress, at which it adopted a definitive name, a statute, and a programme; henceforth it was the Yugoslav National Party, the party of unitarism and centralism.

When Machek and the leadership of the Croatian Peasant Party saw that there was no hope of an early revision of the constitution, they called a meeting with their Independent Democratic allies in Zagreb in November 1932 at which a manifesto was drawn up, calling for a return to 1918 and the elaboration, on the basis of popular sovereignty, of a new constitution to safeguard in association the interests of the three component Yugoslav groups. This, the first important political reaction since the royal coup, attracted over the winter expressions of at least partial sympathy from different quarters, including the Slovenian Populist leadership under Koroshets, who had since been released, and Davidovich's Democrats. At the same time, the Ustashas from abroad stepped up their propaganda denouncing Alexander's rule, calling for an independent Croatia, and instigating terrorism. In September 1932, bands had entered northern Dalmatia from the Italian enclave of Zara, and attempted to incite to rebellion the miserable peasantry of that barren region, particularly sensitive to the deterioration of the economic situation. Police repression was harsh, and was followed by bomb explosions in Zagreb in December. The following January, when Machek, in an interview with foreign journalists on the subject of the Zagreb manifesto, made statements against the royal dictatorship which were considered seditious, he was arrested again, charged under the law on the defence of the state, and sentenced this time, in April 1933, to three years' imprisonment.

The full effect of the world economic crisis hit Yugoslavia just at the time of the political unrest. The winter of 1931–32 was exceptionally severe, and followed by extensive floods. Bewildered by the collapse of their whole economy, the peasants found themselves unable to repay the debts contracted in more prosperous years. State intervention was imperative. In April 1932, the repayment of farmers' loans was postponed and temporarily transferred to the Chartered Agricultural Bank, which was to reimburse creditors at reduced rates. Initially introduced for six months only, the moratorium was eventually kept on until 1936. A banking crisis developed in the summer, and agricultural credit dried up almost completely. Stringent exchange controls had to be imposed that almost paralysed foreign trade, severing old business connexions and cutting off old sources of credit. Agricultural prices reached their lowest levels in 1933–34, and in spite of the deflationary policy by which the government tried desperately to save the currency, the Yugoslav dinar was depreciated by about a third before 1935.

Yugoslavia's trade pattern, furthermore, did not coincide with its diplomatic alignment. Italy was by far the major outlet for its exports, with Austria and Germany following.[26] All three were deficient in the raw materials and foodstuffs that Yugoslavia exported, and these could be shipped to them cheaply by river or sea. In return, they exported to Yugoslavia coke and manufactured products. Yugoslavia's Balkan neighbours had similar economies, and so there was little exchange between them, while France, in spite of its large capital investment in Yugoslavia, had little need of its raw materials.

Although the country's existing alliances had no solid economic foundation, King Alexander's government in no way changed them. On the contrary: in May 1929, the Little Entente states concluded a pact of arbitration and conciliation providing for peaceful adjustment of all their disputes, according to the model recently adopted by the League of Nations, and agreed to an automatic renewal of their treaties. In February 1933, in Geneva (as if to symbolize their close adherence to and co-operation within the League), they signed a formal pact of organization providing for permanent common institutions. By this time, their regional understanding seemed a stabilizing factor in the European balance. Yet Yugoslavia was on increasingly bad terms with Italy and Hungary, and in July 1933, France and Great Britain had joined Mussolini's Italy, and Germany – where Hitler had just obtained full powers – in a four-power agreement to co-operate on the maintenance of peace. This agreement, made without reference to the League, aroused distrust among

[26] In 1930, 57·7% of Yugoslavia's exports went to these three countries (Stavrianos, op. cit., p. 638).

the smaller powers. Preoccupied by this new departure, the Yugoslav government sought to find some greater measure of security and avert outside pressures in south-east Europe by linking the existing Little Entente with the other Balkan states.

Much progress had already been made towards a Balkan understanding. The depression and a certain measure of distrust towards the great powers had undoubtedly contributed. In 1929, Greece had agreed to enlarge the Yugoslav free zone in Salonika. In 1930, a series of unofficial Balkan conferences had started, which laid the basis for much useful social, economic, cultural, and technical co-operation, and paved the way for an official political understanding. In 1933, King Alexander thought that the moment had come to try and promote a political union.

Relations with Bulgaria were tricky, however. Bulgaria was revisionist, feeling sore about Macedonia. In the 1920s, I.M.R.O. bands, using Bulgarian territory as a basis for raids into Yugoslavia, had poisoned relations between Belgrade and Sofia. The Macedonian revolutionary organization had never been monolithic, and although its leadership at that time tended to be pro-Bulgarian, there was tension both between it and the government in Sofia, and between its different factions. Thus relations between Yugoslavia and Bulgaria had never reached breaking-point, and active co-operation had started up again through the Balkan conferences. A series of meetings between King Alexander of Yugoslavia and King Boris in the latter part of 1933 initiated a political *rapprochement*, which domestic events in Bulgaria were going to hasten. Five years after Yugoslavia, in Bulgaria too parliamentary rule was breaking down. Rumours of an I.M.R.O. coup against the government precipitated a counter-coup in May 1934 by army officers, with the backing of a group of politicians and intellectuals, which put an end to both parliamentary government and I.M.R.O. anarchy.

When, at the end of 1933, King Alexander went on a tour of the Balkan states, he found out that the Bulgars were reluctant to commit themselves to joining a formal alliance, which would have implied their giving up all hope of a revision of the territorial *status quo*. Thus, in February 1934, in Athens, Yugoslavia, Romania, Greece, and Turkey joined in a Balkan Entente, without Bulgaria, but with the hope that Bulgaria could be brought in at a later stage. The treaty provided for a mutual guarantee of the partners' frontiers against attack by any Balkan state, and for the co-ordination of their policies. In the autumn, permanent institutions were set up for the Balkan Entente, on the model of the Little Entente. Member countries immediately embarked on a broad programme of co-operation, putting into effect at government level the recommendations of the earlier conferences, and much positive work was accomplished in many fields. In spite of expectations, and of Yugoslavia's entreaties, Bulgaria remained outside, and so naturally did Albania. The Balkan Entente was thus turned from a union to resist foreign aggression into something approaching a pact to prevent Bulgaria from changing the peace settlement. As in the case of the Little Entente, no obligations were undertaken against any of the great powers, and the contracting parties limited themselves to their common interests. Thus, if all the Balkan countries had joined the pact, it could have effectively discouraged outside powers from manipulating them against each other. As it was, the pact seemed at times reduced to a common wish to prevent Bulgaria being encouraged to act against any of the others.

Both King Alexander and his foreign ministers – Marinkovich, followed by Yevtich – aimed at organizing a network gravitating towards France. The French link was obviously all-important, for only this link could hinder Mussolini's aims in the Adriatic and in the Balkans. Such a network, by balancing that gradually being constructed by Italy, would stabilize the situation and facilitate King Alexander's domestic task. France, on the other hand, was more particularly conscious of the rising strength of Nazi Germany and wanted to bring her East European allies and Italy together in a network of alliances designed to check Germany. Barthou, the French foreign minister, went to Belgrade in June 1934 and invited the king to pay a state visit to Paris. This would be a public manifestation of the Franco-Yugoslav alliance and an occasion for French and Yugoslav leaders to carry their discussions a stage further. King Alexander accepted, but before setting off for France, he went on a visit to Sofia, to keep up the Bulgarian link in spite of the fact that Bulgaria had not joined the Balkan Entente, and he was cordially received.

The king's efforts to strengthen his country's external security were obviously closely related to his attempts to consolidate Yugoslavia internally, and there is evidence that, whereas he considered his foreign policy to have been quite successful, he viewed his achievements at home with increasing pessimism. With the suppression of genuine parliamentary representation, the Serbian political parties, because they were parties of individual representation competing for the favours of the electorate, had begun to disintegrate once they had been cut off from their life source. The process of linking the Macedonians, or even the Serbs of the former Habsburg territories, to common institutions through parliamentary parties, had been stopped. On the other hand, that of turning the Croatian Peasant Party from a party of the Croatian peasant masses into a Croatian national movement had been accelerated. More than ever before, the Croats were united against centralism, whatever their views otherwise.

That King Alexander thought of changing course was first indicated in January 1934 by a change of prime minister. Srshkich, who had, after Marinkovich, returned to strong-arm methods that had not proved effective, was replaced by a former Radical prime minister, Uzunovich. The political atmosphere was at once relaxed, and before leaving for Sofia in September, the king contacted Machek and informed him that, as soon as he had returned from France, he would set him free and try to solve the Croatian problem by negotiating with him personally.[27] Because of his relative success in consolidating Yugoslavia's international position, because of indications of impending change, and also because he had become the only authority, the Ustashas decided to strike at King Alexander. In December 1933, a plot to kill him in Zagreb had been discovered, and the trial, in the following March, of those implicated revealed their links with both Pavelich and his Italian hosts.

On 9 October 1934, King Alexander landed at Marseilles on the first stage of his state visit to France. Soon after having set foot on French soil, he was shot dead by an Ustasha agent, along with Barthou who had come to welcome him on behalf of the French government.

Prince Paul's regency

By assassinating King Alexander (who was only forty-six at the time of his death), the Ustashas hoped to provoke a crisis in Yugoslavia, if not actually to break up both his kingdom and his alliances, yet the immediate effect was to unite more closely his subjects and his allies. The murder caused dismay all over the country. Most Serbs had respected their sovereign, even when they had been opposed to his methods of government. Most Croats had approved of his firm policy towards Italy. People everywhere had generally appreciated most of the practical results of his rule, even when they had disliked many of the particular things the king had set out to do single-handed. The grief with which the news was received was a sign that the majority of Yugoslavs recognized that Alexander had become a symbol of their unity and independence, and that he had been removed for that reason.

The constitution of 1931, personally tailored for King Alexander, survived him, although for the next six years it was to function without a monarch. Peter II, Alexander's son, was a child, and a council of regency was set up according to the constitution, its

[27] This is confirmed by several different sources, including Machek himself (op. cit., pp. 153–4).

members having been designated by the late king in his will: his first cousin Paul, and two distinguished though little-known figures.[28] Authority had really been conferred on Prince Paul who, for all practical purposes, was the only member of the royal family who could take over. There was little criticism of the choice of regents, and it was widely hoped that they would inaugurate a return to more representative government.[29] As it was, Uzunovich's cabinet was temporarily retained, reinforced by the inclusion of former prime ministers, until December, when a new administration, headed by Bogoljub Yevtich, who had been King Alexander's foreign minister, released Machek and other political prisoners, relaxed the censorship, and promised new elections.

Both the Little and the Balkan Ententes stood firm by Yugoslavia when it decided to bring a charge before the League of Nations against Italy and Hungary, of complicity in the king's assassination. Feeling ran high in Yugoslavia against the governments of these countries that had tolerated Ustasha activities on their territories, including the running of training camps for saboteurs and terrorists. The French and British governments, however, were anxious that Italy should not be embarrassed, for they needed Mussolini as a counterweight to the rising power of Germany. The Yugoslav government had officially asked the League of Nations for an investigation, but had as yet put forward no charges. Eventually it lodged a complaint against Hungary only. The British foreign secretary, Eden, and the new French foreign minister, Laval, worked out a compromise resolution, which was adopted. This denounced terrorism, and held that the Hungarian government had permitted the Ustashas to operate a training camp, thus facilitating the task for the conspirators. In January 1935, the Hungarian government replied that it had punished some junior officials who had not been vigilant enough with Yugoslav expatriates. The League of Nations took note, and the affair was ended. The Yugoslavs felt bitter and isolated, in spite of the support they had obtained from their Central and East European partners.[30]

[28] Radenko Stankovich, a Serb from Croatia, was an eminent physician, a university professor, and a former minister of education; Ivo Perovich, a Croat from Dalmatia, had been provincial governor in Zagreb.

[29] An appeal, drafted before King Alexander's death and for his benefit, was presented to the regents by leading Croatian personalities from the Church, the professions, the business world, and that of culture. It urged a general amnesty and free elections, and was supported by a similar appeal from the most eminent Serbian intellectuals, headed by the historian and constitutional expert Slobodan Yovanovich.

[30] A French court eventually tried and sentenced three of the conspirators to hard labour for life, and three more (including Pavelich, who continued to live in Italy) to death *in absentia*.

At home the regency had begun auspiciously, and it seems that its aim was gradually to liberalize the régime, while it continued the task of unifying the country. At the same time, Prince Paul believed a solution could be found within the existing constitutional framework. Quite apart from the formal argument that it could not be revised during a minority, the constitution did give the crown powers which must have seemed to him a necessary safeguard for the time being, when Yugoslavia's political structure was still so divided. Thus it was soon obvious, in spite of conciliatory gestures and the more lenient application of laws, that there would be no early drastic overhaul.

The position of the Yevtich administration was not a strong one. The country was tired of veiled authoritarianism and pseudo-representation. The worst had not happened after the murder in Marseilles, and the opposition was raising its head. Although they remained legally forbidden, political parties were now again tolerated within limits. There was some revival, too, of Communist fortunes. The Soviet government estimated that the break-up of Yugoslavia, which could have benefited Russia and communism in the twenties, would now benefit the right-wing totalitarian régimes. The new 'Popular Front' line against Nazism and Fascism coincided with the new political atmosphere in Yugoslavia. Growing emphasis was placed on agitation through legal organizations, and the depression aiding, the Communists succeeded in finding again some audience among the workers in large urban centres, the peasants of the more depressed provinces, and the students, making full use of the confused situation.

Yevtich hoped that he could strengthen support for the government at the elections fixed for May 1935. As the electoral law had been somewhat relaxed, Davidovich initiated a revival of his opposition coalition, in order to obtain a single opposition list which could fulfil the conditions of the law. Croatian Peasants and Independent Democrats, along with Democrats, Serbian Agrarians, and Moslems, presented a single United Opposition list headed by Machek. Whereas the opposition platform was limited to winning the election and reorganizing the state according to a subsequent all-party agreement, the government ran the election as a plebiscite for the dead king. Despite the open voting and much manipulation, the presence of an opposition list attracted 73·7 per cent of the voters to the polls, while it secured almost 37·4 per cent of the votes.[31]

[31] The electoral law had been revised in 1933; conditions for the establishment of countrywide lists were made easier, and the winning list obtained only three-fifths of the seats. This gave the opposition 67 seats out of 370. There were even two more lists, which did not attract enough votes to secure a single seat, that of the old Radicals, and that of Dimitiye Ljotich's Fascist-inspired *Zbor* (Rally) movement. Machek claims (op. cit., p. 160) that the

Encouraged by its performance, the opposition decided not to take up its seats in parliament, and to protest against the electoral law and administrative gerrymandering. It called for a neutral government to organize free elections under a new electoral law. When the newly elected parliament met in June without the opposition, more extreme members of the government attacked the boycotters intemperately. Croatian ministers, followed by some Serbs, resigned and Yevtich's cabinet disintegrated. Machek, as leader of the opposition, was consulted by the prince regent; he advised new elections, but Prince Paul had another plan.

As soon as it had become apparent that the elections had not really solved anything, the prince had asked Yevtich's minister of finance, Stoyadinovich, to survey the possibilities of forming a new government. Stoyadinovich, a former Radical, had built up his own following within the government party. He had approached leading Radicals, Slovenes, and Moslems, and accordingly submitted a memorandum to the prince regent on the organization of a new party which would effectively combine all pro-government elements and stand a better chance of obtaining the country's confidence. On this basis, a new cabinet could be formed which would seek the cooperation of the Croatian Peasant Party and introduce liberal reforms. The programme was an attractive one, and the regency officially invited Stoyadinovich to form a new administration.[32]

Stoyadinovich kept the foreign ministry for himself, brought the Slovenian and Moslem leaders, Koroshets and Spaho, back into the government, and appointed new men to the other ministries. The new government was accepted as one of reconciliation; it further relaxed censorship, amnestied some 10,000 political prisoners, and tolerated the activities of the parties, particularly the Croatian Peasant Party. Its immediate aim, however, was to succeed where Yevtich had failed – to give the government organized popular support. In August, a new government party was formed, the Yugoslav Radical Union, to unite Serbian Radicals, Slovenian Populists, and Moslems. Most of the deputies elected on Yevtich's ticket switched their allegiance to the new party, though a group of about ninety remained loyal to the former prime minister.

Slovenian Populists and the Radicals refrained from joining the opposition because they had been told that the official party would relinquish its monopoly of power after the elections, and bring them into a governing coalition.

[32] Sir Nevile Henderson, who was then British minister in Belgrade, claimed (*Water under the Bridges*, London, 1945, p. 172) that Stoyadinovich owed a good deal of the success of his political career to him, and Hugh Seton-Watson mentions (*Eastern Europe between the Wars, 1918–1941*, Cambridge, 1945, p. 232) Stoyadinovich's connexions with the British business world.

Since there were no signs of the return to true parliamentary government which the remains of the Radical leadership had been expecting, and with which they had hoped for a restoration of their party's fortunes, they too joined the opposition. This removed the Serbian foundation of Stoyadinovich's party and left it with only fragments of the Radical Party, mainly those that had previously joined Yevtich. When a congress of the Yugoslav Radical Union was held in July 1936, it went to the extent of declaring that it respected 'the three names of our nation', as well as their equality and their traditions. But that, with the toleration of the Croatian Peasant Party's activities, was all that Stoyadinovich had done towards 'solving the Croatian problem'. For the time being, and in spite of his failure with the Radicals, his skill in organizing a new government party enabled him to stay in office without having to make constitutional concessions to the Croatian Peasant Party or the Serbian party leaderships.

Croatian public opinion was even more disappointed than Serbian public opinion. The Peasant Party was worried by the radicalization of Croatian student youth and its response to Ustasha influence, with its cult of action, violence, and authority, its racial and religious nationalism. Machek was anxious to keep his hold over the Croatian masses, and worked on developing his party's organization to the point where it gradually came to extend its control over all aspects of national activity. The old Serbian party leaderships continued to co-operate with the Croatian party in opposition, for all shades of opinion agreed that a solution to the Croatian problem must be found before a crisis occurred in Europe which would place Yugoslavia, and all its components, in danger.

Machek kept up his contacts with the regency as well, and there were several meetings between Prince Paul and the Croatian leader, which, however, did not lead anywhere. Machek insisted on a new start in which a new constitution would be adopted by a new Constituent Assembly. Paul answered that he was bound by his oath to the existing constitution, argued that the opposition was by no means united on the nature and the extent of the constitutional revision, and asked if a solution could not be found without altering the constitution. On his initiative, a meeting even took place between Machek and Stoyadinovich, but the prime minister wanted the Croatian Peasant Party to join the government before any concessions could be envisaged. And so nothing was done by the government about the Croatian problem, while under cover of pseudo-parliamentarianism, Stoyadinovich's new course turned out to be one of building the Yugoslav Radical Union into his own ruling party. Stoyadinovich's 'leadership' was not what people had expected, and not likely to please either Croats or Serbs.

It was all the less likely since the foreign policy set-up inherited from King Alexander was becoming shaky. Franco-British policy had led, at the beginning of 1935, to closer links with Italy, which Mussolini had accepted in the hope of being allowed a free hand in Africa. The invasion of Ethiopia, in the autumn, showed that Yugoslavia's policy of relying on France and the League of Nations did not insure it adequately against the risk of aggression. Germany's restoration of permanent armed forces in March 1935, and its reoccupation of the Rhineland a year later, meant that France could not hope to give effective assistance to its East European allies, even if it were willing to do so. Yugoslavia co-operated wholeheartedly in the application of economic sanctions against Italy, voted by the League, but in view of France's eagerness for Italy's friendship and of Great Britain's ambivalent attitude, Stoyadinovich began to doubt the wisdom of denying Mussolini support in Africa. The Yugoslav economy was hard hit by the sanctions. The general staff had warned the government that the army was not strong enough to become involved in any action against Italy without adequate French support. Yugoslavia's regional alliances could not protect it against Italy, and France itself was still trying to eliminate friction between its two potential allies.

Italy had been Yugoslavia's best customer, but with the breakdown of the traditional trade pattern during the depression, German economic penetration began. The deliveries of technical equipment on account of war reparations in the twenties had been followed up by supplying the subsequent demand for renewals. Yugoslavia's trade balance with Germany had been negative until Hitler's advent, but in 1933 it became favourable, and remained so as a result of deliberate German policy. Germany was ready to buy Yugoslav (and, generally, Balkan) produce in large quantities and at high prices, in order to obtain the raw materials necessary for its rearmament, to develop the area as a market for German exports, and to obtain political influence. Trade agreements in 1933 and 1934 increased German purchases from Yugoslavia, at higher prices than those on the world market, and introduced exchange clearing as a method of payment. Germany then stepped into the breach caused by the loss of the Italian market, and in 1936 granted new preferential rates and quotas to Yugoslav exports, while the Yugoslav government placed considerable contracts for machinery in Germany.[33]

[33] Between 1932 and 1936, Yugoslav exports to Germany rose from 11·3 to 23·7%, and its imports from Germany from 17·1 to 26·7% (*La Yougoslavie par les chiffres*, 1937, pp. 74–5).

France and Great Britain were unable to buy more from Yugoslavia, and Yugoslavia lacked the foreign exchange to buy from them. In this way it came to depend upon Germany as its chief customer and supplier.[34] From a purely economic standpoint, the arrangements with Germany were advantageous: the prices of agricultural commodities began to rise again, and the currency to recover. Stoyadinovich's government was able to discard the deflationary monetary policies in favour of more elastic credit, reduce the land tax, and encourage speciality crops again. In October 1936, the pending question of the pre-1932 peasant debts was liquidated. They were transferred definitely to the Chartered Agricultural Bank – to whom they could be repaid over a twelve-year period, the smaller ones being reduced by half. Agricultural productivity increased, but nevertheless only in a very limited and relative way.[35]

The government also stimulated considerable industrial development, and Yugoslavia, with foreign capital investment (about 60 per cent of the capital invested in industry was foreign), was ahead of other Balkan states in industrialization. The country was well endowed with mineral resources which were still very much underexploited, and it was under Stoyadinovich's administration that the foundations of Yugoslavia's mining industries were laid. Textile industries advanced faster, for they required relatively low investments, and had a well protected domestic market. As for the agricultural industries, they naturally had the greatest output, although by 1936 the mining industries had already reached second rank in value.[36] As in the case of agriculture, however, the rate of development was too slow to relieve markedly the pressure of agricultural overpopulation.[37]

The conjuncture in 1936 led Stoyadinovich to draw near to Italy. To support Mussolini's involvement in Africa was perhaps a means

[34] Quite apart from the overall political influence which this situation gave Germany, there were also instances of direct subversive manipulations. J. B. Hoptner (*Yugoslavia in Crisis, 1934–1941*, New York and London, 1962, p. 103) quotes the following instance: in 1937, German representatives bought the entire crop of plums from agricultural co-operatives for 60% more than the current market price, and remitted the difference to the *Zbor* movement.

[35] Between 1934 and 1939, the yield of wheat per hectare increased from 13.7 to 15.2 quintals on the rich soils of Voyvodina, but only from 8.4 to 8.9 quintals at the other end of the scale, in southern Serbia-Macedonia. The national average of 12·1 quintals for 1936–37 compares with 21·9 in Germany (A. Bilimovich, 'Agriculture and Food in Yugoslavia before, during and after World War II', in S. Zagoroff *et al.* (ed.): *The Agricultural Economy in the Danubian Countries, 1935–1945*, Stanford, 1955, pp. 310–11).

[36] *La Yougoslavie par les chiffres, 1937*, p. 48.

[37] Industry was only able to absorb 19% of the new labour force that entered the market between 1918 and 1938 (Stavrianos, op. cit., p. 637).

of keeping him away from the Balkans; it could also release Yugoslavia from exclusive economic reliance on Germany. In September 1936, a commercial agreement reopened the Italian market to Yugoslavia, and in December Stoyadinovich was given an elaborate reception in Rome. Over the winter, the outstanding issues between the two countries were smoothed out. A friendly, united, and independent Yugoslavia now appeared to Italy as a possible check to Germany's southward ambitions. In March 1937, in Belgrade, the two states concluded an agreement of non-aggression and consultation. Italy undertook to respect the territorial integrity of Yugoslavia and not to tolerate any activity against its existing order; Yugoslavia recognized Italy's African empire, and no mention was made of the League of Nations – a novel departure for Yugoslavia.

Before that, in January, Stoyadinovich had taken a step which, though plausible enough, was nevertheless to lead to a loosening of the Balkan Entente ties. Without clearly informing his allies, he had signed a bilateral pact of friendship with Bulgaria. He felt that, in view of the trend of events since 1935, he could look to his country's immediate allies, and still maintain an independent position in international affairs. He had not given up Yugoslavia's friends. At the end of 1937, before going to Rome, he had been to London and Paris, and good work continued to be done by both the Little and the Balkan Ententes in the field of technical co-operation. In fact, in July 1938, the Balkan Entente as a whole reached an understanding with Bulgaria. Bulgaria would still not join its neighbours without specific frontier revisions, but it agreed not to attempt to change its frontier by force, while they agreed to remove all restrictions on Bulgaria's armament.

The agreement with Bulgaria had been prompted by a substantial increase in German power. In March 1938, Austria had been united to the Reich. Germany now had a common frontier with Yugoslavia, as well as control of all Austrian investments in Yugoslavia and a larger share of its foreign trade.[38] Six months later, the partial dismemberment of Czechoslovakia by four-power agreement at Munich relieved Yugoslavia of any obligation to support its northern ally against Hungary: it also exploded the Little Entente. Though the Balkan Entente remained, it was tacitly acknowledged that each member would henceforward have to make its own arrangements with the great powers.

Stoyadinovich's foreign policy claimed to be one of neutrality, well

[38] In 1937, Germany's share of Yugoslav foreign trade was 36% of exports and 32% of imports. In 1938, after the incorporation of Austria, it had become 42% and 39% respectively (Tomasevich in Kerner (ed.): op. cit., p. 212).

suited to ensure the country's safety in view of the heightened tension in Europe. But the growing strength of Germany and Italy, added to material benefits of trade with Germany, and the weakness of what remained of the French security system, made real neutrality difficult. Mussolini had accepted the *Anschluss*, and Hitler had actually welcomed the Italo-Yugoslav agreement as a way of keeping the Balkans quiet. In November 1937, Italy had joined the German-Japanese anti-Comintern pact. The Rome-Berlin 'Axis' was beginning. Large sections of Yugoslav, and particularly Serbian, public opinion were alarmed lest the country be cut adrift from its traditional friends and fastened on to its traditional enemies, at a time when the political machine being fabricated by the prime minister at home assumed an increasingly Fascist appearance.

The Concordat crisis, which broke out in the summer of 1937, suddenly showed the lack of homogeneity of the government party. The Concordat with the Holy See had largely been the work of King Alexander's governments although it had only been signed in July 1935, by Stoyadinovich's administration.[39] If any opposition had been expected, it was from Croats and Slovenes of liberal and anti-clerical tendencies, rather than from Orthodox Serbs. Yet when a bill embodying the terms of the Concordat was tabled in July 1937, it unexpectedly raised a storm precisely in Serbian public opinion. The Orthodox Church started a campaign, not against the Concordat as such, but against its terms which, it complained, granted to the Catholic minority a more favourable position than that enjoyed by the Orthodox majority.

While it could be argued that with its organization and influence, the Roman Catholic Church stood to gain more from a unified régime of relations with the Yugoslav state than the Eastern Orthodox, such an incursion of clericalism among the Serbs would have been strange had it not been that the campaign was used essentially as a stick to beat the government. Elements of the opposition – and more precisely Yevtich's 'loyal' opposition – used it to discredit Stoyadinovich. The Serbian masses followed, because of the general bitterness against his régime, and because they viewed the Concordat with the Vatican as a step towards an alliance with Italy. There were resignations from the government.

The opposition whipped up in Serbia, added to the lack of interest

---

[39] An agreement with the papacy had been necessary to co-ordinate the different legislation and Concordats inherited from the pre-unification period and which regulated relations between the state and the Roman Catholic Church. The Concordat of 1935 was not very different from the old one with the kingdom of Serbia, which both parties had liked, and the settlement satisfied both the Catholic Church and the Yugoslav government.

shown in Croatia, led Stoyadinovich to shelve the Concordat. His policy in delicate domestic issues was to avoid conflict, and let time work for him. This, by the end of 1937, had failed to conciliate a solid majority of Yugoslavs, let alone of the Croats. Only a few time-serving Serbian politicians supported him, while Moslem and Slovenian leaders did so merely to safeguard their own sectional interests – which, in the case of the latter, were particularly exposed geographically. Although he showed an increasing tendency to ape Fascist forms, he had neither a programme to catch the imagination of the masses, nor the technical facilities to indoctrinate them. He had imagined that economic efficiency and diplomatic realism would enable him to achieve, with popular support, what his predecessors had failed to achieve. He had tried to rally government supporters through the Radical Union, but the Concordat crisis had shown how shallow its unity was, and so he tried to turn it into something approaching a Fascist party.

It was around that time, too, that communism once again became respectable as a progressive force against Fascism, and that order was put in the house of the Communist Party of Yugoslavia. In December 1937, Yosip Broz, later known as Tito, had been instructed by the Comintern to take over the Yugoslav Party, purge it, and reorganize its underground network.[40] Tito set about his task efficiently, and applied Popular Front tactics. The strengthening of organized labour, as a result of industrial development and of useful social legislation by Stoyadinovich's administration, enabled the Communists to collaborate with the Socialists in the trade unions, and play a part out of proportion to their numbers. In the universities, and more particularly at Belgrade, they formed a small dynamic group who could always count on wider support outside their ranks. They attempted to reach agreement with other political groups against the Stoyadinovich government, but in this field obtained no more than individual sympathies.

Out of the Concordat storm came forth, not a Popular Front with the Communists, but a more closely United Opposition – a proof that anti-Concordat feelings had not been anti-Croatian. In October 1937, a formal agreement was reached between the opposition

[40] A factory-worker born in Croatia, he had seen active service with the Austro-Hungarian army during the First World War, had been made a prisoner in Russia, and supported the Bolsheviks. In 1928, as secretary-general of the metal-workers' union of Croatia, one of the strongest among the independent (Communist-controlled) trade unions, he had been sentenced to five years' imprisonment. Released in 1934, he had joined the Comintern apparatus in Moscow. When he took over the Yugoslav Communist Party at the end of 1937, its membership was down to 1,500 (Avakumović op. cit., p. 185).

parties, and an appeal was sent out for a national government to work out with the crown a transitional arrangement leading to a new constitution: free elections, based on a fully democratic electoral law, for a new Constituent Assembly which would work out a new structure to satisfy the majority of the Serbs, the majority of the Croats, and the majority of the Slovenes. This programme was supported by a substantial majority in the country, and caused a wave of enthusiasm. Most Serbs then wished to give the Croats satisfaction so as to eliminate the standing argument against the return to real parliamentary government. Never had Serbo-Croatian friendship on a popular level been so close. When Machek came to Belgrade in August 1938, huge crowds turned out to greet him.

Stoyadinovich had parliament dissolved and a general election called for December. The international situation after the Czechoslovak crisis seemed to favour the arguments of the government's propaganda, that it had been right not to count on French and British support and that this was not the time to tamper with the constitution. Stoyadinovich had hoped to come out of the election stronger: he fared worse than Yevtich in 1935, for the United Opposition secured almost 45 per cent of the votes.[41]

By the end of 1938, dissatisfaction with Stoyadinovich, of one kind or another, had drawn most people together. The *Anschluss* had frustrated the hope of being able to play Italy against Germany. The prime minister's increasing authoritarianism provoked adverse reactions even in his own cabinet, and frightened the prince regent. Immediately after the election, Prince Paul initiated confidential negotiations with Machek on the possibility of meeting Croatian wishes without yielding on the constitution. From within the government, one of Stoyadinovich's own ministers, the ex-Radical Tsvetkovich, had been sounding out his colleagues. Apart from his own following, Slovenes and Moslems were also willing to abandon Stoyadinovich for Tsvetkovich. By February 1939, a Tsvetkovich alternative was ready. The cabinet fell apart; Stoyadinovich was not able to reconstruct it; Tsvetkovich's team was sworn in. Stoyadinovich had fallen from power in the same way as he had come to power.

Tsvetkovich's too was a government of the Yugoslav Radical Union. Apart from Spaho, the Moslem leader, it contained no outstanding personality, but it was characterized by a sincere determination to settle the Croatian question by agreement with the Croats. As for the constitution, all that the new cabinet was

[41] 74·5% of the electorate went to the polls, which were public. The *Zbor* list did not obtain the minimum necessary for a seat.

ready to advance was that there would be no formal obstacle to its revision after the coming of age of King Peter II, in September 1941. Talks were resumed with Machek, under the pressure of foreign events. In March 1939, the Czechoslovak republic had been ended. For Yugoslavia, this meant that its most important source of armaments, as well as control over Czechoslovak holdings, had been taken over by Germany.[42] The cry for Slovak autonomy – and independence – echoed across Croatia. Then, in April, the Italians took over Albania, and, in May, Hitler and Mussolini concluded the Pact of Steel.

Popular feelings ran high in Yugoslavia against Italy, and negotiations with the Croats were accelerated. There had been contacts between Machek and Count Ciano, the Italian foreign minister. Playing the card of a unified and independent Yugoslav partner had lost much of its value for Mussolini since Stoyadinovich had gone, but he was still confused as to what to do. Should Yugoslavia disintegrate, Italy could satisfy its territorial aspirations in Dalmatia, but it could also open the way to Germany's expansion to the Adriatic and the Mediterranean through Croatia. So Ciano resumed his links with the Croats, and extended them to Machek, to ensure a wider basis to Italy's influence. For Machek, this was a way of pressing Belgrade to give way over difficulties, a warning not to play into the hands of the separatists. Finally, rumours of the impending German-Soviet treaty got the better of the last hitches.

The Tsvetkovich-Machek agreement instituted a self-governing Province of Croatia covering the old territory of Croatia, Slavonia, and Dalmatia, as well as parts of Bosnia and Herzegovina,[43] with a governor appointed by the crown, and a local executive responsible jointly to him and to an assembly elected by secret ballot. Elections were to be held under a new electoral law, and the Croatian Peasant Party would join the government to carry out the agreement. The agreement was endorsed by the Radical Union's Slovenian and Moslem components, by the Croatian Peasant Party's Independent Democratic partners, as well as by the Serbian Agrarians. All of these agreed to join a new cabinet, with Tsvetkovich as prime minister and Machek as vice-premier. On 26 August, at the same time as the new government was officially appointed, parliament was dissolved, the provisions of the province of Croatia were enacted, and the government was given full powers

---

[42] In 1939, as a consequence of the dismemberment of Czechoslovakia, Germany took more than 50% of Yugoslav exports, and supplied about 50% of Yugoslav imports (Stavrianos, op. cit., p. 639).

[43] Among its 4·4 million inhabitants were included 866,000 Orthodox and 164,000 Moslems.

to modify the electoral law, the law on the press, and the laws on associations.

In spite of the opposition agreement, Machek had come to an understanding alone with the regency. During the negotiations, he had been in touch with the leaders of the Serbian opposition, suggesting that they should trust him and the crown to come to an arrangement that could be carried out quickly, in view of the dangerous situation. The Serbian leaders had refused to be stampeded into half-measures which could have satisfied the Croats but not the Serbs, and argued that an agreement concluded simply between the Croatian Peasant Party and the government was worse than no agreement at all, for it would separate Croats from Serbs at a time when unity was essential. Machek, however, felt it urgent to counter Pavelich's appeal in Croatia before a European war broke out.

Less than a week after the Tsvetkovich-Machek agreement had been formalized, the Second World War started. It seemed that the agreement had solved Yugoslavia's national and constitutional problem just in time. It had certainly started the process of constitutional revision, and was followed by a certain political relaxation which provided all dissatisfied elements with an unprecedented opportunity for increased activity. Yet the whole procedure was extraordinary and provisional, carried out as it was by decree under article 116 of the constitution, on the basis of the crown's reserved emergency powers.

It certainly satisfied the Croatian Peasant Party leadership, and even a minority of the Serbian opposition, but many Croats were disappointed. Because of the rapidly deteriorating situation, nothing was done about elections, either generally or in Croatia, and there was not much time either for implementing the Peasant Party's social programme. The democrats had hoped for democracy, the peasants for social reform, and many, especially in the middle classes of the larger towns, for more autonomy. Fascists used discontent and disappointment to make mischief. In order to take the wind out of Ustasha sails, the Croatian Peasant Party had to leave much freedom of action to the extreme Right, and at the same time, paradoxically, it reinforced in Croatia the law for the defence of the state – when it was being relaxed elsewhere in the country – in order to be able to control Ustashas and Communists. As for the Serbs, they felt frustrated and humiliated. In their view, it was they who had contributed the greatest sacrifices to the cause of the common state and now, after a decade of non-democratic government apparently brought about by the 'Croatian question', the Croats had obtained rights which were still withheld from the Serbs. Many in the ranks of the Serbian opposition were bitter against Machek for dropping his allies in order to share power with Tsvetkovich. The demand was raised for a Serbian counterpart to the Province of Croatia, and Slovenes and Moslems naturally aired similar ideas.

The two acts of aggression, of Germany against Czechoslovakia, and of Italy against Albania, marked the end of Anglo-French appeasement. Between the spring and the autumn of 1939 there had been an intensification of diplomatic activity to attract the governments of the Balkan Entente. The Yugoslav government somehow hoped to keep the country intact, and ward off threats within and without, for as long as possible – at any rate until it could strengthen itself at home, or the West could provide effective help.

By the spring of 1940 Mussolini was itching to attack Yugoslavia. There was general alarm at the fear of a possible Italian invasion. Nervously, the government had Stoyadinovich interned.[44] Confidence was shaken by the inability of the West to make good the loss of Czechoslovak military supplies. Approaches were thus made to the Soviet Union to impress Moscow with Italy's expansionist policies in the Balkans, and to ask for economic relations. These led to the signature of a treaty of commerce in May, and the establishment of diplomatic relations in June. By that time France had fallen, and Mussolini had entered the war on the side of Germany. In Yugoslavia, the defeat of France increased the feeling of helplessness and, particularly with the Serbs, caused a veritable trauma. The Soviets had not expected such a rapid victory in the west; their agreement with Germany had not delimitated zones of influence in the Balkans; they wanted to stake their claims before Hitler could turn east – hence their link with Yugoslavia, and their ultimatum to Romania. By October, this neighbour and ally of Yugoslavia's had been mutilated by the Russians and the German-backed Hungarians and Bulgars, while German troops had been stationed in what remained of its territory.

The outbreak of hostilities in September 1939, with Germany's subsequent victories in the west and Italy's entry into the war, created great difficulties for the Yugoslav economy while increasing its dependence on the Reich.[45] Hitler knew that, by ceasing to buy its agricultural produce, he could bring disaster on the entire Yugoslav economy. Tsvetkovich's government took a series of emergency measures towards economic mobilization which deeply affected the country. Inflation was caused by financing large military outlays

---

[44] He had manifested his opposition to Tsvetkovich, and the government had information which seemed to indicate that the Axis powers had not lost interest in the former prime minister.

[45] Germany acquired partial control over French, Belgian, and Dutch holdings.

through the National Bank, a decrease in supply of civilian goods on the market, and loss of confidence in the currency. During 1940 the cost of living rose, particularly food prices. The harvest that year was inadequate even for the needs of the home market, but Yugoslavia had to provide its quota of exports to Germany in order to obtain the imports required to keep the new industries in operation. In September the dinar was devalued in relation to the mark. The price of bread soared during the winter. This meant a tightening of the belt for consumers in the depressed areas and in the towns. There were demonstrations against the government.

Warned off Yugoslavia by Germany in order not to provoke Soviet protests, Italy invaded Greece at the end of October 1940. Yugoslav opinion was yet further incensed, and the government feared for its outlet through Salonika. There were back-door attempts to sound out the Germans about a possible Yugoslav march on the Greek port – allegedly to prevent the British from forestalling the Italians. The direct result was that Italian planes twice 'accidentally' bombed Yugoslav border territory as a warning, and that the Germans set out to use Salonika as a decoy to bring Yugoslavia into their camp. As the Greek forces stopped the Italian advance and started a counter-offensive in mid-November, the Italian military believed that if Yugoslavs were to join Greeks they could settle accounts with the Italian army. Mussolini asked Hitler to help. Pressure was increased on the Yugoslav government to adhere to the Axis. This was the only way – Hitler told the Yugoslav foreign minister in late November – that Yugoslavia could satisfy its aspirations to peace between Serbs and Croats, protection from Italy . . . and Salonika. But Italy's reverses had temporarily reduced the danger, and the Yugoslav government clung to neutrality, playing for time.[46]

In December, Hitler issued directives for the invasion of the U.S.S.R. the following May, and for helping Mussolini to conquer Greece before that. Early in March 1941, Bulgaria adhered to the anti-Comintern pact and agreed to the presence of German troops, while British troops began to arrive in Greece. Time was pressing. Hitler could not afford to watch Great Britain consolidate its military foothold in Greece while he was preparing to invade Russia. Before he could intervene in Greece, from Romania through Bulgaria, he needed to clear up Yugoslavia's equivocal attitude. In mid-February, he had invited the Yugoslav prime minister and

[46] It even tried to neutralize at least one avenue of invasion by burying the hatchet with its arch-revisionist neighbour, with which no agreement had ever been reached; in December 1940 a 'pact of lasting peace and eternal friendship' was concluded with Hungary.

foreign minister to Berchtesgaden, and had offered to guarantee Yugoslavia's integrity and not to ask for military co-operation. On the other hand, the British government, considering that a Yugoslav intervention against Italy in Albania could transform the situation, pressed Yugoslavia to join Greece.

Yugoslavia's position was weak. Except for Greece, it was surrounded on all sides by countries linked to the Axis. There was no longer a chance of manoeuvring between Mussolini and Hitler. At home, the government did not even have the security of the pseudo-parliamentary support instituted by the constitution of 1931, for the crown had reverted to special powers, and it did not command the loyalty of a substantial portion of the public. Its Serbian members represented not much more than themselves, at best small parties or splinter fragments. Croatian ministers were representative and they considered that the country should try and keep out of the war, even at the cost of some concessions to the Axis, at least until the latter had become involved with Russia and America. They felt this to be in the interests of Croatia, of the country generally, and even of the West, for weak as it was, Yugoslavia's entry into the war at this stage could not appreciably help Great Britain. Underground, Communists and various Fascists were waiting their chance to emerge with the help of one of the two great powers whose rivalry was once again looming over the Balkans.[47]

Throughout March, German pressure grew, and the Yugoslav government stalled until Hitler presented what amounted to a firm, though courteous, demand for a limited adherence to be carried out before 25 March. Prince Paul knew that public opinion was not of one mind. Most Croats and Slovenes were reluctant to provoke the Germans and Italians into invading their geographically indefensible lands. There was no doubt that the prince's sympathies were with Great Britain, but, quite apart from the division in public opinion, he was obsessed with his country's military weakness, with Britain's inability to supply war material, with his fear of communism. He hesitated, consulted the government and the opposition leaders, and, with a feeling of imminent doom, decided to adhere to the pact. It was no guarantee against a future attack by Germany, but if Hitler went against his own word, then the country would be united, which was not the case now.

[47] The government had eased its control over Communist activities since the establishment of diplomatic relations with the Soviet Union, but their propaganda against the French and the British had created a wedge between them and the moderate Left, and deprived them of the greater part of their appeal to university students. From the end of 1937 to the beginning of 1941, Party membership increased from 1,500 to 8,000, whom Tito had wrought into a tightly knit revolutionary minority (Avakumović, op. cit., p. 185).

One last insurance was taken out, to prevent the Axis powers from engineering into authority an administration more amenable to their policies: the British government was asked to admit Stoyadinovich to a British territory.[48] On 25 March, in Vienna, the Yugoslav prime minister and foreign minister signed the protocol of adherence to the anti-Comintern pact. No sooner had they returned to Belgrade than a bloodless military coup overthrew the government and proclaimed King Peter of age – less than six months before the regency was due to come to an end anyhow.

The last days

The feeling of crisis throughout the country had been heightened by the fact that the character of the government did not enable crown and nation to share the responsibility for the crucial decision. The United Opposition front had dissolved. The Croatian and Slovenian parties were in the government, but the Serbian parties that had remained in opposition were no longer organized political forces. Even in the absence of an organized opposition, however, most Serbs believed – and quite a few Croats and Slovenes as well – that, in the long run, their traditional allies would win the war, and that Yugoslavia would then be penalized for what appeared as a betrayal. More immediately, there was the danger that siding with the Axis would encourage, rather than discourage, extreme right-wing Croatian separatism, Fascist trends generally, and Italian territorial claims. The vigour of popular anti-pact demonstrations revealed the strength and the extent of non-Communist and anti-Axis opinion.

During the night of 26–27 March, army and air force officers took control of Belgrade, and, amidst popular enthusiasm, brought together all the party leaders, to form a new and broadly based government. The coup had been carried out in King Peter's name. Prince Paul was not the man to resist such a show of popular feeling, or rebel against his sovereign. He subscribed to the coup, duly resigned along with his co-regents, and left the country.[49] The new administration, uniting the leaders of the Croatian Peasant Party and of the Independent Democrats, of the Moslem Organization and of the Slovenian Populists, of the Radicals and of the Democrats,

[48] He was taken to the Greek border, and thence conveyed by the British to Mauritius.
[49] Prince Paul left for Greece, asking the British government to be allowed to retire to a British territory. A useful complement to the story of the coup, as told in Hoptner, op. cit., is to be found in D. Ristić, *Yugoslavia's Revolution of 1941*, University Park and London, 1966.

of the Agrarians and even of the Yugoslav National Party, under the premiership of General Simovich, had been brought to life by a deep yearning for a fully representative government in an hour of necessity, as well as by a feeling of revulsion against Nazism and Fascism.

Churchill welcomed the coup in a public statement. For Hitler, it turned Yugoslavia into a factor of risk in his plans against Greece. He did not wait to know where the new government stood: the country was basically hostile, and its rulers unreliable. The same day, he gave instructions for Yugoslavia to be invaded along with Greece, and liquidated as a state. Everyone in Yugoslavia now expected aggression. The government had no time to work out a policy. All it could do was to try and win a little more time, in order to prepare to resist as best it could. Some of its members had, anyhow, been in favour of a policy of 'gaining time' even before. It did its utmost not to give Germany and Italy any motive for attack. It assured them that the reasons for the coup had been purely domestic, and that international obligations would be respected. It turned to the Soviet Union, with which it now concluded a treaty of friendship and non-aggression. These gestures, however, failed to alter Hitler's decision.

Nazi propaganda had launched a violent campaign against Yugoslavia, setting Croats against Serbs. On 6 April, alleging atrocities against the German minority, Germany attacked Yugoslavia without an ultimatum or a declaration of war.

PART TWO

The Chaotic Gap

Chapter 3

The Chaotic Gap: 1941–45

Defeat, occupation, and revolt

Hitler had given orders for Yugoslavia to be pulverized 'with merciless brutality . . . in a lightning operation'. The country was already surrounded on all sides except Greece, and the German plan was to prevent any possible Yugoslav contact with Greek and British forces, while a concentric invasion from all other frontiers dealt 'an annihilating blow to the Yugoslav forces'.[1]

Hostilities began on 6 April 1941 with an air bombardment of Belgrade which continued for three days and killed between ten and twenty thousand out of the city's total population of 250,000, while massive air raids on aerodromes destroyed ground installations of the Yugoslav air force. Air operations caused chaos and facilitated the simultaneous attack by land forces. The main weight of the German attack came from Romania and Bulgaria, where its task was to seal Yugoslavia off from Greece and converge on Belgrade. Yugoslav defences in the south held for five days. By 11 April, the Germans had linked up with the Italians coming from eastern Albania. On the 13th, they marched into Belgrade. Sabotaged by psychological action through propaganda addressed to the Croats, the northern front collapsed even more rapidly: on 10 April, the Germans entered Zagreb. The Italians then also invaded Yugoslavia, through Slovenia where they connected with the Germans, and down the coast where, on 17 April, they captured in the Bay of Kotor the remains of the Yugoslav fleet.

Caught half-prepared, ill-equipped, and largely outnumbered, the Yugoslav army had been surrounded and cut off from the outside world, the small air force put out of action, the small navy taken. In spite of local successes against the Italians[2] and of acts of romantic *bravura alla polacca*, by 10 April regular military operations had broken down, Croatia had seceded under the Ustashas, and a similar move had been attempted in Slovenia.

[1] H. Trevor-Roper (ed.): *Hitler's War Directives, 1939–1945*, London, 1964, pp. 60–62.
[2] A Yugoslav offensive in Albania had overrun the whole of its northern tip to Shkodër before being forced back.

The government, losing control of the disintegrating state, had withdrawn from the capital to Bosnia and thence to Montenegro. On 16 April, General Simovich having instructed the chief of staff of the High Command to seek an armistice, the cabinet left by air for Athens where the young king had preceded his ministers. The Germans, however, imposed an unconditional surrender, which was signed on the 17th. Overwhelming German superiority in air and armoured power, backed by the rapid advance of motorized divisions, had hastened the outcome of the 'lightning operation'. Rapid victory had been achieved by aiming at towns and communications, preventing troop concentrations, and encouraging defeatism.

Following the capitulation, the enemy rounded up only those units found on their way. All who opted for the newly-established Croatian state were released, along with those who declared that they belonged to national minorities. Some 300,000 soldiers and 12,000 officers, mostly Serbs, were sent off to prisoner-of-war camps. The greater part of the Yugoslav army had not even seen action, and many officers and men simply made their own way home, some of them seeking refuge in the hills and uplands. Vast quantities of arms lay about, which everyone was gathering up and hiding away.

The Yugoslav state was claimed to have been annihilated along with its army. The Italians claimed Dalmatia, and also wished to supervise a string of vassal states on the other side of 'their' Adriatic Sea. The Germans, for their part, did not want much more than to control the important communication lines and mineral deposits, and thoroughly crush the Serbs. All territorial demands at the expense of regions inhabited by Serbs were accepted. The Slovenes were to be Germanized and Italianized, or dispersed. As for the Croats, it was hoped to find enough support among them to keep them on the side of the Axis. Such were the general lines along which Yugoslavia was partitioned.

The northern half of Slovenia was incorporated into the German Reich. The southern half, with the city of Ljubljana, became part of Italy, along with numerous Adriatic islands and important strips of the Dalmatian littoral, including the port of Split and the naval base of Kotor. Italy also obtained control of a nominally independent Montenegro, and Italian-run Albania was enlarged by the inclusion of most of the Kosovo region and parts of Macedonia. The largest single fragment of the former kingdom of Yugoslavia was the so-called Independent State of Croatia, extending across Bosnia to the gates of Belgrade. The larger part of Voyvodina reverted to Hungary, to which it had belonged in Habsburg times. Romania, however, refused to claim the Yugoslav part of the former Hungarian Banat, with its Romanian minority, or to let Hungary have it, and the Germans thus had to take over its administration. Finally, much of the south-east was annexed by Bulgaria. What remained of Serbia was placed under German military rule.

Although Yugoslavia had been destroyed by the Axis, it nevertheless survived, at least in the opposite camp, as a nominal legal entity and as an idea. Both would be upheld in the years to come by the Yugoslav government in exile, and by the resistance in the dismembered country. No sooner had the government arrived in Athens than it issued a statement that Yugoslavia would continue to fight on the side of Great Britain until the final victory. Unimportant though it may have seemed at the time, this was a warning of things to come. Three facts were to facilitate guerrilla action: the rapidity with which the Yugoslav army had been defeated, the fact that the Balkans were strategically important for the Axis only in so far as they held the main communication lines and mineral deposits, and the constant friction between the two supreme occupation authorities, Germany and Italy.

Different policies were pursued in each of the annexed territories. Germany's share of Slovenia – the industrial north – was appended to existing Austrian administrative provinces and submitted to a policy of brutal Germanization. Many were driven out or fled to the Italian zone, to Croatia, or to Serbia; many more were deported to work all over German-occupied Europe; German colonists were settled on the property of those who had left. Conditions were not so harsh in the more agricultural and woody Italian zone. Although turned into an Italian province, it was accorded a special status which recognized the Slovenian character of the population. While the majority, stunned by the rapidity of the defeat, accepted the fact of Italian rule, albeit without confidence or sympathy, a mushroom growth of small underground groups appeared in the Ljubljana area. Realizing that these people would soon organize themselves, and do so without the Communists who, initially, had no quarrel with the Axis, the Communist Party took the initiative in Slovenia of organizing an underground patriotic Anti-Imperialist Front which attracted left-wingers of all hues. Taking advantage of their existing network, the Communists quickly came to dominate the organization which, after the German attack on the Soviet Union, changed its name to Liberation Front, while, on the other hand, young army officers came to establish contact with their counterparts in Serbia.

In Dalmatia, the Italians again generally recognized the special character of the annexed territory. Opposition, at first concentrated in Split, the main urban centre, was met with rough Fascist methods which, over the summer, made latent tension spread to the whole coast. In the territories annexed to Albania, the Moslem Albanian population welcomed the Italian occupation, which gave them the opportunity of paying off old scores, particularly against those Serbs resettled there between the two world wars. Many Serbs were killed and many more left for Serbia and Montenegro.

The Bulgars strove to settle the ethnic problem in the region they had annexed by treating the local population as compatriots – in so far as they did not insist on being Serbs. Whereas Bulgarian policy tended to be one of wooing the natives, that of Hungary in Voyvodina, where the differences of historical nationalism were too great to allow of similar behaviour, was one of brutal Magyarization.

The collapse of Yugoslavia provided the Fascist-inspired fringe of Croatian nationalism with the opportunity of setting up, under the aegis of the Axis, a Croatian state over all the territories inhabited by Croats. On 10 April, the Independent State of Croatia – better known by the initials of its designation in the original, N.D.H. – was proclaimed, to which several hundred Ustashas returned from Italy with Pavelich, who assumed the title of *poglavnik* (leader). The great majority of the Croats accepted the new régime with the feeling that the worst had been avoided. Of the Croatian Peasant Party leadership, part had stayed in Croatia and withdrawn into passivity with Machek himself, a smaller part had gone abroad with the Yugoslav government, and the right wing had rallied the Ustashas.[3] While the countryside remained distrustful, or at best indifferent to the new settlement, the establishment of an independent state was well received in larger towns. Many Catholic priests tended to view the Ustasha movement favourably, for it had added a religious dimension to racialism and, in the case of the Croats, equated nation with race and faith. Yet, however much they claimed to incarnate Croatian nationalism, the Ustashas remained a minority movement. Although the opposition they faced was itself no more than a minority (the Communists and those of the urban intelligentsia in Dalmatia who were truly Yugoslav in feeling), and the majority force in between, that of the Croatian Peasant Party, seemed to have vanished, the Ustashas suspiciously kept a check on all Croats who had been active in public life before the war and had not joined their movement.

The N.D.H. took its place among the satellites of the Axis,

[3] When the defeat came, Machek resigned his vice-premiership of Simovich's cabinet and hurried to Zagreb, possibly in the hope of salvaging something for Croatia from the shipwreck. The Ustashas had overtaken him. He agreed to issue a statement advising all Croats to accept the new situation peacefully, and was advised to retire to his village. He complied, and was reduced, from then on, in his own words, 'to the role of a helpless watcher' (op. cit., p. 236).

formally declared war on the Allies, and sent troops to the Russian front when Germany invaded the U.S.S.R. It established a regular conscripted army, and Croats who had served as officers in the Yugoslav armed forces were invited to apply for commissions, as well as former officers of the Austro-Hungarian army who had refused to serve Yugoslavia. This army, however, was lukewarm in loyalty to Pavelich, and his government, for efficient action, relied rather on the Ustasha formations, the movement's armed militia.

Satellite Croatia had been planned to fit into Mussolini's Adriatic schemes, yet Germany's interests were specifically safeguarded by the provision of an occupation zone which covered two-thirds of its territory, including Zagreb and Bosnia. Croatia's special relationship with Italy was settled by the Rome agreements of 18 May 1941. Dalmatia was carved up, but those parts nominally left to the N.D.H. were to be kept demilitarized, with a right of transit for Italian troops. It was agreed to prepare a customs and currency union, and the crown of Croatia was offered to an Italian prince. The latter never went to his kingdom nor did he assume his title, but the mutilation of Croatian territory by Fascist Italy was a heavy blow to the satellite régime it had done so much to create.

The Independent State of Croatia could not be truly independent, nor indeed was it a real state, but its leaders were determined to make it purely Croatian. In order to be able to unite all Croats – or at least those who did not live in territories claimed by Italy – Pavelich found himself with almost as many 'aliens'. Catholic Croats amounted to just over half the 6.5 million inhabitants of the N.D.H., the remainder being Orthodox, Moslem, Protestant, and Jewish.

The problem was the existence of just under 2 million Orthodox Serbs.[4] The majority of these lived in Bosnia and Herzegovina, along with Moslems and Catholics; the rest in inner Croatia, with a concentration of half a million in the old Military Frontier. Immediate measures were taken against the Serbs, aimed at eradicating what

---

[4] The Protestants were local Germans, entitled to respect and privileges. The Jews were submitted to the standard measures of Nazi-dominated eastern Europe. As for the 750,000 Moslems of Bosnia, they formed a close and passive society which, ever since the end of Turkish rule in 1878, had looked rather to its own business while coming to terms with the powers that were. They were accepted by the new régime and, as a whole, accepted it in turn. The Yugoslav Moslem Organization had broken up, which enabled Ustashas, Italians, and Germans to play different factions against each other. Its leader, Mehmed Spaho, had died in 1939, and his successor Kulenovich, who had been a minister in both the Tsvetkovich-Machek and Simovich administrations, had gone over to Pavelich.

outwardly distinguished them from Croats. The Cyrillic script was banned, the Orthodox Church officially referred to as the 'Eastern Greek', and the Serbs as 'former Serbs'. A government-sponsored programme of conversion to Catholicism was introduced. The theory was expounded that the Serbs were an alien element who had sought refuge in Croatia a few centuries earlier and would now have to be Croatized or go. By June, government leaders openly announced that the 'Serbian problem' would be solved by conversion, expulsion, and killing, but even before that, Ustasha bands had been let loose to spread terror among the Serbian population, starting with the intellectual and social élite in towns, and then passing to mass extermination. Those who were fortunate or near enough fled over the border into Serbia or Italian Dalmatia. The rest took to the forests and uplands. What began as a panicked flight to avoid horrible death was to turn into a spontaneous rising.

The Ustashas' policy of mass extermination was so ferocious and so blatant that even their protectors were shocked. Italian public opinion reacted strongly[5] and Mussolini was able, early in September, to extend military occupation to the whole of Italy's zone of the N.D.H., in order to put a brake on the massacres. Even the German military in Zagreb feared that Ustasha terror would plunge the satellite state into chaos, to the point of advising Hitler to remove them from power.[6]

Some of the Catholic priests who had adhered to the movement were prominent as theoreticians and propagandists, and some even distinguished themselves as participants in the massacres. Many more just watched with satisfaction the destruction of the Orthodox Church. All this was especially true of the mixed regions, more

---

[5] Carlo Falconi quotes the press in *Le Silence de Pie XII, 1939–1945 – Essai fondé sur des documents d'archives recueillis par l'auteur en Pologne et en Yougoslavie*, Monaco, 1965, pp. 285–6.

[6] The German military commander rebuked the head of the Croatian armed forces. In recent years, he told him sharply, he had experienced many actions of a similar kind, but nothing could compare with the misdeeds of the Ustashas. He contemplated replacing them by a government headed by Machek. In order to play safe, Pavelich had Machek arrested in October. He won the day with the Germans, for their diplomatic representative came down in favour of the Ustashas as the only reliable element in Croatia from the Nazis' point of view. (See U. von Hassel, *The von Hassel Diaries*, London, 1948, p. 186; and Maček, op. cit., p. 240.) Professor Jozo Tomasevich, who is working on this question, gives the figure of 350,000 as a tentative minimum for the number of Serbs killed by the Ustashas during their rule, in their concentration camps, or through action against villages ('Yugoslavia during the Second World War', in W. Vucinich (ed.): *Contemporary Yugoslavia – Twenty Years of Socialist Experiment*, Berkeley and Los Angeles, 1969, pp. 78 and 367).

particularly of Bosnia, where Archbishop Sharich of Sarayevo was an enthusiastic supporter of the new régime. Generally, however, the higher clergy was much less favourable, while some of the bishops were definitely hostile, fearing that Ustasha brutality would do more harm than good to the cause of Catholicism.

Archbishop Stepinats of Zagreb was no Ustasha sympathizer. He was a traditional Catholic prelate, a nationalist Croat, and an anti-Communist. As such, he initially welcomed independence, but his increasing uneasiness about the Ustasha régime quickly led him to hesitations which paralysed the Catholic Church in Croatia almost as much as the Peasant Party. Serious misgivings were especially felt by the hierarchy about the government's campaign of conversions, carried out according to principles and with means that had little to do with religion. After the archbishop's protests against violence and the disregard of established canonical procedure, the government's continued policy of conversions for racial ends, which made martyrs and pseudo-converts, which used the Catholic Church and tinged it with infamy, caused a collective remonstrance, addressed in November to the *poglavnik*.

In May 1941, the pope had received Pavelich, and he had sent a legate to Croatia, but the Holy See had not recognized the N.D.H. and continued to maintain diplomatic relations with the exiled Yugoslav government. Fully aware of the facts, and with an anti-Ustasha lobby in the Vatican itself, the papacy maintained a reserved, and at times even disapproving, attitude towards the boastful Catholicism of the Ustashas. All this in no way changed the attitude of their leadership, and many clerics continued to give them enthusiastic support.

Pavelich had not expected the Orthodox peasants of his state to rise in self-defence, and theirs was not an organized insurrection, nor was it in any way co-ordinated with resistance movements breaking out in other parts of the country. It was not even directed against the foreign armies of occupation. The rising of the Serbs in the N.D.H. was an unplanned reflex of isolated villages in danger of extermination. The urban Serbs had been the first victims of Ustasha fanaticism. The towns, anyway, as well as all the ways and media of communication, were in Ustasha hands. This, as well as the geography and pattern of settlement, isolated the Serbian villages, not only from the outside world, but from each other. Geographically, Bosnia is a series of massifs divided by basins and canyons. The Serbs are mainly settled on the slopes, and their economy is pastoral. Every summer, the flocks are moved up to mountain pastures, and for centuries, whenever there was danger, entire villages retreated up into the mountains. In the summer of

1941, this was the spontaneous reaction once again. Bands were formed, isolated police stations and smaller, lukewarm, N.D.H. garrisons taken over for arms.

Just as in 1875, it was on the borders of Dalmatia that the rising was most developed. It was there that Communists as such began to be noticed after the invasion of the U.S.S.R., making bids for local leadership, with the result that differences emerged between Communists and non-Communists over the distribution of booty, the administration of areas under insurgent control, and the attitude to be taken to Italian troops when they marched into the southern zone of the N.D.H. and put an end to the more acute phase of Ustasha terror. Fighting broke out within the bands, and the Italians withdrew into the towns to watch the civil war developing between Serbs over the winter.

The attempted 'final solution' of the Serbian problem had shaken the whole state of Croatia. Only the armed intervention of German and Italian occupation forces had saved the Ustashas' formal hold over Bosnia and Herzegovina. Croatian disappointment, and even discontent, increased. It still remained below the surface, for the mildest expression of opposition was punished by concentration camp, but units of the regular army were no longer considered reliable enough for action against the Serbs without being accompanied by Ustasha formations. The Communists were, however, the only group to use this disaffection in order to infiltrate the N.D.H. army.

Although a relatively small number of Croats, and even fewer Moslems, had taken a direct part in the massacres, their effect on the future of Yugoslavia was critical, for they started a fratricidal war in the mixed regions which was to put the clock back many decades. Extreme Croatian nationalism had set up a pan-Croatian state from the ruins of Yugoslavia, and attempted to Croatize it by totalitarian terror practised on a national scale. In return, the Serbian insurgents were going to repay atrocity for atrocity whenever they had a chance. Catholics, Orthodox, and Moslems in the mixed regions of Yugoslavia were soon locked in a vicious struggle, each community wishing to eradicate the others from its territories, and forced to turn to foreign conquerors for protection. By giving new life to, and magnifying, all the old ethnic, religious, and political feuds, the Second World War assumed in central Yugoslavia one of its most primitive aspects. The very idea of Yugoslavia, which had survived the state, seemed about to die in this conflagration which was already raging in the centre of the country when the risings in its eastern parts were only beginning.

Serbia was one of the regions of the Balkans over which the

Germans had established their own military administration,[7] and it was not until 29 August that they appointed a 'Serbian government' under General Nedich. A senior general who believed that Germany had definitely won the war, and that it was henceforth the only bulwark against communism, he accepted the task hoping that collaboration might prevent Serbia from disappearing altogether from Hitler's 'new Europe', in order to provide, in the German-occupied rump territory, a refuge for persecuted Serbs from the other regions, and in order to save them from communism. By August, Serbia had indeed been flooded with refugees. The local population lived in a state of increasing nervousness, the more so since many troops were withdrawn as soon as Yugoslavia had been conquered, to be sent against the Soviet Union. The formation of the Nedich government was an attempt to keep Serbia quiet by indirect means. It was authorized to pick up again the threads of the pre-war administrative structure in the region, and to organize a 'Serbian State Guard' for the purpose of keeping internal order.

Gendarmes were enrolled in the State Guard, but it was not easy to find enough officers willing to serve, and the majority of these in due course turned out to be auxiliaries of the resistance rather than of the occupation authorities. The only reliable collaborators the Germans could find were the adherents of Ljotich's small, pro-Axis *Zbor*.[8] Ljotich was allowed to turn his followers into a 'Serbian Volunteer Corps', a para-military political militia much better fitted to Nazi requirements than the half-hearted State Guard.

One of Hitler's aims in the Balkans had been to crush the Serbs, whom he considered an unruly, troublesome, and anti-German element. Most of them realized that they would not get much out of trying to fit into the new Nazi order. Thus it was among the Serbs, generally speaking, that a resistance movement was to start. After the capitulation, many officers and men of the regular army who did not share Nedich's belief that Hitler had definitely won the war just because they too had been defeated, instead of laying down arms or returning home, set off in small groups or individually, hoping that they could make their way to Greece, and eventually going into hiding. One of these officers was Colonel Mihailovich.

[7] Hitler's directive No. 31 had laid down the form of German military control in the occupied areas of the Balkans. Under the commander Armed Forces South-East, with headquarters in Salonika, who was the highest representative of the armed forces in the Balkans, directly subordinate to Hitler, were placed three area-commanding generals – for 'Old Serbia', for the Salonika area, and for southern Greece (Trevor-Roper (ed.): op. cit., pp. 74–5).

[8] See above, p. 89, n.31.

In the army, Mihailovich had been considered a radical intellectual. Like his contemporary Charles de Gaulle, he was considered by his seniors to have too many original ideas, and many did not like him for his views which were not always those of the government of the day. He had been critical of the inadequacy of Yugoslavia's defence dispositions, and there was no love lost between him and his

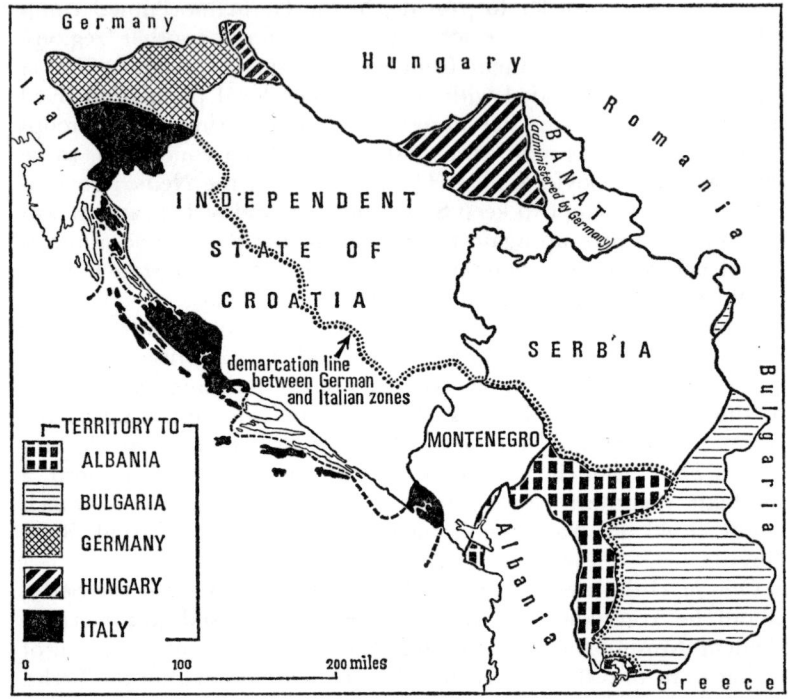

2 The territory of Yugoslavia during the Second World War

one-time superior, Nedich. From northern Bosnia, where he had been chief of staff of an army command, he had refused to accept the capitulation order, and decided to make for Serbia. Towards the middle of May he and his group arrived on Ravna Gora, a plateau in western Serbia, remote enough to escape the attention of the Germans, yet near enough the strategic valley of the western Morava, the main thoroughfare from Serbia to Bosnia.

Mihailovich's was, in May 1941, only one of several armed groups that had sprung up in the confused atmosphere of Serbia, all referred to as 'chetniks'.[9] His idea, however, was to restore some sort of

[9] A *chetnik* is a member of a *cheta* (a 'band' or 'company'). The latter word is that used for a company in the regular army. It had also been used

order, even if it was only an underground order, starting in Serbia, for it was impossible as yet to assess the situation in other regions. He would establish contact with other officers who were in hiding or had formed their own detachments, and organize a network, obtain the confidence of the population, dazed by the defeat, and of the remaining local government authorities, collect intelligence, and prepare for guerrilla action to be co-ordinated with the plans of the Yugoslav government in exile and of the Allies generally. Mihailovich thus began to grope towards an organized network, which he was going to call the 'Yugoslav Home Army', although the armed units were kept to a strict minimum, and although (with the exception of some Slovenian and Croatian officers) all its adherents were Serbs. This would emphasize his wish to react against the destruction of Yugoslavia, and to end the confusion that arose from the very name of *chetnik*, indiscriminately used to describe all irregular Serbian armed formations, even some which the Germans in Serbia were enticing into their service.

Mihailovich believed that the war against Germany would be a long one. His aim was to set up an underground organization, not to launch a large-scale rising there and then; and yet, before the summer was over, just that occurred in Serbia. The rapid withdrawal of many German troops and the very success of Mihailovich's efforts had helped the population to overcome the shock of the rapid surrender. From prostration, the mood passed to exalted optimism. Acts of resistance, such as sabotage on lines of communication, were already being made, when the news that Germany had invaded Russia greatly increased the excitement. Russia – many Serbs believed – was too big a morsel for Hitler to swallow, and an insurrectionary fever rose in Serbia. This was due, also, to the feeling that something had to be done to help the Serbs over the border, in Bosnia.

To the Communist Party, the break-up of Yugoslavia meant the end of a set-up that had persecuted its adherents, or at best restrained their activities, and it enabled them to strengthen their organization during the ambiguous three months that preceded Hitler's attack on the Soviet Union. The Germans left them in peace, and it was in Belgrade that Tito and his Central Committee set up their secret headquarters. With the invasion of the U.S.S.R., for the Yugoslav Communists, as for Communists everywhere, the 'imperialist war' became overnight the 'fatherland war'. While the

in the past to describe the irregular formations that had operated across the Turkish border, and those that had helped the Serbian army in the wars of 1912–18. The veterans of these formations, between the two world wars, were also grouped in a *chetniks*' organization.

Germans and Ustashas began hunting them down, the Comintern instructed them to start guerrilla action 'to alleviate the struggle of the Soviet people'.[10] This was an exacting demand, for the Communists were few and far between,[11] while in Serbia, patriots were already well on the way to organizing themselves without them. At the same time this was a splendid opportunity, for by joining in a popular cause, they would at the same time be helping the Soviet Union and furthering their own revolutionary aims. They believed that Germany would now be defeated, and that they would come to power in the wake of a Soviet victory over Hitler. The Communist Party network was immediately set on a war footing, and a 'High Command of the partisan detachments' formed from its leadership.

Tito's plan was very different from Mihailovich's. It was to force an insurrection, to bring the population out to fight, as quickly as possible. Over the summer, the Communists began to organize their own armed bands in the countryside, and at the end of August, Tito himself left Belgrade for western Serbia and the hills north of the western Morava valley, where tension was at its highest. The Communist partisans wanted to attack the smaller towns, where there were few Germans or none at all, and many of Mihailovich's officers were in the same mood. The Germans started a tactical withdrawal into larger centres, and events unfolded rapidly. Many people were taking to the woods and hills, joining the first guerrillas to be found, all of whom were passing to action in great confusion.

Mihailovich and Tito met for the first time in mid-September and agreed to co-operate in an attack on the towns of western Serbia. Mihailovich's *chetniks* and Tito's 'partisans' (whatever their later official designations, this is what they were to be popularly called throughout the war) successfully fought side by side, though not without rivalry. By the beginning of October, a string of smaller towns were in insurgent hands, road and rail traffic over most of the province had been brought to a standstill, and joint sieges were begun of the larger towns in western Serbia where the smaller

[10] Quoted by Clissold, 'Occupation and Resistance', op. cit., p. 213, and by F. Maclean, *Disputed Barricade – The Life and Times of Josip Broz-Tito, Marshall of Jugoslavia*, London, 1957, p. 128. For the text of the Central Committee's proclamation ('Proletarians from all parts of Yugoslavia – to arms! . . . You cannot stand idly by whilst the precious blood of the heroic people of Soviet Russia is shed. Mobilize all your strength to prevent our country from being turned into a base to supply the Fascist hordes who have unleashed their fury on the Soviet Union, our dear Socialist fatherland'), see S. Clissold, *Whirlwind – An Account of Marshal Tito's Rise to Power*, London, 1949, pp. 30–31.

[11] In a progress report to the Comintern in August 1941, Tito estimated Communist numbers throughout Yugoslavia at 12,000 Party members and 200,000 sympathizers (ibid., p. 34).

German garrisons had retreated. These successes owed much to popular enthusiasm, based on a false feeling of security, spurred on politically by a small but determined group of Communists, and organized mainly by regular officers of the former Yugoslav army under Colonel Mihailovich. Prosaic in a way, for such successes could never have been achieved without the Germans' tactical withdrawal, the story of the first resistance in occupied Europe fired the imagination of the Allied world at a time when it had little good news to sustain it. The Allied public wanted to hear about Mihailovich and the Yugoslav resisters, and Allied propaganda inflated their accomplishments to legendary proportions.

The hasty withdrawal of British troops from Greece did not mean that British authorities – especially those in Cairo – had lost interest in the Balkans.[12] In September a radio link had been established with Mihailovich, and S.O.E. (Special Operations Executive) had landed by submarine a British liaison officer, with two Yugoslav officers, who made their way to Ravna Gora. The Soviet government had urged the British that the revolt should be encouraged, but while it was agreed that everything must be done to keep it going, the Allies were in no position to give any substantial aid. Mihailovich was advised not to exhaust his strength, to keep his movements alive in the hills, and husband his resources in the hope of better times ahead, rather than spread the fighting to towns and cause unnecessary victims. Material aid was promised for the future, but for the time being, very little was forthcoming. Yet this link with the British and the Yugoslav government was a great psychological boost, and it confirmed Mihailovich's views.[13]

Enthusiasm for the bold and open revolt soon abated when the population realized that the Germans were still advancing in Russia, and that neither the Soviet Union nor Great Britain could spare any help. The peasants in Serbia, for all their hatred of the Germans, still had much to lose. Their mood began to change when the enemy reacted by taking measures against the civilian population. The partisans, who appeared to indulge in indiscriminate action irrespective of subsequent reprisals, became unpopular. During October, the alliance between Tito's men and Mihailovich's grew uneasy, and although the two leaders met again towards the end of the month to try and smooth things over, relations at local level took a sharp turn for the worse. The lack of arms, the different approach of the professional officers and of the Communist activists,

[12] J. Butler, *Grand Strategy*, III (in the official *History of the Second World War* series), London, 1968, pp. 11–12.

[13] J. Ehrman, *Grand Strategy*, V (in the official *History of the Second World War* series), London, 1956, p. 77.

the basic lack of trust between them, and the intrigues of German agents, had all contributed.

This situation among the insurgents made things easier for the Germans who began, in mid-September, to take measures to deal with the revolt in Serbia. On the 16th, Hitler signed his famous reprisals order – for every German killed, a hundred native hostages were to be executed, for every German wounded, fifty – and orders were given for the repression of the rebellion. Reinforcements were hurriedly brought in from Croatia, Greece, Romania, France, and even from the Russian front, in order to get communications moving again, relieve the besieged garrisons, and generally clear Serbia of the insurgents. The aim was to try and terrorize the population into submission, in order not to have to bring in too many additional troops. Thousands of hostages were executed in towns still held by the Germans,[14] thousands were confined in concentration camps, and great tracks of Shumadiya laid waste by a punitive expedition. Even so, by the end of November, the insurgents were still active and, as winter set in, the Germans attacked them with armour, air power, and mobile troops. Faced with an overwhelmingly superior enemy, feeling the effects of fear on the population, and divided among themselves, the insurgents had to think how best to save themselves. After consulting together one last time, Mihailovich decided to disperse his formations and lie low, while Tito gave orders to leave Serbia for Italian-occupied Sandjak, the rugged mountainous region which separates Serbia from historic Montenegro.

By the beginning of December, the German operation[15] had achieved its objective. The 'liberated areas' had been reoccupied, and communications restored. The guerrilla bands had been dispersed and put to flight. The revolt in Serbia had been quelled. Yet, in the summer and autumn remnants of the Yugoslav army under Colonel Mihailovich, joined in July by Tito's Communists, had made serious trouble for the *Wehrmacht*, and cleared whole regions of Serbia of German control. It was Mihailovich whom the Allies, the Germans, and the natives considered as the leader of the insurrection, in spite of his reticences and in spite of the part played by the Communists. His influence, his strength, and the activity of his forces had been greatly exaggerated, yet the rising of 1941 in

[14] During a sortie from Kraguyevats in mid-October, ten Germans had been killed and twenty-six wounded. In retaliation, on 20 October, the town's entire male population was rounded up (with help from Ljotichist volunteers) and an estimated 7,000 were shot the next day, including hundreds of schoolboys.

[15] This is known in the official Yugoslav historiography of the resistance movement as 'the First Offensive'.

Serbia was more important than anything which had hitherto appeared in occupied Europe, and the Germans realized it, for they pursued their attempts to get rid of Mihailovich, by force, reasoning, treachery, and bribery.[16]

There was yet a third mass rising in 1941, in Montenegro, which the Italians wanted to reorganize as part of their Adriatic settlement. Their queen was the daughter of the last king of Montenegro, and they believed that with a little kindness, money, and dynastic sentimentality, they could appeal to the region's separate identity and turn it into a sincere satellite. They behaved with goodwill, left the local administration largely undisturbed, released many prisoners-of-war, and enlisted what separatists they could find to help them prepare for the restoration of the kingdom of Montenegro. What they failed to realize was that the handful of elderly and nostalgic separatists with whom they had maintained links before the war had practically no supporters. As soon as the Italians started to make propaganda for a separate satellite state, the inhabitants countered with plans for an insurrection. The purposefully easygoing character of the occupation made it almost easy. Apart from the prisoners-of-war freed by the Italians, most of the soldiers mobilized there had never left Montenegro. This had been the last bastion, where the king and government of Yugoslavia had gone before flying out, and great quantities of arms and ammunition had been left in the mountains. The rising was thus planned in advance by officers, with no lack of arms.

Understandably, the Italian plan did not work out as expected and when, on 12 July, the restoration was proclaimed of a kingdom which neither the heir to the Montenegrin dynasty[17] nor his supposed subjects wanted, the revolt duly broke out. It was a general revolt, and the Communists participated along with everyone else, invoking the prestige of Russia and seizing the opportunity to achieve some of their political aims.[18] By the end of the month,

[16] Emissaries had been sent to Mihailovich to talk him into capitulation. Later, a reward of 200,000 dinars was offered for his capture, by the medium of leaflets as well as through the German-controlled radio and press (*Novo Vreme*, Belgrade, 9 December 1941). The relevant documents are to be found in Records of German Field Commands, Microcopy T-501 (246:000736, and 256:001155) and in the Yugoslav printed collection, *Zbornik dokumenata i podataka o N.O. ratu*, I/1, Belgrade, 1949, pp. 636–7.

[17] Prince Michael, grandson of King Nicholas of Montenegro and nephew of Italy's Queen Helen, whom the Italians wanted to place on the throne, was a staunch Yugoslav and preferred the part of a concentration camp internee to that of a puppet king.

[18] In the poor and mountainous districts of northern Montenegro, there were many sons of peasants with some education, who had failed to get suit-

Italian troops, taken by surprise, had been expelled from the whole region, with the exception of a few urban centres. Disappointed and hurt, they mounted an offensive to re-establish their hold, with their troops from Albania, supplemented by the Albanian regular army, which they controlled, along with Moslem irregulars from Kosovo and Sandjak whose latent anti-Serbian feelings were being whipped up. The Montenegrins resisted until mid-August when, by tacit agreement, the Albanians were withdrawn, Italian troops re-entered the towns, and no attempt was made to disarm anyone.

In spite of this, the revolt was not really stopped until December, by which time Italian reprisals had claimed thousands of victims. As in Serbia, these measures had made the *chetniks* (for here too the insurgents were called by the traditional name) hesitate to undertake more. Echoes of Ustasha terror in Bosnia and of German terror in Serbia had reached Montenegro. It was felt safer to tolerate the Italians than to invite Germans and Ustashas to lend them a hand. The blatant party policy of Montenegrin Communists in the north, where they were stronger, had also aroused in the minds of the leaders of the insurrection doubts as to the desirability of further co-operation. Anyhow, the main aim of the insurrection had been attained. Separatism had been killed stone dead. The Italians now realized that they could not turn Montenegro into a satellite. The best that they could have, if they were not to call for German help, was a territory of occupation, though one in which armed bands were tolerated, and effective occupation was reduced to towns. Neither Mihailovich nor Tito had helped in any way. The revolt of the Serbs in Montenegro was as independent of the revolt of the Serbs in Serbia as it was of that of the Serbs in the N.D.H.

So different were the conditions in partitioned Yugoslavia, that in one year there had been three different mass risings, in three different regions, for three different reasons, against three different enemies. In the N.D.H., the Serbs had risen in self-defence against extermination by Croatian pro-Axis extremists. In Serbia, they had risen against the Germans in an upsurge of patriotic pro-Allied optimism. In Montenegro, they had risen against an Italian formal attempt to put the clock back. Soon divided into Communists and

able employment. There the Communist Party did have rural members, but Communists enjoyed sympathies even among the peasants who did not share their views, as they were pro-Russian, and had suffered from the police. Pro-Russian feelings were still intense among these mountaineers and, proud as they were, they did not like the police, if they were not themselves police-men. The popularity that it had lost earlier in 1941 because of its anti-war line, the Party was able to make up after the German invasion of Russia. Many important Communists were in Montenegro in 1941, including Djilas, a native of the province.

anti-Communists, the insurgents were thereafter to fight a civil war between themselves which, more often than not, took first place over the original aims of their respective risings.

A complex pattern emerges

Yugoslavia also lived on in London where King Peter and his government had arrived in June 1941, via the Near East, to join the gathering of exiled Allied leaders. They were given an enthusiastic welcome. The events of 27 March had impressed British public opinion. General Simovich's prestige was high, and the young king became the symbol of Yugoslavia's struggle to keep its freedom in alliance with Great Britain. The risings in occupied Yugoslavia, and particularly the revolt in Serbia, added further weight. This was felt in a change of the Soviet attitude. After the surrender, the Yugoslav legation in Moscow had been sent away, on the alleged grounds that Yugoslavia had ceased to exist. But when Russia had in turn been invaded, and revolts in Yugoslavia diverted enemy forces, the Soviet government resumed diplomatic relations with the Yugoslav government in London.

The exiled government was indeed impressive as a broadly based coalition of all parties that strove for a solution of Yugoslavia's problems within the context of a representative system. The trouble was that it had been composed, not as a war cabinet or a working team, but as a representation of parties, and that it had not had the time to define a programme, let alone tackle any of the country's accumulated problems. These were still, constitutionally, at the stage where they had been left in 1939 by the regency's emergency half-measures, and much had happened since then. Under the shock of recent events, and in exile, party leaders were faced with the old Serbo-Croatian problem, hideously magnified.

Croatian ministers pressed for a public confirmation of the 1939 arrangement, with its special status for the Province of Croatia. Serbian ministers wanted to reorganize Yugoslavia on a federal basis after the war, but, as a result of the Ustasha massacres, this was no longer so much to satisfy the Croats, as to protect the Serbs. They were not too keen on the way in which the agreement of 1939 had been carried out, or on the extent of the borders of the Croatian unit which included far too many Serbs. At the same time, Croatian ministers, fearing Serbian post-war resentment, wanted to leave as few Croats as possible under Serbian rule. When reports of the massacres in the N.D.H. reached London, some Croatian ministers believed them to be exaggerated, others thought it wiser not to confirm the facts publicly, while all suspected their Serbian colleagues of wanting to use them as a means of discrediting the Croats. To the Serbs, the Croatian suspicions added offence to injury, and some of them really did seize on the massacres as a political stick to beat the Croats.

The refusal of the Croatian ministers to condemn the massacres in loud and clear terms interlocked with the refusal of the Serbian ministers publicly to bind themselves to the 1939 agreement. The result was government crises only remotely connected with the requirements of the resistance in Yugoslavia. For long out of office, and now all together in office, but without a country, the Yugoslav government leaders in London were already, to a certain extent, men with the manners and grievances of another age, who did not realize that their achievements, their ideals, and their followings were being destroyed in the chaos of the war. On one point, however, they soon agreed unanimously: that General Simovich, in spite of his patriotism, was ill-suited politically to preside over them. In January 1942, he was replaced as prime minister by Professor Yovanovich, an influential non-party intellectual and their senior.[19]

In his reshuffled cabinet, Yovanovich included one absentee – Mihailovich, now promoted general, as minister of the armed forces. His second appointment in June 1942, as chief of staff of the High Command of the armed forces, completed the formalization of his Yugoslav Home Army. Mihailovich had expressed his loyalty to the cause of Yugoslavia and of the Allies. He was a professional soldier who had no wish to assume a political role. The new prime minister wanted to link the government to Mihailovich's movement, in order to improve the position of both partners. The link would help Mihailovich to introduce order and unity in the resistance; it would ensure that his essentially Serbian guerrillas remained loyal to Yugoslav unity; and it would place him in a better position to appeal for Allied help. The territory from which Mihailovich operated had become important for the outcome of the war in Africa. By bringing General Mihailovich into the cabinet, the Yugoslav government in London was contributing his resistance organization to the cause of the Allies.

During 1942, the German zone of the Balkans played an important part in the war. Through it ran the important Maribor-Zagreb-Belgrade-Salonika line of communication which carried supplies to Rommel's *Afrika Korps*, and no independent native armed formations could be tolerated near it, hence the brutal repression of revolts. The Germans saw the need for more troops to be kept

[19] He had originally been appointed deputy prime minister on 27 March 1941, along with Machek, as a Serbian counterpart, above the several parties, to the overall leader of the Croatian majority.

permanently in Serbia, but as they could not afford to leave all the reinforcements brought in to put down the insurrection, the Bulgars were asked to help by providing troops that, placed under the German commander of Serbia, occupied the south of that territory.

The Serbs remembered the tremendous blood-letting of the First World War. The Ustasha massacres were on a frightening scale. Coming on top of them, the reprisals now made them obsessed with the fear of national suicide, and the Germans naturally made the most of it. Another general rising could not be envisaged, at least until the enemy was weaker and Allied armies nearer. As Mihailovich told one British officer, he was resolved never again to bring such misery on his country, unless it could result in final liberation.[20] His aim was to create a secret army of men who would live at home and carry on their normal occupations until called upon. Once again, he kept only a strict minimum on active service. The rest were sent home, and some enlisted in Nedich's State Guard. Mihailovich had misgivings about this particular stratagem,[21] but it had its advantages, and was being used by the Communists in the N.D.H. army. It gave people an alibi; it ensured that, rather than act as an auxiliary to the Germans against his network, the Guard would be a protective barrier between it and the Germans; it provided him with intelligence, and also with arms, for what the British could drop was, disappointingly, not what Mihailovich had believed would be forthcoming.

He and his staff had spent several months in hiding in southwestern Serbia until they too, in the spring of 1942, left for Sandjak and northern Montenegro, and it was from there that the organization of the Yugoslav Home Army was pursued. Serbia and eastern Bosnia (where officers had been sent to help the local insurgents) remained the territorial basis of operations, and Mihailovich, that year, was able to build up a good intelligence network which allowed him to know of German transports through Serbia. Such valuable information was passed on to the British in Cairo, and by the summer, the guerrillas in the Morava and Ibar valleys – an important section of the supply line to Rommel – could usefully contribute to the war effort by sabotage action rather than by a general rising. Sabotage was stepped up in the autumn at the

[20] C. Lawrence, *Irregular Adventure*, London, 1947, p. 232.
[21] It was at his specific request that Nedich had been included in the Yugoslav government's official list of traitors broadcast over the B.B.C. (see Yovanovich's letter to *The Times*, 15 July 1946. The request was contained in Mihailovich's telegram No. 310 of 15 July 1942: cf. R. Knežević (ed.): *Knjiga o Draži*, I, Windsor, Ont., 1956, p. 259).

request of the British to stop, as far as possible, all supplies directed to Salonika and Athens, local authorities and railway personnel cooperating. Although there had been no revolt, the price in human suffering was still high, for the Germans sent out punitive expeditions, increased the rate of arrests, executed numerous hostages, deported officers of Nedich's State Guard, and even disarmed a number of units in an attempt to weed out Mihailovichist infiltrations.

Over the winter, German efforts to liquidate Mihailovich were to be pushed to extremes. By then, however, Rommel had been defeated by Montgomery in the Egyptian desert, and Eisenhower had landed in French North Africa. Mihailovich was lauded by the Allies for contributing to the successes in Africa, and their press was again full of praise for him. From the summer of 1942 onwards, and right through the winter, Allied leaders paid their tributes.[22]

The Russians too seemed to attribute great importance to Mihailovich. Their own immediate practical aim in Yugoslavia was to pin down as many German forces as possible, and Tito's partisans were not worth much in the regions where the Germans were concentrated. In August, the Soviet and the Yugoslav governments raised their legations to the rank of embassy, and the Soviets even envisaged sending a military mission to Mihailovich.[23] They must have believed that Mihailovich might turn out to be the leader of a nationwide resistance movement, whereas Tito's purely Communist movement could be liquidated militarily or prove a political embarrassment.[24]

[22] British, American, and Free French commanders sent him telegrams of congratulations, General de Gaulle awarded him the *Croix de Guerre*, the American and British governments expressed their appreciation to the Yugoslav government. In 1948, President Truman awarded him the Legion of Merit posthumously, but this was not generally known before 1967 (*Chicago Tribune*, 5 August 1967).

[23] There were, in 1942, several exchanges between the British, Soviet, and Yugoslav governments on the subject of reconciling the partisans and Mihailovich's movement (V. Dedijer, *Tito Speaks – His Self Portrait and Struggle with Stalin*, London, 1953, pp. 179–80; M. Piyade, *About the Legend that the Yugoslav Uprising owed its Existence to Soviet Assistance*, London, 1950, pp. 18–19; Ž. Knežević, *General Mihailovich and the U.S.S.R. – with Official Memoranda and Documents*, Washington, 1945, pp. 14–17; C. Fotitch, *The War we Lost – Yugoslavia's Tragedy and the Failure of the West*, New York, 1948, pp. 169–73; L. Woodward, *British Foreign Policy in the Second World War*, in the official *History of the Second World War* series, London, 1962, pp. 334 and 336).

[24] Clissold in *Short History*, p. 223. The Communist partisan leaders in Yugoslavia shared the German rather than the Soviet opinion of Mihailovich. E. Kardelj wrote in August 1942: 'We must fight against him by all means' (*Zbornik*, VI/3, 1954, p. 264), and R. Yovanovich-Bradonja, in October, that Mihailovich was 'the main danger to the successful development of the people's liberation struggle' (ibid., I/4, 1954, p. 123).

Mihailovich, during that time, from his secret headquarters in the mountains of Sandjak and northern Montenegro, had indeed greatly extended the range of his activities. Not only was he in contact with Allied commands and governments, he had also made connexions in neighbouring Balkan countries. He had by then established channels of communication with the underground movement in Slovenia, with the Moslem notabilities in the centre regions, with the independent *chetnik* formations of the Italian zone. In Croatia, he had approached former Peasant Party cadres and former army colleagues now serving in the N.D.H. forces, and he had realized something of the extraordinary complexity of the patterns that had emerged across the Yugoslav territory.

In Montenegro, over the winter 1941–42, fighting had flared up again, this time between the insurgents themselves. During the course of the revolt against the Italians, the local Communists, encouraged by the sympathies met with, had begun to suppress all potential political opponents they could lay their hands on. In six months, the Communists' extremism transformed the general popular mood towards them from sympathy to armed revolt. The Italians lost no time in turning this change of attitude to their own advantage,[25] and put out feelers to the leaders of the local 'Nationalist' *chetniks*.[26] Communist excesses, by alienating public opinion, played into the hands of the enemy whose authority was already in fact reduced to the towns. The officers of the former Yugoslav army who had organized the rising, grouped under General Djukanovich, decided to accept the compromise, which left them free with their own independent armed formations in their own territory, on condition that they left the Italians alone in their towns. In the spring of 1942, the Nationalist *chetniks*, backed by the population, began to turn the tables on the Communists, the Italians remaining benevolently neutral or, in some cases, providing arms. Thus, by June, the Communists had been driven out of the greater part of Montenegro, though they retained a precarious footing in the mixed Orthodox-Moslem border region to the east.

In Sandjak, the fighting developed into a cruel and confused civil war, at once political, religious, and ethnic. With the arrival of the Italians, the Moslems had sought to get their own back on the

[25] From February 1942 on, the Communists were instructed to suspend temporarily any action against the Italians in order to concentrate on liquidating *chetniks* (instructions from the partisan command in Montenegro in February, and from Tito himself in March: ibid., III/2, 1950, pp. 210–11; and II/3, 1955, p. 97).

[26] They were known as 'Nationalists' in Montenegro, in the sense that they were opposed to Italian-sponsored separatism, and that they were not Communists.

Serbs,[27] and the occupation authorities had armed a Moslem militia to help them keep some order. During 1942, however, Serbs (both Nationalists and Communists) and Moslems were left by the Italians to fight each other in this virtual no man's land, and with the strengthening of the Nationalist organization in Montenegro, it was the turn of the Sandjak Moslems to suffer horribly at the hands of local *chetniks*.

The situation was even more involved in the western territories. In spite and because of their ruthlessness, the Ustashas had failed to get rid of the Serbs in the N.D.H. They admitted their defeat in the spring of 1942 by creating a 'Croatian Orthodox Church' on paper, which enabled them to save face by henceforth considering the Serbs as Orthodox Croats. In Bosnia they went even further, by actually coming to terms locally with many of the improvised peasant leaders of the Serbian armed bands. The geography of the region made regular military operations practically impossible; the Ustashas were unable to put down the rising there, and feared lest the occupation forces should want to do it for them; as for the latter, they were more concerned with preventing the movement of Serbian self-preservation from turning into a generalized revolt against the Axis. These factors made for concessions, and a series of local, informal, *modus vivendi* settlements were reached which, though concluded with great mental reservations on both sides and often transgressed, in fact put an end to Ustasha power in most of the Bosnian uplands.

Pavelich had already given in to the Italians. He had now given in to the Serbian insurgents in Bosnia. Soon, he was to give in to the Germans as well. The increasing weakness of the N.D.H. made them look closer into the affairs of the Ustasha state, and tension with Italy made the *poglavnik* draw nearer to the Germans: in September 1942, the armed forces of the N.D.H. were placed under the overall command of the Germans.

The Italians really disconcerted Pavelich by their practice of leaving Serbian armed bands unmolested over most of their territory, so long as this did not interfere with their control of the Adriatic. Morale in the Italian army was not particularly high, and the revolt in the N.D.H. was against Ustasha terror, not against the Axis occupation. The Italian forces bought their livestock from the

---

[27] In the nineteenth century, the Ottoman administration had systematically put pressure on Orthodox Serbs to emigrate, and settled Moslems – both Albanians and Slavs – on the best lands of that district, the Sandjak of Novi Pazar, which separated Serbia and Montenegro. When the region was conquered by Serbia and Montenegro and then united to Yugoslavia, Serbs had paid off old scores against these Moslems.

Serbian peasants for special paper currency which the latter used to buy Italian produce to supplement their diet. This influenced the mass of the smallholders not to clash with the occupation authorities so long as lives and property were safe. Furthermore, countless Serbs, as well as Jews, had found a refuge from Ustasha terror in Italian-occupied territory. In this way, the Italians made use of the religious and ethnic war which the Ustasha massacres had triggered off, in order to extend their influence.

Their territory had become not only a haven for Serbian refugees, but also a supply base for Serbian armed bands, who were tolerated and, later, even provided with arms, ammunition, and food to defend Serbian settlements against the Ustashas. These bands operated even outside the Italian zone of occupation, going into Bosnia to protect or avenge their co-religionists.

In the Dinaric region behind the coast, lack of arms, the generous help given by the Italian authorities to the refugees, and the grave blunders committed by Communist zealots, added to a few judicious arrests in Split, had by the middle of 1942 turned the situation against the Communists, and enabled the Italians to restore some sort of rough and ready order. There was a shift of allegiances: many insurgents left the partisans, most *chetniks* withdrew to their villages, and the Italians found ready recruits for an Anti-Communist Volunteer Militia to fight the Communists.

The plight of the Serbs was worst in the former Military Frontier of Croatia, where the N.D.H. could not afford concessions. As, however, neither Ustashas nor Italians could effectively restore their control, they could only agree to send periodical expeditions to ensure that no authority emerged in these parts. The punitive expeditions destroyed settlements to prevent them being used by the guerrillas, and created a conflict of interest between those homeless peasants who had no alternative but to seek food and protection in guerrilla bands, and those as yet spared. Insurgents could not for long fight both the Italians and the Ustashas. Over the winter, internal fighting broke out among the bands. Communist-led partisans eventually predominated in the Serbian regions of inner Croatia, as repeated expeditions made more and more homeless peasants who had no further reason for wanting to avoid a clash with the Italians. Nearer Italian Dalmatia, however, non-Communist bands were supported by those villages that had still not suffered from the expeditions and were anxious not to. With these, the Italians eventually also struck non-aggression bargains.

By the spring of 1942, in the rugged mountainous regions of western Yugoslavia, the occupation forces and their Ustasha protégés had not been able to eliminate the Serbian insurgents. They had either agreed to share power with them, or set rival bands to fight each other. In those regions where some sort of insurgent authority had established itself as a buffer between the Serbian peasantry and the Ustashas or occupants, the Communists could do little. In the no man's land of the Serbian pale in Croatia, however, Communist influence was increasing among the ever more numerous homeless, landless, and bereaved peasants. When, that same spring, Communist-led bands, whom Ustasha and Italian expeditions had not been able to suppress, extended their field of action as far north as the river Sava, the German command in Zagreb decided to take action and ensure that guerrillas would not again get near the Zagreb-Belgrade line. They launched a massive operation which, in June and July, thoroughly devastated the northernmost part of the Serbian area and killed thousands of people.

The initial revolt of the Serbs in western Yugoslavia had been a spontaneous reaction of self-preservation. To the fanatic and terrorist anti-Serbian Croatian nationalism of the Ustashas, the backward and disorganized Serbian insurgents, whether *chetnik* or partisan, responded with narrow anti-Croatian Serbian nationalism. From defending Serbian settlements, at times they passed to seeking revenge on Croatian settlements. When enemy expeditions were sent to rid the Military Frontier region of insurgents, the lack of arms and of co-ordinated leadership prevented these *chetniks* from affording any protection to the population. By the summer of 1942, the Communists had lost many adherents and sympathizers in Serbia and Montenegro, in Bosnia and Herzegovina, but in the no man's land between inner Croatia and Bosnia, where they had infiltrated the chaotic and apathetic N.D.H. administration and army, they had gained in prestige among those populations who had suffered most.

Mihailovich discovered something of the complex situation which reigned in other parts of Yugoslavia when he himself left German-occupied Serbia for Sandjak and northern Montenegro. The *chetnik* leaders of the Italian zone, who had taken up arms independently of Mihailovich and for other reasons, and who had later come to terms with the occupation authorities without asking for his advice, were now anxious to acknowledge him as supreme commander. They saw no contradiction in this double game, for their sympathies were with the Allies, and they considered their arrangements with the Italians as a temporary expedient.

This was straightforward enough in Montenegro, where the population was homogeneous, conscious of a tradition that had led it to union with the rest of the Serbs and Yugoslavs, and guided by its notables, who were anxious to keep alive the legal continuity of the Yugoslav state. Mihailovich disapproved of their tactics, but in the N.D.H., not only were the *chetniks'* tactics alien to him, but even more so their ideological attitude which, more often than not, had become a negative one, anti-Yugoslav, anti-Croatian, anti-Catholic, anti-Moslem, and anti-Communist – the crude response of backward Orthodox peasants to Ustashism. Yet even they looked to Mihailovich as a nominal supreme authority. For most of them Yugoslavia was dead; they ignored the fact that Mihailovich represented a government committed to its restoration in alliance with the Soviet Union; they saw him merely as the representative of the king – the remote symbol of their Serbian nation – and of Great Britain – a remote ideal and ally.

Nevertheless, Mihailovich took the risk and accepted the nominal link, because he knew that all these *chetniks,* quite apart from the fact that they were still involved in countless clashes with German and N.D.H. forces, would never fight with the occupying armies against the British. He believed that the Western Allies would one day land in the Balkans; he hoped that he could in the meanwhile influence the *chetnik* leaders of the Italian zone to change their tactics and their ideas; and he hoped that the Yugoslav government and the Allies would help him in this task. His estimation of these Serbs' feelings towards the Axis and the Allies was shared by Germans, Italians, and Communists alike.[28] These *chetniks* in the Italian zone, even when armed and supplied by the occupation authorities, by their very existence forced the Italians to keep on the Adriatic coast, troops that could otherwise have been sent against the British in Africa; they provided useful intelligence, and through them much Italian equipment found its way to Mihailovich's units. In Bosnia, however, there was a fundamental misunderstanding between the chiefs of most local *chetnik* units and Mihailovich. He believed that because they had no effective organization and because they were not linked to an occupation authority, it would be possible to incorporate them into his Yugoslav Home Army. They only wanted him to help them obtain arms and legitimize their authority in the eyes of the population.

One of the reasons why Mihailovich had accepted the link with the independent *chetniks* of western Yugoslavia was that he hoped to be able to destroy the N.D.H. through them, but they had already

---

[28] Clissold, *Whirlwind,* pp. 86–7. There is some evidence that the British also shared these views, but so far it appears only from Yugoslav sources, both Titoist (in *The Trial of Dragoljub-Draža Mihailović – Stenographic Record and Documents,* Belgrade, 1946, p. 122, and elsewhere in the fuller Serbo-Croatian version) and Mihailovichist (in D. Martin, *Ally Betrayed – The Uncensored Story of Tito and Mihailovich,* New York, 1946, pp. 140–41).

achieved about as much as they could. He quickly found out that, on the whole, outside Serbia and the bordering Bosnian districts, he could not impose his authority, and had to take or leave the situation more or less as he found it. Mihailovich was the organizer of an armed underground movement in one particular province. It so happened that, in the conditions in which he operated, his conceptions were the nearest to those of the Yugoslav government and of the Western Allies, for he stood for the maintenance of the Yugoslav state and the continuation of the struggle against the Axis. In the districts where his influence was strong, his was a resistance movement that openly opposed the occupation forces and their native auxiliaries, and one that, by defending the peasants against their enemies, offered an alternative to seeking the protection of the occupant. At the same time, in other regions, he was now the nominal commander of armed formations over which he had no effective authority, and of whose ambiguous relations with the Italians he really disapproved.

The local *chetnik* leaders outside Serbia, operating in different conditions, theoretically acknowledged Mihailovich's authority in 1942 because he had become a charismatic symbol that could provide the missing moral link between them. But the mass adherence of all Serbian insurgent bands to Mihailovich the symbol, led Croats to believe his movement to be 'pan-Serbian' and anti-Croatian – a belief encouraged by both Ustasha and Communist propaganda – and made it difficult for Mihailovich the effective leader to find any audience among non-Ustasha Croats.

During that time a complex situation also developed in Slovenia, a region which, like inner Serbia, at least had the advantage of a homogeneous population, both by race and by religion. By the winter of 1941, the Communists were making themselves increasingly felt through the Liberation Front, but without any precise political programme, organizing small partisan groups in the Italian province, laying exclusive claim to being the representative underground organization of the Slovenes, and hindering the attempt by regular officers to set up a network linked to Mihailovich's Yugoslav Home Army. In order to counteract Communist action, the local leadership of the majority Slovenian People's Party got together with the other pre-war political parties to set up, in the spring of 1942, a parallel organization, the Slovenian Alliance, intended, like the Front, to be all-embracing, but which the Communists did not join. The Alliance was an underground political front that refused to acknowledge the new order imposed on the Slovenes and Yugoslavia generally, and advocated the union of all Slovenes after the war within a reorganized federal Yugoslav state.

At the same time, it condemned Communist action as being aimed solely at winning support to make a bid for power after the war. It established a radio link with the Slovenian members of the Yugoslav government in London.

The Alliance was handicapped by its belated appearance and the lack of a guerrilla organization to give it effective countenance in occupied territory. Its coming into being, however, was a serious obstacle to the further development of the Communist-led Front, and their partisans answered by attacking, not only Italian installations and native collaborators, but also and increasingly adherents of the Alliance. A wave of assassinations throughout 1942 caused a reaction against the Front among the rural population, and made the peasantry extremely reluctant to expose itself to reprisals.

Disappointed by the lack of co-operation and the spread of armed resistance, the Italian occupation authorities both threatened retaliation and played up the Communist bogy. In order to forestall the setting-up of an efficient pro-Yugoslav underground movement, they rounded up a large number of officers and N.C.O.s of the former Yugoslav army who had not yet been taken into activity – most of them Mihailovichist sympathizers – and then began rounding up hostages. Threatened with reprisals by the Italians if they aided the partisans, and suffering reprisals from the partisans if they did not, the peasants gradually withdrew what support they had given to the Liberation Front and were pushed into collaboration.

The Alliance had begun sporadically to organize the arming of village guards for the defence of the peasantry against indiscriminate attacks by Communist-led guerrillas. This was done initially with arms left over from the war but, as the situation came to a head, the Italians were approached for ammunition. The way was open for successful Italian military operations against the partisans who, by the autumn, had been disorganized and dispersed, although they had in the main escaped destruction and their nucleus had withdrawn into the hills south of Ljubljana. The population was confused.[29]

Out of the complex pattern of 1942, Tito's Communist movement, after having been almost destroyed, was to emerge, like a phoenix,

---

[29] Those regular officers who had escaped internment continued somewhat unsuccessfully their efforts to establish a non-Communist guerrilla network, in co-ordination with Mihailovich (militarily) and the Slovenian Alliance (politically). They had co-operated with the partisans until the summer, then held aloof from the clashes between partisans and village guards, and, after the autumn, tried to infiltrate the latter.

with increased strength. It was only the lack of co-ordination between the two Axis powers that enabled no more than one thousand partisans[30] to slip out of German-occupied Serbia into the Italian zone. They made their way through Sandjak, which had been given up by the Italian soldiery to bitter winter cold and roaming rival native bands, to the remote highlands of south-eastern Bosnia. There, at the end of January 1942, Tito set up his headquarters in the small town of Focha on the upper Drina, and started to reorganize his shattered partisan detachments.

Tension between the three inward-looking religious communities, now strained to its limit, was an obstacle to Communist influence in that region. After the atrocious crimes committed by the Ustashas against the Orthodox, and the contribution of their share of murder by Moslem bands, by the beginning of 1942 bands of armed Serbian peasants had the upper hand. Wanting only to defend their villages and avenge their dead, they were eager for leadership and help. Tito found that Mihailovich's influence was already predominant and that there were practically no Communists among them; yet the local Serbs welcomed Tito's 'Serbian army', in order to drag it into action against Moslems and Croats. It was then that the original partisans and the Communists were reorganized on a firm Party line into 'proletarian brigades', in order to prevent their revolutionary ideals from being contaminated. All the others who wanted to join but who would have winced – to quote Tito himself, reminiscing twenty-five years later – at becoming partisans 'or Communists, as we were called',[31] were formed into 'volunteer detachments'. To all new units, however, political commissars were appointed, to start the political education of the recruits.

In January, with the *chetniks* strengthening their position and Tito's partisans coming into the region, Germans and Ustashas intensified pressure to get rid of this accumulation of guerrillas in eastern Bosnia.[32] Although not liquidated, the two sets of insurgents had been seriously weakened, and each tried to neutralize one of their enemies. Unable to obtain help from Mihailovich, the *chetniks*, through Nedich, offered to stop fighting the Germans if Croatian forces withdrew from the region. Where the *chetniks* were unsuccessful, the partisans were more successful, for they managed to agree

[30] Dedijer, *Tito Speaks*, p. 171, mentions nine detachments. These were formed into the First Proletarian Brigade. Partisan brigades, according to Maclean, *Disputed Barricade*, p. 184, numbered, in the spring of 1942, roughly one thousand men each.
[31] Interview given to the Belgrade daily *Politika*, 28–29–30 November 1967.
[32] The enemy operations in early 1942 are the Second and Third Offensives of partisan military historians.

locally with the Ustashas not to fight each other while both concentrated their efforts against the *chetniks*.[33] In such circumstances, while the latter were even further weakened, the partisans used the relatively calmer atmosphere over the next three months to nurse their forces.

In spite of this, and in spite of the new recruits, the partisans were badly in need of help. Not much ammunition or food was available in these barren mountains, and throughout the spring, Tito kept appealing to the Comintern, but no help was forthcoming.[34] Tito had thought of going to the Communist-controlled free territory in Montenegro, but as a result of the Red terror, that position was destroyed, and it was the defeated Montenegrin Communists who joined Tito's force around Focha. Once again in serious difficulties, the partisan command decided to go west, to another no man's land, the border region between Bosnia and Croatia, from which reports had come of Communist successes. In mid-June, Tito's force[35] started on a long trek which was to last the whole summer, along a route which followed the border between the German and Italian zones, where N.D.H. garrisons were few and weak.

When they arrived in western Bosnia, Tito's units found that the local partisans already controlled a fairly large territory, and had the support of the native Serbian population. The Germans, at this stage, were more worried about Mihailovich's activities in regions of strategic importance than about Tito's in that remote corner of Bosnia. Thus, by the autumn, the partisans more or less controlled a territory almost the size of Switzerland. The seat of what was now officially called the 'People's Liberation Movement' was established in Bihach, a market town on the river Una, after its capture from the Ustashas in November.

The great success of the Communists in these parts was not due to their Marxism. Indeed, revolution was not being mentioned any longer after the lesson learnt from their disasters in eastern Yugoslavia. Experience had taught them that they could not yet stand

[33] Cf. Records of German Field Commands, Microcopy T-501, 247:001030, 001067, 001120, 001155, 001163.

[34] The Soviet government, not without justification, alleged technical difficulties, just as the British did to Mihailovich, but neither of the two resistance leaders would believe that the great power they looked to could not do more to help them in 1942. Furthermore, the Soviets, who at this stage of the war were interested in their own survival more than in the promotion of revolution in Yugoslavia, criticized the Yugoslav Communists for their inexplicable political attitudes. 'Are there really no other Yugoslav patriots – apart from Communists and Communist sympathizers – with whom you could join in a common struggle against the invaders?' one message said in March 1942 (quoted in Maclean, *Disputed Barricade*, p. 180).

[35] Estimated to be some 5,000 men (ibid., p. 184).

against a well-equipped army, and that survival depended on withdrawing and scattering when pursued. Locally, like all other guerrillas, they indulged in various limited, temporary, and mutually convenient arrangements with small enemy garrisons, and exchanged more important prisoners with the German, Italian, and Ustasha commands.[36] Success came to the Communists from their mobile guerrilla force with its Party nucleus, and from their advocating religious and ethnic tolerance, in spite of and against the feelings of local partisans. The partisans in Bosnia in 1942 were always on the side of those who were fighting for their lives, unless these happened to be political rivals. In south-eastern Bosnia, they had been greeted as protectors by the decimated Serbs, but though mostly Serbs themselves, they had also defended Catholics and Moslems from retaliation by Orthodox. Their reputation went ahead of them, it helped them in their march through Catholic and Moslem territory, and when they reached the Serbian regions in the west, they were welcomed once again as a Serbian army who fought the Ustashas, but they were careful to prevent hatred of the Ustashas from turning against the Croats generally. This helped them to develop their infiltration, at local level, of the N.D.H. administration and military.

The sudden development of Tito's movement, after its defeat in the homogeneous Serbian lands of the east, was due to its penetrating the desperate and leaderless struggle against extermination started by the Serbs in the mixed western regions, and to its preventing that struggle from turning to vengeance against Yugoslavs of other faiths. Whereas in most of Bosnia, after the Ustasha capitulation to the local armed bands in the spring, the authorities and soldiery of the N.D.H. had mainly disappeared from the uplands, along the borders of eastern Croatia, Ustasha, Italian, and German expeditions had gone on burning and killing, creating a feeling of hatred for Ustashas, Germans, and Italians alike. The massacres and the expeditions had caused a mass flight to the woods and mountains of young men and women, uprooted and eager to fight, dissatisfied with the compromise solutions welcomed by the older generations and those who had suffered less. These young Serbs flocked to the partisans, but eventually Croats also came, to escape conscription and service on the Russian front.

By taking them out of their respective milieux, the Communist Party turned the adolescents of Bosnia into members of suprareligious units, the only armed units in the mixed territories whose

[36] V. Dedijer, *With Tito through the War – Partisan Diary, 1941–1944*, London, 1951, p. 181; Clissold, *Whirlwind*, p. 153; W. Hoettl, *The Secret Front – The Story of Nazi Political Espionage*, London, 1953, pp. 164–5; and P. Shoup, *Communism and the Yugoslav National Question*, New York and London, 1968, p. 68.

recruitment was not on a religious basis. By the end of 1942, these were not territorial militias defending their own villages against other militias, but the 'People's Liberation Army'. Tito was its supreme commander, and the original partisans who had come with him from the east formed its cadres in a force that had increased tenfold since June.[37]

Life was slowly creeping back into the villages of the partisan territory. After the autumn came a lull in military operations which was used to organize, establish a rudimentary local administration, take over the village schools. Now that they had a territorial basis, the Communist leaders wanted to consolidate their political power as well. They were aware of the need to broaden the basis of the partisan movement, to create a political body which could attract a wider participation than the party's Central Committee. The Soviet government, for whom at that stage of the war the alliance with Great Britain and the U.S.A. was far more important than anything local Communist parties could do in occupied Europe to promote their own position, opposed the setting-up of a political organization which would appear as a counter-government to the existing and internationally recognized Yugoslav government in London, and criticized the Yugoslav Communists for not attempting to make common cause with other resistance groups.

All these considerations were reflected in the composition of the congress of the People's Liberation Movement, which opened at Bihach on 26 November 1942. Fifty-four delegates attended, including some non-Party personalities. This was the first session of the 'Anti-Fascist Council for the National Liberation of Yugoslavia'. It elected as its president an elderly Croatian fellow-traveller, Ivan Ribar, who had been president of the Constituent Assembly after the First World War, and it issued a manifesto on the aims of the movement. This publicly proclaimed that the People's Liberation Movement united all true patriots with the aim of liberating and restoring Yugoslavia as the democratically organized common state of all who lived on its territory. It recognized the religious and ethnic diversity of the population, and did not stress the political,

---

[37] It is impossible to arrive at a reliable estimate of the strength of the partisans in the late autumn of 1942. The Germans put it at 45,000 at the utmost, but Stephen Clissold, who was a British liaison officer with the partisans later in the war, estimates it at 'eight "divisions", each numbering between three and four thousand men, as well as the smaller partisan units proper'. Official Yugoslav sources say 137,000, and even 150,000 (O. Heilbrunn, *Warfare in the Enemy's Rear*, London, 1963, pp. 159 and 164; Clissold in his *Short History*, p. 220; Dedijer, *Tito Speaks*, p. 186). The highest figures seem out of proportion with the manpower and arms available at that time in the 'liberated territory'.

social, or economic aims of the Communist Party. To satisfy the Party's internal needs at that time, as well as the international demands of the Comintern, both the composition and the declared aims of the Bihach congress were meant to give the impression, in Yugoslavia and abroad, that the People's Liberation Movement was a broadly based patriotic expression rather than an instrument of Communist revolution. It was a movement designed to attract to the Communists all those Yugoslavs who wanted to contribute to the restoration of a common state on a democratic basis, but it remained both led and controlled by the Communist Party. Outside it there could be only traitors and collaborators.

The turn of the war

By the end of 1942, with the end of the crisis in North Africa, closer attention was paid by the Western Allies to Europe. In the order of priorities for the attention of the British S.O.E., the Balkans now figured second, after the Mediterranean islands, and before France.[38] The enemy was to be misled about the possibility and whereabouts of an Allied landing in Europe. In Yugoslavia, the arrangements in the coastal region between the various guerrilla groups and the Italians were no longer justified from the British point of view, especially as they turned the local guerrillas to fighting mostly against one another. The first task was to reinforce liaison with Mihailovich's Home Army. However, since the British had not been able to reconcile the two resistance movements, and since they wanted to be sure of support in all the Adriatic hinterland, it was decided to make contact with the partisans as well, since they were now also a force to be reckoned with.[39] During that winter and throughout the following spring, British S.O.E. agents were parachuted into occupied Serbia to be attached to all Mihailovich's unit commanders, and a senior liaison officer was stationed at his headquarters. In the spring, several agents were dropped to partisan units as well, with a liaison officer at Tito's own headquarters.

For the Germans, the sudden threat of a Balkan front made it imperative to ensure absolute control of communications throughout Yugoslavia, and of the Adriatic coast with its hinterland. Early in the new year, Hitler gave orders to suppress Mihailovich's rebels on German-occupied territory, and this was made abundantly clear to the population who were summoned, under threat of drastic sanctions, to co-operate in their destruction. For the Germans,

[38] M. Foot, *S.O.E. in France – An Account of the Work of the British Special Operations Executive in France, 1940–1944* (in the official *History of the Second World War* series), London, 1966, pp. 19 and 234.

[39] Woodward, op. cit., pp. 333–4; and Ehrman, op. cit., V, p. 78.

Mihailovich's remained the most dangerous of all insurrectionary organizations on the territory of the former Yugoslav state, and they feared the possibility of his linking together numerous other formations which, as Hitler believed, were only biding their time to strike a blow against the Axis when the Allies landed.[40]

To clear the Adriatic hinterland of all guerrillas, it was imperative that Italian troops should co-operate with the Germans, and Hitler himself impressed upon the Italian government the need to act urgently.[41] The first phase of this joint operation was to eliminate the partisans of western Bosnia. As soon as the Germans went into action from the north in mid-January, Tito decided to get out of their way. He knew that of all his opponents, Mihailovich was the weakest at that time in armaments and supplies, and also the most dangerous potentially. So he would forestall the Axis encirclement, go east again, there to concentrate all his efforts on destroying Mihailovich and all *chetniks* before an Allied landing. Once again, by quick withdrawal in the middle of winter, and by exploiting the bad co-ordination between Germans and Italians, as well as their links with the N.D.H. authorities, the Yugoslav Communists saved their forces from annihilation. The Italians were unable to close the trap in time from the south, and the People's Liberation Army got away from western Bosnia, with thousands of refugees who preferred to follow the partisans into snowbound uplands rather than remain to face retribution.

From then until May, the entanglement of antagonisms and arrangements between the different sides of occupation and resistance forces was to become increasingly complicated and bloody. Initially, and in spite of German objections, the Italian commanders on the spot had insisted on using local anti-Communist irregulars. They argued that it was impossible to deal at the same time with

[40] 'Among the various insurgent movements which increasingly cause trouble in the area of the former Yugoslav state, the movement of Drazha Mihailovich stands in first place with regard to leadership, armament, organization and activity', assessed a report by the head of German Military Intelligence in eastern Europe in February 1943 (*Trials of the War Criminals before the Nuremburg Military Tribunals*, XI, Washington, 1950, p. 1016).

[41] F. W. Deakin describes in detail some of these top-level exchanges, conferences, and decisions, on the basis of German and Italian documents, in *The Brutal Friendship – Mussolini, Hitler and the Fall of Italian Fascism*, London, 1962, pp. 89–103, *passim*. Ciano reported that Ribbentrop had said 'that not only the rebels but the whole civil population which had any kind of contact with the chetniks must be massacred in their entirety. He also repeated several times that one must exploit the warm relations which existed between some of our commands and the chetnik elements to lay a trap for Mihailovich and to hang him as soon as he fell into our hands' (quoted ibid, p. 97). The Axis operations of the first half of 1943 are known in Yugoslavia as the Fourth and Fifth Offensives.

Communists and anti-Communist guerrillas, and that it was convenient to make use of *chetniks* against partisans before getting rid of the former as well. In reality, they wanted to keep these contacts with the Western Allies, and they did not believe in the success of large-scale 'pacification' operations. The Italian High Command intended to send home as many as possible of its demoralized troops from Yugoslavia to strengthen the defences of Italy itself, holding only the coastal belt across the Adriatic. Leaving the Yugoslavs to fight a multiple civil war in the hinterland was, in Italian eyes, as good a way as any to neutralize all native guerrillas. By mid-February, however, the military situation of the Axis had taken a turn for the worse with the capitulation of Field-Marshal Paulus at Stalingrad, and the Italians' use of their Anti-Communist Volunteers had not been particularly successful.

Concerned about the situation in the Balkans, where the N.D.H. was increasingly weak and the guerrilla bands increasingly restless, Hitler, on 16 February in a personal letter to Mussolini, insisted that all guerrillas should be destroyed, along with their dependants and supporters, as the only way of safeguarding the all-important communications and mineral deposits in Yugoslavia, and of preventing a general revolt in case of a landing. Ribbentrop was sent to Rome to deliver the message and put it across to Mussolini how absolutely essential it was to accomplish the task before a British landing enabled Mihailovich to emerge as the head of a nationwide rising in the rear. To liquidate Mihailovich would not be easy, the Germans were doing their best in their own zone, Hitler concluded, and demanded that the Italians should start by eliminating *chetnik* formations from their zone.[42]

Mussolini undertook to comply with Hitler's request as soon as the operations in hand against the Communists had been completed, but this was precisely where the double game between Nationalists and Italians broke down. By the end of March, the partisans had been able to reach the river Neretva, but only at the double price of great losses and of negotiating with the Germans. On the other side of this important Axis link between Sarayevo and the coast, to the northeast were mountains controlled by Mihailovich, while to the southeast his influence was increasing in that part of the Adriatic hinterland. If he could prevent the partisans from getting across the valley, they would be destroyed by the Italians, and he would then

---

[42] The text of Hitler's letter has been published in *Les Lettres secrètes échangées par Hitler et Mussolini*, Paris, 1946, pp. 143–63 (the passage on the Balkans is on pp. 149–54). For Ribbentrop's mission to Rome and the Italo-German discussions on the situation in Yugoslavia, see Deakin, op. cit., pp. 159–200, *passim*, and 203.

be free to turn against the latter. The Italians, on the contrary, did not mind the partisans being diverted into Mihailovichist territory where the rival factions could be trusted to do each other much harm, but they were anxious to prevent any guerrillas from coming down the coast or blocking the valley of the Neretva. Some of the Nationalist commanders in Herzegovina and Montenegro, unable to appreciate the overall situation, and too dependent on the Italians for their guns and supplies, followed the wishes of the latter rather than Mihailovich's, while in northern Montenegro and Sandjak, local *chetniks*, acting independently of both Italians and Mihailovich, were busy clearing the region of the Italian-armed Moslem militia and, in so doing, burning and killing in Moslem settlements.

Hard-pressed by the increasing tightness of the Axis ring closing in on him in the spring of 1943, Tito in March had contacted the German authorities in Zagreb with the following offer: the partisans would stop harassing the Axis forces in the N.D.H., if they were allowed to return to their homes or withdraw to the east in order to fight the forces of Mihailovich. Discussions were also held about the Communists' attitude to an Anglo-American landing in Dalmatia, and the possibility was envisaged of joint German-partisan defensive action.[43] For once, both the German military and political representatives in Croatia were willing enough to accept such a compromise, which was also favourably viewed by the Italian representatives in Zagreb and in the Croatian government itself, for it now appeared to be the only way of eliminating the partisan movement from Croatia. Hitler, however, rejected the idea of the Germans using Communist against anti-Communist insurgents, just as he opposed the Italians' use of anti-Communist against Communist guerrillas. And just as the British were from that time on opposed to any arrangements between *chetniks* and Italians, so the Russians protested against contacts between partisans and Germans.[44]

[43] Milovan Djilas, in his *Conversations with Stalin*, London, 1963, p. 13, says that the essence of the talks lay in getting the Germans to recognize the rights of the partisans as combatants. The talks on joint action are referred to, on the basis of their own sources, by Clissold (*Whirlwind*, p. 151), Hoettl (op. cit., pp. 168–72), and General Rudolf Kiszling (*Die Kroaten*, Graz and Cologne, 1956, pp. 199–200). Ilija Jukić (*Pogledi na prošlost, sadašnjost i budućnost hrvatskog naroda*, London, 1965, pp. 145–53) was the first to reconstitute the talks as they appear in the German Foreign Ministry records. Professor Ivan Avakumović (*Mihailović prema nemačkim dokumentima*, London, 1969, pp. 112–14) has given a full reconstruction based on the captured German reports and on the Yugoslav published documents. Cf. Records of German Field Commands, Microcopy T-501, 265:001281, and 267:000528.

[44] To which the partisan command replied (not unlike some *chetnik* commanders): 'If you cannot send help, do not send advice either; we have our men and our refugees to think of' (Djilas, op. cit., p. 13).

The Germans anticipated that the partisans would attempt to break through into the no man's land of north-eastern Herzegovina, northern Montenegro, and Sandjak, and what was initially meant to be the second phase of the liquidation operation, reserved for the *chetniks* of the eastern section of the hinterland, was turned against both *chetniks* and partisans. This time, the German command was going to take no risks with the Italians, and assembled Ustashas and Moslems, with its own reliable SS divisions and specially trained anti-guerrilla and mountain units. It was going to turn guerrilla weapons against the guerrillas and, by terrorizing the population, make it impossible for them to subsist.

While the Germans were getting ready, the partisans threw themselves against the Montenegrin and other *chetnik* formations who were still waiting for them at the bend of the upper Neretva. For a full fortnight in March, the two Yugoslav factions fought each other ferociously while Axis forces moved into position to surround the whole area. The partisans eventually managed to cross the narrow gorge of the Neretva, but both they and the *chetniks* were nearing exhaustion. Moving in a gradually narrowing semicircle, from eastern Bosnia to Sandjak, the Germans aimed to capture Mihailovich's headquarters, destroy the Montenegrin *chetnik* forces, and finish off the partisans. The anti-Communist guerrillas suffered heavy losses in May, but while Mihailovich and his staff were able to escape back into western Serbia, several thousand *chetniks* were trapped and sent off to prison camps in Germany and elsewhere.

The partisans, who had managed to break away from the *chetniks* and were making their way up the valleys of northern Herzegovina and Montenegro, found themselves, after the destruction of the *chetnik* screen, exposed to the full pressure of the Axis operation. Surrounded, bombed from the air, shelled from the mountainsides, it was sheer desperation that kept them going, for all prisoners were killed on the spot. In the first days of June, they managed to get out by crossing the narrow gorge of the river Sutyeska and climbing up steep mountains. By the end of the month, they had succeeded in reaching the relative safety of the uplands of eastern Bosnia. Tired after two months of guerrilla fighting, the Germans did not pursue them, and withdrew once more to the north of the demarcation line, leaving the Italians to mop up, and Ustashas, Moslems, and Albanians to vent their rage against Serbs of all political persuasions and hues.

Since the beginning of the year, the Germans had also been active against guerrillas in other regions, and particularly in western Serbia. In July, after Mihailovich's return, their troops combed the region for several weeks, burning and killing throughout the countryside, and using all sorts of stratagems, including dressing up some of their soldiers as *chetniks*. All through the summer, with the help of Bulgarian reinforcements and of Ljotich's volunteers, they organized operations against Mihailovich's units in Serbia, while further waves of arrests and executions of Mihailovichist sympathizers were made, in order to eradicate his organization. Yet in spite of their disastrous losses, both movements survived, for only part of their forces, actual and potential, had been engaged in battle, and their leaders were still at large. The Germans' military solution had failed no less than the Italians' political solution. They were both reduced to offering rewards for the capture or death of Tito and Mihailovich.[45]

Both leaders believed that there would soon be an Allied landing on the Yugoslav coast. For this reason, Mihailovich was anxious to sort things out on the littoral beforehand. It had meant trying to destroy the Communists in that region; it had also meant attempting to end the arrangements with the Italians of the independent *chetniks*, and to integrate them into his Yugoslav Home Army. In Dalmatia, Mihailovich had attempted to take things over directly in the spring and appointed a delegate to go to Split to co-ordinate the hitherto somewhat haphazard action of pro-Allied Serbs and Croats. In the generally confused Dalmatian summer of 1943, much was achieved to improve relations between Croats and Serbs, and to prepare the ground for action against the occupation forces, yet the task was more arduous than it had seemed at first. The Communists had also increased their activities. While Tito considered the link with the British useful, both as a potential source of supplies, and in order to increase his influence over the population, he was desperate about the possibility of an Anglo-American landing which would have strengthened the position of Mihailovich, linked to the government in London. His overtures to the Germans having failed, the Communists went on playing on the anti-Mihailovich prejudices of many hesitant Croats. Many Italians as well as N.D.H. army officers established or strengthened contacts with both resistance organizations, waiting to see whom, Tito or Mihailovich, the Allies would back decisively.

By the time the Allies landed in Sicily and Mussolini fell from power in July, both resistance movements were well on the way to

---

[45] On 28 May 1943, the Italian governor of Montenegro had offered one million lire for Tito, and half a million for Mihailovich (Records of German Field Commands, Microcopy T-315, 67:000726). On 21 July, the German commander of Serbia offered 100,000 gold marks for Mihailovich or Tito, by the medium of posters, and through the German-controlled press (*Novo Vreme*).

recovery, and waiting for the collapse of Italy to take over its spoils. Both were back in their earlier territory: Tito's in the west, still mostly manned by the Serbian peasantry from the western regions and officered by Communist Party members; Mihailovich's in the east, generally made up of Serbian peasants from the eastern parts and commanded by elements of the regular army. They had one aim in common – the renewal of Yugoslavia as a unified and independent country on the side of the Allies.

Since June, Mihailovich was back in his bastion of inner Serbia, soon branching out again into eastern Bosnia, Herzegovina, and Montenegro, with the backbone of his movement functioning once more. Practically all the local authorities followed the orders of Mihailovich's organization, and most of the officers and men of Nedich's State Guard regarded themselves as being on the same side as King Peter's minister of the armed forces, against the partisans and the Germans. It was understood that, when Mihailovich gave the order, the Guard, with the exception of the higher commanders, would go over to the Yugoslav Home Army.

Mihailovich's had been conceived as a purely military undertaking in the service of the Yugoslav state. Ustashism, however, had limited it to a movement which although Yugoslav in name, was almost entirely Serbian in composition. The appearance of a rival movement which did not recognize the legal government and had its own political programme, coupled with the lack of a clear political lead from his government in London, forced Mihailovich to think in terms of acting as a Yugoslav leader on behalf of the Yugoslav government. The remaining representatives in Serbia of the old political parties agreed with him, the more so since many of the younger officers tended to attribute the disasters of 1941 to the treachery of the Croats and the inefficiency of the politicians. Feelings were beginning to subside on both the Serbian and the Croatian sides, Croats were slowly coming over to the resistance, Serbs were gradually becoming aware of the need to co-operate with them, and Tito's movement had already made full use of this. Mihailovich had tried to contact local leaders and parties outside Serbia, but whereas in Serbia such contact was easy, and the views of the non-Communist Left were close to his own, outside Serbia things were no easier than before. Contact with Dalmatia was once again difficult. In Bosnia, Nedich's conception of 'preserving Serbdom' for some vague post-war Greater Serbia was nearer to the local *chetnik* leaders' way of thinking than Mihailovich's talk of friendship with the other communities for a federal reconstruction of Yugoslavia. In Slovenia, he kept trying to come to a working arrangement with the Slovenian Alliance through the army officers who acknowledged his command, but the Italians were back to gentler methods of dividing the Slovenes among themselves, partisans were starting up again, and the Alliance was worried with more immediate and more local preoccupations.

Outside Yugoslavia, Mihailovich had intensified his contacts with neighbouring countries. Both sides of the resistance dreamt of uniting south-east Europe under a new Yugoslavia, and the Communists, too, looked to Bulgaria, Greece, and Albania, across Macedonia, to which Tito paid much attention in 1943. The Communists there had been divided between pro-Yugoslavs and pro-Bulgars, and were not very active. As for the mass of the population in Macedonia, it was indifferent to the relatively meek Bulgarian administration, until it began to find out that it had exchanged Serbianization for Bulgarianization. Neither Mihailovich nor Tito had much success in that region until the latter took up again the idea of playing the card of Macedonian nationalism, in order to make use of the increasing dislike of Bulgarianization, and make communism within a Yugoslav context appealing to the Macedonians. He sent one of his lieutenants to work from the Italo-Albanian zone of Macedonia, in which conditions were similar to those parts of the N.D.H. where the partisans had been successful: Italian control was lax, the Serbs had been revolted by the excesses of the enemy-backed Albanians, while the Moslems feared large-scale Serbian *chetnik* vindictiveness.

Over the summer, Tito's men had worked their way back across Bosnia to their earlier base. In N.D.H. territory, the demoralization of the régime facilitated the partisans' reorganization. Their permanent forces, made up of Party members and uprooted peasants, were very much more mobile than the anti-Communists whose recruitment was always territorial, hence the ease with which Tito could order his fighters from one end of the country to the other. Now that Ustasha power was fast declining, the mass of the Catholics and Moslems began instinctively, though still only passively, to look to the partisans, for they saw Mihailovich's movement only through the local Serbian *chetniks* who claimed allegiance to him.

While Mihailovich's movement had remained predominantly military, Tito's was essentially political, and better armed with propaganda. In order to destroy Mihailovich's prestige, isolate him, and deprive him of Allied recognition, an image of him was projected among non-Serbs as the bearer of Serbian vengeance, and among Serbs as the agent of the British who were simply exploiting them. All opponents were denounced as collaborators. In this campaign, no sooner had the Soviets withstood the first shock of the German invasion, than they started to help the Yugoslav Communists with propaganda, if not yet with arms. As for the British, there were signs that they too, on the eve of the landing in Sicily, were beginning to prefer Tito to Mihailovich.

The fact that they were fighting together against Germany had not yet generated entire confidence between the Soviet Union and the Western Allies. Fearing that the West might let them fight the Germans to mutual exhaustion, the Russians had been asking for the opening of a second front in western Europe, which Anglo-American military strategy had decided could take place only in 1944. In the meantime, the possibility could not entirely be excluded that, once the Germans were turned out of Russia, the Soviet leaders might revert to a policy of keeping out of the war, and of allowing the Western Allies and Germany to fight to mutual exhaustion. Indirect immediate help could be given to the Soviet Union, and the ground prepared for a cross-Channel invasion, by secondary action in and around the Mediterranean which would force the collapse of Italy, and compel Germany to divert forces both from the eastern front and from western Europe. In Yugoslavia, consequently, the British would tend to support the guerrilla movement which appeared to be pinning down the greatest number of enemy troops, especially if, notwithstanding Foreign Office warnings, that same movement appeared to be viewed more favourably by the Soviet government.

The Yugoslav government in London was also losing prestige in British eyes. Owing to the endemic deadlock of the Serbo-Croatian disagreement, it was unable to provide united leadership for the pro-Yugoslav moderate forces in the country which, wedged between Fascism and communism, looked to their exiled leaders. A further factor complicating the political life of the government was King Peter's wish to marry, which his advisers opposed as inopportune. Blown up out of all proportion to reality in the rarefied atmosphere of London, this provoked the resignation of Professor Yovanovich in June 1943. After a transitory successor, the appointment in August of Purich, a senior diplomat, marked the end of the all-party government that had at least had the merit of being so representative of the Yugoslav political spectrum on 27 March 1941. Purich's, though it kept General Mihailovich, was a cabinet of civil servants, with no political authority. Its existence now depended on the confidence of a twenty-year-old monarch who wanted a cabinet to approve his marriage, and on the toleration of the British prime minister.

It was in that period that Mihailovich lost British confidence. The recently arrived S.O.E. operatives had been trained in demolition work, but not in the intricacies of the Yugoslav situation. They had been instructed to increase the former, and avoid the latter.⁴⁶ Eager for action, they demanded more and more sabotage action, and, in order to obtain it, promised help that never came, for the problem of supply was a real one, and what was dropped after their arrival was disappointing. Mihailovich, like everyone in the Balkans, expected a British landing, and he was preparing for it, but meanwhile, in the light of past experience, he thought it best to limit action to essentials only, so as to avoid renewed slaughter and premature destruction. His movement had been so inflated by Allied propaganda that the British officers were disappointed by a reality which they found to be below their expectations, and they tended initially to brush off the magnitude of reprisals as excuses or exaggerations. So much praise had been lavished on General Mihailovich through the B.B.C. that it was found puzzling among Serbs, now that British officers were actually to be seen with all guerrilla units, that they were not the advance guard of direct military intervention, or at least of large-scale parachuted help. Tension developed between Mihailovich's headquarters and the British liaison officers.⁴⁷

On the other hand, liaison officers sent to the partisans arrived to find enemy action against them at its height. Their training and experience were as inadequate as that of their opposite numbers with Mihailovich's units, but they were able to witness the ordeals of the crossing of the Sutyeska. Captain Deakin, an Oxford don who had helped Winston Churchill with his historical writings,⁴⁸ had come to Tito's headquarters in northern Montenegro in late May; he was wounded along with him, and was moved by the partisans' resilience. This was the first direct contact between S.O.E. and Tito, and Deakin's reports of the partisans' heroic deeds made a deep impression on the military authorities in the Middle East. Tito was quick to take advantage of British exasperation with his political rivals, and of the first favourable impressions gained by the British officers.

⁴⁶ C. Thayer, *Guerrilla*, London, 1964, pp. 122-3, and J. Rootham, *Miss Fire - The Chronicle of a British Mission to Mihailovich, 1943-1944*, London, 1946, pp. 3-4.

⁴⁷ See Rootham, op. cit., chapters 1-5, *passim*. In the rank-and-file, there was growing suspicion, fanned by Communist propaganda, that Great Britain was coldly planning to use Yugoslav flesh and blood to further its own ends, and growing fear, encouraged by German propaganda, that Great Britain was gradually selling out to Russia in the Balkans. In a speech delivered in February 1943, in the presence of British officers, Mihailovich complained: 'Since France is no more, we have no one in the world; we are alone, and our allies behave as if they were merchants of human flesh.' This caused a diplomatic incident in London, and further estranged the British.

⁴⁸ F. W. Deakin, the historian, author of *The Brutal Friendship*. In 1969 he received from President Tito two high Yugoslav awards 'for special services in the People's Liberation War'.

Mihailovich allowed facts to speak for themselves, and facts often spoke wrongly, badly, or not at all to British operatives who, anyhow, did not always understand them. Tito spoke up and interpreted facts – those that spoke well in his favour, and those that the British wanted to hear.

The opinion could have been formed in British policy-making circles that, if Tito assumed power, he might want to have friends in the West to offset the friendship of the Soviet Union, which was then not giving more than moral help, and could in the future become heavy-handed. To support Tito might help to remove Soviet suspicions of Western intentions, and make Tito responsive to British influence. To this possibility should be added the fact that, to many people near the British policy-making centre, distance, lack of real knowledge about Yugoslavia, left-wing tendencies, Communist propaganda, and the constant discord of the Yugoslav government leaders in London, all combined to make the exiled ministers appear as reactionary, the horrors of the ethnic and religious massacres as exaggerated, and Mihailovich as synonymous with *chetnik* anti-Communist monarchism, anti-Catholic anti-Moslem Serbian nationalism, and accommodation with the enemy. In 1943, the B.B.C. started to soft-pedal Mihailovich and place more emphasis on Tito. By the end of the summer, Tito had been placed as hero of the Yugoslav resistance on the pedestal once built for Mihailovich. The Allied press sang the praises of Tito's forces with as much exaggeration of exploits and numbers as it had done for Mihailovich, who had now become the villain of the Balkans.

Militarily, the Allied invasion of Italy made it necessary to exploit every opportunity of involving the enemy on the Yugoslav side of the Adriatic as well. During the summer, it was decided to increase again the scope of the British missions to both movements, to place each of them under an officer holding the rank of brigadier, and to attach American observers to them. The two new heads of mission were to report on the relative value of each force's contribution, and make recommendations as to how it could be increased.

By the time Brigadiers Maclean and Armstrong had reached their respective destinations, Italy had already surrendered. Germany had been prepared for this eventuality, and from 8 September 1943 to early October events moved fast in Yugoslavia. Native guerrillas joined Germans in a scramble for Italian territory and equipment, but German troops took over from the Italians key positions and lines of communication, although in some instances they had to do it by force. Some Italians surrendered to the guerrillas, but most of them were removed as prisoners to Germany. During October, the Germans formed a special administration for the Adriatic littoral, grouping the Julian region around Trieste, the province of Ljubljana, and the Dalmatian coast, and proceeded to exploit Italo-Slav animosities in order to make their task easier.

When the Germans moved into the province of Ljubljana, the struggle between Communists and anti-Communists had been going on for a year under the Italians. The partisans had clear political aims and discipline. The anti-Communists gave their support to the Yugoslav government in London and recognized General Mihailovich's nominal command over all Yugoslav armed forces in the country. Otherwise their direct political leadership remained in the hands of the Populist- (Catholic) dominated Slovenian Alliance, their potential military strength in the village guards, and their actual military strength in small underground armed groups under Mihailovich's officers. Taking for granted a military landing in Istria, they planned to take over and concentrate the village guards, and join the advancing Allies. Not only was their premise false, but the partisans were quicker. Within one day of the armistice, claiming to be the only force recognized by the Allies, and helped in that by the British liaison mission,[49] they had obtained the surrender of many Italian arms and become the best-equipped force in the region. While the village guards hesitated to rally Mihailovich's officers, the partisans were able to defeat, destroy, or disperse, first the latter's smaller concentration, then the former. In Ljubljana, the Germans set up a native Slovenian administration under the former Yugoslav General Rupnik, who was allowed to build up an anti-Communist Home Guard of what remained of the village guards. In Montenegro, where the Germans only came to control the coast and some key positions, more fighting broke out between Nationalists and Communists. By the end of October, the Montenegrin partisans were once more in control of parts of the territory; they had succeeded in capturing and killing General Djukanovich together with most of the Nationalist commanders, though not in eliminating the local *chetnik* units, who were now left mostly undisturbed by the Germans. In Dalmatia, as everyone anticipated an early Allied landing, Communists and Nationalists joined forces and a spontaneous, united movement took over the cities, but only for a short time, for German forces moved in quickly to recover control of the coast.[50]

For the Ustashas, the disappearance of Italy meant the end of the

---

[49] Cf. W. Jones, *Twelve Months with Tito's Partisans*, Bedford, 1946, pp. 101–4.
[50] German operations in the Italian zone in September and October 1943 are known as the Sixth Offensive in Yugoslav historiography.

endemic tension with one of their co-protectors. While their pro-German wing gained in ascendancy, others were beginning to think that they should try and follow Italy's example, and defect while there was still time. The idea that the Western Allies might be willing to sponsor the survival of an independent Croatian state rather than see it form part of a Communist-dominated Yugoslavia now had credence both within the Ustasha leadership and outside it. The majority of Croats, however, were less worried about saving an independent Croatian state, Ustasha or not, which they saw as doomed, and more about which side of the resistance to go over to.

Although no formal decision had as yet been taken by the Allies against Mihailovich, Italian troops in Yugoslavia had been instructed to surrender to the partisans. Whereas a few Italian garrisons did surrender to Mihailovich's forces in Sandjak and Montenegro, Tito's had been able to disarm at least six divisions,[51] and obtain much from the great military depots of the coastal towns before the Germans moved in. This was the first time that either of the two resistance movements had been able to arm itself properly, but it was merely one of several factors which contributed to strengthening Tito's position in the western regions of Yugoslavia.

The B.B.C. had done for Tito morally at least as much as Italian armament achieved materially. All who wanted to join the victors on the eve of victory threw in their lot with the partisans. Thousands of members of the N.D.H. army went over to the People's Liberation Army, in which officers were given equivalent rank.[52] The Croatian youth began to adhere to the partisans, especially in Dalmatia, where even Serbs looked to them since the collapse of Italy had brought about the moral collapse of the local *chetniks*.

An important reason for Tito's success in western Yugoslavia was the failure of sectional nationalisms. Their rejection of the common state and their mutual antagonism had led them to seek the support of the Axis powers who had destroyed Yugoslavia, and who were now losing the war. In the backward and mixed regions which had so much suffered from the settlement of accounts between Catholics, Moslems, and Orthodox, the new political order of the Communists, which proclaimed the 'equality and brotherhood' of communities and faiths, was especially attractive. Mihailovich, far away in Serbia,

---

[51] Ehrman, op. cit., V, p. 79.
[52] One partisan general whom Maclean came across had held commissions in the armies of the Austro-Hungarian monarchy, the kingdom of Yugoslavia, and the N.D.H. in turn, before being accepted in the People's Liberation Army (*Eastern Approaches*, London, 1949, p. 352).

had failed to establish any significant appeal in those parts, except as a vague and misinterpreted symbol for one of the communities. Tito now felt stronger than Mihailovich.

In the east, however, in Serbia with eastern Bosnia and Montenegro, the situation was very different. The population was homogeneous, and its disappointment with the events of 1941 had thus never taken on a violently anti-Yugoslav aspect. It was opposed to the Axis, it stood behind Mihailovich, and Tito's appeal was negligible. The collapse of Italy had had consequences for Mihailovich as well. When he had learnt the news, he was still in the mountainous corner bordering on Sandjak and Bosnia, and intense activity followed for about a month. Although it brought him only a small part of Italian spoils, it did rally to his orders the remains of the local *chetniks*, and enabled him to attack German positions in eastern Bosnia.

It was at that time that Brigadier Armstrong took over as the new overall head of the British mission, with instructions to obtain a steep rise in sabotage action, so as to keep the Germans guessing, and to test Mihailovich. In late September, operations had reached Vishegrad on the Drina, an important point on the Sarayevo-Belgrade line, well garrisoned by Germans and Ustashas, which Mihailovich's forces were able to take while putting the railway line out of action, before proceeding towards Sarayevo in pursuit of the Germans. Soon, however, the partisans from Montenegro were attacking in the rear. Placed between Germans and partisans, as partisans had once been between Germans and *chetniks*, Mihailovich's units had to retreat. The Germans came back, and it was the turn of the partisans to retreat, by following Mihailovich across the Drina into western Serbia. Mihailovich moved his headquarters further north into Serbia where, during the autumn months, action had also been stepped up, especially in the Morava valley, with its all-important railway.

The capitulation of Italy had greatly increased optimism in German-occupied Serbia, where the population also turned *en masse* to the representative of the victors, in this case General Mihailovich, minister of the London government. Allied propaganda had a completely different effect in Serbia than in Croatia; it caused indignation among people who knew Mihailovich's organization at close quarters. Now that he could recruit as many eager young men as he pleased, Mihailovich was at last able to form a permanent mobile force which could be sent anywhere, to fight the occupation forces, and give more cohesion to his movement. Time, however, was against him, for not only was Tito well ahead of him in western Yugoslavia in terms of mobility and centralized command, of armament and Allied support, but in Serbia itself, the Germans once again worked at undoing his efforts.

One year after the Bihach congress, the Communist leadership felt sufficiently strengthened at home and abroad to set up a counter-government. At Yaytse, a small town in Bosnia which had been captured by the partisans, 142 delegates met for a second session of the Anti-Fascist Council. On 29 November 1943, it took a number of decisions which virtually set up a new state there and then. In order to give satisfaction to all ethnic groups in the country, including those who had laid claims to separate identities and whom the Axis had used against Yugoslavia, and in order to obviate the fear of imbalance due to Serbian predominance, Yugoslavia was to be a federation of six units – Serbia, Croatia, Slovenia, Macedonia, Montenegro, and Bosnia-Herzegovina. The question of the monarchy was to be settled by the people after the complete liberation of the country. Meanwhile, the government in London was denied any rights, and King Peter forbidden to return from exile. The Anti-Fascist Council assumed legislation functions and gave its executive, the National Committee for the Liberation of Yugoslavia, the character of a provisional government. Tito was made its president and given the title of marshal.

Mihailovich's position was by that time distinctly weaker. Two of his commanders, wedged in between Germans and Communists, concluded temporary cease-fire arrangements with the former on their own initiative, in order to gain time. Interpreted by them as a sign of German weakness, the arrangements were seen as a sign of Mihailovich's weakness by the Germans, who tried to extend them. The opposition of both Hitler and Mihailovich, however, put an end to them before the winter was over. But there was another weakness to Mihailovich's position. Linked to the government in London which, however moderate, had been unable to offer a constructive lead on the question of inter-communal relations, he had not himself attempted to give any political unity to his movement, beyond loyalty and obedience to that government. With Zhivko Topalovich, the leader of the small Yugoslav Socialist Party, whose influence at his headquarters was increasingly felt, Mihailovich agreed that the time had come to answer the Communist challenge with a radical programme compatible with, yet more positive than, mere attachment to legal continuity.

The answer to the Yaytse congress was the Ba congress of January 1944. There, in a village of western Serbia, 274 delegates gathered, including refugees speaking on behalf of the Slovenian political parties and the Yugoslav-orientated Croats. Topalovich was elected president, and, on 27 January, resolutions were passed calling for the reorganization of Yugoslavia as a federation of three units – Serbia, Croatia, and Slovenia – each of which would in turn provide within it autonomies for its different communities. All changes were, however, to be carried out after the liberation, once the state had been restored by legal means and democratic methods. Until then a Central National Committee, representing political groups and regions in Yugoslavia, would embody the political aspect of the movement, and co-operate with the Allies and the government in London. The congress deplored the Communist Party's unilateral attempt to change the constitutional order, and appealed to it to unite with other political forces. Soon afterwards, the political organization set up at Ba attempted to contact Machek again, this time with a plan to co-ordinate the action of moderate Serbian, Croatian, and Slovenian forces, while in the territories under Mihailovich's command, local committees began to function as organs of civilian political control.

The expected victory of Yugoslavia's allies now meant that the country would be restored as an independent and united state. This simplified the nature of the civil war. Those native forces of separatism which had thrown in their lot with the occupants were fast declining, and would collapse along with Germany. The religious and ethnic aspect of the war was receding. The average Yugoslav, whether he sympathized with the one movement or the other, and even the average fighter in each camp, wanted a state based on a new order, and no return to the past, but they did not think in terms of a revolution, especially not one affecting their peasant land tenure. Hence the relative restraint of the Titoists' Yaytse programme, and the relative radicalism of the Mihailovichists' Ba programme.

Tito's 'army' lorded it over western Bosnia, parts of eastern Croatia, and most of inland Dalmatia; Mihailovich's over Serbia, Sandjak, parts of Montenegro, eastern Bosnia and Herzegovina, and a smaller part of inland Dalmatia. The Germans' aim was to control those stretches of Yugoslav territory which they considered of decisive importance – areas with mineral deposits, vital communication links, and the coast. This they were able to do, even without Italy's help, but only at the price of practically giving the rest over to guerrillas. Rather than attempt to crush them, the Germans now resorted to political warfare with ever greater emphasis. To fan the flames of civil war, as a means of preventing the Allies from gaining in the Balkans any solid advantage from the collapse of Italy, German propaganda depicted one set of guerrillas as sinister agents of Red terror, and the other as deluded hangers-on of the perfidious Anglo-Saxons. To Slovenes, Croats, and Serbs, the Germans were presented as the only effective protectors against each other, the Italians, the British, and the Russians, at the same time as they continued with reprisals, thus much reducing the activity of both resistance movements over the winter. For both movements, the fight against the Germans, whose defeat at the hands of the Allies was a question of time, was more than ever before secondary to the civil strife. The contenders could tie down a certain number of German troops. They could not free Yugoslavia from German control.[53]

After a month with Tito, Brigadier Maclean was the first British liaison officer with the Yugoslav guerrillas to return to the outer world and personally deliver a full report on the situation in Yugoslavia. Of the two heads of mission sent out in September, he was obviously the nearer to the prime minister. Churchill had instructed him 'simply to find out who was killing the most Germans and suggest means by which we could help them to kill more. Politics must be a secondary consideration.'[54] Maclean knew little about the background situation. He was a Conservative M.P. with a varied experience of diplomatic and military service, a taste for adventure, and a romantic enthusiasm for action. He had arrived in Yugoslavia in time to see the partisans take over Dalmatia, briefly but efficiently. He does not appear to have witnessed much fighting, nor to have known anything about Mihailovich except from partisan sources.

---

[53] A precise count of the strength of both movements at the end of 1943 is impossible, yet some attempt must be made at least to compare figures from different sources. 300,000 armed fighters is the figure adopted for the partisans by the official histories of the war in Yugoslavia (e.g. *Enciklopedija Jugoslavije*, V, Zagreb, 1962, p. 138). Allied propaganda in the autumn of 1943 mentioned 250,000. The Foreign Office thought that the British military authorities exaggerated the value of partisan forces (Woodward, op. cit., pp. 335 and 338), and the Yugoslav government, naturally, did not accept these estimates (ibid., p. 339; Martin, op. cit., p. 45; and K. Pavlović's review article of the Macmillan war memoirs in *Glas kanadskih Srba*, Windsor, Ont., 25 April–30 May 1968). Sir Fitzroy Maclean, in the account of his mission published in 1949 (*Eastern Approaches*, p. 331), estimated Tito's forces at 150,000. A correspondent of the London weekly *The Tablet* ('Tito's Military Achievement: The Legend and the Fact', 28 April 1945, pp. 196–7), in an analysis based on partisan communiqués of the time, cross-checked them against each other, and against enemy communiqués, and arrived at a total of 60,000–80,000. On a tour of Mihailovich's units in Serbia at the end of 1943, a group of British and American officers estimated that, given arms, he could throw into battle at least 250,000–300,000 trained men, but that only about 72,000 were actually in active service in Serbia, 10,000–11,000 of them fully armed (A. Seitz, *Mihailović – Hoax or Hero?*, Columbus, Ohio, 1953, p. 81). These figures are slightly below those that can be gleaned from the accounts published abroad since the war by participants in Mihailovich's movement. The Yugoslav military encyclopaedia (*Vojna enciklopedija*, VI, Belgrade, 1964, p. 111) puts the figure at 60,000.

[54] *Eastern Approaches*, p. 281.

The gist of his report was that the partisans were 'killing the most Germans'. They refused to co-operate with Mihailovich, and only armed intervention on a large scale could prevent them from taking power after the German withdrawal. On the ruins of the old order, which had already been destroyed by the war, they must be expected to set up a totalitarian and Moscow-orientated form of government. Maclean concluded that it was advisable to establish satisfactory relations with them and help them kill more Germans. All this confirmed the views of the British prime minister who, moreover, believed that if British influence was established with the partisans, it could redress the political situation after the war through free elections.[55]

The new trend, which had been visible since the beginning of the year, became official and fully operative by the end of 1943. On 8 November, the Allied supreme commander in the Mediterranean, General Wilson, broadcast a message denouncing all those forces in Yugoslavia who were dishonouring the name of *chetnik* by acting against the forces of freedom, and claiming to be acting with British approval. At Teheran, between 28 November and 1 December, Churchill, Roosevelt, and Stalin agreed to give all possible help to the partisans in Yugoslavia. Early in December, in Cairo, concrete steps were taken to carry out the agreement. It was decided to increase substantially the despatch of supplies to Tito from bases in Italy, and to extend both the size and the scope of the British mission. Orders were sent to all British officers with Mihailovich's units to leave them.

From Drvar to Belgrade, via Bari and Moscow

Pavelich's N.D.H. was well suited for Tito's movement to grow in. The more obvious the coming defeat of Germany became and the nearer the break-up of the satellite Ustasha state, the greater the number of Croats who wanted to leave that sinking boat.[56] The People's Liberation Movement offered them a way out. It was in such an atmosphere that Tito's movement expanded, especially since over the winter 1943–44 Allied support was now at last forthcoming. Thirty-two bombers were placed at S.O.E.'s disposal in the Mediterranean, while in January 1944 both the Americans and the

[55] On Maclean's views and his reports, see his *Eastern Approaches*, pp. 338–41, and Woodward, op. cit., p. 338.
[56] Even among the Ustashas, some wanted to break away from Nazi Germany. A conspiracy, led by two ministers, hoped to offer an alternative to Tito by getting rid of the *poglavnik*, and bringing the N.D.H. over to the Allies. It was detected in the summer of 1944, and Pavelich applied Ustasha terror to the Ustashas themselves.

Russians decided to establish independent missions with the Yugoslav partisans. Tito was hailed as the acknowledged leader of the Yugoslav resistance. Allied support, material and moral, caused many Croats to believe that Tito would moderate his communism, and this was confirmed by the fact that, in Croatia, his movement welcomed almost everyone who would co-operate.

In eastern Yugoslavia, however, the great majority of the population was solidly behind Mihailovich, and Tito's influence was negligible in Serbia. It was not only that Allied propaganda could not change the stubborn Serbian peasants' opinion of a movement they had seen at work in their midst. It was felt that in Tito's new Yugoslavia, such as it had been sketched out at Yaytse, the Serbs would be more partitioned than ever, and the bulk of them in Serbia separated from those in Macedonia, Montenegro, and Bosnia-Herzegovina, not to mention those further west. The British loss of confidence in Mihailovich, and the Serbs' disappointment with the British, played into the hands of German psychological action.[57]

In 1944 the Germans renewed operations to clear the territory between Belgrade, the Danube and the Greater Morava valley, and the littoral with its hinterland – of both partisans and *chetniks*. The occupation of many islands by the partisans, in particular, was a constant threat to German sea communications and a possible springboard for an Allied landing. As for the control of the former territory by Mihailovich's men, it threatened German land communications, and their eventual retreat routes. This last major attempt against the Yugoslav resistance also aimed at capturing the heads of both movements.

There were not, however, enough occupation troops available for manning coastal defences, keeping communications clear, and waging anti-guerrilla warfare, at a time when more and more troops were required on the eastern front. Thus, in January, although they considered it necessary to mount a major offensive against Mihailovich, finding their forces insufficient for the task, the Germans had to settle for a number of smaller actions.[58] No sooner had they found out that a political congress had been held at Ba under their very noses, than they resorted once more to large-scale arrests in order to get at the organizers. A particular

[57] From the end of September 1943, more and more action had been demanded of Mihailovich, and less and less said abroad about the resulting activity. Of the German offers of rewards for the capture of Tito and Mihailovich, only the first had been spoken of. The B.B.C. even attributed to Tito's forces action by Mihailovich's units. The action at Vishegrad was thus attributed to the partisans, on the strength of Titoist sources, in spite of the reports sent in by the Allied officers present (Seitz, op. cit., pp. 27–35).

[58] Heilbrunn, op. cit., p. 163.

effort was made to force native auxiliaries to co-operate in tracking down Mihailovich. This caused a crisis at the top of the collaborationist administration of Serbia. Most of Nedich's ministers and his Guard commanders were against taking part in this drive with the Germans, for they knew that all their men would desert, and they were now fighting shy of blatantly unpopular action. Pressed, Nedich tried to resign. He was not allowed to, but from that moment on, although he remained formally head of the 'Serbian Government', all vestiges of his influence disappeared. Mihailovich escaped capture and withdrew to eastern Serbia.

The Germans also missed Tito, but this was a much nearer miss.[59] During the latter part of 1943, his headquarters had been nomadic in middle Bosnia. By the beginning of 1944, he was back in western Bosnia, in the small town of Drvar. On 25 May, the partisan High Command was surprised by an airborne attack. Tito with his staff, the Allied missions, and their escort barely escaped capture, and lost touch with their forces. It was then that the Russians, fearing for the co-ordinated control of his movement, advised Tito to get out of Yugoslavia, to Allied-occupied Bari on the Italian side of the Adriatic. Early in June, having reached a partisan-held air strip, Tito was evacuated, yet he was as anxious to return to a firm base in Yugoslavia as the British were anxious not to have yet another exile in their care.

By that time, of all the islands, only Vis, more than 50 kilometres away from the Yugoslav mainland, had not been retaken by the Germans. It had been turned into an Anglo-partisan base, through which may of the Allied supplies reached Yugoslavia. It was to Vis that Tito was taken from Bari by a British destroyer. Large-scale intervention by the Western Allies, in the form of air support and supplies from Italy, saved the partisans,[60] but for the first time

[59] The 'Seventh Offensive'.

[60] Between June 1941 and June 1943, few British supplies had reached either Yugoslav resistance movement: 23 tons of material were dropped to Mihailovich and 6½ tons to Tito. With the supply of aircraft to S.O.E., the volume of airborne supplies rose in the third quarter of 1943 to 144 tons to both movements. At the end of September 1943, naval coastal forces were diverted to help the bombers, and more than 2,000 tons were landed in the last quarter of the year on partisan-held islands, in addition to 125 tons of airborne supplies. During the first quarter of 1944, over 6,500 tons were either landed or dropped, increasing in the second quarter to some 8,500 tons (Ehrman, op. cit., V, pp. 79–80 and 273). 'The following figures for supplies during 1944 give some idea of the scale on which the Western Allies were now helping the Partisans: over 100,000 rifles; over 50,000 light machine guns and sub-machine guns; 1,380 mortars; 324,000 mortar bombs; 636,000 grenades; over 97,500,000 rounds of small-arms ammunition; 700 wireless sets; 175,000 suits of battle-dress; 260 pairs of boots' (Maclean, *Eastern Approaches*, p. 461).

since he had taken the field in the summer of 1941, Tito and his High Command were separated from the bulk of his forces.

The problem for the British government during the first half of 1944 was how to reconcile its *de facto* military alliance with the People's Liberation Movement, and its *de jure* obligations to the Yugoslav government abroad. Short-term considerations had originally made the military authorities in the Middle East turn their attention to the partisans. The liaison officers sent to them had become enthusiastic promoters of the partisans' cause.[61] Brigadier Maclean argued that the partisans were of such military value that the British government should subordinate political to military considerations. Furthermore, he did not believe that the monarchy was any longer a unifying factor in Yugoslavia, and assumed that the ultimate success of the partisans would be in accordance with British interests in so far as it would lead to the establishment of a strong and independent Yugoslavia. He advised dropping Mihailovich and giving full support to Tito, while maintaining only formal relations with the king's government, until the time when the question of Yugoslavia's form of government could be freely settled by the Yugoslavs themselves after liberation. The Foreign Office, on the other hand, kept warning that such a policy would prejudice the question of the post-war régime by handing over control in advance to the Communists; it thought that Brigadier Maclean exaggerated the strength of the partisans outside the N.D.H., and it did not neglect the reports from the liaison officers with the other movement which spoke of massive and uncompromising opposition to Tito among the peasants in eastern Yugoslavia.[62]

[61] Twenty-five years later, five of the survivors, including Sir Fitzroy Maclean, were awarded Yugoslav honours on the occasion of the visit to London, in February 1970, of the chairman of the Yugoslav Federal Executive Council.

[62] Even General Wilson was opposed on purely military grounds to a complete breach with Mihailovich. (On the different, and often clashing, British points of view, see Woodward, op. cit., pp. 338–45.) It is still impossible to establish the numerical strength of the partisan forces in mid-1944. According to data supplied at the time by partisan headquarters to the Soviet military mission, and published in the Soviet Union in 1960, they amounted to 300,000 men, of whom 190,000 were armed. Yugoslav figures published since the war range from 300,000 to 750,000 (S. Bosnitch analyses these figures in 'The Significance of the Soviet Military Intervention in Jugoslavia, 1944–1945', *Review of the Study Centre for Jugoslav Affairs*, 8, London, 1969, p. 696). Stalin doubted the figures given by the Yugoslav Communists. He is reported to have said in November 1944: 'I know those partisan figures. They are always exaggerated' (Dedijer, *Tito Speaks*, p. 267). Maclean's estimate is 250,000 (*Disputed Barricade*, p. 282). German appreciations also vary, from 80,000 to 120,000 (German sources quoted by Heilbrunn, *Partisan Warfare*, London, 1962, p. 72, and Bosnitch, op. cit., p. 696).

The prime minister was by now enthusiastic about Tito and antipathetic to Mihailovich, but he wanted to save the monarchy in Yugoslavia. He felt a moral obligation to King Peter who had thrown in his lot and that of his country with Great Britain in an hour of need; he also imagined that he could moderate Tito's movement, and safeguard British interests, by linking it to the monarchy. Churchill believed that Tito could be made to accept the monarchy if King Peter dropped Mihailovich. In January 1944, he opened a personal correspondence with Tito on that subject[63] to try and reach a compromise which would protect the king, and a series of steps was taken in the following months to win Tito over. In February, the prime minister revealed to the House of Commons the government's dissatisfaction with General Mihailovich, and its decision to back Marshal Tito and his partisans 'with all the strength we can draw'. In a broadcast in March, he included a reference to 'the heroic struggle of the partisans of Yugoslavia under the leadership of Marshal Tito'. In April, one of Tito's generals was received in London by Churchill. Finally, on 24 May, the prime minister announced in the Commons that the supply of arms and support to Mihailovich had ceased, while the largest possible supplies were being sent to Tito.

During these months, parallel action was taken with King Peter. In March, he was advised by the foreign secretary to change his government and give up General Mihailovich after his marriage had been celebrated. After the king's wedding on 20 March, pressure was increased. He had been advised to include some personalities favourable to Tito in his new cabinet and a prime minister was even suggested – Shubashich, one of the leaders abroad of the Croatian Peasant Party. Losing his patience with King Peter, Churchill wanted to threaten him with branding his minister of the armed forces as a collaborator, with attacking his prime minister in the Commons, with granting recognition to Tito's committee. Finally, in the speech of 24 May, he announced in anticipation that King Peter had accepted the resignation of Purich's cabinet, and that he was in the process of forming a new government, without Mihailovich, in which Dr Shubashich would be an important factor. After three months of such pressure, the king gave in, but it was not until 1 June – almost a week after Churchill's announcement, and without the previous resignation of the Purich administration – that he entrusted Shubashich with the task of forming a new cabinet.

The twenty-year-old monarch who had tried for ten months to

[63] The letters are reproduced in full in Churchill's memoirs (*The Second World War*, V, London, 1952, pp. 416–21).

play a political role over and above the heads of the representatives of his country's traditional parties, now became a simple instrument. Shubashich's 'government' had been called into being by the British for the express purpose of coming to an arrangement with Tito. It did not include Mihailovich, nor did it include anyone else for the time being. Ten days after his appointment, Shubashich left for Vis. The negotiations were almost completely one-sided. Tito was ready to make certain formal, limited, and tactical concessions to obtain a measure of political recognition from the Allies, and possible benefits at home from the appearance of an arrangement with the exiled government. He granted, in writing, that the issue of the monarchy would not be raised while the war lasted, and gave a verbal assurance that he did not intend to impose a Communist system on Yugoslavia. For the rest, it was Shubashich who gave in. The royal government recognized the provisional administration set up by the People's Liberation Movement as the only authority on Yugoslav territory, and the People's Liberation Army as the only fighting force. Shubashich would form a cabinet made up of progressive elements that had not taken a stand against the People's Liberation Movement, and Tito put forward the names of two personalities whom he wished included. The main task of this cabinet would be to organize support for the partisans from abroad. On this basis, an agreement was drawn up and signed on 16 June, both leaders undertaking to issue statements on the subject of their co-operation.

The British government did not feel enthusiastic about the agreement it had sponsored. On his return to London, Shubashich set about implementing his side.[64] From Tito, however, there was immediate evidence that he was trying to elude the agreement, quite apart from the fact that its very substance did not satisfy the Foreign Office. It contained little which could appease Mihailovichist Serbia, and the British government was worried about the inability of the partisans to get any support there.

Churchill, who in the summer of 1944 was becoming alarmed at the approach of the Soviet armies, thought it desirable to take the opportunity of a visit to Italy in August to put the British point of view directly to Tito. The Yugoslav Communist leader came reluctantly, on Soviet advice, this time to Caserta. The British prime minister made it clear to him that he could expect no political recognition until he had come to a true political arrangement with the

[64] He appointed a very small cabinet, made up of a few London politicians who agreed to co-operate with Tito's movement, supplemented by some personalities who had come from Yugoslavia and were already linked to the partisan cause; and he issued an appeal to the nation to unite around Tito.

king. He reminded Tito that the Allies were not providing him with arms to fight a civil war and impose communism. He asked the Yugoslav leader whether he would meet King Peter on Yugoslav territory, and make a public statement that he did not intend to impose communism. Tito was adamant that he would do neither.[65]

In view of the country's impending liberation and of the necessity of having a single united government, further steps were taken to appease Tito. The High Command of the armed forces was abolished by royal decree in August, thus withdrawing from Mihailovich his remaining office, that of chief of staff of the High Command. Finally, on 12 September, King Peter personally appealed over the B.B.C. to Yugoslavs to rally round Tito, adding that the 'stigma of treason' would stick to all those who did not.

During this politically crucial period of the summer of 1944, there was, on the whole, no large-scale action against the Germans in Yugoslavia. For Mihailovich's forces in particular, left without supplies and having to face increasing partisan attacks, this was the nadir of their military activities against the occupant. Nevertheless, Mihailovich held down Axis forces in Serbia; he had systematically organized the saving of Allied airmen shot down over eastern Yugoslavia during their raids on south-east Europe; final touches were made to his organization, discipline was tightened up, rail sabotage pursued, and collaborators increasingly brought to heel. Among prominent collaborators executed by order of Mihailovich was the head of Nedich's secretariat. Uncomfortably wedged between the Germans and Mihailovich, Nedich turned to Mihailovich. In order to show his goodwill, he had General Damyanovich freed from captivity in Germany, and offered him the recently vacated position of head of his secretariat. Mihailovich, whom Damyanovich contacted for instructions, told him to accept, and thus acquired a source of intelligence working under his orders, at the top of the collaborationist structure. Both sides were trying to exploit each other's predicament to save their positions, for while Mihailovich's organization, through its agents, obtained as much equipment and money as the puppet administration could yield in these difficult times, Nedich went on to offer to place his Serbian State Guard under the command of Mihailovich who alone could save Serbia from communism, now that Germany was breaking up, and the Soviet army approaching.

[65] The statement which Tito, on his return from Caserta, issued as a counterpart to Shubashich's, merely stated that the aim of the agreement was to strengthen the struggle for liberation, and to prevent traitors such as Mihailovich from taking cover under the authority of a legitimate government.

Serbia was important to Tito, politically and militarily, but the partisans were out of sympathy with the population there. Nevertheless, if they were going to link up with the approaching Red Army, they had to get through Serbia. Thus, although there was not much fighting between guerrillas and Germans, there was more and more of it between partisans trying to get into Serbia, and *chetniks* trying to fend them off. Serbia had also once again assumed its full importance for the Allies, as the Belgrade-Salonika corridor was the Germans' principal potential line of retreat. Mihailovich's *chetnik* having been abandoned, everything was done to build up Tito's partisans in a territory whose loyalties were with the former and against the latter. No British troops were to be used in the area, but a plan was agreed on to harass the German retreat through coordinated attacks on communications by the partisans and by Allied air forces. With the material aid dropped by the Allies, and the moral support of British and American liaison officers, the partisans were able to increase their foothold in south-eastern Serbia.[66]

During that summer the Americans took a somewhat independent stand on the question of Mihailovich. Some of their liaison officers had returned to Washington and reported both fully and favourably on his movement. Robert Murphy, their representative in Italy, had made it clear to Tito at Vis that he could not be considered the sole representative of Yugoslav resistance.[67] Above all, the U.S. air force was seriously concerned about evacuating its airmen from eastern Yugoslavia before large-scale operations started up again, and this could not be done without some link with Mihailovich's organization. Landed in August, an American liaison team organized the evacuation of several hundred Allied (mainly American) airmen, in co-operation with Mihailovich's movement.[68] The mis-

---

[66] The air support given by the Anglo-American air force which bombed objectives indicated by Tito's headquarters, was too often an unconscious form of help for the Communist cause. The bombing of larger towns, often on feast days and solemn occasions, demoralized the population, the best-known instance being the bombardment of Belgrade on the Orthodox Easter Sunday (16 April) and Monday, three years after it had been partly destroyed by the German bombardments.

[67] Even the Russians, right until February 1944, had wanted to have direct liaison with both Tito and Mihailovich (Ehrman, op. cit., V, pp. 275–6).

[68] See the statement by former Vice-President (later President) Richard Nixon, in *Tributes to General Mihailovich* (Windsor, Ont., 1966, p. 14). The story is told, in particular, in Fotitch, op. cit., pp. 268–71. J. Inks, *Eight Bailed Out*, New York, 1954, the diary of an American officer whose bomber was forced down over Yugoslavia in July 1944 and who subsequently spent ten months with Montenegrin *chetniks*, is an unsophisticated and unprejudiced record of the entangled loyalties of one particular group of guerrillas at the end of the war.

sion, under Colonel McDowell, of the U.S. Office of Strategic Services (O.S.S.), also served as a channel for the surrender proposals to the Western Allies that came from the Germans in the Balkans in the spring and autumn of 1944.[69]

Not much notice, however, was paid by the Supreme Allied Command to these German offers, or to Mihailovich's plan to place both resistance movements under overall Allied operational control, and give them specific tasks in separate zones of action. Since the Tito-Shubashich agreement, the partisans were being built up in Serbia under the personal supervision of Brigadier Maclean. Their reinforced attempts to make headway into the Mihailovich-held uplands of southern and central Serbia imposed civil war again on that region, and made it easier for the Germans to hold.

Realizing that this was the decisive battle for Serbia, Mihailovich concentrated his forces on the western Morava, to prevent the partisans from breaking into Shumadiya. September was a crucial month. Soviet troops were in Romania; Bulgaria had withdrawn from the war on 23 August and evacuated its troops from Yugoslav territory. While Titoist and Mihailovichist guerrillas fought for Serbia, the Germans, holding on to communication lines, were evacuating troops from Greece with surprising ease. Considering that the time had come to launch a decisive attack on the German positions and communications in co-ordination with the Soviet advance, on 1 September, Mihailovich proclaimed general mobilization, to rid Serbia of the occupation forces. All officers of the Serbian State Guard who were already linked to the Home Army, and an important part of the soldiery, openly went over to him. According to his estimates, several hundred thousand men presented themselves at his recruiting centres, but there were weapons

[69] The parley has been recorded by all three sides involved; Hermann Neubacher, the German Foreign Ministry representative for south-east Europe (*Sonderauftrag Südost, 1940–1945 – Bericht eines fliegenden Diplomaten*, Göttingen, 1956, pp. 207–9); Zhivko Topalovich, the president of Mihailovich's Central National Committee (Ž. Topalović, *Pokreti narodnog otpora u Jugoslaviji, 1941–1945*, Paris, 1958, pp. 124–7, and *Srbija pod Dražom*, London, 1968, pp. 107–28); and Colonel McDowell, the head of the American liaison mission ('Statement by Colonel Robert H. McDowell' in *Report of Commission of Inquiry of the Committee for a Fair Trial for Draja Mihailovich*, New York, 1946, p. 16, reproduced in *General Mihailovich, the World's Verdict – A Selection of Articles on the First Resistance Leader in Europe Published in the World Press*, Gloucester, 1947, pp. 36–9). The story of Neubacher's initiative and of his attempt to create an anti-Communist front of Nedich's State Guard, Mihailovich's Home Army, and the Montenegrin Nationalists, has been reconstructed from German sources by Avakumović *Mihailović prema nemačkim dokumentima*, pp. 151–4. The latter initiative was wrecked by the opposition of both Hitler and Mihailovich.

for only about 40,000.⁷⁰ On 6 September Soviet troops reached the Yugoslav border, and it was to them that Mihailovich now tried to put his plan of keeping the two guerrilla forces separated until the complete liberation of Yugoslavia. Not surprisingly, the Russian command in Romania took even less notice of it than the Anglo-American command in Italy.

With the Red Army on the eastern borders of Yugoslavia, Tito could now turn to the Russians, and away from the British, for this last stage of the civil war. In the night of 21 September, he 'levanted' – as an indignant Churchill described his disappearance from Vis.⁷¹ The airfield on the island was occasionally used by Bari-based, Soviet-leased planes. It was on one of these that Tito had originally left the Yugoslav mainland. It was on one of these again that he went off, without warning the British, for Marshal Tolbukhin's headquarters in Romania, before going on to Moscow to confer with Stalin – their first meeting since Tito had returned to Yugoslavia in 1937 to take over control of the Communist Party. In spite of help – political, moral and material – from the Western Allies, he had not been able to wrest Serbia from Mihailovich. There was the risk that the latter might be able to entrench himself there after the Germans had withdrawn. Tito needed the direct intervention of the Red Army to help him conquer Serbia quickly.⁷² On 28 September, it was announced in Moscow that the High Command of the Yugoslav People's Liberation Army had agreed to a request from the Soviet High Command for Soviet troops to cross Yugoslav territory bordering on Hungary in pursuit of retreating German forces, but that in the areas where the Russians operated, the civilian administration would be that of Tito's National Committee.

Soviet troops entered Yugoslavia from Romania, in the direction of Belgrade, and from Bulgaria, into the heart of Serbia. In eastern and central Serbia there were practically no partisans, and Soviet commanders initially co-operated with Mihailovich's commanders. There was a brief period of fraternization before the Soviet forces

⁷⁰ Just before the mobilization, the Germans estimated his forces at 60,000–70,000 (Heilbrunn, *Warfare in the Enemy's Rear*, p. 163).

⁷¹ Maclean, *Eastern Approaches*, p. 498.

⁷² According to the official Soviet history of the Great Patriotic War, Tito had been invoking Soviet help ever since July 1944, and, early in September, asked for the entry of the Red Army into Yugoslavia (quoted in Bosnitch, op. cit., p. 697). In a speech on 8 August 1945, Tito also stated that he had gone to Moscow to ask that the Red Army enter Yugoslavia 'to help our units liberate Serbia and Belgrade' (J. Broz Tito, *Govori i članci*, II, Zagreb, 1961, p. 10). From the account of Tito's conversations with Stalin given by Dedijer (*Tito Speaks*, pp. 232–5) it could be deduced that the Soviet leader would have preferred, rather than provide troops to help conquer Serbia, a gradual takeover with initial acceptance of King Peter's return.

turned to disarming the *chetniks*, while Tito's administration set itself up in liberated towns, hunting down Mihailovichists. Then the Bulgarian army returned, to help liberate, under Soviet command, the territories which they had helped occupy, under German command, until just over a month before. There were thus strange fighting partnerships in Serbia, for a short spell at the turn of September-October: Soviet troops co-operating with Mihailovichist guerrillas against the Germans; Bulgarian troops co-operating with Titoist guerrillas against Mihailovichists; Titoists fighting both Mihailovichists and Germans. Engaged against the retreating Germans, attacked from three sides by the advancing Soviets, Bulgars, and partisans, Mihailovich resorted to the old guerrilla tactics: during October, he withdrew from Serbia.

He was not stopped, for the partisans and their Soviet allies were hurrying to Belgrade. This was an important point on the Germans' withdrawal route from the Balkans, and they had concentrated troops in and around the well-defended capital. In spite of the part played by the partisans in the liberation of Belgrade, it would no doubt have been impossible, at that stage, for them or any other guerrilla force to free the city from the Germans without the Soviet contribution in tanks, artillery, and heavy armament. Even so, it was only after a week-long battle that Belgrade was liberated on 20 October 1944. After that, the Red Army went on into Hungary, and the Yugoslavs were again left to liberate themselves and fight their civil war to an end. Before the end of November, the Germans had stabilized the front in Yugoslavia, protecting their positions in the central mountains, and stopping the partisan advance west of Belgrade, in the plain between the Sava and the Danube. Even in Macedonia, they stopped Bulgars and partisans until the last of their troops had left Greece.[73]

[73] They had also ceded much of the Dalmatian coast in October, in the face of attacks by Allied-backed partisans, but whereas in Serbia, the Yugoslav Communists had welcomed and indeed called for Soviet troops, they regarded with dislike the possibility of Anglo-American forces operating on the littoral. When asked by Stalin how he would react in case of a British 'invasion' of Yugoslavia, Tito answered: 'We should offer determined resistance' (Dedijer, *Tito Speaks*, p. 235). In his war diary, published in 1955, a partisan leader, R. Cholakovich, commented that the agreement about the entry of Soviet troops meant that no Allied force could henceforth land without the consent of the partisans. 'This was of great importance to us, since there had latterly been some talk of a disembarkation on the Dalmatian coast. . . . Now such a step, if not excluded, was at least much more difficult. Any attempt would amount to an infringement of our rights. Even the most diehard reactionaries were unlikely to try it' (quoted from the abridged English version, R. Čolaković, *Winning Freedom*, London, 1962, p. 400). When in answer to a request for some field artillery, the British, at the end of October, also landed a small contingent of marines, since the partisans had no

Now that the Soviet armies not only controlled Romania and Bulgaria, but were helping Tito to liberate and conquer eastern Yugoslavia, the British feared that the Russians intended to install in Belgrade a purely Communist government, under Soviet influence, which would ignore both the wishes of non-Communist Yugoslavs and British interests. Earlier, in May, the idea had already been put by the British to the Soviet government of a temporary division of spheres of action in the Balkans – the Russians being recognized as having a leading role in Romania, in return for non-intervention in Greece. The Americans had approved, provided it applied to military operations only, and was limited to three months. In October, on Churchill's urging, the British and Soviet leaders attended a conference in Moscow, President Roosevelt being kept at home by the American presidential campaign. The earlier agreement on the Balkans was extended and clarified, in terms of percentages of influence in the control of events – understood for the duration of the war – and Yugoslavia 'went fifty-fifty'.[74] On this basis, it was agreed to recommend jointly to Tito and Shubashich the constitution of a united government.

Back in liberated Belgrade from Marshal Tolbukhin's headquarters in Romania, Tito concluded with Shubashich, who had joined him from London, a second agreement on 1 November. Pending a plebiscite to decide on the future form of government after the complete liberation of the country, the king would remain abroad, and delegate the exercise of the royal prerogative to a regency council appointed in agreement with Tito. A provisional government would be set up, from Shubashich's cabinet and Tito's committee, to supervise arrangements for the plebiscite, and the Anti-Fascist Council would continue to act as a temporary legislature. Five weeks later, they agreed to drop the plebiscite in favour of elections for a constituent assembly, which would decide the organization of the post-war régime.

When Shubashich returned to London, King Peter refused to accept the new agreements. His prime minister, he claimed, had gone to Yugoslavia to assess the possibilities for the formation of a united government. Once there, he had agreed not only to a delegation of the royal prerogative, but to an arrangement which generally gave power in advance to one party, before the final decision by popular vote. The British government pressed the king to accept the realities of the situation, while Churchill told the

experience of handling such weapons, the former were made most unwelcome and were withdrawn after protests that the entry of British or American troops had not been authorized (Ehrman, op. cit., VI, 1956, pp. 53–4).

[74] Churchill, op. cit., VI, London, 1954, pp. 198–204.

Commons on 18 January 1945 that, 'if we were so unfortunate as not to be able to obtain the consent of King Peter, the matter would have, in fact, to go ahead, his assent being presumed'. At the end of the month, under strong British pressure, the king reluctantly gave way, and in mid-February, Shubashich and his ministers left London for Belgrade. A few days earlier, at Yalta, the Big Three had agreed to recommend to Tito and Shubashich that the arrangement between them be put into effect immediately. It was also recommended that the Anti-Fascist Council should be enlarged to include those members of the last pre-war Yugoslav parliament who had not compromised themselves with the enemy.

Another fortnight elapsed before final agreement was reached on the composition, according to Tito's wishes, of the regency council and of the united government. More British pressure got the regents appointed by royal decree. On 7 March, on the proposal of the presidency of the Anti-Fascist Council, they entrusted Marshal Tito with the formation of a new government. In the final merger, Tito, prime minister and minister of defence, had a majority of twenty-five ministers to three; Shubashich was in charge of foreign affairs. The new government was granted formal recognition by the Allies. The role of the British in Yugoslav affairs, over the winter, had been confined to 'that of a, somewhat unhappy, intermediary, in an effort to induce King Peter to comply with Tito's demands'.[75]

After the capitulation of Italy, most of the Serbian anti-Communist formations in the formerly Italian-held littoral had retreated to German-held Slovenia, whence they had been directed to the Julian region – the area between the pre-1918 Italo-Austrian border and the pre-1941 Italo-Yugoslav frontier, which comprises the Istrian peninsula and its extension inland to the present Austrian border. The Germans themselves had left its southern part largely unoccupied. They were anxious to protect the southern approaches to the railway lines from Trieste, but they did not trust these *chetniks* with whom they still occasionally clashed, and who pined for an Anglo-American landing.[76] In October 1944, therefore, they were reinforced by the better-trusted corps of Ljotichist volunteers

---

[75] Ehrman, op cit., VI, p. 55.

[76] The partisans in the Julian region, attacked by Germans and Italian Fascists, by Slovenian and Serbian anti-Communists, had survived only by resorting to all the guerrillas' stock-in-trade, including an agreement with the Germans, in the summer of 1944, to the effect that the former would not attack rail connexions from Trieste, while the latter would leave the Communists alone north of the city. Like all such agreements, this one too did not last long. (B. Novak, *Trieste, 1941–1954 – The Ethnic, Political, and Ideological Struggle*, Chicago and London, 1970, p. 106.)

from Serbia, while the now utterly useless Nedich was despatched to German territory.

Having disbanded the mass of recently acquired recruits, Mihailovich himself, with his staff and several thousand men, had crossed the Drina into Bosnia, while the main body of his troops had withdrawn southwards into Sandjak, accompanied by a great number of refugees. As he was regrouping his forces in the mountains of southeastern Bosnia in the autumn, he offered to place his force of 50,000 men at the disposal of the Supreme Allied Command for the Mediterranean, to be used anywhere against the Germans, while at the same time he rejected soundings from the retreating Germans for possible common action against the partisans.[77] Mihailovich did not yet think that the Communists had won the civil war. He had not been defeated; he had popular backing; like Tito, he had grounds to believe that, since Soviet troops had entered Yugoslavia, Anglo-American troops would do so as well. When the American officers finally left him in November, Mihailovich refused an offer to be evacuated, and decided to stay where he was for a while, to be at hand should there be an Allied landing. The troops gathered round him, with many civilian refugees, were, however, becoming prey to disease and hunger. They had to go north in search of food, and over the winter, their slow progress to the Sava was constantly interrupted by desultory clashes with Ustashas and partisans.

The Germans still held on to most of Montenegro, Bosnia, Croatia, and Slovenia, and although the three-cornered fight between Ustashas, *chetniks*, and partisans continued, the German retreat was, on the whole, undisturbed. Although strengthened by Allied aid, a secure rear, a solid strategic basis, and mass conscription in Serbia, the partisan army found it difficult to switch to regular warfare in the open country west of Belgrade, and the Germans held their own.

Early in March, however, the Germans withdrew troops from southern Bosnia to support an unsuccessful counter-offensive in Hungary. The partisans south of Bihach were thus able, later in the month, to attack the weakened German positions in an operation which had been prepared in conjunction with, and made possible by help from, the British and Americans. At the same time, both Ljotich and the independent *chetnik* commanders in Istria attempted to link themselves to Mihailovich, and possibly to get his units to join theirs. The former had wholeheartedly served the

[77] 'We have always been enemies, and shall remain enemies,' Mihailovich answered. 'That we now have the same enemies, that we are both fighting the partisans is a sad coincidence, which I regret' (*The Trial of Dragoljub-Draža Mihailović*, p. 268).

Germans against Mihailovich and the Allies, the latter had played a double game between the Italians and Mihailovich. They all now needed him to reorganize them into an efficient anti-Communist force acceptable to the Allies, and did not realize that his patronage could not help them any more with the victors. Rather than joining former collaborators and semi-collaborators on the borders of Yugoslavia, Mihailovich was in favour of dispersing his men into smaller guerrilla groups which would have kept resistance alive throughout the country, while he himself would again establish his base in Serbia. Nevertheless, he did not reject Ljotich's overtures, for the Yugoslav prisoners-of-war in Germany were his last hope. The Julian region was a convenient area on the borders of Italy and Germany to which ex-prisoners-of-war could make their way after the final collapse of Germany, where possible contact could be established with non-Communist forces in Slovenia, as well as with British and American forces. He decided to send General Damyanovich, with a nucleus of officers and men, to take over command in Istria. All who wanted to go, however, were left free to do so. Many left him to try and get to Istria, but only a small percentage of survivors reached their destination. The rest were destroyed by Ustasha forces, or died on their way from sickness and hunger.

Mihailovich's Istrian plan was a failure. The different units there took orders only from their own commanders, who paid lip-service to Damyanovich's formal command on behalf of Mihailovich, but listened only to Ljotich, who now kept away from the limelight and remote-controlled this motley force from Vienna with German money. As for the prisoners-of-war, by the time they were freed, there was no more 'national force' to go to in Istria or Slovenia.

To most non-Communist Slovenes, the belief that the Tito-Shubashich agreement had been concluded with the full agreement of the Western Allies seemed to offer a guarantee that the Communists would not be allowed to take over completely, and in the summer of 1944 the Liberation Front appeared to be well supported. The development of the situation, however, brought the moderate political forces grouped around the Slovenian Alliance to take a more positive stand. The blow the partisans had delivered to the non-Communist forces just after the capitulation of Italy, and the establishment of the Home Guard, had paradoxically brought more cohesion to the Alliance. The Slovenian Home Guard now had a unified command, a good military organization, and a single aim – to defeat the partisans.[78] Like the men of Nedich's State Guard at

---

[78] By the end of the war, it numbered 10,000–15,000 men (Novak, op. cit., p. 84).

that time, those of Rupnik's Home Guard, while nominally collaborating with the Germans, were in sentiment for the Western Allies. They believed that they were serving the cause of the British and Americans, as well as their own, in fighting the Communists. The Alliance itself, while giving moral support to the Home Guard, avoided collaboration and remained underground, in contact with the Yugoslav government in London, with General Mihailovich, and with the Vatican through Bishop Rozhman of Ljubljana. In the autumn of 1944, it issued a statement setting down as its aims, when the war came to an end, the unification of all territories inhabited by Slovenes in an autonomous Slovenian unit within a Yugoslav federation. The plan, worked out over the winter, was for an assembly of all Slovenian members of the last pre-war Yugoslav legislature to meet as soon as feasible, proclaim a provisional government of Slovenia within a federal Yugoslav monarchy, invite King Peter to come to Ljubljana, take over the Home Guard, obtain the capitulation of German troops, and call on the Anglo-Americans to send troops from northern Italy. Mihailovich's delegate for Slovenia, who retained a small underground organization, co-operated closely with the Alliance. The establishment of a united government under Tito, recognized by the Allies, had come as a setback, and although, in the spring, arrangements had been made for Damyanovich's force to link with the Slovenian anti-Communist forces and take over from the Germans, there were many obstacles to the establishment of an anti-Communist alliance between a potential Slovenian front and Mihailovich's force in northern Bosnia.

In Slovenia itself, the Slovenian Alliance failed to come to an agreement with General Rupnik who was reluctant to hand over his Guard before the Allies actually came. There was not much unity between Damyanovich's incongruous force and the confused Slovenian Home Guard commanders who were not sure whom to obey. Last, but not least, they were all separated from Mihailovich, by the armed forces of the N.D.H., which, in spite of large-scale desertions, were still much stronger in numbers and arms than all that the two groups could muster. Mihailovich tried to get round this obstacle by sending emissaries to Machek in Zagreb, to try and get him to win over the N.D.H. army to a broad anti-Communist front after the collapse of the Ustasha state. Machek, however, feared an Ustasha trap, and the Ustashas themselves intercepted the mission, which thus came to nothing.

At the end of April 1945, as Allied and Soviet forces drew near to each other in Germany, as the Allies advanced in northern Italy and the Russians in western Hungary, the final German withdrawal started from western Yugoslavia, and a parallel partisan advance rolled up the anarchic N.D.H. As the Germans moved out of Croatia, all sorts of people fled in panic – Pavelich and the Ustasha leadership, the remnants of their army, and masses of civilians (Machek among them). Their common aim was to reach Austria, and the protection of Anglo-American troops, before Soviet and partisan forces cut off their retreat routes. On 9 May, the Yugoslav partisans entered Zagreb.

In the last days of April, the partisans had also attacked in Istria and, by the 30th, were fighting in the suburbs of Trieste. During that day and the following days, General Damyanovich's mixed force crossed the river Isonzo near Gorizia, after the partisans had done their best to capture it. His troops were immediately disarmed and interned by the British. On that same day, 3 May, unaware of these events, an assembly called by the Slovenian Alliance met in Ljubljana to proclaim the prearranged plan. The German general, however, refused to hand over to the new authority, the partisans were moving to encircle Ljubljana, and on learning that Damyanovich's force was no more, the Slovenian Army, newly so-called, also headed for Austria where its units, too, were disarmed and interned by the British. The partisans entered Ljubljana on 7 May. In those early days of May 1945, all sorts of refugees were converging on British-occupied Carinthia, armed units and civilians, fleeing the Communists. Thousands were turned back and were summarily executed by the partisans, before confirmation of the massacre made the British bring an end to indiscriminate return *en masse*.

Tito's forces pursued German occupation and native anti-Communist forces across Yugoslavia's pre-war boundaries, to establish a claim over Yugoslav-inhabited border territories of Italy and Austria. The British and Americans took a firm stand in order not to allow what they considered a unilateral Yugoslav anticipation of the decisions of the peace conference. Units of the People's Liberation Army had entered Trieste a week before Ljubljana and Zagreb, so anxious had they been to get there before the Western Allies. Under pressure, Tito soon gave way, both in Austria and in the Trieste area.

Berlin had fallen on 2 May, on the same day the German surrender in Italy had taken effect, on the 9th the German terms of general surrender had been ratified in Berlin, but in Yugoslavia, German forces held out until 15 May, reluctant to surrender to 'irregulars'. Left to native forces, the war in Yugoslavia had gone on for seven months after the liberation of Belgrade, and for a full week after the end of the war on other European fronts.

The civil war, however, was not quite over. No anti-Communist front had been set up in western Yugoslavia, there had been no Anglo-American intervention, and all those Serbian, Croatian, and Slovenian armed units which had been formed, armed, fed, or simply tolerated by the Axis powers to fight communism, had fled abroad. There still remained Mihailovich with his guerrillas. In mid-April they had set out from northern Bosnia on a long march back to Serbia, with the aim of starting everything once again, this time against the new Communist order. In order to give his opponents – Ustashas to the west, partisans to the east – the impression that he too was going to make for Slovenia, Mihailovich moved westwards to start with. The Ustashas tried to stop them, and only after suffering great losses did the Mihailovichists break through, to begin their progress southwards into the mountains.

The Communists soon found out the manoeuvre. Pressing in from east, north, and west, they were able to harass the columns. Mihailovich nevertheless managed to capture Travnik on 1 May, where he regrouped his men before starting off again for Herzegovina. During the first half of May, his units, already much reduced, went through all that Tito's partisans had gone through, two years earlier, in these same mountains of northern Herzegovina. Between the Neretva and the Drina, strong, well-equipped, air-supported partisan forces set for the remnants of their rivals' army the same trap that the Germans had once set for them. Over the Neretva and across the Sutyeska, in narrow defiles and up steep and woody mountainsides, they battled. The survivors who squeezed out of the trap were too exhausted to attempt to cross the Drina, where fresh partisan troops had been massed to meet them. Of some 30,000 who were still assembled under Mihailovich's orders in March, at the end of May there were no more than 2,000 left.[79] The Yugoslav Home Army had ceased to exist.

Of Tito's armed opponents, only disorganized bands of guerrillas were left, and a special corps of flying squads was created to deal with that problem, while the winning party in the civil war pursued the setting-up of the new régime.

[79] Estimates by Zhivko Topalovich, on the basis of information provided by survivors (Topalović, *Pokreti narodnog otpora u Jugoslaviji*, pp. 201–14, *passim*).

PART THREE

Reunification, Revolution and Beyond

Chapter 4

Stalinism–Titoism: 1945–50

The setting-up of the Communist régime

Marshal Tito's provisional government, formed in March 1945, was one of the transitory concessions made by the Communist leadership of the People's Liberation Movement to satisfy the Western Allies. Five non-Communist members – two of them fellow-traveller adherents of the Movement – sat alongside twenty-three Communists, under the premiership of the leader of the winning faction in the civil war. This arrangement for the executive was complemented by a similar one for the legislature when, according to a recommendation of the Yalta Conference, the Movement's Anti-Fascist Council was enlarged to include some members of the last pre-war parliament, and turned into a provisional legislature. It was not too difficult to allege that not so many members of Stoyadinovich's parliament, elected in 1938 and dissolved in 1939, were entitled to join partisan resisters in a pre-parliament for liberated Yugoslavia, and on 7 August 1945, at a third and last session of the Anti-Fascist Council, 318 delegates co-opted 118 additional members, only thirty-six of whom had sat in the last pre-war parliament.[1]

In this way international recognition and formal sanction were given to a whole governmental structure which had already been

[1] Fifty members of the Anti-Fascist Council were absent from that meeting. Of the co-opted members, apart from former M.P.s, 69 were members of non-Communist political parties and 13 were non-party personalities. Later, a few more non-Communist members were co-opted. (On the Tito-Shubashich agreements and the Yalta recommendations, which the formation of the provisional government and of the provisional legislature were supposed to implement, cf. above pp. 166–7.) Tito justified these concessions to the fifth Party congress in 1947 as follows: 'We had to accept this [the Tito-Shubashich] agreement because the Western Powers stubbornly insisted on it. . . . We decided to do so because we were aware of our strength.' Twenty years later, during the 25th anniversary celebrations of the decisions taken by the Anti-Fascist Council at Yaytse, Tito in his speech of 29 November 1968 again stressed that these concessions had been made 'primarily for reasons of foreign policy', in order to strengthen the international position of the new régime.

set up by the Anti-Fascist Council, and which operated under the control of the Communist Party, with its administrative apparatus, its armed forces, and its security forces – in fact a veritable state known as Democratic Federative Yugoslavia. In the new federated units, the local people's liberation committees simply became governments without further addition or ceremony.

The Provisional Assembly ratified all the legislation of the Anti-Fascist Council, and adopted further legislation – to set up people's courts, to confiscate the property of collaborators and enemies of the people, to carry out a new agrarian reform, to control the press, to withdraw Yugoslav citizenship from certain categories of refugees. It also legislated on elections to the Constituent Assembly. It extended the franchise to all above the age of eighteen, including women, and to everybody, regardless of age, who had fought with the partisans. On the other hand, it disenfranchised all those deemed to have collaborated with the enemy, all who had adhered to 'fascist' organizations, and all those condemned to the loss of their political rights. Finally, for the purpose of these elections, a People's Front was constituted at a congress held in Belgrade that same month of August 1945, not as a coalition of parties, but as the coming together, with the Communist Party, of various partisan organizations and of individuals of non-Communist background who had once belonged to other political parties and were now willing to collaborate with the new régime.

There was no confrontation between non-Communist parties and the Communist Party, for the former had no political organizations, the Front had absorbed shadow splinter-groups claiming to represent them, and those party leaders who had returned from abroad found themselves unable to reorganize their followings. Milan Grol, the leader of the Democratic Party, had returned from London and joined the provisional government as deputy premier, along with the former prime minister Ivan Shubashich and his friend Yuray Shutey, both of the Croatian Peasant Party leadership, believing they could exercise a moderating influence from within the government. They soon realized that the only role they were allowed to perform was to follow Tito's majority. Grol resigned on 19 August,[2] followed in September by Shubashich and Shutey. An attempt was then made to try and influence developments from the outside. Grol and the former Radical prime minister Trifunovich, who had also returned from London, planned to present a United Democratic Opposition list of candidates, independent of the People's Front; an attempt was made in the same direction by Peasant Party circles in

[2] Grol's letter of resignation to Marshal Tito, not published at the time, is given in J. Korbel, *Tito's Communism*, Denver, 1951, pp. 351–7.

Zagreb; and each of the two groups started a newspaper. Shubashich, however, was ill and kept under house arrest in Zagreb, so his party's paper went no further than its first issue. Grol's weekly in Belgrade survived a little longer, until thuggery, arson, and a printers' strike eventually stopped it as well, while opposition meetings were set upon by Communist militants. Finding it impossible to run a campaign, Grol and Trifunovich decided, a month after starting their venture, to boycott the election.

On the government side, the campaign was organized as a plebiscite for Tito and the Front, and a referendum against the monarchy – presented as the symbol of all opposition which was, by definition, anti-national and counter-revolutionary. The whole network of the partisan administration was mobilized to secure an impressive result. It was reinforced by the visible presence of a large Communist-controlled partisan army and the visible and invisible action of the O.Z.N. (Department for the Protection of the People), founded during the war as the partisans' intelligence and security agency, and turning into an ubiquitous political police patterned after that of the U.S.S.R.

No less than 164,000 anti-Communist Yugoslavs were dispersed throughout Europe[3] and another 250,000 had been officially deprived of the vote in the country, so an unredeemably oppositional 5 per cent of the electorate was out of the way. With the reins of

[3] R. Knežević, 'Podaci o jugoslovenskoj emigraciji', part i, in *Poruka*, 52, London, December 1958, pp. 11 seqq. This is the only comprehensive study attempting to estimate the numbers of Yugoslav 'displaced persons' in the aftermath of the Second World War. It is based on a collation of data provided by J. Vernant, *The Refugee in the Post-War World*, New Haven, 1953; M. Proudfoot, *European Refugees, 1939–1952 – A Study in Forced Population Movement*, London, 1957; J. Tannahill, *European Voluntary Workers in Britain*, Manchester, 1958; and the first Yugoslav post-war census in 1948. The estimate of no less than 164,000 (p. 17) is for the autumn of 1945 and represents the hard core of the 0.5 million Yugoslavs who had been 'displaced' by May 1945 – those who had refused to be repatriated, with the addition of the first post-war refugees. It excludes some 360,000 members of the German minority, who had been expelled to Germany, deported to the Soviet Union, or simply escaped, as well as the Ustashas who left Yugoslavia and about whom there are no available figures. The final laws on citizenship made it clear that the loss of citizenship was only at the discretion of the authorities. The law on citizenship of 5 July 1946 made the possession of Yugoslav citizenship prevail in Yugoslavia over any other citizenship an individual may have acquired, unless he had been released from or deprived of his original status. Even the law of 23 October 1946, which finalized the loss of citizenship of certain categories of refugees, did not automatically deprive these of their Yugoslav status, but merely made them liable to be deprived of it by individual administrative decisions. Their provisions enabled the government to regard refugees as being Yugoslav citizens, or not, according to its convenience in individual circumstances.

power firmly in the hands of the Communists, a single list of candidates presented by the People's Front and headed by the prime minister, Broz Tito, the opposition in trammels and shambles, and after a terror-backed campaign, no obvious intimidation was necessary to turn out the voters on 11 November. To stay at home required courage. Once at the polling station, there was no one else to vote for but Communists and fellow-travellers. Over 88 per cent of the electorate voted, and the People's Front received over 90 per cent of the ballots cast.

The Constituent Assembly met on 29 November[4] 1945, and its first act was, by acclamation, to abolish the monarchy and proclaim the Federative People's Republic of Yugoslavia. It then ratified all earlier legislation passed by the Anti-Fascist Council and the Provisional Assembly. On 31 January 1946, it unanimously approved the draft constitution which had been prepared by the government.

The constitution of 1946 was modelled on Stalin's constitution of 1936. It sanctioned Yugoslavia's new structure as a multi-national federation of six units, 'a community of peoples equal in rights who, on the basis of the right of self-determination, including the right of secession, have expressed their will to live together in a federative state'. The right of self-determination having thus been exercised, the constitutional instrument delegated extensive powers to the federation, leaving the theoretically sovereign component republics with but negligible remains. A pyramid of people's councils, similar to soviets, was capped by the Federal People's Assembly, the supreme organ of authority. This was composed of a Federal Council of representatives elected by universal and direct suffrage, and a Council of Nations delegated by the legislatures of the federated units. All other organs of the state were chosen by and subordinated to the People's Assembly, the most important being its presidium, combining the functions of a parliamentary steering and standing committee, and those of a corporate Head of State. Supreme in theory, the role of parliament was in fact limited almost exclusively to the approval of bills submitted to it by its executive.

As if to follow the precedent of 1921, the Constituent Assembly turned itself into the first regular legislature of the new régime, and elected a presidium, under the chairmanship of Dr Ribar, which in turn appointed a cabinet under the premiership of Marshal Tito. Both the presidium and the new government contained a number of safe non-Communist fellow-travellers, but whereas the cabinet was placed in the hands of the head of the Communist Party and real head of the new régime, the ceremonial and empty functions of

[4] A date already considered festive by the new régime as the anniversary of the decisions taken at Yaytse in 1943.

chairman of the Assembly presidium went to the elderly fellow-traveller who had already served in that capacity with the Anti-Fascist Council.

The constitution made no mention of the Communist Party, and yet all power emanated from the Party at the head of which was its secretary-general, Tito, assisted by Edvard Kardelj, Milovan Djilas, and Aleksandar Rankovich. Control by the Party leadership was exercised through a number of channels. The head of the Party was head of the government, minister of defence, commander-in-chief, member of the presidium, and head of the People's Front. He was being built up as legendary hero whose cult was consciously organized. Other Party leaders held the chief positions in the government, and loyal Communist partisans had been appointed to all key posts in the administration and the economy. Special Party schools were set up for the ideological education of Communist cadres, and Party cells organized in every place of abode and work. Through the People's Front, the Party sought to control the population at large, for it was made to include individual non-Communists favourable to the new order, as well as collective organizations such as youth and women's unions, labour and writers' unions, and many others. Thus, in spite of its newly acquired federal structure, the Yugoslav state was, in its concentration of real power, no less a unitary state than in the days of monarchical centralism.

The army remained a political force with an elaborate network of Communist control and education through political commissars and ideological courses. It was, however, through the security forces and the judiciary that ultimate Party control was guaranteed, for in that revolutionary period, when the country had not yet been pacified, Yugoslavia was a Stalinist police state. The constitution guaranteed a set of rights, but specified that these could not be used for the purpose of changing or infringing the constitutional order. A total break had been made with the old legal system, and as new legislation, designed to protect the new socialist order, gradually replaced it, the only rules of law were the Communist judges' interpretation of the principles of the revolution and of the notion of collaboration with the enemy – at best, their common sense of justice. Judges were elected by and subordinate to the political authorities, and the corner-stone of the judiciary was the federal public prosecutor, chosen by the Federal Assembly, who in turn appointed the other prosecutors. The O.Z.N. – reorganized after a few years as the Direction of State Security or U.D.B. – operated both as an auxiliary to the judiciary and independently, carrying out thousands of arrests, meting out secret administrative sentences quite apart from those of the regular courts, establishing personal files on most people, and generally maintaining the population in an atmosphere of terror.[5]

Although the Communist régime was both an accomplished and a legalized fact, disorganized bands of guerrillas were still operating, in particular the remains of Mihailovich's forces. To deal with them, a specialized élite National Defence Corps had been set up, most of whose efforts, backed by the security apparatus, were bent on capturing Mihailovich himself who was still at large and continued to believe that all was not lost. This hope was based on the idea that the Allies would either intervene to enable the holding of free elections, or refuse to recognize the results of elections that did not correspond to the Yalta Declaration on political rights in liberated Europe. It appears, furthermore, that this lingering hope was fairly widespread in the country at large.[6] At the Potsdam Conference in July–August 1945, the British and the Americans did make another attempt to bring about the implementation of the earlier agreements on liberated Europe generally, and the Balkan differences between the Big Three were considered. The Soviet determination to get the new governments in eastern Europe recognized by the Western powers, and the rather confused attitude of the latter, led the question of Yugoslavia eventually to be dropped.[7]

[5] None other than Rankovich himself, minister of home affairs and head of the security police, testified to the extent of its ruthlessness in 1951, when the restraints were first relaxed. He admitted that local Communist cells provided the police with blank judicial decisions imposing labour camp sentences, and that people were punished for collaborating with the enemy who had in fact been in enemy concentration camps. More revelations and admissions were to come after Rankovich's disgrace in 1966.

[6] See Korbel, op. cit., pp. 29–31. It explains the attitude of the representatives of the old parties who had joined Tito's provisional government. When they resigned, and then decided to boycott the elections, it was in order not to participate in, and thus give a veneer of approval to, the system. During the electoral campaign, they were accused of having acted on instructions from abroad. At the time of the Potsdam Conference in July 1945, Shubashich had suggested to the British government that the Big Three should remind Tito of his obligations (Woodward, op. cit., p. 558). In August, alleging that the Tito-Shubashich agreements had been disregarded in Yugoslavia, and that the regents had not been allowed to carry out the constitutional duties for which they had been appointed, King Peter in London had withdrawn the authority delegated to them earlier in the year. Political leaders abroad had appealed to Allied leaders for the great powers to supervise the holding of free elections and, later, to withhold formal recognition from the new government.

[7] Churchill had admitted to King Peter his disappointment and helplessness (Woodward, op. cit., p. 516). After the elections, the U.S. State Department had presented the Yugoslav government with a note to the effect that the establishment of diplomatic relations did not mean the sanction of the

The Western powers, however disappointed or reserved, could at that stage do little beyond trying to protect what interests could still be saved. Furthermore, the opposition tendencies in Yugoslavia, though widespread, were disconnected, broken up, and leaderless. While armed resistance slowly shrank to terrorist acts by tracked bands, a series of widely publicized political trials eliminated those personalities who could still have been considered as major potential anti-Communist rallying-centres, even if disorganized and disjointed.

On 24 March 1946 it was announced that Mihailovich had been captured ten days previously. His trial in Belgrade, which lasted from 10 June to 15 July, was the first and the most dramatic of a long series. It was held in an atmosphere of organized hostility, and was more in the nature of the principal battle in a violent campaign waged against non-Communist political and military leaders, than of a judicial case. General Mihailovich was tried along with many other co-defendants. These included a certain number of political leaders, former ministers, and officials of the wartime government in London, tried *in absentia*. Actually present in court were some of Mihailovich's commanders and members of his movement's Central National Committee, personalities who could be linked to the Radical and Democratic parties and who had been arrested in Yugoslavia, as well as a group of officials of Nedich's administration and armed units, and of Ljotich's militia. All were charged together with war crimes and collaboration with the enemy, opposing resistance, and having been encouraged in their action by Great Britain and the United States. All having duly been found guilty, General Mihailovich and ten others were condemned to death, the rest to terms of imprisonment with hard labour. Mihailovich's execution on 17 July marked the final defeat of the losing side in the civil war, the removal of a potential danger among the peasantry of Serbia, and, more generally, of a powerful symbol that, in spite of all the adverse propaganda, and whatever its drawbacks, still carried great prestige, both in Yugoslavia and abroad. It also served to discredit the pre-war political parties, particularly the Serbian-based ones, and to show that the Western Allies had supported collaboration with the Axis to prevent the victory of the partisans.

Two months after Mihailovich's execution, Mgr Stepinats, archbishop of Zagreb and head of the Roman Catholic Church in Yugoslavia, was arrested. His trial, held in Zagreb from 30 September to 11 October, was also a political one, staging a prejudged case in an atmosphere of organized hostility. This time, it marked the removal of the potential danger of the Catholic Church which had come to policy or methods of the new régime which had not as yet respected or fulfilled the Yalta Declaration.

symbolize the hopes of non-Communists in Croatia. It served to deal an irreparable blow to the Churches, particularly the Catholic Church among the Croats, and to show that the papacy had supported a policy of pro-Axis extremist sectional nationalism. Archbishop Stepinats was accused of collaborating with the enemy, of complicity with Ustasha crimes, of sanctioning compulsory conversions, of associating with Mihailovich, and of conspiring with foreign powers to secure their intervention in Yugoslavia. According to the technique already established, in order to give weight to these accusations and confuse the issues, the prelate was tried along with other defendants – Roman Catholic priests and Ustasha officials. They were all found guilty. The archbishop was sentenced to sixteen years' hard labour, two others to death, and the rest to lesser terms of imprisonment with hard labour. Stepinats had been tried and sentenced, allegedly for collaborating with the Ustasha régime, in fact for not collaborating with the Communist régime.[8]

The régime then went on to deal with the non-Communist politicians who had initially co-operated to a certain extent, or had at least been willing to act as a legal opposition within the system, but who were now increasingly insisting on their right to dissent. The best-known case is that of Professor Dragoljub Yovanovich, a left-wing Serbian Agrarian dissident who had been elected to parliament on the People's Front list, and even to the presidium. Gradually, during 1946, he began, within the precincts of parliament, to criticize many aspects of the government's policy. Recalled from the Assembly by his constituents, he was the target of a campaign of abuse before being arrested in March 1947. Along with Franjo Gazhi, a Croatian Peasant Party dissident who had also given his support to the People's Front, he was tried for conspiring with the British intelligence service to organize a peasant opposition. Both were sentenced to terms of imprisonment with hard labour.[9] During 1947 other political trials, held in Belgrade, Zagreb, and Ljubljana, sent to prison (and even to death) a series of personalities prominent in pre-war political parties – Radicals, Democrats, and

---

[8] These two trials in a way had an opposite effect to that intended. They did not so much discredit the Serbian general in the eyes of the Serbs, or the Croatian archbishop in the eyes of the Croats, as strengthen myths already believed by the ones about the others. Accepting the evidence presented at the Belgrade trial, most Croats were confirmed in their belief that the Serbs, under Mihailovich and the monarchy, had been planning revenge and hegemony, whereas most Serbs read in the evidence presented at the Zagreb trial proof that the Croats had betrayed the state in 1941, and that the Catholic Church had been instrumental in planning massacres and conversions.

[9] Of Dragoljub Yovanovich, Djilas told the Czechoslovak minister frankly: 'We had to silence him' (Korbel, op. cit., p. 166).

Socialists, Croatian Peasants, Slovenian Populists and others, all accused of conspiring with and spying for British or American intelligence services. Right up to the spring of 1948, there were many more trials of lesser-known and unknown people, sentenced with much publicity for conspiring to overthrow the constitutional order, helping terrorist bands, spying for foreign powers – British or American, Greek or Turkish. Articulate opposition had ceased, and yet, right down to the 1950s, special security forces were kept busy dismantling the remains of Mihailovich's wartime network, and local Party bosses were still being killed in rural areas.[10]

After the elimination of the political opposition, the Churches remained the only organizations outside complete Communist control. Although most Yugoslavs had little time for clerics, religion played a large part in their traditional way of life and in their several forms of collective historical consciousness. The Churches were, by their very nature, hostile to communism, whatever their actual attitude to the régime. The constitution had declared religion to be the individual's private concern, and the religious communities free in the performance of their religious affairs and rites, in so far as their doctrines and activities were not contrary to the new order. Within this context, the Churches had to be made harmless before they could be tolerated.

The Serbian Orthodox Church was a local Church. It had no canonical links with the West. More often than not it had taken a stand against the occupiers and had thus emerged from the war with great prestige, which had, however, been obtained at a heavy price, in so far as persecuting it had been part of the Axis policy of thoroughly crushing the Serbs.[11] Despite its prestige, it was a war invalid. Yet, both as a Christian Church and as an integral part of the national consciousness of the Serbs, it remained an implicit obstacle to the new order, and alongside the Catholics, the Orthodox had their share of difficulties. The régime encouraged the demand for local autonomous ecclesiastical units corresponding to the new federal structure, in order to dismantle the patriarchal jurisdiction, and it sponsored the formation of associations of clergy as a counterpart to the authority of the episcopate. Patriarch Gavrilo, the head of the Serbian Orthodox Church, whom the Germans had deported to Dachau, returned to Yugoslavia at the end of 1946. He had talks

[10] Cf. the revelations of a serial in the Belgrade daily *Politika*, 28 March–14 April 1969, and in *Ilustrovana Politika*, 17 November 1970. The subject of Lawrence Durrell's *White Eagles over Serbia*, London, 1957, is the same. Durrell was press attaché at the British embassy in Belgrade in 1951.

[11] In some dioceses, 90% of the clergy had been killed and 75% of the churches rendered unusable (S. Pavlowitch, 'The Orthodox Church in Yugoslavia', part ii, in *Eastern Churches Review*, II/1, London, 1968, p. 31).

with Tito, and did his utmost to use his great authority to reach some settlement with the government. The Orthodox espiscopate accepted the facts of the situation, but it wanted to be free within its own domain. Such was the gist of a memorandum presented to the government in February 1947, and a new statute, enacted by the hierarchy in June 1947, adapted the Church's constitution to the principle and fact of separation from the state.

The authorities nevertheless persisted in their attempts to reduce the authority of the Orthodox episcopate. They acted directly against a number of bishops; material incentives were used to increase membership of the government-sponsored associations of clergy; latent pressure was maintained for the separation of the Church in Macedonia. These levers were, nevertheless, considered sufficient to keep in check the Orthodox Church against which the Communists never undertook a campaign of the kind that was directed against the Roman Catholic Church.

It was the latter which bore the brunt of the new régime's policy of rendering religion harmless, and it was with the Catholic rather than with the Orthodox hierarchy that the real conflict was waged. The Catholic Church, because of its ties with the West, was considered an agency of the Western powers. Because of its better organization, greater wealth, and social involvement, it was regarded as a greater danger. Furthermore, the Roman Church had generally adopted an outspoken anti-Communist stand; its hierarchy in Yugoslavia opposed the principle of separation; and political movements had, directly or indirectly, claimed inspiration from it in Slovenia and Croatia.

For a brief initial period, the Catholic Church was spared. Tito met Archbishop Stepinats in the spring of 1945, and invited him to co-operate with the new government in running the Catholic Church in Yugoslavia more independently of Rome. Whether intended as an act of blackmail or a tactical concession, the move misunderstood the nature of the Roman Catholic Church, and it failed. Mgr Stepinats accepted the new government as the new secular authority, but insisted on upholding his Church's rights. In September, the Catholic episcopate protested against the principle of separation, the nationalization of ecclesiastical property, and the pressures to which the clergy was being submitted. A campaign of abuse was then unleashed against the Catholic Church and the government asked the pope to replace Mgr Stepinats. The aim was to discredit the Roman Church as one affiliated with Croatian Fascism and foreign powers, in order to drive a wedge between Catholic Yugoslavs and their Church. It failed utterly, and merely succeeded in turning the Catholic Church, for the first time among the Croatian masses, into a symbol of their national tradition. In such circumstances, the imprisonment of Mgr Stepinats was the only way out.

The Holy See retaliated by excommunicating all those concerned with the trial, and thereafter the Catholic Church was considered for a number of years as a foreign-inspired, almost subversive organization. Anti-Catholic propaganda was harsher than the general anti-religious propaganda. Pressures against the episcopate, including direct action, remained strong. Many clerics were imprisoned – whether as former Ustashas or as unsubdued Catholics was never quite clear. Associations of Catholic clergy were also tried, but for a long time they failed to overcome the opposition of the bishops.

The absence of a real Moslem 'Church' explains the initial concentration of the Communists' anti-religious effort on the Christian ecclesiastical structures, but the structure of the organized Islamic faith turned out to be no less recalcitrant, until in 1947 the authorities had to adopt against the Moslems the same forms of pressure as against the Christian Churches. This led the Islamic Religious Community to capitulate in August 1947, adopt a new statute, and elect more subservient leaders.

The Churches as such were never persecuted. Provided they remained passive and loyal, and did not oppose the official anti-religious propaganda, they were tolerated. Thus, it was anticipated, religion would gradually die out with the older generations, at the same time as younger ones were being raised in a new ideology through the youth organizations, the schools, and the army.

Much of the success of the Communists during the war had been due to their ability to advocate the liberation and reconstruction of a common Yugoslav state on a basis of religious and ethnic tolerance. Profiting from the failure of the monarchy to weld the separate identities of Serbs, Croats, and Slovenes into one Yugoslav national consciousness with the help of a centralized state structure and a government-fostered 'Yugoslavianism', the Communists had federalized the country,[12] and emphasis was placed on equality between all the different ethnic and religious varieties to which the inhabitants of Yugoslavia chose to belong. To the three established groups of Serbs, Croats, and Slovenes were added the Macedonians, and the inhabitants of Montenegro were encouraged to think of themselves as Montenegrins rather than Serbs.[13]

[12] This solution had been put forward as far back as the Constituent Assembly of 1919–20. It had not won the day then but was later repeatedly and increasingly advocated by various personalities and political trends as the 'Serbo-Croatian question' loomed larger.

[13] In the census of 1948, out of a total of 15·8 million, 41·5% registered as Serbs, 24% as Croats, 8·9% as Slovenes, 5·2% as Macedonians, and 2·7% as

All in all, the aim of the Communist 'founding fathers' was to create an equilibrium between the different ethnic groups and prevent the expression of sectional intolerance. One of the cornerstones of their early legislation was the prohibition of 'incitement to national, racial and religious hatred and discord'. The Macedonian region was set up as a separate republic and a separate nation.[14] Montenegro recovered its historical identity, thus going back on the age-old tendency for the unification of these two territories whose inhabitants had traditionally regarded themselves as belonging to one nation. The two autonomous regions of Kosovo and Voyvodina – each had, respectively at the beginning of its mediaeval and of its modern development, been the home of the Serbian national idea – were also carved out of Serbia. All this was meant to keep Serbia from being disproportionately larger than Croatia, and to bring about a balance between Serbs and Croats, while giving satisfaction to the differences that existed in all the units separated from Serbia.

The establishment of an equilibrium and the prohibition of intolerance seem, however, to have marked the limit of the new régime's contribution towards solving Yugoslavia's national problem, apart from the form of the federal system itself. The latter served as a lightning conductor for national emotions without limiting the power of the Communist Party.[15] Everyone was allowed to call himself by whatever ethnic name he wished, and to develop his own harmless cultural and linguistic idiosyncrasies within their own,

---

Montenegrins. 5·1% were 'undeclared', plain Yugoslavs, and these were mostly Moslems. The percentage of minorities was 12·6, and included 750,000 Albanians and 496,000 Magyars, the Germans having been practically eliminated. Generally speaking, each of the Yugoslav national groups recognized as such was concentrated in one republic, with the historic entity of Bosnia-Herzegovina added for good measure so as to avoid the difficulty of partitioning it between Serbia and Croatia, and in order to satisfy the nationally undecided Moslems. There were in Bosnia-Herzegovina in 1948, 44% Serbs, 24% Croats, and 31% 'undecided' Moslems. Voyvodina and Kosovo, as regions of mixed Yugoslav and non-Yugoslav ethnic groups, were given a special status as autonomous regions within the republic of Serbia.

[14] Nationalism in Macedonia grew rapidly in the immediate post-war period – as a consequence of latent genuine popular feeling, and of politically motivated decisions reflecting aims both domestic and foreign. The introduction of an official and literary Macedonian language was a popular move which did much to win the allegiance of the population to the new Yugoslav régime, although its implementation took some time, for there was no single manner of speech which could be called 'Macedonian', but rather a spectrum of dialects from Serbian to Bulgarian from which a new written language had to be first created, and then taught to the people.

[15] Cf. Shoup, op. cit., p. 113.

ideologically limited confines. The feeling of inequality and of humiliation felt by some sections of the population before the war was reduced – that, for instance, of the Macedonians towards Serbianization, of the Serbs of Croatia towards the Croats, of the Croats towards the impression of Serbian hegemony, and of the minorities against the Yugoslav state generally. For the rest, the national problem was not so much solved in the immediate post-war period by the new revolutionary régime, as paralysed. Its final solution was tied to the victory of communism over the remnants of attitudes created by the old social order. No attempt was made to integrate the sectional national feelings into an overall Yugoslav consciousness, since this was associated with the practices of the old régime, but rather the aim was to harness them to a common ideological cause. The slogan of 'brotherhood and unity' contained a large dose of genuine optimism, based on the belief that communism was going to make the problem redundant.

Meanwhile, behind the façade of the slogans, it remained. People did not speak of it, because it was forbidden to do so, because it evoked painful wartime memories, and because they were preoccupied with the more immediate worries of everyday life. Yet the feelings of national differences remained. If anything, they were destined to be sharpened by the impossibility of fostering anything common to all Yugoslavs other than communism, and by the lack of contact between the different nationalities, religious communities, and cultures. Embittered by the war, and then swept under the carpet without the possibility of being rationally examined and explained, nationalism in Yugoslavia was soon reduced to something very primitive and emotional.[16]

Economic reconstruction and transformation

Once again, the country had emerged devastated from the conflict. Indeed Yugoslavia was one of the European countries which had suffered most during the Second World War, chiefly as the result of internal strife. The figure of 1·7 million is that generally mentioned for its population losses – over 10 per cent of the pre-war popula-

[16] Croats came to believe that communism was the work of Serbs because the original partisans in Croatia had been Serbs and consequently played an important part, in the post-war period, in the administration and police of the republic of Croatia. Serbs came to believe that communism was the work of Croats because the Serbian element had been so systematically weakened by the new régime; because the flower of Serbian youth had been sent to their death by the partisan command in the last stages of the war against the Germans; and because so many of the latter-day partisans were turncoats from the N.D.H. army.

tion[17] – besides which allowance should be made for an increased mortality, the fact that the average age of those killed was in the early twenties, and the heavy encroachments of the losses in the groups with better education or skills. The territory had disintegrated as an economic unit; it had been exploited and plundered by the occupying powers, and its productive facilities had been destroyed. One-quarter of the population was homeless, more than half the livestock had been lost, the industrial potential was reduced to a third of its pre-war value, the communications system was utterly destroyed, agriculture was disrupted.[18] In addition, Yugoslavia's gold reserves had been deposited abroad for safe-keeping on the eve of the war, mostly in the U.S.A.

With no exportable goods, no foreign exchange, and no credit, there was only one source of help – the United Nations Relief and Rehabilitation Administration. But UNRRA was essentially American, and relations between it and the Yugoslav revolutionary authorities were not altogether smooth. Although shipments of relief food had begun to arrive at the end of 1944, the agreement with UNRRA was not signed until late March 1945. The Yugoslav government was suspicious of UNRRA officials who, in turn, were critical of some of the ways in which the Yugoslav authorities distributed the supplies, for these were mostly sold to finance the government's own rehabilitation activities.

UNRRA's immediate task was to provide food for the population to survive. Over the winter of 1945–46, it fed 3 to 5 million people and provided additional food for many more. It was the only source of civilian clothing and medical supplies. Furthermore, it sent livestock and tractors to help with local food production. Altogether Yugoslavia obtained more than 14 per cent of UNRRA's total budget of nearly $428 million for slightly over two years, or more than half the value of all the country's imports in the period 1934–38. Even so, in the first post-war years there was undernourishment in almost all regions and sectors, and partial starvation in

[17] This places Yugoslavia second in that unhappy category, after Poland (22%), and just before the Soviet Union (10%). Yugoslav official sources explicitly say 1·7 million dead (cf. Dedijer, *Tito Speaks*, p. 224), to which should then be added the refugees and the expelled (M. Meken, in R. Byrnes (ed.): *Yugoslavia*, New York, 1957, p. 77; and Tomasevich in Kerner (ed.), op. cit., p. 390). George Hoffman and Fred Warner Neal, however (*Yugoslavia and the New Communism*, New York, 1962, pp. 86–7), consider that the figure of 1·7 million covers *all* losses, and that 1·1 million should be taken as the number of those who actually lost their lives.

[18] For more precise figures, based on UNRRA estimates and those of the Allied Reparations Commission, see Tomasevich in Kerner, op. cit., p. 391; R. Wolff, *The Balkans in Our Times*, Cambridge, Mass., 1956, p. 323; Hoffman and Neal, op. cit., p. 87; and Bilimovich in Zagoroff, op. cit., p. 345.

some of the poorest and worst devastated. UNRRA could not, overnight, make up for wartime losses. All it could do was to help prevent the death of millions from starvation and disease, and provide the basic assistance without which the new régime could never have re-established the flow of agricultural produce, or maintain any form of price control and rationing.

Food rationing was introduced in the summer of 1945, and a year later the total ration-receiving population was 8·5 million. Of the different categories of rations, only the highest would have been sufficient if they had been actually available. Full rations, however, were rarely issued, and, in so far as they could afford it, people were forced to turn to the black market. In such circumstances, it was hardly surprising that speculation and corruption were widespread among employees of the supply organizations, in spite of severe punishment.

The first requisite for stabilizing prices and fighting the black market was a currency reform, for at the time of liberation in 1945, the money in circulation was forty-two times the pre-war amount.[19] and in a whole range of currencies issued by the different powers and authorities that had, at one time or another, ruled over different parts of the country during the intervening years. In April 1945, new dinars were issued at the rate of one for twenty pre-war units.[20] Individuals were allowed to convert up to 10,000 old dinars. All holdings above that amount were to be declared and deposited with banks, where they were blocked. Part of these was confiscated, according to a rate rising with the size of the holding to 70 per cent, the rest being placed at the disposal of the state for a number of months. Before the year was over, what remained of the blocked accounts was freed after further reductions for the government's reconstruction fund. The aim of the reform was threefold – to check inflationary tendencies by reducing the amount of money in circulation,to provide resources to finance state investments, and to destroy at least the monetary part of existing fortunes.

The destruction of the property-owning classes was naturally one of the aims of the Communists' economic policies on gaining control of the state apparatus. If the urban bourgeoisie was no great obstacle, the peasantry was a formidable one. The new government's land-policy was marked by the ideological desire to introduce socialism

[19] N. Spulber, *The Economics of Communist Eastern Europe*, Boston, 1957, p. 105.
[20] The new dinar was officially based on gold, and a theoretical exchange rate fixed at the pre-war level of 50 to the dollar. In practice this had little significance, for no foreign transactions were conducted in dinars and a monopoly of foreign exchange transactions was given to the nationalized, currency-issuing central bank.

in the countryside, and the political desire to reduce this obstacle. It was not, however, thought possible to introduce a policy of immediate collectivization of the land. Yugoslavia was essentially a land of smallholders, and the produce of their land was badly needed. Furthermore, the partisans themselves were peasants. For this reason, the Communist leaders could not afford to unite the peasantry in open opposition against the revolution. Caught in the whirlwind of war and revolution, the reaction of those peasants who had kept their land was to cling to it and survive. On the other hand, those from the poor and devastated areas, who had been forcibly uprooted and had become a significant element in Tito's army, were after a new deal, but not one which affected their independence and their traditional frame of mind.

A new agrarian reform was enacted in August 1945. Since there was no appreciable body of richer landowners left after the land reform carried out between the two world wars, the law of 1945 was aimed at the non-farming owners. As a general rule, it expropriated without compensation all estates above 30 hectares owned by non-farmers,[21] and land owned by farmers in excess of that amount. To the land expropriated under the agrarian reform was added that confiscated from expelled German farmers, enemies of the people, and refugees. All in all, about 1·6 million hectares – slightly less than half expropriated and slightly more than half confiscated – were acquired by the state. Just under half of it was distributed free to 330,000 poor or landless peasant families, primarily of veteran or dead partisans, the rest being kept for state-owned enterprises or for the first collective farms. Most of these transfers occurred on the rich, formerly German-owned farms of Voyvodina, where land-hungry peasants from the bare and overpopulated mountainous core were resettled, both on private holdings or in the first collective farms. To complete the 1945 agrarian reform, all peasant debts were cancelled later that year.

Comprehensive legislation on the collective sector in agriculture was not issued until July 1946, when separate provisions were made for 'general agricultural co-operatives', in which private farmers associated to perform a variety of economic functions, and for 'peasants' working co-operatives', to which the private farmer turned over his land. Whereas the former were claimed to be merely extensions of the pre-war system, the latter were in effect Soviet-type *kolkhozes*, although the word – and indeed any mention

---

[21] Individual non-farmer owners of less than 30 hectares were allowed to keep up to five. Religious institutions were allowed to keep up to ten, and if of major historical or architectural importance, up to 30 hectares of arable land and 30 of forests.

of socialism – was carefully avoided. Membership of both types was voluntary, and no open coercion was employed, for the authorities left it to other means to induce the peasants gradually to give up private farming.

The government was in a position to exercise considerable pressure on the peasantry, first and foremost through the officially controlled collection, distribution, and sale of foodstuffs, then through its tax policy. As early as the summer of 1945, the compulsory sale of surplus production to the state was introduced, the quotas and prices being fixed in advance. Prices were well below what the farmers could have obtained on the market. Non-delivery was severely punished, often by confiscation of the land. No credit was available to the private farmer; he paid higher taxes; it was made difficult for him to obtain consumer goods, basic tools, and equipment. Although no fundamental blow had yet been struck at the old rural structure, by mid-1948 the Yugoslav Communist government had moved faster than any other East European government. His standards diminished by the war, increasingly apprehensive of the new authority – whose policy he now saw as an attack on his traditional independent way of life and means of livelihood – the Yugoslav peasant chafed under pressure. He chose to cultivate only the minimum for his own needs, and there was little that could be done in face of his passive resistance. It was little wonder, in such circumstances, that agriculture was at the mercy of climatic conditions.[22]

With the exception of the land, the initial post-war period was marked by the radical transformation of property relations through the processes of confiscation, expropriation, and nationalization. In so far as they were not already German-owned, most big firms had been taken over by the Germans in the course of the war, in one way or another. As early as November 1944, the property of enemy nationals, war criminals, and collaborators was placed under government control in liberated territory. Since most commercial and industrial enterprises had fallen under some form of enemy control, it was easy to stigmatize their owners as collaborators, if they had not been killed or fled abroad. There was thus not much left to expropriate when in December 1946, industrial enterprises and mines, wholesale and foreign trade enterprises, banks and transport

[22] In contrast to 1945, in 1946 farmers were allowed to sell a percentage of their surplus on the market. If the quantities delivered exceeded the prescribed quotas, they were allowed the privilege of buying rationed goods. These measures, intended to induce the peasant to produce, declare, and deliver more, had only a limited success. The grain harvest, which in 1945 had been down to about half its normal pre-war level, increased somewhat in 1946, and again in 1947, until in 1948 it was back at its pre-war level.

facilities were formally nationalized.[23] As for retail trade, it too was progressively liquidated by the issue of new licences. By the time of the expropriation law passed in April 1947, which provided for the expropriation of any private property if made necessary by public interest, the only larger group of survivors of private enterprise, apart from the peasants, were the craftsmen.

It was in the year 1947 that the government moved to long-range planning. In June, UNRRA operations were concluded. In July, an international conference was summoned in Paris to examine the American Marshall Plan of aid to Europe. Yugoslavia refused an invitation to take part. In the spring of 1946, Boris Kidrich, head of the government of Slovenia, had been sent to Moscow to study the Soviet economic system. On his return, he was put in charge of the country's economy, and in April 1947, under his guidance, a five-year plan was introduced in Yugoslavia – almost two years before any other Communist-ruled country in eastern Europe.

The Soviet Union under Stalin had relied on heavy industry as the carrier of change. Yugoslavia under Tito was going to do the same. The declared aim of the five-year plan was to turn the country into an independent industrial power. Rapid industrialization would free Yugoslavia of its old dependence on foreign capital. It would shift the large passive surplus of agricultural labour into higher-income-yielding activities. Political and ideological considerations were also involved. The plan would socialize the economy, create a strong industrial proletariat, and make Yugoslavia a powerful partner in the Communist alliance. The idea of eliminating the disparities in economic development among the different regions was closely linked with that of rapid industrialization. The industrialization of the politically unstable backward areas would help to stabilize them, since their predominantly peasant population was not satisfied with the government's agricultural policy.

On the basis of the 1939 levels, the national income was to be doubled in five years, industrial production almost trebled, and investments more than trebled, to absorb over 27 per cent of the national income. Investments would follow the Soviet pattern, according to which industry grew faster than agriculture, heavy industry faster than other industrial sectors, and machine industry

---

[23] Boris Kidrich, the government's chief economic planner, told the fifth congress of the C.P.Y. in 1948 that in the course of the first year after liberation, 35% of industry had already come into the hands of the state, while another 27% had been placed under sequestration, which was tantamount to nationalization. Private banks were already in fact liquidated before the law of December 1946 by the process of revision of licences.

Many artistic influences cross in and enrich the artistic landscape of Yugoslavia
1 The Romanesque portal of Trogir cathedral (mid-thirteenth century)

2 The Turkish mosque of Mustafa-Pasha, Skopye (late fifteenth century)

3 The monastery church at Visoki Dechani, near Pech (mid-fourteenth century)—a late example of the blend of Romanesque, Gothic, and Byzantine, characteristic of the mediaeval Serbian monarchy

4 Dushan of Serbia with his wife and son—a fresco at Visoki Dechani

5 Orthodox Baroque—the altar screen in the church of St Nicholas, Zemun

6 Catholic Baroque—the façade of the Ursuline church in Ljubljana

7 The Byzantine church of Staro Nagorichino, near Skopye (early fourteenth century)

8 Nineteenth-century 'historic' painting—*The Migration of the Serbs* (1896), by Paya Yovanovich

9 Twentieth-century 'naïve' painting—*Eclipse of the Sun* (1964), by Miyo Kovachich

10 Ivan Meshtrovich (1883–1962), *Mother at Prayer* (1928)

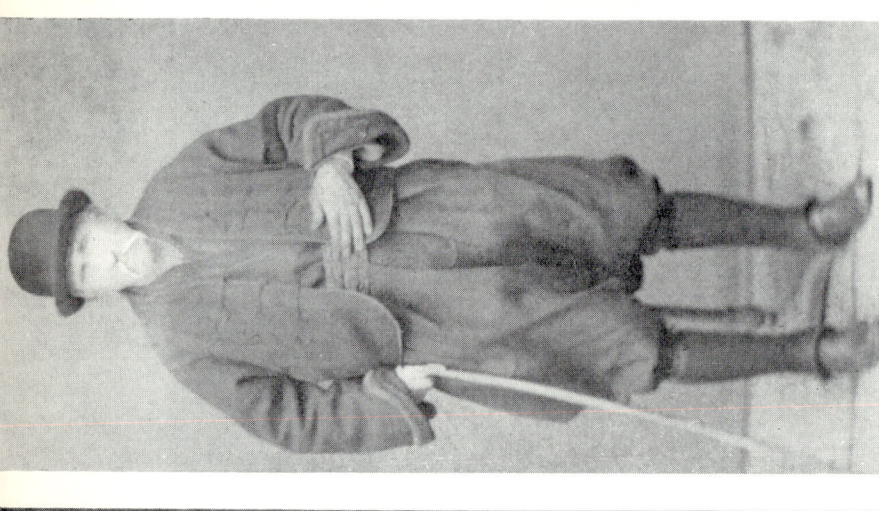

11, 12, and 13 Turkish influence was widespread and long-lasting. From l. to r. a Moslem noble of Bosnia, posing for the photographer (early twentieth century); a merchant in a provincial town of Serbia—from 'Turkish' to 'European' (late nineteenth century); and Croatian soldiers ('Turks' as the soldiers against whom they had once defended the Habsburg lands (early nineteenth century)

14 The official painting of the proclamation of the Kingdom of the Serbs, Croats, and Slovenes—1 December 1918

15 The preliminaries to unification included Serbia's military contribution to the Allied cause (above: Serbian war graves, 1915), combined with the realism of the leaders of the Habsburg Yugoslavs within the Monarchy, and the idealism of those who had gone abroad to propagate the cause

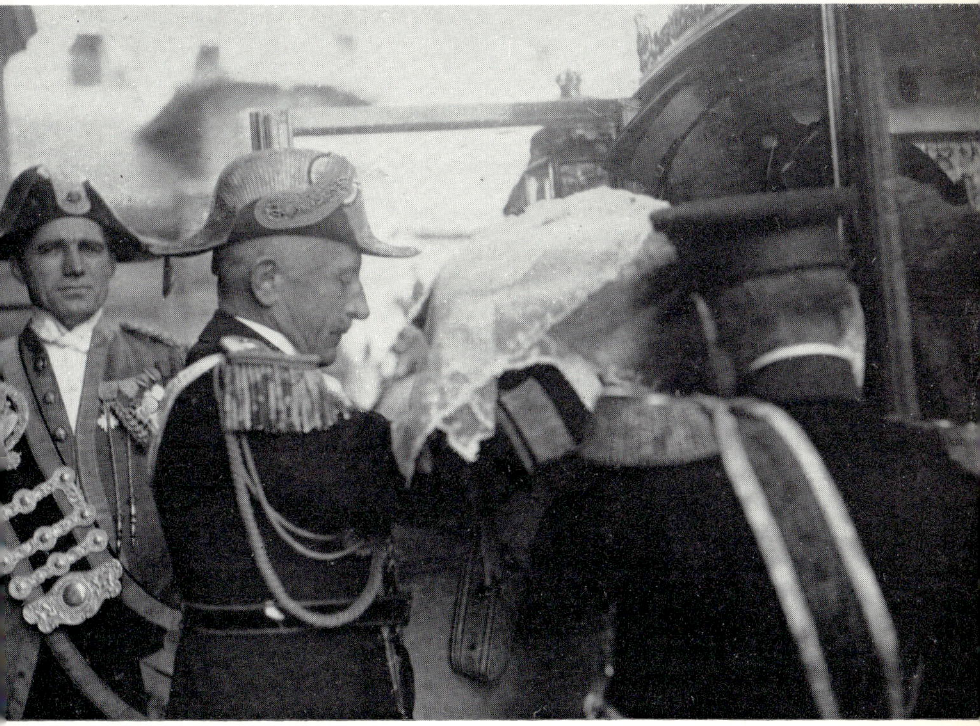

Yugoslavia between the wars

16　The uncrowned king of the Croats—Stjepan Radich addressing a political meeting

17　The future last Karageorgevich king makes his official debut—the infant Crown Prince Peter being taken to his christening

18 The men who founded the first Yugoslav state—members of the Serbian government and of the Yugoslav Committee, Corfu 1917. Seated third from l., Trumbich, with Pashich next to him; Davidovich on the far r. Standing third from r., Marinkovich; Drashkovich on the far r.

19 The men who founded the second Yugoslav state—members of the Communist leadership in their mountain headquarters, 1943. Second from l., Rankovich, with Djilas (head and shoulders); Tito in the centre, with Zhuyovich behind him and Hebrang next to him; Piyade and Kardelj on the r.

The resistance that was also a civil war—the German ransom in gold for Tito and Mihailovich (*Novo Vreme*, Belgrade, 21 July 1943)

The strong men of Yugoslavia

21 King Alexander—he tried to impose ethnic unity
22 Marshal Tito—he tried to impose ideological unity. (Pictured here with his wife and the Belgian royal family on a state visit to Brussels in 1970.)

Humbler approaches to unity
23 Church leaders—Cardinal Sheper and Patriarch Gherman (Karlovtsi, spring 1968)
24 The up-and-coming intelligentsia—university students (Belgrade, spring 1970)

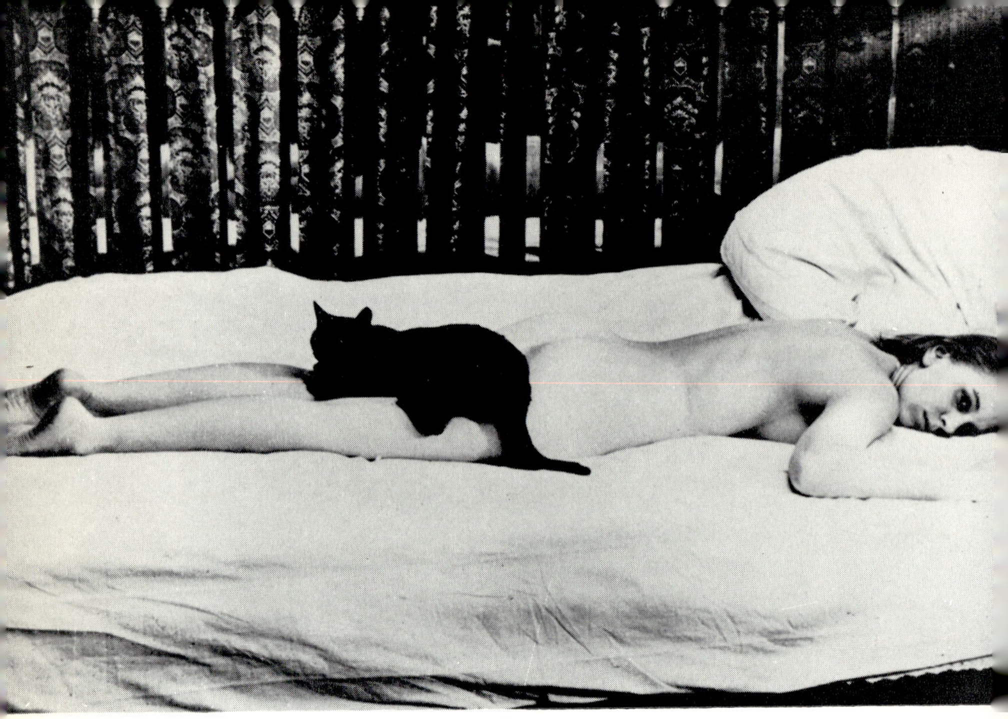

Yugoslavs in the 1960s. Did they think of unity, or simply of the good things in life?
25 The young heroine of Makaveyev's film, *Switchboard Operator*
26 An elderly peasant tasting plum brandy

fastest in heavy industry. The whole process was controlled by the government through a highly centralized and detailed system of planning and administration, which defined all levels of production and employment, channelled all investments through the budget, physically allocated goods, fixed prices, and conducted all profits back to a central investment fund.

The plan would have been a formidable undertaking in the best of circumstances. As it was, in 1947 production was not yet back to pre-war levels, which made the indices of growth, based on 1939, even more daring. The first two post-war years had hardly begun to heal the wounds of war. The capital equipment and industrial materials needed to realize the plan were far beyond the country's capacity to produce, nor could they possibly be paid for by the exports of a war-battered, distrustful, and under-financed agriculture. There was an almost complete lack of trained technicians.

Nevertheless, the powerful tools placed in the hands of the state did enable the government to increase capital formation, and achieve economic growth at an unsurpassed pace, though at a price. Confiscation, expropriation, and nationalization measures provided a start. Full use was made of taxes and prices policy. An already hungry population was made to forego consumer goods and keep belts tight. Reserves were squeezed out of the country's natural resources. Foreign trade was orientated chiefly towards the Soviet bloc, which took most of Yugoslavia's exports of metals and minerals, with the result that in 1946 and 1947 its balance of trade was positive. War reparations from enemy countries – mainly Germany – were once again extremely useful,[24] and the contribution from UNRRA should not be forgotten. The Yugoslav government also counted on aid from the U.S.S.R. Some credits and loans were indeed promised for the purchase of capital equipment, and Soviet technicians were sent.

Above all, the Yugoslav planners had faith, they believed that revolutionary ardour would see them through. The country was potentially rich, enthusiasm in the service of the plan would do the rest, with help from the Soviet Union. General mobilization, it was thought, could make up for the lack of equipment and experience. A massive propaganda campaign was launched by all the officially sponsored organizations of the People's Front. Any lack of faith or courage was denounced as treachery. The tasks of the new Communist-led Trade Union Organization were to arouse the zeal of the working class, to raise productivity and instil discipline, to convince workers to accept necessary sacrifices, and to educate them in the

[24] Yugoslavia was allocated 10% of the German reparations in capital equipment, and over 6% of German assets abroad.

spirit of Marxism. Last, but not least, much use was made of unpaid labour, voluntary as well as penal or semi-penal.[25]

Several of the premisses to the plan were not, however, entirely sound. The Soviet Union was interested not so much in seeing a small-scale Yugoslav reproduction of its economic structure, as in exploiting Yugoslav agricultural and mineral resources. Soviet economic relations with the Communist régimes it had helped to install were rapidly turning to exploitation of the latter's economies through trade agreements and joint companies. The Soviets bought at lower and sold at higher than world prices. As for the joint companies, the Russians barely invested anything in them except German capital declared prize of war, and through them they dominated and exploited whole sectors of the partner country's economy. Most of the Yugoslav output of mineral ores went to the Soviet bloc for low prices, in exchange for an inadequate supply of heavy equipment and industrial goods, expensive, often of poor quality, and slowly delivered. By the beginning of 1948, the foreign trade balance was negative. Negotiations for the joint-stock companies dragged on, and eventually only two were set up – for air transport and for river shipping. As for Soviet credits, by 1948 Yugoslavia had received only under $1 million, or slightly over 6 per cent of what had been promised.[26]

Voluntary, pressed, and convict labour could in no way make up for the lack of skilled labour, just as the revolutionary zeal and political loyalty of the ex-partisans rewarded with jobs in the economy could not make up for the lack of trained staff and technicians. Factories were erected in less time than was needed to train skilled labour and experts. One of the plan's most apparent results was the lavish use of unskilled labour on large-scale building projects which involved little capital equipment.

In introducing the five-year plan, Tito had denied that it marked a step towards the abolition of private ownership of land. In so doing he was trying to allay the fears of the peasantry, whose economic performance was also one of the premisses to the plan. But the low priority of investment accorded to agriculture, added to the pressures on the farmers, and their apathy, meant that agricultural production could hardly rise to cover domestic needs, let alone provide exports. It was not only the farmers who saw no incentive to work. The lack of consumer goods, low wages, high prices, and material hardship of all sorts affected the will to work in most

[25] Apart from convicts, there were the people sent to do 'socially useful work' by order of the police – mostly peasants who had failed to deliver their quotas.
[26] Wolff, op. cit., p. 337.

sections of the population. At the same time, the massive investments needed for the plan increased the currency in circulation, and by the end of 1948, inflation had accelerated again. As Tito was to recognize himself at the sixth Party congress in 1952, the first five-year plan was a grandiose programme built on unrealistic premisses and enthusiastic overestimations of existing conditions.

Foreign policy

The new régime's foreign policy was, like its domestic policy, full of revolutionary dynamism. As a partner of the victorious Allies, Yugoslavia could have expected to round off its ethnic domain to the north-west by obtaining those Yugoslav-inhabited territories left over the border after the First World War, in Austrian Carinthia and in the Italian Julian region. During the war, the Allied powers had not been unfavourable to these Yugoslav claims.[27] But Tito's attempt to force the decisions of the peace conference as soon as he had secured all he could usefully obtain from the Western Allies,[28] his close adherence to the Soviet Union, and his increasingly hostile attitude to his wartime friends in the West, changed the attitude of both Great Britain and the U.S.A. By taking a strong stand, they brought Yugoslav ambitions across the north-western frontier to a halt. The Soviet government, anxious not to be involved in a major conflict with its Western Allies at that time, advised the Yugoslavs to back down. Early in May 1945, Field-Marshal Alexander's forces secured the lines between Italy and Austria. Later that month, the Yugoslav partisans withdrew from Austrian territory, having been requested to respect the frontier of 1937. On 9 June, an agreement was signed in Belgrade between Great Britain, the United States, and the Yugoslav provisional government, establishing an Allied military administration over the whole disputed area of the Julian region pending a final settlement by the peace conference. In the meantime, the territory would be divided into Yugoslav and Anglo-American zones of occupation, the port of Trieste being included in the latter.

Negotiations for the peace settlement were protracted. By the summer of 1946 the foreign ministers of the four European Allied powers had finally agreed on a French compromise between the Anglo-American pro-Italian, and the Soviet pro-Yugoslav, lines. This left roughly the same number of Italians and Yugoslavs on the

[27] The British government in particular, in discussions with the exiled Yugoslav cabinet in London, had expressed itself favourably regarding claims on Istria and Trieste (Maclean, *Disputed Barricade*, pp. 337–8).

[28] Cf. above, p. 171.

'other' side of the border and turned Trieste with its immediate hinterland into a free territory. As the Peace Conference opened in Paris in July, relations between Yugoslavia and the West were tense. Distressed at the Four-Power plan on Trieste, which they attributed to American influence, and increasingly suspicious of Western intentions, the Yugoslav authorities constantly complained of territorial violations by American transport planes flying between Italy and Austria. In August they forced down one such plane and shot down another, while Tito publicly accused the U.S.A. of sending squadrons of military planes over Yugoslavia. Under threat of an immediate reference to the Security Council of the newly formed United Nations Organization, the Yugoslavs released the first crew and paid indemnities to the families of the victims in the second case.

Tension between Yugoslavia and the West had nevertheless been dangerously raised. While all the other Allies accepted the recommendations of the 'Big Four', Yugoslavia threatened not to sign a treaty embodying those regarding Trieste. The treaty with Italy having been finally drafted and the Security Council having agreed to take over responsibility for the Free Territory of Trieste, Yugoslavia eventually gave in.[29] On 10 February 1947, the peace treaties with Italy, Romania, Hungary, and Bulgaria were finally signed in Paris. Yugoslavia obtained all the territory up to and including the upper valley of Isonzo (Socha), including the actual Istrian peninsula, with the exception of Trieste and its immediate hinterland – altogether an addition of some 7,760 square kilometres with 600,000 inhabitants. Italy, Hungary, and Bulgaria were to pay reparations to Yugoslavia.

The peace settlement did not solve the whole problem, for Trieste became a pawn in the Cold War, and the clauses on the Free Territory were never implemented. While the Soviets and the Western powers vetoed each other's candidates for the post of Security Council governor of the F.T.T., the town itself with the area to the north (about 300,000 inhabitants, some 15 per cent of them Yugoslavs) remained under Anglo-American military occupation and administration, and the rest (just over 60,000 inhabitants, slightly over half of them Yugoslavs) under Yugoslavia.[30]

[29] The Soviet government probably exercised pressure on the Yugoslav leadership in the expectation of the Communists coming to power in Italy soon, and the leader of the Italian Communist Party, Togliatti, visited Belgrade in November 1946.

[30] These figures are based on statistics of 1950–53 and 1945 respectively (H. Kostanick, 'The Geopolitics of the Balkans', in C. and B. Jelavich (ed.): *The Balkans in Transition – Essays on the Development of Balkan Life and Politics since the Eighteenth Century*, Berkeley, 1963, pp. 22–3; and Novak, op. cit., p. 268).

In 1948, soon after the Communist *coup d'état* in Prague, general elections were to be held in Italy, the first under the new republican constitution. The issue was a clear one between communism and anti-communism. With a violent campaign under way, the Soviet Union suggested the return to Italy of its African colonies, and the Western powers proposed that the whole of the F.T.T. be returned to Italy, since the Yugoslav authorities had, in their zone, disregarded the clauses of the peace treaty which guaranteed the liberties of the inhabitants of the territory. Needless to say, both Yugoslavia and the Soviet Union rejected the latter proposal, but it strengthened the hand of the anti-Communist parties in the Italian election in April. The Trieste stalemate continued, but the Western powers now seriously favoured ousting the Yugoslavs entirely. As for Yugoslavia's claims against Austria, they could merely be reasserted, with Soviet support, without getting very far, however, since the West was not able to get the U.S.S.R. to agree on a treaty with Austria.

If Communist Yugoslavia's policy towards Italy and Austria could be considered as one aiming at completing the unification of its ethnic territory by bringing in the last remaining *irredenta*, its policy towards the south-east was well and truly expansionist. During the war, all the armed movements which had been generated in defence of the Serbian population had met with the hostility of the Albanian minority, and had returned like for like. This went for partisans as well as for *chetniks* of one kind or another, in spite of the help given by the Yugoslav Communists to the Communist partisans in Albania. Initially, communism did not alter in any way Yugoslav-Albanian relations over the Kosovo region. The Albanian Communist leadership took up its country's claims over it, while the Yugoslav Communist authorities adopted towards this hostile ethnic minority measures which differed little from those used by the occupation authorities against the Serbs in the same region. The result, inspired by Albanian irredentist resentment against Yugoslav Communist terror, was an uprising which broke out in December 1944, and was not finally put down until the following summer.[31]

It was only then that the Yugoslav leadership took a different attitude towards the border region with Albania. In recognition of its mixed ethnic character, Kosovo was declared an autonomous province in the constitutional settlement, and Albanian was introduced as one of the official languages – an arrangement similar to that made for Voyvodina, the province bordering on Hungary. A more moderate approach to the Albanian question could be envisaged, for the Albanian Communist Party, now safely in power, had

[31] On this little-covered episode, cf. Shoup, op. cit., pp. 104–5.

purged itself of the elements opposed to Yugoslav influence, and Communist Yugoslavia was taking over the role formerly played by Fascist Italy – that of the richer patron which Albania, unable to produce enough food to feed itself, had always had in its modern history. The new Albanian government was remodelling the country according to the hardly more ancient pattern of its bigger neighbour, who granted considerable economic assistance, sent ever-increasing numbers of Yugoslav experts of all kinds, established joint-stock companies on the model of those being foisted by the Soviets upon eastern Europe (and resisted by the Yugoslavs), and intervened directly in Albania's domestic affairs. In July 1946, Albania signed with Yugoslavia a long-term treaty of friendship and mutual assistance, and a year later, by another agreement, Yugoslavia granted credits corresponding to over half the entire Albanian budget, with no stipulation regarding repayment. No matter how generous, the Yugoslavs had come to treat Albania as their satellite, and both their government and that of the Soviet Union agreed in principle that Albania ought to unite with Yugoslavia, which would at least have solved the question of the Albanian minority in Yugoslavia.[32]

The federal arrangements had hardly been adopted for the existing territory of Yugoslavia, as a first step towards reducing sectional friction between different historic regions and ethnic groups, than plans were made to expand it. The very concept of federation left it open to additional members, and the Yugoslav Communist leaders were so confident that the revolution in the political, economic, and social orders would solve, or rather dissolve, the problem of sectional friction, that they did not hesitate to contemplate extending the federal formula. Indeed expansionism and federalism went hand in hand in more ways than one, for an expansionist foreign policy helped to satisfy most Yugoslavs, either by enabling fringe groups to unite with their kin over the border, or by satisfying the bigger groups at the expense of traditional, non-Slav ethnic rivals.

With the recognition of a Macedonian nationality and the establishment of a republic of Macedonia, the new régime aimed not only at showing the local population that its interests were best served within a Yugoslav state directed by the C.P.Y. in Belgrade, but also at providing a structure around which the Bulgarian and Greek portions of Macedonia could be united. The different steps devised to appeal to the feelings of the inhabitants of Macedonia, the rejection of the Serbian heritage, the cultivation of a Macedonian national consciousness, and the support given to the principle of

[32] Djilas, op. cit., p. 121.

Macedonian unification, all aided the Yugoslav Communist leadership in consolidating its hold over a traditionally difficult region.

The Macedonian Slavs were only a transition between Serbs and Bulgars, or an ethnic element which could, for a large part, have been moulded into either Serbs or Bulgars. The latter, across the border, were a fellow South Slav nation whose separation from the others, united in the Yugoslav federation, appeared illogical now that communism was removing the political and social forms of the past, as well as the foreign interferences, which were held responsible for the disunity between Serbs and Bulgars. The Yugoslavs acted quickly, as soon as Bulgaria had capitulated. They did not wait for the weak Bulgarian Communist Party to consolidate itself in power, strengthen its international position, and perhaps even take over the nationalist policies of its predecessors. Plans were immediately drawn up, first to unite Bulgarian Macedonia with Yugoslavia, then to extend the Yugoslav federation to the whole of Bulgaria. Negotiations were started between the Communist Parties of Yugoslavia and Bulgaria as early as the autumn of 1944.

In November, the Yugoslavs put it to the Bulgars that they should become the seventh unit in the Yugoslav federation. The Bulgarian Communist leaders were not averse to making a fresh approach to the Macedonian question within a wider Communist framework. They had already acknowledged the existence of a separate Macedonian nation. But they feared that, since Tito and the C.P.Y. were at the height of their international prestige, while theirs was at its nadir, they would be simply swallowed up by Tito's Yugoslavia. They submitted a counter-proposal for a union between Yugoslavia, as one partner, and Bulgaria, as the other, to be negotiated at parity between the two existing sovereign states. To this the Yugoslavs retorted that some of the units in their federation had also been sovereign states in the past, and well before Bulgaria. The Bulgars then retreated behind a new proposal for a defensive and mutual assistance pact to be concluded as a preliminary step. The Yugoslavs had tried to exploit the temporary disparity between the fortunes of the two parties, but they had failed to obtain rapid results when the going was good. As no further progress could be achieved in the talks, both sides went to Moscow, in January 1945, to put their differences to Stalin, just as earlier in the century, Serbs and Bulgars went to the tsar to arbitrate on their Macedonian differences. Not only were they advised to delay plans for federation, but even the substitute treaty had to be postponed. Bulgaria was a defeated country with whom peace had still not been signed, and as such it was not empowered to conduct foreign negotiations without the authorization of the Allies. Alarmed at the rumours of an impending union between the two Soviet-backed states both neighbouring on Greece, the British, backed by the Americans, objected to any such treaty being concluded before peace had been formally restored – an objection no doubt welcomed by Stalin.

Tito and his C.P.Y. headed a more powerful machine and were better established than any other East European Communist Party; they could be expected to promote Soviet interests in the Balkans. There was thus no apparent reason to frustrate their plans regarding Albania and Bulgaria, two small Balkan countries emerging from the Axis orbit, but it would have been difficult for the Russians to sanction the consummation of such plans as early as 1945. The Soviet Union was not yet completely master in eastern Europe, nor were the local Communists yet completely masters in Yugoslavia and Bulgaria. In the former, the Communist régime had not yet been constitutionally installed or internationally recognized, while the latter was still under Allied three-power control. In such circumstances, the Soviet Union could not afford to disregard entirely the views of its Western allies. Even less could it disregard the sensitiveness of its Bulgarian protégés, at a time when so many people in Bulgaria, both outside and inside the Communist Party, were strongly opposed to making any concessions to the Yugoslavs over Macedonia.

The Yugoslavs did not insist. Although in January 1946, their new federal constitution legally came into force, the government was more cautious over Macedonia than over Trieste or Carinthia. There were the interests of other Communists to take into account, and national feelings were not as clear-cut on the borders of Bulgaria as they were on the borders of Italy and Austria. To start with, not all the inhabitants of the People's Republic of Macedonia were keen Macedonians. Refugees from the Bulgarian occupation, who had left because they felt themselves to be Serbs and who returned to Macedonia after its liberation, were not welcomed, especially those whose land had been taken over by squatters who did not feel themselves to be Serbs at all. Among them were most of the colonists who had been resettled between the wars on land expropriated from Moslem estate-owners. To prevent clashes, and give satisfaction to the Macedonians, measures were taken in the spring of 1945 according to which most colonists were deemed to have forfeited their holdings.[33]

---

[33] These included *émigrés*, officials of the old régime, and all who had been granted land in return for services to the old régime, and they constituted the majority, since most colonists were Serbian ex-servicemen and volunteers of previous wars. The decrees applied to all such holdings, both in Macedonia and in the Kosovo region.

The government in Belgrade was not entirely certain to what extent it could rely on the Macedonian nationalism it was encouraging. Macedonians had been poorly represented in the central organs of Tito's movement during the war, because Macedonian Communists had joined the struggle rather late in the war and had contributed relatively little. The man placed at the head of the Skopye government, Kolishevski, though born in Macedonia, was closely associated with the Serbian Communists. Around him, the new republic had attracted to its Communist Party a variety of figures who had played active parts in Macedonian politics of old, though not always as Yugoslav or as Communist as they were in 1946. For this reason among others, the Yugoslav leaders were chary of going ahead too fast alone, but this in turn was a potential source of discontent among the more nationalist-minded Macedonian Communists. One of the leading figures in the Skopye government, Antonov-Chento, was soon to resign, apparently disillusioned, and was quickly arrested, allegedly on his way to put before the Peace Conference a plea for an independent Macedonia. He was tried and sent to prison in November, and sufficient evidence is available to indicate that the Yugoslav Communist government came across serious difficulties in Macedonia in 1946 and 1947.[34]

In the summer of 1946, just after Antonov's resignation and in conjunction with that crisis, the Yugoslavs once again broached the subject of Macedonian unification. This time the initiative was made to come from Skopye. In a speech delivered there in August, Kolishevski said that to raise the question of uniting all Macedonians outside the framework of the Yugoslav federation was not in the interest of the Macedonian nation, and was meant as a provocation to both Yugoslavia and Bulgaria. He expressed the hope that the two states, now that they had similar political systems, could come to an agreement on the basis of allowing Macedonians on both sides of the border to develop as they wished. A simultaneous move was made on the Bulgarian side, when the Central Committee of the Bulgarian Communist Party adopted a resolution to the effect that

[34] There were more trials in 1947 and early 1948 of groups of Macedonians accused of conspiring to separate Macedonia from Yugoslavia. In 1949 the Macedonian Home Ministry revealed that, in the initial post-war period, the O.Z.N. had to combat members of armed bands and counter-revolutionary groups (*Nova Makedonija*, Skopye, 14 May 1949). All these opposition groups were alleged to have been linked to the West, and working for the creation of an independent Macedonia under Western protection. It is difficult to say whether this was really so, or whether they were made to appear as pro-Western anti-Communists rather than pro-Bulgarian Communists, in order not to spoil the chances of a friendly settlement with a Communist-led Bulgaria at a future date.

the question of unification of the Macedonians of Bulgaria and Yugoslavia was one to be achieved by the Macedonians themselves and the Communist Parties of the two countries, on the basis of a treaty of alliance and of a policy of cultural *rapprochement* between Macedonians on both sides of the frontier. Although this resolution, which was never published, was meant as little more than a friendly gesture towards the Yugoslavs, by the end of that year authoritative public statements had been made in Bulgaria about the possibility of an autonomous status for Bulgarian Macedonia. This was the time of the peace negotiations: the Bulgars needed to cultivate Yugoslavia generally, and more particularly in view of their interest in Greek Thrace. If the Yugoslavs could have helped them obtain western Thrace, they would probably have agreed to cede their portion of Macedonia to the Yugoslav republic of Macedonia.

By that time, however, the Macedonian question was further complicated by a new outbreak of the civil war in Greece. In the autumn of 1946, after the electoral victory of the anti-Communist parties and the plebiscite in favour of King George's return, the Greek Communists went into rebellion again, this time in the mountainous northern region of Greek Macedonia, where they could have the backing of Communist-ruled countries. Albania, Yugoslavia, and Bulgaria all helped the Communist-led Greek People's Liberation Front, because they wanted it to come to power, and also because they were all interested in Greek territory.

The question of Greek Macedonia was, from a strictly ethnic point of view, different from that of Bulgarian Macedonia. The linguistic difference between Greek and Slav dialects of Macedonia was complete, without the sort of transitional no man's land that had existed between Serbophones and Bulgarophones. Whereas it was easy for a Macedonian Slav to be turned into a Serb or a Bulgar, to change from the one to the other, and to switch from the one to the other language, in Greek Macedonia, in so far as a Slav became Hellenized, there was no easy slipping back. Between the wars, the Greek part of Macedonia had indeed been Hellenized to a great extent, as a result of the departure of most Slavs who thought of themselves as Bulgars, and of the resettlement there of the Greek refugees from Turkish Asia Minor.

Towards the end of the war, the Yugoslav Communists had established contacts with the Greek Communist partisans and encouraged, within their movement, the formation of Yugoslav-orientated Slav Macedonian units. At the end of the war, the new Yugoslav régime had seemed willing enough to suspend further activities in the direction of Greek Macedonia, but with the beginning of the new uprising, the Greek Communists needed not only the support of the now established Yugoslav Communists, but that of the local Slav minority as well. The Yugoslavs extended military assistance to the guerrillas. They also sent political and military advisers, and revived a Slav 'Macedonian' movement as a direct instrument of their policies. Although this organization asked for no more than equality of rights for the Slavs in Greek Macedonia, and the Greek People's Liberation Front had officially adopted such a policy, distrust prevailed between the rank-and-file of the Greek guerrillas and the adherents of the Yugoslav-sponsored Macedonian Front, between the Greek Communists and their Yugoslav or Bulgarian helpers, between Bulgarian and Yugoslav Communists.

By the time that the peace treaties were signed in February 1947, the Bulgarian authorities were already allowing Macedonianism to be freely propagated, and the Yugoslav government had decided to renounce its share of war reparations from Bulgaria. In August, the Bulgarian Communist leader and Comintern veteran Gheorghi Dimitrov went on a visit to Tito at Bled in Slovenia. The full story of what was said and decided at that meeting is not yet known. The published announcements made no mention of either federation or the unification of Macedonia, but merely of a pact of alliance that was in the making. In the meantime, a series of protocols were concluded, on economic co-operation, common policy towards Greece, and cultural autonomy for Bulgarian Macedonia. By collating what both sides revealed after 1948, it seems that agreement was reached on the principle of federation, to be achieved gradually, while the groundwork was being laid; that the Bulgars agreed to Macedonians from Yugoslavia conducting a cultural and educational programme in Bulgarian Macedonia; but that they refused to consider any more concrete steps towards the unification of their portion of Macedonia with Yugoslav Macedonia prior to the formation of a federation.

At any rate, Yugoslav propaganda poured over the now open border, agitation for unification of the two sides within the Yugoslav republic of Macedonia gained momentum, and Yugoslav 'cultural workers' took to quarrelling with local Bulgarian officials. It all looked very much like the old struggle between Serbs and Bulgars, through priests and schoolteachers, for the loyalty of the Macedonian Slavs in Ottoman times, except that the Yugoslav propaganda had become more subtle than the Bulgarian in so far as it advocated Macedonianism within Yugoslavia.

In November, Tito paid a return visit to Dimitrov in Sofia, and the long-talked-of Yugoslav-Bulgarian treaty of alliance was signed. Tito announced, 'We shall establish co-operation so general and so close that federation will be a mere formality', and Dimitrov proceeded to develop the theme in a series of articles. The Bulgarian Communist leader was certainly keen on closer ties with Yugoslavia, as so many Bulgarian leaders of the Left had been in the past, and he was even attracted by the vision of a powerful South Slav federation in which Communist internationalism would triumph over petty nationalist rivalries, but the Bulgarian Communists had not suddenly become converts to the idea of a federation in which the Yugoslavs would have the upper hand. It was rather that Tito was at the height of his triumph, as the strongest, the most solidly established, and the most reliable of the East European Communist leaders. Following his visit to Moscow in May–June 1946, he had built a network of alliances with the Communist-dominated régimes of eastern Europe and, in 1947, been on a tour of their capitals. The treaties concluded at the end of that year with his Bulgarian, Hungarian, and Romanian neighbours guaranteed his rear, and gave him the necessary backing for the next great step in his Balkan policy. It was from Radio Belgrade that the formation of a 'Provisional Democratic Government of Greece' was announced in December 1947. By the end of that year the dream of a Yugoslav-centred Balkan federation seemed to be moving towards reality. Not only was the incorporation of Bulgarian Macedonia closer than ever, and Bulgaria getting used to the idea of federation, but the prospect of being patron to a successful Communist revolution in Greece was also being opened to Marshal Tito's mind.

Excommunication

The Yugoslav Communists had emerged from the war fanatically devoted to the Soviet Union and to Stalin personally,[35] and they were dynamic in promoting the aims of communism in their own country, in the Balkans, and even further afield. They had successfully turned a foreign war into a revolutionary one, and brought their country solidly into the Soviet camp, thus reducing to scraps of paper (as far as Yugoslavia was concerned and with only little, though decisive, Soviet help) both the British 'fifty-fifty' formula and the American-inspired Declaration on Liberated Europe. They were full of self-confidence, proud of their wartime hardships and successes, and tended to be forgetful of the help they had received.

[35] 'In no country in the world, in no Communist party outside the Soviet Union was that devotion (to the Soviet Union and to Stalin personally) so powerful as in Yugoslavia during the war' (Dedijer, in preface to *With Tito through the War*).

They had been the first Communist Party in eastern Europe to eliminate all competitors, to take over the state, to organize a political machine and an economy on the Soviet model, to start the process of collectivization of the land. Nowhere else outside the Soviet Union was there as yet such a solidly united native Communist leadership in command of the Party apparatus, of the security apparatus, and of the military apparatus. At its head, Tito was the first Communist dictator in eastern Europe, the first to have followed Stalin's example in being at once head of the Party, of the government, and of the armed forces, with a specially created unique rank above that of all the other military chiefs, in being considered as an ideological and cultural inspirer, elected to scholarly academies, and the object of a personality cult. He commanded the emotional loyalty of the Communist hierarchy and held undisputed sway over its organs of power.

Indeed, in the early post-war years, Yugoslavia was the first and only Communist-ruled country which approximated to the Stalinist pattern. This explains why its leaders were proud of their achievements since the war, no less than of their achievements during it. They felt themselves to be the strongest Communist Party outside the U.S.S.R., hence its best ally. Tito himself viewed his position as that of the foremost exponent of Communist policy outside the Soviet Union. As such, ever since 1945, he had been calling for the re-establishment of the old Communist International. Stalin, however, was looking for a more subtle approach, and when Tito visited him in Moscow in June 1946, he put to him instead the idea of an agency to facilitate the co-ordination of views among Communist parties. The idea duly ripened, and in September 1947, ostensibly at the invitation of the Polish Party, representatives of the Communist Parties of Bulgaria, Hungary, Romania, Czechoslovakia, and Yugoslavia met in Poland with representatives of the Soviet and Polish Parties, as well as those of France and Italy, and founded the Information Bureau of Communist Parties, or Cominform.

The aim of the Soviet leadership was to establish both a unification of purpose, and a veiled control over the main Communist Parties among those ruling in eastern Europe and those that were playing an important political role in the West. After the parenthesis of the war and of the liberation, it was necessary for the Communists to emerge again as a separate force, united and disciplined in a co-ordinated front. It was important, too, that the co-ordinating, disciplining, and initiating of policy should appear to come, not from the Soviet leadership alone, but from all the major Communist Parties. The need to close ranks at home and against the West was the result of Communist Parties having come to power in several East European countries with various degrees of help from the Soviet armed forces. It was also the answer to such American initiatives in 1947 as the Marshall Plan and the Truman Doctrine – the former meant to put Europe generally on its economic feet again, so as to make it less vulnerable to communism, the second granting direct aid to Greece and Turkey in particular, to prevent them from being taken over by communism.

Only the Yugoslavs were decidedly enthusiastic about the new organization, in which they were given an important role along with much attention. It was their delegates who were asked to criticize the Communists of western Europe who had played at being governmental parties instead of resisting American imperialism, and it was in their capital that the seat of the Cominform was established. Yugoslavia was indeed a model to follow, and the Soviet leaders could count on the Yugoslavs to be their seconds, hence the role assigned to them. At the same time, this was good camouflage for Soviet control, and it helped to harness the Yugoslavs' self-satisfied dynamism to the collective aims of the Soviet camp. Both to the Yugoslavs and to the world at large, it seemed that Yugoslavia's position as the leading ally of the Soviet Union was more firmly established than ever.

Yugoslavia was certainly the most important of the new countries that had come within the Soviet pale in Europe. It was also the geopolitical advance guard of Soviet power. It bordered on, and had territorial interests in, three countries not as yet dominated by the Communists, but which could become so: Austria, with its undecided status and Soviet occupation troops; Italy with its large Communist Party; Greece, in the throes of civil war. With its sub-satellite Albania, it controlled the whole of the eastern Adriatic littoral. Its geographical position, looking out to Central and western Europe, to the Mediterranean, and to Africa, was as important as ever. It also had the military potential of a strong and loyal Communist-dominated army, natural riches, and almost 16 million inhabitants.

Yet the very combination of this unique position with the success of the régime contained potential complications. The superiority complex of the Yugoslav Communists did not make Tito and his lieutenants so very popular with the leading groups of the other Communist Parties, especially those of their immediate Balkan neighbours. Part of the Albanian leadership was not reconciled to Yugoslav domination, chafed under it, and looked to the Soviet Union. Some of the Greek Communists felt much the same about Yugoslav advice and patronage; as for the Bulgars, they were far from satisfied at having had to accept Yugoslav infiltration into their part of Macedonia, and it is doubtful whether the majority were eager at the prospect of a federation in which the Yugoslavs would have had the upper hand. Even Dimitrov made clear their reluctance to enter into simple union with Yugoslavia by indicating the need for a wider union, which would embrace other Balkan countries under Communist rule, and then by proposing publicly, in January 1948 in Bucharest, a broad Danubian customs union in place of the Balkan federation which he thought as yet premature.

It is easy to look for the origins of the quarrel between Stalin and Tito in the light of what was said and done after all hope of a settlement had vanished, when both sides began to recall as undoubted indications of coming treachery those moments of strain which, at the time, were but dissonances no greater than those experienced in relations with other leaders of eastern Europe. The Russians did to Yugoslavia very much what they did to the other satellites. The difference was that, with the others, they did it to a larger extent, that it did not lead to a break, and that it was not made public. Soviet troops behaved in Yugoslavia as in conquered territory from the autumn of 1944 to the spring of 1945, but they did so as well in other countries, where they stayed far longer. The Yugoslavs had expected, and failed to obtain, Soviet support over Trieste and Carinthia, but they failed to understand the reasons that made the Soviets want at that time to avoid a major conflict with the West, and other East European countries had actually lost territory to the Soviet Union. In international conferences, Soviet delegates behaved haughtily towards the Yugoslavs, but they did so with Czechoslovaks and Poles as well, not to mention the representatives of former enemy states such as Romania, Hungary, and Bulgaria. Soviet military advisers and civilian experts behaved no more contemptuously in Yugoslavia than in other countries. As for the Soviet attempt to control and exploit the economy, Yugoslavia got away very lightly compared with some of its neighbours.

The real differences between the Yugoslav régime and that of the other Communist-led countries of eastern Europe had been created by geography, and by the war. They lay in Yugoslavia's geopolitical position, bordering on the Mediterranean and on non-Communist Europe. They lay, too, in the extent of Tito's hold over his Party and his state. In other countries, either because of the more massive military and political backing given to weaker Communist Parties, or because of tension between different personalities and groups within the several Parties, the Soviets were able to follow and control developments closely without giving cause for obvious grievance and real disappointment among local leaders. In Yugoslavia, they had to resort to petty espionage and intrigue, which, more often than not, scandalized and disappointed pro-Soviet feelings.

The crisis eventually arose from Tito's extra-Yugoslav ambitions. It was difficult enough to keep any control over his domestic set-up, but this was nothing compared to the difficulty – and the liability – which the Kremlin would have to face if this set-up, however loyal, succeeded in creating a vast Balkan power complex and expected to share in the formulation of the overall Soviet-bloc policy, and that with a naïveté which disregarded the power-structure at world level, over-estimating both its own strength and that of the Soviet Union. If Yugoslavia's foreign policy caused too much opposition from other Communists, if it divided more than it unified, and if it became a generally uncontrollable force, then it had to be cut down to size, and its dynamism made to serve Soviet and Communist aims as planned in the Kremlin, not as interpreted independently by Tito and his lieutenants.

By the beginning of 1948, tension between East and West was rising, and both the U.S.S.R. and the U.S.A. were becoming convinced of each other's essentially aggressive designs. The failure of the last Four-Power conference, in December 1947, to find a settlement for the German question, forewarned of an approaching showdown over Berlin. At the same time, the backing given by the Communist-led states to one side in the Greek civil war, countered by the backing given by the U.S.A. to the other side, threatened to turn the Cold War into hot confrontation in that country, while in Italy too, the approaching elections threatened other forms of confrontation. Yugoslavia was placed between Greece and Italy, and involved in both directions, especially in the former.

Did Stalin feel that Tito was dragging the Soviet Union into greater risks than he was willing to assume? Or was it Tito who felt that Stalin was pushing Yugoslavia into a dangerously exposed situation without sufficient backing? Not enough has been revealed for an answer to be given.[36] Whatever the view adopted, it seems

[36] Most authors assume, on the strength of the Yugoslav version of the events leading to the break with Moscow, that it was Stalin who wanted to prevent any more adventurous moves by Tito in Greece and Italy. Both Dedijer (*Tito Speaks*, p. 331) and Djilas (op. cit., p. 164) have recorded Stalin as saying, in February 1948, that the Greek revolt would have to be folded up as it appeared to have no chance of success. Ilija Jukić, however (*Tito between East and West*, London, 1961, pp. 8–13, *passim*), in spite of this piece of concordant evidence on at least one point, thinks that it was Tito, not Stalin, who wanted to stop the fighting. Tito's complete estrangement from the West after the end of the war does add plausibility to the view that the Soviet Union might have thought it easy to manipulate him against the West, and Hamilton Fish Armstrong (*Tito and Goliath*, New York, 1951, p. 68) believed that one of the Soviet objectives early in 1948

certain that the Soviets, because of the increasing tension in Europe, wanted to prevent the development of a situation likely to cause trouble in the Communist camp itself, and be able to control Yugoslavia more directly in view of its important strategic position. The inception of a Balkan power structure under Tito had to be stopped, and it was necessary to exercise more leverage within the Yugoslav power structure itself so as to make it more immediately responsive and disciplined.

Tito's foreign policy was getting into deep waters: he was trying to obtain Bulgaria as well as Albania, at a time when Greece was becoming explosive, and the Bulgars, in order to wriggle out, were proposing an even broader, looser form of association. Stalin called a halt to all these schemes, and Yugoslavs and Bulgars were once again summoned to a meeting in Moscow in February 1948. If there was an element of pique in Stalin's action, there was some as well in Tito's reaction, for he did not himself go to Moscow, thus refusing to be treated as a subordinate in constant need of instructions.

In Moscow, the Soviet leaders expressed dissatisfaction with Dimitrov's publicly aired scheme, because it involved Romania and its economy (a Soviet *chasse gardée*), and they pressed for implementation of the Yugoslav-Bulgarian federation plan. At the same time, the Yugoslavs were rebuked for taking important foreign policy moves without always closely consulting Moscow, and they were made to sign an agreement about mutual consultation on questions of foreign policy.

Although Stalin's blessing had been given to union with Bulgaria, and Albania as well, it was obvious that he was determined to have a deciding say in the timing and the manner of the plan. The Yugoslavs feared that this sudden pressing for implementation meant that Stalin hoped thereby to stir up even more trouble between them and the Bulgars, or even control them through the Bulgars. They decided not to be pushed and, in March, informed the Bulgars that they would not pursue the federation plan any longer. At the same time, however, they pursued with greater insistence the more immediate plan of incorporating the Bulgarian portion of Macedonia into their own republic of Macedonia. The Bulgars resisted, and their reaction was to try and halt the spread of Yugoslav influence over the border altogether.

At home, too, Tito responded by removing Andriya Hebrang, the

was to make sure that the road to the West would be open through Yugoslavia. Another certain fact is that Yugoslavia did not rush to recognize Markos Vafiades's counter-government, although its formation had been broadcast from Belgrade.

man known to have been the direct agent of Soviet plans to undermine his position in the Party. Hebrang was first demoted from his position as chairman of the Planning Commission to a minor economic ministry, although he kept his place on the Party's Central Committee, as did his associate Sreten Zhuyovich – an altogether lesser figure.[37] Later, when it became clear that the discussions held by the Yugoslav leaders after the Moscow meeting had been leaked to the Soviet government, Hebrang was expelled from the Central Committee, and both ministers failed to appear at the March session of parliament.

In order to press their point home, the Soviets also delayed concluding new trade agreements to replace the existing ones with Yugoslavia due to expire in April 1948, and on 18 March, they stepped up the pressure by ordering their military advisers and civilian experts to withdraw. When Tito complained, Stalin wrote on 27 March, laying charges of Trotskyism, Menshevism, revisionism, and imperialism, accusing the Yugoslav Communists of covertly criticizing the Soviet Communist Party, and singling out for personal attack four of Tito's trusted lieutenants – Djilas, Vukmanovich-Tempo, Kidrich, and Rankovich. The Yugoslav Central Committee was summoned to examine this document. On 12 April, it decided to write back, to deny the charges which it blamed on inaccurate information, and to invite the Soviet Central Committee to send a delegation to come and examine the situation on the spot. Zhuyovich, who alone opposed this answer, was in turn expelled. It would seem that both Stalin and Tito entertained illusions. The Soviet dictator probably thought that he had built up a sufficiently strong agency within the Yugoslav power-structure for the leader-

[37] Differences between the two, on the one hand, and the rest of the leadership, went back to 1946, when Hebrang had given way to Kidrich as chief economic planner on the eve of the five-year plan. Several authors, taking the cause of the differences at their face value, see them as purely economic. Doreen Warriner (*Revolution in Eastern Europe*, London, 1950, p. 53) has put forward the theory that Hebrang and Zhuyovich were rationalist economists who opposed Tito's 'romantic' and 'heroic' economic policies. François Fejtö repeats this, translated into more masculine and French intellectual terms ('le parti de la prudence' and 'le parti de l'optimisme': *Histoire des démocraties populaires – L'Ere de Staline, 1945–1952*, Paris, 1952, p. 165). Maclean (*Disputed Barricade*, pp. 343–4) writes that Hebrang had wanted to steam-roll the peasants into submission. There is clearly a contradiction between Professor Warriner's interpretation of the two characters who appear as anti-romantic 'realists' in matters of economic planning, and Sir Fitzroy Maclean's where they appear as even more 'heroic' than Tito in matters of agricultural policy. Not enough is known of these differences of 1946, but it seems more probable that the economic issues were subordinate to political ones, and that Hebrang and Zhuyovich's criticisms of Yugoslav economic policies were simply an element of direct Soviet leverage.

ship as a whole to accept being disciplined and reduced to size, or failing this, that his letter of accusation would cause a palace revolution. The Yugoslav dictator, on the other hand, probably believed that there was a certain amount of misunderstanding, due to petty intriguers, which could be put right by a frank explanation with Stalin.

The Yugoslav leadership had the situation in its Central Committee well in hand and, to be on the safe side, even carried out a minor purge. Not only was it announced that Hebrang and Zhuyovich had been expelled from the Party, and then arrested, but in April, members of the Communist Party were put on trial for the first time.[38] The situation was deteriorating. On 4 May, Stalin wrote again: the Soviet Central Committee reminded the Yugoslavs that their services were not, after all, so much greater than those of the other Communist Parties; it would not send a delegation to Belgrade; instead, it announced its intention of putting the case to the Cominform at its forthcoming session. The Yugoslavs decided not to attend, for the Soviet Union had already prejudiced their case by feeding the other politburos with its own version of the dispute.

The Cominform thus met in Bucharest, without the Yugoslavs. They, who only nine months earlier, at the Information Bureau's founding session, had attacked the 'moderation' of Communists in the West, were now not only accused of ideological deviation, but actually expelled from the community, and the Cominform's seat was transferred to Bucharest. The resolution, published on 28 June 1948, brought the conflict into the open and startled the outside world. It personally castigated Tito, Kardelj, Djilas, and Rankovich for the un-Marxist line taken by the Yugoslav Party on major questions of domestic and foreign policy, for its undemocratic organization, and for its unfriendly attitude to the U.S.S.R., as well as for their personal ambition, arrogance, conceit, and nationalism. At the same time it called on the 'healthy elements' within the C.P.Y. to overthrow their leadership.

Stalinism without Stalin

The idea that Tito's régime broke with the Soviet-led Cominform is a latter-day one developed by Yugoslav propagandists and wishful-thinking Western journalists. It was, perhaps, subconsciously helped

[38] Fifteen Communists were tried in Ljubljana as traitors who had been Gestapo agents during the war and British Intelligence agents since. Eleven of them were sentenced to death, and the rest to long terms of imprisonment with hard labour.

into being by the dates of Stalin's original letter of accusation and of the Cominform resolution. Both spelt defiance in Yugoslav folklore, the first – 27 March – against the Axis only seven years earlier, the other – 28 June – against the Turks some five and a half centuries earlier, and against the Habsburgs in 1914. This imaginative interpretation, developed after the events, should not be read back into the time preceding the events.

The men who ruled Yugoslavia had not seen the break coming; they had not contemplated such a possibility, let alone wanted it. They had only three years' experience in statecraft. Their training had been one of guerrilla and revolutionary warfare and, for the older generation, one of clandestine activity, illegal agitation, and prison. Their policy reflected their ideals, their faith, their ambitions, and their pride. Tito, however, had been hand-picked by the Comintern to purge the C.P.Y. in 1937. He and the group that had been brought to the fore in those years knew what had happened to their predecessors who had given in to Moscow's demands after they had been charged with various deviations. They realized that, if they acknowledged the mistakes which they were alleged to have made, they would lose their grip on the Party, perhaps have to step down, at worst be physically liquidated.

The nucleus of political power was essentially in the hands of the men singled out by the Cominform resolution: Tito; with Rankovich in charge of the security apparatus; Djilas in charge of propaganda; and Kardelj in charge of foreign policy; with, around them, the veteran Piyade, their *doyen d'âge*; Kidrich, in charge of the plan; Leskoshek in charge of heavy industry; General Goshnjak, the Party chief of the armed forces; some of the regional heads of Party and government organizations – Neshkovich of Serbia, Bakarich of Croatia, Kolishevski of Macedonia. All were long-time friends and collaborators of Marshal Tito's. The younger ones among them had literally been brought up by him as political figures. All were linked to him by personal affection and self-interest. Under them, the Party numbered slightly less than half a million members, the core of whom had spent their formative years as partisans under Tito's command, and the People's Front, through collective membership, claimed 7 million by 1948.

Tito and his friends at the top of the Yugoslav Communist hierarchy instinctively clung to power. This reflex, rather than revolt, ideological disagreement, or nationalist resentment, is the clue to the stand that they took. They stuck to their positions with a mixture of naïveté and shrewdness. They knew that the slightest sign of weakness would have a negative psychological effect on their own followers, but they did not realize that their defiance would lead to a rupture with the Soviet Union.³⁹ Rejected by the Communist countries, they felt betrayed and isolated,⁴⁰ and not even altogether sure of their hold over their own followers. In order to carry their own Party and show their innocence, they publicized the correspondence with the Soviet Central Committee, and proceeded to hold a congress of the C.P.Y.

Held in Belgrade at the end of July, the fifth congress of the Communist Party of Yugoslavia was the first to meet since the Party had come to power.⁴¹ It was meant as a demonstration – to the Soviet and other Communist Parties, but also to the Yugoslav Party itself – that the C.P.Y. and the Yugoslavs generally were united behind their leaders. It was devised so as to avoid anything which might lend substance to the Soviet charges or shock Party opinion, and to show that the Yugoslav revolution had been the result not only of Communist internationalism and Soviet help, but of popular backing as well. This was indeed the gist of Tito's nine-hour report on the history of the C.P.Y., which, by linking the resistance with the revolutionary struggle, Soviet help with the achievements of the partisans, orthodoxy with the magnitude of post-war achievements, answered and partly met Soviet criticism, appealed to the Yugoslav Communists' wartime solidarity, and, indirectly, to the country at large. The crisis was treated as if it did not involve the Soviet Union, but only the Cominform organization and Yugoslav traitors. Tito, Djilas, Kardelj, and Rankovich were confirmed in office as members of the Party Secretariat, and joined in the renewed Political Bureau by Goshnjak, Kidrich, Leskoshek, Neshkovich, and Piyade.

No chances were taken in consolidating the position of the régime. Some of the more irresponsible, and of the more extremist, elements among the *émigrés*, had thought of taking advantage of the crisis by trying to establish contact with the armed bands still at large in parts of Yugoslavia. Strengthened and reorganized, the security police increased its efforts to eradicate these remains of the civil war. Throughout 1948 and 1949, the number of political trials increased, involving all sorts of charges of illegal and subversive activity. Most of the non-Communist fellow-travellers still left in positions of relative importance were eliminated. The number of refugees making their way to non-Communist neighbouring countries rose.⁴²

³⁹ Cf. A. Ulam, *Titoism and the Cominform*, Cambridge, Mass., 1952, pp. 105–6.
⁴⁰ 'Yugoslavia was alone in the world.... Never in history had a small country been in a more desperate position' (Dedijer, *Tito Speaks*, p. 375).
⁴¹ Indeed, it was the first to meet for twenty years. The previous congress had been held at Dresden in 1928.
⁴² By May 1946, the number of registered Yugoslav refugees, as estimated by the Intergovernmental Committee on Refugees, had been reduced to

The security services now turned their attention to the 'counter-revolutionary' activities of Communists, as well as to those of anti-Communists, and to Eastern- as well as to Western-inspired subversion. A Party purge to eliminate potential anti-Titoists had preceded the congress, and fear of the police was one of the factors which kept the C.P.Y. united – along with partisan solidarity, loyalty to Tito, indignation at the treatment inflicted by the Soviet Union, and atavistic patriotism. The unanimity displayed at the congress was not, however, quite as genuine as made out, for a handful of higher officers attended and took part in the work of various commissions, who, it soon turned out, were involved in a military conspiracy.

Khrushchev in 1956 told the twentieth Soviet Party congress that Stalin had believed he would overthrow Tito by lifting his little finger. The words sound more Khrushchevian than Stalinist, but even if they were not historically pronounced by Stalin, they no doubt corresponded to his frame of mind. Not enough has been revealed of how much subversion was inspired by the Soviet Union, and how much of it was weeded out by Yugoslav security forces, but the Soviets certainly tried to penetrate the two main instruments of power – the Party and the army. Having failed to provoke a palace revolution through the Central Committee, Stalin seems to have tried a military conspiracy. One of the highest-ranking officers of the Yugoslav army, General Arso Yovanovich, a pre-war officer who had gone over to Tito, who had been the partisans' chief of staff during the war, and who had only just returned from specialized training in the U.S.S.R., was shot dead trying to cross the Romanian border one night in August with two other higher officers. One other general succeeded in fleeing the country. The fact that they decided to leave Yugoslavia soon after the Party congress can only indicate that they did not think a military coup possible. Not a few senior officers were subsequently arrested and tried.

The army and the administration appear to have been well purged,[43] and, according to the figures revealed by Rankovich himself at the sixth Party congress in 1952, over 11,000 pro-Cominform sympathizers were expelled from the Party, arrested, and punished by the police, over and above the 2,500 sentenced by regular courts. For them the desolate Adriatic island of Goli Otok, south of Riyeka,

135,000 (Vernant, op. cit., p. 31), due to the repatriation of many of the displaced persons. By the end of that year, however, this return movement had been almost exhausted (R. Knežević, art. cit., part i, in *Poruka*, 52, p. 17), and in 1948 there was once again a sudden upsurge in the number of refugees from Yugoslavia.

[43] Numbers, ranks, positions, and the most important names are listed in the Cominform-inspired *La Jugoslavia sotto il terrore di Tito*, Rome, 1949.

was turned into a 'perfect miniature reproduction of a Stalinist Siberia'.[44] Although there were no doubt many Cominformist sympathizers in the ranks of the C.P.Y., they remained leaderless and disorganized, and so easily exposed to the Stalinist methods of the Yugoslav police. On the whole, the instruments of power remained firmly in the hands of Tito and his group. Vigilant and on the defensive, for more than a year after the exchange of letters the Yugoslav régime did not counter-attack, however, partly because of the leaders' genuine inability to face the strange new facts, partly not to shock their followers. Perhaps it would be more correct to say that they waited for the rank-and-file to be gradually and spontaneously shocked into placing the full responsibility squarely on Stalin's shoulders. The anti-Titoist propaganda coming from the Cominform was so far-fetched that it became the best propaganda weapon of the Titoist régime.

If the direct impact of the Cominform's attitude was relatively modest, the indirect impact was so great as to be immeasurable. The defects of the five-year plan were already appearing when the Soviet Union and other East European countries began to apply economic pressure. The Soviet Union delayed renewing its trade agreements with Yugoslavia until the last day of 1948, and then drastically reduced exchanges. The following month, the member states of the Cominform set up a Council for Mutual Economic Assistance – to be known as Comecon – to which Albania was admitted. The Yugoslav government, which had also applied, was told its application would be considered only if it abandoned its hostile attitude. Following that, all the members of Comecon gradually slowed down, reduced or stopped deliveries to Yugoslavia, and suspended, annulled, or did not renew their trade agreements, so that, by the summer of 1949, Yugoslavia's trade with its principal partners was seriously jeopardized. Contracts were cancelled; transport and postal services were reduced or even cut. By the end of the year, trade with the Soviet bloc had come virtually to a standstill. The realization of the five-year plan depended on the Soviet camp in so many ways that the blockade, together with the military pressure applied on the borders, forced the Yugoslav government to re-adapt its programme of economic development.

The plan, however, was not abandoned. The leadership itself did not believe that this situation would last; having intoxicated the Party on the plan's virtues, it could not now urge moderation and risk giving the impression that there was any truth in the Cominform's accusations. Industrialization was, after all, the basic aim of its whole economic policy. The only concessions made were in

[44] V. Dedijer, *Izgubljena bitka J.V. Staljina*, Sarayevo, 1969, pp. 420–21.

extending by a year the realization of the plan, and in gradually reducing it to 'essential projects'. The military threat from the Soviet bloc induced the government to shift important resources to defence industries. For the rest, industrial development was mainly restricted to heavy industrial projects already started. This meant that the pattern of investment became even more top-heavy, that agriculture was even more starved of capital, and that not much could be done by way of eliminating disparities between regions. Even before the crisis, priority had been given to expanding in the more developed areas, where existing structures made growth cheaper. This had been intended as a precondition of industrial expansion elsewhere. Now, however, since the crisis, expansion elsewhere could not be envisaged any more, except in so far as defence industries were to be located, for security reasons, in the less accessible central mountainous regions.

All the other economic processes which had been initiated for ideological reasons were, nevertheless, now accelerated for political reasons – to meet some of the Soviet criticism, and prevent sedition in the Party. In April 1948, Kardelj told parliament of the need to 'modify the socio-economic structure', and announced the forthcoming 'liquidation of the capitalist remnants in the village'. A second nationalization law was passed that session, affecting catering, lodging, and cultural and medical establishments. Private retail shops were henceforward allowed only if needed to supplement state shops. As for private craftsmen, a law of June 1949 submitted them to licensing at the discretion of local authorities. By that time, only 1·5 per cent of the total retail trade was still in private hands.[45]

It was in agriculture particularly that there remained much to be done, for almost 94 per cent of the arable land was still in private hands in 1948.[46] The income-tax law enacted that August, which explicitly stated that peasants' working co-operatives should be fostered by lower taxation, marked the beginning of the drive for land collectivization.[47] All the methods used hitherto were stepped up, and by the summer of 1951 almost 430,000 peasant households, with 2·6 million hectares of land, had been coerced into working co-operatives.[48] The situation in the collective sector was chaotic. Collectivized peasants sabotaged production by all imaginable means. In order to obtain anything at all from them, and maintain

[45] Spulber, op. cit., p. 157.
[46] Hoffman and Neal, op. cit., p. 271.
[47] According to Dedijer, there was a veritable rush to collectivize, out of straightforward dogmatism, 'which was still then very strong among us, in order to show the Informbureau how unfounded their accusations were' (Dedijer, *Izgubljena bitka*, p. 409).
[48] Wolff, op. cit., p. 431.

some discipline, an extensive administrative apparatus was attached to the collectives – an additional item, onerous and unproductive, to be covered by the meagre sums invested in the land. Agricultural production which, in 1948, had just about returned to pre-war level, slipped well below it again by 1950. The disasters of Yugoslav agriculture in these years were attributed to climatic conditions, but rainless summers were not a new post-war occurrence. It was rather that all the other non-climatic factors gave climatic factors a fatal importance which they would not have had otherwise. By sustaining a Stalinist system, the Titoist régime was unable to halt the exorbitant increase in food shortages, prices, and foreign debts, and the country soon found itself on the verge of economic collapse.

In foreign affairs, the Yugoslav government also tried at first to continue outwardly as if nothing had happened. The peace settlements had confirmed the freedom of navigation on the Danube, and a conference was due to be held to revise the treaties governing the international waterway. Representatives of the great powers and of the riparian states met in Belgrade in 1948. The Soviets, who controlled the majority, pushed through their draft which nullified all previous treaties and established a new international commission of riparians only. The Yugoslavs voted with the Soviet bloc, and thus maintained the common front in international affairs. The Soviet Union, however, was quick to break it. While still insisting that an Austrian treaty must await the solution of the German problem, it now accepted the Western argument that Austria should lose no territory, and, in August, told the Yugoslavs that it would no longer support their claims, for it regarded their government as inimical.

No sooner was the Danubian conference over than the full blast of Soviet propaganda was turned on Tito. The Russians now encouraged neighbouring Communist countries to revive and press their claims against Yugoslavia. It had become almost historical practice – for it had seventy years' standing – to revive in periods of crisis inter-Balkan territorial aspirations kept dormant in more serene periods. The Soviet Union and the Axis powers had in turn, before the war, used revisionism and separatism to harm the Yugoslav state whenever a strong unified Yugoslavia was not to their liking. The Soviet Union did so again after 1948. As a matter of fact, neither Bulgars nor Albanians needed encouragement. Permission was enough. Their leaders and those of the other Communist countries were not at all sorry that Tito had at last been taught a lesson by Moscow. Though not a member of the Cominform, Albania saw in the Cominform's denunciation the chance to throw off Tito's tutelage, and was the first to respond. It denounced its economic agreements with Yugoslavia barely three days after the publication of the Cominform resolution. It was easy for the Albanian government to stir up trouble in the Kosovo region of Yugoslavia, where the Albanian population remained alienated from the Yugoslav Communist régime.

The Bulgars could now say out loud how unhappy they had been at all they had had to accept. Not only was all Yugoslav propaganda in Bulgarian Macedonia brought to an end, but the initiative on Macedonia also changed hands. Bulgarian propaganda did not go so far as to deny the existence of Macedonians, but it stressed their close connexions with the Bulgars, and passed to the offensive by advocating the establishment of a united, Bulgarian-sponsored Macedonian unit within a democratic Balkan confederation. Now that the Bulgars were associating themselves with the idea of Macedonian unification, the Yugoslavs soft-pedalled it and, the roles being reversed, became defenders of the *status quo*. Both sides denounced each other's sincerity in supporting the Macedonian national movement, and new pressures were generated on the loyalties of Macedonians on both sides. With Bulgarian propaganda accusing the Yugoslavs of maltreating unredeemed Macedonian brothers, and Bulgarian agents fomenting subversion in Yugoslav Macedonia, a serious situation developed there, and was checked only after numerous arrests.[49] It induced also a further 'Macedonianization' of Yugoslav Macedonia, by a massive drive to educate the population in the newly codified Macedonian language (purified of Bulgarian elements), and in the newly written Macedonian history. The overall result was to encourage many Macedonians to take a more favourable view of the Yugoslav federation than earlier, and Bulgaria was not without problems in its part of Macedonia, presumably from pro-Yugoslav elements.

Hungarians too, and even Romanians, set about inciting their minorities in Yugoslavia, and persecuting the Yugoslavs within their own borders. To all this the Yugoslav authorities responded by organizing anti-Cominformist bodies among the nationals of neighbouring countries in Yugoslavia. There were signs again of highhanded treatment of the Albanian minority by the Yugoslav authorities, and of Soviet attempts to use existing latent strains among the Yugoslavs themselves.[50]

The dispute between its backers was, of course, fatal to the Greek

[49] Cf. E. Kofos, *Nationalism and Communism in Macedonia*, Salonika, 1964, p. 193.

[50] In 1950, a group of highly placed Serbs in the Communist Party of Croatia declared for the Cominform and attempted to rally support among the Serbs of Croatia. Maclean writes (*Disputed Barricade*, p. 396) that there were Soviet attempts to encourage separatist tendencies in Croatia and Montenegro as well as in Macedonia.

Communist uprising. By the end of the year, its leader, Markos Vafiades ('General Markos'), who had been closely connected with Yugoslav support, was replaced. As a large proportion of its fighting force was made up of local Macedonian Slavs, and the new Greek Communist leadership could not afford to antagonize both them and the Yugoslavs, in January 1949 it declared itself in favour of the Bulgarian-sponsored project of a unified Macedonia within a Balkan confederation. This potential cession, albeit tactical, of Greek Macedonia played into the hands of the Athens government.[51] In July 1949, alleging that the Greek Communist Party was conspiring with the Cominform to break up Yugoslavia, the Belgrade government announced that it was closing the border and withdrawing all support – thus publicly acknowledging what was already accomplished fact. With the well-equipped Greek government forces closing in for a decisive summer offensive, the uprising in Greek Macedonia ended in confusion. The Slav minority in Greece had, on the whole, collaborated with Bulgarian and German occupation authorities during the war, then looked, through the Greek Communist movement, to Yugoslavia and Bulgaria. Friction between their militants and the Greek Communists had been intense in the closing days of the rebellion. The mass exodus to Yugoslavia and other Communist countries of all those Slavs who felt anti-Greek (estimated by the Greek government authorities at 35,000), not only contributed to ending the civil war: it also solved the Macedonian problem as far as Greece was concerned.

In 1949, the Cominform's propaganda warfare against Yugoslavia was intensified. In all the other Communist countries also, the crisis precipitated the process of communization and of the tightening-up of discipline, domestic and bloc-wide, which had been started at the end of 1947 – a process in which Yugoslavia was well advanced, domestically at least. All the tendencies and tensions which, in the case of Yugoslavia, had led to the crisis, existed potentially in the other Communist-ruled states as well, though conditions for their coming to a head were less favourable. These were rooted out in all the countries of the Soviet bloc, by purges, trials, and executions which surpassed similar proceedings in Yugoslavia, in both extent and intensity.

The trial of the veteran Hungarian Communist leader Laszlo Rajk,

[51] According to Kofos (op. cit., pp. 178–9), 'General Markos' was replaced not simply because of his pro-Yugoslav attitude. He seems to have come to the conclusion that, without Yugoslavia, the Greek Communists stood no chance of winning unless the Soviet Union intervened, whereas the Soviets apparently wanted a pro-Cominform force on the Greek-Yugoslav border as well. Markos also objected to raising the Macedonian issue precisely for fear of playing into the hands of the Athens government.

in September 1949, served to provide allegations of Yugoslavia's hostility to the U.S.S.R. and a pretext for the Cominform states to denounce their political treaties with Yugoslavia. Already in August, protesting against the treatment of Soviet citizens in Yugoslavia, the Soviet government had threatened to resort to 'other more effective measures'. No sooner was the Rajk trial ended, than it abrogated the Soviet-Yugoslav treaty of friendship, mutual assistance, and co-operation which had been signed as early as April 1945. Its satellites followed suit, and the Cominform met in Budapest for a third session, when the leaders of the C.P.Y. were described as 'fascist beasts' and 'assassins and spies'. There were troop movements along Yugoslavia's borders, and frontier incidents.

All methods – save military intervention – had been tried by Stalin, first to discipline, then to overthrow, the Yugoslav leadership. If he did contemplate armed aggression as a final weapon, it was essential to disgrace Tito beforehand as an enemy of communism, and not to turn him into a national hero. Yet the more the Soviets waited, the greater were the risks, for, in spite of the ideological and economic shocks received, Tito had been consolidating his position. The Soviet threat, following on their denunciation of the Yugoslav leaders as (among other deviations) nationalists, enabled the Yugoslav government to capitalize, in the country at large, on a patriotism derived from fear of the Russians. By the end of 1949, Soviet action had strengthened Tito's position among non-Communists in Yugoslavia more than it had weakened it among Communists. Also by that time, the U.S.A. was certain to intervene in favour of Yugoslavia if the Soviet bloc attacked.

The break had come to the world at large as a surprise, and generated in the West initial reactions of distrust, soon to be followed by exaggerated hopes. The attitude of the Yugoslav government was, at first, far from encouraging. Many influential people in Belgrade were, at the time, really more afraid of a Western than of a Soviet intervention. The West was, for the Yugoslav leaders, synonymous with reaction and imperialism. Even if there had been no other danger from the West, turning to the enemy for help would have alienated many of their own supporters at a time when no one foresaw how deep the cleavage would become. At the same time, there are indications that Tito felt, when Soviet threats had become more pressing, that the division of Europe was already so advanced that the Americans would not allow the Soviets actually to intervene by force of arms.[52] Certainly as early as

[52] Maclean (*Disputed Barricade*, pp. 397–8) is of the opinion that, from the first, Tito was encouraged in his resistance to Soviet pressure by the feeling that there was an alternative. Djilas, when in America in 1968, re-

July 1948, two days before the opening of the Yugoslav Party Congress, the U.S.A. signed an agreement with Yugoslavia for the release of the latter's gold assets, blocked because of the Yugoslav refusal to pay compensation for nationalized American property. The Yugoslav government, in return, agreed to pay compensation.

The American and West European governments were faced with a dilemma. Should they help a now weak and isolated, but otherwise successful, instance of communism, while 'containing' communism generally? The Yugoslav régime was defiantly Communist and anti-Western in both its internal and its external policies: there was doubt as to whether it would not, sooner or later, make its peace with Moscow. The materials needed to help the Yugoslav economy were still needed as well by the countries of western Europe, engaged in rebuilding their war-battered economies, and there was even more doubt as to the efficiency with which Western aid would be used by the Yugoslavs. And yet, if Yugoslavia were left to collapse, only the Soviet Union would benefit. If, on the other hand, Tito's régime were helped to survive economically, his rift with Moscow could be widened to the point where no reconciliation was possible any longer, and his independent position could then entice other East European régimes to follow his example. Thus, at the same time as the states of western Europe and North America were grouping together to constitute the North Atlantic Alliance, it was decided, as a calculated risk for a long-term advantage, to assist Yugoslavia without asking its government to alter its domestic policies in any way.

To avoid economic collapse the Yugoslavs began, in 1949, to turn to the West for raw materials and credits, realizing that no other concessions were demanded but the payment of some compensation for nationalized foreign assets. Trade agreements were concluded with several West European countries. The American government agreed to relax, in the case of Yugoslavia, its otherwise rigid control of exports to Communist countries, and the American Export-Import Bank granted a loan to enable Yugoslavia to purchase mining equipment in the U.S.A. The U.S.A. and its allies had gradually moved into the position of granting trade facilities and credits, and the Yugoslav government of accepting them, but the sums provided were still only drops in the ocean, so great were Yugoslavia's needs.

An element of political co-operation also gradually crept in with economic contacts. In May 1949 Tito had privately given the British government assurances that he would extend no further help to the

vealed that Tito believed, and said privately, that the Americans would never allow the Russians to invade Yugoslavia ('A Conversation with Milovan Djilas' on National Educational Television, New York, 2 December 1968).

Greek Communist guerrillas.[53] That summer, in return, the U.S.A. and Great Britain pressed the Greek government not to pursue its offensive into Albanian territory, so as not to cause embarrassment to the Yugoslav government, which was still linked to Albania by treaty commitments, and it was Yugoslavia that subsequently denounced its alliance with Albania. Later that year, as the Yugoslav press toned down its attacks on the West, Western statesmen and officials made statements to the effect that their governments would not remain indifferent to aggression against Yugoslavia.

The Yugoslav economy was near the point of collapse. Tito's government had had to turn to the West to obtain credits to help it complete some of the projects started under the five-year plan. It had also had to abandon – at least for the foreseeable future – its foreign ambitions, particularly that of acquiring the whole of Macedonia. Nevertheless, both the country and the régime had survived. Before 1950, Stalin had expected that he could generate internal convulsions which would overthrow Tito. He had failed, and only military intervention was left; but this, by 1950, had become too dangerous.

[53] Maclean, *Disputed Barricade*, p. 401.

Chapter 5

Titoism: 1950–60

Rapprochement with the West

By 1950, the world appeared divided into two blocs, each one believing the other bent on aggression. That summer, two events changed the attitude of Yugoslavia and of the West towards one another. The eruption of war in Korea increased the fears of the Yugoslavs in their isolation, and the determination of the Western powers to prevent a similar war elsewhere. More locally, a devastating drought in Yugoslavia diminished the harvest, caused agrarian unrest, threatened starvation, and precipitated the economic crisis. Only the West could mitigate its effects. The Yugoslav government asked for help, and the United States, through the Export-Import Bank and the Economic Co-operation Administration, forthwith provided over $31 million-worth of food and cash,[1] and smaller amounts were supplied from West European sources. Before the end of the year, the Yugoslav Emergency Relief Act had provided another $38 million of American aid, and the Yugoslavs agreed both to give full publicity to the fact that the U.S.A. were helping them and to let the Americans observe the distribution.

It was obvious, however, that Yugoslavia was virtually bankrupt, and that the Western powers would have not only to continue their aid, but also to co-ordinate it. In spite of favourable weather, the harvest in 1951 again did not meet the needs, and the following year there was a drought worse than in 1950. The U.S.A., Britain, and France agreed in the summer of 1951 on a programme of tripartite aid to subsidize Yugoslavia's current trade deficit, and the International Bank for Reconstruction and Development advanced $28 million for investment. In 1952, the U.S.A. again made $30 million available to offset the new drought, and tripartite aid became regularized until 1955, some 65 per cent of it being provided by the Americans. With this injection, the 1948 level of total trade was once again reached after 1952, this time with western Europe and the U.S.A., and only the flow of Western aid enabled Yugoslavia to

[1] This and other figures for aid in the following years in Wolff, op. cit., pp. 412 seqq.

withstand, during that period, its large annual deficits in trade and finance. All in all, throughout the 1950s, Yugoslavia must have received some $2,000–2,500 million in one form or another, most of it up to 1956 in the form of outright grants.[2]

The immediate and unqualified economic aid from the U.S.A. made easier the gradual acceptance of military aid. In the autumn of 1950, as a first step, the Yugoslav government accepted a $16 million American loan for army rations. In the January 1951 agreement formalizing American assistance, Yugoslavia undertook not to transfer it to any other government without consent, and to supply the U.S.A. with materials it required. The following month, while the three Western governments issued warnings against threats to Yugoslavia, Tito publicly announced his country's intention of resisting aggression but, on the same occasion, still rejected the idea of receiving arms from the West. Yet in April, it was announced in Belgrade that increased border incidents and the intensive arming of neighbouring states had made it necessary to accept arms from the West. These were French small arms in the first instance, and the U.S.A. advanced $29 million from Mutual Defence Assistance funds. In June, it was known that the chief of the Yugoslav general staff was in Washington to discuss the acquisition of modern weapons, and the first light equipment was then delivered from U.S. excess stocks. The Yugoslavs were by then anxious to re-equip their army with up-to-date equipment, and obtain Western aid, but they were reluctant to have it under an assistance programme, or to admit an American military mission. It was thus not until November that an agreement was actually concluded on arms delivery. Since Yugoslavia could not afford to obtain them otherwise, these were going to be supplied in the framework of the 1949 Mutual Defence Assistance Act and the 1951 Mutual Security Act. In lieu of a mission,

[2] It is difficult to arrive at even an approximate total of Western aid – tripartite aid, International Bank and other loans, American military assistance, agricultural surpluses from the U.S. administration, gifts of relief food from the American Red Cross and other private organizations. No overall figures have been published, nor have the exact amounts of military aid been released. Vido Arnez ('Aid and Trade: the Pattern of Tito's Economic Relations with the World', in *Review of the Study Centre for Jugoslav Affairs*, 1, London, 1960, p. 35) tentatively reckons not much less than $2,000 million over 1950–55, about nine-tenths of which came from the U.S.A. Hoffman and Neal (op. cit., pp. 347 and 354) estimate that, between 1950 and June 1959, Yugoslavia received $1,157.6 million U.S. economic aid (of which more than half was in foodstuffs), and a further $724.2 million military aid to 1958, as well as roughly $219 million from West European countries to 1959 – totalling to just under $2,200 million. Phyllis Auty puts it even higher at $2,400 million (*Tito – A Biography*, London, 1970, p. 256), and even $2,517 million ('The Post-War Period', in Clissold's *Short History*, p. 250).

a small distribution staff was to be assigned to the military attaché in Belgrade. Yugoslav officers would visit the U.S.A. to be trained in the use of new arms.

Earlier in November, President Truman had notified Congress of the urgent need, in the interest of the security of the U.S.A. 'and also of the free world', to strengthen the Yugoslav armed forces. That year, the situation on Yugoslavia's borders had grown more threatening than ever, and the Yugoslav government stressed the country's danger. Yugoslavia was clearly afraid of becoming a Balkan Korea, for only such fear could have made Marshal Tito accept arms from the U.S.A. On the other hand, the Soviet leaders knew (and the Yugoslavs knew that they knew) that it was now too risky to intervene militarily against Yugoslavia, and to stress the danger the country was exposed to was in the interest of the Yugoslav government: it tapped the potentialities of American assistance, and closed the ranks at home. Aid from the West had certainly made it possible to withstand both the consequences to the imitation-Stalinist economy of the Cominform's economic pressure, and its military pressure on the borders.

Circumstances had already put limits to Tito's foreign policy ambitions even when Yugoslavia was still *la fille aînée* of the Cominform. Being reduced to leaning on his former arch-enemy against the pressures of his former mentor made the Yugoslav leader now painfully aware of his country's position as a small power. As relations between Yugoslavia and the Western powers improved of necessity, the latter wanted to integrate the former in their plans for European defence. In October 1951, Greece and Turkey formally joined the North Atlantic Treaty Organization, after having been associated with its military planning in the Mediterranean for a year. They were, however, separated from western Europe, not only by the Soviet bloc, but also and more directly by Yugoslavia. On the other hand, American, British, and French troops in Austria had an exposed right flank which could be protected effectively only if Italy and Yugoslavia linked their forces. Thus the Western powers encouraged Yugoslavia to settle its differences with Greece, Turkey, and Italy, and to link itself in some manner to NATO.

Relations with Turkey had been unfriendly until, in January 1950, Yugoslavia agreed to pay compensation for nationalized Turkish property, and a trade agreement was concluded, after which relations gradually improved as trade developed. To settle with Greece was both more important and more difficult. Greece offered a gap in a hostile encirclement, but the Macedonian question coming on top of ideological enmity was a difficult obstacle, the overcoming of which necessitated much American mediation behind the scenes, with pressures on both sides. The Greek elections of the spring of 1950 resulted in the formation of a government of the Centre, and that was a good opportunity to start with the announcement of the forthcoming exchange of ambassadors; but the Yugoslavs brought up the question of the 'Macedonian minority' in Greece, no doubt thinking that, since they were anxiously being asked to come to terms with the Greeks, they could expect serious concessions. Getting rid of the Macedonian issue was, however, precisely one of the advantages which could induce the Greek government to make it up with those who had supported the Communist rebellion. The war in Korea, accompanied by border incidents with Bulgaria over the summer, made the Yugoslav government quietly shelve the question, and ambassadors were exchanged in December.

Throughout 1951 relations improved, as rail and air links were restored and trade resumed, and by the end of 1952, friendly visits, delegations of one kind or another, interviews, and talks had multiplied to the extent that a Yugoslav military delegation had been to Greece, and the Yugoslav Party Central Committee called for joint defence measures with Greece and Turkey. Eventually, in February 1953 at Ankara, Greece, Turkey, and Yugoslavia signed a treaty of friendship and co-operation which provided for consultations, at diplomatic and military level, on problems of mutual interest, as well as for economic, technical, and cultural co-operation. In spite of a general agreement that regional co-ordination of their several defence efforts would be advantageous in case of local war, it was some years before the pressures of the Cold War brought the three non-Soviet-controlled states to overcome their differences and enter into a marriage of convenience. Greece and Turkey (who themselves were not without differences) first wanted to be fully protected by NATO before undertaking commitments to Yugoslavia, and then felt satisfied or restricted by their membership of NATO. Yugoslavia, on the other hand, was afraid lest a formal treaty should attract hostility before it had time to improve the country's defences. Informal arrangements would have suited Tito better; they would have corresponded more closely to what was considered an unsavoury and temporary (however necessary) adjustment. Early in 1954, Tito, now Head of State under a new constitutional law, went on state visits to Greece and Turkey, and that August, at Bled in Yugoslavia, the treaty of Ankara was turned into a twenty-year alliance which provided for permanent common institutions, mutual consultation in the event of crisis, and mutual armed assistance in the event of aggression.

In September 1952, the British foreign secretary, Eden, had paid a visit to Yugoslavia, an occasion on which Marshal Tito had first appeared socially with his third wife Yovanka married earlier in the year, and who was thereafter increasingly to play the part of Yugoslavia's first lady. In March 1953, Tito had been on a return visit to London – his first visit to any foreign country since 1948 – travelling in state aboard his yacht and lunching with the royal family, all of which had both delighted and impressed him. Yet many influential people in the West still had to be fully convinced that Yugoslavia could be trusted. This, along with the need to strengthen their country's position *vis-à-vis* Italy, was no doubt among the reasons which made the Yugoslav leaders agree to the treaties of the 'Balkan Pact'. For similar reasons, large-scale manoeuvres had been staged in Croatia in September 1953, to which NATO observers had been invited. Their theme was to stage an effective defence against an attack from Hungary in the direction of Riyeka.

The Trieste area was a harder bone of contention between Italy and Yugoslavia than Macedonia between Greece and Yugoslavia. The Yugoslav leaders still saw themselves as victorious allies, and did not realize just how much the defeated enemies across the Adriatic had become part of western Europe. The latter were not enthusiastic about American military assistance to Yugoslavia, or the military clauses of the Balkan Pact, both of which they feared would strengthen the bargaining position of Tito's government in the Trieste dispute. Thus Trieste continued not only to impede the efforts made to connect Yugoslavia to NATO, but even to hamper Italy's own contribution to it.

In May 1952, in order to give practical recognition to the predominantly Italian character of their Zone A of the territory of Trieste, and give the Italians some compensation for the increasing integration of Zone B by the Yugoslavs, Great Britain and the United States agreed to reduce the scope of their Allied military government, and associate the Italians with its administration. Fearing that Italy might obtain Trieste without first renouncing its claims to Zone B, the Yugoslavs reacted furiously. There were mass demonstrations and inflammatory speeches. The Yugoslav government protested against what it considered to be violations of the peace treaty and, in order to weigh the scales down on his side, Tito loudly told the West that, in case of war, Yugoslavia would contribute more than Italy.

In October 1953, Great Britain and the U.S.A. tried to impose a simple solution by announcing their intention of withdrawing their troops and relinquishing the administration of Zone A to the Italian government. Yugoslav reactions were even more furious than previously. To anti-Western demonstration, Tito added a threat that, if Italian troops entered Zone A, Yugoslav troops would march in simultaneously. Faced with a threat of war between two countries deemed essential to Western defence, the American and the British governments backed down. They assured the Yugoslav government that they would not surrender Trieste to Italy without its agreement,

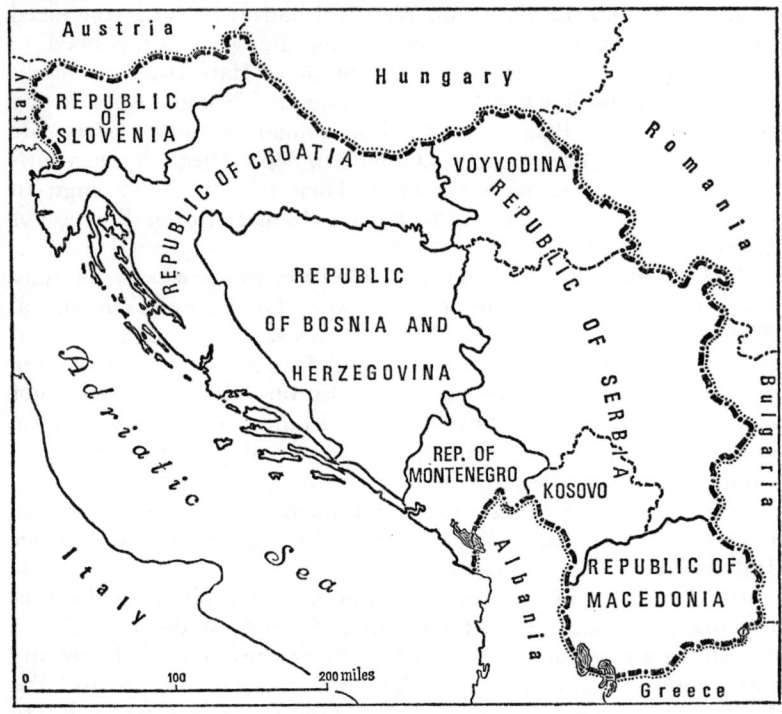

3 The federated units of Yugoslavia since the Second World War

did not withdraw their troops, and continued to mediate between the two contenders in search of a settlement. The tempest abated and, seeing that it could obtain no better, the Yugoslav government eventually accepted a compromise. In October 1954, a Memorandum of Understanding, signed by Great Britain and the U.S.A., Italy and Yugoslavia, terminated the military government of the F.T.T., and thus placed Zone A under Italian administration, calling for Zone A to go to Italy and Zone B to Yugoslavia. This was no formal arrangement of international law; it involved no transfer of sovereignty and no renunciation of claims; it was an allegedly provisional arrangement. In effect, the four governments agreed to recognize *de facto* what had already begun to take effect. The final obstacle to Yugoslavia's incorporation in the Western defence system had been overcome, and many in the West indeed felt that Yugoslavia was about to become one of them, so close did the co-operation appear, both political and military.

Decollectivization, decentralization, relaxation

The drought had somewhat concealed to the outer world the extent to which peasant antagonism against the régime had mounted. In 1950, the drought destroyed any chance the private farmers ever had of being able to meet delivery quotas, at the same time it led the authorities to try and extract the utmost from them. There were serious peasant riots. By 1951, peasant sabotaging of agricultural production was nationwide and, with the help of another drought in 1952, made it drop that year to about half the 1939 output. Threatened by the Soviet bloc, and completely dependent on American aid, the Yugoslav government was faced with imminent collapse of the country's economy, widespread peasant revolt, and dangerous exposure to foreign pressures.

The intrinsic error of the government's agricultural policy had been to try and force an overpopulated rural structure into collectivization, while starving it of capital. Many peasants had joined collective farms for an initial three-year period during which they did not lose their title to the land. In 1951, the widespread withdrawal of those who had joined in 1948 was stopped only by means of threats and arrests. The government, however, forced to recognize the crisis, began to make concessions. The drive towards collectivization was relaxed, compulsory deliveries were gradually discontinued, and a series of measures were taken to make membership of working co-operatives more attractive. Those operating at a loss in particularly poor regions were even allowed to disband.

Although it was made clear that such measures did not mean any fundamental change in the government's rural policy,[3] economic necessity and peasant resistance forced further and major concessions. A decree in March 1953 allowed the peasants to withdraw freely from the working co-operatives, with the land, livestock, and implements they had brought with them. Although the terms of the decree clearly made it anything but easy to withdraw from the

[3] 'Without victory for the socialist sector in our villages, there can be no ultimate victory for socialism in our country,' Tito told the sixth congress of the C.P.Y. in 1952.

collective farms, peasants took on all the conditions, left *en masse* and quickly. Of the peak number of about 7,000 collective farms in June 1951, almost one-fifth had been disbanded even before the decree. By May 1953, there were only 4,800 left, and less than 1,200 by the end of the year. It was officially stated that of 2·6 million hectares once collectivized, more than 2 million were back in private hands. The movement continued and, by the end of 1956, the 'socialized' sector amounted to 22·9 per cent of the total agricultural land.[4] In 1953, too, investments for agricultural developments were somewhat increased, and the increase continued in the following years.[5] In 1954, a new system of taxation was introduced, to induce farmers to produce more.

However helpful, the concessions did not solve the agricultural problem, for the first object of the government's policy continued to be ideological: to integrate the peasantry. Productivity remained but a secondary objective: overall production did increase somewhat, but not enough even to catch up with the increase in population. In order to prevent the growth of 'capitalist tendencies in agriculture' after the decree of March 1953, in May the government enacted another land law which expropriated property in excess of 10 hectares of arable land – the new maximum for individual private holdings. The expropriated land went into a 'people's land fund' from which allotments would be made to agricultural co-operatives and other economic organizations. Although this law affected only a small section of the peasantry,[6] it came as a shock to all farmers, and considerably reduced the psychological effect of the earlier decree. Many official statements let it be known that collectivization had not been abandoned as a long-term aim, and that the government would continue to encourage it, on a voluntary basis, through its planning, credit, price, and fiscal policy.

In the meantime, the rural population in absolute figures had remained stationary since before the war, which made nonsense of collectivization, while in the private sector, the increase in the number of unprofitable smallholdings, along with discriminatory taxation, prevented the private peasant from accumulating any

[4] This last percentage in *Stanje poljoprivrede i zadrugarstva i perspektive njihovog razvoja*, an official publication of the Yugoslav Federal People's Assembly, Belgrade, 1957, p. 15. Other figures in official Yugoslav statistics for 1955 and 1959, as well as in Wolff, op. cit., pp. 431 and 435, and A. Meister, *Socialisme et autogestion – L'Expérience yougoslave*, Paris, 1964, p. 138.

[5] From 4·1% of total investment in 1952 to 4·9% in 1953; 10·4% by 1957 (figures in Hoffman and Neal, op. cit., p. 282, and Meister, op. cit., p. 139).

[6] Of all private farms (representing 28% of the arable land), 9·6% were still above 10 hectares in 1953, and their average size was 16·9 hectares (Wolff, op. cit., pp. 436–7).

capital for productive investment. Any improvement in the government's agricultural policy was reserved for the socialized sector, and the farmers' continued lack of confidence kept production low. The fact that, far from having an agricultural surplus to pay for the capital goods needed by its growing industry, Yugoslavia had to import food to feed an increased population,[7] explains the constantly growing trade deficit in the early 1950s.[8]

Less obvious to the population at large and the superficial foreign observer, there were pressures, none the less real, calling for readjustments in every single other branch of the economy. Industrialization had been imposed, just as collectivization had, but to make the apparatus productive was more difficult than to force it into being. The Stalinist model, with state ownership of means of production, central command planning, capital without price, and concentration on heavy industry, had created productive capacities which could not be used, at the same time as it produced goods which were not in demand, caused inflation, and kept personal consumption low. After 1948 appeared the threat of a loss of all imports, which would have meant an end to the industry the system was trying to create. The steadily rising cost of living had greatly reduced most employees' purchasing power, with consequently widespread dissatisfaction. In industry as in agriculture, the government had to postpone (without abandoning) the ultimate aim, adopt a less straining pace, and make concessions to realities. Furthermore, it was able to make such changes appear, not as a retreat, albeit tactical, but as an advance towards socialism.

In 1950 the first of a series of steps were taken to decentralize the economy generally. Announced in January, workers' self-management was introduced by law in June. In each state economic enterprise, all employees would every year elect a workers' council which would, in turn, choose a management board to act as its executive. While the board would generally undertake all the current functions of management on the basis of laws and regulations and of decisions of the council, the technical day-to-day running of the enterprise would be in the hands of a professional manager chosen, from applicants, by the local authorities. Within the overall framework supplied by the state, the board would prepare the production plan for approval by the council, which would also decide on the distri-

[7] From 15.8 million in 1948 to just under 17 million in 1953 (census figures).

[8] The maximum foreign trade deficit was in 1953: $209 million; in 1951 and 1953, the deficit was greater than the entire value of exports (figures in Wolff, op. cit., p. 446, and B. Pešelj, 'Yugoslavia's Economy Looks to the West', in *Law and Policy in International Business*, II/1, Washington, 1970. p. 54).

bution of that portion of the profits which remained at its disposal. The measure was announced as the passing on to a higher form of socialist ownership of the means of production – from state ownership to 'social' ownership – and was gradually extended to collective farms and collective urban dwelling-houses.

That year, too, control of several branches of the consumer goods industry was transferred from the central government to the several federated units, the federal authorities retaining only regulating functions. This was subsequently extended to other branches and industries, until direct central control remained only over building, transport, and those producer goods industries to which the régime had given pride of place since the beginning. All these measures aimed at transferring much of the decision-making process from the central to the local authorities and to the industries themselves, in an attempt to debureaucratize, and thus give more efficiency to, the whole planning system which was grinding to a halt. At the same time, however, not only was the extensive character of the economy kept untouched, but the concentration on heavy industry was, if anything, intensified.

By 1951, the five-year plan had failed to achieve its original aim of 1947. Its extensive character had restored unity to the country's economy, industry – and especially heavy industry – had been greatly developed since before the war, and the rate of investment had reached the planned percentage of the national income. But the national income itself, far from having doubled since 1939, had risen by less than 15 per cent, and the following year it was to fall back to the pre-war level.[9] The break with the Cominform had initially caused hardship, but as the loss of Eastern aid had since been more than balanced by Western aid, the Soviet bloc could not be saddled with the whole responsibility, and the Yugoslav government in 1951 became concerned at the failure of the Soviet economic model to produce expected results. After a first effort to

[9] Lj. Sirc, 'State Control and Competition in Yugoslavia', in A. Seldon (ed.): *Communist Economy under Change*, London, 1963, pp. 140–41. The same economist has calculated that the average worker earned in 1952 slightly more than before the war (although the white-collar worker's income was only about half its pre-war level), and the number of workers had naturally increased. The peasants' income before taxation was less than half of what it had been, whereas the land tax had increased from 2%–3% of income, before the war, to 10%–20% after the war, and 50%–90% in the period 1951–53 ('Inflation in Jugoslavia', in *Review of the Study Centre for Jugoslav Affairs*, 5, London, 1965, p. 308). The head of the Trade Union Organization stated at the end of 1954 that *per capita* commodity consumption that year was running at about pre-war level (quoted by E. Neuberger, 'General Survey of the Yugoslav Economy', in Byrnes (ed.): *Yugoslavia*, p. 196).

make management less bureaucratic by decentralizing it, the search for greater efficiency led to a partial restoration of the market principle in 1952. At the sixth congress of the C.P.Y., in November that year, it was publicly admitted that the Yugoslav economy had been built on unrealistic bases, and Kidrich, who was still in charge, talked of the need to submit plans to the 'checks and correctives of economic law'.

Rationing had been gradually abandoned after 1950, and price controls for most goods abolished in 1952. In 1951, individual enterprises were given the right to engage in foreign trade, within limits. The following year, the dinar was devalued, from the theoretical parity of fifty to the dollar to the more realistic one of 300, and enterprises engaged in foreign trade were allowed to keep part of the currencies thus earned for direct buying abroad, or for selling on an official foreign exchange. Also, starting with 1952, detailed long-term economic planning was replaced by annual 'social' plans, meant as a framework and guide for the local governments and enterprises to follow in determining their own individual plans. The centralized budgetary system of investment was given up in favour of a system which set apart a proportion of every enterprise's income for ploughing back. Otherwise, investment credits were to be distributed to the highest bidders, and interest paid on them. Collective and personal incentives, profitability, and credit were to be used to foster the desired amount of production, under the general control of the government, exercised through monetary and fiscal policies, as well as various kinds of political and social pressures.

The introduction of workers' self-management had been neither immediate nor spontaneous. The régime had hitherto been busy remodelling society rather than the minds of the workers, for the vast majority of whom communism had meant a change in management, and little more in terms of ideology. Taken over from private ownership, the wage structure helped to preserve the traditional dominance of wage problems in workers' minds. To the majority, self-management appeared as a nominal exercise, in which collective decisions and elections of councils would be mere formalities. The task of the trade unions remained that of educating the workers and they were given a privileged position in drawing up lists of candidates for elections of workers' councils.

Since the average Yugoslav worker did not respond, and was in no way equipped to manage his factory, more often than not the authorities – and even the central authorities – continued to control the factories, indirectly, through the local people's committees, Party units, and trade unions, and through their general policies. To a large degree, influential Party members continued to run the factories, not so much through the cells of the enterprises as directly from positions of influence at the head of, or above, the enterprises. Often the same individuals were on the workers' council and the management board, in the trade union, the Party organization, and even the local authority. Communists were not in a majority on the councils, or even the boards, but the majority of managers still had the right political qualifications rather than the necessary professional qualifications.[10] The same management personnel, it appears, remained in charge, which was yet another form of control over the economy.

In so far as workers' councils did initiate anything new, it was to increase the price of their products, and even reduce their labour force, in an effort to keep profits up, and to vote disproportionate increases for the administrative staff and highly skilled workers who provided the vocal elements in councils, boards, trade unions, Party units, and local government bodies. So in 1952, the distribution of profits had to be drastically limited, and in 1953, inspection committees were instituted to supervise the financial activities of enterprises. But even those powers the workers' council did originally get and retain were limited, for wage-scales had to be established in conjunction with, and with the approval of, the trade unions and local authorities, production planning depended in most cases on obtaining credit from the banks, and even after 1952, the bulk of industrial investments continued to be controlled by the government through grants from the investment fund.[11]

On the whole, the changes instituted in 1950–52, while correcting some particularly objectionable features of the Stalinist system, had little immediate effect, because they did not change much in the relationship between government and economy, between labour and management. The same people who had been formed by the Stalinist system and placed their faith in it, continued in charge of the Yugoslav economy, and operated the changes. Decentralization had not been a radical break, but more simply a correction in the scope and

[10] In the 1954 elections to workers' councils, over one million workers voted (and there were only 200,000 workers in the C.P.Y. at the time). Of the 158,000 elected to councils, less than 30% were Communists; of the 42,000 elected to boards, only a third were Communists (these figures according to *Borba*, Belgrade, 14 March 1954). In 1951–52, over 90% of managers were Communists, and only just over 20% had adequate technical qualifications (*Borba*, 13 February 1952).

[11] In 1957, from this fund were still financed a third of all economic investments, including more than half of all industrial investments (F. E. I. Hamilton, *Yugoslavia – Patterns of Economic Activity*, New York, 1968, p. 239).

scale of planning. Basic economic decisions were still made by the central political leadership, which also decided how much and when to delegate. The alleged advantages of heavy industry were so ingrained that they continued to attract major investment, and all that went with it: the transfer of unskilled and untrained peasant labour, which reduced efficiency, and the importing of raw materials, which increased costs. Heavy industry, which had hitherto lived off the budget, certainly did feel the pinch of the new measures, and no sooner were enterprises required to submit to the test of profitability than the uneconomic state of many of them, hitherto hidden by inflation, appeared in full light. But since it was precisely in the most cherished branches that investment was being curtailed, the auctioning of investment funds was divided up into sectors, according to a planned overall scheme, and irresponsible borrowing resumed. After a pause, inflation returned as from 1953.

In 1950, in order to survive, the Yugoslav régime had begun to look for Western backing – financial, diplomatic, military – and for a way to inject efficiency into the economy. That year too, the conflict with the U.S.S.R. began to be expressed in ideological terms, and the Yugoslav Party press began to attack the Soviet system. Milovan Djilas, the member of the top Party secretariat in charge of propaganda, whose writings after the war had been inspired by infinite love of the Soviet Union, published a series of articles branding the Stalinist order as being no longer socialist. The Soviet Union was no longer the ultimate guarantor of the Yugoslav Communist leaders' hold over their country; it was against them. After having sustained its fire for two years, it was now necessary to return it, and denounce the Stalinist system as having deviated from Marxism. At home, this meant seeking support from a broader section of the population and using persuasion as an alternative (or, at least in the beginning, as an auxiliary) to intimidation.

Most members of the C.P.Y. had joined in conditions fostering solidarity with the Yugoslav rather than with the Soviet leadership, many of them since 1948, while obvious Cominformist sympathizers had been not only expelled but persecuted. Yet the Party remained a minority of cadres,[12] and moreover of cadres increasingly interested in privileges, decreasingly in militancy. Such a Party not only could not really act as the 'conscious vanguard' of anything, but the blatant privileges enjoyed by its rank-and-file even threatened to offset in the population at large the new support granted to the leadership for what appeared as its defiance of Stalin. This also

[12] Membership had increased from 468,000 in 1948 to 779,000 in 1952 (membership figures for the fifties quoted in this chapter from Hoffman and Neal, op. cit., pp. 174 and 196–7, and Meister, op. cit., pp. 212–13).

pointed to the need for a wider consensus. Lastly, there was no apparent attempt by the Western powers to attach political strings to their aid, and the Yugoslav government was careful never to appear as wanting to court the former with political concessions; but it could not have been entirely oblivious of the need to build for itself a more favourable 'image' for consumption by public opinion in the West.[13]

Thus, in 1950, the Yugoslav government began to experiment with persuasion and less offensive methods of control, in relative freedom from outside interferences, since neither of the power blocs could afford to destroy or dominate it. The experiment started mildly, with the elections of March 1950. A new electoral law enabled candidates to stand with the backing of a hundred voters, and the campaign was conducted with slogans of decentralization and participation, but also with Tito's corrective that there could be but one political programme, that of the People's Front which was that of the Communist Party. At the polls, more than 90 per cent of the electorate supported the unopposed candidates of the People's Front. More significant was the announcement, made in October, by the Party's Central Committee – ostensibly because of the drought – that the special privileges of food and housing enjoyed by Party members and officials of all sorts would be abolished.

In February 1951, a new criminal code adopted the principle that there could be no crime or punishment unless specified by law, and legally ended arbitrary action by the police. In June, Rankovich issued a sensational report to the Party's Central Committee, both admitting the atrocities which his political police had been committing and castigating them. The following year, the U.D.B. was turned into a plain-clothes agency, and the National Defence Corps[14] into a frontier guard. The U.D.B. was maintained as an instrument of control, and mention of administrative sentences continued, but the total number of arrests was more than halved between 1950 and 1952.[15] In September 1953, a new code of

[13] Charles McVicker, who was then U.S. consul in Zagreb, writes that, just prior to the close of the food negotiations, the American ambassador reminded Marshal Tito that it would be well to remember that Congress would eventually have to authorize the expense of the food which the government of the U.S.A. had agreed to send, and that Congress had been openly critical of the lack of civil and religious liberties in Yugoslavia (*Yugoslavia – Pattern for International Communism*, New York, 1957, pp. 24–5).

[14] Cf. above, p. 180.

[15] From over 36,000 in 1950 to 15,500 in 1952 (Hoffman and Neal, op. cit., p. 389). In December 1951, admitting to no more than 50,000 *émigrés*, Rankovich invited them to return with the promise of an amnesty, which would not, however, apply to 'war criminals'. By that time, some 14,000 had returned to Yugoslavia since 1946, less than half after 1948. On the other

penal procedure reformed and codified investigation proceedings and prison conditions.¹⁶ The following year, the judicial reform was completed. Although still elected by political assemblies, professional judges were to have legal qualifications and could only be removed for reasons stipulated by statute. Public prosecutors, henceforth also required to have legal qualifications, were placed under the jurisdiction of the courts.

All this did not amount to creating an independent judiciary. The presidents of courts and a large percentage of the judges continued to be members of the Communist Party, and those who were not, were invariably affiliated with the People's Front. Socialist legality was designed to strengthen the socialist system. A whole range of ill-defined petty offences were still punishable directly by the local authorities, and the stipulations concerning political offences were made so general that the government retained, now strictly according to the letter of the law, virtually unrestricted reserved authority in that field at least.¹⁷ Yet even with these qualifications, the judicial reforms of the early fifties, by placing greater emphasis on legality, and by pushing the administrative security services into a more discreet background, went a long way towards making the régime more secure. As ordinary people gradually became accustomed to receiving justice from the courts in ordinary matters, their feeling of security would grow, and with it, their respect for the law, and the government could rely more, for the protection of its system, upon the nature and scope of its laws, and

---

hand, nearly 5,000 had escaped after 1948. The total number of Yugoslav refugees in the world at the end of 1951 has been estimated at more than 150,000 (Knežević, art. cit., part i, in *Poruka*, 52, pp. 14 and 18).

¹⁶ Torture was forbidden; persons in custody were entitled to at least eight hours' uninterrupted rest in every twenty-four; confessions had to be corroborated by evidence.

¹⁷ The 1951 penal code defined 'hostile propaganda' as propaganda in favour of 'fascist and other ideas hostile to the people and government', aimed against the state, the social organizations, and the people's authorities, or against political, economic, military, and other important measures taken by them. 'Intent to undermine' the authority of the working people, the defensive power of the country, the economic bases of socialism, and the brotherhood and unity of the peoples of Yugoslavia, was deemed sufficient to establish guilt. In 1959, a revised penal code somewhat narrowed the definition to calling for or inciting 'violent or unconstitutional changes', and representing 'maliciously or untruthfully' conditions in the country – 'in writings, speeches or otherwise'. Rankovich had explained in 1951 that the courts could not be independent 'from the achievements of our revolution', nor separated 'from the political and social developments of our socialist system' (A. Ranković, *Izabrani govori i članci*, Zagreb, 1951, p. 402). On Yugoslav legal theory, cf. I. Lapenna, *State and Law – Soviet and Yugoslav Theory*, London, 1964.

less on arbitrary police action.[18] Although arrests for pro-Cominform activities continued throughout the first half of the decade, at the same time several thousand Cominformist sympathizers were released. While it was announced in 1952 that Hebrang had committed suicide in prison, his companion Zhuyovich recanted publicly in the Party daily *Borba* at the end of 1950 and was set free to return to private life. Several of the non-Communist figures condemned in post-war years were also freed. By 1952 also, passports were beginning to be issued to private persons, especially the elderly with relatives abroad.

Towards the end of 1950, there were several concessions to religious feeling. After Patriarch Gavrilo's death, Marshal Tito in September paid an official call on his newly elected successor, Patriarch Vikentiye, who issued a statement on the good relations between the state and the Serbian Orthodox Church, while the government returned to that Church certain important properties. In November, it publicly offered to release Archbishop Stepinats if he would leave the country, or retire to a monastery. The archbishop, who was ill, had become an embarrassment to the government in the development of its relations with the West. The prelate himself did not want to leave Yugoslavia, and the Holy See would not accept anything less than rehabilitation, so that, at the end of 1951, the Yugoslav government took a unilateral half-step as a concession to opinion at home and abroad: it released the archbishop of Zagreb but confined him to his native village, and did not allow him to resume his duties.

Nevertheless, relations with the Churches remained tense. Refusing to meet the Yugoslav government halfway, Pope Pius XII made Stepinats a cardinal in November 1952. The Yugoslav government reacted indignantly by breaking off diplomatic relations with the Vatican. With the Orthodox Church too, relations were not as smooth as appeared from the niceties exchanged at the time of Patriarch Vikentiye's election. In order to prevent the Orthodox bishops from being tempted to elect the more anti-Communist Metropolitan Yosif of Skopye, the latter had been arrested on a charge of plotting against the state. Two bishops (an Orthodox and a Catholic) and many priests, particularly Roman Catholics, were still in prison, and anti-religious propaganda had not abated. There were still people sentenced in 1952 as Vatican spies; bishops of both Churches were attacked for spreading hostile propaganda. As late as 1953, both the Roman Catholic and the Serbian Orthodox bishops were expelled from Banjaluka by the police, and the Orthodox

[18] McVicker, op. cit., p. 208.

Metropolitan Nektariye of Bosnia was beaten up by a mob of Communist hooligans. In 1952, the government stepped up its efforts with the associations of clergy, and in 1953, a fundamental law on the legal position of religious communities was enacted to regularize existing practice on the basis of the government's own conception of separation – one in which the state confined the Church to the performance of religious rites, but did not renounce its own influence on religious affairs.[19]

By 1953, 'socialist realism' was given up as the official doctrine in literature and the arts, when the Communist writer Krlezha, in Zagreb, and those of the pre-war surrealists who had rallied the Communists, in Belgrade, same out resolutely against its conceptions. Thereafter literature and painting developed more freely, and although polemics between 'formalists' and 'realists' continued right through the decade, non-utilitarian themes gradually became predominant. Characteristic was the success obtained by naïve peasant artists with the directness and fantasy of their creations.[20]

The new atmosphere was not without its effect on education. In 1953, university students were allowed freely to choose their courses of study, although their choice could still be indirectly influenced by the grants made available. In 1954, a law reorganized the universities,[21] which were to be administered by elected academic bodies, but controlled by mixed councils of faculty representatives, student representatives (for long silent), and representatives of the republican parliaments, where non-academic members outnumbered the academics, and Communists predominated. Teachers had to be re-elected every five years, and could be removed from their position at any time by the university council. All anti-Communist lecturers had been eliminated in the immediate post-war period, and as the fifties progressed, more and more academics were simply apolitical. There were courses in Marxism but, except in those disciplines which lent themselves to Marxist interpretation, ideology tended to fade, although Party influence remained strong enough to prevent anything which smacked of political deviation. The reform, while giving greater independence to the teaching staff in administrative

[19] According to the census taken in 1953 (which noted religious adherence), there were 7 million Orthodox (41·4%), 5·4 million Catholics (31·8%), 2·1 million Moslems (12·3%), and 2·1 million non-believers.

[20] Among the better known are the painters Ivan Gheneralich (b. 1914), of the village of Hlebine in Croatia, famous for its school of peasant painters, and Miyo Kovachich (b. 1935), his pupil, with the wood-carver Bogosav Zhivkovich (b. 1920), from Serbia.

[21] To the three pre-war universities of (in order of foundation) Zagreb, Belgrade, and Ljubljana had been added the University of Skopye in 1946, for Macedonia, and that of Sarayevo in 1949, for Bosnia-Herzegovina.

and academic matters, was so devised as to keep universities under the eye of the authorities.

It was the whole system of education which was being slanted so as to convince its products of the superiority of communism as it was evolving in Yugoslavia. The new law on education, passed in 1955, stressed the need to form conscious citizens capable of contributing to the development of socialism. In 1950, eight-year general compulsory schooling was introduced, but it was not until 1953 that the number of primary schoolteachers rose above that of 1939. Many of the pre-war teachers had been eliminated for political reasons. Low pay discouraged new entrants generally, while working conditions in the least literate regions were a further handicap. The result was that, while the number of university students had increased from 18,000 in 1939 to 55,000 in 1952 and 70,000 in 1955, that of primary schoolchildren had remained more or less static at under 1.5 million. In 1953, the illiteracy rate was still 25 per cent, as in 1948.

By gradually shifting the emphasis from intimidation to persuasion, the Yugoslav leaders were able to evolve institutions which aimed at giving the working people (at any rate those integrated in the system) the feeling that they participated in the local day-to-day decision-making process, without discontinuing the careful direction of the overall line of development. Local government was thus reorganized so as to enlarge its area of authority, and encourage wider public interest. In 1952, people's committees were made bicameral by adding to the local councils, directly voted in by the general electorate, a council of producers elected by those employed actively in 'producing material goods' – which excluded the professions and the majority of peasant farmers outside collectives and co-operatives. Each people's committee elected a president as its political chief, and a professional secretary to head its executive administration. Three years later, in 1955, the main emphasis was placed on the communes which became the key local units. Apart from running the usual municipal services, the local authority supervised the economic life of the commune, and played its part in establishing wage-scales, in appointing and dismissing managers of enterprises, in underwriting their loans, and in having the right to suspend a management board or to demand the election of a new workers' council. Fairly autonomous financially, local committees could enact their own by-laws subject to the approval of the higher echelon. Last but not least, local authorities participated in the 'social management' of a whole gamut of public institutions.

Whereas direct workers' self-management had been introduced in 'productive' economic enterprises, in 'non-productive' enterprises –

such as educational and cultural establishments, professional associations, social insurance and health institutions, newspapers, and broadcasting stations – the self-management mechanism was capped by a mixed board representing both employees and the local political authority.

In 1956, specialized citizens' commissions were attached to the communal authorities to make recommendations on such matters as town-planning, housing, education, or health. Their members were chosen by the people's committees from names put forward by voters' meetings which were called at regular intervals as public forums to discuss local affairs, nominate candidates for these commissions, and candidates for elections at all levels.

Local government authority was emphasized not only in content, but also in size, by concentrating a smaller number of units over larger areas,[22] with the whole propaganda apparatus mobilized to glorify self-government through territorial communes as ushering in, together with self-government through economic enterprises, a free society of free producers. Participation in self-management and social management was to be a more advanced form, or a *succedaneum*, of political democracy.

Hitherto, local government had been little more than an extension of the Party organization. Thereafter, a wider variety of citizens was drawn into semi-governmental sectional activities; freedom of expression slowly crept into local, non-political affairs; local Party secretaries were instructed not to cumulate their functions with the presidency of local government bodies. Yet communal government continued to be strongly influenced by the Party. Members of social management bodies were drawn almost exclusively from the People's Front, with a strong backbone proportion of Communists, many of whom served on several boards at the same time, and the low educational standard of local civil servants made it impossible for any really effective decentralization to be carried out overnight.

On the whole, decentralization meant, in fact, decentralization within the C.P.Y., with more devolution to its lower strata, coupled with an effort to increase Party consciousness and reduce careerism.[23] To endorse the changes, a Party congress was held in November 1952. In contrast to the fifth congress, the sixth was devised as a solemnization of the C.P.Y.'s new role in the further development of Marxism, and as an anti-Stalinist demonstration. While accusing Stalin of every imaginable crime, Tito described the transfer of factories to workers' self-management as 'an epoch-making historic

[22] 7,102 communes and 360 districts in 1950; 1,103 communes and 91 districts in 1959.
[23] 180,000 members were expelled between 1950 and 1954.

act', and defined the Party's role as that of inspiring political and ideological action. To symbolize is moving on to a higher phase of development, where the emphasis would be placed on educating the masses in the spirit of socialism, the Party's name was changed to League of Communists of Yugoslavia. Members would henceforth be expected to exert their responsibilities as Communists, not through the Party as an organization, but as individuals within the institutions in which they were employed, through their positions as citizens and producers. The leaders, however, were careful to emphasize that the Party would not renounce its responsibilities, lose its cohesiveness, or be turned into a mass organization, and that it would not countenance Western influences.

The Political Bureau, renamed Executive Committee, was enlarged by the inclusion of General Vukmanovich-Tempo, Bakarich, Kolishevski, Salay (head of the Trade Union Organization), and Putsar (head of the government of Bosnia-Herzegovina) – Neshkovich being dropped allegedly for pro-Cominform sympathies apparently manifested since the fifth congress. Tito, Kardelj, Djilas, and Rankovich were again confirmed in the Party secretariat, to which were also promoted both Kidrich (still in charge of economic policy, but soon to die) and General Goshnjak.

Three months later, in February 1953, the People's Front also held its congress – to adopt a new name, and a new role. The name was the Socialist Alliance of the Working People of Yugoslavia. The role was explained to the congress by Kardelj. With the Party as the educator, the inspirer, the vanguard, the Front or Alliance was to become a mass public forum, broad enough to admit all citizens who accepted the aims of socialism and performed their social duties, the mechanism through which Communist ideas were to be put into practice and transmitted to the people at large. It would supervise elections as well as the working of local government and social organizations. The congress elected a presidency of twenty-five Party personalities, nineteen of them from the League's Central Committee (including seven members of its Executive Committee), with Kardelj as its secretary-general and Tito as its president. It was difficult to tell where exactly the functions of the League ended and those of the Alliance began.[24] Not only did the Alliance, as an organization, remain dominated by the Party, but, however wider its membership (and it claimed to represent half the total population), it functioned only through its Communist members.

[24] In 1954, *Borba*, the Party's daily organ, was handed over to the Alliance, to which also belonged many other newspapers, including the two main dailies, the Belgrade *Politika*, as organ of the S.A. of Serbia, and the Zagreb *Vjesnik*, as organ of the S.A. of Croatia.

In January 1953, a new constitutional law correspondingly adapted the constitutional machinery of 1946 to the needs of the régime's experimental phase. Since the original constitution, it had been official theory that the Yugoslav peoples, by uniting into a federation, had made use of their right to self-determination. Furthermore, it was thought by the framers of the constitutional law of 1953 that the construction of a socialist society through self-management at all levels would absorb the old sectional, regional, and ethnic interests. Consequently, less stress was placed on the theoretical sovereignty of the nations and republics, and more on the rights of the working people expressed through their self-government institutions. The Council of Nations – which had never exercised any initiative on behalf of the republics – was thus merged with the Federal Council,[25] and replaced as a second chamber by a Council of Producers, delegated indirectly by different categories of producers.

The executive organs were also reorganized. The Federal Executive Council was instituted as the supreme policy-making body. Elected by the Federal People's Assembly, it was relieved of administrative responsibilities, it initiated and enforced legislation, and controlled the federal administrative apparatus. It was capped by secretaries of state in charge of the fields of predominant concern to the federal government.[26] The office of president of the republic was introduced, whose holder, the highest executive officer, would be Head of State, head of the government, and head of the armed forces. The whole constitutional structure – minus the president – was reproduced in the federated units.

The system was already beginning to be defined as one of 'socialist direct democracy',[27] leading towards a society in which the working people would themselves directly make the political decisions affecting their lives, by their participation in all the organs of local government, social management, and workers' self-management. The state would thus be able in time to wither away, although it remained meanwhile as an instrument to safeguard the revolutionary process and the country's independence. The system rejected not only Stalinist state socialism, but also bourgeois democracy with its plurality of political parties and its indirect parliamentary representation. A plurality of parties was not only

[25] It could still meet separately to debate certain types of acts affecting the component republics.

[26] The theoretical separation of political and administrative executives was vitiated from the start by the appointment of members of the F.E.C. to head the secretariats of state. In 1956 this practice was formalized by law.

[27] Cf. extracts from the lecture delivered by Kardelj in Oslo on 8 October 1954 ('The Practice of Socialist Democracy in Yugoslavia') in C. Wright Mills, *The Marxists*, London, 1963, pp. 401 seqq.

meaningless in the long run (since there was no clash of economic interests in the Marxist sense), but immediately dangerous (for Yugoslavia was still in the process of revolutionary change). Because it was leading to complete socialism, the system could not allow anti-socialist action, or even criticism; it discriminated against those of its citizens (as yet the majority) who were not integrated in the social sector of production; and its legality was intended to protect the achievements of the revolution.

New elections had originally been announced for the spring of 1953. The question was to decide on the greatest possible freedom of form and substance compatible with obtaining the right results, and there had been much talk of experimenting with more than one candidate in most constituencies. The new electoral law, however, was not enacted until September, thus allowing the decollectivization decree of March 1953 to be turned into a political asset.

However great a departure from the previous single-list method, the new electoral procedure – which turned the nominating process into the most important part of the elections[28] – made it almost impossible, in practice, for anyone not sponsored by a 'conscious socialist' organization or group to be nominated. When polling took place in November 1953, less than 10 per cent of national constituencies had more than one candidate. At the level of republican elections, less than a quarter of the seats were contested, but only four of these contestants were 'non-official' – local Communists who had fallen out of grace, and managed to get nominated without the approval of local Alliance or League organizations. There was less pressure on voters to turn out, and 10·6 per cent of the electorate failed to do so.

The new parliament elected a Federal Executive Council of thirty-eight – all but two of them members of the Party's Central Committee. The presidency of the republic had been tailor-made

[28] In each commune, the president of the People's Committee summoned a voters' meeting (the quorum being 10% of the registered voters) which elected a nominating committee, and submitted to it names of candidates backed by at least ten voters. Those candidates endorsed by the nominating committee were then submitted for the approval of at least one-third of the number of voters present at the meeting – as signified by a show of hands. Candidates could also be nominated directly by a petition signed by any group of 200 voters. Finally, nominees had to be confirmed by a constituency electoral commission. A similar procedure was followed for producers' elections in their economic enterprises. Representation of industry and agriculture in producers' councils was in proportion to each category's contribution to the national income, based on somewhat arbitrary price lists. These tended to undervalue the contribution of agriculture, which thus had only 67 representatives at federal level, compared with industry's 135. Private farmers were not entitled to vote as producers.

for Tito, and he was duly elected – with one dissenting voice. In a very real sense, he had himself built the Party of which he was the senior member and head; he had directed the establishment of the new régime and personified Yugoslav communism at home and abroad. The consequences of 1948, the removal of Stalin as the transcendent inspirer, the need for the régime to have a symbol larger than the Party, had all contributed to building up Tito's position, and to increasing, rather than reducing, the cult of his personality.

Reconciliation with the Soviet Union

By the time that the final obstacle to Yugoslavia's incorporation into the Western defence system had been overcome, its rulers had already begun to move away from such a close association. On 5 March 1953, two days before Marshal Tito embarked on the Mediterranean cruise that was going to take him to London, Stalin had died in Moscow. His uneasy successors quickly showed signs of wanting to reduce the tensions with the West, and the following summer, the Yugoslav government cautiously accepted their suggestion that ambassadors be reappointed.

By that time, however, the Yugoslav government had also begun to establish closer contacts with some of the newly (and not so newly) independent states of Asia and Africa. Faced with the need to mobilize all their capacities in order to develop their economies and raise their standard of living, some form of socialism seemed to them more appropriate to their needs than unmitigated private enterprise. They were, anyhow, suspicious of the once colonial West, but at the same time not enthusiastic about Soviet communism, and fearful of Chinese communism. Alarmed at the increasing bi-polarity of international relations, their foreign policies were moving towards a position soon to be known as non-alignment. To the Yugoslavs, this appeared as a field in which they could promote their new brand of independent and progressive democratic socialism, and where they could find less compromising company. By associating with the states of the 'third world', Tito could hope to reduce his increasing dependence on the West, and even to satisfy the foreign policy ambitions which events had curtailed since 1948.

In the summer of 1954, Emperor Haile Selassie of Ethiopia visited Belgrade. President Tito's intention was, no doubt, to give a demonstration of solidarity with another victim of Italian imperialism at the time of the thorny negotiations over Trieste. Later that year, he went on an eight-month tour of Asia, where he was presented as a guerrilla hero of the Second World War and a symbol of national independence. Tito praised the Bandung Conference which, in April 1955, brought together for the first time twenty-nine Asian and African states. The success of his Asian trip enabled Yugoslavia's leaders both to start playing down their association with the West, and to ensure that a reconciliation with Stalin's heirs would not affect their independence.

The question of Soviet relations with Yugoslavia was bound up with that of rising discontent in the satellites – and both were bound to the struggle for power in the Kremlin. Khrushchev appears to have headed a group which wanted to reintegrate Yugoslavia – under Tito – into a less rigidly organized Communist bloc, and thus increase the credibility to the outside world of the new Soviet leadership's peaceful intentions. He also appears to have met with misgivings and reserve among other Communist leaders, both in the Kremlin and in other capitals.

Since the reappointment of ambassadors, there had been a slow but steady improvement of relations between Yugoslavia and the Soviet Union, and with the Soviet bloc generally. The borders had been opened, traffic resumed, the economic blockade lifted, and the propaganda campaign ended. By the spring of 1955, the improvement had reached the stage where a meeting between Soviet and Yugoslav leaders could be arranged to settle the future basis of their relations: on 14 March it was made public that Khrushchev and Bulganin – by then respectively first secretary of the Communist Party and prime minister of the U.S.S.R. – would shortly lead a Soviet delegation to Yugoslavia.

On landing at Belgrade airport on 26 May, Khrushchev, as head of the Soviet Communist Party, read a statement which rehabilitated the Yugoslav Communist Party with Tito at its head, and blamed Beria, the Soviet police chief executed a few months after Stalin's death, for the mistaken policy which the U.S.S.R. had pursued towards Yugoslavia after 1948. At the end of the visit, on 2 June, after a week spent in the capital and on the Yugoslav president's island residence of Brioni (off the west coast of the Istrian peninsula), Marshals Tito and Bulganin, on behalf of the two governments, signed a joint declaration which formalized the reconciliation and amounted, in substance if not in form, to a real treaty of friendship and co-operation. It established as principles which would govern their relations: non-interference in the internal affairs of other states; respect of the sovereignty, independence, territorial integrity, and equality of socialist countries; and peaceful co-existence among nations, regardless of ideological or social differences. The two governments agreed on a common attitude to be adopted on certain important international questions (such as the admission to UNO of the Communist government of mainland China, and aid to the underdeveloped countries), and undertook to extend, as well as regulate by further agreements, their co-operation in different fields – economic, cultural, and others, including co-operation between 'social organizations' of both countries in the 'exchange of socialist experience'.

There was, at the time, much confused and superficial reporting to the West of the Belgrade talks and declarations. It was said that, in going to Belgrade, the Soviet leaders had capitulated to Tito, that they had 'gone to Canossa'. It was also said that the Yugoslavs wanted the reconciliation to be kept strictly on the level of the two governments, that Khrushchev, without warning, had tried to drag the Parties in as well in his airport speech, but that tough bargaining by the Yugoslavs had made them win the day in the final declaration. It is difficult to believe that issues as important as these had not been well prepared in advance, the more so since over nine weeks had elapsed between its announcement and the arrival of the Soviet delegation. Even without knowing what happened behind closed doors, the Belgrade settlement clearly appears as a reconciliation on equal terms, without either side capitulating. The Yugoslav leadership was rehabilitated and obtained recognition of its independent position. On the other hand, before finalizing and formalizing the reconciliation with Tito, the new Soviet rulers gathered together the other Communist-ruled states of eastern Europe into a formal political and military alliance, the Warsaw Pact, signed on 14 May, which not only strengthened the cohesion of the Cominform bloc, but included Albania, to which no formal guarantees had ever been given by Stalin, and made possible the continued maintenance of Soviet troops in Hungary and Romania when they should have been withdrawn following the imminent conclusion of the Austrian state treaty.[29] As for the Party issue, the very presence of Khrushchev implied it, and it was included in the final declaration.[30]

In other words, an attempt was made – unconsciously by Western commentators to their audiences, but consciously by Yugoslav interpreters to Western commentators – to minimize the importance of the settlement in the eyes of the West, for the Yugoslav government was concerned that its good relations with the West should continue. These, even more than the building of new relations with third-

[29] As for the parallel with Canossa, it was not only misleading ('going to Canossa' implies capitulation and humiliation), but unhistorical (Tito would have 'gone to Canossa' if he had gone to Moscow to make amends to Stalin; it was not Gregory VII who went to make amends to Henry IV; and anyhow, Khrushchev was not quite the 'pope' Stalin had been, even if we assume Tito to be the 'emperor').

[30] Part III, clause 7, on the co-operation between 'social organizations'.

world countries, provided a sort of guarantee that, in the process of its *rapprochement* with the Soviet Union, Yugoslavia would not be trapped into renewed subordination. They also provided much-needed aid. In spite of apprehensions in the U.S. Congress, aid was not discontinued. The American secretary of state, Dulles, went to see Tito in November, and they issued a joint communiqué on the importance of the independence of East European states.

Economic and financial reasons also played a role in the reconciliation. In September 1955, an economic agreement with the Soviet Union increased trade exchanges on favourable conditions, and provided a substantial loan which enabled the Yugoslav government to meet interest payments on short-term credits from the West. Normalization of economic relations with the Eastern countries produced in the year 1955–56 a series of agreements which provided Yugoslavia with credits to a total value of $646 million.[31] The Soviet Union held out the prospect of large-scale investment credits, and the Yugoslavs hoped to find in eastern Europe a market for the goods which their industry was now turning out in increasing quantities, but in qualities which were not yet up to the requirements of Western markets. Taking a leaf out of the American book, the Russians attached no strings to their offers.

Opposition to reconciliation with Tito among the Soviet leadership seems to have been checkmated by the time of the twentieth congress of the Soviet Communist Party, in February 1956, which accepted the peaceful co-existence of different social systems, and that of different forms of socialism. The news was greeted with joy in Belgrade, as was Khrushchev's denunciation of the crimes and errors of Stalin. All this was interpreted by the Yugoslavs as the final victory of Khrushchev over Molotov, as the revenge of Titoism over Stalinism. Other Communist governments made gestures of appeasement by removing or downgrading some personalities. When, in April, the dissolution of the then useless Cominform was announced, the Yugoslav leaders interpreted it as the proclamation by the new Soviet leadership of its renunciation of Stalinist hegemony over other Communist Parties. To Tito more particularly, there appeared once again the possibility of his taking a more active part in shaping the world policies of communism. By being the main ally of a Khrushchevian Soviet Union, he would, no doubt, increase his stature in eastern Europe.

Tito's return visit to the Soviet leaders in June 1956 was a warm and uninhibited display of friendship renewed. The day before his arrival, it was announced that Molotov had been relieved of his post

[31] Arnez, art. cit. in *Review of the Study Centre for Jugoslav Affairs*, 1960, p. 37.

as foreign minister. Speaking in Stalingrad on 11 June, the Yugoslav president said: 'In time of war as in time of peace, Yugoslavia marches shoulder to shoulder with the Soviet people towards the same goal – the victory of socialism'. On 20 June, another joint declaration was issued which formally and explicitly resumed fraternal relations between the two Communist Parties on the basis of freedom to determine the manner and form of socialist development. At the same time, the similarity of the two governments' views on a number of international questions was announced.

After his visit to the U.S.S.R., Tito believed with characteristic pride, but not without reason, that the conceptions which his régime had of necessity evolved, had come to be adopted by the Soviet Union. Khrushchev certainly wooed Tito, and was ready enough to acknowledge for the Yugoslavs (and the Chinese – both of whom had already acquired it in fact) the right to their own socialist ways; but this was done in order to consolidate the weakened Soviet hold over the satellite states.

Khrushchev's estimation of Tito was not, however, entirely to the taste of the other East European Communist leaders: 'de-Stalinization' discredited them, who had so faithfully toed the line, and once again gave the place of honour in their family to the ambitious, prodigal, and unrepentant son. If they followed the new line, they were bound to erode the basis of their own authority, which was Stalinist and anti-Titoist. If they did not, they risked facing an opposition which could claim to be both Titoist and faithfully Kremlinist. Of Yugoslavia's Communist neighbours, the Romanians found it least difficult to conciliate the restoration of traditional friendship with adaptation to the new Soviet model. The Bulgars, in spite of strong reservations, both ideological and nationalistic, agreed to drop their claims on Macedonia, and to acknowledge the existence of ethnic Macedonians – even in their own country. Dimitrov's successor, the once Stalinist and anti-Titoist Chervenkov, stepped down. Bridging the gap with Hungary was more difficult, for the leadership there was divided, the once Stalinist and anti-Titoist leader Rákosi remained in charge, and the partisans of effective de-Stalinization looked to Tito, who wanted Rákosi removed. With the Albanians, relations remained frankly bad, for their leaders were apprehensive lest they should again be made to pay the price of Yugoslavia's special position in the Communist camp.

For Tito, Yugoslavia's reconciliation with the Soviet Union on equal terms was not only useful, in that it brought hope of regaining a leading position in the international Communist movement: it was also necessary, to end the complete confusion which had spread within his own Party. The ideological level of Yugoslav Communists was generally low. Instructed to switch from intimidation to persuasion, but to carry on in leading the fight for socialism, and against Western ideas, at a time when friendship with the West was being fostered, and the Soviet Union denounced for practices which had been their own, few could find their bearings. Some of them viewed the changes without enthusiasm, and ignored them. Others took them up with enthusiasm, and read into them more than was intended. Many, baffled, sank into passivity.³² Outside the Party, many people felt freer (too free, some believed) to relax.

Towards the end of October 1953, a series of articles by Milovan Djilas, on the future of the Party, began to appear in the Party organ, *Borba*, and they continued throughout November and December, until the middle of January 1954. The author argued that, since the class struggle in Yugoslavia had been successfully brought to an end with the liquidation of all effective enemies of socialism, the country was entering the post-revolutionary phase. In such conditions, the dictatorship of the Communist Party was not only obsolete, but dangerous, for its now meaningless bureaucratism could only hinder the development of socialist democracy, without which self-management could not prosper. 'If it is to survive, the revolution must transform itself into democracy and socialism.'

Djilas's articles were received with ever-increasing enthusiasm. They caught the imagination of people, both within and outside the Party, and, coming from so important a source,³³ they were taken to be official doctrine. For many within the Party who would not otherwise have shared such advanced ideas, they had to be accepted, at least for the time being, as the new line. For many more Communists and non-Communists, it was the sign that things were indeed beginning to change. Everywhere, people began to give rein to their long-repressed wish for political expression. Djilas had coined the term 'socialist democracy' in an election campaign speech of the spring of 1950. He had conceived the idea of workers' self-management. He had been the main impulse behind the changes. He believed in them integrally with the continued faith of a Communist

³² In 1953, 72,000 members were expelled, and 32,000 resigned; total membership fell from 779,000 to 700,000.

³³ Still only forty-two years old, Djilas had been a member of the Party's Political Bureau since before the war. As minister in charge of propaganda after the war, he had made for himself the reputation of a fanatic whose hatred of the West was second only to his love for the Soviet Union. He was, with Kardelj and Rankovich, at the top of the hierarchy, just behind Tito. One of the four deputy chairmen of the F.E.C., one of the six members of the L.C.Y.'s secretariat, he had no routine administrative duties, but was the régime's leading propagandist. At the end of December 1953, he became, moreover, president of the newly elected Federal People's Assembly.

and of a revolutionary who wanted them carried to their logical end, once the old order had been destroyed, if political power was not to become an end in itself. That Djilas wanted to force the issue now seems obvious, and only Tito could have prevented him from so doing, but Tito, during these critical weeks at the end of 1953, was away in his castle in Slovenia. The *Borba* articles were a *crescendo*; the more that were published, the more difficult it was to bring them to an end without embarrassment.³⁴ When, in the January issue of his magazine *Nova misao*, Djilas published a ferocious satire of life in the new aristocracy of the higher Party circles,³⁵ the scandal it caused precipitated a crisis. A ban was placed on any further publishing, and the Central Committee was called to examine his case.

The Central Committee of the L.C.Y. met on 16 and 17 January 1954. Djilas was accused in turn of mysticism, existentialism, political pornography, reactionary deviation, and revisionism. Only Vladimir Dediyer, head of the Central Committee's press and propaganda section, and Djilas's divorced wife, Mitra Mitrovich, ventured, if not to defend the accused, at least to explain his stand. 'I was the first to speak of the withering-away of the Party,' Tito explained,

> but I did not say it should happen within six months, or one year, or two years. . . . Before socialist consciousness has permeated all layers of our population, there can be neither a withering-away, nor a liquidation of the L.C. . . . The class struggle does not come to an end with the armed struggle. It is a lengthy process which lasts all through the construction of socialism, until we arrive at the higher stage of communism – a very lengthy process indeed, and various hostile forces will oppose and obstruct us in the most diversified ways, especially if we take into account the strength of Western influence.

Finding everyone arrayed against him, Djilas gave in: he admitted his errors, and was unanimously expelled from the Central Committee.

In order to prevent one of the group from leading part of the L.C.Y. into the heresy of pushing their new version of communism to its extreme logical conclusion, the other Yugoslav leaders resorted

---

³⁴ One can only list suppositions as to why Tito did not intervene earlier: he trusted Djilas, and did not realize how far he would go; he did not bother to read the drafts of the first articles; he wanted to test the ground with Djilas's articles, in order to see how far one could safely advance with reforms; he wanted to open Djilas's eyes to the difficulties of further reform; he distrusted Djilas's reformist zeal, and wanted a pretext to eliminate him; he thought that the reforms had gone too far, and wanted a pretext to restore order; he wanted to make a scapegoat of Djilas, to facilitate reconciliation with the Soviet Union.

³⁵ This later appeared in English as *Anatomy of a Moral*, London, 1959.

to the only method they knew: the Stalinist practice of morally discrediting the dissenter before condemning him. The publicity given to the proceedings (they were broadcast, and also reported verbatim in the press) and the mildness of the punishment were, nevertheless, characteristic of the effort made to use the old methods only in so far as this was deemed necessary. Djilas was not prosecuted, nor even expelled from the Party. He resigned his official positions, his constituents deprived him of his seat in parliament,[36] and he retired into private life, where he was ostracized. When even Dediyer joined in condemning him,[37] Djilas resigned from the Party.[38]

Djilas's sympathizers within the L.C.Y. must have represented as great a force as the antipodal pro-Cominform tendency in earlier years. Furthermore, his ideas also appealed to many younger people outside the Party who, almost a decade after the establishment of the régime, and following Stalin's death, no longer feared or hated communism as their elders did. But his calm acceptance of his disgrace can only have discouraged any potential following. When, at the end of 1954, he recovered and attempted to resume the fight, he did so divested of all influence on the Party, and with Dediyer as his only supporter. The two of them had to turn to Western newspapers in order to be heard, and so exposed themselves to the accusation of seeking support from the class enemy.[39] A campaign was started to denounce them as traitors, while they were put on trial *in camera* for 'hostile propaganda'. In January 1955, they received suspended prison sentences – eighteen months for Djilas, and six for Dediyer. Feeling that it had to resort yet again to Stalinist practice, the Yugoslav government still did it as lightly as possible.

There had been a real attempt to experiment with persuasion, accompanied by no less real warnings that the new ways could be checked if they proved too slippery. The attempt had caused much confusion. Within the Party, and right up to the very top, some had wanted to take the experiment to its extreme limits. Diplomatic, economic, cultural, and even military, contacts with the West had

[36] Less than two months earlier, they had returned him with a 98·8% majority, which was higher even than Tito's 97·7%.

[37] Maclean, *Disputed Barricade*, p. 428.

[38] For Djilas's version of his political 'trial' before the Central Committee, cf. his *The Unperfect Society – Beyond the New Class*, London, 1969, pp. 172 seqq.

[39] Maclean (ibid., p. 434) says that Djilas and Dediyer petitioned Tito to be allowed to found a new political party based on socialist principles. Dediyer complained to *The Times* correspondent that he had been submitted to pressures, and taken to task for not boycotting Djilas. The latter then told the *New York Times* correspondent that he wanted a second, socialist party, to compete with the L.C.Y., and explained the pressures on Dediyer as an attempt to frighten off their potential supporters within the Party.

partially opened Yugoslavia to the outer world. These experiments and contacts had deeply shaken the Party: membership, through expulsions, resignations, and slackening of recruitment, continued to drop, and did so alarmingly.[40] Concessions had been made, partly in order to seek popular support and a closer association with the West, then partly from a realization that Stalin's policies after 1948 were endangering the development of communism as a world movement. With Stalin's death, there was once again the possibility of change in the Soviet Union and its satellites, which could enable Yugoslavia to influence developments in the Communist camp. The reform movement came to a standstill. Tito began to issue, at regular intervals, warnings against the danger to socialist development of infiltrations from the West. In May 1954, the tenth anniversary of the foundation of the security police was celebrated with emphasis, and in the following four years, there were almost 2·2 million cases of imprisonment by simple 'administrative' decision, that is to say without trial.[41]

In the economic sphere as well, the more flexible policies introduced in the early fifties did not develop quite as envisaged. The year 1954 brought a greater emphasis on agricultural production, to the point of making some credit, however limited, available even to private farmers. The socialized sector, however, continued to receive the lion's share of what the government did grant to agriculture, at the same time as it developed its role as intermediary between the private agricultural producers and the consumer. From those smallest holdings which yielded no marketable surplus, or could not even provide subsistence for a whole family, the young took industrial employment for additional income, leaving the land to be worked by progressively fewer and older relatives. By the end of the decade, labour had become a critical factor on these very small farms, and many of their owners were ready to sell or lease out. This opened up a new avenue of growth for the socialized sector, but it also left much arable land uncultivated. Production was getting more costly in the minority socialized sector, while it remained difficult in the majority private sector.

In industry, vested interests, irresponsibility, and ignorance distorted the reforms. The network of unqualified managers, who had

[40] In 1954–55, 273,000 members were expelled; total membership dropped to 636,000 at the end of 1955.
[41] According to a statement by President Tito to the F.E.C. (*Borba*, 20 April 1958). The return to police methods, and the ideological disappointment of the Djilas anti-climax, help to explain the sudden rise in the number of people who escaped from Yugoslavia in the next few years (3,700 in 1954, 3,600 in 1955, 11,000 in 1956: Knežević, art. cit., part ii, in *Poruka*, 55–6, p. 14).

been rewarded for political services, with all their connexions and protections, often meant that little more than lip service was paid to real workers' management. What interested most workers, anyhow, was participation in profits rather than participation in management.[42] When (and in so far as) it got under way, decentralization had unexpected negative results. As wages had been linked to prices in ratios fixed by the government for every industrial sector, prices continued to be boosted by enterprises even, and especially, after the limitation brought to the distribution of profits in 1952. The passage from state to 'social' ownership reduced the feeling of respect for property which belonged to everyone, yet to no one in particular. Social management and decentralization was accompanied by a lowering of social discipline at work. Local authorities, with their independence increased, often favoured uneconomic prestige investments and Party politicians, now more anxious to please local interests, protected those enterprises which had been set up to satisfy political ambitions, or reward services.

Thus in 1954, the government began to tighten the controls again, in the economy as in the political field, and to seek corrections to some of these flaws – in matters of wages, prices, foreign exchange, and investment. Wages were then included among the costs of enterprises, and thus fixed independently of prices, the proportion of the profits which could be distributed as bonuses was reduced, and in 1956, commune and trade union were brought in as legal partners with the enterprise for the contracting of wages. The government decided to fix the prices of some final products – a measure which affected mainly industrial and wholesale prices but which, by 1956, extended to 52 per cent of home-produced raw materials and 27 per cent of gross industrial production.[43] Participation in foreign trade was limited to registered firms and, by 1956, all export enterprises were made to surrender to the National Bank practically all their foreign earnings. Banks were given a major role in credit and investment policies, by administering investment funds, by controlling the estimates of future profits, and by checking the utility of projects for which credits were sought. Whereas the National Bank henceforth combined the functions of a central bank with those of a department of the budget, and those of a commercial bank, communal banks were instituted to act as local budget offices and commercial banks. Specialized banks were also created for

[42] The average worker's part in the self-managing process was reduced to voting – often not even that. He was not prepared to stay on after work for meetings, and thus not only did not participate, but knew little or nothing about the mechanism of participation, especially when he lived far away, in the country.

[43] Sirc, in Seldon (ed.): op. cit., p. 147.

carrying out the government's credit and investment policy in particular sectors.

Starting in 1954, enterprises were encouraged to group themselves into vertically linked organizations, not unlike the corporations of Fascist Italy. Voluntary at first, membership of these chambers became obligatory in 1958. They provided the government with a good communications network, and were soon assigned semi-official functions in preparing and enforcing governmental regulations.

By 1956, something had been achieved. In agriculture, the total area of land available had finally caught up with the devastations of the war,[44] but little had been done to intensify its use or to overcome the distrust of its users. Although a basis had been laid for an improvement in production, it was still so fragile as to be at the mercy of climatic conditions, and the output could not rise above pre-war levels. Industrial output had risen by 62 per cent since 1953,[45] but this resulted from the completion of many plants started in the Stalinist era, and from the restored availability of machinery and raw materials – all of which had been made possible by foreign assistance. Many of the new industries produced goods which were still of low quality, yet expensive, because based on imports, and which could be exported only with government subsidies. Neither devaluation nor tighter import controls had been able to arrest the constantly increasing trade deficit. Agricultural stagnation made Yugoslavia a net importer of foodstuffs, and the structure of its industrial production made it import to produce goods which it found difficult to export.

At least geographically, an effort had been made to invest money where it would give best results, and so, generally speaking, the more advanced northern regions had continued to develop, rather than the backward south. Left to operate freely, decentralization would have acted against the backward regions, whose poor resources and structures did not generate much profit for investment. These were all, however, regions which the government was anxious not to antagonize. Macedonia and Kosovo could not be made to feel like foster-children of the Yugoslav federation lest they should look to Bulgaria and Albania. On the other hand, Montenegro, Bosnia-Herzegovina, and the poorer, Serbian-inhabited belt of Croatia had provided Tito's movement with many good fighters during the war, and his government with many loyal servants since. For different reasons, the government was anxious that these should not be antagonized. Feelings in some of these regions were already sore, and agrarian unrest had been serious there in 1950, particularly in the

[44] Hamilton, op. cit., p. 126.
[45] Ibid., p. 123.

'have-not' Serbian belt of the otherwise 'have' republic of Croatia. The central government thus allocated part of its General Investment Fund for guaranteed free investments, to finance plants in the backward areas. Decentralization of the economy, however, by thrusting new responsibilities on regional and local organs of authority, encouraged the reappearance of the hidden sectional national feelings at many levels, and not least within the Party. Thus the national problem soon emerged once again, combining old emotional feelings with new economic grievances.

A reconciliation difficult to consummate

A week after Tito had ended his tour of the U.S.S.R., the serious rioting which broke out at Poznań in Poland indicated to the world the extent of the tension which de-Stalinization was causing in eastern Europe. The situation was particularly tense in Poland and Hungary where divisions within the Party leadership enabled public pressure to be felt. It was with neighbouring Hungary that Tito was more particularly concerned. In July 1956, in order to try and satisfy the Yugoslav president, Rákosi had been replaced by Gerö – a compromise which removed a once Stalinist and anti-Titoist leader, but did not replace him by Nagy, the reformists' candidate. By early September, however, the deteriorating situation made it necessary for the Soviet Central Committee to remind satellite Party leaders, by a secret circular, of the Soviet Party's leading role, and to warn them that to follow the Yugoslav example might be dangerous.

On 19 September, it was announced that Khrushchev had suddenly arrived in Yugoslavia for a holiday with Tito at Brioni, and then, no less suddenly, came the news that he had left, with Tito, for another holiday, in Crimea. Tito had come to know of the secret circular, and had been shocked. Furthermore, he had not been satisfied with the choice of Gerö in Hungary. Khrushchev found it necessary to come and personally explain his reasons to Tito. Gerö also joined them in Crimea. Khrushchev, clearly, had asked Tito to meet him, and accept a compromise over Hungary which would help to stabilize the situation there. By his return, on 5 October, Tito must have agreed to Khrushchev's suggestion, for less than ten days later, Gerö arrived in Belgrade at the head of a Hungarian delegation, to settle all outstanding questions with Yugoslavia.

Throughout the summer and autumn of 1956, Khrushchev and Tito were in close contact over developments in the satellite states.

The Yugoslav leader was consulted on questions which did not directly concern Soviet-Yugoslav relations. Khrushchev needed Tito's help, and this gave the latter, once his position in relation to the Soviet Union had been recognized and accepted, the possibility of influencing his neighbours. On returning to Belgrade in October 1956, Tito must have thought that he stood a fair chance of attempting anew to realize his ambitions of regrouping the Communist states of south-east Europe around Yugoslavia, for Bulgarian and Romanian delegations came to Belgrade, as well as Gerö's Hungarians.

Both Khrushchev and Tito were anxious for the de-Stalinization process to be ordered and channelled. If Tito agreed to resume relations with the satellites without insisting on their first purging themselves of Stalinists, this allowed him to influence them, yet at the same time, they remained under Soviet control. Struggling with Stalin's heritage, the Soviet leaders were in search of practical solutions for the problems they were faced with, and they were not all of one mind. Khrushchev needed Tito's help to back him up against his more conservative colleagues in the Kremlin who, on their side, were supported by the old-line Stalinists in eastern Europe. He must have had some plan of his own to channel de-Stalinization, one which unavoidably entailed some amount of reorganization, in order to maintain Communist rule and overall Soviet supremacy. On the other hand, Tito needed Khrushchev, and the Soviet Union, in order to restore the foundations of his own Party's faith, and be accepted by the leaders of other parties. He believed, however, that after the Belgrade and Moscow declarations, the Soviet leadership had completely accepted his own answers to their problems – a polycentrist system of equals, with Belgrade and Peking, along with Moscow, first among equals, a more flexible system which would reinforce Communist rule and the Communist movement, restore Yugoslavia to a leading position in it, and increase its international appeal.

There was much misunderstanding, not only between Tito and the Soviet Union, but also between Tito and the satellites. Before 1955, the Yugoslavs had done much to publicize their reformed system, although what they 'promoted' was not so much what was actually being carried out in Yugoslavia, as its ideological justification. What they wanted was to give themselves more importance in the world Communist movement, and attract more attention. As soon as they envisaged the possibility of extending their influence over East European governments, they became less interested in promoting their model. Yugoslav propaganda, however, had been successful to the extent that the model was, by that time, taken most seriously in the satellite states. Reformists looked to it, Stalinists dreaded it. This could be dangerous for the L.C.Y., for in both Poland and Hungary, public feeling backing the reformists was increasingly anti-Russian, and even anti-Communist. Events were moving fast. At the end of October, Polish reformists won the day with Gomułka's return to power, and proceeded to carry out a controlled revolution. In Hungary, on the day that Gerö returned from Belgrade, Nagy was swept into power by a popular movement which quickly turned against both Russia and communism.

People in Yugoslavia were seized with emotion. There was widespread sympathy for the Hungarian insurrection, even among some of the Communist rank-and-file, whereas others panicked. The government was frightened by the turn of events which had actually started an anti-Communist revolution across the northern border. Tito's contention, that more autonomy for local ruling parties would not lead to the setting-up of anti-Soviet or even anti-Communist régimes, was being disproved. His attitude towards Hungary changed as soon as the new government in Budapest announced a return to the system of multi-party democracy.[46] It seems that he was consulted by the Soviet government before it decided to crush the revolution and install a new team. With no assurance that either the anti-Communist revolution or the Soviet military intervention would stop at the Yugoslav border, Tito gave his assent to intervention, and his support to Kádár's new Hungarian administration.

Conservative Communist circles throughout eastern Europe, nevertheless, privately blamed Tito for releasing the forces of bourgeois democracy and nationalism by his talk of pluralism, while in Yugoslavia, the Party was completely confused, and public opinion sided with the insurgents. To preserve at all costs his link with Moscow had been Tito's preoccupation on the eve of the Soviet intervention of 4 November, but, as a result, his position at home and abroad appeared so contradictory that he felt it necessary to give some public explanation in the speech delivered at Pula on 11 November. In it he maintained that Stalinism, rather than Titoism, had caused the insurrection in Hungary. 'Socialism has been dealt a terrible blow' by the intervention, yet this was a lesser evil than civil war and counter-revolution. 'If it saves socialism in Hungary, then we shall be able to say, although we are against intervention, that Soviet intervention was necessary.' On these premises, he both

---

[46] On 30 October, he had written, on behalf of the Yugoslav Central Committee, to the Hungarian Party leadership, to say that it would not be in the interest of socialism, or of the Hungarian people, if the legitimate discontent of the Hungarian people against the errors of the past were allowed to undermine the workers' faith in socialism.

assured Kádár of his support, and attacked inveterate Stalinists elsewhere.

Although the Soviet press, and that of some other Communist states, commented on the speech critically, Khrushchev, preoccupied with internal problems, and acting on the assurance that Tito did not intend to disrupt the system, was willing to push matters no further. Tito, on his side, was anxious to avoid being once again reduced to complete dependence on the West. In July 1957, when Molotov had been expelled from the executive of the Soviet Central Committee, along with the rest of the group generally considered Stalinist, both Khrushchev and Tito considered that they could resume the dialogue which the Hungarian revolution had interrupted.

Each of them still thought that he could win the other over. Tito still hoped that he could influence developments in the U.S.S.R. and the Communist movement through Khrushchev, by helping him strengthen his position. At the same time, he was preparing a new congress of his L.C.Y. – originally scheduled for 1956, and then postponed because of the uncertainty of the situation – as a manifesto of Yugoslavia's bid to participate in the leadership of the movement. As for Khrushchev, he still hoped that he could restore order in the satellites through Tito, and get him to return to the fold under Soviet leadership, by maintaining the close link that had been established, and absolving the Yugoslav leader of any responsibility for Hungary. At the same time, he was preparing a great gathering of Communist Parties in Moscow – the first of its kind since the dissolution of the Comintern – to celebrate the fortieth anniversary of the Russian Revolution, and recognize the Soviet Union's leading role. Kardelj and Rankovich went to Moscow to arrange for a meeting between Tito and Khrushchev. Khrushchev seems to have laid down conditions for renewing the relationship, and consummating the reconciliation initiated two years previously. Yugoslavia could certainly claim to be recognized as a full member of the Communist movement, but after what had happened in Hungary, it was not possible to allow complete equality and diversity for all – even though there was going to be no return to Stalinist control. At least in public speeches during a visit to Czechoslovakia in July, Khrushchev made his position quite clear by giving priority to the unity of the Communist camp under Soviet leadership. He also gave a limited interpretation to the clause on 'different roads' contained in the Belgrade declaration, by saying that there were indeed several roads, but only one general direction – somewhat 'like a big river with tributaries'.

Khrushchev and Tito met in Bucharest at the beginning of

August. As a result, it was agreed that the Yugoslav president would personally attend the November gathering in Moscow at which the ruling Communist parties would sign a declaration of solidarity; an end was put to the public quarrelling between the Soviet and the Yugoslav Parties, while the Soviet aid programme was confirmed and amplified. The impression was given by both sides of their firm intention to reach final unity, whatever differences still remained to be bridged.[47]

For the sake of a full implementation of his participation in the world Communist movement, Tito realized that, after what had happened in Hungary, he had to make further concessions. Gomułka of Poland, who, no less than Tito, had been impressed by Khrushchev's victory within the Soviet Party leadership the previous summer, and who was also interested by the position which the Yugoslav leader had been able to obtain for himself in his own country, helped to bring the latter nearer still to the Soviet first secretary. When the Polish leader visited Belgrade in September, Tito publicly reduced the differences at Bucharest (they were not over principles), debunked 'so-called national communism' ('sheer nonsense'), emphasized the strongly internationalist position of the L.C.Y., and partially acknowledged the leading role of the Soviet Union ('the first country of socialism'). In the following month, he proceeded to give his full support to the foreign policy of the Communist camp. He joined it in the U.N. General Assembly in opposing a resolution condemning the Soviet intervention in Hungary, he recognized East Germany,[48] and backed Poland and Romania in their moves for establishing a neutralized belt between the two blocs.

In spite of all this, the fortieth anniversary of the Russian Revolution did not see the consummation of full reconciliation. Soon after the Bucharest meeting, Khrushchev circulated the draft of the

[47] It is difficult to say to what extent Khrushchev actually laid down at Bucharest specific conditions for implementing full reconciliation, and to what extent he tried, in his Czechoslovak speeches, to disarm the suspicions of which he was the object because of his lenient attitude towards Tito. It is no easier to say to what extent Tito agreed to comply with any new conditions, and to what extent he obtained from Khrushchev an understanding to have the 'different roads' principle endorsed. Later public recriminations on both sides naturally give only extreme, hence contradictory, interpretations of the Bucharest agreement, whereas both men had an intrinsic sympathy for, and mutual faith in, each other, which probably helped them to gloss over differences at a time when they both were anxious to come to an agreement.

[48] No state outside the Soviet bloc had done so. In recognizing the G.D.R., Tito risked serious retaliation from the Bonn government – such as an end to credit and reparation arrangements. In fact, the West German government limited itself to breaking off diplomatic relations.

declaration to be put to the ruling Parties at the commemorative meeting. In a world divided into two diametrically opposed systems, it stressed the need for discipline and the danger of revisionism. Tito had not expected so much. Feeling that the coming meeting in Moscow was being used to press him back into the flock on terms he was not ready to accept, he backed out. He decided that it was not possible for the Yugoslav delegation to subscribe to the document. Furthermore, pleading ill-health, he cancelled his personal participation, sending Kardelj and Rankovich in his stead. On the occasion of the Moscow celebrations in November 1957, all ruling Communist Parties, with the exception of the L.C.Y., signed the declaration circulated by Khrushchev, and the larger gathering of sixty-eight Parties – including the Yugoslav and all the other ruling Parties – signed a manifesto calling for peace, and endorsing the foreign policy positions of the Soviet Union.

Both Yugoslavia and Poland had hoped that China would cooperate in encouraging Khrushchev towards a more flexible relationship among the Communist Parties. Yet however much it wanted equality for itself, the Chinese leadership distrusted Khrushchev's conception of co-existence with the West. No sooner had the Chinese seen the reformist trend in Hungary heralding a multi-party system and neutrality, than they decided that it was time to end all further compromises, both within the Communist camp and on the international stage. They pressed for a return to rigid centralism and revolutionary militancy. They were able to play a decisive part because they could exploit a favourable conjuncture. After the Hungarian rising and its repression, communism had become contested and hated, both within and outside the camp, to the extent where all its leaders – including Tito – agreed on the necessity of drawing together, and were ready to do something about it. When the Chinese called for a strictly anti-revisionist stand and an anti-co-existence strategy, they found a ready audience among Soviet and East European Stalinists. The Soviet leadership, now frightened of being drowned by the wave of de-Stalinization, was already putting the accent on international solidarity, and Khrushchev himself had seen the need to restore order in eastern Europe. The Soviet Union was still quite able to clamp down on its European satellites without Chinese help, and had proved it.

The Chinese leaders, however, considered that the whole approach of Khrushchev to the problems of Stalin's inheritance was a dangerous one, and that Tito had a harmful influence on him. It was they who had insisted on giving the declaration of solidarity an anti-Yugoslav formulation which would make it unacceptable to the Yugoslavs. Because of the impression made on Soviet and East

European conservatives by Chinese firmness in an atmosphere of crisis, Khrushchev had in part to accept the Chinese formulation, which effectively prevented the expected implementation of the reconciliation with Yugoslavia. The 1957 Moscow declaration did not, however, identify Yugoslavia as revisionist. Its formulation was a compromise between the Chinese and Khrushchev, who still hoped to be able to bring Tito back to the fold – on his own Khrushchevian terms, which although they might not be entirely Tito's, were nevertheless not Mao's either.

The Yugoslavs, too, viewed the November 1957 failure as no more than a temporary setback. They were disappointed more by the Chinese than by Khrushchev, and continued with what concessions they could make to the common cause. At the beginning of 1958, not only did they reject charges of being influenced by Western aid, but began to be cautious in accepting it, while Tito again denounced the bad influence of the West on Yugoslav youth. Yet, forced back on their original positions, they also went ahead with their Party congress. In mid-March, a draft programme was produced, and circulated to other Communist Parties. Although this contained nothing new, appearing as it did after the 1957 Moscow declaration, it sounded rather too much like a polycentrist manifesto. Some alterations were made to meet Soviet objections, but its substance remained, with its particularly objectionable condemnation of *both* military blocs. Early in April, Khrushchev informed Tito that no Soviet delegation would attend. The Poles again tried to act as mediators, and failed. The Soviet Party periodical *Kommunist* severely criticized the draft as being 'nationalistic', and the other Communist Parties in turn decided to boycott the Yugoslav congress.

By the spring of 1958, the attempt to close the gap between Tito's and Khrushchev's conceptions of reorganization of the post-Stalinist Communist world had failed – although both men were still determined ultimately to succeed. What Tito does not seem to have realized, is that the relatively great influence wielded by Yugoslavia in 1955–56 had been the consequence of a unique period of emergency, and that for several years after that, as an anti-climax to the emergency, China was wielding that same sort of influence. Soviet criticism had remained moderate until the Chinese launched their attack on Yugoslav revisionism in May. The Peking press attacked Titoism for splitting the Communist movement, and expressed the opinion that the Cominform resolution of 1948 had been 'basically correct'. It was then that Khrushchev gave in, and found himself making pronouncements and taking decisions which undoubtedly went beyond his original intentions. Before the end of May, the Yugoslav government was informed that the implementation of credit arrangements, to the amount of some $285 million, had been postponed. In June, at the Bulgarian Party congress, Khrushchev blamed Yugoslavia for its part in the Hungarian events, and denounced Yugoslav revisionism as 'the Trojan horse of imperialism'. The following month, at the East German Party congress, he called Tito a renegade who had sold himself for American money. Back in Moscow, he used matrimonial metaphors: there had been a divorce, because one of the partners had not carried out his marriage pledges.

Attacks followed from other Communist capitals. It was the Chinese who attacked most vehemently, and it was mainly against them that the Yugoslavs returned their fire. Having been accorded in the summer of 1957 a title of equality not unlike that accorded to the Yugoslavs a year earlier, it was the Chinese who now envisaged the possibility of rising to a leading position in the Communist movement – indeed, perhaps *the* leading position, if they could discredit Khrushchev who had tried to bring the Yugoslavs back. The Albanians joined the Chinese in violent polemics, and took up again the issue of the Albanian minority in Yugoslavia. They feared that they would have to pay the price of a reconciliation between Tito and Khrushchev, and automatically allied themselves with those who seemed most determined to prevent it. Another neighbour who took the chance of raising a burning national issue was Bulgaria – with Macedonia.

The Soviet government certainly made indirect use of such issues between Yugoslavia and some of its neighbours, in order to keep its leaders in their place, but direct Soviet polemics were, on the whole, lukewarm. As early as July 1958, at the very same East German congress where he had denounced Tito as a renegade, Khrushchev suggested that the anti-Yugoslav campaign be kept within reasonable limits. The 'second dispute' never assumed the threatening tones of the first one. The U.S.S.R. was satisfied with Yugoslavia's foreign policy; it refrained from any steps which would force Yugoslavia to seek anew military aid from the West; and interstate relations continued normally. Tito had lost his battle for a major role within the Communist movement, yet Khrushchev's strategy was designed, not to overthrow him, but ultimately to bring him back to the Soviet-led family.[49]

On the Yugoslav side too, moderation was shown. No great interest was felt by the population for the new conflict with the U.S.S.R., and Tito's influence in south-east Europe had deteriorated

[49] 'We and Tito are Communists, and somehow we will settle this affair. It is an internal affair,' Khrushchev told Adlai Stevenson (as reported by Stevenson himself in the Washington *Evening Star*, 3 October 1958).

sharply after 1956. At the same time, the Yugoslav government did not lack information on the growing difficulties in Sino-Soviet relations, and directed its hopes to the day when the Soviet leadership would once more be in need of help. All this made Tito bear Khrushchev even less of a grudge than he deserved, and attribute to the Chinese more than their fair share of blame.

An additional reason for Khrushchev's toning down of the anti-Yugoslav campaign in 1959 was his wish to create a calmer atmosphere before his meeting with President Eisenhower. When the 'summit' meeting proved to no avail, Tito, in May 1960, publicly blamed America for its failure, and the following month, a Yugoslav diplomatic spokesman described the Balkan Pact as having 'effectively ceased to exist'. By that summer, Russo-Chinese relations, and alongside them Russo-Albanian relations, were deteriorating; the Soviet Union had begun to marshal support in view of the possibility of a serious rift. In August, Kardelj wrote in *Borba* a series of articles on the theme of socialism and war which were a detailed criticism of Chinese theses, expressed with humility. The Yugoslav government was, in this way, offering its help to Khrushchev, with words that could make it acceptable should he want to take it up. The offer was not yet taken up, but it was not rejected either, and in September, at the U.N. General Assembly, Khrushchev even met Tito. He announced that their points of view were 'very close on all questions' – which Tito later confirmed to his own parliament.

Nevertheless, in November 1960, a conference of eighty-one Communist Parties which the Soviet leadership had organized in Moscow to discuss the differences with China, ended with another Sino-Soviet compromise, toned against Yugoslav revisionism. Yugoslavia, however, was almost beside the point, for the situation was evolving rapidly in another direction. Indeed, the Yugoslav leadership realized this, for in rejecting the charges, they blamed the Chinese and avoided a direct attack on Khrushchev. The Albanian delegation walked out of the Moscow conference, and thereafter relations worsened between Albania and the U.S.S.R., until the Soviet government, a year after that conference, broke off diplomatic relations. Stalin had not gone that far with Yugoslavia. Needless to say, relations between Albania and Yugoslavia also took a sharp turn for the worse.

During all this difficult period, while the Yugoslav government was seeking for ways to re-establish its position *vis-à-vis* Moscow, or patiently waiting for the moment when it could again be useful to the Soviet Union, it also worked to safeguard its immediate interests. This called for a tricky relationship with the West, one which could help it when it was left isolated on the doorstep of the Communist camp, but did not embarrass it when there appeared the possibility of contacts with Moscow. In 1956, there was in the West, after Tito's tour of the Soviet Union, much criticism of the aid given to Yugoslavia. The U.S. Congress, in July, voted to halt aid to Yugoslavia under the Mutual Security Act the following year, unless the president decided that its continuation was in the best interest of the United States. In October, President Eisenhower decided that it was in the country's interest to continue to provide at least limited assistance, which turned out to mean a curtailment of military assistance in 1957.[50] Increasing Yugoslav criticism of Western – particularly American – foreign policy in 1957 led the State Department to notify Belgrade that the U.S. aid programme was undergoing review. The answer, in October, was that if it was to be constantly reviewed, the aid programme might as well be stopped altogether, and Yugoslavia spared further humiliation. In January 1958 came public announcements from Vukmanovich (who had been placed in charge of the economy on Kidrich's death) that Yugoslavia needed no more gifts, and from Tito himself, that no more military assistance would be accepted. Military assistance was effectively ended by the spring, although American agricultural surpluses continued to be sent on long-term credit.

By the spring of 1958, however, the quarrel with the Communist camp had flared up again, and it did not prove difficult to make it up with the West. One of the aims of the L.C.Y.'s seventh congress was to reiterate Yugoslavia's independence to the West. The Soviet bloc went back on its promises of large-scale aid precisely at the time when a poor harvest threatened disaster for the coming winter. The Yugoslav government again turned to the West, and that summer, asked Great Britain and the U.S.A. for economic aid to the value of some $200 million. Before the end of the year, the U.S. administration had decided on a new aid programme, with loans, and more agricultural surpluses to be delivered either free or on favourable terms. British, West German, Italian, and French credits followed.

The Yugoslav government had been able to obtain Western aid when it needed it, and to reject it when it preferred to do without it, because its Western creditors believed that they could help it financially to remain at some distance from the Soviet Union; but

[50] At the same time, in order to offset this, and encourage Yugoslavia in its independent stand, Eisenhower invited Tito to visit America. Coming as it did in October 1956, the invitation was ill-timed, however much the Yugoslav president had tried to obtain it before 1955. He was able to seize on the uproar caused in America by the news of his expected visit as a pretext to decline for the time being.

for how long would it be considered worth aiding? The Soviet danger did not seem particularly pressing. West Germany had broken off diplomatic relations when Yugoslavia had recognized East Germany. Relations with France were none too easy because of the support given by Yugoslavia to Algerian nationalists.[51]

Several reasons led Yugoslavia to strengthen its connexions with the third world. It wanted to overcome its somewhat isolated position between the two blocs, and to maintain its character as a noteworthy country. It wanted to expand the circle of socialist countries, because its leaders genuinely believed it was possible to find new peaceful ways of expanding communism, and because in a loosened Communist system they could not only find their place more easily, but even a leading role. The third world could perhaps offer an adequate power basis (which had not been found in the Balkans) to force Moscow to take Yugoslavia more seriously, for longer.

As relations with the Soviet Union improved in 1955–56, Tito's policy towards Asia and Africa was in no contradiction with Khrushchev's. Both were interested in promoting the growth of forces fighting for socialism. Yugoslavia's active involvement increased as its relations with Moscow became more difficult in 1958. For three months at the turn of 1958–59, Tito went on a second tour of Asia and Africa, which took him to Indonesia, Burma, India, Ceylon, Ethiopia, Sudan, and Egypt. Frozen out of the Communist camp, Tito needed to promote his image, both in Yugoslavia and abroad, as a leader of world opinion outside the two blocs. Also for fear that the two super-powers would come to an agreement at the expense of the countries that were not in their blocs, he set out to establish a league of the neutralist states.

In order to achieve this, Tito was ready to perform all kinds of services for the non-aligned. He concentrated on Egypt, and by 1960, had met Colonel Nasser on eight separate occasions. He supported his pan-Arab plans, and it was to please the Egyptian leader that he jeopardized Yugoslavia's relations with France in helping the Algerian nationalists. Itself in receipt of aid, Yugoslavia extended aid to more underdeveloped countries, in the form of credits, loans, technical assistance, and study grants at Yugoslav universities. At the 1960 U.N. General Assembly, Tito dramatically took the lead in bringing together the heads of the non-aligned states, to formulate independent and common proposals. Then, from February to April 1961, he went on yet another extended tour through West and North Africa, returning by way of Egypt.

[51] In a press conference in 1959, President de Gaulle had included Yugoslavia among those countries of eastern Europe whose régimes, imposed by Russia, would be swept away if their peoples could express themselves freely.

Yugoslav influence in the underdeveloped world culminated in the Belgrade conference of non-aligned states in September 1961. The collapse of nuclear talks had generated enough tension to provide the Yugoslav president with a first-class opportunity of appearing before the world as the leader of the neutralists. The choice of Belgrade certainly testifies to the prestige that Tito's activities had earned him. The conference, however, was not widely representative of neutral states. It was predominantly African, and Yugoslavia was the only European of the twenty-five participants, selected on the whole on the basis of their none-too-favourable feelings for the West. The Yugoslav government exploited its position as host to give the conference as much of an anti-Western and pro-Soviet tone as possible. Tito's successful cultivation of relations with neutralist states of Asia and Africa had provided him with an important platform from which yet again spontaneously to offer his help to Moscow.

An uneasy period of stricter controls

Characteristic of the gloomier atmosphere in Yugoslavia after 1954 was the pressure exercised on the Churches to prevent them from turning to their account their limited but surviving influence. Associations of clergy continued to be used to promote official policies within the religious communities, and as a check to the authority of the episcopate. From time to time, clerics were associated with a narrow and exclusive form of sectional nationalism, with some form or other of 'hostile propaganda'. In 1954, the Orthodox metropolitan of Montenegro was gaoled on a charge of interference with local elections; in 1960, the Catholic bishop of Skopye was sentenced on a charge of illegal currency deals. Occasionally, an issue of a religious periodical was seized. In 1958, renewed tension with Bulgaria over Macedonia led the government to encourage the setting-up, by a local council of clergy and laity, of an autonomous Macedonian Orthodox Church, to strengthen the framework of a separate Macedonian nation. Although canonical links with the patriarchate in Belgrade were retained, the government had in fact finally succeeded in dividing the major Christian Church in the country, placing a smaller part of it under its close dependence, and using it for its own political aims.

The increasingly top-heavy structure of its educational system – whereby some primary schools in remoter rural areas were actually closing down for lack of teachers, secondary schools remained where the war had left them, and the number of university faculties constantly rose[52] – made the government adopt in 1958 various measures to discourage indiscriminate attendance at universities. A formal entrance examination was introduced, whereas previously the school-leaving examination had been the only matriculation requirement. In spite of this, and other deterrents (such as quotas, compulsory attendance, and periodical examinations without resits), universities continued to be overcrowded. Inadequate grants and living conditions led, in May 1959, to riotous student demonstrations in Zagreb and Skopye, which Tito blamed on 'class enemies from abroad'.

The question of nationalities, too, needed checking, for under a régime committed to disregarding it, the problem was taking a turn for the worse by appearing within the Party itself. With the growing role of the federated units, sectional nationalism had found its framework, and become the one available mode for the emotional expression of dissatisfaction with issues of all sorts – from bureaucratic centralized control to economic differences, through Marxist cultural inspiration and discouragement of religion. Having thus found its channel, local nationalism appeared among artists and intellectuals as well. Socialist realism was on its way out, and no other common Yugoslav foci had been allowed for regional centres to look to, other than at a Marxist, or administrative, level, so that Belgrade and Zagreb had begun to look separately to Paris, Rome, Munich, London, or New York for cultural inspiration, but hardly ever at each other. More disturbing still, such attitudes appeared among the young, simply as attitudes of protest.

This led the government in the middle fifties to attempt, with all due caution, to restore respectability to the cause of 'Yugoslavism', which it had so thoroughly discredited. Such a move appeared necessary, to counteract the combined effects of Moscow- or Peking-inspired internationalism without, and economic-ethnic-regional nationalism within. Avoiding all rashness, prudent en-

[52] Of children of school age, only just over 80% actually attended in 1957–58, and only 60% completed the last four of their compulsory eight years. It has been estimated that, by the mid-sixties, over 70% of those adults who had been made literate since the war had reverted to illiteracy. (This figure, quoted by R. Staar, *The Communist Régimes in Eastern Europe – An Introduction*, Stanford, 1967, p. 228, is based on press and broadcast reports.) In 1961, there were about 20% registered illiterates, which does not account for the relapsed, or the future potential relapses among those children with only four years' schooling. The number of secondary schools had risen from 205 in 1938–39 to 219 in 1959–60. But the total number of university faculties had grown from 23 just before the war, to 56 in 1955, and 77 at the end of the fifties. A sixth university had been founded at Novi Sad, Voyvodina, in 1958. The student population had doubled in the latter half of the decade, to 140,000 in 1960.

couragement was given to the possibility of eventually merging the several existing related cultures into a single Yugoslav culture, thus taking up the ideas propagated by progressive young intellectuals of all the Yugoslav regions in the early years of the century. In 1954, a Council of Cultural and Educational Unions of Yugoslavia had been formed as a co-ordinating body, and that same year leading Serbian and Croatian writers and philologists met to establish the basis of a common dictionary and grammar of the Serbo-Croatian language. In 1958, Kardelj gallantly attempted to justify the effort in Marxist terms, with a new edition of his pre-war work on the Slovenian question. In a lengthy theoretical introduction, he not only criticized the incarnation of nationalism in the several republics, which were simply local organs of government, but introduced the notion of an overall 'Yugoslav socialist consciousness' as a contender for the loyalty of the inhabitants. The year 1958, with the seventh congress, marked the highest point of the careful attempt to create a climate in which some measure of 'Yugoslavism' – this time socialist – could again begin to grow.

No more had been heard of Djilas, who had retired from any sort of activity under threat of his suspended sentence, until the Hungarian insurrection when, in a statement to a French news agency, and in an article published in America, he charged the Yugoslav government with having deviated from its position against intervention in the internal affairs of other countries, and hailed the rising as the beginning of the end of communism – thus indicating the extent of his personal evolution. He was arrested and indicted. The charges were of conspiring against the government and the people, and of helping hostile propaganda. He was tried *in camera*, and given a three-year sentence. Before his arrest, however, he had sent abroad the manuscript of a book, which was published in the West after he had gone to prison. *The New Class*[53] did more than map out his evolution from revolutionary communism, through increasing estrangement from the reality of contemporary communism, to democratic socialism. It was the first systematic denunciation of Stalinist Communist régimes and of their ruling apparatus by one who had reached the top. The author was immediately put on trial for a third time, in October 1957, and his sentence increased to ten years.

Precautions were taken all round, among all categories known not to be following the Party line – disappointed reformist Communists, nostalgic conservative Communists, and non-Communists of one sort or another. In 1957, several Communist or ex-Communist

[53] *The New Class – An Analysis of the Communist System*, New York and London, 1957.

intellectuals (including Dediyer), who indicated sympathy with Djilas, or objected to making up to Moscow, were denied passports, or harassed in other ways. In Slovenia, where non-conforming views among intellectuals had been able to find a relatively more open forum, because of their linguistically limited audience, harsher measures were taken against a few periodicals and individuals. Anti-Communists of different species, some of whom had already served prison sentences immediately after the war, received new ones, for hostile propaganda, or for deeds going back to the civil war.[54]

The case that attracted most attention was the trial, in Belgrade at the beginning of 1958, of a group of elderly gentlemen charged with actually plotting to overthrow the régime. The accused were two Socialists and two academics: Aleksandar Pavlovich, one of the founders, before the First World War, of the old Serbian Social Democratic Party, who had, in the Second World War, been a member of the Central National Committee of Mihailovich's movement, and had already served a seven-year sentence; Bogdan Krekich, a pre-war trade union personality; Milan Zhuyovich, a law professor, whose brother – then living in Paris – had been prominent in Mihailovich's movement; Dragoslav Stranjakovich, an eminent historian, who had also participated in that movement, and had paid for it by being expelled from the university and sent to prison, just after the war. Their specific misdeeds were that they used to meet from time to time to exchange anti-government feelings, that they had tried to establish contacts with *émigrés*, and that one of them had written a book critical of Tito which they had tried to get published in the West. They received prison sentences of four to eight years. It was deemed useful, on the eve of new elections, to discourage potential non-Communist authors of anti-government books from imitating Djilas, or, indeed, from doing anything else by way of political action, however limited.

Since the sixth Party congress, there had been an alarming drop both in total membership and in the proportion of peasants, workers, and young people. Pending the seventh congress, the Central Committee took drastic action in March 1956. It decided to establish 'actives' wherever there had previously been cells which had been discontinued, to start a recruitment campaign, substantially to increase professional Party cadres, and to reopen Party schools for their training. All this was, in a way, putting the clock back to before the sixth congress. By the beginning of 1958, many Party

[54] In 1957, there was a great increase in the number of refugees from Yugoslavia (26,000 according to Hoffman and Neal, op. cit., p. 86; 25,000 according to Knežević, art. cit., part ii, in *Poruka*, 55–56, p. 14), although by that time it was difficult to distinguish political from economic motives.

officials had only too easily and too happily resumed their old practices, and this reversal had generated such discontent, at a time when many feared too close a return to the Soviet Union, that in February, before the elections and the congress due later in the spring, the Executive Committee found it safer to warn Party organizations against bad old Stalinist habits which were having 'extremely harmful political consequences', and also against *petit-bourgeois* anarchist conceptions of democracy, and attacks on socialism disguised as attacks on bureaucracy.

Elections were held in March 1958.[55] At federal level, there were rarely more candidates nominated than seats to be filled, and 'unapproved' candidates were even rarer than in the previous election. Only six out of over 300 federal constituencies were contested, although the proportion was greater at republican level, and the practice was regular at communal level. Only 6 per cent of the electorate abstained from the polls, and Tito himself was re-elected with a 99.3 per cent vote.

The long-delayed seventh congress of the L.C.Y. (the numeration was continued in spite of the change of name) was held the following month, boycotted by Communist Parties – except for a Scandinavian or two – and by Western Socialist parties. Tito, Kardelj, and Rankovich were the main speakers. The Yugoslav president spoke harshly of 'the revisionist and anarchist ravings of that lunatic', Djilas, 'traitor and renegade, who spat at the finest achievements of the revolution'. He denounced Western influence, and limited individual freedom to that which could promote the cause of socialism: 'Anything that in any way opposes this aim is retrograde and reactionary.' Kardelj amplified by adding that 'only those forms of democracy can be suitable instruments of social progress which allow ... socialist relationships to "rest" comfortably.' The Party's new programme stated that 'Communists will continue the struggle to keep key positions of authority in firm revolutionary hands', and Rankovich was able to confirm that a large majority of those occupying such positions were members of the L.C.Y. Measures were taken for tightening the Party's cadres, its ideological and propaganda activities.

In contrast with this strictly monopolistic position at home, for the world at large the congress adopted a broad Djilasist view of socialism. The programme laid down that 'the opinion according to

[55] A more indirect nomination procedure had been introduced. In each constituency, there was a nominating assembly to which every voters' meeting delegated a representative. Candidates were named there by any five delegates, and those names who had obtained the approval of more than 40% of the assembly were submitted to voters' meetings.

which Communist Parties possess the monopoly of socialist development, and that socialism finds its expression in and through these Parties only, is theoretically wrong, and in practice extraordinarily harmful.' Tito, in his address, blamed Stalin's power-policy for the existence of the Atlantic bloc, and Rankovich talked of the right to equality among Communist countries.[56]

Once again, patriotism and partisan solidarity were invoked to obtain an enthusiastic manifestation of unanimity and solidarity behind Tito, who now trod a binary path – one foot in the narrow path of monopolistic communism at home, the other in the broad path of multifarious socialism abroad.[57] Of the thirteen-man Executive Committee elected at the sixth congress, Kidrich and Piyade had since died, while Djilas was in prison. Five new personalities were promoted, thus enlarging the Executive to fifteen: Blazho Yovanovich (head of the L.C.Y. in Montenegro); Marinko (Party head in Slovenia); Stambolich (who had succeeded Neshkovich in Serbia, and had become, after the last election, president of the Federal Assembly); Veselinov (now Party chief in Serbia); and Vlahovich. Veljko Vlahovich, who had edited the Party's press organs, was, at forty-four, by far the youngest member of the leadership. The secretariat was reduced to the survivors of the original tetrarchy – Tito, with Kardelj and Rankovich.

Following the congress, the L.C.Y. entered a phase of intense and widely publicized organizational and propaganda activity. Renewed polemics with the U.S.S.R. helped the recruitment drive, which brought in 100,000 new members before the end of 1958, and thus caught up with the 1952 record.[58]

The lack of immediate success in Tito's policy towards the U.S.S.R., coupled with the relative restoration of order in Yugoslavia, contributed to yet another change of climate before the decade was over. The Yugoslav government was back to a position where it needed to make its rule acceptable. The autumn of 1959 brought an improved revision of the penal code, and before the end of that year, Dediyer was once again in possession of a passport which took him to the West and a new career as a scholar. At the beginning of 1960, in order to re-establish a measure of co-operation with the

[56] At this point, the Soviet ambassador, who attended the proceedings as an observer, walked out, followed by his Communist colleagues, with the exception of the Polish ambassador.

[57] The congress chanted: 'Comrade Tito, we swear to you that we will not deviate from your path.' More than half the delegates had joined the Party during the war.

[58] By the end of 1959 there were 936,000 members. The percentage of workers and young members had been increased, but that of peasants continued to drop.

West European Left, Krekich and Pavlovich, Stranjakovich and Zhuyovich were released on parole. Kardelj, in February 1960, declared that intellectual life should not be interfered with by politics, and in the new year 1961, Djilas himself was freed on parole.

Having come to accept that it would take several generations before religion actually died out, the government was beginning to appreciate that useful and different links could be established with the outside world through the country's religious communities – through the Islamic Community, with the Near and Middle East; through the Orthodox Church, with the Soviet Union, Romania, and Bulgaria, with Greece, with the Anglican world, and even with Ethiopia. Important changes were beginning to take place in the Catholic Church. With the death of Pope Pius XII in October 1958, the accession of John XXIII, and the calling of the Second Council of the Vatican, a new attitude to communism was made possible. On 9 February 1960, on the occasion of his eightieth birthday, the acting president of the Roman Catholic Episcopal Conference of Yugoslavia, Mgr Uychich, received a high award from President Tito. The next day, Cardinal Stepinats died. There was now the possibility of a *modus vivendi* between Catholicism and communism in Yugoslavia, and the way was being opened by the visits which several Catholic bishops had been able to make to Rome since 1958. An intransigent prelate of the Orthodox Church, too, had died in 1957: Metropolitan Yosif. Having pushed through a *de facto* autonomous status for the Church in Macedonia, the government had Metropolitan Arseniye of Montenegro released from prison in January 1960. In May, President Tito decorated the newly elected Patriarch Gherman, successor to the deceased Patriarch Vikentiye. On his accession, the new head of the Orthodox Church had recognized that there was freedom of religion in Yugoslavia, and his words had been reported in the press. The following autumn, the Catholic episcopate submitted to the government a memorandum with proposals for improving Church-state relations. In April, the head of the Islamic Community had likewise been decorated. A new relationship between the political and the spiritual powers could be envisaged, and this was not the least of the factors which contributed to improving the atmosphere in which the next decade was to start.

At the end of 1956, ten years had passed since the first five-year plan had set its aims of heavy industrial development. By then, these aims had been attained for the most part, but far from solving Yugoslavia's economic problems, the achievement had accumulated difficulties – low agricultural production, low productivity, low consumption, high deficit in the balance of payments. The government decided to try and increase the scope of economic criteria while maintaining overall control. In 1957, it introduced a second five-year plan, more realist and more flexible than that of 1947 – following the model established by the annual plans of the interim period. It reduced the proportion of the national income allocated to investments, and changed their pattern, by placing greater emphasis on consumer goods and agriculture. It set itself to ensure a regular growth of national income and of production – by 68 per cent for industry and 43 per cent for agriculture – to reduce the deficit in the balance of payments by increasing exports more than imports, to improve the standard of living, and, so far as possible, to aid the development of the poorer regions.

As some 90 per cent of the total agricultural area was back in private hands, it was essential to allay the mistrust of private farmers, and in May 1959, Kardelj publicly promised them that they need no longer fear collectivization by force.[59] The policy was henceforth one of encouraging co-operation with the socialized sector through the general co-operatives. Fiscal incentives to improve techniques, and the introduction of new types of higher-yielding Italian wheat, added to greatly increased investments and an improved psychological climate, did enable the planned growth of agricultural production, although erratically. The harvest in 1957 was the best since the war, but a drought made 1958 a bad year; 1959 had another record-breaking harvest which more than made up for the previous year, but weather conditions brought production down in 1960, and another bad drought in 1961 reduced it again to pre-war level, making it necessary to return to U.S. assistance and large-scale imports of cereals. Yet on the whole, Yugoslavia was removed from the list of net agricultural importers.

This, however, was at a price, for although the Yugoslav government had publicly renounced forced collectivization, it was still committed to ultimate socialization of the countryside, and the main feature of the new agricultural policy was its concentration on the small socialized sector, which gave growing returns at growing

[59] The ownership of urban real estate, in so far as it had survived post-war confiscations and expropriations, had been left untouched by law, although it had long ceased to be profitable. Owners were allowed only 10% of excessively low rents, and had virtually no other right to their property but to live in part of it, although the sale and purchase of privately owned real estate had been freed in 1954. In December 1958, as an ideological consolation for having renounced the immediate collectivization of rural property, all privately-owned residential houses with (as a general rule) more than two dwelling units, and non-residential premises and sites, were declared social property. In compensation, owners would continue to receive 10% of the rents for fifty years.

costs. The tendency was to pump investments into highly productive state farms and collectives, run at increasing expense, relatively overfertilized and overmechanized, at a time when agriculture as a whole still suffered from overemployment. On the other hand, the individual peasant was given little chance to improve his status. The amount of arable land which he could own was limited to 10 hectares; the prices he could obtain for his produce declined relatively to the cost of manufactured goods. There had developed among younger peasants, and those living on the smallest holdings, a desire to escape from agriculture. Many more continued to leave agriculture for industry than industry could, for the time being, absorb, or indeed, in view of the pattern of agricultural production and of the rural exodus, than agriculture could afford. The flow was facilitated by the possibility of combining work in the factory with residence in the village, or even industrial with agricultural work.[60]

Responsibility for the location of industrial growth had been shifted to local authorities and enterprises, by making them participate in the planning process, and, especially, by enabling them to compete for a larger share of loans from the General Investment Fund, while richer communes and enterprises could invest in new plants from their own available funds. At the same time, the government retained sufficient control over investment allocations to direct industrial development.[61] Too many industrial projects were, however, still fathered by a desire for local prestige rather than by genuine economic considerations, which could often be disregarded because of many fixed prices and abundant cheap labour.

In order to help the poorer regions overcome their initial handicap, direct allocations continued to be made from the General Investment Fund, in the form of global subsidies to each of the scheduled underdeveloped areas. Yet such assistance was not always put to best use. These areas were as poor in technical personnel as they were in capital, and their squandering on prestige projects, while in no way confined within their borders, became a source of irritation to the more developed regions, who contributed most to the General Investment Fund, got the least out of it, and felt that

---

[60] Over 2·8 million people migrated from villages between 1948 and 1961. By the beginning of the sixties, approximately half of Yugoslavia's industrial workers lived in rural areas and commuted, and peasant-worker households owned almost a third of all agricultural land (J. Halpern, *A Serbian Village – Social and Cultural Change in a Yugoslav Community*, rev. edn, New York, 1967, p. 317).

[61] After 1957, 42% of industrial investments still came directly from central government sources, and with the added indirect control of loans from federal sources, the government in Belgrade actually controlled 70–75% of all industrial investments (Hamilton, op. cit., p. 244).

their resources were being wasted. The government thus became more reluctant to continue providing large sums for investments which did not serve very productive purposes. The result was tension between those who thought they were not receiving enough, and those who thought they were giving too much.

The shift of investments from heavy to light industry, greater freedom in production, a qualified increase in the supply of skilled labour and raw materials, added to considerable foreign technical assistance, explain the continued high rate of industrial growth, as planned. This too, however, was at a cost, for it was achieved, to a considerable extent, by the construction of many uneconomic small factories, depending on foreign countries for the supply of technical licences, machinery, parts, and raw materials, producing too great a range of articles, of relatively low quality and relatively high cost, so that new products, to be launched on the market, often had to be subsidized.

To ease foreign trade, a multiple system of exchange rates had been introduced in 1956, from the official basic parity of 300 dinars to the dollar, through various premium and settlement rates, to over 600 for exports. Exports did rise, but it was not until 1958 that they surpassed in value their pre-war level, and imports rose in the same proportion. The Yugoslav government was anxious to increase the share of manufactured goods in its exports, but found it had to undersell them, at best to credit their sale, in foreign markets as well, in order to make their price match their quality. The developing countries of the third world did offer potential markets, but the export subsidies and the large-scale capital projects with long-term credit seem to indicate that Yugoslavia's promotion of its finished goods on the markets of Asia and Africa was ancillary to its diplomacy. However valuable in purely economic terms, the share of the third world in Yugoslavia's trade remained small throughout the fifties – 14 per cent of its exports by the end of the decade, and less of its imports. Eastern European markets, too, had their possibilities, and when trade relations with other Communist countries returned to normal after 1956, the Yugoslav government did envisage them, concurrently with a decrease in certain imports from the West. Thereafter, they certainly contributed a significant share of Yugoslavia's total foreign trade, but they stagnated at about 25 per cent – slightly in favour of Yugoslavia – and were generally disappointing because of their bilateral rigidity.

Western Europe remained by far the most important single trading area, but Yugoslavia's trade balance there was negative, and increasingly so, reaching a deficit of over $65 million in 1958, and of over $72 million in 1959. Yugoslavia's favourable trade balance with eastern Europe and the third world was useless, for it was tied down by long-term credit arrangements or strict bilateralism, and was anyhow nowhere near to making up for the deficit in the West, even on paper. Invisible exports, such as shipping services, remittances by Yugoslavs or people of Yugoslav origin living abroad, and tourism (which, by 1955, had regained its pre-war importance), were beginning to assume a greater importance, but could not yet compare with the trade deficit. Exports certainly rose, but the deficit in industrial trade continued to rise so rapidly that it could not be balanced by the modest surplus in agricultural trade, and by invisibles. Balance of payments problems were aggravated by the lack of gold or exchange reserves. Import of capital goods to build up an industrial base, and imports of foodstuffs to feed the population, had produced a recurring foreign exchange crisis. The Yugoslav government, for a long time, saw the problem as a temporary one which would disappear in the long run, when both industrial and agricultural production had increased to the point where the trade deficit could be eliminated. Rather than attempt to reduce imports, they thus increased both imports and exports, trying simply to increase the latter more. Meanwhile, grants, credits, and loans (increasingly the latter) saw them through. Meanwhile, too, thirteen years after the end of the war, in 1958, personal consumption had overtaken the pre-war level, though not necessarily for everyone. Great differences remained, and their pattern had changed since before the war.

The labour force began to be noticed in the period of the second five-year plan. New regulations in 1957 and 1958 specified the rights of self-managing enterprises and the rights of individual workers. All net profits were left exclusively to the enterprises, partly to be paid into different amortization funds, partly to be distributed as bonuses to employees, the only limitations being the basic wage-scales prepared according to legal prescriptions, a special tax imposed on the enterprise when the minimum wage was increased by more than 60 per cent in bonuses, and discretionary legal penalties should profits not be allocated according to principles of 'socialist morality'. After 1958, the trade unions lost their legally privileged position in drawing up lists of candidates for elections to workers' councils. Yet more than ever, emphasis was placed on their role as the watchdogs for national economic policies, when Vukmanovich, chief economic planner after Kidrich's death, took over the presidency of the Trade Union Organization on Salay's death in 1958.

In so far as they were given freer rein, enterprises again tended to raise salaries. But since bonuses were distributed in proportion to wages, they increased differences between classes of employees, and since enterprises in the richer regions had greater profits to distribute, the system also increased salary differences between regions. By 1960 the accepted span was 1:7, although there were actually cases (as revealed by the press) of much greater inequalities, reaching 1:17. A movement swept through the enterprises, originating from unskilled workers everywhere, and in the poorer regions, in favour of a reduction in the differences; it was resisted by the trade unions on the grounds that it would destroy incentives. This was the cause of the first strikes, which appeared in 1958, as unprecedented, spontaneous manifestations, for which no provisions had been made, and which embarrassed the government.[62]

At the end of 1960, it was announced that the second five-year plan had been accomplished one year in advance. This was hailed as a great success, which indeed it was up to a certain point. National production had increased as planned, but the balance of payments deficit had also increased. The period had enabled significant progress to be achieved – and at the same time it had made the internal difficulties of the system glaringly evident. The compromise between long-term planning and free competition was not always a combination of their more positive features. Enterprises were given more freedom on the market, but they were still protected from the sanctions of the market. In spite of its growth-rate, industry could not absorb quickly enough the excess labour coming from the land, in a country whose rate of population increase[63] was the highest in Europe, save Albania.

The very abundance of cheap labour kept wages down, reduced productivity and employment by forcing unskilled labour to keep two jobs or work on the land as well, and thus increased unemployment. This was another new phenomenon, unknown before the early fifties. The stress on capital-intensive industry had limited the capacities of labour expansion, and the consequences began to be felt at the time when a similar trend in agriculture started a rural exodus: unemployment increased from 67,000 in 1952 to 233,000 in

---

[62] The first strike occurred in February 1958 – a three-day sit-down strike in a large coal-mine in Slovenia, where the pit workers demanded an increase which their workers' council would not grant and their trade union would not support. The head of the Slovenian government, Miha Marinko, rushed to the spot, and alternately threatened and pleaded. After an investigation, the authorities came to the conclusion that the strike was just a spontaneous outburst against wage conditions recognized as unfair, and no action was taken against the strikers who, in the end, got a rise. The Party, however, did take disciplinary action against those Communists who had struck.

[63] 14.7% in 1958, as compared with 10.5% in 1933, with the poorer territories providing most of it: Macedonia and Montenegro over 22%, Bosnia-Herzegovina over 25%, Kosovo over 31%.

1961. The government was gradually closing its eyes to illegal border crossings, thus contributing to the great exodus of refugees from Yugoslavia, which, by the end of the decade, contributed more refugees than any other Communist country except East Germany.

By 1960, the economic integration of western Europe was already beginning to hurt Yugoslavia's exports, and its lack of foreign exchange had become acute. While politically it looked to the East, economically the Yugoslav government had to look West. That year, it decided to appeal to the West for financial assistance which would help it make its currency convertible, and liberalize its foreign trade, in order to be able to draw nearer to the West European economic system. Yugoslavia was on the threshold of new economic reforms.

PART FOUR

Monocratism and Polyethnism

Chapter 6

Reformists and Conservatives: 1961–67

The reforms of 1961

Yugoslavia followed anxiously the movements for economic integration taking shape in both eastern and western Europe. Comecon (Council for Mutual Economic Assistance), the Soviet rejoinder to the Organization for European Economic Co-operation (O.E.E.C.), had in 1960 agreed, in principle, to co-ordinate the long-term economic plans of its member states. In 1959, the six West European states of the European Economic Community (E.E.C.) had made their first cuts in duties paid on imports from one another. To minimize negative effects of these moves on its own exports, Yugoslavia had tried to secure a footing in each camp, and had become interested in international trade organizations. In 1964, it was accepted into a loose relationship with Comecon. More important to Yugoslavia was its trade relationship with non-Communist Europe where it found the best markets for its farming products, particularly livestock. In 1955, it had been able to secure observer status in the O.E.E.C., and in 1959 was admitted as an associate member to the General Agreement on Tariffs and Trade (G.A.T.T.). In the spring of 1960, the Yugoslav government appealed to the West for financial backing to enable it to liberalize its foreign trade, and qualify in time for full membership of G.A.T.T.

By the end of 1960, as the O.E.E.C. became the O.E.C.D. (Organization for Economic Co-operation and Development) with the adherence of the U.S.A. and Canada, it was announced that over $275 million would be made available to Yugoslavia in grants, loans, and credits, from the International Monetary Fund and from American and West European sources, to help its economy adjust to freer trade and convertibility in foreign economic relations.

From January to June 1961, a series of reforms were enacted to that end. While technically leaving the official parity of 300 dinars to the dollar, a uniform clearing rate of 750 replaced the previous multiple rates for all practical purposes of foreign trade. Free trade was allowed for about one-third of imports. Generally speaking, it was intended that fiscal and monetary policies should completely supplant direct price-fixing over the next few years. For this reason, enterprises were placed, in relation to banks, in a position not unlike that in capitalist countries. The banking system was accordingly reorganized to make credit control a more effective instrument of economic policy, with the main role going to the communal banks.[1]

Enterprises were closely linked to communal authorities, who could set up enterprises and provide them with initial capital, dissolve them, suspend their organs of self-management, appoint and dismiss their managers. At the same time, enterprises were to have a much freer hand in disposing of their net income. Having covered their general expenses – including interest on credit and depreciation on invested capital – and paid their contribution to the local and central governments, enterprises could henceforth use their net profit as they wished. The old fixed wages were abandoned as a basis of workers' incomes, in favour of a share in the profits of the enterprise based on productivity criteria fixed by the enterprise itself.

Simultaneously, however, a third five-year plan, adopted in December 1960 to cover the period to 1965, marked a partial return to old ways. While it was now granted that market indications should form the basis for short-term decisions, it was still thought that long-term economic developments should be based on conscious options and planned direction, because of the ingrained belief that industrial development would eventually solve the problems of foreign trade. There was a reversion to stepping up investments in general, more particularly in industry, and even more so in heavy industry. The plan aimed to increase industrial production by 84 per cent, and agricultural production by 42 per cent.

The reforms of 1961 were a halfhearted attempt to remedy the country's economic ills, an experiment which the government wanted to be able to control, so that it should not detract from the long-term aims. Administrative interferences checked market indications of the most effective allocation of resources and, in effect, continued to protect favoured industries. These interferences took the form of refunds, bonuses and subsidies from central and local budgets, reduced interest rates, and the outright non-repayment of bank loans. They created, in the favoured economic sectors, an illusion of profitability, but could only have a negative effect on other sectors.

[1] All enterprises deposited their funds with the local communal bank whose services they used, and it was through the agency of the communal banks that the specialized banks granted credit to enterprises. In turn, communal banks deposited their reserves with the National Bank which ensured that they adhered to the framework of the plan by restricting or facilitating credit. The National Bank itself no longer acted as a commercial bank.

This was notably the case with agriculture, which still employed half the total active population; it led to renewed stagnation in production, and to further losses in the socialized sector.

Credit and investment policies continued to follow criteria more political than economic. A large proportion of investment resources was still in the hands of political bodies. The central government still maintained dominant control over the allocation of funds for the development of heavy industry, to mention only one such important sector. Quite apart from the planned investment pattern, many local authorities and enterprises indulged in reckless, and often uneconomic, investments. The general relaxation of plan discipline, the nervousness arising from the reforms, the competition for easier money, and the thirst for consumer goods all added to such an atmosphere. So much of the enterprises' income was being creamed off for investment in new ventures that there was not enough money left to improve their productivity, and more often than not, barely enough for wages. The Yugoslav economy was producing beyond its means, expanding under-utilized capacities, and stock-piling unsold goods.

Since the domestic economy was not yet able to satisfy the demand for consumer goods, nor yet indeed the demands of the growing industrial structure, imports rose much faster than exports. Soon, multiple exchange rates returned through the back door in the form of rate manipulations to save the policy of exporting highly manufactured goods.

However apathetic and unqualified most workers still were for management, they were interested in increasing their earnings, and given the new possibilities, workers' councils tended to raise nominal incomes out of all proportion to productivity. Often, however, workers had to wait for cash payments until their enterprise had obtained the necessary credit, and meanwhile went ahead purchasing consumer goods on credit. The insolvency of many enterprises was thus hidden by bank advances and unpaid debts.

The action of workers' councils was essentially an effort to catch up with the prices, which had rocketed following the reforms. It certainly contributed to inflation, though its principal cause was the continued issue of money, which grew faster than the national product, and reached the economy through credits to various extra-budgetary funds and banks.

Price controls had to be reintroduced gradually while reform measures were still being enacted – starting in April 1961, and extending until they covered about half the industrial production. They were announced as temporary measures, to check inflationary pressures stemming from the reforms during the period of transition to the new price system. In June, more stringent credit conditions were introduced, while local authorities and enterprises were encouraged to invest in working capital rather than in new capacities, and to set apart some of their revenues as reserves. There was also a certain amount of revision of the policy of aid to underdeveloped regions. The sudden constrictions had the effect of slowing down production, and began to expose the latent insolvency and unprofitability of certain sectors.

Yet inflation continued to accelerate, and with it the size of commercial stock and of the balance of payments deficit. By the spring of 1962, the Yugoslav economy was in a state of serious crisis, a situation angrily made public by President Tito in a speech on 6 May in Split. In July, the Central Committee met to discuss the crisis. Frightened by the effects of its halfhearted attempt at more serious economic reform, the government decided that it was necessary to return to a certain amount of stricter central controls. The plan due to end in 1965 was given up, and a transitional plan adopted for 1963, based on a more modest growth aim of 9·7 per cent, while a new seven-year plan would be studied, to start in 1964. A series of deflationary and restrictive measures were adopted.

Officially, the blame for the inflationary surge was placed on the workers' councils' lack of 'socialist morality' in distributing profits, and as early as April 1962, a law had established, at every level of government, supervisory commissions appointed jointly by the corresponding political authority, the producers' council, and the Trade Union Organization, to control all individual incomes. In fact, this amounted to transferring incomes from the competence of workers' councils to that of supervisory semi-official bodies.

That was also the time to start a campaign against private enterprise. Further curbs were imposed on some of the remnants of private business, such as owners of taxis and haulage lorries. Tito, in his Split speech, made it clear to peasants that, whatever prosperity they could get out of their individual holdings, they should not count on it as a lasting factor, and that they were to pool their efforts. The following autumn, when a 45 per cent increase in agricultural prices was announced because of losses in the socialized sector and of generally low production, private farmers were prevented from benefiting from this increase by a corresponding increase in taxation. Fears were again raised in the private sector of agriculture, and peasants were discouraged from investing in improvements any profits they could have made.

The economic situation continued to deteriorate, for the government shrank from carrying out measures which would make large portions of industry idle. By concentrating on the misuse of the power given to workers' councils, it had merely singled out one of the many reasons for the crisis, and not the main one at that. Indeed, the share of personal incomes in the net income of enterprises was to decrease thereafter, while inflation continued.[2] Inflation had so far superficially mitigated Yugoslavia's economic difficulties, and inflation was not taken all that seriously by the government as long as capital flowed in from abroad. But after 1962, the pace of inflation quickened so much that the danger was envisaged of foreign aid coming to an end.

The working class was beginning to express dissatisfaction with the partial reimposition of political controls, to the point where trade unions could no longer be counted on, to the same extent as hitherto, to act as watchdogs of the economy. It was precisely that minority of the working class which really held self-management in its hands, through the local trade unions and Party organizations, which had most benefited from the relaxation of controls. In so far as these worker-managers aimed at obtaining better wages and more consumption, all the working class stood behind them. By 1964, strikes and unemployment were openly discussed among Communists, in the press and in parliament. Viewed in the theoretical perspective of self-management, factory-workers were striking against themselves, and 'stoppages of work' were thus symptoms of serious defects in the mechanism of the system. However much it was argued that strikes were due to workers' misunderstanding of broader economic problems, or to 'backward' industrial relations in some enterprises, strikes tended to occur mostly in the older industrial centres with a tradition of labour organization and industrial action, and among skilled workers.

Unemployment had steadily risen throughout the fifties, mainly as a result of the generally poor performance of agricultural production which, added to rural overpopulation, led surplus agricultural labour to seek work in industry.[3] Unable to provide enough jobs at home, or to stem the tide of the rural exodus, the government gradually opened the borders to western Europe, where economic expansion created a demand for Yugoslav surplus labour. This was done, at first quietly, in the early sixties, then more publicly when surplus labour

[2] Lj. Sirc, art. cit. in *Review of the Study Centre for Jugoslav Affairs*, 1965, p. 286.
[3] The number of unemployed rose from 67,000 (0·8% of the total labour force) in 1952, to 450,000 (7·1%) in 1966. More than three-quarters of these were unskilled workers, and the highest rates of unemployment were to be found in the least developed regions. Ian Hamilton estimates that, in 1965, there was a 'real surplus' in agriculture of 1·4 million (op. cit., pp. 128–9).

from the more developed regions, as well as skilled and highly qualified personnel, had begun to follow into emigration the unskilled and those from the less developed regions.[4]

The position of the underdeveloped regions had grown more difficult as funds became harder to obtain, and regional disparities in the level of economic development had grown rather than diminished. By 1965, the difference in level between the most developed region – Slovenia – and the least developed – Kosovo – was twice as great as it had been in 1945.[5] Decentralization had not been to the advantage of backward regions. The central government had less money to distribute, the plan of 1961 had cut back on assistance, and what remained of federal aid went primarily to projects in construction.

Industrial production had multiplied sixfold since before the war, but the Yugoslav market itself remained small. It was the least developed in Europe, with the exception of Portugal and Albania – those two economic blind alleys of western and eastern Europe respectively. Half the consumers gained a precarious living from a relatively backward agriculture. The generally impressive growth-rate of the economy – mainly the industrial growth-rate – had been possible because it was easy to produce unsaleable goods, and to erect underutilized factories. It was essential to step up exports, but Yugoslav investment goods were hardly competitive, in terms of either price or quality, and so the trade deficit and the balance of payments deficit continued to grow.[6] In 1964, exchange-rate manipulations, in terms of export subsidies alone, cost the economy 270,000 million dinars.[7] Yugoslavia's debts, by 1965, amounted to over $1,000

---

[4] Bakarich admitted the brain drain in an interview to the Belgrade weekly *Nin* (8 March 1964), when he stated that 110,000 workers, including highly skilled technicians, had emigrated to western Europe (mostly West Germany) because the Yugoslav economy offered them no 'decent prospect'. The Croatian Party leader also added that he believed the government could not stop this economic emigration.

[5] Hamilton, op. cit., p. 138. In 1961, the average *per capita* income in Slovenia was six times that in Kosovo: Frits Hondius vividly spotlights these Yugoslav extremes when he notes that, on the rough and ready basis of the official exchange rates, Slovenia was then more or less on the level of Italy, and Kosovo on that of Thailand (*The Yugoslav Community of Nations*, The Hague and Paris, 1968, p. 29).

[6] The trade deficit had increased from $260 million in 1963 to $430 million in 1964, when the balance of payments deficit was over $166 million. In 1963–64, Yugoslavia did manage to increase its exports to East European countries, but its main trade partners were highly developed countries in western Europe, and however much it forced exports to the latter, imports from them increased more rapidly.

[7] G. Macesich, 'Major Trends in the Postwar Economy of Yugoslavia', in W. Vucinich (ed.), op. cit., p. 216.

million.[8] Some of the foreign loans became due that year, and the dates for others loomed dangerously close.

Economic reforms had started in the early fifties, and yet by the middle sixties, Yugoslavia faced all the shortcomings of the post-Stalinist era that the rest of Communist-dominated eastern Europe was facing. In those fifteen years, all sorts of forces had been released in the economy. The government could not afford, for political reasons, to let them completely loose. On the other hand, was it possible, economically, to brake the trend, as had been attempted in 1962? The situation was worse in 1964 than in 1962. Slowly the government came round to the view that the source of difficulties lay not in what limited reforms had been adopted, but rather in the earlier system, and returned to economic reform measures. During 1964, most planning powers were handed over to the regional governments, the General Investment Fund was swept away, credit conditions were gradually tightened, fixed prices were removed, the limitations on the distribution of net incomes by workers' councils were abolished, and the emphasis placed instead on increasing their ability to save.

Party trends and regional trends

If the government's economic policy in the early sixties was half-hearted, and seemed to be going to and fro, it was because the leadership itself was hesitant and divided. It was increasingly evident to many Communists that the political institutions were likely to be affected, sooner or later, by the economic reforms. They knew that the whole system of self-management and direct democracy could not run smoothly along the lines established by the revolution until the majority adhered more or less to the ideology propagated by the L.C.Y. Even in purely economic terms, they failed to see how one could avoid the dangerous increase in the consumption rate which was bound to follow the changes, unless there was such an ideological adherence among producers. The question which they asked was whether the cart was not being put before the horse.

All down the line, changes met with fear, dissatisfaction, and opposition, from those who were concerned with their vested interests, from lower Party functionaries who feared for both their own and the Party's authority, from workers who were not too sure of the possible effects of the reforms on wages and job security. Right at the top, there were those who paid lip-service to the need for change

[8] Sirc, art. cit. in *Review of the Study Centre for Jugoslav Affairs*, 1965, p. 297.

while engaged in delaying manoeuvres. Considerable differences of opinion had developed within the leadership itself, between the reformists – those who wanted more decentralization, more economic change – and the conservatives – those who wanted to tread more carefully and more slowly, or even to go back on what had been started. To the fundamental economic issues was linked that of the autonomy of local governments. The question of nationalities came up for good emotional measure, and personalities clashed. In 1961, the differences crystallized, and the two groups stood face to face. Public rumour and foreign commentators identified the two *chefs de file* as Kardelj for the reformists and Rankovich for the conservatives.[9] Since Tito, who did not usually deal directly with economic questions, had not yet spoken *ex cathedra*, open discussions were carried on down the line.

Before the end of 1961, the economic situation had given the conservatives their chance to press for a tightening of the reins, and Tito came out on their side, because it removed the prospect of a split within the Party, but also because it removed obstacles to a *rapprochement* with the Soviet Union. The previous spring, Soviet-Yugoslav relations had shown signs of improving. In April, it had been announced that the Yugoslav foreign secretary would visit Moscow, and Moscow's East European allies stopped their criticism of Yugoslavia. Defied by China and Albania, Khrushchev could not insist on discipline which he was not able to exact. His confidence shaken by a deteriorating domestic situation, Tito could no longer advertise the Yugoslav model which no one was then particularly anxious to imitate. Both were under attack from Peking for their foreign policy. The joint communiqué issued at the end of Popovich's visit to Moscow in July stated that relations were developing normally between the two countries, whose positions on fundamental international issues were similar.

In October 1961, at the twenty-second congress of the Soviet Communist Party, the Sino-Soviet dispute had come out into the open, and thereafter Chinese support had replaced Soviet aid to Albania. This was Tito's chance to move closer to Khrushchev. He spoke strikingly on 13 November, in Skopye. He stressed the importance of the recent Soviet congress as a contribution to 'progressive development, not only in the Soviet Union, but in

[9] The terms 'liberal' and 'dogmatist', which have been used at times by Western commentators, are both pejorative in official Yugoslav ideological phraseology. Furthermore, they are misleading. Victor Meier has rightly pointed out how 'dogmatic' Kardelj could be in putting the case for reform and decentralization, whereas Rankovich's power approach was so empirical that it could, out of sheer realism, touch on more 'liberal' interpretations (art. cit. in W. Griffith (ed.): *Communism in Europe*, pp. 65–6).

general'. He attacked those in the West who, because of its position at the Belgrade conference of the non-aligned states, had tried to put pressure on Yugoslavia at a time when it was in economic difficulties. These difficulties Tito described in an unprecedented way, for it had always been the practice to minimize them. At the time of the Belgrade conference, President Kennedy had, it is true, stated that in planning its foreign aid, the U.S.A. should give greater attention 'to those nations who have our view of the world crisis', and stronger reactions had been expressed in America. The rift with the West had, however, been deliberately exaggerated. Yugoslavia's internal troubles and its inability to obtain further economic or financial concessions from the West were forcing Tito to accelerate the movement leading to closer links with the Soviet Union – a development he had anyhow been hoping for.

Before the Soviet foreign minister returned Popovich's visit in April 1962, trade relations had been intensified, and credit facilities restored. Soviet tanks, the first to be obtained by the Yugoslav armed forces since 1948, figured in the May Day march-past that year, and at the end of September, it was the Soviet Head of State who visited Yugoslavia. In December, Marshal Tito was again in the Soviet Union to return the visit. Granted the privilege of addressing the Supreme Soviet, the Yugoslav president told the Soviet parliamentarians that their two countries had identical aims, while Khrushchev, reporting on the state of Yugoslav-Soviet relations, delivered to Tito a public testimonial of socialism.[10] On returning home, at a public speech in Split on 29 December, Tito confirmed the identity of aims between Yugoslavia and the U.S.S.R. There was no such thing as 'national' communism in Yugoslavia, he stressed, and he had no need for the compliments paid by certain people to the so-called Yugoslav brand of socialism.

Relations were further intensified in 1963 when it was authoritatively and in several instances stated that the L.C.Y.'s position was within the international revolutionary workers' movement, and that the country's foreign policy was one of co-operation with the other socialist states. At the May meeting of the Yugoslav Central Committee, Tito praised Khrushchev as the chief architect of de-Stalinization, and castigated those Yugoslav Communists who, because of unpleasant experiences in the past, still mistrusted the U.S.S.R. This was by way of preparing the visit of the Soviet first

[10] 'If Yugoslavia is not a socialist country, what is it? . . . I must say that the steps undertaken in recent times by the Yugoslav Communists, by their leaders, in their domestic as well as in their foreign policy, have removed much of what we regarded as wrong and detrimental to the building of socialism in Yugoslavia.'

secretary himself who, in August, came to spend a holiday with Tito, thus rounding off the series of exchanges, and sealing the relationship on the ultimate, personal, and Party level. During this summer visit, Khrushchev praised his hosts' system of workers' councils, and described the *rapprochement* as extending to practically all fields of state and Party relations.

In order to muster support against the Chinese leadership, Khrushchev had had to draw nearer to Yugoslavia, and also to give the other Communist states of eastern Europe some measure of satisfaction. For them, the Sino-Soviet rift was to offer opportunities of relative emancipation, thus giving Tito the chance of playing a mediatory role between them and Moscow. Such was particularly the case with the Romanians, whose relations with Yugoslavia had developed well. When, in April 1964, the Romanian Central Committee adopted its resolution on the 'rights of every socialist state to elaborate, choose, and change the forms and methods of its socialist development', Tito intervened to put things right between his Romanian and his Soviet friends. In 1964 and in 1965, he was busy offering his services to Soviet and East European leaders to help them find their bearings in the new circumstances.

When, in October 1964, Khrushchev had to step down from power, the Yugoslavs feared that it might have been a concession to the Chinese at Tito's expense. It removed the element of personal intimacy with the Yugoslav president, but otherwise Yugoslav fears were soon allayed. In December, Yugoslavia was duly granted observer status in Comecon, as had been announced shortly before Khrushchev's resignation. In June 1965, Tito was in Moscow again, for talks with Brezhnev and Kosygin, Khrushchev's successors, when he obtained the postponement of debt repayments, and additional credit facilities.

Tito had wanted to return to the Communist family which, he believed, had under Khrushchev considerably changed its character, and in order to do so, he had been ready to make extensive concessions. Such as it appeared in 1962–63, the *rapprochement* suited him, for it entailed no hierarchic or organic link, and there really was agreement between Belgrade and Moscow on a whole range of international problems. The arrangement, however, depended on just the right amount of tension between Moscow and Peking. If this became too strained, there was the possibility that the U.S.S.R. might want to press its European friends to excommunicate China, and attempt to discipline its satellites, semi-satellites, and former satellites.

The Yugoslav government was thus anxious not to put all its eggs in the Soviet basket. The West was a useful protective shield in case of emergency, and although considered not generous enough, it generally remained an invaluable source of benefit. Alarm in the U.S.A. at Yugoslavia's apparent realignment certainly reached a climax in 1962, and so did criticism of the administration's aid policy. In the end, all that the opposition in Congress could achieve was a further tightening of the conditions under which the president could extend assistance to some Communist countries, and to deny Yugoslavia (as well as Poland) the most-favoured-nation treatment which it had enjoyed. In May 1963, Secretary of State Rusk went to Yugoslavia to meet Tito and his foreign minister. With some Western states, however, relations were noticeably cooler.[11]

Non-alignment remained the established basis of Yugoslavia's foreign policy. It was the only one acceptable both to those who wanted a yet greater partnership with the U.S.S.R., and to those who desired closer relations with the West. It enabled Yugoslavia, when moving closer to one diplomatic family, to avoid giving the impression that this was directed against the other. It satisfied the pride of the Yugoslav leadership, and of its president in particular. By consorting with, gathering, and touring the non-aligned, Tito with his country continued to attract attention. All this activity culminated in the second conference of non-aligned states which met in Cairo in October 1964. Although the number of participants had risen to forty-seven, they were all Afro-Asians, except Cuba and Yugoslavia, and what had been latent at the Belgrade conference became obvious in Cairo – that most delegates were primarily concerned with their own immediate problems and quarrels. Non-alignment as such was not a sufficient basis for unity of action, except to condemn imperialism and colonialism. Yugoslavia itself had failed to offer India more than polite verbal support against China, as had indeed all of India's non-aligned friends. Similarly, however much they contributed to the glamour of Yugoslavia's diplomacy, its Afro-Asian friends could be of little value to its security.

Of the three contending socialist influences, the Yugoslav was probably closest to the nationalists of the 'three continents'. Yet Tito had been somewhat coolly received in Latin America, and

[11] Relations with France had become more tense. When Yugoslavia extended *de jure* recognition to the Algerian nationalists' provisional government, the French diplomatic mission in Belgrade was shorn of its ambassador. President de Gaulle had never been attracted to Marshal Tito's régime, quite apart from Yugoslavia's interference in what was considered to be a French internal problem, and in his 1964 New Year message, Yugoslavia was again included among the 'Communist totalitarian régimes that still constrain captive peoples'. If friendship with the Soviet Union had improved relations with Bulgaria over Macedonia, it made up for a worsening in relations with Greece: statements again issued forth from Skopye about the Macedonian minority in Greece and its ill-treatment.

had failed to get any of his hosts there to participate in the Cairo conference. Yugoslav diplomacy concentrated on Africa, more particularly on the Mediterranean states and the Left-inclined, whose nationalistic sensitiveness and suspicion of great powers thrived even without Yugoslav encouragement. Yugoslavia, however sympathetic, was a European country with problems very different from those of the African countries. Other European countries that could provide aid without being suspected of political afterthoughts were viewed with no less friendliness – capitalist Sweden and Switzerland, and even that member of NATO and former colonial power in Africa, Italy.

It was Yugoslavia's economic weakness that prevented its influence from being anything more than superficial. The realities of Yugoslav socialism, as opposed to its slogans, were never seriously envisaged by Afro-Asian economists as a practical model for their nationalized or semi-nationalized economies. To bolster its influence, Yugoslavia had to promote trade links which appeared somewhat extravagant in the light of its increasing trade deficit with western Europe. In order to make its socialism credible to those countries that offered Yugoslavia the basis for a continued prominent role in world affairs, it had to put its economic house in order.

To the change in foreign policy corresponded changes at home which belied the hopes with which the new decade had opened. At a meeting of the Central Committee's executive in March 1962, the differences in the top Party leadership broke out almost openly. No documents were published, but heated exchanges were later admitted, and Tito must have come down on the side of the conservatives, for it was then that a certain amount of back-pedalling started in the economy.

As if to symbolize the readjustments in both foreign and domestic policies, Djilas was returned to prison. He had written a book on his meetings with Stalin, and mailed the manuscript to his American publisher. Its existence was no secret, and in March 1962, a Yugoslav equivalent of the Official Secrets Act was passed, whereupon Djilas was arrested and put on trial *in camera* under that law. Another five years were added to his previous sentence, and his book was duly published in America.[12] And yet, only a fortnight before Djilas's arrest, a general amnesty had been announced on 13 March for political crimes committed before 1952, which applied also to some 150,000 *émigrés*. A great amount of publicity, directed to the West, was attached to this act, as if to indicate that the *rapprochement* with Moscow did not affect the continued liberalizing trend in Yugoslavia. The amnesty was intended both to show the stability of

[12] *Conversations with Stalin*, New York, 1962; London, 1963.

the régime, and to destroy the emigration as a political phenomenon, at a time when economic difficulties were forcing a new wave of Yugoslavs to emigrate.[13]

What retrogression there was in 1962 did not signal a reactivation of the whole paraphernalia of mass intimidation which had, since 1950, gradually been put aside. The government intended to preserve the authority to control the scope of such changes in methods of planning and management as economic necessity had pressed upon it. For this it was sufficient, but also indispensable, to restore discipline among all those who might be tempted to separate from the flock, and to remind everybody that the L.C.Y. would remain 'a strong and monolithic organization'. These were the words used by Tito in his Split speech of May 1962, and such was the tenor of all his speeches, as well as of Central Committee pronouncements thereafter.

The reimposition of discipline on the intelligentsia had actually begun in 1961 when a new method of financing cultural institutions placed them under tighter control from social organizations, and when voices were heard from members of the government to warn intellectuals against cutting themselves off from the workers, or questioning the ethical values of the revolution. At the July 1962 Central Committee meeting, Tito personally opened fire on liberal trends in cultural life, and throughout the year, his speeches contained stern criticism of the pro-Western inclinations of Yugoslav intellectuals. The last warnings, couched in terms of quasi-Stalinist dogmatism and quasi-Khrushchevian philistinism, were given at the beginning of 1963, and the authorities thereafter moved into action.

All that year, there were cases of a play being stopped here, a film there, a literary magazine closed down, a novel banned, allegedly for lack of funds, or distortion of facts, or pornography. And so it went on into 1964. The case that caused a real public outcry was that

[13] In 1951, when the first amnesty was announced, Rankovich had admitted to no more than 50,000 *émigrés*. The 1962 amnesty was the culmination of a campaign which had started in June, to convince Yugoslavs living abroad of the need to 'normalize' their relationship with Yugoslav diplomatic and consular agencies, i.e. to resort to their services, and thus lose their status as political refugees. The effects of the amnesty law were more limited than appeared at first sight. In Yugoslavia it applied to only about 1,000 people, in prison for at least nine years (sentenced before 1952). The exceptions were left conveniently vague: the amnesty did not apply to those who had indulged in collaboration, committed war crimes, murdered representatives of the people's authority, or to those who were engaged in action against the constitutional order. A year after its enactment, only 823 expatriates had returned to take advantage of it (*Borba*, 15 March 1963). In May 1962, the law of 1946 under which some 6,000 *émigrés* had been deprived of their citizenship was rescinded, thus doing away with what had been an anomaly in Yugoslav post-war legislation – that of actually removing anyone from the jurisdiction of Yugoslav laws.

of the Ljubljana periodical *Perspektive*, which had been the voice of non-conforming intellectuals since 1959. Its mounting radicalism reached the point of emitting the Djilasist thought that genuine democracy was possible only through the institutionalization of opposition tendencies, upon which it was closed down in May 1964, and two of its editors were held under arrest for a while. Then, in September, young Communist academics of the Philosophical Society of Croatia, in Zagreb, founded *Praxis*, which quickly became the most forward critic from the ranks of the radical intelligentsia, demanding a thorough revision of Marxist thought and practice. Far from being intimidated, radical intellectuals had actually answered back, so much so that, at the Party congress held in December, it was Rankovich who denounced the 'petty bourgeois self-styled champions of freedom' who had lately tried to attract attention, thus implying the threat of methods attached to his name.

In order to fix and harmonize the entire complex of social, economic, and political developments of the past ten years, a new constitutional statute, promulgated in April 1963, both enshrined a political programme and established the framework for one of the most complicated political systems in existence. First canonized in the constitutional law of 1953, socialism was not only reaffirmed, but entrenched all through the new constitution. The name of the state became 'Socialist Federal Republic of Yugoslavia' ('socialist' coming before 'federal'); the League of Communists was recognized as the 'fundamental motive force of political activity for the protection and further development of the achievements of the socialist revolution'; and the Socialist Alliance as the 'basis of the social-political activity and of the social self-management of the working people'.

The constitution designated the 'working people' (an expansion of the concept of 'producers') and the 'nations' (the ethnic entities) as the carriers of the supreme political power. Their sovereign rights were to be exercised through the federation and through the component republics, according to a theory of double sovereignty, no less theological in its diphysitism than the first Yugoslav constitutional theory had been, forty years earlier, in the trinitarianism of its 'one nation with three names' theory. The basic concern of the federation was to safeguard the country's independence, unity, and established order.

The Federal Assembly was turned into a complex, corporatist-type multicameral structure, by the expansion of the previous Council of Producers into four corporative chambers, representing different categories of the 'working people' – the economy, education and culture, social welfare and health, and the administration. The Federal Council was retained intact, along with its incorporated

Council of Nations. All bills were to be considered by the Federal Council, in conjunction with the relevant corporative chamber. The new constitution did away almost entirely with direct elections, replacing them by an elaborate filtering system. The electoral emphasis was completely shifted from the 'formal act of voting' to the nominating process, in which all citizens could participate as members of a commune, while those who were also members of 'working communities' (which excluded private peasants and private entrepreneurs) had another vote as members of their corporation.[14]

Several innovations were introduced in the executive which tended to elevate the position of the president of the republic, and provide him with increased help in exercising his functions. He was given a vice-president of the republic and a deputy supreme commander of the armed forces, a Council of the Federation as a privy council of notables, a Council of National Defence, and a separate chairman of the Federal Executive Council to act as head of the federal administration. Nominated to the Assembly by the president, the chairman-elect in turn nominated the members of the F.E.C., a procedure which made it, according to the letter of the constitution, more the president's than the Assembly's Executive Council. A more important innovation in the president's powers of nomination was that of the Constitutional Court of Yugoslavia – with counterparts in the republics – to act as administrative tribunal and custodian of

[14] In public elections, the procedure began with the summoning of voters' meetings to nominate candidates for communal councils of communal assemblies (formerly people's committees). Nominations were made either at the meeting, by any voter with four seconders, or by a petition signed by fifty voters. The meeting then decided, by a show of hands, on each name thus put forward. The same procedure was applied in corporative elections, at meetings of members of working communities. Voters' meetings also made a first selection of candidates for regional and federal legislatures. As, however, parliamentary constituencies usually comprised more than one commune, these lists were circulated and submitted to other voters' meetings in the constituency. All names accepted by 10% of the total number of registered voters in the constituency were then screened by the electoral commission, to check whether they fulfilled legal conditions, and whether they had been regularly nominated.

The progressive concentration of local government units continued throughout the decade. By 1961, the number of communes was down to 782, and to 501 by 1967. Districts were virtually to disappear in the sixties. Communal assemblies remained the only representative bodies to be elected directly. Once constituted, they selected from among themselves delegates for the district assembly, and from the candidates nominated by corporative meetings they elected deputies to the corporative chambers. Finally, from the candidates nominated for the single-member parliamentary constituencies, they selected those whom they wanted presented to the voters who, on polling day, eventually 'elected' or 'confirmed' according to whether one or more candidates had been presented to them.

constitutionality. All elective functions were limited to one or, in the case of the more important, two four-year terms, so as to bring in younger personnel, avoid the sterilizing effect of permanence in office, and ease the elimination of unwanted personalities. At the top, however, personnel rotation was often, inevitably, destined to be more in the nature of a game of musical chairs.

The first elections under the new constitution were held in June 1963. No great effort was made to provide voters with a choice on polling day,[15] and Tito was re-elected president. The constitution of 1963 virtually made Marshal Tito life president and mentioned him by name: article 220/2 explicitly stated that the limitations of office did not apply to Yosip Broz Tito who, by now, enjoyed quasi-monarchical attributes. He was supreme commander of the armed forces; stamps and gold coins were issued with his portrait; he had an official birthday, celebrated as the Day of Youth; he had the use of a number of palaces, castles, and villas, with the island residence of Brioni becoming a second, secluded, capital.[16] Tito had become a legend and a symbol, as well as the animator of policy. It was he who set the line, whether political or social, economic or cultural, on which others would gloss and amplify. He was above criticism, and people were encouraged to complain to him personally. Like the monarchs of old, he was not responsible for the errors of his ministers and agents.

Having entered his seventh decade in 1963, Tito tended to be conservative, contrary to the legend. Indeed he has often not been as 'Titoist' as imagined. He does not innovate, but rather adopts as his own, integrates, and preserves what innovations are accepted by the

[15] For the Federal Council, there were only as many candidates as seats, and even for communal assemblies, no more than a third of seats had more than one candidate. When half the seats came up for renewal in 1965, the situation was slightly better. At federal level, a few constituencies did have more than one candidate, while at the other end of the scale, at communal level, there were about twice as many candidates as seats to be filled. The most important part of the entire nominating process takes place within the political apparatus of the Party and of the Alliance, prior even to the 'formal act' of nominating. Participation at the polls continued to be massive, though the trend was towards a slight reduction (95.5% in 1963, 93.6% in 1965).

[16] Marcel Prélot, in his preface to Djordjević, *La Yougoslavie, démocratie socialiste*, thus describes Tito's place in the Yugoslav régime (pp. 1–2): 'Comme la personnalité d'Ataturk, celle de Tito domine le régime: il est, lui aussi, le "Victorieux", le "Libérateur"; il est le chef de l'armée, objet de tous ses soins; il est l'homme qui a tenu tête à Staline et qui a le premier dénoncé ses propensions dictatoriales; il est le diplomate que les chancelleries sollicitent et que les capitales attendent; il est surtout le chef du parti unique qu'il tient fortement en ses mains et dont lui-même dirige l'appareil. Au vrai, toute la politique yougoslave dépend de lui, y compris la composition et l'orientation des assemblées auxquelles il est, en principe, soumis.'

leadership as a whole. His is the last word, or the first, when state policy or his own interest wants it. Because of his ever more elevated status, because of the increasing complexity of the affairs of state, because of his age as well, Tito began to withdraw from the day-to-day running of business. Like some Eastern counterpart to General de Gaulle, he had his *domaine réservé*, which included foreign policy, world affairs, and the prestige of Communist Yugoslavia, but not the economy.

After him, Kardelj and Rankovich had second place. At the time of the enactment of the new constitution both were in their early fifties, both were secretaries of the L.C.Y., both were vice-chairmen of the F.E.C., both were survivors of the original team. In 1963, they were given the two second highest functions in the state, Rankovich the vice-presidency of the republic, Kardelj the presidency of the Federal Assembly. There had been no hint of Tito's possible retirement, and he was irreplaceable, but many foreign observers interpreted elements of the new constitutional arrangements in the light of the succession problem, and placed the odds on Rankovich, since Tito had sided with the conservatives.

The total Party membership had, in 1964, fallen to 1,019,000 from its 1961 peak of 1,035,000 as a result of the purges in the drive for more discipline. Long-standing members still provided the backbone for the ruling element, hence the real need for rejuvenation. The emphasis of the eighth congress of the L.C.Y., held in December 1964, was thus placed on youth. The average age of the delegates was down to 35.9. Salay had died since the previous congress, and Leskoshek (67) retired from the Executive Committee for no other reason than to make way for younger people: six new members, aged between 43 and 51, were added to the remaining thirteen. Right at the top, Tito (71), Rankovich (54), and Kardelj (53), brought in Vlahovich (49) to join them in the secretariat.

This was an undramatic congress, attended for the first time by delegations of the Soviet and allied Parties, and concerned mainly with domestic questions. Even Tito's opening address (greeted by chants of 'We are Tito's; Tito is ours'), although it criticized the Western powers and China, dwelt much more on the problems of self-management, complicated by those of nationalism, and tried to steer a middle line between the individuality of the several nations and their unity. New statutes were adopted in an effort to adapt the Party to new conditions without diminishing its monopoly of control over the decision-making process. Personnel rotation was to be introduced in Party functions as well. Members were authorized to hold, and manifest, opinions contrary to decisions adopted, as long as this did not slow down their implementation, and the former provision that members should not belong to any Church was dropped.

The attempt to encourage the gradual blending of the several related cultures had met with resistance, and so strong had been the reactions to any centrally sponsored 'Yugoslavism', however socialist, that the government, in the early sixties, had been forced to retreat, under pressure from local leadership in the republics. Certainly because Serbo-Croatian was the language spoken by about three-quarters of the population, and the *lingua franca* for the whole country, Slovenes and Macedonians feared they would be handicapped. Moreover, because there were more Serbs than Croats, the latter again complained of the former's cultural hegemony. Yet it was not cultural particularism, but rather the decentralization of the power-structure, coming on top of the economic differences, which had led to rivalry between territorial units.

Yugoslavia, in terms of economic development, presents a sharp contrast between north and south which, in Europe, can only bear comparison with that of Italy. The 'economic north' comprises the area north of the Sava and the Danube, with the Morava-Vardar axis, and the more important coastal ports as southern appendices. It has better infrastructural facilities, and commercially more viable production units, which often go back to before the war, and which have in turn facilitated greater expansion in a naturally better-endowed agriculture, in transport, trade, and services. The south, besides poorer agricultural resources and a higher rate of population growth, has extractive and basic processing industries which give lower-value products, employ fewer skilled workers, and expand less rapidly than manufacturing industries.

With decentralization, local Party leaders had gained more responsibility, and wished to be supreme within their own territories, especially in the richer regions where they were less dependent financially on the central government. It was only in the early sixties that the idea arose of the regions performing significant economic functions, and in 1964, many such functions which had previously belonged to the federation or the communes were handed over to the republics. Many particularistic forces stemmed precisely from the transitional, compromise character of the economy. The completely centralized command had been dismantled, and yet the economy had not been freed from political control. Partially controlled, and partially market-orientated, it had become partially controlled by a decentralized political structure, and partially orientated towards territorially limited markets.

The richer republics wanted to retain as large a part as possible of the national product produced in their areas, and as much as possible of the state revenues for use within their borders, so as to increase their self-sufficiency. The poorer wanted to duplicate economic facilities in reckless disregard of feasibility and of their own resources, hence their demand for more federal aid, at a time when there was less of it to be had. These economic and local-power rivalries turned for support to the existing nationalistic feelings, raising economic differences to the level of questions of national honour, while pent-up local feelings found new channels in which to flow. The two fed on each other.

National feelings clashed when there was controversy among the republics over the allocation of investment funds. They all had in common their dissatisfaction with the centre. Having given up its short-lived and discreet attempt to return to the concept of an over-all Yugoslav, albeit socialist, consciousness, the central government was left with no clear-cut policy to deal with the problem of relations between the several existing and multiplying nationalities,[17] except for the continued development of socialism which, in that field, was at best only a very long-term policy.

Serbia, which represented the average Yugoslav level of development, had no particular economic grievance. The complaint there was rather one of national neglect, that everything which expressed Serbia's tradition had been curtailed in order to satisfy the other units. Serbian feelings fed on nostalgia and empty romanticism, expressed mostly in emotions and words. Local leadership did not develop as much as elsewhere, because it was too near the central leadership and tended to look up to it, with the result that the conservatives at the centre, in so far as they were Serbs, made use of such dissatisfaction for their own ends.

In Croatia, too, there was emotional nationalism, of a type which fitted into the tradition of dissatisfaction with higher-level government in distant capitals. But Croatian particularism had been discredited after the war, and pressures against it had been stronger because it was considered more dangerous for the existence of a unified Yugoslavia. The older generation had a grudge against the Serbs in Croatia and in Bosnia-Herzegovina because they, as resisters against the Axis-backed Fascist version of Croatian nationalism, had originally obtained a larger share in the administration of these two

[17] The census of 1961 listed twenty-four ethnic categories. Out of a total of 18·5 million, 42% registered as Serbs, 23·1% as Croats, 8·5% as Slovenes, 5·6% as Macedonians, and 2·8% as Montenegrins. A new ethnic category, that of 'Moslems by ethnic affiliation', was provided, in which were registered nearly 1 million (5·2%) who had previously registered as 'Yugoslavs, unspecified'. The latter were now reduced to 317,000 (1·7%). National minorities amounted to 11% of the total population, with nearly 1 million Albanians and more than 0·5 million Hungarians.

republics than was warranted by their numbers. Yet it was the younger generation, gradually freeing itself from the post-war complexes, who provided support for the local leadership in its efforts to become more economically independent of Belgrade. For Croatia was a richer republic, and complained of being exploited for the benefit of the eastern areas in the interest of the central government in Belgrade.

Yugoslavia is geographically slanted north-west to south-east, and it is interesting to note how the economic difference between north and south is often turned to a political difference between west and east. The complaint against economic exploitation was even stronger in Slovenia, which was both northern and western, even more developed, further away from the centre, and different too on account of its homogeneity, ethnic and religious. Having survived the age-old threats of Germanization and Italianization, and attained Central European rather than Balkan standards, their economic development was as precious to the Slovenes as their ethnic distinctiveness, and the two interacted.

Macedonia and Montenegro had been consciously built up by the régime for reasons of political expediency, and they had drawn great benefits from it. The trend to particularism was no longer the preserve of the larger and older groups. If the Montenegrin national consciousness still existed more on paper than in the hearts of the Montenegrins, and was a disputed fact, that of the Macedonians had become undisputed, and both republics wanted more, not less, federal aid.

In the 1961 census, the Moslems had been recognized as a separate ethnic entity, and the 1963 constitution of Bosnia-Herzegovina expressly named Moslems, alongside Serbs and Croats, as one of the peoples living on the territory of that republic. Like the Macedonian nationality, that of the Moslems was going to fill a void, and give an ethnic label to people who felt neither this nor that. Around this newly acquired status began to pile up arguments about a separate community between Serbs and Croats, grown out of a traditionally Balkan combination of historical and religious factors – Islam and the Ottoman Empire, and before that, Bogumilism and the mediaeval monarchy. Finally, greater efforts were made to get Albanians and Hungarians to feel at home in Kosovo[18] and Voyvodina respectively.

By the end of 1964, the question of nationalities had come to occupy a place in the domestic concerns of the Yugoslav leadership second only to that of economic reform. It had caused divisions

[18] Kosovo remained a problem, for it was difficult to satisfy a minority growing at the rate of 29·6% (1961) in the most backward region of the country, and incited against Yugoslavia by the government of Albania.

within the Party which cut across those between reformists and conservatives. All the measures taken in the early 1960s had resulted from compromises that sought, above all, to preserve unity within the L.C.Y., and they had solved none of the problems.

The reforms of 1965

When, in the latter part of 1964, the Yugoslav leadership decided to return to the economic reform movement of 1961, all the shortcomings of the economy were exposed to the eighth Party congress, along with the benefits of a freer play of market mechanisms. Since the need had been recognized in the early fifties of aiming at economic efficiency, reformists had realized it was necessary to put an end to expansion at any price, and thought in terms of measures to stabilize the economy. The objections of the conservatives were not so much to the economic reforms themselves, as to their political consequences. Indeed, the division was essentially one between economic realists and political realists, with the result that reform measures had hitherto always been half-measures to start with, that they had been incompletely carried through, and that brakes had been applied at the first signs of difficulties.

The promoters of economic reforms now argued that it was not possible to avoid initial difficulties, but that success would be apparent after a transition period, if only the measures adopted were carried through to the end. Just as political necessity had made Tito side with the conservatives three years earlier, so now economic necessity made him accept the arguments of the reformists. After their general framework had been adopted by the Central Committee in June 1965, a new set of reform measures were enacted in July. In connexion with them, an initial foreign exchange reserve of some $140 million was established with Western, mainly American, assistance, and Yugoslavia was accepted as a full member of G.A.T.T. in August 1966.

A massive devaluation brought the official parity to 1,250 dinars for the dollar. Import regulations were liberalized. Subsidies were drastically reduced. At the same time, important alterations in the structure of taxation now left enterprises with a share of their net income raised from 51 to 71 per cent. By leaving them with the bulk of available funds, and exposed to foreign competition, it was intended to get enterprises to modernize their existing capacities rather than build new ones, and to specialize in what they could profitably sell. The general level of wages was raised by about 23 per cent over the summer of 1965, to meet the general readjustment of prices, the general level of which rose by about 25 per cent. Prices of farm products were raised in greater proportion to those of industry, so that agriculture should particularly benefit from the price adjustment. Finally, at the end of the year, a new dinar was put into circulation, of the value of 100 old dinars, in order to restore confidence in the currency.

The system of open competition for capital was swept away, central planners retained investment initiative only for certain industries, responsibility for the management of resources being on the whole transferred to local government authorities, to banks, and to enterprises themselves.[19] Planning was anyhow demoted to an analysis of market conditions and an indicator of general trends. The seven-year plan announced in 1962 for 1964 had never materialized, and annual plans had again followed the transitional plan for 1963, until the adoption of the 1966–70 plan.

A special fund for crediting the economic development of poorer regions was set up as an autonomous institution, through which a percentage of the total national product could be channelled into long-term economic assistance to the underdeveloped areas. Funds were made available through a levy on the income of enterprises, and through loans, and given out on favourable, though strictly business, conditions.

The reforms introduced in 1965 not only went back to, but also went much further than, the previous attempts of 1961 and 1952. They broke the back of centralized state control over the economy, gave up discrimination against the private smallholders, reduced the over-ambitious subsidies to underdeveloped regions, and slashed into unproductive personnel – on paper, at least, but even in practice, to a certain extent. They cut back the share of investments in the national income from 25 to 17 per cent in 1966, and produced smaller, but on the whole better-managed, investments. Taxes and prices had given little incentive to the private peasant after decollectivization, and progress in agriculture, following the record-breaking harvest of 1959, had been slow. A new start was made in 1965, when smallholders were allowed to benefit fully from the new policy. With the added help of favourable weather conditions, 1966 was another record year in agricultural production.

The government, however, could not quite bring itself fully to

[19] Whereas banks had hitherto operated within precisely defined specializations and territorial limits, in 1966 they were given the right to compete with each other on a wider scale. All banks were then refounded with industrial enterprises as quasi-shareholders, putting up capital, receiving a corresponding share of profits, and participating in management – with only one vote each, however. The National Bank continued to supervise the activities of all banks.

accept private enterprise as an equally valid contributor to the economy in those sectors where it survived. On the eve of the reforms, 88 per cent of the arable land and 91 per cent of all livestock were owned by over 2·6 million private landowners producing 76 per cent of the total farm output. Although these were tiny holdings, worked with primitive techniques, and with little marketable surplus, their average yields had risen between 1959 and 1966, whereas production had actually stagnated in the collective, or social, estates, so that the former had put in more effort for the record harvest than the latter.[20] Yet the success of 1966 was attributed to the socialized sector because yields remained much higher on the larger, richer, and mechanized collectives, but only at very high costs which forced the government to keep raising agricultural prices. On these, the private peasant now flourished, and was no longer prepared to sell his land to social estates as easily as earlier. Indeed, in 1966, much less land was sold thus than in 1965, and at much better prices.[21]

Another sector in which private enterprise survived was tourism. Since the number of foreign tourists had in 1955 overtaken the 1939 figure of 276,000, it had passed the million mark in 1961. In terms of nights spent by foreign tourists, it had been a 10-million mark. The government was quick to see the possibilities of the country's abundant 'tourist assets' as earners of foreign currency. In 1965 it started to relax visa regulations, until all tourist visas were unilaterally abolished in 1967. Already one of Europe's cheapest tourist countries, Yugoslavia became even cheaper after the 1965 devaluation. The number of nights spent there by foreign tourists jumped to 14·7 million in 1966 and 16·1 million in 1967, bringing in $160 million and $185 million respectively. This development came at a critical time, when it could help to offset the trade deficit and create employment, and private initiative was quick to exploit the inadequacies of socialized accommodation and catering facilities.[22]

[20] *Ekonomska politika*, Belgrade, 15 October 1966. As the total farmland had only returned to its 1939 level of 15 million hectares in 1956, and had actually been slightly reduced since 1961, the record was due entirely to higher yields.

[21] *Privredni pregled*, Belgrade, 12 January 1968.

[22] There were again over 3,000 private family restaurants in 1963, and a thousand more by 1965. Innumerable people took foreign lodgers – with or without the knowledge of the authorities, who did not look too closely into such activities, even when they did not actually encourage them. To the official foreign currency receipts should be added those cashed and exchanged for dinars by private individuals. Some Yugoslav sources thus estimated that the real intake from tourists in 1967 reached about $280 million (P. Lendvai, 'Continued Increase in Tourist Traffic', in the *Financial Times* survey on Yugoslavia, London, 4 March 1968).

The great demand for service activities also created possibilities for the development of small private enterprise. By 1964, private crafts and trade employed some 145,000, and could have absorbed more but for the ideological objections which imposed legal limits, harsh taxation, and social pressure.

By moving nearer to a parity of prices and costs, the reforms of 1965 exposed the inefficiency of many enterprises which had depended on semi-arbitrary prices to turn out a wide range of products, in small quantities, with poorly productive labour and high-cost equipment. It was estimated in 1965 that 600,000 people were employed in enterprises which operated at a loss amounting to the annual aggregate of $600 million, and in 1966 that 30 per cent of all enterprises should be closed down to achieve consistency.[23] Moreover, the period of extensive economic development had left behind many uncompleted projects. To close down so many plants, and to stop so many projects in a short time, would have been political suicide. Although most investment decisions had been transferred away from the federation, they were still concentrated in the hands of a few important banks which were under the influence of various levels of government. On that account alone, the economy could still be distorted if, when, and where this was considered politically necessary. In 1966, enterprises were still allowed to lay hands on large amounts of additional revenue, and it was still possible for them to obtain credit towards goods yet to be paid for, yet to be sold, or even yet to be produced.

Another handicap to the reforms was management itself, for the effective management was slow to change its methods, to turn to intensive investment, specialization, and linkages, to learn business reflexes. But on account of self-management, it was the workers who were being made to pay, in terms of wages, not only for current production decisions which their elected councils had ratified without understanding, but also for original investment decisions made outside their enterprises.

Even when and where it had been hoped to establish immediately a free market, such hopes had to be postponed, for no sooner had the reform measures been put into operation than prices rose so high and rapidly that the government again had to step in. The rise was caused partly by short-term transitory adjustments due to the reform, partly by such long-term inflationary pressures as had not been affected by the reforms. Within a fortnight of the first reform acts, the government had reimposed temporary price ceilings on certain goods and services; within a month, nearly all prices were

[23] Hamilton, op. cit., p. 252; and *The Economist*, London, 3 and 31 December 1966.

under some form of administrative control. And the freeze was not as temporary as had been imagined, for it was not until the beginning of 1967 that it was allowed to thaw.

If the drive for greater profitability did not lead to the closing-down of all unprofitable factories, it did mean the end for a certain number of them, and the dismissal of a surplus of unqualified labour. The unemployment figure was still under 260,000 at the end of 1966, but only because work was available in western Europe. That year, the government finally recognized that therein lay part of the answer to the problem of unemployment during the period of adjustment, and to that of the balance of payments deficit. It removed most restrictions on the right to seek employment abroad, and began to conclude immigration agreements with foreign governments. By the end of 1966, there were 380,000 Yugoslavs recently arrived in the West to work – 120,000 of them that very year.

In 1966, there was an inevitable amount of belt-tightening, which affected the weakest regions and the weakest categories of the population most. A certain amount of social discontent followed on regional discontent, and was reflected in a greater number of spontaneous strikes, since there was no genuine labour organization to take up the interests of the working class in a system of workers' self-management. However imaginative and forward-looking, self-management had come from the top, and operated as it was through official trade unions and the Party, it still appeared very paternalistic. For as long as business and earnings seemed to be good, the professional management had been left to do the effective planning and running, along with the trade unions, and little more than a rubber stamp from the workers' councils. But when it stopped being so, and the workers were made to feel the pinch of decisions which they did not feel to be theirs, they vented their anger on the management. These strikes were still not very frequent, and they involved only a minute proportion of the labour force,[24] but they were considered important enough to be discussed in parliament and in the press.

The greatest immediate achievement of the reform was deemed to be the improvement in the trade balance in 1965, with exports amounting to 85 per cent of imports. Unfortunately, this was no more than the temporary result of pressures on enterprises to import less and export more, for in 1966, exports were back to 77 per cent of imports – the same proportion as in 1964 – and further down to 73 per cent in 1967. For the first time since the war, the balance of

[24] There were 134 strikes in 1966 (*Borba*, 24 December 1966) involving 11,000 men (*The Times*, London, 7 December 1967). Altogether, by that year, there had been 1,365 strikes since 1958 (*Nin*, 29 October 1967).

payments showed a slight surplus in 1965, but in 1966, there was again a deficit of some $50 million – even though this was a great improvement on the $166 million of 1964.

In 1966, a quarter of Yugoslavia's foreign trade was with the area of the European Economic Community, and another important proportion with the European Free Trade Area, but the expansion of exchanges with both groups was slowing down as their integration made more difficult the conditions under which Yugoslav exports competed in these countries. Yugoslav agricultural exports were affected. President Johnson had, in 1964, reapplied to Yugoslavia the most-favoured-nation treatment which had been withdrawn in 1962, and full membership of G.A.T.T. in 1966 entitled it to the same treatment in dealing with co-members. Yugoslav officials, however, were critical of the restrictive trade policy of Western countries, and, duly assisted by credits, trade with the Soviet Union increased in 1966 to the point where the latter rivalled Italy for the first place among Yugoslavia's trade partners.

The reforms of 1965 had been intended, and applied, more seriously than their predecessors, but much compromise had attended their conception, and much lip-service their carrying-out. While some of the resulting pains were due to the treatment, others came from the fact that not enough medicine had been prescribed or administered. What measure of reform was carried out generated the need for more as it exposed negative results of the over-ambitious investments of the past. The enormous expansion of higher education, for instance, was beginning to be seen as too expensive in comparison with its efficiency, and even the graduates turned out at such cost were finding it difficult to obtain employment.[25]

The fall of Rankovich and its effects

Disturbing to different sections of the population, these difficulties provided ammunition for the opponents of the reforms. The reticences of conservatives were reinforced by the fact that the reforms

[25] A seventh university had been founded at Nish (Serbia) in 1964. In 1966, with 95 students to every 10,000 inhabitants, Yugoslavia, for the relative number of students, ranked just after the U.S.A., U.S.S.R., Canada, the Netherlands, Australia, Japan, France, and Denmark. (In 1967 the proportion had risen to 105 to every 10,000, leaving France and Denmark behind.) Only 14% of these managed to complete their studies at all, and only 2% within the prescribed period. In 1965, 15,700 university teachers had turned out no more than 23,000 graduates, at a cost of 8% of the national income (cf. *Ekonomska politika*, 15 October, 5 November, and 4 December 1966). In 1965–67, 9.9 doctors to every 10,000 inhabitants compared badly with Yugoslavia's neighbours (Italy 16.8, Austria 18, Hungary 17.4, Romania 13.9, Bulgaria 16.8, Greece 14.7).

implied the gradual transfer of much of the decision-making powers in the field of micro-economics to the new professionally trained managerial class, whose ideological qualifications would, in order of professional priorities, rank after their technical qualifications. Even within the Party organization, veteran officials were being replaced by younger and updated cadres. The many ex-partisans and Party bureaucrats retired before their time formed a dissatisfied network within the L.C.Y. itself, with energy and leisure to devote to their dissatisfaction. Again within the Party, two categories who mattered much more to the leadership, the young and the workers, were becoming disaffected, owing to growing inequalities of income, the failure to eradicate material abuses among higher cadres, and even the revival of private enterprise.

It was not only the Party conservatives who made the most of the confusion and discontent which accompanied the reforms. The coincidence of this state of affairs with the flow of migrants going to work in the West acted as a tonic on the ageing extremist fringes of the expatriates. The Yugoslav authorities had done their best to deprive the *émigrés* of their political significance, and time, probably more than the efforts of the Belgrade government, had gone some way towards achieving this by the early sixties. It was soon discovered, however, that among the mass of new, young, and utterly non-political migrants in search of a better living in the West, there were some whose virgin discontent with the state of affairs at home could be exploited by totalitarian terrorists and propagandists of another age. Discontented people in Yugoslavia were feeling freer to write to relatives and friends abroad to complain of the situation, and some of this material found its way into the *émigré* press. By the middle sixties, occasional Ustasha contacts were being apprehended on Yugoslav territory, and occasional outrages perpetrated on Yugoslav missions in the West. In 1964, several trials had sent to prison people convicted for contacts with *émigrés* of all sorts. This, too, was an argument used by the conservatives against the reforms.

In 1954, political imperatives had forced Tito to strike at Djilas and exclude him from the top leadership, in order to destroy the incipient formation of a forward-looking, imaginative, radical force disruptive of Party unity. In 1966, it was economic imperatives which forced him to strike at Rankovich, and exclude another close friend and lieutenant, in order to destroy the incipient formation of a backward-looking, unimaginative, conservative force, equally disruptive of Party unity. After simmering below the surface for several years, the crisis erupted and was overcome that summer.

On the evening of 1 July 1966, the news was broadcast that vice-president Aleksandar Rankovich had offered his resignation at a full

Central Committee meeting which had been held that day in Brioni. The main accusation against him was that he had built up the S.D.B. – the state security service, successor to the U.D.B. – as a personal power basis. The substance of the accusations linked a struggle for power with opposition to reforms and Serbian nationalism. Along with Rankovich, the Central Committee implicated his right-hand man, Stefanovich, the captor of General Mihailovich and chairman of the government's Commission for Internal Affairs.

Rankovich's disgrace was a complex affair, many elements of which are still unknown because of the secrecy with which the operation was carried out. He had always been essentially an executor of policy, and there is no real evidence, or even likelihood, that he was plotting to take over in any way. Nevertheless, more than one simple reason must have made him look askance at the continued liberalization of the economy.

He knew that the regions which had given most fighters for the Communist revolution, hence those most linked to the Party and its traditional image, were also the least developed economically. He feared that the reforms would make the underdeveloped regions even poorer, and thus create dissatisfaction in the most Party-minded areas. This was not so much the republic of Serbia itself, as the poorer territories outside their republic where Serbs were to be found – Bosnia-Herzegovina or the less rewarding parts of Croatia, as well as Montenegro, still Serbian enough, or Macedonia, now hardly Serbian at all. It has been said superficially that Rankovich stood for Serbian interests, but police pressure was generally much stronger in the less developed regions, and there was much less freedom near to the centre of power. For this reason, the Communists of Serbia, unlike their counterparts in Croatia or Slovenia, had developed no strong local leadership, and because they had such an eminent representative at the very top, they tended to look up to Rankovich, so that many of them were carried away by his opposition to reform. The Party in Serbia was divided on this issue, but generally speaking all the conservatives in the L.C.Y. looked to Rankovich.

Rankovich had attained a lofty position, and his public image had been growing of late. His special interest in security matters, which had been kept within the prerogative of the federation, gave him a potential advantage. This was another reason that made his colleagues join forces in order to remove him from a position which might give him an advantage over them in a bid for Tito's succession. Quite apart from any question of reform, one of their aims was to take the security apparatus out of the hands of the man who had created it.

In the absence of conclusive evidence, one can but interpret in the light of probability. A counter-conspiracy to anticipate a conspiracy was unlikely. Less sensational but more probable was a conspiracy to remove a colleague, at that time complacent in high office, but who could become a dangerous rival. It hit the coalition of all those who impeded economic change, a coalition effective on account of its dead weight rather than its organization, and this was symbolized, rather than led, by Rankovich. It also provided a ready scapegoat upon whom to heap the blame for the failure of the reforms, and against whom to turn the grievances of every group, class, or category.

The pronouncements of Brioni had the effect of taking the lid off the cauldron. That summer in Yugoslavia was one of purge and criticism, which the leadership attempted to keep within bounds. It was necessary, for instance, to stop Rankovich's disgrace from being interpreted in terms of ethnic rivalries. Serbs were thus chosen to succeed to Rankovich's positions. It was also necessary to prevent him from being made a martyr. He duly resigned from all his government posts, and was duly expelled from all his Party posts, but no judicial proceedings were taken against him or his associates, and they were allowed to retire, on pensions, into obscurity. At the same time, as if to redress the balance, Djilas was released after nine years off and on in gaol – although still under a five-year ban on public activities. Both acts of clemency had been deemed necessary to calm things down before the next elections.

The aim of those who removed Rankovich had been not to dismantle the security police, but to place it fully under their control and ensure that it be used for the right purposes only. Tito hastened to make this clear, and called for an end to indiscriminate attacks on the security service. A new law, enacted in December, placed the S.D.B. under the Federal Secretariat for Internal Affairs, as a specialized intelligence agency with the exclusive task of unmasking and combating all subversive activities against the constitutionally established order.

A series of warnings was issued in the summer of 1966 that criticism was going too far, and that no weakening of the Party's grip was to be expected while it was in the process of adapting itself to changing circumstances. President Tito publicly decried those in the West who interpreted events in Yugoslavia as a victory for liberalism, and warned those in Yugoslavia who longed for something other than socialism that there would be no leniency for them. No right of opposition to the system itself was to be allowed. This being clarified, the government continued to allow a gradually widened area of permissible expression, and to foster an increasing emphasis on legality.

By the middle sixties, the average citizen of the S.F.R.Y. did not think of challenging the régime or its policies, which were accepted, at least passively, by the majority of the population. A wide variety of views could increasingly be found in the press on every issue which did not challenge the régime's foundations or leadership, and on which no official line had yet been taken. No formal censorship was needed in a situation where most publications operated under the aegis of the Socialist Alliance, most journalists belonged to the L.C.Y., and the press was subsidized by grants from the political authorities. An official news agency handled government news, and in individual papers, special correspondents of political reliability dealt with important issues where an authorized line did exist.

Yet at the same time, elements of truly independent opinion were growing in non-political, and especially cultural, institutions. At the most accepted level, there were the intellectuals who used the established press to express independent criticism within authorized limits. In literature, the arts, and scholarship, the mood was increasingly one of total disinvolvement. For a while, since the controversy between 'formalists' and 'realists'[26] had died out in the early sixties as the new forms became generally accepted, the maturity of Yugoslav letters had been symbolized to the outside world by Andrich and Krlezha, the grand old men of the literary scene, respectively in Belgrade and Zagreb. Now entering their seventies, they appeared as great writers of a bygone age. Two new trends had appeared, neither of which was welcome to the Party. One of romantic nostalgia for the past, attempted to satisfy the need for historical roots; the other of anti-romantic nihilism, wanted to destroy all myths, of past and present. The cinema, hitherto, had lagged behind as a vehicle of socialist realism, producing edifying illustrations of the partisan war, but the new war films tended to be unedifying and anti-heroic, and many directors switched to contemporary social and psychological, non-political, issues.

In their struggle against Party conservatives, the reformists had tolerated from the intellectuals much more than they would have done otherwise, and the disgrace of Rankovich had unwittingly reduced the authorities' capacity to inspire awe. With Rankovich out of the way, it was necessary to get the public expression of independent opinion back into its accepted limits.

It was on its own academic fringe, among Communist philosophers and social scientists, that the Party had to face a real, though limited, political challenge. These were younger men who believed

[26] See above, p. 239.

that political liberalization could, and should, come about within a Marxist context, through constructive criticism within the Party.[27] All of them were agreed on the necessity of obtaining total freedom of opinion within the L.C.Y., but some went on to ventilate ideas for a two-party system within socialism, and even of indirect democracy through representative bodies, as opposed to the official ideology of direct democracy. These ideas were put across in literary and philosophical journals which did form the beginnings of a free press. However limited the number of their readers, such ideas did reach a larger public, if for no other reason than the reactions of authority.

As a result of financial discrimination, and a public campaign led by Tito himself, *Praxis* went out of circulation from the summer of 1966 to the following spring. It was then that two Belgrade periodicals, *Gledishta* and *Knjizhevne novine*, took over, going on throughout 1967 and into 1968, though attacked by the press and reprimanded by the Party. All such publications were indeed attacked, threatened, and at times silenced, but they emerged again in one form or another, and no more drastic action was taken against their editors than short periods of detention, because, however dissident, they did not stray beyond broadly interpreted Party limits.

The case that showed to what extent the government felt that the intelligentsia was a potentially disruptive force, was that of Mihaylo Mihaylov, a young non-Marxist university teacher of Russian. On returning from a cultural exchange visit to Moscow, he began to publish his impressions of the new literary trends there in a well-known Belgrade literary monthly at the beginning of 1965. By publicly rebuking the prosecutors for not having noticed this travelogue, Tito himself made a full-blown case out of it. The magazine was seized, the press attacked Mihaylov, his faculty suspended him. He was then arrested and dismissed from the university, but not before he had personally circulated an open letter to the press, denouncing the nostalgic Stalinism of some of the attacks against him. The whole procedure raised so many protests abroad that the authorities then backed down. Mihaylov was found guilty of having painted an offensive picture of the Soviet régime and of having sent his manuscript abroad. After appeal, he was left with a suspended

[27] The Yugoslav neo-Marxist school was influenced by the Polish neo-Marxists and by new Western thinking on Marxism, but also by the French and German philosophers of existence, and, in particular, by British empiricism. Several of these philosophers and sociologists had done post-graduate work in Western universities in the fifties. Cf. the international edition of *Praxis* (published in Zagreb since 1965, in English, French, German, and Italian), contributions in E. Fromm (ed.): *Socialist Humanism*, London, 1967, and G. Petrović, *Marx in the Mid-Twentieth Century*, Garden City, 1967.

five-month sentence on the second count alone, jobless, and without passport. It was hoped that the case would be forgotten.

Mihaylov, however, decided otherwise. He was going to make the best of the generally favourable climate of the reformists' struggle against the conservatives, and of the publicity he had been given by the authorities, in order to test the extent of legality and constitutionalism. He appealed against his dismissal; he complained that his mail was being tampered with; he wrote, for the New York *New Leader*, articles on Djilas and on the need for political freedom in Yugoslavia. At the same time, he took the necessary legal steps to start an independent newspaper which was intended to become, eventually, the rallying-point for a democratic socialist movement within the existing constitutional framework. His action was well-timed. It coincided with the general free-for-all criticism of July 1966. It skilfully exploited Yugoslavia's liberal image abroad. It embarrassed the government. There was the risk that, in such circumstances, his plan might crystallize some opposition tendencies, and seriously handicap the government. Some way had to be found of stopping him before he went too far, but without infringing his constitutional rights at a time when the 'Rankovich faction' was accused of having done just that.

Eventually, he was arrested on charges that bore no relation to his intended newspaper – his publications abroad. His friends were intimidated into calling off the whole project. The press spread the idea that they were agents of foreign interests, while Tito turned harshly against discontented intellectuals, in two speeches, on 22 August and 1 September. In September, while the Soviet C.P. first secretary, Brezhnev, was in Yugoslavia, Mihaylov was tried a second time, and sentenced to one year's imprisonment. In order, however, to discourage non-Communists from being tempted into any sort of political action, Mihaylov was to be given an even stiffer sentence, and be discredited as linked with Fascist expatriates. On the eve of the last round of the elections, in April 1967, he was brought out of prison for a third trial. Accused of distributing to his friends texts of his articles published abroad, and *émigré* pamphlets he had received, he was sentenced to four and a half years, with an additional four-year ban on any form of public activity. When all the dust of the two-year case had settled, there remained an unknown young academic who had frightened and confused the authorities, simply because he had, at an awkward period, revealed the contradictions of the situation.[28]

[28] For some of the original texts in which the ideas and opinions of Mihaylov and his friends were expressed, see 'The Dossier of the Mihajlov Case', in *Review of the Study Centre for Jugoslav Affairs*, 6, 1967.

In a way, an independent press completely outside the influence of the L.C.Y. did exist, although it was not a political press: it was the religious press which had gradually established itself in the sixties. It was not subsidized; it took a completely independent stand on matters relating to faith, ecclesiastical organization, and religious life; it was even, in its field, beginning to argue with the Communist press, with the authorities, and with the Marxist intellectuals. That such an independent voice was being heard was a sign of the increasing independence of the Church.

In the middle sixties, the Serbian Orthodox Church was well on the way to recovery. Since the late fifties, all sees had been regularly filled, and the quality of the episcopate, headed by Patriarch Gherman, was generally of a high standard. A tremendous effort had been made to rebuild churches destroyed during the war, reorganize the training of priests, restore a parochial network, and revive monastic life. In some dioceses, considering the amount of destruction, the effort can be described as miraculous. Because of its tradition of other-worldliness, Eastern Christianity had never opposed the civil authority, and this had certainly helped the Serbian Church to come to terms with the new society, however hostile. By 1967, although much remained to be done, the fabric had been rebuilt in a rough and ready way, and many new elements had, moreover, been modestly introduced, in religious instruction, general welfare work, and the use of the press. During these years, the Serbian Orthodox Church had been active not only in the pan-Orthodox movement, but also on a wider oecumenical level, by establishing closer contacts with other Christian denominations.

The Roman Catholic Church had started off with a tighter organization, a better-trained clergy, a tradition of social involvement, and international backing, which gave it better material foundations in more difficult political circumstances. In many ways it had shown the Orthodox how to go out to the faithful, just as the Serbian Orthodox Church had shown the Catholic how to find its place in a hostile structure. It was the Second Vatican Council, however, more than anything else, which helped the Catholic Church find its due place in the Yugoslav society of the sixties. By 1965, under the newly elevated Cardinal Sheper, it was led by a hierarchy that had been almost completely renewed, and was ready to face the realities of the situation. The Yugoslav bishops took an important part in the work of the Council and, inspired by its spirit, kept the Church free from any political commitment, in order to militate for a better implementation of its constitutional rights. Contacts were renewed between the Yugoslav government and the Holy See which resulted, in June 1966, in the signature of an agreement, whereby the Yugoslav government recognized the jurisdiction of the Roman See in dealing with the Catholic hierarchy in Yugoslavia, and the Church agreed not to allow its priests to misuse their office for political ends. The arrangement stopped short of a complete restoration of diplomatic relations: there was to be an apostolic delegate in Belgrade, and a Yugoslav special envoy to the Vatican.

Bridging the gaping abyss created by the war between Orthodox and Catholics had been an arduous and unenviable task. One may truly wonder which was the more painful act of humility – for the Catholic hierarchy to recognize the criminal errors of a part of its flock, or for the Orthodox to step down from the pedestal of martyrdom. It was a Catholic prelate, Bishop Pichler of Banjaluka, who had taken that first and major step, in his Christmas pastoral of 1963.[29] The two Churches gradually began to lean on, and learn from, each other in order to face common difficulties. The increasing solidarity, in the middle sixties, on a strictly religious level, of the two major Christian Churches seemed to be taking the religious sting out of the Serbo-Croatian problem. By April 1968, when Cardinal Sheper left for Rome to take up his new appointment as head of the Congregation for the Doctrine of the Faith, the new spirit of day-to-day co-operation on a practical basis had so progressed, that his meeting with Patriarch Gherman was much more than an exchange of oecumenical niceties. It was, on a Yugoslav level, as important an occasion as the first meeting between Pope Paul and Patriarch Athenagoras.

This religious drawing-together was all the more significant for taking place against a background of continued clashes of ethnic susceptibilities. The middle generations – those in their forties to sixties – were the country's backbone, yet in spite of more than

[29] 'In this country, during the last war, many of our brethren of the Orthodox faith lost their lives simply because they were Orthodox. Those who killed them held Catholic baptismal certificates, and called themselves Catholics. These Christians killed other men, who were also Christians, because they were not Croats and Catholics. With pain in our hearts, we admit the horrible error of these depraved men, and we beg our fellow Christians of the Orthodox faith to forgive us as Christ forgave all from the Cross.' (Quoted in S. Pavlowitch, 'The Orthodox Church in Yugoslavia', part iv, in *Eastern Churches Review*, II/3, 1969, pp. 278–9.)

In Banjaluka, a town of three faiths, there is now a solid tradition, not only of toleration but also of mutual co-operation, between Orthodox and Catholics, and between Christians and Moslems as well. Mgr Pichler and his Orthodox colleague Bishop Andrey, continuing the work initiated by their respective predecessors just after the war, had, by the end of the sixties, set up – discreetly and modestly – a model Christian fellowship about which not enough is known elsewhere in Yugoslavia, let alone abroad. Churches are open to the faithful of both confessions, and the two bishops in many ways act as joint pastors of a common flock.

two decades of communism, their subconsciousness and much of their consciousness were pre-Marxist. Since they could not be satisfied with old-fashioned political freedoms, they were allowed to indulge in nationalist self-satisfaction. This was a dangerous policy, for these emotions were passed on to the following generation, whose intellectuals and Communists now began to air their nationalism without the guilt complex of their elders.

In so far as the expression of such feelings was directed against the centralist Party conservatives, the decentralizing reformists, however internationalist, had given it full rein, and it was particularly meaningful in the richer republics of Slovenia and Croatia, where self-sufficiency made more sense than elsewhere. Complete homogeneity gave such strength to Slovenian isolationism that in March 1967, the local Central Committee felt it necessary to denounce not only isolationism, but separatism as well.[30]

In Croatia, the problem was more complex. Most Croats who had lived through the period of Ustasha rule still felt an uneasy and repressed sensation of guilt. The authorities in that republic could not afford to probe too much into the past, especially as the Party there contained too many members, even in the cadres, who had come over to it out of passive resistance towards the end of the war, or after. Outright separatism made little sense, for there were too many Croats outside the republic of Croatia, and too many Serbs in it.[31] However suspicious of Belgrade, of centralism, and of Yugoslavism, Croatian Party leaders did not want to run the risk of being taken for Serbophobes, or of reviving anti-Croatian feelings elsewhere, especially among the Serbs of their own republic. Publicly at least, Croatian particularism still expressed itself through non-political forms, notably emotional and unscholarly discussions on language and literature.

These culminated in a storm that blew up in the summer of 1967 when over a hundred Croatian intellectuals presented a declaration to parliament asking that a separate Croatian language be recognized, so as to protect their tongue from the danger of Serbianization under the mask of the common Serbo-Croatian. Published in the press, this declaration provoked a counter-statement from forty-odd

[30] Of the Slovenes of Yugoslavia, 96% lived within the confines of their republic where they made up 95·9% of the population. (These and other percentages, below, according to the 1961 census.)

[31] There were 26·8% of Croats living outside the republic of Croatia; in it, Croats amounted to no more than 80% of the population. Dreams of an independent Croatia continued, however, to haunt these 'outer' Croats, especially in Bosnia-Herzegovina – Party officials in both Zagreb and Sarayevo told Georges Chaffard, of *Le Monde* (cf. his 'Yougoslavie 1969 – un socialisme humain', in *Le Monde diplomatique*, Paris, July 1969).

Serbian writers demanding, among other things, an equal status for the Serbian language and Cyrillic script for the Serbs in the republic of Croatia. As this was taking place on the eve of a general election, and many of the signatories on both sides were Communists, the leadership had to react to such verbal excesses taking place within the Party. All media were used to condemn the language statements; there were expulsions and resignations (including that of the writer Miroslav Krlezha) from the L.C.Y.

Communists in Serbia complained that, in its struggle to implement the reforms, the Party had allowed too much irresponsible talk about the Serbs being conservatives, and getting too large a slice of the federal cake: it had ignored the consequent upsurge of anti-Serbian feelings. There were ruffled feelings, whose expression produced perhaps even more hot air than elsewhere, but it was even more difficult in Serbia than in Croatia to think of separatism. The proportion of Serbs outside the republic, and that of non-Serbs within, was even larger than corresponding proportions for the Croats.[32]

Over the winter of 1967–68, efforts were again made towards encouraging a separate Montenegrin national identity, by building up – not very successfully – at least the concept of a separate culture. The most conspicuous and unashamed nation-building, however, continued to be that in Macedonia, particularly during 1967. A separate Macedonian Academy was instituted, as an addition to the three well-established scholarly institutions of Belgrade, Zagreb, and Ljubljana. More important still, the Church in Macedonia took the plunge into autocephaly, which was unilaterally proclaimed in July, after an application to the patriarchate in Belgrade had been rejected. Government intervention was blatant. Little trouble was taken to vest this act in the garb of ecclesiastical respectability, but it was a way of giving full satisfaction to the local Macedonian Party leadership within Yugoslavia, and of making the Macedonian beacon shine fully towards Bulgaria and Greece.[33] Culture and Church are traditional attributes of nationhood in the Balkans, but the fact that it was now becoming difficult to exploit for political

---

[32] There were 27% of Serbs living outside the republic of Serbia, while in the republic 25% of the population was non-Serbian. The large minority groups of Albanians and Hungarians were concentrated in Serbia. Only 56.5% of Serbs lived in inner Serbia.

[33] For opposite reasons, it was opportune to do so towards both countries. Because of the closeness of relations between Belgrade and Moscow, the Sofia government was anxious to draw closer as well, and so could be indirectly pressed to give more recognition to its own 'Macedonians'. On the other hand, the Yugoslav government was upset by the *coup d'état* of April 1967 in Athens, and did not object to the making of Macedonian noises at the new Greek government.

ends the ancient mistrust between the Eastern and the Western Churches, might well have been another reason for wishing to create a breach within the Orthodox Church itself.

There was yet another reason for wishing to satisfy the Macedonians. No more than 71 per cent of the population of their republic was registered as Macedonian, and the ratio of Albanians to Macedonians in their republic was greater than that of Albanians to Serbs in Serbia. The proportion of Albanians was constantly increasing, yet because of tension with Albania, police rule in Kosovo remained much more in evidence than elsewhere. Kosovo was, in fact if not in law, a security region. After the fall of Rankovich, there were promises of reform, more Albanians were appointed to positions of responsibility, and tales of S.D.B. brutality were revealed, in order to relieve tension. But the removal of police pressure, coinciding with the tide of nationalism rising all over the country, made Albanian nationalism, egged on by the government in Tirana, an inflammable element.

Judging by what was officially said and printed, it seemed that all measures in favour of the Albanian minority had been dead letters, and many other measures as well, simply because the whole system had, all along, been controlled by Rankovich and the S.D.B. All the glorified and publicized changes since the early fifties, which had caused so much admiration in the West, and so much fright in the East, appeared as so many words and illusions never put into practice. Rankovich had been easily removed, in spite of the alleged strength of the combined forces that had stood behind him and imposed their will on the government for so long, but so anxious were Yugoslavia's leaders to blame everything on Rankovich, and to appear innocent of all that was objectionable, that they made the former vice-president appear, in retrospect, much stronger than he had been. By contrast, they appeared much weaker themselves. Moreover, most foreign observers not only accepted all Yugoslav claims at their face value, but so interpreted them as to make the government appear liberal.

The image of weak liberals which had emerged as a result was bad publicity, and the leaders took pains to redress the impression, both at home and abroad. Tito himself, on no less than five separate occasions between the spring and the end of 1967, reaffirmed that Yugoslavia was not going 'liberal' or 'Djilasist'. What was being initiated, he explained, was a long-term process in which the Party was becoming the controlling force of the country's evolution to socialism, until such time as the Communist consciousness of citizens had developed to the point where a guiding force was no longer necessary. Meanwhile, it was necessary to keep the Party strong, united, and disciplined. It was ridiculous to speak of a reduced role, since it was Communists who initiated and carried out policy, who sat in parliament, in all institutions of government, and in all political forums. There could, however, be no differences of opinion concerning vital issues, and there could be no room in the Party for those who did not really belong to it. As for those who were outright against socialism, there was no place for them in the machinery of direct democracy, and they were right to be afraid.[34]

Even the most reformist members of the leadership had no intention of dismantling as yet the one-party dictatorship. What they believed was that the day-to-day implementation of policies decided by the Party could, and should, be left to the existing institutions of local and corporate government, and to the Socialist Alliance, through the Communists who participated in and guided them. The exercise of direct democracy through corporate self-management would be sectional and technical rather than general and political. It would be carried out within the framework of a long-term policy, and under the guidance of a leadership, neither of which could be questioned.

In applying this system, the government faced several problems. To start with, the system did not make sense unless it attracted wide participation. It was thus continually 'sold' through mass media, through mass manifestations, through mass organizations, and last but not least, through the non-toleration of all other ideologies, which were denounced as anachronistic or alien. Yet in spite of these efforts people were increasingly apathetic to ideology and politics in general, and even contemptuous of politicians. All changes had been initiated and handed down from above; they had all been empirical or tactical, but were always presented to the accompaniment of high-sounding formulas which quickly lost their value; as such, they were not likely to capture the imagination of anyone in Yugoslavia. At the same time, the intolerance of any discussion attempting to question the basis of the system allowed for no other way of participating than to express approval, or obtain technical responsibilities for the management of collective property. The coincidence of monopolistic political power, police relaxation, and collective property, encouraged not only indifference to the system, but also the pursuit of personal material advancement within it, while avoiding responsibility. The inherent contradiction of the system was that it needed mass participation while it incited to indifference.

[34] Cf. Tito's speeches of 28 March, 17 April, 5 July, and 1 September 1967, and his New Year message for 1968. Other leaders took up the theme, both in public speeches and in interviews.

There was contradiction, also, in the Party which ran the system. Too many things had happened too quickly, not to have a debilitating effect on the Party, in spite of efforts to the contrary. Purges from mid-1966 to early 1968 had rid the L.C.Y. of tens of thousands, and as many had left voluntarily, with the result that membership dropped in 1967 to little over a million. The Party's new role was defined as one of guiding an evolution, but the Party was not agreed on the nature and extent of this evolution, nor on the character and degree of this guidance. Only the Party could provide the driving force for the reforms, but the leadership knew that the L.C.Y., such as it then was, could not fulfil this duty, and the population knew that the same Party, now advocating reform, was responsible for the situation which called for reform. Since it could not be said for how long the majority of the population would passively accept the leading role of the Party, and since the needs of the economy pressed, time did not permit a pause for a radical reformation of the L.C.Y. itself.

The leadership was thus forced to go on with economic reform and Party reform simultaneously; to act as if the League were qualified for the job, while separating itself from many loyal servants who had become useless hangers-on. The group in power realized that as a direct organ of power, the Party had become an anachronism because of its rigid structure. The reformed Party it appeared to be aiming at would allow for greater flexibility in formulating and implementing new policies. It would replace dismissed policemen, prematurely retired officers, impoverished partisans, frustrated local secretaries, and all ignored disillusioned members, with the children of the régime – the new technical and managerial cadres. It would be deprived of direct power in its apparatus, but would nevertheless be a tool for implementing the programme of the ruling élite through the discipline and zeal of its new-model members.

The Brioni meeting of July 1966 had deplored that the Party had not kept up with the country's social and economic evolution. As a result anarcho-liberal tendencies had developed and, by way of reaction, strengthened the Party conservatives. By October, a set of temporary measures to reform the structure of the leadership was ready, pending the next congress. The reorganization of the Romanian Party executive carried out in July 1965 provided the model. The secretariat was abolished. Tito became president of the L.C.Y., and a new thirty-five-member presidency was elected as the supreme policy-making body, composed of the most renowned leaders, of representatives of all the republics, of the largest ethnic minorities, and of the army. A new eleven-man Executive Committee was selected as the actual administrative executive agency. One aim was to bring up more and newer people from the Central Committee, thus handing over administrative duties to a younger generation of well-trained Party administrators, leaving the older ruling group to lead from behind. The other was to prepare for a smooth succession. It brought together all the old leaders who, together, could bridge the gap, bolstering them up with representatives of the regional leadership groups and of the armed forces. At the same time, it made it difficult, by introducing as much division of functions as was practicable, for any one personality to accumulate excessive power.

Special emphasis was again suddenly placed on the 'enemy', more than twenty years after the end of the civil war. The cause of communism in Yugoslavia was made to appear as being still in its revolutionary phase, where it had to face numerous hidden enemies from within and without. The ghost of the old bourgeoisie was revived and attacked, and all the pre-war and wartime ideologies, parties, and movements were bandied about in speeches and articles, as if they were still active and powerful political forces. Political expatriates, whom everyone believed to be but helpless remains of a breed on the way to extinction, were remembered, as the link between the class enemy in Yugoslavia and foreign reactionary circles and intelligence agencies.

In fact, the bourgeoisie had been well and truly destroyed economically, humiliated socially, and suppressed politically, and since this had been accomplished over twenty years earlier, many of its former surviving members in the country had even died. The peasantry, though a class as yet unsocialized, had also been weakened to the point where it hardly represented a greater danger. There was, however, the fear of potential anti-communism lying buried in all those who were ideologically and politically disorientated, who still nourished vestiges of old ideas and instinctively looked to the West.

There were the masses of penniless and unlettered workers in western Europe who could be contaminated by the crudest and loudest of the *émigrés*, those belonging to the extremist anti-Communist and anti-Yugoslav fringes. There were thousands of Yugoslav citizens working on overseas aid and contractual projects in Asian and African countries, exposed to fresher and less pretentious nationalist and revolutionary ideas. There were the products of the brain drain, scholars, scientists, research workers, professionals, to be found in centres of learning and in professional undertakings throughout western Europe and North America, exposed to a way of life and to political attitudes which could bring back to life the old bourgeois origins of many of them, or better suit the new bourgeois status of all of them.

There had been, since the end of 1966, a string of unsavoury acts of terrorism committed against Yugoslav missions in western Europe and North America, and even in Yugoslavia. In most cases, the planners appear to have been those past masters of terrorist anti-Yugoslav action, the Ustashas, and the perpetrators, Yugoslav citizens recruited mainly for mercenary reasons among the new migrants, who also provided recruits for the totally unpolitical illegal activities of the local underworld in host countries.

There was a veritable onslaught, after the 1967 elections in Yugoslavia, against the *émigrés*, whose activities were magnified and attributed to the patronage of Western right-wing circles, police, and intelligence agencies. The French police and the C.I.A. were openly mentioned by name. Actual and potential C.I.A. agents were discovered everywhere. The population was warned against all Western scholars (particularly social scientists) interested in Yugoslavia, but all Americans working in the country, all foreign tourists, and, for that matter, all Yugoslavs working abroad, as well as all expatriates, were to be considered potential agents.

As a result of the events in the eastern Mediterranean in April and June 1967, there was a genuine fear in Yugoslav ruling circles of a shift in the balance of power there and, possibly, of C.I.A. manipulation of dissatisfaction in Yugoslavia. To work up a real persecution mania was, nevertheless, also an act of policy, useful to divert attention from the all-too-real immediate domestic problems. It was useful, too, to help identify Party, state, and country. In this way, security arrangements could be tightened up, and the S.D.B. rehabilitated by stressing its role in the defence of the fatherland. Western and *émigré* influences could be denounced as anti-Yugoslav, and Western governments pressed to be harsher against all Yugoslav expatriates.

Throughout this period, the tone of official or officially inspired pronouncements was openly anti-Western, directed against Western influences on intellectuals and young people, against Western imperialist reactionary circles, Western intelligence agencies, Western governments that tolerated *émigrés*, and even NATO summer manoeuvres in Italy and Greece, allegedly aimed at Yugoslavia. Quite apart from an element of genuine fear, this was the inevitable complement of a reaffirmed relationship with the Soviet Union, which went together with reaffirming the power of the Party at home. The collective strength of the Communist community and of the U.S.S.R. itself was, after all, the ultimate safeguard of the Yugoslav régime. Tito did not feel any contradiction in striving for both that and equality between the Communist Parties, just as he did not see any contradiction between wanting to lead the non-aligned and wanting to play an important role in the family of Communist parties. He considered himself the best propagator of socialist ideas among the underdeveloped nations, and also hoped to influence the evolution of the Communist states. Brezhnev and Kosygin had not changed Khrushchev's policy towards Yugoslavia. Tito's visit to Moscow in June 1965 had been marked by great cordiality, and had been returned by Brezhnev, in his new capacity as head of the Soviet Party, in September 1966.

In 1966, Yugoslav diplomacy had attempted to revive the declining influence of the non-aligned in world affairs. Events in the Near East the following spring and summer had, however, placed a particular emphasis on the eastern Mediterranean and on the Tito-Nasser link. Both men reacted to the Greek coup of April 1967 in a similarly anti-American way. From the start of the Near Eastern crisis, Yugoslavia supported Egypt without reserve. For Tito, this was part of his efforts at promoting Yugoslav, and thus socialist, influence in the Mediterranean, without a strong Soviet presence which would call for a yet greater American presence. Since the Greek *putsch*, Tito wanted to avoid anything likely to increase the American involvement.

Coming so soon after the change of régime in Athens, the Israeli victory greatly disturbed Tito. He saw it as the beginning of an American action to alter the balance of power in the Near East, and as a threat to Communist-ruled Yugoslavia. He feared Nasser's fall which would have greatly reduced Yugoslavia's influence in the Arab, and more generally in the non-aligned, world. Tito's total solidarity with the Arab, and with the Soviet-led, states, against Israel and the U.S.A., in the name of socialism and non-alignment, was much too extreme for the liking of many Yugoslav Communists.

Shortly after the end of the fighting, Tito went to Moscow for a meeting of the East European leaders which, on 9 June, issued a very strong condemnation of Israeli aggression in collusion with imperialist forces. In line with the Soviet bloc, Yugoslavia broke off diplomatic relations with Israel. Soviet ships visited Yugoslav ports in June. For reasons of his own, domestic and foreign, Marshal Tito made Yugoslav policy in the summer of 1967 coincide with that of the Soviet Union much more than the latter could have hoped for, and certainly more than Romania's leaders, who had neither signed the Moscow statement of 9 June nor severed relations with Israel.

Soon, however, Yugoslav diplomacy stopped seeking *revanche*, in order to rescue Nasser from the wreckage of defeat. The Soviet leadership was not particularly anxious for a confrontation with the U.S.A. In the L.C.Y. itself there was a noticeable lack of ardour for its president's truculent verbal displays against Israel and Western imperialism which, if anything, increased mutterings against the extravagance of Yugoslavia's economic links with Africa and Asia. The interests of Yugoslav security, of its trade balance, and of its migrant labour, were not well served by a deterioration in relations with Italy and other West European countries. Mediation too could satisfy pride, since during the crisis in June 1967, President Johnson had made use of Yugoslav diplomacy as a channel to reach the Egyptian president. The new line, that of negotiation, was confirmed by two further East European meetings in July, with Yugoslavia, but without Romania. In August, Tito was off to Egypt, Syria, and Iraq, to act as mediator, and busy writing letters to many statesmen, trying to mobilize world opinion in favour of Egypt, before yet another East European gathering in September, in Belgrade.

In the autumn of 1967, and during the following winter, Yugoslavia was the prime promoter of a series of meetings of Communist and progressive parties and movements of the Mediterranean, held behind closed doors in Yugoslavia or Italy, and working up to the January 1968 resolution, sponsored by Yugoslavia, calling for the removal of every form of foreign military presence in the Mediterranean. In this way, the Yugoslav government tried to redress the balance of its non-alignment to a certain extent, before Tito left, at the beginning of 1968, for yet another tour in Asia and Africa, and plans for a third conference of the non-aligned were revealed.

By then, too, the Yugoslav government was being careful to cultivate relations with its main West European economic partners. In January, as diplomatic relations were re-established with West Germany, the chairman of the F.E.C. went to Rome for talks with the head of the Italian government and, on that occasion, called on the pope as well.

During this period, but more particularly in the summer of 1967, Western observers talked about an increased role played by the army in Yugoslav policy considerations. Such reports were often inconsistent, and it is still impossible to say whether there was any truth in the rumours they conveyed.[35] Much attention was certainly lavished on the army, which was a successful instance of what was being tried out with much less success on other institutions: it was the child of the revolution, yet it had been constantly rejuvenated, and brought up to date technically. The stress on the army was a

[35] In the summer of 1966, at the time of Rankovich's fall, the army was supposed to have been Western-orientated, but the following summer, at the time of the Near Eastern crisis, it was supposed to be so pro-Soviet.

sign of the tendency to emphasize the role and the prerogative of Tito, while awaiting the revitalization of the Party. The army symbolized the power of the state behind the historic leader.

In a climate of general change, Tito appeared as the sheet-anchor, with his prestige as a military leader, a revolutionary leader, and an international statesman. In 1967, while the debate on reforms was going on, his powers and his personal involvement seemed greater than ever. Foreign policy was entirely his own. At home, he was the moderating element, and the supreme arbiter between different trends, but in spite of all his political realism and adaptability, his mentality was in many ways that of an old revolutionary turned conservative, just as in terms of international preferences, in spite of non-alignment, he personally remained pro-Soviet and anti-Western. Attacks on the conservative elements came to an end, as the press accentuated the importance of the army, of the security services, and of Party veterans. Not only was President Tito on the move and making pronouncements on world affairs, he was similarly involved at home, touring the country before the elections, denouncing the class enemy, stressing democratic centralism, making gestures to please all ethnic groups and to discourage extremists among them. The cult of Tito's personality was strengthened in the great celebrations, in December 1967, of his thirty years at the head of the C.P.Y.

Characteristically, when a number of constitutional amendments were enacted in April 1967, before the elections, the presidency was left prominent as the only personal institution in the constitution. The offices of vice-president of the republic and of deputy supreme commander were abolished, thus making it impossible for any personality to build up a constitutional position from which to be more advantageously placed to succeed Tito. On the other hand, the position of the component republics was strengthened in several ways, in the first place by making the Council of Nations, though technically still part of the Federal Council, in fact a fully fledged chamber in so far as it wanted to act as such.[36]

The elections held in April 1967 for partial renewal of all assemblies were hailed as introducing a new climate of freedom and democracy. Although there was no change in the established filter process to ensure that only candidates deemed worthy of trust were selected, there was more open discussion in the choice of

---

[36] The federation would henceforth finance from its own resources only such investments as were specified by federal legislation, republics were made co-responsible with the federation in matters of state security, and republican public prosecutors were to be appointed locally instead of by the federal public prosecutor as hitherto.

candidates eventually put up for endorsement by the Socialist Alliance, and where there were competing candidates, they reflected different approaches to local issues, or conflicts of generations. The campaigning was vigorous, and often passionate. The largest number of competing candidates was allowed at the lowest, communal, level. At regional level, there were 425 candidates for 325 constituencies, and at federal level, 81 for 60. All in all, at these two levels, there were 86 contested constituencies, of which a dozen were federal. In fact, a number of these candidates had managed to get nominated in spite of the opposition of the Socialist Alliance – old-time Communists with good connexions who were officially frowned upon in favour of younger, new-style activists. Not all of these 'unofficial' candidates were able to battle on until election day, but of those who did, twenty-four were returned, three of them at federal level.[37] The proportion of voters who went to the polls dropped again, by 4.5 per cent to 89 per cent.

The first large-scale application of the rotation of personnel, introduced by the constitution of 1963, now took place when new executives were instituted after the 1967 elections. The Party elders were freed from administrative office, and appointed to positions of non-administrative political leadership in the 'presidential councils' – the Council of the Federation and the Council of National Defence. Their duties hence consisted in collectively assisting Tito in the formulation of policy, and also in leading parliament. On the eve of his seventy-fifth birthday, Tito was re-elected president,[38] and appointed Mika Shpiljak to constitute a new Federal Executive Council, in succession to Stambolich. The former head of the executive of Croatia thus took over from a former head of the executive of Serbia to balance the two major nationalities. The federal administration was almost completely renewed, along with the regional executives, bringing in the élite of the next Party generation. The average age of the F.E.C. itself was forty-seven.

In the turmoil that followed the fall of Rankovich, much less was

[37] The most awkward case was that of a wartime partisan general, Radivoye Yovanovich (mentioned above, p. 126, n. 24), elected for Lazarevats (Serbia) in a five-cornered contest, with an overall majority of 12,000, defeating the secretary for foreign trade. Since he refused to submit to pressure, the Serbian Central Committee met to discuss his case, and accused him of having been elected with the support of reactionary forces. He was eventually 'recalled' by the voters of his constituency in December 1967. Another interesting case in these elections was that of a sixty-five-year-old lawyer from Nish (Serbia) who was sentenced to three years' imprisonment, also in December, for hostile propaganda: he was found guilty of having sent pamphlets to peasants calling on them not to vote for candidates of the Socialist Alliance. The case for the defence rested on alleged mental unbalance.

[38] Two blank ballot papers impaired the traditionally unanimous vote.

heard of economic developments, although they had led to his fall, and had been much more real than any of the political changes. The harvest in 1967 had still been good, though farm production that year was slightly below 1966, and industrial production remained level. The proportion of exports to imports was falling again, so much so that in 1967 the balance of payments deficit had risen to $464 million – almost three times the deficit of the year before the reforms. Investments, scheduled to be scaled down, had actually begun to rise sharply again, with no corresponding growth in productivity. In the autumn of 1966, after having been stable for some months, prices resumed their upward trend in spite of controls. A new credit squeeze in 1967 managed to stabilize them, and by the summer, about 40 per cent of industrial production had actually been freed of price control – but growth had stopped altogether.

By the spring of 1968, there were 400,000 unemployed in Yugoslavia, and as many Yugoslavs employed abroad whose remittances were an important source of hard currency.[39] Apart from stepping up emigration, another solution to unemployment which was beginning to be envisaged, even in certain government circles in 1967, was employment in the private sector. Here the republic of Slovenia was particularly forward looking, since it had, as far back as 1964, legalized catering and the taking of paying guests on a family basis. In 1967, the use of up to three paid employees by private caterers, and of up to five by private craftsmen, was legalized throughout the country. By the autumn of 1967, the press was discussing the advantages of enlarging the private sector. Indeed, in 1968, a total of just over 400,000 people were engaged in the private sector outside agriculture – in private workshops, restaurants and cafés, letting of sleeping accommodation, road haulage, and taxis, apart from lawyers, and even architects. In fact, there were probably more, for the five-employee limit was not always rigidly enforced, and many local authorities closed their eyes to breaches of the rules since they obtained more rapid service from private contractors.

Another significant development was the limited opening of the

[39] The proportion of graduates among unemployed and emigrants rose. They were considered expensive, unproductive, and potential rivals for management by those who had entrenched themselves in management boards. The situation in the 'non-economic' sectors, such as teaching or health, was not brighter. Pay rises lagged behind in these categories, which were nonproductive, run on deficits, and not yet inclined to strike. At the end of 1966, there were 20,000 unemployed graduates (*Borba*, 27 December 1966); a year later, their number had risen to 60,000 (*The Times*, 15 November 1967). Remittances from Yugoslavs working abroad had increased from $32 million in 1965 to $135 million in 1968 (C. Bird, quoting data obtained from the National Bank, in *Problems of Communism*, XVIII/4–5, *Washington*, 1969, p. 78).

Yugoslav economy to foreign capital. From a purely economic point of view, the need for foreign investment, with its concomitant technical know-how, had been acknowledged earlier, but it was not until the summer of 1967 that ideological scruples were overcome. Under legislation adopted that July, foreign capitalists could enter into investment contracts with existing Yugoslav enterprises, within certain conditions.[40] Lack of capital and lack of efficient management had been correctly diagnosed as the two outstanding factors which limited the effect of the reforms attempted after 1965. In many ways, the Yugoslav economy was still too backward for some of the experiments to which it was being subjected.[41] Thus, to a great extent, the success of the reform depended on outside aid.

In November 1967, the head of the F.E.C. had stated in parliament that the Yugoslav economy was in a state of ferment because of the changes. The liberalization of the economy had given birth to all sorts of economic pressure groups. One of the most interesting of these developments was, doubtless, the development of the trade unions during 1967. With the working class becoming more conscious of itself in spontaneous industrial action, the Trade Union Organization hesitantly began to follow the movement, and to establish itself, at national if not at shop-floor level, as a force pressing for a more forward policy in favour of the workers. The rash of strikes from the middle of 1966 and throughout 1967 followed a simple pattern. Workers struck against wages lagging behind, against redundancy dismissals, against decisions of their nominally elected management boards, against pay according to work performed, against the closure of uneconomic plants or pits. They even used violence: there were instances of works occupied by striking workers, of managers thrown out of their offices.

[40] The foreign investor could either invest directly in his Yugoslav partner, or in a new jointly formed enterprise. All investment contracts had to be officially registered. Some sectors (such as banking and insurance, domestic communications and commerce) were not available to foreign investment without F.E.C. approval. The foreign partner could not own more than 49·9% of the capital of a given enterprise, nor withdraw more than 80% of the tax-paid profit received. Capital once invested could be transferred, but not withdrawn from Yugoslavia. If assets as opposed to money were invested, they were to be amortized over a prescribed period, after which the foreign partner no longer had any rights over, or profits from, the joint venture. The foreign partner could partake in short-term managerial responsibility through a joint business committee, but had no control over labour relations or internal profit distribution. (Cf. Pešelj, art. cit. in *Law and Policy in International Business*, II/1, 1970, pp. 69 seqq.)

[41] A Czechoslovak economist commented sarcastically on the Yugoslav economic reforms: 'You have to have an economy before you can start talking about economic reform' (quoted in J. Brown, *The New Eastern Europe – The Khrushchev Era and After*, London, 1960, pp. 123–4).

The official point of view was that the answer to all difficulties lay in the full implementation of the reforms including the full implementation of self-management. The reforms themselves were obviously to be blamed only in so far as they had exposed the consequences of the previous system, but there remained the problem of management *per se* – whether by workers or otherwise – and of its responsibilities. There were other problems which the economic reforms by themselves could not cure, such as that of Yugoslavia's isolation from Europe. Moreover, the new economic policy was being carried out with the same people in charge – in spite of purges and rejuvenation – who had had, for almost two decades, to be forced into accepting it during the long process of trial and error, of plunging ahead and pulling the reins, to which the Yugoslav economy had been subjected.

Chapter 7

Crisis and Beyond: 1968–70

The crisis of 1968

Although it had aligned its diplomacy with that of the Soviet Union during the Near Eastern crisis, Yugoslavia did not associate itself with the preparations for a meeting of Communist parties planned for the autumn of 1968. During the first half of that year, it multiplied friendly contacts with two other Communist-ruled states that were showing signs of wanting to follow their own line – Romania and Czechoslovakia. Furthermore, when a new meeting of Mediterranean progressive movements, held in May 1968 in Rome, moved closer towards Soviet positions than Yugoslavia was prepared to do, the latter, which had been the prime mover of these meetings, refused to vote for a resolution directed solely against the American presence in the Mediterranean.

On his return from Asia at the end of April 1968, Tito had gone to Moscow to make his position clear to the Soviet leaders: the Yugoslav government was now worried about the negative influence that a Soviet naval presence in the Mediterranean, or Soviet pressure on its European allies, might have both on the strength and the credibility of the Communist community. It feared that, far from strengthening socialism in the world, it would harden opposition to it. Another factor, about which Tito was probably not so frank, was that the wish of Romania and Czechoslovakia to pursue different courses gave Yugoslavia a further chance of making its influence felt in eastern Europe.

If Yugoslavia supported the reforms being introduced in Czechoslovakia after Dubček succeeded Novotný as the head of the Party there, it was not out of anti-Sovietism, but because its leaders believed they were acting in the best interests of socialism.[1] After

[1] The Yugoslav government took great care to advise the Czechoslovak leadership on how far it could safely go (cf. Tito's interview with *Paris-Match*, 16 November 1968). Public opinion, and even the press, went much further than the government in its enthusiasm for developments in Czechoslovakia which, the Yugoslavs felt, enabled that country to break through restrictions which still existed in their own country after twenty years of independent

the apparent compromise reached between the leaders of Czechoslovakia and the U.S.S.R. in the first days of August, the Yugoslav government wanted to believe that a solution had been found. Either it did not think that the Soviet Union would intervene militarily, or it tried to exorcize such a possibility. When Tito went to Prague ten days before the invasion, far from offering the Czechoslovaks full moral support against the U.S.S.R., he spoke only of the dangers of Western imperialism, and of reaction and counter-revolution.

When Warsaw Pact troops entered Czechoslovakia on 21 August, the Yugoslavs suddenly felt that they too were in danger. Among the developments that the Soviet Union wanted to nip in the bud, there were perhaps – in addition to those developments in the Czechoslovak power-structure that it regarded with apprehension – Romania's diplomatic heterodoxy and the potential 'Little Entente' of the dissident Communist states generally. Yugoslavia had again tried to play too big a role among the East European Communist Parties; it lay on the shortest route between the Warsaw Pact territory and the Soviet build-up in the Mediterranean. All its efforts at being the European head of Afro-Asian non-alignment suddenly seemed useless: Yugoslavia felt isolated, and Tito seemed cast as Franco's frightened East European opposite number.

The highest political bodies immediately met. Tito condemned the intervention as a serious blow against socialism, and expressed Yugoslavia's determination to defend its own independence. Romania was, of course, in a much more vulnerable position, and no sooner had Yugoslavia's position been clarified than Tito and Ceauşescu – Gheorghiu-Dej's successor at the head of the Romanian Party – met at the border on 24 August, and again on 4 September when they declared their determination to resist any aggression. By so doing, the heads of the Yugoslav and Romanian ruling Parties were warning the Soviet government against any possible intervention in either of their two countries, in the hope that the risks the Soviets would run should appear greater than they had turned out to be in the Czechoslovak adventure. They were also out to reassure their own cadres and populations, as well as calling for the attention of international opinion. Tensions rose in late September and early October. In the Soviet press, and elsewhere in eastern Europe, the Yugoslav political and economic system came under attack, and the Yugoslav president himself was accused of having helped the counter-revolution in Czechoslovakia.

development (cf. *The Times*, 29 March 1968). This was a further reason for the Yugoslav government to keep a check on the progress of reforms in Czechoslovakia, so as not to allow them to go further than in Yugoslavia.

With the formulation of the so-called Brezhnev doctrine of the limited sovereignty of socialist states, Yugoslavia again turned to the West, which alone could provide serious cover. A vice-chairman of the F.E.C. was despatched to Washington, while official and private contacts were multiplied. In order both to reinforce the plea for support, and to impress Western opinion favourably, Djilas was granted a passport to travel to the U.S.A., and while abroad he duly stressed the need for the West to support Yugoslavia against a Soviet invasion. In answer to these appeals, in mid-October President Johnson issued a statement about America's 'clear and continuing interest in Yugoslavia's independence, sovereignty, and economic development', and a destroyer of the Sixth Fleet put in at Dubrovnik. At its November meeting in Brussels, the NATO Council gave warning signals meant to deter the Soviet government from any move against Yugoslavia, whilst the U.S. secretary of state, Dean Rusk, spoke of a 'grey zone' including Yugoslavia that was to be shielded by the alliance.

From Yugoslavia itself came vastly exaggerated reports of mobilization and troop movements, aimed at giving the impression, at home and abroad, of alarm and resolution. Some reservists were, in fact, called up, and available troops were moved about, but it was not until late October that a series of legislative measures were passed, increasing defence estimates and introducing the military training of civilians within their working communities. In February 1969, further legislation brought into being a Territorial Defence Organization, which was to be set up by the regional governments to help maintain order and defend the local communities against every possible form of enemy action. The defence of the independence, territorial integrity, and established order of Yugoslavia was proclaimed by law to be the duty of all citizens, ethnic groups, and organizations. In the following July, the first Territorial Defence units began to function.

Meanwhile, the psychological mobilization undertaken by the government was greater than all its military mobilization, real or presumed. The flag of patriotism was waved just as when the C.P.Y. had been expelled from the Cominform in 1948, or when it had entered the resistance after the German attack on the Soviet Union in 1941. The country's military virtues and traditions were extolled. There were great celebrations, in November 1968, to mark the twenty-fifth anniversary of the Yaytse resolutions,[2] the victories of the partisan army at the end of the Second World War, and the foundation of the Communist régime. These were even extended to coincide with the fiftieth anniversary of the victories of the Serbian

[2] See above, p. 152.

army at the end of the First World War, and the foundation of the first Yugoslav state.

It was soon apparent, however, that both the Soviet and the Yugoslav sides were anxious to avoid a breach. Only a few weeks after the NATO Council had discussed the possibility of a Soviet attack on Yugoslavia, the Soviet defence minister had sent a warm message to his Yugoslav counterpart on the occasion of the Yugoslav Army Day on 29 November, while the following day, Tito had lessened the tension with the U.S.S.R. and rejected the American secretary of state's idea of a 'grey zone' in Europe. If attacked, Yugoslavia had no need for outside help, Tito declared, adding that he had no reason to believe that any attack was being contemplated.

In reality, however, there was serious doubt whether the country could resist an invasion in 1968 any better than in 1941. Yugoslavia had sounded the alarm because it had felt isolated and weak. No sooner had its leaders convinced themselves that the U.S.A. would not countenance a Soviet intervention, than they were anxious not to provoke the U.S.S.R. any further. The same reasons that had made the government turn to the West in the summer made it eager to find a new *modus vivendi* with the Soviet Union in the autumn – the more so since a drastic separation would again require greater reliance on the West, and lead to unwelcome political influence.

The Soviet danger had also been used to restore the domestic position of the government, which was strengthened by its defence posture. The alarm had already been given before the invasion of Czechoslovakia, but then it had been done against the West and American imperialism. The Yugoslav leadership genuinely feared the extension of American influence, and it had intended to ease domestic strains by attributing all difficulties to Western intrigues. The country at large had not been convinced. When, however, the alarm was raised against the East, after the intervention in Czechoslovakia, it sounded more convincing. All difficulties were then traced back to Soviet and East European action, and the threat from the East successfully united most Yugoslavs behind their government. For a time, the predominant theme was the defence of the fatherland, and since that year also happened to mark the fiftieth anniversary of the unification of the Yugoslav lands – something not celebrated usually – the coincidence was used for a timid attempt to cement national unity.

Yet one cannot but agree with Marshal Tito when he said at Yaytse on 30 November 1968 that he had no reason to believe that the Soviet Union was contemplating an attack on Yugoslavia. Nothing had changed in his country. Tito himself was no rebel, in spite of his reputation, and in spite of his ambition. The Soviet leaders knew that there were limits beyond which Yugoslavia would never go so long as he was at the helm. They appreciated the advantages of Yugoslavia's contribution to common aims, and the Yugoslav president could even be relied upon to advise other Communist leaders from going ahead too far. They knew that – however much he needed the West for economic reasons and, when necessary, to resist Soviet pressure – for political reasons he was anxious to avoid too close a relationship with the West. Yugoslavia had long been accepted as being militarily on the periphery of the Soviet camp, and the Soviet leaders had never said whether the Brezhnev doctrine applied to it or not. Indeed, they probably wanted to leave it in an imprecise 'grey zone'. To try and exclude it formally from the 'socialist commonwealth' risked upsetting the latter's, and Yugoslavia's, already uncertain equilibrium. To attempt to bring it back in by force would, if nothing else, have ruined the chances of coming to any accommodation with President Nixon's new administration. Keeping the Yugoslavs guessing was also a way of exerting pressure on them, not so much to change their government, or to frustrate the development of their system, as to trim their ambitions down to size. Doubtless, the aim of the Soviet leaders was also to be in a position to control the situation in their favour, or at least to prevent it from being used to their disadvantage, in case of a serious crisis in Yugoslavia, or a serious change in its orientation. Soviet pressure on Yugoslavia had not started in the summer of 1968, but it had been mounting for some time. Both the tension with Bulgaria over Macedonia and the trouble with the Albanian minority were, most probably, used by the Soviets as instruments of such pressure.

By giving more satisfaction to the Albanian minority in order to ensure its loyalty to Yugoslavia, the government also helped it to become more conscious of its rights and of its strength. The Albanians had been used, within the L.C.Y., as a stick with which to beat the conservatives, and the leaders of the Albanian community had, in turn, used the Party to promote their own cause. The rising pressure of their nationalism was backed by the physical pressure of their demography, which had made Albanians the majority in Kosovo, with an important overspill outside the region.[3] As difficulties piled up in 1968, Albanian agitation rose until, in October, the authorities took fright. Tito met regional leaders, and offered both

---

[3] According to the 1961 census, there were 915,000 Albanians in Yugoslavia, and they formed 67% of the population of Kosovo. Since then, their total number has been estimated (cf. G. Chaffard, art. cit. in *Le Monde diplomatique*, July 1969) at over 1 million: over 850,000 in Kosovo (as against 250,000 Serbs, adding up to under 300,000 when joined by the Montenegrins, and some 27,000 Turks), and 230,000 in western Macedonia.

more economic aid and more autonomy, although the demand for a separate Albanian republic within Yugoslavia was turned down. At the end of November, nevertheless, the situation exploded. Thousands of Albanians demonstrated in the streets of Prishtina, the provincial capital, and other towns in Kosovo, calling for union with Albania, acclaiming the name of Enver Hoxha, the Albanian Party leader, shouting their hatred of Serbs, and clashing with the police. The situation was hushed up, and no foreigners were allowed in the trouble area, but there were reports that the army had been sent to restore order, and many Albanian nationalists were arrested. All the same, by the end of December the agitation had spread to Macedonia, and similar demonstrations, though on a smaller scale, were organized in Tetovo.

Albanian nationalism in Yugoslavia has several facets. The union of all Albanians is a dream and a good slogan, but the Tirana régime is not to the liking of all Yugoslav Albanians. Albanian peasants in Yugoslavia wish to give up neither their land nor their religion, and there was more than one hint of anti-communism in the demonstrations of 1968. The Albanians in the Kosovo Party leadership and the young Albanian cadres in the province realize that, although their region is the most backward in Yugoslavia, it stands to gain more from Belgrade than from Tirana. The radicals among them want an Albanian republic within Yugoslavia, made up of Kosovo and western Macedonia, which could then look out to Albania with the hope of one day uniting all the Albanians in an Albanian republic within the federation. This version of a 'greater Albania' would enable the leaders and young cadres of the Kosovo Party, with their better training and wider outlook, to play the decisive role, while it would, moreover, fit in with Tito's old dream of a greater Yugoslavia.

Differences with Bulgaria flared up again in 1968 with the celebrations by the Bulgars of the ninetieth anniversary of the Russo-Turkish Treaty of San Stefano which had, on paper, created a large Bulgaria extending over the whole of Macedonia. Throughout the year, the dispute ranged over history and language, on a level reminiscent of similar exchanges between Serbia and Bulgaria in earlier times. The Bulgars wrote about their mediaeval rulers whose writ had prevailed in Macedonia, analysed the nature of the Macedonian 'dialect', and stressed the part played by the Bulgarian forces in the liberation of Macedonia from the Germans in 1944. Both sides indulged in mock-scholarly controversy about the 'nationality' of mediaeval saints, rulers, lords, and heroes. Belgrade accused Sofia of casting a covetous eye on Yugoslav territory, and Skopye again accused Sofia, for the first time in almost a decade, of denying rights to its own Macedonian minority. At the same time the Bulgarian government's emphatic denials in the autumn of any territorial claims, accompanied by statements in favour of improved relations, did indicate that however much the Bulgars wanted to put pressure on Yugoslavia, they did not want to press too hard.

Renewed Bulgarian pressure, followed by Albanian agitation, made the Macedonian Party leaders realize more clearly than ever that solidarity with Yugoslavia was essential to the existence of a distinct Macedonian nation. In their own republic, a little over one million ethnic Macedonians lived with 230,000 Albanians and 180,000 Turks, not to mention those who still felt more or less Serbian (or, for that matter, Bulgarian). They could not afford to give way to their own Albanians in Macedonia, as the Serbs had in Serbia, and were ready to oppose any attempt to limit their national rights or to divide them. One way of doing this was to keep alive the dream of uniting the whole of Macedonia within a greater Yugoslavia.[4]

The trend towards identifying the republics with ethnic groups increased the Serbian malaise, since, of all ethnic groups, the Serbs had the largest proportion living outside 'their' republic. The separation of Montenegro from Serbia, which had its historical, administrative, and political *raisons d'être*, was an artificial one on ethnic grounds. In the republic of Serbia itself, Voyvodina in the north and Kosovo in the south had been given special status, because of their mixed ethnic composition. The latter, however, was rapidly becoming a national home for the Albanian minority in Yugoslavia. Serbs also lived in every other republic except Slovenia. For that reason, Serbian opinion was not keen on giving yet more power to the republics at the expense of the federation, and the Serbian Party leadership was in an awkward situation, trying to avoid being identified with either Yugoslav centralism or Serbian nationalism. Devoid of official channels and of leadership, Serbian nationalism could only express itself in nostalgia and empty talk. Traditionally linked as it was with the ups and downs of the Serbian nation, the Serbian Church found itself gradually tempted to provide, if not leadership, at least a more satisfying form of expression for these feelings.

The Croat Bakarich and the Slovene Kardelj had led the

[4] Although they did not do so loudly, Yugoslav Macedonian Communists did talk, off the record, of a greater Macedonia at the same time as Bulgarian Communists started their San Stefano year. One personality in Skopye told the correspondent of *Le Monde* (31 January 1968) that, whereas the short-term minimum programme was to work for the cultural rights of Macedonians outside Yugoslavia, the long-term aim remained the union of all Macedonians.

decentralizing tendency because they realized that the economic decentralization demanded by Croatian and Slovenian Communists in the interests of their respective territories could not be fully carried out without some political decentralization; also because it was a way of giving satisfaction to these regions and of making the Communist Yugoslav state more acceptable there. Nevertheless, in their republics they resisted the more particularist trend which was directed against the Serbs. The policy of the Communist leadership at the centre had become one of trying to keep a delicate balance between satisfying and resisting the centrifugal pull of local Party leaderships.

It had tried, and was still trying, to integrate the different groups, regions, and traditions on an ideological basis, that of communism; but it would not, or could not, allow them to unite on any other basis, and so preferred, in all other fields, to give free rein to the expression of their separate identities. The former aspect of the government's approach was an extremely long-term one, and it was in no way helped in the short term by the latter, which meanwhile separated rather than integrated. Although resisting the more extreme, the government continued to give satisfaction to various local demands. In 1968, two important concessions touched on the hitherto exclusively common domains of diplomacy and the army. Local parliaments were allowed to set up their own commissions for foreign affairs, and one-fifth of all recruits were allowed to do their military service within their own region, while all personnel in the federal administration were now recruited according to an 'ethnic scale'.

Nationalism, which was not permitted to grasp at anything positive – except the danger of foreign invasion – increasingly developed its negative aspects. Stirred by disappointment in the present, fear for the future, and nostalgia for the past, it poured itself into old moulds, and most local Communist leaders looked to the past for a model which would place them in a historical perspective while they worked towards the realization of a Communist society. The leaders of Slovenia looked back to the nationalist-clerical leadership of old when they struggled for freedom to look after their own region efficiently and with little or no interference from the central government. In Croatia, nationalism of one kind or another had been the major ideology of the modern era, and legalism the major political weapon. The stress was now again on a legal framework within which an autonomous Croatian political entity could function in dualism with the central government of the common state, and nationalism was the natural sequel to relaxation. In Montenegro, the Party leadership could only imitate the former dynasty in its more selfish moments, by stressing the traditions of a separate political existence against the deeper-felt tradition of being part of the Serbian nation in every other way. Even the newer nationalism of Macedonia expressed itself in forms ridiculously reminiscent of the nineteenth century. In Serbia, where the political leadership could not afford to indulge in such exercises and stuck to the central leadership, culture and religion took over the old structures left unoccupied by politics, and private nationalism became wordy and lachrymose.

Such a state naturally strengthened the hands of those who, in government circles, believed that only strong centralism could save the régime. It also strengthened the hands of those in the ranks of the clergy who thought it unwise to go against the sectionalist mood of the faithful. Finally, it led extremist expatriates to dream of a *politique du pire*, adding a destructive note – given full coverage by the mass media in Yugoslavia – to the already dominantly negative tone of nationalism within Yugoslavia.[5]

Their wishful thinking would not have been worthy of mention had it not been that they were able to find recruits among the migrant workers to execute their plans. Many of these, dissatisfied with conditions at home, uprooted from their traditional environment, and unable to adapt themselves to the industrialized urban society of the West, were a ready prey for the hard-core survivors of the civil war and the old terrorists who had, before the war, tried to destroy another régime in Yugoslavia. From their American or West German armchairs, aged terrorists and guerrillas from another age raved in their publications and urged the need for action. In times of tension, emotional people are tempted to perform what they think are acts of heroism. In Yugoslavia, authority was being challenged by writers, students, and local Communist groups, but also by violent strikes, increased criminality, and general hooliganism. Violence, as a way of expressing dissatisfaction, was catching on in the West anyhow. Bombs exploded in Yugoslav diplomatic and consular missions in Paris, Klagenfurt, and New York, then in Belgrade itself, causing damage, injuries, and loss of life, all between February and October. The Yugoslav press inveighed against *émigrés* and made them all appear as terrorists. More people were tried for hostile propaganda, and official pronouncements lumped all opposition tendencies into one vast conspiracy, at once Stalinist, Maoist, neo-Cominformist, bourgeois democratic, anarcho-liberal, reactionary, collaborationist, fascist, nationalist, and clerical.

[5] There were variations on the dream. Serbian extremist *émigrés* dreamt of a collapse of the Communist régime which would free the Serbian people; their Croatian counterparts, of a collapse of the Yugoslav state which would allow Croatia to slip to the West.

More difficulties confronted the Yugoslav government that year. Corruption was so rampant that it was found necessary to implicate relatively important personalities, as a sacrifice to public, especially worker, opinion. The working class spoke out against the widening gap between rich and poor, and the privileges of the bureaucracy, so much so that when the sixth congress of the trade unions was held in Belgrade at the end of June, an unexpected storm blew up. The carefully prepared agenda was disregarded, and delegates spontaneously voiced shop-floor feelings. In a passionate discussion in which government policy was freely criticized, demands were made for independent trade unions that would really stand up for the working class.

The problem for the government was to keep within limits all these independent pressure groups – nationalisms and Churches, workers and intellectuals – which had been growing in importance. As long as they remained sectional, they were useful safety valves, but in 1968 there was the danger that they would all be activated at once and influence each other. The student body, sensitive to the discontent of all sections at home and to events abroad, was by now unprejudiced and vocal, and potentially troublesome. The material conditions for students were difficult.[6] The opportunities of employment for graduates were limited and poorly paid. The proportion of Party members among students was declining fast.

Trouble in the universities had been building up since the beginning of 1968. It was known that all the controversial writings of intellectuals were being avidly read by students, and that their own union papers were also becoming more controversial. In the early months of 1968, there were embarrassing political and legal skirmishes with students' unions in several universities. Nevertheless, the revolutionary conflict that exploded at Belgrade University on 2 June came as a surprise to everybody. Under the impulse of the French 'events', and acting upon an insignificant pretext, Belgrade University students revolted. The actual revolt lasted for a week, but its rumblings went on for a whole year. They took over the university buildings where they staged an eight-day sit-in. They attempted to march from their *cité universitaire* on the outskirts to the centre of Belgrade, and were driven back only after a pitched battle with the police involving the use of firearms.[7] There were

[6] Grants had not increased on a par with the number of students or the cost of living. The proportion of grant-holding students had diminished from 25% in 1962 to 14% in 1966 (*Borba*, 19 May 1968). Only a small minority of students – about a third – could benefit from social insurance (*Politika*, 29 May 1968).

[7] The injured numbered 134 students, 21 policemen, and 14 others, according to the figures officially released.

echoes of solidarity in all the other universities, and support for the students came not only from their teachers and non-conforming intellectuals, but was also expressed in numerous meetings in factories, enterprises, and offices. The students' revolt in June 1968 and its reverberations presented the régime with its most significant challenge since it came to power.

The motives for the revolt were varied, contradictory, and confused. They reflected the general disquiet of the younger generation, the special disquiet of the Yugoslav students, and indeed the disquiet of all Yugoslavs generally. On the one hand, the students' demands indicated an obvious wish to improve their own material situation and the number of openings available to them, as well as expressing the wish to extend the opportunity to go to a university and to increase student participation in the way universities were run. On the other hand, they constituted a more general reaction against a system which tried to disguise abuses and evils allegedly peculiar to capitalism under empty socialist slogans. The movement, which reflected at the same time a yearning for egalitarianism and liberalism, was interesting in that it showed a surprising awareness of the Belgrade University tradition of opposition, and no sign of sectional nationalism.

The reaction of the authorities was no less varied, contradictory, and confused than the challenge they had to face. The students had no firm organization or leadership, but it was feared that they might provide a link between intellectuals and workers. The initial reaction was for some authorities to express approval of the students' academic demands, while ignoring the rest, and for other authorities to denounce the students for having naïvely fallen into the trap of the anti-Communist opposition. While a ban was imposed on further meetings in Belgrade, and student magazines were confiscated, a series of measures were taken concerning the management of halls of residence and canteens, the health insurance of students, and the employment of graduate trainees.

Since the only organized movement among the students was the Communist Party, and control over this was quickly restored, the authorities manoeuvred so as to allow it to take over the direction of the student movement. By 9 June, the stage was set for Tito's direct television appeal to the students. His approach was avuncular rather than paternal. He placed himself on the side of the students, recognized the justification of much of their criticism, pledged himself to solve their problems (and to resign if he failed). He appealed to them to help him fulfil his pledge and root out opposition to reforms, but warned them at the same time to beware of infiltration by hostile elements. A fortnight later, he took a similar line with the workers in his speech to the trade union congress. By that time, calm had been restored, the movement had fizzled out, and a campaign in support of President Tito was already under way.

The government had managed to turn the explosion of disaffection among workers and students into a movement of support for Tito's revolutionary leadership, while private entrepreneurs and intellectuals, transmogrified into scapegoats past redemption, were made responsible for the return to capitalist practices and the poison the students had taken. The intelligentsia, in particular, was accused of wanting to take over as the vanguard from the working class. In July, the Central Committee met to denounce the academics who had grouped into political opposition to the L.C.Y., and all the reactionary forces that had tried to profit from the disorders. Thereafter for the rest of the year, there were expulsions of writers and dons from the Party and university, and many issues of periodicals, in Belgrade, Zagreb, and Ljubljana, were banned for having given distorted interpretations of the June events.

For a while, the intellectuals grouped around the literary-political journals appeared to be coalescing into a recognizable minority, and the students, too, seemed ready to act in accordance with some sort of programme of their own. What emerged, to be most vehemently denounced, was the call for pluralism and for the institutionalization of opposition. Yet, however much the intellectuals influenced the students, and the students expressed grievances which elicited sympathy from the workers, no common front was established.

The Party had the organization, the power, and the ability to manoeuvre within and around opposition trends, which were confused, disorganized, and not consciously synchronized. However divided otherwise, the apparatus of the L.C.Y. was united on the fundamental political issue of power itself. The intelligentsia had no striking power, and was not organized for action. It could only make gestures, with little impact on public opinion at large. It expressed itself through individuals who were not politicians, yet many of them were members of the Party and of the establishment and thus subject to disciplinary action, so they could not really put up an effective defence when blamed for all the country's ills. As for the workers, they were busy with their immediate material problems. Their grievances received organized expression only through the hierarchy of trade unions which were still fundamentally organs of the established system rather than the voice of the workers. Confined as they were to the limits of their enterprises, in the management of which they were allowed to play a role, the workers could not really, on their own, turn their interests into class interests.

Beyond the political issue of power, however, by the beginning of 1968 the L.C.Y. no longer represented an effective force able to deal with any other problem. It had ceased to be much of an organizational whole, since it had developed into a plurality of regional leagues. It did not even provide a unifying force, for most regional leaderships had jumped on to the nationalist bandwaggon, although it still effectively prevented any coming-together of people and groups outside the Party. In reforming itself, the Party was so determined not to let freedom of political expression get out of hand that official spokesmen often seemed more intent on criticizing their opponents within the Party than on making their programme attractive to the population. The L.C.Y. was so divided within itself that it was not very clear to members themselves, let alone to the country at large, what the Party's role really was. Its compromise policies and devalued slogans had failed to generate widespread enthusiasm. The economic reforms themselves were not generally considered a success, so much had they been presented as the panacea for all the country's ills, and so difficult was it to enforce them. The result was growing distrust in the régime – among reformists and conservative Communists, and among Communists and non-Communists alike – and a growing impatience in all sections of the population.

Could the leadership readapt the Party quickly enough, if at all, to lead the country forward towards the fulfilment of communism, before the sectional, disorganized ferment within and outside its ranks combined on a widely based front to challenge its monopoly of power, or before it blew the country itself to pieces? That was now the question facing the leadership. In the summer of 1968, the answer had almost been negative, and yet a series of stop-gap measures, blending concessions here with threats there, had managed to restore some measure of calm, while the real or imagined dangers of American and Soviet imperialism, magnified and lumped together into a gigantic anti-Yugoslav plot, had even managed to close the broken ranks for a while.

When the Federal Assembly met at the end of the year, classical parliamentary democracy was strongly condemned, and more constitutional amendments were enacted. The Federal Council was abolished and finally divided into its two separate political components: the Social and Political Council, directly elected by the citizens in the communes,[8] and the Council of Nations, representing

---

[8] The corporative chamber representing the administration was abolished. Elections for the three remaining corporative chambers were to be indirect, through electoral colleges composed of communal councillors and delegates of the working communities. The electoral role of the Socialist Alliance was further strengthened by the new electoral law of 15 January 1969, according

the regional parliaments. The functions of the Federal Council were taken over by the Council of Nations, which became the first and most important chamber. The status of the two autonomous provinces within Serbia was made tantamount to that of the republics,[9] while the minorities, promoted to 'nationalities', were given full cultural and linguistic equality with the 'nations'.

Holding the system together

With the feeling of having Western support against the danger of a Soviet invasion, a fragile unity between the Party line and public opinion had been achieved. It was in this atmosphere that the ninth congress of the L.C.Y. was held in March 1969 to restore the balance between continued economic reform and the authority of the Party – which then numbered 1·1 million members. Some seventy foreign Communist, Socialist, and other 'workers' and progressive parties and movements' were represented, but of the ruling East European Communists, only the Romanians came. Tito's opening speech set the tone for the congress by its insistence on the continued revolutionary nature of the L.C.Y. It had gone too far in liberalization and decentralization. Yugoslav 'socialist democracy' and 'socialist patriotism' were to be defended against all their enemies. There was to be strong leadership at the centre which would bring in younger people, 'because some of us are already getting on, and we need to ensure continuity in the highest leadership'.

The latter was the main issue of the congress. The temporary changes introduced in 1966 were superseded by a new permanent structure designed so as to give the central leadership authority, strength, and ability to face and solve the complex tasks ahead. More federalization and the injection of new blood would ensure not only continuity, but also that decisions were implemented locally. The Central Committee was abolished, and replaced by a Permanent Conference of representatives of regional leagues. The presidency

to which it both nominated and confirmed candidates. In every constituency, the Socialist Alliance now set up an official electoral commission to examine the lists of candidates nominated by voters' meetings, with the right to veto and replace any candidate. Alterations could be made in the list drawn up by the commission only if agreed on by either one-third of all voters' meetings in the constituency, or 10% of all registered voters. All chambers were now to be renewed entirely every four years.

[9] Now called 'socialist autonomous provinces', they were to have their own constitutions and supreme courts, the financial competence of republics, greater legislative prerogatives, and separate representation on the Council of Nations.

would also be composed of representatives of the local parties – six from each republic, three each from Kosovo, Voyvodina, and the army – with the Party's president and the presidents of local central committees as *ex officio* members. It would elect an Executive Bureau, to work collectively and permanently in Belgrade.

Tito was re-elected president of the L.C.Y., and twenty-two members of the 1966 presidency, including General Goshnjak, were quietly dropped from the new body, without dishonour. Tito himself proposed that the Executive Bureau should be made up, besides himself, of two prominent leaders from every republic, with one each from Kosovo and Voyvodina, and these he nominated.[10]

The Party congress was followed by general elections under the new electoral law. Although the trend towards more candidates was maintained, great care was taken to avoid the personal electioneering of the 1967 election, and the presence of unauthorized candidates.[11] On 12 April 1969, polls were held at all levels for the representatives of the communes, and 87 per cent of the electorate voted – a further 2 per cent drop since 1967. In spite of the care taken, there were still a few off-beat happenings. A Catholic priest was elected to a communal assembly in Slovenia. Another priest, this time an Orthodox, caused a milder sensation in his rural constituency in Serbia by predicting the end of Communist rule, and was duly sentenced to twenty days' imprisonment even before polling day. In some constituencies, where the turnout had not been high enough for any of the candidates to get the minimum number of votes required, a second poll was needed. In one federal constituency in Bosnia, the only candidate could not be returned because 80 per cent of the ballot papers cast were blank. Finally, at federal and regional

---

[10] The members of the Executive Bureau were: Tito (president), N. Dizdarevich and Ts. Miyatovich (Bosnia-Herzegovina), V. Bakarich and M. Tripalo (Croatia), K. Gligorov and K. Tsrvenkovski (Macedonia), B. Shoshkich and V. Vlahovich (Montenegro), M. Pechuylich and M. Todorovich (Serbia), S. Dolants and E. Kardelj (Slovenia), F. Hodja (Kosovo) and S. Doronjski (Voyvodina) – average age fifty, excluding Tito. Of the sixty-three personalities elected to the Central Committee at the 1948 congress, only ten were still among the fifty-two members of the latest presidency (V. Bakarich, Y. Blazhevich, R. Dugonjich, E. Kardelj, L. Kolishevski, Ts. Miyatovich, M. Popovich, P. Stambolich, V. Vlahovich – and Tito). Of the nine members of the 1948 Political Bureau, only Tito and Kardelj were left in the new Executive Bureau. Of the others, Neshkovich, Djilas, and Rankovich had been expelled, Piyade and Kidrich had died, Leskoshek had retired because of old age, and Goshnjak had just been left out.

[11] At federal level, 624 candidates stood for the 360 seats of the corporative chambers, but there were only 179 for the 120 seats of the directly elected Social and Political Council.

levels, four unauthorized candidates managed to get on the lists, and two of them were returned, both in Serbia, one of them to the federal parliament.[12]

In May, when the new Federal Assembly was fully constituted, a new Federal Executive Council was formed. After a Serb and a Croat, it had been expected that the new chairman of the F.E.C. would be a Slovene, but Tito's choice of Mitja Ribichich came as a surprise. The new 'prime minister' had never been in the limelight and, moreover, had made a career in the S.D.B. His 'cabinet' was neatly balanced according to the needs of ethnic and regional representation, age and sex, and specialization and rotation. Although the whole ritual, and even the terminology used, now tended to recall classical parliamentary forms, it was obvious that the F.E.C. was the executant rather than the executive, the formal administrative agency of the Party's Executive Bureau that was all the more the real government for being made up of different people.

Tito's personal involvement in all fields greatly increased in 1969, the year following the crisis. Now seventy-seven years old, he mobilized all his energy to hold the system together while it was being readapted. Not only did he go on an extensive tour of the country in the summer and autumn of 1969, to put across the new policy of hardening the line, but he was off at the beginning of 1970 on yet another long journey to Africa, and ended that year with a series of visits to the countries of the European Common Market. On several occasions, he defined what the right trends should be in literature, the arts, learning and science, and attacked specific works and backed others.[13] The dogmatic tone of his pronouncements, ranging from those on American foreign policy to those on the cinema, and from Marx to cattle-breeding, had an increasingly anachronistic ring – paternalism turned into patriarchalism. More

[12] The outgoing federal M.P. for Chachak was rejected by local League and Alliance organs for having tried to lead some Communists away from the Party line. He was re-elected by 78,277 against 29,346 for the officially backed candidate. At Nish-II, for the parliament of Serbia, a local farmer was confirmed by voters' meetings although the electoral commission had vetoed him on account of his judicial record. He was returned in a three-cornered contest by 11,745 votes, against 11,661 and 11,531 for the two other, approved, candidates. In both cases, many peasant voters openly said that they had voted for the unapproved candidate out of bravado, or because he must be the best since he had been attacked so much.

[13] Tito personally backed the official super-production, *The Battle of the Neretva*, a three-hour epic of the partisan war, with the participation of the Yugoslav army and an international star-studded cast which seemed to reflect Yugoslavia's links with the two super-powers and its two main trade partners (Silva Koscina, Yul Brynner, Sergei Bondarchuk, Kurt Jurgens, and Orson Welles – as the *chetnik* villain).

than ever, the régime and the country were linked to his personality, turned into a living myth.[14] Next to him, the only other survivor of the original team, Kardelj, now occupied the second place in the order of real precedence, less as an heir apparent groomed to succeed Tito, than as an heir presumptive who could, in case of need, be trusted to superintend a smooth transition after Tito had gone. Tito wanted, after 1968, to ensure that power should be located in the Party, to prevent the further disintegration of the authority of the central leadership and the further dissolution of Communist ideology.

The direct consequence of this policy was that the federal administration was henceforth no more a source of power than the American president's administration. It was staffed by people formed by the Party rather than by men the Party had been formed by – technicians rather than politicians. It was headed by someone who had all the advantages and none of the disadvantages once offered by Rankovich. Ribichich's record was that of a faithful and pliable executant, who had held important positions in the security apparatus of his native region; but he had neither created nor headed the S.D.B., nor even served in the central administration. He had no personal prestige, and did not belong to the major ethnic group.

The downgrading of General Goshnjak can be explained simply by the same concern that there should be no source of power outside the top collective leadership of the L.C.Y. Both the security services and the armed forces were such potential sources. Rankovich had been removed because of his direct control of the police apparatus. In order to eliminate this possible threat, the Party leadership had been helped by Goshnjak and the army, who had played a useful role between 1966 and 1969, in a period of domestic and foreign stress. Now that the crisis had been overcome, it was necessary, not so much to reduce the role and the prestige of the army, as to ensure that it was fully under the top leadership's control, and to prevent it giving any one of the leaders any potential independence.[15]

[14] Speakers at the ninth congress referred to 'Tito's epoch'. The message addressed to the president by the youth of Yugoslavia on his seventy-eighth birthday in 1970 spoke of 'Tito's Yugoslavia'. Recent biographies have glorified the legend for domestic and foreign consumption (V. Vinterhalter, *Životnom stazom Josipa Broza*, Belgrade, 1968; Auty, op. cit.). Tito the man is stressed in these biographies as much as Tito the hero, and the former aspect came through in the conversations with his son which appeared on the eve of Tito's seventy-eighth birthday in the popular Belgrade weekly *Politika-express*, under the title 'My Father Yosip Broz'. Schoolchildren learn his life and his achievements by rote, and confectioners sell cakes moulded in the shape of his head.

[15] General Goshnjak was 'rotated out' of the top leadership, but he was kept in the Council of National Defence, and was awarded a high decoration

The *grande peur* of the Soviet Union had disappeared, and Tito's speeches, followed by a series of meetings of the Party presidency, defined the new line over the summer and autumn of 1969: unity through the Party, around the Party, and within the Party; no leniency towards those who wished to stray away from socialism such as it was implemented in Yugoslavia. Even before he had been officially appointed, Ribichich had, at the end of April 1969, threatened with 'methods of revolutionary pressure' those who tried to stand in the way of 'revolutionary achievements'. In May, the twenty-five years of the S.D.B. were officially celebrated, with both Tito and Ribichich, the latter now formally installed, stressing the need to bolster it up and make it more efficient.

This was essential in view of the fact that opposition trends were openly acknowledged. Within the establishment, a conflict of generations was developing on the traditional Balkan pattern, according to which the ideology of the ruling class fails to satisfy the aspirations of its children. It was admitted that anti-communism was spreading.[16] With the passage of time, past ideologies and movements no longer appeared as so many taboos to those old enough to remember them.

on his sixtieth birthday in June 1969. At the same time, General Hamovich replaced General Shumonja as chief of the general staff. The same generals first described by Western commentators, in the summer of 1966, as Tito's anti-Soviet stalwarts who had removed Moscow-backed Rankovich, were then rumoured in the West, in the spring of 1969, to have been 'purged' because they were too pro-Soviet. When General Hamovich was in turn replaced in January 1970 by General Bubanj, there was more talk in the Western press of generals plotting to take power with Soviet help. Warmed up for every change at the head of the Yugoslav armed forces, the same unimaginative theory of a Soviet-backed conspiracy failed to explain why, no sooner had one set of Soviet-backed plotters been removed, than their removers and successors in turn started plotting for Moscow – unless all Yugoslav generals were involved in a gigantic conspiracy of which the Party leadership had no inkling, and played a game of hide-and-seek in order to confuse Tito.

[16] There have actually been open manifestations of anti-Communist opposition reported in the press. Thus, in some rural areas of Shumadiya, in Serbia, private farmers organized unofficial purchase and sale co-operatives which soon began to form pressure-groups at voters' meetings, and which were then accused of being really political groups accepting only anti-socialist members. The climax of this activity was reached in March 1970, when 150 demonstrators (which the press described as private farmers, craftsmen, and café-owners) came to the communal assembly at Kraguyevats with anti-Communist placards. Personal criticism of Tito and reactions against the Tito cult have also begun to surface. In March 1970, the home secretary for Serbia referred to personal attacks against the president. In April, an issue of a Youth League paper in Zagreb was banned for reproducing a film poster with a caption so styled as to be insulting to the president. In May, there were complaints in a Belgrade literary paper that the Tito cult was in danger of turning into a mockery ('Mercy for the President', in *Književne novine*, 23 May 1970).

As for the others, they had never learnt, read, or heard about the Cominform and Djilas, or non-Communist wartime or pre-war movements, except in terms of superficial, generalized, dogmatic, and of late none-too-convincing denigration. Sectional nationalism had also helped in part to whitewash the old movements of each ethnic group, in so far as they were opposed to those of the other groups. Yugoslavia was increasingly open to the outside world. Hundreds of thousands of Yugoslavs managed to travel to western Europe on a $30 annual travel allowance. Travellers and emigrants heard abroad different versions of the events that had preceded the coming to power of the C.P.Y. *Emigré* publications were smuggled in or even sent by post to Yugoslavia.

To counter these trends and influences, the old Stalinist technique was resorted to of uniting the opposition – from Ustashas and *chetniks* to Stalinists and new-Left radicals, including sectional chauvinists and Yugoslav unitarists, Rankovichists and Djilasists, clerical reactionaries and bourgeois remnants, liberals and anarchists. This heterogeneous coalition was linked to all those forces abroad that (for one reason or another) resent the existence of socialist Yugoslavia. Official statements and press articles have lumped together all those who disapprove of Yugoslavia in its present form, territorially or politically, turning them into a kind of hydra engaged in enemy activities against it, by magnifying its domestic difficulties and using the old political *émigrés*, now partially revivified, as sources of information and instruments of subversion. All foreign newspapers which spoke of crisis, of division, or of dissatisfaction in Yugoslavia, were seen as forces engaged in this psychological warfare.[17]

Greater emphasis was once again placed on ideology. Efforts were made to halt the disindoctrination of the young. The centenary of Lenin's birth was solemnly celebrated. There was, in 1970, a discreet renewal of lower Party cadres, and of membership generally, through expulsions, resignations, and new enrolments. Attempts were made to check and restore order in all possible channels of ideological influence, whether the press, the intellectuals and students, or the Church.

Not many newspapers are read in Yugoslavia because of the still low rate of literacy, but within that limited market, the non-

[17] The correspondent of the Hamburg *Der Spiegel* was arrested in March 1970 on a charge of espionage for an unidentified foreign power, linked to 'the political underworld and opposition circles in Belgrade'. Even Sir Fitzroy Maclean has been included in this 'enemy action' for repeating, in his foreword to the picture-book *Yugoslavia* (London, 1969), the worn-out cliché of centuries-old antagonisms and East-West divisions between the peoples of Yugoslavia ('Who, and for Whom, now Revives the Ghost of Yalta, and Hopes for the Division of Our Country', in *Vus*, Zagreb, 13 May 1970).

subsidized press has increased its circulation to the detriment of the official Party or Alliance press.[18] In June 1969, Tito warned journalists that they should follow the Party line and carefully check their information. Following that, in November, the Party presidency adopted the general principles of a new press law to prevent the misuse of the freedom of expression. By May 1970, about a dozen periodicals had been banned, suspended, confiscated, or closed down in various ways for political reasons, and even the foreign press had been threatened.[19]

A new generation of Communist writers, dramatists, and film directors had come to the fore in the late sixties, out to shock all their elders, of whatever ideology, including their own, with a boldness that was no longer one of form, but of content, and a realism no longer socialist, but licentious. If in 1965 Miodrag Bulatovich had to publish abroad *Hero on a Donkey*, his pornographic novel debunking the resistance in Montenegro, by 1968 it had found a publisher in Yugoslavia as well. At that time, Slobodan Selenich's *Memoirs of Pera Bogalja* or Dragoslav Markovich's *When the Pumpkins were in Bloom* were best-sellers. Selenich's 'hero' was an upstart ex-partisan who lived a cushioned life and was addicted to sexual orgies, and Markovich's, an ex-boxer turned *émigré* as a result of adventures that had nothing to do with politics, but which had given him a taste of secret police methods. While Selenich's novel obtained a literary prize in 1969, Markovich's, no sooner than dramatized for the stage, had to be taken off because Tito had censured it as a 'counter-revolutionary attempt'. Similarly in the cinema, the prevalent mood was dark and disenchanted, cynical and critical, anti-political and totally 'permissive'. While the government encouraged war epics, the great successes that earned hard currency abroad were films like Dushan Makaveyev's *Switchboard Operator* (1967) and *Innocence Unprotected* (1969), which proclaimed that trivialities rather than progressive political ideas were the ultimate values in life.

After the challenge from the Zagreb philosophers came the challenge from those in Belgrade. At the turn of November-December

[18] In 1968, of the dailies, the Belgrade evening *Vechernje novosti* had the highest circulation with 341,000, followed by the morning Belgrade *Politika* (263,000) and Zagreb *Vjesnik* (99,000). *Borba*, the official organ of the Socialist Alliance, came only seventh with 86,000. *Glas Koncila*, the Zagreb Catholic fortnightly, had a circulation of 150,000–200,000 (as much as the nudist monthly *Adam and Eve*), and the Belgrade Orthodox monthly *Pravoslavni misionar* 50,000.

[19] After the London *Daily Telegraph* had published a letter from an expatriate Yugoslav telling of his prison encounters with Ribichich as an U.D.B. official, a letter appeared on 6 August 1969, from the manager of a Belgrade newspaper import-export enterprise, threatening to cancel his orders if the *Daily Telegraph* should again publish anything similar.

1969, the Philosophical Society of Serbia, whose members were Communist Marxists who had contributed to *Praxis* and *Knjizhevne novine* and participated in the events that had shaken the university, organized a public debate on 'socialism and culture'. The aim was to discuss the whole issue of cultural freedom in the light of the series of recent official interventions and judicial sentences. Several hundred philosophers, social scientists, writers, artists, and actors gathered to protest against politicians meddling with culture and to demand full freedom of expression. Throughout December, both the organizers and the participants were subjected to slashing attacks in officially inspired articles and at Party rallies for having organized an anti-Communist opposition gathering.

Many books had begun to appear in private editions. Several of these attracted attention for dealing with historical questions from an approach that was not strictly according to official interpretations. They were attacked by political organizations, and at times even banned. The problem of how to control private publishing was discussed in the press. Tito once again intervened, in June 1970, to remind intellectuals of the strict Marxist role assigned to learning, which was not to explain, but to change. In a socialist society, learning was the handmaid of the working class. Officially inspired exegeses expanded this into the following reasoning: what was politically right was historically true, what was historically true was aesthetically valid. Printers were warned to keep a sharp eye for 'private' historical writings and political pamphlets.

It was characteristic of the atmosphere in 1969–70 that all sorts of works which drew their inspiration from sectional nationalist feelings managed to appear in print – at times even under the imprint of a regular publishing enterprise of the socialized sector – but no works of independent political critical analysis. When in the U.S.A. at the end of 1968, Djilas, who was still under an injunction preventing him from publishing anything until 1972, had handed over to his American publisher the manuscript of a new book which duly appeared early in the new year, soon after the author had returned to Yugoslavia.[20] Whereas *The New Class* had been a Marxist critique of contemporary communism, *The Unperfect Society* went 'beyond *The New Class*'. This was an analysis of Marxism at the end of the cycle in which it had started as stimulating and penetrating sociological analysis in the nineteenth century, only now to end as sclerotic scholasticism. The book provoked no reaction in Yugoslavia until almost six months after its publication, when the new harder-line course had been well and truly launched. At the end of October 1969, the work was banned in Yugoslavia, in all its editions and

[20] *The Unperfect Society – Beyond the New Class*, New York, 1969.

serializations. The decree was interpreted so widely that even issues of foreign newspapers with only reviews of *The Unperfect Society*, or indeed with any article on or by Djilas, were likewise banned. No reprisals were taken against Djilas himself, however, until he was due to leave on another visit to the U.S.A. in March 1970. No sooner had he obtained his air-ticket than his passport was confiscated on the grounds that his behaviour abroad on his previous journey had allegedly harmed the country's interests.

The new generation of Communist intellectuals were dangerous in so far as their ideas found a welcome among students. Naturally, not all of Yugoslavia's quarter of a million students were potentially troublesome, but the arts faculties could be, and in Belgrade they were. Belgrade University had a tradition of radicalism, and the wider regional recruitment of its students made them less prone to ethnocentrism and thus more open to political thinking. The events of June 1968 had left a deep impression on all of them. In spite of the promises that had been made, their worries – political and academic – had not been allayed. In the spring of 1969, as the anniversary of June 1968 grew near, there was a feeling of restlessness among the more politically-minded students of Belgrade University. *Student*, the Belgrade students' union paper, had been banned several times in 1968, and by the following spring it had become almost an opposition paper,[21] attracting many readers outside the university.

To bring the militants back to order and to get *Student* out of their hands were not easy tasks. Its editors, although expelled from the Party, remained in charge. Early in May, there were serious incidents when four students were arrested. In Belgrade, leaflets were distributed and posters stuck up, protesting against the arrests and accusing the Party of using every possible form of coercion to suppress *Student*. Whilst demonstrations were being organized for the June anniversary, a special presidency meeting under Tito was convened to discuss the situation. Owing to strong government and Party pressure, nothing happened, but only after university buildings had been closed as a precaution. The arts faculty union was singled out as an anti-Communist opposition nucleus, and all student agitation was labelled subversive. The rector declared it intolerable that *Student* should still be in the hands of a small group of non-Communists. In spite of action through the university Communists, through the printers, through union meetings endlessly adjourned because of disorders or the frequent lack of a quorum, and attacks of

[21] During the ninth congress, a journalist on the staff of *Politika* had written an open letter to the congress, protesting against the lack of freedom in the press, and had sent it to all newspapers. *Student* had been the only one to print it.

all sorts,²² *Student* continued until January 1970, when a resolution was manoeuvred tortuously through a marathon general union meeting which eventually got rid of the *Student* team. Incidents continued to occur, such as occasional demonstrations of sympathy with strikers, until the chairman of the arts faculty union – a radical, militant, and popular figure of the student movement since 1968 – was brought to trial and sent to prison in October 1970 for hostile propaganda, his sentence triggering off more demonstrations in Belgrade and elsewhere.

Specific faculties and academics were reprimanded in parliament that year, and a debate was started on university reform. The aim of the plans under discussion was to link the university more closely to working organizations and trade unions. This would both tie academic production to the needs of the economy, and prevent the academic world from developing its own alien political consciousness which could contaminate society.

Religions and nations

The Orthodox and Catholic hierarchies had begun to co-ordinate the demands they put to the government in 1969 for time on radio and television, for giving seminarists the same status as other students, for making Christmas a public holiday, and for preventing the liberalization of the abortion law. The religious press was expanding; religious books found a ready market, as did both live and recorded religious music. The Church was increasing its social activities, especially among the young, as well as its charitable work among the old, the sick, and the needy. Although urbanization, industrialization, emigration, and indoctrination had destroyed much of the traditional religious pattern, and even caused the de-Christianization of specific sectors or areas, the Church satisfied many needs which the Party and Party-backed activities could not. It naturally helped to satisfy people's spiritual needs, but it also offered some form of participation in world events outside official channels, through world Catholicism or world Orthodoxy. It appealed to many of those who were dissatisfied with the present, and were attracted to something else which could provide a link with another world, whether that after death, or that before communism. For the young, it had the added attraction of being not quite accepted by the establishment.

Both Churches derived inspiration from traditional sources which

²² *Student* was even attacked for propagating the ideas of Herbert Marcuse and Karl Jaspers!

they adapted to present needs. Whereas with the other ethnic groups, local Party leadership had canalized the cause of national and regional emotions and interests, in Serbia it went hand in hand with the central leadership. The Serbian Orthodox Church found it natural to tell its faithful to leave politics to those who wanted a reward in this world and to unite around the Church which stood alone in caring for their real interests. The mass of the faithful – and not a few clergy as well – who identified Serbianism and Orthodoxy, wanted a framework within which freely to express their ethnic identity, and therefore turned readily to the Church. This conjuncture gave particular emphasis to the great celebrations, held in the autumn of 1969, of the 750th anniversary of the establishment of the autocephalous Serbian Orthodox Church.

If the Orthodox Church had a tradition of providing at once a refuge from the world and a structure for preserving the cultural and spiritual unity of the nation, the Catholic Church had a tradition of involvement in this world. It multiplied its contacts with other Christians, with Moslems, and with Communist intellectuals. It protected its rights and tried to extend them. By demanding to put its own point of view, it contributed to the pressure for more freedom of expression. In the traditionally Catholic Slovenian countryside, the clergy were again an influence to be reckoned with, even if not a directly political one any longer. Where the local Party leadership had taken up the cause of ethnic and regional particularism, there was no crying need for the Church to satisfy such requirements, and yet in Croatia too, people wanted to express their nationalism outside the established Communist framework – including, naturally, some of the clergy.

The Serbs could create their own home-made saints. The Macedonians simply nationalized the great apostles of the Slavs. The Croats had to wait for the pope to grant them a saint. However much the hierarchy stressed the religious aspect of the event, the proclamation by Pope Paul in Rome, in June 1970, of Saint Nicholas Tavelich, a fourteenth-century Franciscan from Shibenik in Dalmatia who died a martyr's death in Jerusalem, was turned into a manifestation of nationalism. The pride felt by the Serbs in the seven and a half centuries since Constantinople had granted them their own Church, was nothing compared to the ecstasy the Croats felt at Rome granting them their own saint.

Oecumenism came to a standstill as each Church busied itself with its own problems again and popular conceptions identified Church and nation. Not only was there a partial reversal of the earlier trend towards *rapprochement* between Eastern and Western Christians: each Church divided into ethnic compartments. The

Orthodox were already divided by the Macedonian schism, which divided two conceptions as well as two nations. The Macedonian Church, established in all but name, promoted as an auxiliary to the state what it considered to be the interests of the Macedonian nation – in true nineteenth-century style. The Serbian Church similarly promoted what it considered to be the interests of the Serbian nation, but in spite of the state, and increasingly to its distaste – in seventeenth- and eighteenth-century style. For most practical purposes the Catholic Church now had two organizations, one for the Croats and another for the Slovenes; and the Holy See, which had acquiesced in the ethnic compartmentalization of the faithful in Yugoslavia, appointed an Albanian bishop to take charge of the Catholic Albanians in that country. As for the Islamic Religious Community, it did not lag behind. Quite apart from increasing its building, educational, and social activities, its adherents in Kosovo identified it with Albanianism, and those in Bosnia-Herzegovina with Moslem Slavism. Its decision, in November 1969, to shorten its name to the Islamic Community, in order to get rid of a pleonasm, has also been interpreted as a wish to be identified with the budding Moslem 'nation'.

In order to counter the increasing role of religion, the government resorted to different means. From time to time, a specific issue of a religious paper has been banned. There have been repeated attempts to exploit, or to create, differences between sections of the clergy and the hierarchy. Party organizations, the press, and regional governmental commissions for religious affairs have, in every region except Macedonia, attacked the Church for going beyond the state interpretation of its constitutional rights. In June 1969, there was talk in parliament of the need for a new law to define more closely the boundary within which religious communities could operate.

The militant students of Belgrade were almost right when they asserted that there had been no further reforms since the events of June 1968. The only important reforms since then had been the constitutional affirmation of ethnic parity at federal level, and greater autonomy both for the republics and for Serbia's associated provinces. Further concessions had been made to Slovenian and Croatian governmental autonomy, to Macedonian 'statehood', to changing the character of Kosovo from that of a multi-ethnic to that of a predominantly Albanian province, to building up a separate Montenegrin entity, and to recognizing the Slav Moslems as a distinct ethnic group.[23]

[23] In the republic of Macedonia, however, according to a ruling by the secretariat of the local Central Committee on 11 September 1970, Macedonian-speaking Slav Moslems are 'historically and scientifically' Macedonians.

The result was that a further effort had to be made simultaneously to check the growing tendency to ethnocentrism. After the summer crisis of 1968, the slogan used was that of 'Yugoslav socialist patriotism', defined as socialist proletarian internationalism within the Yugoslav territorial framework. The logic of this new concept of Yugoslavism[24] was to link the common state with the socialist system and the role of the L.C.Y. In the summer of 1969 a great campaign was started against nationalism in all its manifestations and forms. It was made clear that the new trend in Kosovo would have to stop short of turning the province into a republic. Nationalist tension was played down. In Serbia, local political leaders bore down upon Serbian nationalism, and the Serbian Orthodox Church was treated increasingly as the local Church of that republic. For the benefit of the more ethnocentric Croatian Communists, Milosh Zhanko, the Croatian vice-president of the Federal Assembly, wrote in *Borba* castigating the unchecked manifestations of nationalism in Croatia which were provoking fears in Serbia. In Bosnia-Herzegovina, the Central Committee warned against the trend towards setting up a Bosnian national entity, with its own historical, linguistic, cultural, and religious framework.

The campaign had hardly been started in the summer of 1969 than a storm blew up in Slovenia over the priorities in a road-extension programme to be financed out of a loan from the International Bank for Reconstruction and Development. The completion of a project in Slovenia was among those postponed when the bank had asked the Yugoslav government to cut down on the number of projects to be financed at that stage. The Slovenian Executive Council protested and demanded that the federal government's decision be revised. The Slovenian demand was rejected, and Tito, in several speeches, did not mince his words about the whole affair. Without naming names, he attacked the lack of discipline among Party leaders, and threatened the Slovenian leadership with retribution. Kardelj himself had to be despatched to Ljubljana to bring the Slovenian leaders back to reason. The crisis ended in compromise: the Slovenian leadership failed to have their way, but no one was removed.

The roads issue had been no more than a pretext. It had served to show the extent of dissatisfaction in Slovenia with the amount of federal control over the region, and the lack of Slovenian control over the federation. The intensity of Slovenian particularism, with undertones of separatism, could be measured from the exhortations of the Party leaders who felt it necessary to argue, in terms of

[24] 'Tito's Yugoslavism', as described by M. Tripalo, one of the two Croatian members of the Executive Bureau, in April 1970.

material advantages and in so many words, the case for a continued union of Slovenia with the rest of Yugoslavia and its participation in the general development of the country.

The government of Croatia had initially backed that of Slovenia on the roads issue, and six months later the Croatian leadership in turn challenged the centre. In mid-January 1970, the Central Committee of Croatia met for a well-prepared and fully reported onslaught on Zhanko. Attacked for having exaggerated the danger of nationalism in Croatia, he was accused of undermining the local Party leadership and of bolstering up centralism. The Central Committee decided that he could no longer represent it on the Permanent Conference of the L.C.Y. A campaign was then got under way to press him to resign from all his functions. As Zhanko rejected this criticism, and refused to resign, the campaign was stepped up to have him ousted from his posts and even expelled from the Party, until in April the Zagreb parliament voted to recall him from the Council of Nations in Belgrade.

The case of Milosh Zhanko, like that of the Slovenian roads, was one which simply crystallized an atmosphere. In 1970, emotional nationalism was no less extravagant in Croatia than in Serbia. The republic had the lowest birth-rate in Yugoslavia – indeed, one of the lowest in Europe – and the highest number of emigrants. 'The Croatian nation is dying', was the dramatic cry echoed everywhere. Soon, it was added by some, the ethnic character of parts of the land would be altered. There was not so much a wish to break away, as a feeling that the taboos on the expression of nationalist feelings in Croatia – discredited by the wartime link with Fascism – had been lifted. The central government was once again openly identified with the power of the Serbs.

In Serbia, however, it was not felt that the Serbs gained anything by the solidarity of their republic's leadership with the federal government, so much so that in July 1970 the secretary of the local Central Committee felt it useful to answer charges that the Serbian leadership was 'a-national', and to proffer discreet criticism of those Communists who allowed nationalism to be rejuvenated through them. In October, the same secretary stressed the fact that all republics were becoming multi-national – even in Slovenia, usually considered the exception, there were 120,000 workers from other regions – so that there had to be equal facilities for all ethnic groups everywhere. The inference seemed to be: if all minority groups were to be granted linguistic facilities in Serbia, Serbs should be entitled to similar opportunities in regions where Serbo-Croatian was not spoken. If there were special schools for the 30,000 Ruthenes in Voyvodina – nominally part of the republic of Serbia – there were none for the 50,000 registered Serbs in Macedonia. If the Croats feared that parts of Croatia would lose their Croatian character, the Serbs knew that Kosovo was fast losing what little remained of its Serbian character. There was sabotage on the railways, monasteries complained of attacks, life was being made generally difficult for the Serbs in Kosovo, and they moved out in increasing numbers. To keep this backward region as satisfied as it could, and to provide more and better work for its Albanian population, multiplying at Asian rates, the federal government laid special emphasis on its development, both economic and cultural.[25]

Macedonia celebrated 'twenty-five years of Macedonian independence' in August 1969, but nation-building exercised itself particularly in Montenegro from then on. From the summer of 1969 to that of 1970, a storm raged over the tomb of Peter II Petrovich-Njegosh, prince-bishop of Montenegro who died in 1851, one of the greatest Yugoslav poets and a precursor of the Yugoslav idea. Montenegrins worship his memory, as indeed do all Serbs. In order to pay their own tribute to Njegosh, the local Party leaders had decided to erect over his tomb on Mount Lovchen a gigantic mausoleum. The little chapel in which his remains lay buried had, however, become something of a national shrine, and was Church property. The Serbian Orthodox Church opposed its removal or the transfer of the bishop's remains, and the Party accused it of political action aimed at denying the existence of a Montenegrin nationality. In July 1970, the Montenegrin Central Committee met to attack the Church and to formulate a programme of action to solve the still unsolved Montenegrin national problem.[26]

In April 1970, the Party presidency met to discuss the aggravation of friction between the republics and the growth of nationalism. It laid down that the role of the federal government was to maintain and develop a unique and uniform political and social system, as well as to ensure the equality of all peoples in Yugoslavia. Otherwise, its direct competence was limited to diplomacy and defence in consultation with the regional governments. It was decided to accelerate the introduction of ethnic quotas for all branches of the federal administration, as well as the application of the constitutional principle of equality between all languages and scripts in the

[25] A university was opened at Prishtina in November 1969.

[26] The programme was to promote Montenegrin culture, with a university in Titograd, and textbooks written specially for schools in Montenegro according to the Montenegrin pronunciation and with emphasis on Montenegrin history. This, strangely enough, was expected to rehabilitate the Italian-backed pre-war Montenegrin separatists. All notions of Yugoslavism, of Montenegrins as a branch of the Serbs, and even of unity within the Orthodox Church were rejected as being anti-Montenegrin.

federal administration, in the armed forces, and even in the conduct of international relations.

In August, officially inspired articles began to appear in the press on the need to embody in the constitution the new relationship between the federation and the republics which had been laid down in April. The process of constitutional revision was publicly initiated by President Tito in a speech the following month, and endorsed by the Party leadership after a more lengthy *exposé* by Kardelj. In order to ensure unity, the highest institutions of the state would be reorganized so as to be brought into line with the structure previously adopted for the Party leadership. The spheres of activity and the prerogatives of the federation and those of the republics would be clearly set out anew according to recent developments, so as to avoid further friction. The presidency of the republic would be turned into a collective body that would bring together the best people in the several regions, wield the real authority in law as well as in fact, and prepare for a smooth succession. Tito would naturally head this body for as long as he was there, and thereafter it would be chaired by rotation.

Since 1967, state security has been shared between the federation and the republics, and the S.D.B. has been thoroughly reorganized. It has certainly been active in tracking down all sorts of 'enemy activities', for in the twelve months following April 1969 – a period of time taken at random – some two dozen political trials were recorded in the press.[27] Acts of terrorism continued in 1969, including an attempt on the life of the head of the Yugoslav military mission in West Berlin, and yet another bomb in Belgrade railway station, and that same year saw a new development – the assassination of expatriates. A wave of unsolved murders and unsuccessful attempts at murder – mostly in West Germany, but also in France,

[27] The charges were: hostile propaganda, spreading of false rumours likely to alarm the public, espionage on behalf of unidentified foreign powers, membership of *émigré* organizations, spreading of ethnic hatred, and terrorism. The cases include that of a worker who had written verses to incite his fellows to demonstrate against a shut-down; a former Cominform sympathizer who had made public statements against the régime; returned expatriates or migrant workers who had been members of *émigré* organizations while abroad; people who had been in correspondence with *émigré* organizations, who had written and distributed opposition pamphlets, or who had sung 'enemy songs'; a group of former inmates of Goli Otok who had organized a Ljotichist cell in that penitentiary; and a man who had been telling a fellow-traveller in a train that the Croats were under Serbian domination. The terrorists arrested on Yugoslav territory and brought to trial as 'Ustashas' had, in fact, all been infants in 1945, and left Yugoslavia in the sixties to work abroad. In 1969 and 1970 several people were arrested for actions committed during the civil war, and in July 1970 a British tourist was arrested for aircraft-spotting and kept in custody for a month.

Spain, and Sweden – were explained in the Yugoslav press as part of a Mafia-type war between rival *émigré* groups. The Western press hinted at retaliatory action by the Yugoslav security services, and in Yugoslavia officials and newspaper articles boasted that the S.D.B. did not limit its activities to Yugoslav territory exclusively.[28]

Diplomacy and sales promotion

If this was really so, a tentative explanation might be the wish to deal with the *émigré* danger, real or potential, without impairing relations with West European countries, for non-alignment remained the only foreign policy acceptable to all factions of the L.C.Y.. In Tito's interpretation of it, leading and influencing the uncommitted states, it was both a diplomacy of prestige for Yugoslavia and a contribution to the propagation of socialism. Plans for a third conference of the non-aligned countries had been stopped by the Czechoslovak crisis. The uncommitted were divided in their attitudes to the Soviet invasion, and whatever their attitude, they had been shown to be of no practical use to Yugoslavia. In 1969 Tito had to start again from scratch, and it proved a difficult task. There were by then as many definitions of non-alignment as there were non-aligned governments, not to mention the growing scepticism about the usefulness of such gatherings. Preparatory meetings held in July and September had fallen terribly short of Yugoslav expectations.

And so Tito, at the age of seventy-seven, went off personally to canvass African leaders. In November 1969, he was in Algiers. In January-February 1970, he worked his way up through East Africa, from Tanzania to Egypt – where he had his twenty-third meeting with Nasser in fifteen years – with a stop in Libya on his way home. From February to May 1970, other Yugoslav personalities toured among other potential participants in a non-aligned conference – in the Far East, Latin America, and West Africa. The result was another preliminary meeting at Dar-es-Salaam in April, which decided to hold a conference in Lusaka before the twenty-fifth anniversary meeting of the United Nations in the autumn, and was otherwise a complete disappointment. Institutionalized non-alignment no longer had any *raison d'être*, but no one wanted to be the first to say so. Meanwhile it survived through the resoluteness of Tito alone, and the third conference of non-aligned states was duly held

[28] Several probabilities come to mind, such as the rivalry between the services of different republics, the action of parallel agencies, and the double involvement of agents, to help explain the less obvious cases.

in the Zambian capital early in September, with fifty-four participants. Cuba had been joined by three other West Indian states and Yugoslavia remained the only European member. Appropriately enough, it was Tito who, together with President Kaunda of Zambia, opened the proceedings. Past were the days when earlier conferences tried to act as 'non-aligned' mediators between existing blocs. The Lusaka conference frankly concentrated on the only issue around which all participants could be aligned: the opposition to minority European régimes in southern Africa.

Non-alignment in these terms had brought Yugoslavia considerable diplomatic prestige for as long as there had been clearly defined blocs,[29] but it had been economically extravagant and did not correspond to the régime's needs or possibilities. What Communist Yugoslavia needed at the end of the decade was not to lead a third bloc, but to be on good terms with the other Communist countries, as well as with the West. This was another interpretation of non-alignment. The Yugoslav government was anxious to improve its relations with the Soviet government in order to check the advance of non-Communist influence in the country. Yugoslavia did not attend the World Communist conference which the Soviets at last managed to hold in Moscow in June 1969, but on the eve of the conference, it made gestures to please the Soviet Union, and the conference in effect accepted the diversity of socialist models, thus opening the door to Yugoslav participation.

By the beginning of August, in a speech in Skopye, Tito could say that relations with the U.S.S.R. and its allies were progressing well, and could express the hope that mutual efforts would gradually eliminate the consequences of the 'events of August last year'. Although there was no attempt to ignore the differences, the enormity of the French-style euphemism used was characteristic. Soon afterwards, it was announced that the Soviet foreign minister would come to Yugoslavia. On the eve of his arrival, the latest issue of *Knjizhevne novine*, with an article by its chief editor on the delicate issue of the Soviet occupation of Czechoslovakia, was banned as a deliberate attempt to sabotage the *rapprochement*, and its author was brought to trial and forced to resign. Gromyko's visit early in September provided the first occasion for high-level talks since the polemics which followed the invasion of Czechoslovakia. Both sides stressed what linked them, rather than what divided

[29] Even as late as 1970 it brought satisfaction to Tito to be asked to pass proposals on to President Nasser in different peace initiatives, such as when he crossed paths in Addis Ababa in February with U.S. Secretary of State Rogers, or when Dr Goldman, president of the World Jewish Congress, went to see him discreetly at Brioni in June.

them, and the Yugoslavs obtained what amounted to a Soviet recognition of their special status, based on the Belgrade declaration of 1955.

Thereafter, gradually if not spectacularly, the atmosphere improved. In November, an important delegation of the L.C.Y. went to Moscow for Party talks. In January 1970, another Party delegation attended in Moscow a conference of European Communist Parties on the question of European security. In February, the L.C.Y. was represented at an international ideological conference of twenty-seven Communist Parties. In April, on the occasion of the centenary of Lenin's birth, Bakarich led a Party delegation to Moscow, and *Pravda* published an article by President Tito. Complaints continued in the press on both sides about the attitude of the other's press, but in no way did they prevent the careful preparations for Ribichich's visit to Moscow in June 1970, which was marked by the same frankness about existing differences combined with the will to overcome them. Yugoslavia acknowledged the eminent role of the U.S.S.R. in world affairs, and the Soviet Union recognized that its relations with Yugoslavia were based on principles of equality, mutual respect, and non-interference. A similarly cautious normalization was established with East Germany, Hungary, and even – though only to a certain extent – with Bulgaria. With Romania, relations continued to be very close, although the two governments did not see eye to eye on the Middle East and relations with Israel.

The normalization of relations with the Communist world went even further. At the time of the Czechoslovak crisis, China stopped its press attacks on Yugoslavia and expressed a wish to renew trade contacts. In March 1969, a trade agreement had been signed, and by August 1970, the two governments having agreed to appoint ambassadors once again, the envoys had taken up their posts. This was the beginning of a gradual Chinese diplomatic comeback everywhere. As a result, Albania also showed signs of wanting to come out of its isolation, and a slight improvement in relations with Yugoslavia was felt by the end of 1969. The disorders in Kosovo had not been exploited by either government; crossing points had been opened on the border, and a trade agreement signed. A conciliatory speech by Enver Hoxha in June 1970 had been welcomed in Belgrade. Tito's answer came in a speech at the beginning of August suggesting the re-establishment of normal relations. A cultural agreement followed at the end of the year, and in January 1971, it was officially announced that ambassadors would soon be exchanged between Belgrade and Tirana.

Although anxious to restore normal relations with Eastern

countries, the Yugoslavs wanted to make it appear that they were not desperate and that they were willing to leave the initiative to the other side. With the West, however, it was they who, unabashed, were taking the initiative, in order to ensure better outlets for their goods and better opportunities for their workers. This was easy in the case of a traditionally neutral country like Switzerland, whose foreign minister came to Belgrade in October 1969 to discuss precisely those points. In the case of another neutral, Austria, there were good neighbour relations to be fostered, and President Jonas's visit in September 1968, just after the Czechoslovak crisis, had been welcomed as a sign of friendship with a non-Communist yet neutral neighbour.

This policy of 'active and positive co-existence' was naturally applied to Italy – the neighbour whose goodwill was the most important of all, for Italy was a bridge to NATO the E.E.C., and the Vatican.[30] Italy was interested in helping Yugoslavia to place its goods in the Common Market, for Yugoslavia was also Italy's principal trade partner, and the balance was in Italy's favour. In two decades, relations between the two had advanced from being abysmally bad to being as good as they could be between a Communist one-party state, and a parliamentary régime dominated by a Christian Democratic party that was also a member of the North Atlantic Alliance. The relationship was all the more interesting for not being able to rely on convenient myths of traditional friendship. It was based unashamedly on mutual interest. Having, in the summer of 1967, denounced NATO manoeuvres in Italy as being aimed against Yugoslavia, a year later Marshal Tito's government found itself wanting on the one hand a stable parliamentary Italy in NATO to give protective backing, and on the other a developing industrial capitalist economy to absorb Yugoslavia's agricultural exports, and to help with investments and technology. President Saragat's visit to Yugoslavia in October 1969 was a great success; Tito hinted that Yugoslavia would be ready to consider small adjustments of the border to please its neighbours.

[30] The Yugoslav government was even anxious to improve its relations with the Vatican to give satisfaction to its own Catholic subjects, and keep some check over at least one manifestation of nationalism. Full diplomatic relations between Yugoslavia and the Holy See were restored in August 1970. The Yugoslav press, however, felt it necessary to interpret the event as resulting exclusively from an initiative of the Vatican whose positions on non-alignment, the Near East, Vietnam, colonialism, and underdevelopment were similar to those of Yugoslavia itself. The note was then forced into total disregard of historical evidence when it was said that the Holy See had originally broken off relations and that it was now, for the first time, entering into diplomatic relations based, not on a Concordat with the other party, but on respect of the latter's constitution!

The Federal German Republic was another West European state whose goodwill Yugoslavia was anxious to obtain for many reasons: German credits, capital investments and technological co-operation, Yugoslav migrant labour, the Common Market, and the exiles. Several ministerial visits were exchanged between February 1969 and March 1970. Unlike Italy and West Germany, France was not a major trade partner of Yugoslavia's, but it was an important member of the E.E.C. and not too well disposed to any economic leniency towards Yugoslavia. These reasons made it imperative for Yugoslavia to win its goodwill. Again unlike Italy and Germany, in the case of France there was no lack of mythology of past friendship to provide the necessary lubricant to the machinery of *rapprochement* which was started in September 1969, not long after General de Gaulle's resignation. In 1970, ministerial visits were also exchanged with Belgium and the Netherlands. In all these Common Market countries, the aim was to encourage investment, technical co-operation, and greater purchases of Yugoslav produce.

Over and above all the Yugoslav government's interest in the Common Market, the chairman of the F.E.C., Ribichich, went to London in February 1970 to attract capital, tourists, and technology. To lend glamour to his efforts, Ribichich invited Princess Margaret and Lord Snowdon to visit Yugoslavia as Marshal Tito's personal guests – which they did on an eight-day whistle-stop tour in June. In August, the chairman of the F.E.C. went on informal visits to Norway and Sweden, and in October the Danish foreign minister was in Belgrade to recruit Yugoslav labour for his country's economy.

Tito himself – in order to give full backing to his ministers' efforts in Europe and to destroy the impression that his concentration on the third world had made Yugoslav diplomacy lag behind in Europe – went on a round of visits to five Common Market countries: Belgium, Luxembourg, West Germany, the Netherlands, and France. He did so in October, soon after returning from Lusaka, but not before he had received President Nixon. In order to be available at that particular moment, Tito even stayed away from the funeral of President Nasser, so great was the importance attached to the American president's visit: indeed, all Yugoslav objections to many aspects of the latter's policy were well outweighed by the public demonstration of the U.S.A.'s continued interest in Tito's Yugoslavia, as well as by the incentive to American investments it was hoped it would provide. Tito had visited all E.E.C. countries except Italy, the visit to Italy having been cancelled because of nationalist demonstrations in both countries.

This pragmatic aspect of non-alignment went to the extent of being on good and trading terms with the southern, *junta*-ruled, Greek neighbours, and even with Spain, where Franco's régime had never recognized Tito's. In the sense of wanting to be friends with everyone, as indeed in the sense of taking a lively interest in world affairs, the Yugoslavs were internationalists. Otherwise, Yugoslavia's position in international relations since the ninth congress had been one of refusing to accept any limit to its own sovereignty, of whatever kind, and for whatever reason – a position as nationalist as that of any British anti-Common-Marketeer or French Gaullist, if not more so. While denying anyone the right to be interested in the affairs of others – and least of all of Yugoslavia – it overstressed its own mission in international developments, apportioned praise and blame, and delivered pronouncements on the rights and wrongs of other states.[31]

Yugoslavia's foreign policy had been, of late, a compound of megalomaniac tendencies, natural ideological inclinations, political necessities, reflexes of fear, and, last but not least, economic realities. In spite of all reforms, a measure of centralized political control over investments and their maintenance at a high level had remained characteristic features of the economy. The policy of reflation, adopted in mid-1968, directed in particular towards export-producing industries, had allowed industry to resume its growth. The trend, no sooner restarted, got out of control, going beyond what had been intended and leaving agriculture to continue its erratic course, at the mercy of the climate. While the lack of a real market for capital failed to ensure its mobility, and thus greatly reduced the efficiency of the money invested in industry, the private sector of agriculture continued to consolidate itself, though short of capital on which to base any sustained growth. Imports of farm produce were reduced to a minimum, and by 1968 there were actually important surpluses of meat and maize available for export. With easier credit, consumption grew faster than production, and the inflation spiral started anew.

[31] Cf. Tito's dramatic Riyeka speech of 3 May 1970: 'In the name of all the nations of Yugoslavia, in the name of our workers . . . I protest against, and most loudly condemn, aggression in Cambodia, in Vietnam and in the Near East. . . . Israel is but a tool in the hands of those who have interests in the Mediterranean. . . . It has the most modern American armament.' The Yugoslav president repeatedly attacked 'technological colonialism' in 1970 while his ministers toured capitalist countries to attract industrial, technological and capital investments. While complaining of the activities of foreign intelligence services, Yugoslavia was not above spying on powers whose goodwill it was anxious to obtain. (A Frenchman was sentenced in Paris to fifteen years' imprisonment for spying for the Yugoslav S.D.B., and an Italian, arrested on similar charges, hanged himself in his cell in Padua, both in April 1970.)

Restrictive measures had to be introduced again at the beginning of 1969, and they disclosed the insolvency of many enterprises. By July, 10 per cent of enterprises employing 14 per cent of labour in the social sector were found to be working at a loss which had accumulated to a total of over $300 million. By October, over a third of all enterprises were insolvent. Paying salaries became an acute problem. In order to avoid mass bankruptcy, shut-downs, dismissals, strikes, and serious political consequences, over the summer some temporary relaxation of the tighter monetary policy was necessary, but in the autumn, the government squarely faced the problem of investments, at least in words. In his speeches Tito put the blame for the insolvency crisis on uncovered long-term investments, which would not be allowed any more until the reforms had enabled the economy to afford them again. Meanwhile, priority would be given to those investments which could be realized soon, and strictly according to market indications.

Management was, however, ill-suited to provide rapid responses to these indications. Self-management functioned in conditions where two workers out of three had not completed their primary schooling, and one out of eighteen was completely illiterate.[32] Too often, workers' councils simply reacted to defend their own immediate interests, or management boards turned into instruments of domination. Local political bosses continued to have a decisive voice in the choice of managers, many of whom were thus still qualified politically rather than technically. There were all sorts of conflicts within enterprises, between unqualified labour and technical staff, between workers and their elected board, between labour and the manager, and between the manager and the technical staff. In industry at large, there were conflicts between enterprises competing in the same market, between workers as producers and workers as consumers, and between social enterprises and self-employed craftsmen. Corruption,[33] strikes,[34] and the first symptoms of a change of attitude in the trade unions were sure signs that self-management, such as

[32] *Borba*, 17 September 1969.
[33] Between the beginning of 1965 and the end of 1967, 422 people were tried for corruption, and 2,784 for misusing their official position.
[34] Two strikes have left a particularly deep impression. In June 1969, a strike paralysed the port of Riyeka and shook the town. The management and staff were beaten up, and police reinforcements were rushed in to cordon off the port area. Twelve months later, police had to prevent striking miners from Bosnian coal-mines from marching to Sarayevo. In November 1969, the Party presidency rejected a request to recognize the right to strike as yet another manoeuvre by the opposition against socialist democracy, where the workers had all rights, in order to slide gradually back into a system where the working class simply had a few formal 'rights', such as the right to strike, while political decision-making belonged to the élite.

it had evolved in twenty years, could protect neither the interests of social ownership, nor those of the working class, let alone those of the economy.

Among the constitutional amendments adopted at the end of 1968, the fifteenth amendment had been hailed at the time as a step forward, for giving workers' councils greater discretion in deciding on the internal structure of enterprises. In the following year, quite a few enterprises had delegated wider powers to their managers, with the simple aim of improving business. Several enterprises had replaced their management boards by business committees elected from the technical staff, with the responsibility of making operative decisions within the policy framework adopted by the workers' council. Politicians soon raised the alarm that workers' self-management was going to be reduced to a fiction, and Tito denounced the technocratic tendencies as being part of a general attempt to reduce the role of the producers to the advantage of the intellectual élite.[35]

At the beginning of 1970, the official unemployment figure was still 375,000. Continued emigration was one ready remedy. In 1969, 200,000 new emigrants brought the total of Yugoslav workers abroad to 700,000, half of them in West Germany. By the end of 1970, a million Yugoslavs – one in 20 of the country's total population – were earning their living abroad. They tended to come from two different sources. One was the poorest regions with the highest demographic expansion. The other was those regions where contacts with western Europe were easier, and which produced more qualified workers who could find better-paid employment abroad. Whereas migrants from Kosovo moved out first and foremost to neighbouring inner Serbia and Macedonia, and also, to a certain extent, to other regions of Yugoslavia, half the emigrants originated from Croatia. By 1968, the percentage of the qualified, highly qualified, and graduate emigrants had risen to 30 per cent, and by 1970 to almost 50 per cent. Emigration was also a remedy for the balance of payments. During 1969, Yugoslav workers abroad sent home over $200 million.

Throughout 1969, the debate continued about extending the limits within which private employment was still confined, but ideological opposition was too strong. The Party continued to back

[35] Speech on Republic Day, Sarayevo, 29 November 1969. On 9 September, however, in Sisak, he had argued in favour of the need to keep a wage-scale as an incentive to skills, and given advice which sounded very much as if it had been taken out of one of the speeches of Louis-Philippe's conservative prime minister, Guizot: 'Let everyone make an effort to acquire greater skill, to work better, to contribute more to the collectivity, and thus to earn more money.'

the development of a socialist agrarian policy, and to encourage private smallholders to leave the countryside. Political and fiscal pressure at communal level kept the number of paid employees in private service well below limits. In 1969, the number of private entrepreneurs and professionals, and of their employees, which had slowly but constantly risen since 1965, actually fell.[36]

Yugoslav diplomacy in the West had, to a large extent, been a promotion campaign for the country's spare capacities, surplus labour, and general potential, in order to attract foreign capital and technology. By the beginning of July 1970, twenty foreign firms had concluded joint-venture contracts with Yugoslav enterprises, and had invested a total of over $44 million – almost half of it by Italian firms. This was well below Yugoslav expectations: the rush of foreign capital, which many Communists had feared and others advocated, but all expected, had not materialized. The possibility was being examined of liberalizing the conditions of foreign capital investment.

A special effort was made on tourism as the ideal sector in which to invest, for it gave quick results, helped underdeveloped regions, earned much hard currency, and could attract foreign investors. The whole coastline was being rapidly turned over to it. Culture, history, and religion, as well as climate and scenery, were mobilized as auxiliaries to the tourist industry. New hotels were built, old palaces and monasteries converted, churches restored, and ruins rebuilt as fast as possible. The number of nights spent by foreign tourists in Yugoslavia had risen to over 18 million in 1969, and through them the economy earned that year $241 million in foreign exchange – slightly less than through its half-million emigrants.[37]

[36] There were in 1969, 297,000 private entrepreneurs and professionals (3·6% less than in 1968) who employed another 83,000 (16% less than in 1968). Within that total, accommodation and catering actually continued to rise that year, but crafts and services shrank dangerously.

[37] Because the income from tourism was so important, there was extreme sensitivity to anything which might deter foreign tourists from Yugoslavia. In the summer of 1969, the press reacted brutally to foreign press reports of inadequacies in the Yugoslav tourist industry. *Politika* (19 and 28 August, 18 September, 1969) immediately unearthed a great plot, engineered and paid for by the Italian tourist industry, and obviously part of the general reactionary conspiracy against socialist Yugoslavia, to fight off competition from that country. Tito, however, soon after admitted and criticized some practices which did tend to put off foreigners (Split, 28 September), while Italy was, in fact, interested in plans to develop the Yugoslav tourist potential (*The Times* Business News, 19 November 1969). At the end of the 1970 summer season, one which had disappointed expectations, the inadequacies of the tourist industry were severally probed into by the Yugoslav press itself only a year after it had reacted sharply against similar criticism in the foreign press.

Invisible exports were indeed essential partly to offset the trade deficit, for if Yugoslavia 'sold' to the world much more tourism and man-power than it could 'buy' from it in terms of capital and technology, its foreign trade in goods was largely in deficit. Both showed the dependence of the Yugoslav economy on western Europe. In 1969, the trade deficit was up to $656 million, and the balance of payments, in spite of the invisible earnings, was still uncovered by $125 million. Both deficits continued to rise in 1970; Yugoslavia's foreign trade was relatively small – not more than 20 per cent of its gross national product – and its deficit grew along with its expansion. Foreign trade enterprises on the whole knew too little about foreign markets. To import was easier anyhow, so that, with the liberalization of foreign trade, the low labour productivity and archaic technology of Yugoslav manufacturers became apparent. Pressure to protect them from foreign competition made the government gradually go back on this liberalization in the course of 1969, while exporters were again given facilities which enabled them to sell at an effective exchange rate higher than the official parity.

Trade with East European countries was still carried out through bilateral clearing agreements, and since it had provided Yugoslavia with a surplus, the government asked that, as from 1970, trading with Comecon states should be based on convertible currency. But in 1969, the Eastern share of Yugoslav exports had fallen by 4 per cent to 30 per cent, and that of imports by 3 per cent to 24 per cent – with a small deficit for Yugoslavia. At the same time, trade with Common Market countries continued to increase, absorbing in 1969, 33 per cent of Yugoslavia's exports and providing 39 per cent of its imports. Of its total trade deficit of $656 million, $363 million was the negative balance for the E.E.C. alone.

The E.E.C.'s economic integration had made it increasingly difficult for Yugoslavia to step up its exports in that direction. Although Yugoslavia was a member of G.A.T.T., it had not as yet achieved unrestricted trade and thus was at a disadvantage even in relation to other G.A.T.T. members. By 1968, the coming into operation of the E.E.C.'s common agricultural policy hit Yugoslav exports particularly hard just at a time when its agriculture was beginning to show an interesting surplus in some exportable commodities: meat exports had become as vital to Yugoslavia in the late sixties as they had been to Serbia in the early years of the century. Exports to the Common Market area fell that year by $18 million. The problem of coming to some arrangement with the Community had become urgent. In March 1970, after a year and a half of negotiations, an agreement was finally concluded. Yugoslavia was granted certain preferential conditions, the E.E.C. lowering its levies on some products, notably beef.

The problem of hard-currency scarcity was made more difficult by foreign debts which, by the beginning of 1970, amounted to $380 million. Many long-term debts came up for payment that year which had hitherto been put off, while the developing countries to which Yugoslavia had extended credit could not pay back their debts in time. Repayment of foreign debts, along with short-term crediting of regional development and export development funds, and the payment of the federation's part in remaining infrastructural investments, were expenses which stood outside the regular budget. They were intended to be balanced from extra-budgetary sources, such as foreign loans, turnover taxes, interest levied on the business funds of enterprises, and interest on various kinds of short-term credit. In 1970, the government's 'extra-budgetary balance' showed a deficit of almost $240 million, double what it had been in 1968. In order to try and meet its obligations, which were intended to disappear by 1975, but which meanwhile were growing alarmingly, the government went back to the traditional solution and increased the amount of money in circulation.

The economic situation at the beginning of 1970 was particularly serious because it coincided with preparations for the new 1971–75 plan. This aimed at bringing to an end the role of the state as an accumulator of investment resources. It would keep the industrial growth-rate relatively high for employment purposes, but direct it towards producing what could be profitably sold. Increase of exports – both visible and invisible – would be encouraged. In the first six months of the year, however, the situation deteriorated: compared to the same period in 1969, food prices had increased by over 11 per cent and services by more than 15 per cent, the trade deficit by 32 per cent,[38] and investments by 47 per cent.

By the middle of 1970, it seemed as if the reforms had achieved little. The essential cause of continued inflation continued to be the issue of money reaching the economy through credits to various extra-budgetary funds and advances to hand-picked sectors. For political reasons, the government shrank from fully carrying out measures which increased unemployment, exposed the inefficiency of industrial management, and exerted more pressure in favour of private enterprise. It turned out that money was back in the hands of the state, but this time at the levels of republics and communes, and as misinvested as ever. Insolvency thus went hand in hand with inflation: the distinctive feature of the Yugoslav system, satirists

[38] In July, after a record-breaking monthly import figure which increased the trade deficit by $100 million, a temporary 5% import tax was introduced.

said wryly. Credit was exhausted – the solvency rate of business banks was below the legal minimum of 3 per cent since August – and there were rumours that enterprises would not be able to pay wages in the autumn. Inflation had seriously reduced the value of industrial wages which was also indirectly affected by the ever-increasing trade deficit. Tourist earnings had increased by 37 per cent in the first six months of 1970, but it was obvious that they would not reach the figure of $400 million planned for 1970. At the end of the season, the deficiencies of the tourist industry were very frankly analysed in the press: it had tried to get too much out of the foreign tourists too quickly; new and hastily erected hotels and other structures were defective; and service had deteriorated while prices had rocketed. Remittances from emigrants had increased by 113 per cent in these first six months, but if the mass exodus of labour continued with so big a proportion of skilled, technical, and graduate manpower, it would soon create almost as many problems as it solved, for there was already a shortage of technicians in Slovenia.

For lucid critical analyses of the causes of the economic crisis, it was sufficient to read the Yugoslav press. By mid-October, the Party presidency came round to issuing a warning that the economic situation was more serious than it seemed. Unless the position was stabilized – Ribichich stated in an interview[39] – political and social conflicts could break out. Government leaders now gave top priority to finding ways of stabilizing the economy. The International Bank for Reconstruction and Development, which had already credited Yugoslavia to the amount of $306 million over the sixties, and with another $98 million in the first five months of 1970, was approached for yet bigger advances, for infrastructural projects as hitherto and for crediting industrial exports to developing countries – a way of helping both them and Yugoslav industry. But especially, as Kardelj told the presidency on 16 October, it would be necessary to reveal the full truth, to consent to sacrifices, and to undertake unpopular measures. The submission to parliament of the new five-year plan, due to come into operation at the beginning of 1971, but postponed since June because of disagreements, was now left until after the stabilization of the economy and the changes in the constitution had been carried through. In the meantime, restrictive measures were introduced again at the end of October, along with a temporary price freeze, and in January 1971, a new devaluation brought the dinar down by 20 per cent to 1,500 for the dollar.

[39] *Politika*, 11 October 1970.

Chapter 8
Conclusion

'La fureur et l'ivresse d'Érôs se retrouvent ainsi dans cette volonté démiurgique qui, cherchant à réorganiser la genèse des êtres et l'histoire des hommes, prend souvent la notion de progrès pour alibi afin de justifier les rages de vivre et les érostratismes où s'exprime le désir de parcourir le champ de l'altérité avec le maximum d'intensité, de vitesse et de violence....'

(Jean Brun, *Le Retour de Dionysos*)

Drawn together yet drawn apart

The development of Yugoslavia – the land of the South Slavs – evinces one long historical contradiction. On the one hand, there is the process whereby its populations have tended gradually to blend together, thanks to their common linguistic origins, the absence of anthropological racial differences, and the various direct or indirect influences that have come together in this important geopolitical area. On the other hand, because of their natural antipathy, the dominant influences – in so far as they appeared in the shape of conquering powers – prevented the blending process from ever reaching completion. Conquerors moved or harassed populations, they mixed or divided them, but never integrated them. Moreover, the geography that attracted intervention from outside also prevented any one native power from expanding from a centre, growing, attracting, unifying, and checking foreign interference.

The first great turning-point to affect modern developments came at the end of the fifteenth and the beginning of the sixteenth centuries, when the Ottoman conquest also marked the beginning of the Habsburg reconquest, destroyed much of the indigenous development, and cut off most of the territory from contact with Europe. What remained of the mediaeval Serbian and Croatian monarchies under the rule of the Turks and the Austrians – respectively the Serbian Church and the Croatian nobility – continued in their several ways the process of evolving a historically conscious entity, thus facilitating the transition from mediaeval antecedents to modern nationalism. Both these forces were much weakened by the time of the second turning-point, which occurred at the end of the eighteenth and the beginning of the nineteenth centuries and marked the start of the modern era.

The nineteenth century witnessed a long-drawn-out revolutionary process, at once national, social, and political, which removed the vestiges of the pre-existing order stage by stage and region by region. It inaugurated a new order, based upon the principles of freedom for the nationalities, security of property, equality before the law, and social mobility through competition. It established institutions resembling those that had only recently been introduced into western Europe itself: written constitutions and codes, political parties with a variety of ideologies, educational facilities for an increasingly widening public – all of which, however much they were mere pale imitations of their models, nevertheless brought about a slow return to the mainstream of European culture.

Among the Serbs, the expansion of the nucleus of a state again provided the framework in which nationalism and politics could develop and look forward to the liberation and unification of kindred populations as yet unredeemed, according to the possibilities afforded by changing circumstances. Among the Croats, the legal framework, however precious, was largely a formal one existing within the historic dynastic state of the House of Habsburg, in which national and political progress tended to be more erratic; as a result, the development of a national and political consciousness continued to be the work of an élite, the Croatian middle class having taken over the role from the nobility.

The Yugoslav idea was born within the confines of the Habsburg Monarchy, in whose territories South Slavs lived intermingled; but it had its prophets among all ethnic groups and in all lands, both in and outside Austria. It originated among intellectuals – ethnologists, linguists, and poets – who were the first to recognize a common identity characterizing both the way of life and the speech of the kindred populations, and who looked ahead to the achievement of the romantic ideal of a greater national entity that would link all their peoples together, and each one with its glorious past. Reacting against the Yugoslav idea, Austria-Hungary created a Serbo-Croatian problem by manoeuvring Croats and Serbs against each other in order to help maintain its loosening hold over them, as it did with the Czechs and the Slovaks. Thus the South Slavs could not afford, from within the Monarchy, to propagate the idea of political unity cutting across the territorial divisions that existed at the time, and so they concentrated instead on cultural unity. In the

1860s, the diet of Croatia decided that the official language of its proceedings should be *Yugoslav*, and the newly founded *Yugoslav* Academy in Zagreb adopted a statute declaring that its main aim was to cultivate the *Yugoslav* language and literature. In Serbia, the Yugoslav idea was conceived in more political terms, as a way of escaping from the close watch of neighbouring powers, and of weakening both the Ottomans and the Habsburgs – the vision of a bigger population, a wider territory, a more powerful economic unit, with a coastline giving on to the outer world.

The Yugoslav idea led to the fact of Yugoslavia, surely but only slowly, partly because the power-structure did not favour it, and partly because common action was reduced to intellectual dreaming or political scheming, put to practical use when it suited the Serbian or the Croatian side, but rarely by the two simultaneously. The political reality behind the idea remained malleable, and so did its linguistic counterpart. By adopting the principle of a literary idiom based on the language spoken by the people, linguists paved the way to unity in the near future, for the South Slavs could understand each other once the speech and writing of their educated classes had been purified of foreign adulterations. In the remoter future, however, there was the seed of possible disunity if that principle was pushed to the extreme of codifying regional variants – a possibility which could never have been envisaged by any of the intellectuals intent on working out a common cultural approach.

The First World War, which precipitated the process, came too early for the Yugoslav idea, but 1918 became a turning-point when it suddenly made real what had been merely a dream, an ideal, a speculation, a subject for research, or simply a talking-point. Willy-nilly the idea had become a polity. The approaches to it were widely divergent, because circumstances had kept them apart, and there had been no time for them to draw nearer to one another. All the negotiations, declarations, resolutions, and proclamations of governments, committees, councils, assemblies, rulers, and politicians on the subject of a unified state had been full of good intentions, but as far as the actual populations were concerned, such affirmations corresponded to vague feelings rather than to a clearly expressed national will. Not even the élites, let alone the masses, were ready for unification when the powers which had kept them apart collapsed. Instead of changing their respective attitudes to suit a new set of circumstances, they went on as if 1918 had simply been the outcome of the limited aims each had realistically been struggling to achieve. For the Serbian state, this was the final liberation of all the remaining enslaved regions. For the Croatian political class, it was the ultimate improvement on Croatia's autonomous status. Yugoslavia, however, was neither an extension of the Serbian state nor a Yugoslav version of Austria-Hungary. Federalism might have helped to smooth the transition from old to new, but although it was invoked, there was complete misunderstanding of this peculiarly Anglo-Saxon combination of the rule of law and representative government, and of give and take between the parties to a contract.

The common enterprise would have been a difficult one even if attempted under the best possible conditions; but it was in difficult times that the revolution, initiated in the first years of the nineteenth century, reached its climax as a result of the First World War, in the creation of a state of all the Yugoslavs, from which the political and social power of the alien ruling classes had been finally eliminated. Equality before the law and the free interplay of political parties had been instituted through a fully fledged parliamentary régime. Economic inequalities, however, were not and could not be abolished; moreover, they were aggravated by the population increase which had left the peasants with less and less land as they became 'more and more equal'.[1] The governments of the inter-war period, unlike their successors after the Second World War, were able to obtain only moderate amounts of foreign capital for economic development. Furthermore, since possibilities for emigration did not exist, and since the urban economy grew only at a slow rate, the excess rural population, forced to stay in the villages, lessened the good effects of agricultural improvement. The abnormal strains created, not only by the population growth and the multiplicity of traditions, but by the world economic crisis and the appearance of new totalitarian ideologies in central and eastern Europe, imposed impossible burdens on the clumsy grouping-together in imitation of West European forms. The Balkan revolution of the nineteenth century did not have the time to achieve the social structure that might have managed to withstand the strains of the 1930s.

Serbs and Croats were the two largest historically conscious groups, and the nearest to each other, both culturally and territorially. The Serbs, however, reacted as a satisfied majority. The combined state had inherited many of the characteristics of their own limited pre-war Serbian state. They themselves saw it as the achievement of what had been started in 1804 when they first rose up against the Turks in the sandjak of Belgrade, and so they naturally wanted to preserve and defend its framework. The Croats reacted as a dissatisfied minority. The unified state had not turned out as they had envisaged it, and since they were not numerous enough to change its structure through constitutional methods, they shifted their attention to extra-parliamentary means. Feeding on the disillusionment

[1] T. Stoianovich, *A Study in Balkan Civilization*, New York, 1967, p. 162.

of most Croats, a fraction was soon to turn to violence. The crown failed to find any solution that would satisfy the Croats without changing the structure of the state, and therefore brought the parliamentary régime to an end. Having dealt impatiently with a Serbo-Croatian problem inherited from Austria-Hungary, it attempted to impose a negative solution by forbidding the expression of sectional nationalism, and encouraging a feeling of Yugoslav patriotism to overcome it.

In the difficult decade of the thirties, the Serbo-Croatian problem was driven outside the channels of open political dialogue, and was discussed only through contacts between Serbian and Croatian opposition parties wanting to combine in order to challenge the authoritarian régime, or between the crown and the Croatian opposition in order to divide the opposition. It was on this basis, as the Second World War was about to break out, that the Yugoslav monarchy tried one last emergency solution which, unfortunately, made possible a recrudescence of hard feelings on both the Serbian and Croatian sides. The other smaller ethnic groups presented no such problem, either because the unified state seemed to them necessary for their survival, or because they had not yet developed a separate consciousness.

It had taken a world war for Yugoslavia to come prematurely into the world, and however shaky its condition, it took another world war to destroy the kingdom of Yugoslavia. In the Second World War, the foreign conquerors destroyed the common state; they also set its components against each other in an unprecedented way, for never before had there been any physical conflict among the Yugoslav peoples. The violence was not exclusively due to strife between different ethnic groups, but occurred much more significantly between groups siding with the Axis and other groups siding with the Allies, then later between Communists and anti-Communists. Even what appeared as a fratricidal war between Serbs and Croats was much more of a struggle fought by an ethnic minority of Serbs – Communists and non-Communists – on the territory of an Axis puppet state, against the enemy-established régime of an extremist fringe of Croatian nationalism. The war which introduced this tragic innovation also revived some older themes of Yugoslav history, such as migratory movements, and the identification of nation and religion. The comings and goings of guerrilla forces with their dependents, together with all kinds of expulsions and displacements, caused people to be shifted about in the course of the war. In its immediate aftermath, the participants on the winning side in the civil war moved from the mountains down to the plains, and from the villages into the towns, whereas many of the losers left the country altogether – not to mention the expulsion of half a million Germans. These migrations intermingled yet again the people from different regions, but they hardly contributed towards bringing them nearer to each other in feeling, and in consequence the identification of religious denominations with ethnic groups made still further progress. Whereas in pre-war Yugoslavia all Orthodox were identified with Serbs (though the inverse was not necessarily true), in the Ustasha state of Croatia, Catholicism was identified with Croatism, and religious differences between Eastern and Western Christians loomed larger than they had ever done between Christians and Moslems.

The chaos of the Second World War caused such bloodshed that latter-day foreign observers, unable to see below the surface, came to believe in a mythical fratricidal tradition. In point of fact, the attempted genocide of 1941 caused more harm than if Serbs and Croats had really fought internecine wars down the centuries. One single Drogheda is, after all, more difficult to efface than centuries of Anglo-French wars. And yet, without the war and without the resistance (however confused), Yugoslavia and the other countries that Hitler wanted to erase from the map of Europe would probably have disappeared. The outcome of 1945, as of 1918, led to a united Yugoslavia, even though, once again, there was no national consultation. The defeat of the Axis powers had destroyed the chances of those native movements and forces that had thought of a solution in terms of putting the clock back, and of withdrawing into the confines of narrow, sectional nationalism. The resistance, on the other hand, had been led by people who wanted to maintain a unified Yugoslav state against all odds – even if it had not always been fought locally with that aim in mind. The more they resisted, the more they came to look at the enemy occupation as a temporary phenomenon, and the more they became concerned with one another – one side with the threat of a Soviet-backed Communist revolution, the other with the threat of the moderates coming to power backed by England and America. As much blood was shed in fighting between Yugoslavs for the restoration of Yugoslavia, as had been shed earlier in the war in the fighting between Yugoslavs that had threatened to destroy Yugoslavia for ever.

The rise to power of the Communists marked the last turning-point. In some ways one has to go back to the Ottoman conquest for a precedent. Once again, the mixture of foreign invasion and domestic dissension enabled the invaders in the Balkans to proclaim themselves the deliverers of the common people. Once again, a new order was imposed which cut the territory off from Europe and allowed some of the more ancient elements of the old order to survive. In other ways one has to go back to the nineteenth-century revolution, of which the Communist revolution was the antithesis. In order to abolish the power of money, with its concomitant economic and social inequalities, it also abolished the principles of equality before the law and the political liberties which had been the proclaimed ideals – if not always the practice – of the old order. Bourgeois society, which had not had time to establish a stable integrated social structure throughout Yugoslavia, was rejected as a whole. What could not be brushed aside, however, was the question of national identities. Apart from its general Communist, political, economic, and social aims, the new régime had one specifically Yugoslav aim, and that was to solve the problem of national identity in the territory over which it ruled. It was declared that this would be achieved immediately on the basis of the 'brotherhood and unity' of all the ethnic groups, and in the long run, it would be consolidated on the permanent basis of proletarian internationalism. The Communist attempt at solving the problem was no worse than the previous – monarchical and bourgeois – attempt. As internationalists, the Communists could have been expected to forget national feelings, just as their opponents could have been expected to overcome similar feelings on their part in order to close their ranks.

The polarization of Party and society

The new régime achieved the difficult task of restoring a unity that had been torn to pieces. Its contribution towards solving the national problem was, however, limited to reducing the feeling of inequality or humiliation felt by some sections of the population before the war, establishing an equilibrium between Serbs and Croats, prohibiting the public expression of intolerance, and introducing the form of a federal system. For the rest, the problem was not so much solved as anaesthetized. The attempt of the old régime to harness all local feelings to a common Yugoslav nationalism was condemned, both as a failure and because it had been attempted by opponents of the new régime. In contrast, the Communist rulers allowed the expression of different local feelings, provided they were not directed against each other, or against the community or the new order, and they proceeded to harness them all to a common ideology in the belief that communism was going to make that problem, and many others as well, merely redundant.

The solutions to the problems of rural overpopulation and of dependence on foreign capital were also to be found in communism: in the nationalization of the means of production, and in forced

CONCLUSION 379

extensive industrialization through a centralized command economy. It has been said that the Communists were the first in eastern Europe to run the sort of risks that 'conquering bourgeoisies' had taken in western Europe – and with the same lack of concern for the human material involved. Having taken the risk, they had succeeded in achieving an industrial 'take-off' by the late fifties. The success, however, was not due to communism alone, but to its association with Western capitalism. The C.P.Y.'s expulsion from the Cominform led the U.S.A. and western Europe to offer massive economic aid, which enabled Yugoslavia in the fifties to preserve its independence of the U.S.S.R. and to lay a new groundwork when the system of command economy was seen to be grinding to a halt.[2] The rural problem, in the end, was on the way to being solved, not by a combination of collectivization and industrialization, but by a combination of industrialization and emigration. By the late fifties, the system of command economy had outlived any economic purpose it had ever served. By gradually introducing a policy of reforms, the Yugoslav government started to drag the economy off the sandbank into which it had been wedged by the speed of its acceleration, but not all of the many problems which had piled up could be cured by internal economic reforms. Some of them derived from the country's isolation in Europe.

The workers' self-management of economic enterprises was a brilliant idea from the point of view both of ideology and of public relations. It might also have provided a good motive force with which to get the economy moving away from its original Stalinist conceptions. But everyone in Yugoslavia is now agreed that self-management remained purely formal for the fifteen years up to 1965. No sooner were efforts made to adapt industry to more real and more modern requirements, than the workers' councils reacted – in so far as they initiated anything at all – to defend what had been acquired. With small margins of profit, it turned out to be contradictory to introduce at the same time the self-financing of enterprises and workers' participation in their profits. Workers' councils, had they been allowed to be fully operative in the fifties, could have played a valuable part within a framework of small and medium-sized enterprises. When the imperatives of efficiency began to call for integration into larger units and for global economic decisions, it became difficult for workers' councils to be the sources of real decisions, especially in view of the level of education among Yugoslavia's industrial labour. The régime had given prominence to the notion of *struggle* rather than that of *competence*. In placing the emphasis on the people's liberation struggle, on the class struggle,

[2] Ibid., pp. 105–6.

on the struggle to implement socialism, on the struggle to implement the plan, and on the struggle to defend the achievements of the revolution, the Communist Party had not trained the working class for the competent management of a socialist society.

Starting from the conditions of education in 1970, it will still be a long time before enough workers are able to participate – if indeed they are interested in so doing – in order to make self-management an efficient proposition. By that time, workers' self-management may be totally superseded by a tightly organized, market-geared, highly industrialized economy, for which, in its present form, it can hardly be considered a model. Meanwhile, it is for the government a way of giving the workers something to work on; it is a good slogan, and a way of sharing responsibility for past economic failures. It is also developing into a stick used by many people – in the Party, among nationalists of different nations, and among the 'new Left' – to beat everyone else. As for labour, it is groping its way back to old forms of industrial action, in rebellion against both its own elected management and bureaucratic trade unionism – so much so that the latter, which had started by condemning strikes, has slowly been forced to back down without, however, having yet found its role.

Reforms have started to undermine the economic basis of the monopoly of political power, and the extension of self-management has started to erode totalitarianism. Through economic necessity, the Yugoslav leadership has had to throw overboard many tenets of a faith which has become detached from reality. At the same time, Yugoslavia's rulers have been careful to maintain the semblance of a coherent continuity so as to appear to the world at large as true Marxists, and to wrest from those who had condemned them an acknowledgement that theirs was also a valid road to socialism. Every change, every new phrase, has been justified in relation to the past, and has in turn justified the past.[3] President Tito, in January 1954, put the rhetorical question:

> Has there ever been any other revolution whose leaders have liquidated so courageously the conditions which they have themselves promoted, and which they now find to be obsolete and erroneous, so that they might bring into being conditions which are new and better?[4]

They have acknowledged their errors, but also explained them *a posteriori* and attributed them to objective factors. The very people who make the mistakes later try to put them right, without having to go through a salutary period of opposition in which to reflect on them. Yet every time that they condemn any one of

[3] Cf. Meister, op. cit., pp. 284–8.
[4] Quoted in Wolff, op. cit., p. 409.

themselves or of their servants, or indeed anything in their past, they condemn a little bit of their collective self.

Theory may originate as hardly more than the conceptualization of practice, and practice may not always follow theory. Yet it would be a mistake to think that the Yugoslav Communists do not believe in their theories. Ideology may be weaker among the middle than among the older generations, and weaker still among the younger generations, but it does afford an insight into the thinking of at least the leadership. However empirical it is, policy, both at home and abroad, remains 'socialist', and one which has to be carried out by the 'conscious action of organized socialist forces'. Over the past twenty years, the Yugoslav Communists have come to envisage an ideal socialist world of equal socialist forces, with an important role for themselves in helping the spread of socialism. Since it is always fashionable to talk of communism in ecclesiological terms, one could say that the Yugoslav conception of socialism is more Orthodox than Catholic, and that they view Moscow as Constantinople rather than as Rome, but that the multifariousness and subtlety of their missionary activity remains more Latin than Greek. Such an analogy explains behaviour which – to return to more socialist metaphors – has become almost social democratic internationally, but has remained semi-Stalinist nationally.

No other organization is allowed to challenge either the Party or its policies at home. The political leadership in power recruits and supervises the élite, and controls the mass communication media and education. Weakened though the ideological guidelines may be, they have managed so far to offset any ideological challenge from within, and have avoided a complete change of course. The Communist régimes of eastern Europe are, until further notice, viable and effective totalitarian structures. Time and experience have allowed them to improve on the techniques of all their predecessors. They are not simple dictatorships of a single man, a group, an oligarchy, a caste, or a class. They are much more complex power-structures – the dictatorship of an apparatus guided by an ideology and embodied in the Party. Hence their continuity, and their relative stability to date, especially in Yugoslavia, where the régime has not only lost the stigma of having been helped into power by the Soviet Union, but has actually acquired the aura of having resisted that power.

The systematic rotation of personnel involves the transfer of the administration of the state to a new generation, endowed with better technical qualifications, yet with less strength to operate the totalitarian techniques. The extension of self-management from economic enterprises to all social institutions and territorial units brings in more and more citizens to participate in the smaller technicalities of government. These two changes are important, although they do not necessarily lead towards greater efficiency or liberalization. The systematic dislocation of the administrative personnel every four years, and its reconstruction on the principle of musical chairs, does not contribute to the continuity of a system which needs to appear continuous. As for 'socialist direct democracy', even if and when it functions best, with little or no outside interference, the fact that its authority never extends beyond one enterprise, institution, or territorial unit means that it cannot take part in the decision-making process on important national issues.

Direct democracy functioned within the narrow limits of the free élites of some city-states of ancient Greece. It has been known to function in insurrectionary circumstances among insurgents, and in tribal societies among warriors. It still functions in three Swiss cantons that are mountainous and sparsely populated. In the large and advanced societies of the twentieth century, it either functions only occasionally through referendum, or it is turned to corporatism in the case of Fascist or semi-Fascist régimes – to replace, distort, or counterbalance countrywide constituency representation. In the large and less advanced societies of the twentieth century, corporatism and village-council democracy are occasionally used by modern enlightened despots who need some apparent representative backing of sorts, but who cannot afford classical parliamentary representation. In an exercise of direct democracy in 1969, the French rejected General de Gaulle's senatorial reform which would have introduced representatives of social and professional categories on an equal footing with those of the citizens in their parliamentary constituencies. The electorate rightly considered that the principle of democracy could not allow delegates of particular groups to have the same powers as the political representatives of citizens. The former can offer a useful point of view, express a consultative opinion, or even participate in the legislative process, but the last word must belong to the latter.

The practice of political democracy is as necessary to socialism as to any other social and economic system. It is hard to understand how a régime which has used violence to obtain power and to establish the foundations of its achievements, which has institutionalized authoritarianism to ensure the permanence of these achievements, can ever condition its citizens to anything other than violence and authoritarianism. What the Yugoslav ruling élite is now doing is to split up the body politic and the body social into their component professional, economic, and territorial sectors, and to reorganize them into hierarchies. It has distributed little portions of

CONCLUSION 383

authority which have made every unit and corporation responsible for its own difficulties. Whereas the system can be democratic enough at its lowest, smallest, least relevant, and least advanced level, at any higher level it can offer no more than an illusory participation in decisions already made, and that amount of individual freedom which does not threaten the leadership's plans, its direction of fundamental policies, or its choice of top personnel.[5]

To facilitate their task, the rulers have used, or even fostered, all sorts of apparent dangers and diversions. There has been the danger of the political and class enemy of the civil war, linked first to the Axis powers, and then to the Western powers. There has been the threat of Western imperialism and that of Soviet imperialism, each patronizing its own fifth column, separately at first, but now combined one with the other and both with the rejuvenated political and class enemy of the civil war. There have been the scapegoats: the old régime, the occupying powers, the Cominform, the liberals, and the conservatives.

Slogans and cults are also commonly used. Mere words tend to be repeated instead of real solutions being found. The current slogans since 1968 are those of the permanent revolution and of self-management leading to non-party direct democracy. Since the 'new' Yugoslavia is now older than its 'old' predecessor when it expired, it is becoming difficult to put the blame for all that is wrong on people, forces, and events that pre-date 1941, 1945, 1954, and 1966, and criticism, especially from the young, has begun to turn on people, forces, and events that post-date 1966. In answer to such criticism, the latest slogan is that Yugoslav self-managing socialism is the only genuine opposition to the two great established power blocs which rule over the world, each with its own sphere of influence, but neither with the ability to change the condition of contemporary man, except in such a way as to increase his alienation. The Yugoslav system claims to break through the blocks on progress; and to oppose it – to be in opposition to opposition – is to betray a sympathy with either of the two established dominating positions, if not with both at the same time. It is obvious that such slogans cannot generate any great enthusiasm in the man in the street, who is increasingly apathetic about politics and contemptuous of politicians. For many of the young, the workers, and the intellectuals, such

[5] A strip cartoon in the Belgrade weekly *Nin* (26 April 1970) shows an artist arguing with another artist, a politician with another politician, a journalist with another journalist, and a worker with another worker, with the caption: 'See, Pete – artists criticize artists, politicians criticize politicians, journalists criticize journalists. This means I can criticize only you, and you can criticize only me.'

slogans have become not only meaningless but ridiculous. It was to a large extent against slogans that both students and trade unions stood up in 1968, chafing at the stupidities of old leaders who went on repeating outworn dicta.⁶

Marshal Tito's birthday is the Day of Youth. 'The cult of youth is an adults' way of deceiving themselves into thinking that they have not grown old', Raymond Aron has written, of other old men in other circumstances.⁷ While youth has provided slogans for the leadership – slogans which went sour between June 1968 and June 1969 – the cult of one old man is what the youth of Yugoslavia is nourished on. The cult of Marshal Tito is one of the elements which enable the Yugoslav leadership to maintain a continuity, and to profit from his prestige in the East where he is known and esteemed, in the West where he is less known and more admired, and among the non-aligned governments to whom he has extended some material help, rather more diplomatic help, and a certain significance in world affairs. The personality cult of Tito is a unique survival in the Communist world of today, and surpasses that of his western European counterpart, Franco. Streets are named after him everywhere, and so is one mountain peak; Titograd is the name of the capital city of the republic of Montenegro; and three other towns have their name preceded by the predicate 'Tito's'. His name is enshrined in the constitution.

Psychologists will no doubt, one day, be interested in two emotional aspects of the cult. One is the fan-like adulation, even the love, of Tito being fostered among crowds, particularly the young. The other is the admiration, at times the love, felt for Tito by many intellectuals in the West. While the former facilitates mass manipulation, the latter answers a basic need for hero-worshipping repressed in a less emotional atmosphere.

Tito is a politician of genius who has worked his way up, and consolidated his position by skilfully using the circumstances he found himself in to eliminate all his rivals, both in the Party and out of it: first at the time of Stalin's Comintern, then during the resistance to the Axis conquerors and in the civil war, and finally when holding out against Stalin's Cominform. He has known how to modify the style and methods of his rule for the sake of what he has created – the Yugoslav Party machine that controls the

---

⁶ Within the context of the government's programme, even Kardelj had to say, at a public meeting in Slovenia as late as 7 June 1970, that there was too much delay in implementing what had been decided at the ninth congress – that it was high time to pass from words to action.

⁷ *La Révolution introuvable – Réflexions sur les événements de mai*, Paris, 1968, p. 41.

territory of a reunited Yugoslavia – without ever renouncing either the cause of proletarian internationalism or his personal ambitions. Simultaneously, for the sake of the same creation, the same cause, and the same ambition, he has always resisted any moves to lead his régime away from strict Party rule. He has consciously held on to the absolute monopoly of the Party apparatus. Tito, by virtue of his age, has in many ways remained a dogmatist and become a conservative, suspicious of free scholarship, of free artistic expression, of free enterprise, and of free contacts with the outer world.[8] Although he came out against the conservatives in 1966, his attitude of mind can only help the authoritarian trend within the L.C.Y. which is united, behind and through Tito's authority, on the question of power, whereas the reformist trend is hopelessly divided into nationalities and republics.[9]

In some respects, Tito is not unlike a Communist Yugoslav de Gaulle. With a personal prestige going back to his role in the war, he has not renounced either his grand design or a certain mythology,

[8] Marshal Tito's conception of freedom, judging by his public pronouncements, invites comparison with that of Oliver Cromwell when he wrote to the governor of Rosse in Ireland on 19 October 1649: 'For that which you mention concerning liberty of conscience, I meddle not with any man's conscience. But if by liberty of conscience you mean a liberty to exercise the mass, I judge it best to use plain dealing, and to let you know, where the Parliament of England have power, that will not be allowed of. (W. Abbott (ed.): *The Writings and Speeches of Oliver Cromwell*, II, Cambridge, Mass., 1939, p. 146.) As for his conception of art, it is not unlike that of Colonel Ioannis Ladas, secretary-general of the Greek Ministry of Home Affairs, who in a speech at Xanthi on 16 September 1970 expressed the opinion that, as a military man, he felt qualified to speak on art, since letters and the arts were components of social life – 'These cannot leave indifferent the guards who have responsibility for security and order in the social life of the nation' – and stated: 'Art, if it does not benefit society and does not promote man, is no longer art.' (*The Times*, 18 September 1970.)

[9] Political trials for hostile propaganda against the people and the state, for spreading false rumours likely to cause anxiety among the citizens, for sending out leaflets or making statements critical of the established order, for writing false and exaggerated reports on the situation, are a characteristic not merely of the Yugoslav régime, but something it shares with a variety of authoritarian régimes of all shades. According to reports in *The Times*, a man who urged the Greeks to vote against the new constitution proposed by the military *junta* was sentenced to imprisonment on 25 September 1968 for 'anti-national declarations', while at the other end of the Mediterranean, a Spanish theologian was awaiting trial on charges involving 'illegal propaganda'. On 31 March 1970, the publisher of an Athens daily was tried for 'spreading false reports likely to evoke anxiety among citizens', and with 'engaging in anti-national propaganda'. On 14 August 1970, two Sino-Filipino journalists, deported from the Philippines, were found guilty by a court in Taipeh of writing 'propaganda articles for the benefit of the Chinese Communist rebels', and 'false and over-exaggerated reports' on China.

both of which are part of his formation and of his ideals. Some of his attitudes have come more and more into conflict with the realities of Yugoslavia's development, and his world role has hardly helped to solve his country's internal problems. Tito's action as a world leader, his preoccupation with uniting a bloc of the non-aligned; his denunciation of imperialism, colonialism, and technological colonialism; his pronouncements on the problems of Asia, Africa, Latin America, and even of North America and Europe – all these are in contrast with Yugoslavia's more down-to-earth policy of trying to export meat and labour, of attracting foreign capital, technology, and tourists, of buying foreign armaments, of balancing its trade and its payments, and of being friends with everyone from Chairman Mao to the Greek colonels.

For the time being, Tito's presence at the head of Yugoslavia keeps the Party leadership together, attracts international attention, and makes direct Soviet intervention improbable. After his departure, one can only hazard the guess that, if the Party divides, its different sections will have to look for support outside its ranks, perhaps even outside the country, whilst in a serious crisis the Soviet Union will not allow the situation to deteriorate to its disadvantage. Much of what is distinctively 'Titoist' in Yugoslavia's foreign policy will probably fade after Tito's passing, and perhaps also much that is still dogmatic in character in domestic policies – including self-management. Self-management was one of Djilas's ideas which made sense in the context of its author's idealistic thinking. It is now increasingly used as a slogan rather than a technique, and in the more advanced regions its main attraction has lain in helping to maintain local funds.

Something which could become much more a part of Yugoslav communism than self-management, and towards which Yugoslavia seems to be heading rather than to any form of direct democracy, is socialist pluralism – or, in the words of Professor Alec Nove (not written apropos of Yugoslavia), 'a kind of centralized pluralism, or pluralistic centralism'.[10] The Party could become a real league, in fact as well as in name – a *Bund* of the various pressure-groups generated by economic reform, with perhaps even a legalized opposition within the institutionalized framework of a participatory, pluralistic, corporative, *and* authoritarian system that enabled this or that interest group to fight any decision of the ruling élite which threatened to affect the vital interests of its members.

Although these changes can be sensed, they cannot be mapped or forecast, for in the absence of a fully open and rational discussion of

[10] 'The Way the Cookie Crumbles', in *Problems of Communism*, XIX/1, Washington, 1970, p. 18.

the real issues to be faced and of the real choices available, the changes brought about by modernization take place not only in a very serious economic situation, but also in an ever more fragmented political and social system. The aggressive pursuit of sectional interests and their conflicting demands cannot easily be reconciled by the bargaining methods usually associated with interest-group policies, because they are allowed to express themselves in no other framework than that of official communism – which is losing the confidence of the people. With no common aim to cling to, it is difficult for all the differentiation to lead to political liberalization, the more so since Yugoslav society is still so penetrated with the idea of social promotion that any other urge is bound to take second place.

The end of the sixties might mark the approach to yet another turning-point, brought about through the strains of what Milovan Djilas describes as the polarization of the economy and official policy within society.[11] The evolution of society has created problems which are becoming too big for the small ruling group to solve. However limited, the existence of private landownership and enterprise, of foreign capital and technology, of labour strikes and of anti-communism, clashes with an ideology of socialization, self-sufficiency, and producers' self-government. The problems of economic reorganization, of management efficiency, of the links with Europe, of constitutional arrangements, and of national identity, merge into political problems. Many of them call for a spontaneous and time-consuming process to take place outside the framework of government, and for the formation of an independent public opinion and the confrontation of conflicting views within legally guaranteed and socially accepted forms.

When all the grievances came to a head rather than coalesced in 1968–69, the impression grew that they were linked in a co-ordinated movement, and it certainly united the people in power in the simple reflex of the preservation of their power. For as long as the established order holds together, the 'haves' will support it in order to defend their own situation, whilst the 'have-nots', the 'haves-no-more', the 'haves-not-yet', and those after something other than mere 'having', will continue to lack ideas or common aims. Since the régime has established the production of material goods as the ideal of society, it has divided the intelligentsia from the producers, quite apart from the ethnic divisions and the contrasting interests of economic sections. All are kept in their separate reservations, to busy themselves with immediate problems, or to make gestures which cannot really affect institutions or public opinion – in so far as it exists. The régime's ability to manoeuvre, together with its organization and its control of

[11] *The Unperfect Society*, London, 1969, p. 151.

force and of the mass media, have enabled it to survive from crisis to crisis, though its unity and its authority are becoming increasingly difficult to maintain under the repeated assaults of society.

'What is thy name? And he said, Legion'

The mutation of Yugoslavia is taking place in an atmosphere saturated with the emotions produced by the Yugoslavs' unsettled national identities. The Communist régime is being weakened by the sterile pattern of ethnic conflict no less surely than its predecessor. The less political freedom there is to discuss the country's important problems, including that of its national identity, the more the question of national identity, because of its outstandingly emotional nature, tends to permeate all the others. In so far as the psychological urge for greater freedom of expression is not prevented from expressing itself through any ideology but the established one, it turns to nationalism, which in Yugoslavia is by its very nature fragmented. That being so, it represents no great danger to the establishment so long as it does not become destructive, and it is tolerated within these bounds. The urge for greater freedom of expression is thus reduced all too often to no more than an urge to call oneself by the name of one's small and (either genuinely or not so genuinely) ancient nation. Coming on top of the general social and economic differentiation, and giving it an aura of spiritual satisfaction, sectional nationalism joins forces with social advancement to take precedence over the need for political freedom. Not only does nationalism not lead to the liberalization of the political structure, but, in so far as it goes too far, it reinforces the conservative tendencies in the L.C.Y.

Yugoslavia is neither a homogeneous nation-state like Italy or Greece, nor a fully multinational state like the Habsburg Monarchy of the past or the U.S.S.R. today, but is something in between, grouping together several South Slav ethnic groups whose kinship and common interests have been strong enough to foster a Yugoslav movement, to transcend the political and religious obstacles that kept them apart and made them develop distinct historic entities; strong enough too, so far, to keep them together for over half a century despite their differences, the recurring crises, and interferences from outside aimed at separating them. It is a state of different groups that have, at different stages and at different speeds, evolved from the feeling of belonging to a biological community, to an awareness of a common cultural heritage, and then on from that to the creation of a political framework and to its continued improvement. To the South Slav groups one must add the non-Slav minorities, and bear in mind the fact that all of them have been shifted around and mixed up together by foreign conquerors.

The national problem of Yugoslavia centres on the crucial Serbo-Croatian problem that existed before the creation of a common unified state, in the provinces of Austria-Hungary where Serbs and Croats lived together, where neither Serbian nor Croatian (and even less any form of Yugoslav) nationalism was allowed free political expression, and where they were used against each other to facilitate the task of their rulers. In the unified Yugoslav kingdom, after a decade of free if clumsy political interaction, a single integrating Yugoslavism was fostered from above which, with the help of the powers that wanted to destroy Yugoslavia, ended by driving both of them to extremes. Now, in a reunified Communist Yugoslavia, the lack of any means of free political expression for Serbian and Croatian nationalism has once again acted to sensitize them.

Nationalism, as a historical phenomenon, is in itself neither a blessing nor a curse. However, when considered as totem – or taboo, it can distort or ossify other national developments. It raises questions which can only be answered by the healthy growth of various national functions outside the sphere of state action. Governments can, by their policies, contribute to the solution of these questions; they cannot solve them by decrees, slogans, declarations, and constitutions. The Yugoslav state was first set up on the basis of the national unification of the Serbs, the Croats, and the Slovenes. After the last war, Yugoslavia was reunified as a multinational state of related nations on which there was imposed, nevertheless, an integrating unity of power and ideology. Once the break-up of the family had been avoided, fraternal co-existence was declared to be the programme of the new régime. That this could be done at all was considered little short of a historical miracle. It meant that – on whatever sides they had fought – the victims of those movements and powers that had sought to liquidate Yugoslavia had not died in vain. For a long time it was thought that the common aims and interests inside the ranks of the Communist Party, coupled with a common subjection to the same form of rule in the country at large and a subsequent span of years together, had gone a long way towards blending the various nationalities together, and had contributed significantly towards making the reasons that had brought them together in the first instance outweigh their differences.

The Communist régime has introduced a form of federalism; it has divided the country according to different criteria in order to establish a balance between the different nationalities. The form could have facilitated the elimination of various ethnic obsessions, for it rid the Serbs of their self-satisfaction at being in the majority, and freed the Croats from their dissatisfaction at always being in the minority. The experience of inverting positions under the rule of the Axis powers had been at best disappointing, and at worst tragic. Communist rule, however, replaced the aim of ethnic uniformity with that of ideological uniformity, and until the end of the fifties, the centralized rule of the Party prevented federalism from being much more than an empty shell.

According to A. J. P. Taylor, 'Marshal Tito was the last of the Habsburgs'.[12] By bridging the gap between Habsburg dynasticism and Communist partyism, the formula disregards the force of nationalism in eastern Europe, which, with the help of other factors, for better or worse brought the one to an end and still keeps the other in existence. It also seems to betray that weak spot which many people have, north of the Alps and west of the Böhmer Wald, for any system which 'reins in' the troublesome peoples on the other side. Written in 1948, the *mot* has, in two decades, acquired an unwittingly prophetic ring. Within the confines of a succession state which at one time had been thought a nation-state, communism has declared that this was never the case, and in its place set up an ideological state that recalls some aspects of the old dynastic state. The Austro-Hungarian Monarchy was Catholic-inspired; in theory it was a personal union of different historic territories; it linked their different populations through a common loyalty to the dynasty and the cult of the emperor-king who ruled by historically sanctioned right, by means of a social and political ruling class that had overcome its ethnic origins in order to safeguard its material position and its political order. In Yugoslavia today, the Party leadership, Marxist-Leninist-inspired, governs what in theory is the union in revolution of different nationalities, by virtue of historically sanctioned rights. It links the different populations through a common loyalty to the Party and the cult of the marshal-president, by means of a ruling class that could be described in similar terms. Like the imperial and royal authority, that of the L.C.Y. has learnt to divide and balance nationalities, thereby using them against each other so as to acquire the support of one in order to restrain another. It too is careful that they should not unite in any other way than in loyalty to the historically established order. Would Tito be Francis Joseph? There were, after all, two other 'last Habsburgs' whose model could, for the sake of argument, be envisaged: Francis Ferdinand, who planned to restore a strongly centralized monarchical rule; and

[12] *The Habsburg Monarchy, 1809–1918 – A History of the Austrian Empire and Austria-Hungary*, revised edn, London, 1948, p. 260.

CONCLUSION 391

Charles, who gave in to everybody to try and save the dynasty, and who failed in his belated attempt.

Having discarded integral Yugoslavism, the Communist régime has placed excessive stress on the ethnic exclusiveness and cultural individuality of the different Yugoslav peoples, and thus kept them aware of their differences. Although not intended to do so, the stress on ethnic separateness has worked counter to the desire to foster ideological integration. No sooner had economic and social developments led to a pluralistic reaction against ideological and political uniformity, than the government was confronted with the growth of the very kind of nationalism it had hoped to discourage. It had, furthermore, successfully thwarted any attempt at fostering integration on any other level than that of official ideology – such as that which was taking shape between the Orthodox and Catholic Churches in the middle sixties. When the Communist rulers' policy of imposed ideological integration appeared to have been no more successful after two decades than the monarchical policy of imposed ethnic integration before them, it was seen that Yugoslavia's national question was worse in the sixties than it had been in the thirties, because what had been an essentially political and constitutional question had now taken on economic, social, and cultural aspects as well. There had developed a confused, negative kind of nationalism, with inter-ethnic antagonisms that affected the ruling Party and consequently found their way into the shell of federalism. With decentralization, or rather with the switch from monocentralism to polycentralism, the local Party leaderships started to reduce the strength and the significances of the Yugoslav community.

It was then that Serbs seriously began to reflect on the consequences of such a development, for – together with the Montenegrins who were being taught to think of themselves as having a separate nationality – they were dispersed over seven different regions, and almost half of them lived outside their own stronghold of inner Serbia. The territorial units adopted in 1943 by the leadership of the People's Liberation Movement were acceptable to most of them as the framework for a federal administrative structure, but not as a basis for the development of mini-nation-states within the Yugoslav community. Serbian nationalism began to resemble opposition to the régime, just as Croatian nationalism had done before the war. And just as before the war, when the rulers of the state and the leaders of the Serbian political parties had realized that a policy which went directly against Croatian opinion could not in the long run be implemented, so now the rulers of the state and the Croatian Party leaders came to realize that the same was true of a tendency that flouted Serbian opinion, and tried to contain its more extreme manifestations. On both sides, nationalism shows itself backward-looking. The process of identifying nationality with religion is finally being completed under a régime whose aim it is to create conditions that will gradually eliminate the religious needs of men, and in a society which is already to a large extent de-Christianized.[13] But whereas among the Serbs, the defence of the historic identity seems to have been actually taken up again by the Church, among the Croats its main champion is as before the political class, now the Party cadres that have succeeded the bourgeoisie and the nobility in that role.

At the same time, in the outer regions, the juvenile nationalism of the Macedonians and the sedate nationalism of the Slovenes have contrived to turn their units into 'nation-republics', the Macedonians on such romantic bases as languages, pseudo-scholarly history, and the Church, and the Slovenes on the much more realistic bases of economic growth and *per capita* income. Whereas Macedonian nationalism knows that it needs a strong Yugoslav community in order to survive, Slovenian nationalism wonders whether a weaker community would not give its own economic development wider scope.

In the Party itself, three tendencies exist. One of them still hopes to rally all Yugoslavs around a Serbo-Croatian cultural nucleus; another sees nationality as virtually a metaphysical category; and a third holds firm to the official line in which, through the fulfilment of socialism, nationalities and religions will fade away. Meanwhile, Yugoslavia can develop neither as a supranational state, nor as a simple league of independent states. The official basic definition offered by Party leaders – neither one nation nor separate states – at times seems to have been inspired by the hybrid that the powers contrived in August 1858 for 'the United Principalities of Moldavia and Wallachia'.

Before the last war, while the official policy attempted to integrate

[13] The better knowledge that Orthodox and Catholics now have of each other in Yugoslavia has not led them to imitate only what is best in their 'separated brethren'. Whereas the Orthodox Church has, in the late sixties, begun to display most un-Eastern elements of clericalism, the Catholic Church is catching the nationalist fever of the Orthodox. Ever since the 1860s, Orthodoxy in the Balkans has tended to distort the concept of local Churches by looking at it through ethnic lenses. A century later, the post-conciliar trend to local Churches in the Western Church has encouraged Yugoslav Catholics to ask that, in a multinational state such as theirs, the local Church should be not territorial but national, for it is linked not to the state but to the people. Religion, like everything else in Yugoslavia, is in danger of becoming tribal, and the universal morality of Christianity is in danger of being lost sight of at a time when the tribal morality of nationalism has become, for most people, the only alternative to the class morality of Marxism.

CONCLUSION 393

them into a single nation, Yugoslavs could still express themselves, within limits, as Serbs, Croats, and Slovenes, but no other category was allowed to take its place besides those three historic entities which, it was hoped, would soon be no more than historical memories. Similarly nowadays, while official policy is working to complete the integration of all the inhabitants into a socialist international consciousness, they can still express themselves, within limits, as belonging to one of several accepted ethnic categories, but not to any which lacks official approval. The difference, apart from the new aim of the integrating process, is that more and more nationalities have been acknowledged, in order to break the population down into smaller categories and thus expedite their integration. Nationalities are encouraged in inverse proportion to their size and age. The post-war policy of nationalities started by recognizing Macedonians, then created Montenegrins, and went on to turning Moslems from a religious into a recognized ethnic group. It also satisfied the largest minorities, Albanian and Hungarian, before turning to all sorts of smaller ones – down to Italians, Gipsies, and Ruthenes. Moreover, Yugoslavism – the aim of the previous integrating process – has been discouraged to the point of being now almost forbidden.[14]

In 1970 Yugoslavia's leaders are on the verge of saying that their country is no longer the land of the South Slavs, as it is etymologically, but the country of all those who live within the territory of that socialist state. In the light of some recent pronouncements, one wonders why 'Yugoslavia', the name officially adopted for his country by King Alexander, is still used to designate what started life as the kingdom of the Serbs, Croats, and Slovenes (though generally and unofficially known already as Yugoslavia), and which has now (although still generally and officially known as Yugoslavia) in fact become the socialist republic of the Serbs, Croats, Slovenes, Macedonians, Montenegrins, ethnic Moslems, Albanians, Magyars, Turks, Slovaks, Romanians, Bulgars, Italians, Czechs, Ruthenes, Gipsies, Germans, Vlachs, Russians, Poles, Jews, Greeks, Austrians, 'undecided', 'various', and 'unknown'.[15]

On paper or in some rarefied ideological atmosphere, such an

[14] There is no special 'Yugoslav' category in the census of 1971, and people are being actively discouraged from registering as Yugoslavs. Yugoslavism – it is authoritatively stated in political forums and officially inspired articles – was not a historical process which stemmed from the consciousness of similarities and links among different nationalities: it was simply a mask to cover up the face of ethnic hegemonism. Those who insist on putting down 'Yugoslav' as their 'nationality' are classified as 'various'. ('Nationality' in Yugoslav terminology is distinct from 'citizenship': thus one could be a Yugoslav citizen of Welsh nationality.)

[15] These were the ethnic categories listed in the last census, which, moreover, still had a category of 'Yugoslavs, nationally undecided' (317,000).

attitude would solve all problems. Yugoslavia would be a name with vague historical associations, kept for the sake of convenience – a name no better or worse than 'Ivory Coast' or 'Netherlands' – since current practice requires a state to have a name, a flag, a coat of arms, a national anthem, a seat in UNO, and an airline. On that given territory, ethnic proportions could vary in time without upsetting any balance, for all inhabitants would be socialist citizens of the S.F.R.Y. with rights to schools, universities, academies, churches, dubbed films, and simultaneous translations into whatever literary language they chose to develop out of local linguistic peculiarities. Such a stand would ensure, on the one hand, that not a square inch of that socialist territory would ever be ceded, for no neighbouring nation-state could ever lay claims to co-nationals who, on the Yugoslav side of the border, were simply Italian-, Albanian-, Greek-, Bulgarian-, Romanian-, Hungarian-, or German-speaking socialist citizens of the S.F.R.Y. On the other hand, it would enable the Yugoslav government to take an interest in the fate of those co-nationals of the majority groups who lived over the borders, and, if circumstances permitted, perhaps even add a square mile or two to its socialist territory.

The snag in the pattern is that, since 1963, nationality has become more closely associated with locality, and that until such time as all are equally socialist, it is not clear to what extent Yugoslavia is to be a federation of lands and to what extent a federation of nations – South Slav or otherwise. The present federal division was adopted on the basis of both ethnic and historic regions, in order to give every one of the *Yugoslav* ethnic groups a centre, to establish a balance between them, to avoid the impossible division of ethnically intertwined territory, and to cater for regions with a mixed population of Yugoslavs and non-Yugoslavs. On these grounds, Kosovo and Voyvodina were set up as autonomous provinces because of their mixed population of Yugoslavs and non-Yugoslavs; Montenegro was given the status of a republic on the basis of its separate historical development in order not to have too big a Serbian unit; and Bosnia-Herzegovina was also kept as a historic region in order to avoid its division between Croatia and Serbia, and to create a centre for the Slav Moslems. The assumption was that Yugoslavia was the land of the South Slavs, and that South Slavs of different groups, when living outside their own respective units, needed no special provisions. Now, however, that Yugoslavia is no more the land of the South Slavs, but that of fifteen or so nations and nationalities, the question is being asked whether one or more autonomous units should not be set up in these areas of the republic of Croatia which have a large Serbian population.

CONCLUSION

All sorts of questions spring to mind in the confusion which breeds nationalities as socialization proceeds. Which has precedence – the rights of the soil, or the rights of man? To what extent can ethnic rather than territorial nationality be recognized as a legal category – somewhat on the lines of the old Ottoman *millet* system of religious-ethnic jurisdictions which started the identification of religion and nation in the Balkans? The Turkish system worked with a static society and a subsistence economy. It worked also with a super-élite of the Ottoman Moslem governing class which transcended ethnic barriers. Could this be an answer to Yugoslavia's intermediary stage, between nationalism and socialism? There would be a Serbian, a Croatian, ... a Gipsy, and a Ruthenian *millet*, all inward-looking and slowly disintegrating, while the state was ruled by the super-élite of the Yugoslav Communist government class according to socialist law. Tito has been described as the last of the Habsburgs. As ruler of a country where both Habsburg and Ottoman influences have left deep and lasting traces, could he be the last of the sultans?

In the West, until recently, it was not always easy to understand how nations could exist without territorial frontiers or political frameworks. In the Near and Middle East, the overthrow of the mediaeval monarchies and the conquest by large foreign empires, together with shifting frontiers and frequent migrations, often prevented the formation of integrated units, even when the principle of the nation-state and of the self-determination of nationalities had received its full consecration in the Versailles settlement. Nations had survived, re-emerged, or even been born in circumstances somewhat different from those normal in western Europe. The sectional and ancient nationalism of Basques and Catalans, the sectional and newer nationalism of Flemings and French Canadians, the identification in Ireland of religion and nationality, and Scottish and Welsh nationalism, have brought such instances nearer at hand. Yet while they may help the Western reader to approach the complexity of the Yugoslav national phenomenon, they will not help him all the way, for the rulers of Yugoslavia claim to have superseded it. Nationalism is all right for the Palestinian Arabs whose rights the Yugoslav government supports, but for the Yugoslavs, it has found a higher ideological *raison d'être*. Marxism, however, is not taking root, or – if it is – is doing so only very slowly; the Yugoslav idea has almost entirely evaporated; and since the Palestinians (for the sake of argument) are recognized as having the right to formulate their own identity, every Yugoslav group wants the luxury of a separate identity, if not actually of a separate state. It is less and less clear what constitutes the spiritual cement unifying the Yugoslav nationalities. Is present-day Yugoslavia as vulnerable as pre-war Yugoslavia, which attempted and failed in its experiment in national integration? Is it as vulnerable as the old-time ideological states that ruled over Yugoslav lands – the Habsburgs and the Ottomans? Is Tito the last of the Habsburgs or the last of the sultans, or is he the last king of Yugoslavia, the last of the Karageorgeviches?

Tito's ambition, in fact, is certainly not to be the last of anything, but the first of many things. Even if one takes the pessimistic view that proletarian internationalism is at best a very long way off – at least as long a way off as Yugoslav integral nationalism was in 1929 – and that there is no other feeling of spiritual solidarity running all the way from Slovenia to Macedonia, there are nevertheless forces holding together the lands and populations of Yugoslavia. At the lowest level, there are external pressures – the common fear of foreign aggression and interference. There is the fact of economic interdependence: the poorer territories cannot develop without help from the richer territories, and the latter cannot develop without the former's sources of raw materials and outlets for manufactured goods. Serbs and Croats are linked by a common language and a common mentality, which makes them bicker so well – not to mention the bond of a completely intermingled population which, short of a radical reordering, is indivisible. The Slovenes, however well off by Yugoslav standards, cannot really want to become a cul-de-sac to northern Italy and Austria. The Macedonians, however flamboyantly they proclaim the sovereignty of their republic, can want to be neither a rump state nor the prey to Bulgarianization. In spite of everything, they both feel more akin to other Yugoslavs than to Latin Italians, Germanic Austrians, or even Slav Bulgars.

It is recognized that the splintering into separate nation-states, even if it could be carried out physically, would place the 'succession states' at the mercy of more powerful neighbours, and at loggerheads with each other. Those who attempted separatist solutions during the last war enabled others to see the tragic consequences of their attempts, even if they themselves did not always see them. More generally, all those who counted on foreign powers to achieve their aims during the war were, sooner or later, disappointed, whether they looked to Germany or Italy, to the Western Allies or the Soviet Union. Furthermore, although different regions and nationalities may be regressing to autarkic economies and autarkic cultures, they cannot – nor do they want to – go back to the economic and social structures of Habsburg times, let alone Ottoman times, for they are all eager for economic advancement and social promotion. Generally speaking, however strong the centrifugal pull, a counteractive centripetal attraction is simply the absence of any viable alternative to unity. All that is far from the Yugoslav idea which led to the unification of the Yugoslav lands, but it is better than nothing.

In his book *Le Retour de Dionysos*, Professor Jean Brun has analysed the 'erotic' fury of systems that want to reorganize man and history, in order to force reality into their conceptual moulds. Although the author does not refer to Yugoslavia, students of Yugoslav affairs can find more food for thought on several pages of that book than in many a commonplace volume devoted entirely to Yugoslavia's problems. Philosophers are, at times, more useful than social scientists! Ever since Yugoslavia was prematurely brought to life in 1918, it has been the victim of those who 'want to make the forest come alive, and who forget that it is made of trees'.[16] First the Yugoslav ideology, then the Communist ideology, tried to force existing realities into their conceptual stereotypes instead of examining the realities and working through them. Unity – whether ethnic or ideological – has always been imposed, through dogmas, slogans, and paper solutions, because those seeking it had the backing of a formal majority, or of force, or of history.

What Yugoslavia needs, now that it is over fifty years old, is something that it has never had: freedom from slogans and a hard look at realities; a rest from emotional reactions divorced from reason and from conceptualizing reasons divorced from feeling; less demiurgic inspiration and perhaps less power for those at the helm; more humanity and less talk about humanism. This was what Alexander Dubček tried to offer Czechs and Slovaks. Serbs, Croats, Slovenes, Macedonians, and whatever else the Yugoslavs choose to call themselves, all need to know and understand their own sectional history, each other's history, and the history they have in common. Too often they have been made to break with the real past and learn a mythical past, at the behest of those who wanted to build only on chosen elements of the past, who wanted to rewrite the past, or who wanted to obliterate the past altogether.

In 1970 a generation that has not known any war is twenty-five years of age. It is a long time since that last occurred in the Yugoslav lands, and it is not the least of Yugoslavia's present assets. The older generations, who have known the pre-Communist order and who fought, or simply witnessed, the civil war, are defeated, disappointed, passive, or tired. The middle generations, who have grown up in chaos, terror, and hunger, have turned materialist or opportunist. The younger generations have been brought up in relatively easier times and have had a relatively better education. They are more

[16] *Le Retour de Dionysos*, Paris, 1969, p. 139.

sensitive to what is happening in Yugoslavia, and in the world at large. They are confused and rebellious; they have no political experience. For them, the Cominform and Djilas belong to the past, let alone the war and the old order. For their sake, it might be worthwhile to remember one forward-looking tradition which was interrupted in 1914 – that of the role of the intelligentsia as the vanguard of political progress. The tradition is anti-Marxist; authoritarian governments of all colours have, to say the least, discouraged it; and the intelligentsia itself has often betrayed it. It nevertheless remains true that, prior to 1914, in several instances, the strivings of intellectuals rescued the Yugoslav peoples from blind alleys into which they had been pushed by mythologizing ethnocentrism and political sclerosis. These intellectuals wanted to know about the past – the historical, not any mythical past – in order to have a better understanding of their times, and they looked to Europe – the Europe of civilization and not the Europe embodied in this or that power. If the young were taught how to think, Yugoslavia could perhaps be exorcised of its demons. A countrywide psycho-analytic therapy is the necessary concomitant to economic reform.

Suggestions for Further Reading

The following is not a complete catalogue of books about Yugoslavia, nor a bibliography of titles used by the author. It is simply a list of suggestions for further reading, chapter by chapter. It is confined to works in English and French.

Chapter 1: The Yugoslav lands until their unification

Section I: The beautiful photographs by T. Schneiders, T. Dabac, and others in the Thames and Hudson picture-book on *Yugoslavia* (London, 1969) are an admirable visual introduction to Yugoslavia. J. Cvijić, *La Péninsule balkanique – Géographie humaine* (Paris, 1918) is still the great scholarly work on the geopolitics of the region. Chapter 12 on Yugoslavia in N. Pounds, *Eastern Europe* (London, 1969), and A. Blanc, *La Yougoslavie* (Paris, 1967), provide the geographical background. There is no satisfactory general history of the Yugoslav lands in English or French. E. Haumant, *La Formation de la Yougoslavie* (Paris, 1930), though dated, is still the best reference for facts. H. Temperley, *History of Serbia* (London, 1919), and L. de Voïnovitch, *Histoire de la Dalmatie* (2 v., Paris, 1934), are dated and limited geographically, though both remain historiographical landmarks. The readable, though broken-up narrative of H. Darby's chapters 1–8 in the Cambridge *Short History of Yugoslavia* (S. Clissold ed., 1966; New York, 1968) will provide useful additional information on the history of the South Slavs before their unification, and so will the relevant sections of L. Stavrianos, *The Balkans since 1453* (New York, 1963). On the Middle Ages, also F. Dvornik, *The Slavs in European History and Civilization* (New Brunswick, N.J., 1962), A. Vlasto, *The Entry of the Slavs into Christendom – An Introduction to the Medieval History of the Slavs* (Cambridge, 1970), and D. Obolensky, *The Bogomils – A Study in Balkan Neo-Manicheism* (Cambridge, 1948), as well as G. Millet, A. Frolow, and T. Velmans, *La Peinture du moyen âge en Yougoslavie* (4 v., Paris, 1954–69).

Section II: Apart from the general works mentioned above, T. Stoianovich, *A Study in Balkan Civilization* (New York, 1967), G. Rothenberg, *The Austrian Military Border in Croatia, 1522–1749* (Urbana, Ill., 1960), and *The Military Border in Croatia, 1740–*

1881 – *A Study of an Imperial Institution* (Chicago, 1966), H. Bjelovučić, *The Ragusan Republic – Victim of Napoleon and its Own Conservatism* (Leiden, 1970), L. Hadrovics, *Le Peuple serbe et son Eglise sous la domination turque* (Paris, 1947), and G. Noyes (trans. and ed.), *The Life and Adventures of Dimitrije Obradović* (Berkeley, 1953). For the sixteenth century it is essential (particularly for Dubrovnik) to read F. Braudel, *La Mediterranée et le monde méditerranéen à l'épogue de Philippe II* (second edn, 2 v., Paris, 1966).

Section III: Apart from the general works, M. Ibrovac, *Claude Fauriel et la fortune européenne des poésies populaires grecque et serbe* (Paris, 1966), D. Wilson, *The Life and Times of Vuk Stefanović Karadžić, 1787–1864 – Literacy, Literature, and National Independence in Serbia* (Oxford, 1970), N. Iorga, *La Révolution française et le sud-est de l'Europe* (Bucharest, 1934), D. Djordjević, *Révolutions nationales des peuples balkaniques, 1804–1914* (Belgrade, 1965), G. Yakschitch, *L'Europe et la résurrection de la Serbie, 1804–1834* (Paris, 1907), L. Edwards (trans. and ed.), *The Memoirs of the Prota Mateja Nenadović* (Oxford, 1969), M. Pivec-Stele, *La Vie économique des Provinces illyriennes, 1809–1813* (Paris, 1931), G. Castellan, *La Vie quotidienne en Serbie au seuil de l'indépendance* (Paris, 1967), J. Mousset, *La Serbie et son Eglise, 1830–1904* (Paris, 1938), S. Pavlowitch, *Anglo-Russian Rivalry in Serbia, 1837–1839* (Paris and The Hague, 1961), M. Djilas, *Njegoš – Poet, Prince, Bishop* (New York, 1966), W. McClellan, *Svetozar Marković and the Origins of Balkan Socialism* (Princeton, 1964), M. Stojanović, *The Great Powers and the Balkans, 1875–1878* (Cambridge, 1939), D. Mackenzie, *The Serbs and Russian Pan-Slavism, 1875–1878* (Ithaca, 1967), C. Jelavich, *Tsarist Russia and Balkan Nationalism – Russian Influence in the Internal Affairs of Bulgaria and Serbia, 1879–1886* (Berkeley and Los Angeles, 1958), P. Sugar, *Industrialization of Bosnia-Hercegovina, 1878–1918* (Seattle, 1963), R. Seton-Watson, *The Southern Slav Question and the Habsburg Monarchy* (London, 1911), C. Macartney, *The Habsburg Empire, 1790–1918* (London, 1968), L. Voïnovitch, *Dalmatia and the Yugoslav Movement* (London, 1920), W. Vucinich, *Serbia between East and West – The Events of 1903–1908* (Stanford, 1954), V. Dedijer, *The Road to Sarajevo* (New York, 1966; London, 1967), and – for economic developments, 1878–1914 – J. Tomasevich, *Peasants, Politics and Economic Change in Yugoslavia* (Stanford, 1954).

Chapter 2: The Yugoslav Kingdom

Section I: General works become even less satisfactory for the post-unification period. Dealing with contemporary issues, their authors cannot find enough documentary sources or detachment to write works of real scholarship. The chapters on 'The Formation of the Yugoslav State' by R. Seton-Watson and R. Laffan in *A Short History of Yugoslavia* (Clissold ed.) are informative, though already dated, being abbreviated reissues of the historical sections of a Naval Intelligence handbook originally produced for service use. Surveys on the frontier settlement, constitutional, agricultural, economic, and diplomatic developments, by R. Kerner, M. Graham, B. McCown, J. Tomasevich, and H. Howard in R. Kerner (ed.), *Yugoslavia* (Berkeley, 1949). W. Vucinich's chapter 'Interwar Yugoslavia' in *Contemporary Yugoslavia – Twenty Years of Socialist Experiment* (Vucinich ed., Berkeley and Los Angeles, 1969), based mostly on official and semi-official histories and encyclopaedias published in Yugoslavia since the Second World War, is better on economic and diplomatic than on political aspects, a characteristic it shares with all general works. For economic and social developments, J. Tomasevich, *Peasants, Politics and Economic Change*, relevant chapters by A. Bilimovich in S. Zagoroff et al. (ed.), *The Agricultural Economy in the Danubian Countries, 1935–1945* (Stanford, 1955), and – though very different – O. Lodge, *Peasant Life in Jugoslavia* (London, 1941). Also I. Lederer, *Yugoslavia at the Paris Peace Conference – A Study in Frontiermaking* (New Haven and London, 1963), and I. Avakumović, *History of the Communist Party of Yugoslavia*, vol. I (Aberdeen, 1964).

Sections II and III: Apart from the general works mentioned earlier, S. Graham, *Alexander of Yugoslavia – Strong Man of the Balkans* (London, 1938), a British point of view favourable to King Alexander; S. Pribitchévitch, *La Dictature du roi Alexandre* (Paris, 1933), the point of view of a Yugoslav opponent; V. Maček, *In the Struggle for Freedom* (New York, 1957), the memoirs of Radich's successor at the head of the Croatian Peasant Party. For a sample of the cultural developments mentioned, N. Rice (ed.), *The Sculpture of Ivan Meštrović* (Syracuse, 1948), the catalogue of the Meshtrovich exhibition at the Musée Rodin (Paris, 1969), and H Kapidžić-Osmanagić, *Le Surréalisme serbe et ses rapports avec le surréalisme français* (Paris, 1968).

Sections IV and V: One addition to the general works, J. Hoptner, *Yugoslavia in Crisis, 1934–1941* (New York and London, 1962).

Chapter 3: The Chaotic Gap

This chapter is a cross between a bet and an experiment, for there is not as yet a single scholarly work on Yugoslavia during the Second World War. On the other hand, there is a flood of official histories, memoirs and diaries, apologetic, tendentious, and controversial interpretations, from all sides involved (and at various levels) in the war – a war that was at the same time regular, irregular, and civil. The records of German field commands have been microfilmed under the auspices of the American Historical Association's Committee for the Study of War Documents, and microcopy series T–315 (Divisions) and T–501 (Rear Areas, Occupied Territories, and Others), deposited at the National Archives, Washington, contain much essential material. Also microcopy series T–175 (Reichsführer-SS). Many German and Italian documents are also available in print. American, British, and Soviet documents are quoted in official histories. Many Yugoslav documents have appeared in apologetic or inquisitorial collections and interpretations, published under official auspices in Yugoslavia, and at haphazard all over the *émigré* world. By collating all these, impressions can be gained of the kaleidoscopic chaos of the period which do much to destroy the deceptively neat simplicity of the published narratives. In the absence of a detailed scholarly book, this is what is attempted in Chapter 3. A few titles will be given to enable the reader to confront for himself some of the more readily available interpretations.

Section I: The accounts of Allied liaison officers with the Yugoslav resistance – S. Clissold, *Whirlwind – An Account of Marshal Tito's Rise to Power* (London, 1949), C. Lawrence, *Irregular Adventure* (London, 1947), F. Maclean, *Eastern Approaches* (London, 1949) and *Disputed Barricade – The Life and Times of Josip Broz-Tito, Marshal of Jugoslavia* (London, 1957), J. Rootham, *Miss Fire – The Chronicle of a British Mission to Mihailovich, 1943–1944* (London, 1946), A. Seitz, *Mihailović – Hoax or Hero?* (Columbus, Ohio, 1953). Clissold is also the author of the chapter on 'Occupation and Resistance' in the *Short History* edited by him. The 'Titoist' case is made out in V. Dedijer, *Tito Speaks – His Self Portrait and Struggle with Stalin* (London, 1953) and *With Tito Through the War – Partisan Diary, 1941–1944* (London, 1951), M. Piyade, *About the Legend that the Yugoslav Uprising owed its Existence to Soviet Assistance* (London, 1950), and in *The Trial of Dragoljub-Draža Mihailović – Stenographic Record and Documents* (Belgrade, 1946). A. Djonlagic, Ž. Atanacković, and D. Plenča, *Yugoslavia in the Second World War* (Belgrade, 1967, trans. by L. Edwards) is the drastically abbreviated translation of the Serbo-Croatian original (*Jugoslavija u drugom svetskom ratu*) which puts forward the official view of the People's Liberation War. The 'Mihailovichist' case is made out in D. Martin, *Ally Betrayed – The Uncensored Story of Tito and Mihailovitch* (New York, 1946), B. Lazitch, *The Tragedy of General Mihailovitch* (London, 1946), E. Yourichitch, *Le Procès Tito-Mihaïlovitch* (Paris, 1950), C. Fotitch, *The War we Lost – Yugoslavia's Tragedy and the Failure of the West* (New York, 1948), and in *General Mihailovich, the World's Verdict – A Selection of Articles on the First Resistance Leader in Europe published in the World Press* (Gloucester, 1947). Also the early chapters of B. Novak, *Trieste, 1941–1954 – The Ethnic, Political, and Ideological Struggle* (Chicago and London, 1970) which survey the background of events in Slovenia.

Sections II–IV: In addition to the works mentioned for Section I, O. Heilbrunn, *The Soviet Secret Services* (London, 1956), *Partisan Warfare* (New York and London, 1962), and *Warfare in the Enemy's Rear* (London, 1963; New York, 1964), with C. Thayer, *Guerrilla*

(New York, 1963; London, 1964), are all monographs which contain material on the Yugoslav resistance.

Chapter 4: Stalinism-Titoism

Section I: For the post-war period, the reader will have to turn from the historian and historian of sorts, to the social scientist and the publicist. These will be apt to have preconceived ideas in their study of Yugoslav affairs, particularly for the early post-war period – which does not diminish the value of their contribution, but merely qualifies it. Chapters 9–12 in R. Wolff, *The Balkans in Our Time* (Cambridge, Mass., 1956) provide a general framework for the first decade, along with R. Byrnes (ed.), *Yugoslavia* (New York, 1957), and the more recent G. Hoffman and F. Neal, *Yugoslavia and the New Communism* (New York, 1962). Maclean (*Disputed Barricade*) and Dedijer (*Tito Speaks*) carry the story of 'Marshal Tito's rise to power' and 'his self-portrait' into the post-war era. F. Fetjö, *Histoire des démocraties populaires – L'Ere de Staline, 1945–1952* (Paris, 1952), and B. Lazitch, *Tito et la révolution yougoslave* (Paris, 1957), deal with the Yugoslav revolution from other angles. J. Korbel, *Tito's Communism* (Denver, 1951) is an eyewitness report by the Czechoslovak minister in Belgrade in the immediate post-war years. R. Pattee, *The Case of Cardinal Aloysius Stepinac* (Milwaukee, 1953) gives a Croatian nationalist and Catholic viewpoint.

Section II: Apart from the general works listed under Section I, the chapter by Bilimovich on 'Agriculture and Food Supply in 1945 and 1946' in Zagoroff et al. (ed.), *The Agricultural Economy in the Danubian Countries*, and that by Tomasevich on 'Postwar Foreign Economic Relations' in Kerner (ed.), *Yugoslavia*.

Sections III–V: In addition to the general works, E. Barker, *Macedonia – Its Place in Balkan Power Politics* (London, 1950), and E. Kofos, *Nationalism and Communism in Macedonia* (Salonika, 1964), on the all-important Macedonian question; for the Trieste question, Novak, *Trieste, 1941–1954*; for the Soviet-Yugoslav dispute, M. Djilas, *Conversations with Stalin* (New York, 1962; London, 1963), E. Halperin, *The Triumphant Heretic – Tito's Struggle against Stalin* (London, 1958), and A. Ulam, *Titoism and Cominform* (Cambridge, Mass., 1952), along with *The Soviet-Yugoslav Dispute – Text of the Published Correspondence*, published by the Royal Institute of International Affairs (London, 1948).

Chapter 5: Titoism

Sections I–III: Fetjö continues his history of Communist-ruled Europe into the post-Stalin era with *Histoire des démocraties populaires – Après Staline, 1953–1968* (Paris, 1969). Along with Hoffman and Neal, *Yugoslavia and the New Communism*, three authors offer three different points of view on Yugoslav developments in the fifties: C. McVicker, *Titoism – Pattern for International Communism* (New York, 1957), A. Meister, *Socialisme et autogestion – L'Expérience yougoslave* (Paris, 1964), and J. Djordjević, *La Yougoslavie – Démocratie socialiste* (Paris, 1959). The last two chapters of P. Blumberg, *Industrial Democracy – The Sociology of Participation* (London, 1968) give an account of the framework of Yugoslav self-management and a rapid estimation of how the system works, on the basis of second-hand sources in English. On economic developments, I. Hamilton, *Yugoslavia – Pattern of Economic Activity* (New York, 1968) is sympathetic, and Lj. Sirc's chapter ('State Control and Competition in Yugoslavia') in A. Seldon (ed.), *Communist Economy under Change* (London, 1963), critical. Also Novak, *Trieste, 1941–1954*, J. Iatrides, *Balkan Triangle – Birth and Decline of an Alliance across Ideological Boundaries* (The Hague and Paris, 1968), A. Rubinstein, *Yugoslavia and the Nonaligned World* (Princeton, 1970), P. Shoup, *Communism and the Yugoslav National Question* (New York, 1968), and J. Halpern, *A Serbian Village – Social and Cultural Change in a Yugoslav Community* (revised edn, New York, 1967). From 1954–55, statistical year-books have been published by the Yugoslav Federal Institute of Statistics, with an English edition as well.

Section IV: In addition to the works mentioned above, the chapter by V. Meier on 'Yugoslav Communism' in W. Griffith (ed.), *Communism in Europe – Continuity, Change and the Sino-Soviet Dispute* (Cambridge, Mass., 1964), along with V. Beneš, R. Byrnes, and N. Spulber (ed.), *The Second Soviet-Yugoslav Dispute – Full Text of the Documents, April–June 1958* (Bloomington, 1959), and D. Zagoria, *The Sino-Soviet Conflict, 1956–1961* (Princeton, 1962).

Chapters 6 and 7: Monocratism and Polyethnism

Most of the books listed for the previous chapter deal with the early sixties as well. M.-P. Canapa, *Réforme économique et socialisme en Yougoslavie* (Paris, 1970) is a useful monograph, and B. Johnson (ed.), *New Writing in Yugoslavia* (Harmondsworth and Baltimore, 1970), a vividly personal anthology. For the rest the reader will have to turn to specialized journals and to the daily press, *Socialist Thought and Practice* and *Review of International Affairs*, in Belgrade, *Review of the Study Centre for Jugoslav Affairs*, in London, contain interesting descriptive, documentary, and analytical material on contemporary developments, for English-reading Western students of Yugoslav affairs – the first two from an official Yugoslav point of view, the latter by expatriate scholars with contributions from American and British scholars. The Paris daily *Le Monde* (with its monthly *Le Monde diplomatique*) fully covers developments – political, economic, diplomatic, cultural, and religious – and usually manages to steer clear of the sketchy, the superficial, the sloppy, the fashionable, and the sensational.

Index

Adriatic, 25, 27, 29, 31, 36, 41, 48, 49, 51, 54, 75, 86, 98, 108, 111, 121, 128, 131, 138–40, 148, 149, 157, 206, 214, 227
Aegean, 25
Africa, 92–4, 124, 126, 131, 138, 197, 206, 245, 246, 266, 267, 276, 293, 294, 325, 346, 360, 361, 386
Afrika Korps, 124
Albania, 51, 55, 75, 86, 98, 100, 102, 107–9, 122, 145, 197, 198, 200, 202, 206, 209, 215, 217, 218, 222, 247, 249, 255, 263, 264, 278, 288, 290, 302, 319, 336, 362
Albanian language, 197
Albanian minority in Yugoslavia, 55, 56, 185, 197, 198, 218, 263, 301, 302, 318, 319, 335–7, 355, 358, 362, 393
Albanians, 38, 49, 56, 109, 110, 128, 142, 145, 336
Alexander Karageorgevich, reigning prince of Serbia, 41, 45
Alexander (Karageorgevich), king of Yugoslavia, 52, 65, 67–70, 72–4, 77, 78, 80–9 passim, 92, 95, 393
Alexander (Obrenovich), king of Serbia, 45
Alexander, Field-Marshal, 195
Algeria, 266, 293, 366
Allies in First World War, 50–5 passim, 57, 60, 103
Allies in Second World War, 103, 111, 117, 119–27 passim, 138–140, 143–57 passim, 160–75 passim, 180, 181, 195, 199, 200, 376
Andrey (Andrej), Bishop, 316
Andrich (Andrić), Ivo, 312
Ankara, treaty of, 226
Anti-Communist Volunteer Militia, 129, 139, 140
Anti-Fascist Council for the National Liberation of Yugoslavia, 137, 152, 166, 167, 175, 176, 178, 179
Antonov-Chento, 201
Armstrong, Brigadier, 148, 151

Aron, Raymond, 384
Arseniye (Arsenije) III, Patriarch, 36
Arseniye IV, Patriarch, 36
Arseniye, Metropolitan, 267, 273
Asia, 202, 245, 246, 266, 267, 276, 293, 294, 325, 386
Athenagoras, Patriarch, 316
Athens: German supplies directed to, 126; Yugoslav government in exile in, 108, 109
Australia, 308
Austria, 26, 28, 43, 46, 48, 52–4, 84, 94, 95, 97, 109, 167, 171, 195–197, 200, 206, 217, 225, 247, 308, 363, 396
Austria-Hungary, 43–64 passim, 73, 75, 79, 86, 96, 108, 111, 150, 167, 212, 373–6, 388–90, 395, 396
Austrian Monarchy, 31–3, 35–52 passim, 372
Axis powers, 95, 100–3, 108–10, 115, 122, 128, 131–3, 139–42, 150–2, 161, 172, 181–3, 200, 212, 217, 301, 376, 377, 383, 384, 390

Ba congress, 152–6
Bakarich (Bakarić), Vladimir, 212, 242, 288, 337, 345, 362
Balkan conferences, 85
Balkan Entente, 85, 86, 88, 94, 100
Balkan leagues, 43, 47, 48
Balkan Pact, 226, 227, 264
Baltic, 25
Banat, 55, 108, 109
Bandung conference, 246
Banjaluka: tradition of religious co-operation in, 316; bishops expelled from, 238
Bari: Soviet planes based in, 164; Tito's escape to, 157
Barthou, Louis, 86, 87
Basques, 395
Battle of the Neretva, The, 18, 346
Belgium, 100, 364
Belgrade, 27, 108, 156, 162, 164, 165, 168; conference of non-aligned states, 267, 291, 293;

405

conference on Danube, 217;
Declaration, 247, 257, 259;
Germans enter, 107; local elections
(1920) in, 60; Machek's 1938 visit
to, 97; Ottoman province of, 36,
38, 40, 375; partisans and Soviet
forces enter, 171; proclamation of
Kingdom of the Serbs, Croats,
and Slovenes in, 52; radio station,
204, 209; railway lines, 124, 130,
151; surrealist school in, 74, 239;
Tito's secret headquarters in, 117;
treaty of, 36; Turks enter, 31;
University, 96, 239, 340, 341, 352
Beria, Lavrenty, 246
Berlin: Allies enter, 171; crisis, 208;
congress, 44
Bihach (Bihać), 168; Anti-Fascist
Council session in, 135, 137, 138,
152
Blazhevich, Yakov (Jakov Blažević),
345
Bogumils, 28-30, 33, 302
Bohemia, 37
Bondarchuk, Sergei, 346
Borba, 250, 251, 264, 356
Boris III, king of Bulgaria, 85
Bosnia, 28-31, 33, 35, 38, 44, 47,
60, 64, 108, 111, 113, 114, 116,
117, 122, 125, 128-32 passim,
134-6, 139, 142, 144, 145, 151-3,
157, 168, 170, 172, 345, 366
Bosnia-Herzegovina, 46, 48, 49, 53,
55-7, 152, 156, 186, 239, 255,
278, 301, 302, 310, 317, 355, 356,
394
Brezhnev, Leonid, 292, 314, 324;
doctrine, 333, 335
Brioni, 246, 256, 298, 310
British armed forces during Second
World War, 101, 107, 119, 131,
162, 165, 169, 171
British Broadcasting Corporation,
147, 148, 150, 156, 161
British Foreign Office, 146, 154, 158,
160
Broz, Yosip (Josip), *see* Tito
Broz, Mme Yovanka (Jovanka), 227
Brun, Jean, 397
Brynner, Yul, 346
Bubanj, General, 348
Bucharest: Cominform transferred
to, 211
Budapest: Cominform meets in, 220
Bulatovich (Bulatović), Miodrag, 350
Bulganin, Marshal, 246
Bulgaria, 33, 45, 47, 49-51, 54, 74,
85, 86, 94, 100, 101, 107, 109,
110, 125, 143, 145, 163-6, 196,
198-207 passim, 209, 217-19,

226, 249, 255, 257, 263, 267, 273,
293, 308, 318, 335-7, 363, 396
Bulgarian language, 47, 186, 202
Bulgars, 26, 29, 199, 202, 218, 393,
396
Burma, 266
Byzantine Church, *see* Orthodox
Church
Byzantine empire, 26-9

Cairo conference of non-aligned
states, 293, 294
Cambodia, 365
Canada, 283, 308
Canossa, 247
Carinthia, 29, 54, 171, 195, 200, 207
Carniola, 29, 46
Catalans, 395
Catholic Church, 18, 26-35 passim,
46, 88, 95, 112, 113, 181, 182,
184, 185, 238, 267, 273, 315, 316,
319, 345, 350, 353-5, 390-2
Catholics in Yugoslavia, 33, 35, 43,
46, 55, 63, 73, 95, 110-14, 131,
136, 145, 149, 150, 183, 184, 239,
316, 363, 377, 392
Ceylon, 266
Charles VI, German emperor, 37
Charles, emperor of Austria, 75, 391
Chartered Agricultural Bank, 79, 84
Ceauşescu, Nicolae, 332
Chervenkov, Vlko, 249
Chetniks, 116-18, 122, 127-35
passim, 139-45 passim, 148, 150,
151, 155, 156, 162, 165, 168, 197,
346, 349
China, 245, 247, 249, 261-4, 268,
290, 292, 293, 299, 362, 385
Churchill, Winston, 104, 146, 147,
154, 155, 159-61, 164, 166, 180
Ciano, Galeazzo, 98, 139
Cominform, 205, 206, 211, 213-15,
217-20, 225, 232, 238, 242, 247,
248, 252, 262, 333, 349, 379, 383,
384, 398
Comintern, 59, 60, 65, 68, 69, 96,
118, 135, 138, 203, 205, 212, 259,
384; Anti-Comintern Pact, 95,
101-3
Common Market, *see* European
Economic Community
Communist Party of Yugoslavia
(C.P.Y.), *see* Communists in Yugoslavia
Communists in Yugoslavia, 60-2,
64-7, 76, 78, 89, 96, 99, 102, 103,
109, 110, 113, 114, 117-22, 125-
127, 129-53 passim, 158, 160-72
passim, 175-80 passim, 182-7
passim, 189-94 passim, 197-207

INDEX   407

passim, 210–16 passim, 220, 221,
226, 229, 233–7, 239, 241, 242,
245, 250–62 passim, 265, 268–72,
278, 287, 289–91, 294–6, 298–
300, 303, 309–23 passim, 326,
327, 333, 335, 337, 339–60 passim,
362, 368, 369, 376–81 passim,
384–6, 389–92; *see also* Independent Workers' Party; Partisans;
Workers' and Peasants' Republican Alliance
Congregation for the Doctrine of the Faith, 316
Conservative Party of Serbia, *see* Constitutionalist Party of Serbia
Constantinople: Patriarchate of, 31, 32, 38, 354; crusaders enter, 28; Dushan's expedition against, 29
Constitutionalist Party of Serbia, 41, 42, 44
Corfu, 51
Corinth, 29
Council for Mutual Economic Assistance (Comecon), 215, 283, 292, 369
Croatia, 27–31, 34–9, 41–4, 46, 47, 49–52, 57–9, 64, 66, 72, 73, 80, 83, 88, 96, 98, 99, 102, 107, 109–113, 120, 127, 129, 130, 135, 136, 141, 150–3, 156, 168, 171, 184, 186, 187, 212, 218, 227, 255, 256, 301, 302, 310, 317, 318, 327, 338, 354–8, 367, 374, 394
Croatia, Independent State of (N.D.H.), 107, 108, 110–14, 127–131, 135, 136, 139–41, 143, 145, 150, 153, 155, 158, 170, 171, 181, 187, 377
Croatia, self-governing Province (*Banovina*) of, 98, 100, 123
Croatian Bloc, 65, 66
Croatian language, 317
Croatian nobility, 31, 34, 35, 37–9, 372
Croatian Orthodox Church, 128
Croatian Party of the Right, 43, 44, 46, 47
Croatian Peasant Party, 47, 59, 61–73 passim, 80, 82, 83, 86, 89–91, 98, 99, 103, 110, 113, 127, 159, 176, 182, 183
Croatian realm, 27, 31, 34, 35, 39, 41, 46, 48, 70, 372
Croatian-Slavonian realm, 43, 46, 47, 52, 53, 55, 57, 372
Croatian Union, 59, 63, 64
Croato-Serbian Coalition, 47, 48, 51, 59, 60
Croats, 26, 27, 31, 33, 35, 37, 39, 41–3, 46–8, 50–2, 55–9, 61, 63,

64, 66, 67, 70, 72, 73, 78–81, 83, 87, 88, 90–2, 94, 96–104 passim, 107, 108, 110–14, 117, 122–4, 130–2, 134, 136, 143, 144, 150, 152, 153, 155, 156, 172, 182, 184, 185, 187, 269, 300–2, 316–18, 338, 329, 354–6, 358, 359, 373–8, 389–96 passim
Cromwell, Oliver, 385
Cuba, 293, 361
Cyril, Saint, 26, 29
Cyrillic script, 112, 318
Czechoslovakia, 75, 81, 94, 97, 98, 205, 207, 259, 331, 332, 334, 360, 361
Czechs, 373, 393

Dalmatia, 25–30 passim, 33, 34, 36, 38, 41–4, 46, 47, 49, 52–6, 83, 88, 98, 108–12, 114, 129, 141, 143, 144, 149, 150, 153, 154, 165
Damyanovich (Damjanović), General, 161, 169–71
Danilo, reigning prince of Montenegro, 45
D'Annunzio, Gabriele, 54
Danube, 25, 26, 29, 38, 39, 156, 165, 217, 300
Dar-es-Salaam conference, 360
Davidovich (Davidović), Ljubomir, 67–9, 73, 75, 82, 83, 89
Deakin, F. W., 147
Dediyer (Dedijer), Vladimir, 204, 251, 252, 270
Democratic Party, 60–73 passim, 82, 83, 89, 103, 176, 181, 182
Denmark, 308, 364
Department for the Protection of the People (O.Z.N.), *see* State Security Service
Dimitrov, Gheorghi, 203, 204, 207, 209, 249
Dinaric region, 25, 27, 129
Direction of State Security (U.D.B.), *see* State Security Service
Dizdarevich, Niyaz (Nijaz Dizdarević), 345
Djilas, Milovan, 122, 179, 182, 210–213, 235, 242, 250–3, 269–73, 294, 309, 311, 314, 333, 345, 349, 351, 352, 386, 387, 398
Djukanovich (Djukanović), General, 127, 149
Doronjski, Stevan, 345
Drashkovich (Drašković), Milorad, 65, 66
Dresden congress of the C.P.Y., 213
Drina, 134, 151, 168, 172
Drvar, 157
Dual Monarchy, *see* Austria-Hungary

Dubrovnik (Ragusa), 41; republic of, 28, 30, 33, 36, 39, 40
Dubček, Alexander, 331, 397
Dugonjich (Dugonjić), Ratomir, 345
Dulles, J. F., 248
Dushan, Emperor, 29

East Germany, *see* German Democratic Republic
Eastern Church, *see* Orthodox Church
Eastern Roumelia, 45, 47
Eden, Anthony, 88, 226
Egypt, 126, 266, 324, 325, 360
Eisenhower, General, 126, 264, 265
Ethiopia, 92, 266, 273
European Economic Community (E.E.C.), 283, 308, 369, 370
European Free Trade Area (E.F.T.A.), 308, 364
Export-Import Bank, 221, 223

Ferdinand I of Habsburg, King, 31
Fiume, *see* Riyeka
Flemings, 395
Focha (Foča), 134, 135
France, 37, 39, 41, 53, 75, 84, 86–8, 92, 93, 95, 97, 100, 102, 120, 126, 138, 147, 223–5, 265, 266, 293, 308, 360, 364, 365, 377
Francis Ferdinand, Archduke, 50, 390
Francis Joseph, emperor of Austria, 50, 51, 390
Franco, General, 17, 332, 365, 384
Frank, Yosip (Josip), 46
Frankish empire, 26, 27
Frankists, *see* Pure Party of the Right
Frankopan, Fran Krsto, 35
French Canadians, 395

Garashanin, Iliya (Ilija Garašanin), 41
Gaulle, General de, 116, 126, 266, 293, 299, 364, 382, 385
Gavrilo, Patriarch, 183, 238
Gay (Gaj), Ljudevit, 41
Gazhi (Gaži), Franjo, 182
General Agreement on Tariffs and Trade (G.A.T.T.), 283, 303, 308, 369
Geneva: signature of pact of Little Entente in, 84; talks between Serbian government and National Council in, 52
George II, king of the Hellenes, 202
German armed forces and occupation authorities in Yugoslavia during Second World War, 107–28 passim, 131, 134–44 passim, 147–57 passim, 161–72 passim, 183, 187, 191, 336
German Democratic Republic, 260, 263, 266, 279, 362
German empire in the Middle Ages, 27, 28
German Federal Republic, 260, 265, 266, 288, 325, 339, 360, 364, 367
German minority in Yugoslavia, 55, 104, 111, 177, 186, 190, 377, 393
Germans, 27, 28, 34, 35, 44, 46, 55, 109, 111, 302, 396
Germany, 42, 48, 50, 51, 54, 75, 84, 86, 88, 92–8 passim, 100–2, 104, 108, 109, 111, 117, 118, 142, 145, 146, 148, 153, 155, 161, 169, 170, 193, 194, 208, 217, 333, 396
Gerö, Ernö, 256–8
Gheneralich (Generalić), Ivan, 239
Gheorghiu-Dej, Gheorghe, 332
Gherman (German), Patriarch, 273, 315, 316
Gipsies in Yugoslavia, 393
Gledishta (Gledišta), 313
Gligorov, Kiro, 345
Goldman, Naum, 361
Goli Otok, 214, 359
Gomułka, Władysław, 258, 260
Goshnjak (Gošnjak), General, 212, 213, 242, 345, 347
Great Britain, 84, 88, 92, 93, 97, 102, 103, 109, 119, 123, 125, 126, 135, 137, 138, 141, 145–9, 153, 154, 156–60, 162, 164, 166–8, 171, 180–3, 195, 200, 204, 211, 221, 222, 223, 225, 227, 228, 265, 365, 377
Greater Morava, 156
Greece, 74, 85, 101–4, 107, 115, 119, 120, 145, 163, 165, 166, 183, 198, 200, 202–4, 206, 208, 209, 218, 219, 222, 225–7, 273, 293, 308, 318, 323, 324, 365, 385, 386, 388
Greek Church, *see* Orthodox Church
Greek language, 202
Greek People's Liberation Front, 202, 203
Greeks, 26, 27, 38, 47, 202
Gregory VII, Pope, 247
Grol, Milan, 176, 177
Gromyko, Andrei, 361
Guizot, François, 367

Habsburg dynasty, 28, 29, 31, 32, 34, 35, 37, 41, 54, 75, 372, 373, 390, 395, 396; *see also* Austria-Hungary; Austrian Monarchy; Charles VI; Charles of Austria; Ferdinand I; Francis Ferdinand;

INDEX

Francis Joseph; Joseph II; Leopold II
Hadjich (Hadžić), General, 72
Haile Selassie, emperor of Ethiopia, 245
Hamovich (Hamović), General, 348
Hebrang, Andriya (Andrija), 209–11, 238
Helen, queen of Italy, 121
Henry IV, German emperor, 247
Hero on a Donkey, 350
Herzegovina, 30, 32, 33, 40, 41, 56, 60, 97, 111, 114, 130, 141, 142, 144, 153, 172; *see also* Bosnia-Herzegovina
Hitler, Adolf, 20, 84, 95, 98, 100–2, 104, 107, 112, 115, 117, 118, 120, 138–41, 152, 163, 377
Hlebine school of peasant painters, 239
Hodja, Fadilj, 345
Holy See, *see* Rome
Hoxha, Enver, 336, 362
Hungarian minority in Yugoslavia, 55, 186, 218, 301, 302, 318, 393
Hungarians, 26, 27, 39, 41, 42, 44, 46, 55
Hungary, 27–38 passim, 42, 43, 46-8, 50–4, 60, 74, 75, 80, 84, 88, 94, 100, 101, 108, 110, 164, 165, 168, 170, 196, 197, 204, 205, 207, 218, 227, 247, 249, 256–61 passim, 263, 269, 308, 362

Ibar, 125
Illyrian language, 36
Illyrian Provinces, 39
Independent Democratic Party, 67, 69–72, 83, 89, 98, 103
Independent Workers' Party, 67, 69
India, 266, 293
Indonesia, 266
Innocence Unprotected, 350
Internal Macedonian Revolutionary Organization (I.M.R.O.), 68, 85
International Bank for Reconstruction and Development, 223, 224, 356, 371
International Labour Office, 81
International Monetary Fund, 283
Iraq, 325
Ireland, 395
Islam, 32, 33, 35, 38, 185, 302; *see also* Moslems in Yugoslavia
Islamic Religious Community, 185, 273, 355
Isonzo (Socha, Soča), 171, 196
Israel, 324, 325, 365
Istria, 26, 29, 34, 54, 149, 167–9, 171, 195, 196, 246

Italian armed forces and occupation authorities in Yugoslavia during Second World War, 107, 109–12, 114, 121, 122, 127–43 passim, 145, 148–50, 154, 167, 169
Italian language, 54
Italian minority in Yugoslavia, 195, 196, 393
Italians, 46, 54, 108, 149, 195, 302, 396
Italy, 26, 28, 29, 34, 37, 42, 48, 50–4, 57, 58, 75, 80, 83–8 passim, 92–5, 97, 98, 100–4, 108–11, 140, 144, 146, 148–51, 153, 155, 157, 164, 167, 169–71, 195–7, 200, 206, 208, 225, 227, 228, 245, 255, 265, 288, 294, 300, 308, 323, 325, 363, 368, 388, 396

Japan, 95, 308
Jaspers, Karl, 353
Jews in Yugoslavia, 111, 129
John XXIII, Pope, 273
Johnson, President, 308, 325, 333
Jonas, President, 363
Joseph II, German emperor, 37, 39
Julian region, 149, 167, 169, 195
Jurgens, Kurt, 346

Kádár, János, 258, 259
Karadjich (Karadžić), Vuk, 40
Karageorge, 40, 41, 45
Karageorgevich (Karadjordjević) dynasty, 18, 47, 67–9, 396; *see also* Alexander, Prince; Alexander, King; Karageorge; Paul; Peter I; Peter II
Kardelj, Edvard, 126, 179, 211–13, 216, 242, 250, 259, 261, 264, 269, 271–4, 290, 298, 337, 345, 347, 356, 359, 371, 384
Karlovtsi (Karlovci, Karlowitz): Metropolitanate of, 37, 44; treaty of, 36
Kaunda, President, 361
Kennedy, President, 291
Khrushchev, Nikita, 214, 246–9, 256, 257, 259–64 passim, 266, 290–2, 324
Kidrich (Kidrič), Boris, 192, 210, 212, 213, 233, 242, 265, 272, 277, 345
Kiev, 25
Knjizhevne novine (*Književne novine*), 313, 351, 361
Kolishevski (Koliševski), Lazar, 201, 212, 242, 345
Kommunist, 262
Kopitar, Yerney (Jernej), 40
Korea, 223, 224, 226

Koroshetz (Korošec), Mgr, 72, 73, 75, 77, 82, 83, 90
Koscina, Mme Silva, 346
Kosovo (Kosovo Polje), battle of, 30, 31, 38
Kosovo region, 38, 55, 56, 108, 122, 186, 197, 200, 218, 255, 278, 288, 302, 319, 335–7, 344, 345, 355, 356, 358, 362, 367, 394
Kosygin, Alexei, 292, 324
Kotor, 107, 108
Kovachich, Miyo (Mijo Kovačić), 239
Krbava (Krbavsko Polje), battle of, 31
Kraguyevats (Kragujevac): anti-Communist demonstrations in, 348; German massacre in, 120
Krekich (Krekić), Bogdan, 270, 273
Krlezha (Krleža), Miroslav, 239, 312, 318
Kulenovich, Djafer (Džafer Kulenović), 111

Ladas, Colonel, 385
Latin America, 293, 386
Latin Church, *see* Catholic Church
Laval, Pierre, 88
Lazar, Prince, 30
Lazarevats (Lazarevac), electoral contest (1967) in, 327
League of Communists of Yugoslavia (L.C.Y.), *see* Communists in Yugoslavia
League of Nations, 75, 81, 84, 88, 92, 94
Lenin, centenary of his death, 349, 362
Leopold I, German emperor, 36
Leskoshek, Frants (Franc Leskoshek), 212, 213, 299, 345
Liberal Party of Serbia, 41, 42, 44
Liberation Front of Slovenia, 109, 132, 133, 169
Libya, 48, 360
Little Entente, 75, 84–6
Ljotich, Dimitriye (Dimitrije Ljotić), 89, 115, 143, 168, 169, 181; *see also* Zbor
Ljotichists, *see* Zbor
Ljubljana, 108, 109, 133, 171; Italian province of, 109, 132, 149
London: Yugoslav king and government arrive in, 123; Tito's visit to, 227, 245
Louis II, king of Hungary, 31
Lovchen (Lovćen), Mount, 358
Lusaka conference of non-aligned states, 360, 361
Luxembourg, 364

Macedonia, 25, 27, 29, 32, 33, 38, 47–51, 54, 56, 57, 61, 85, 108, 145, 152, 165, 184–6, 198–202, 204, 207, 209, 212, 218, 219, 222, 225, 227, 239, 249, 255, 263, 267, 278, 293, 302, 310, 318, 319, 335–337, 339, 355, 358, 362, 367, 396
Macedonian Academy, 318
Macedonian language, 186, 218, 336
Macedonian Orthodox Church, 267, 273, 318, 355, 392
Macedonians, 32, 47, 49, 61, 86, 93, 145, 156, 185, 187, 198–203 *passim*, 218, 219, 226, 249, 293, 300–2, 318, 319, 337, 354, 355, 392, 393, 396
Machek (Maček), Vlatko, 69, 70, 73, 78, 80, 81, 83, 87–91, 97–9, 110–112, 124, 153, 170, 171
McDowell, Colonel, 163
Maclean, Brigadier, 148, 154, 155, 158, 163
Magyars, *see* Hungarians
Makaveyev, Dushan (Dušan Makavejev), 350
Mao Tse-tung, 262, 386
Marcuse, Herbert, 353
Margaret, Princess, 364
Maribor railway line, 124
Marinko, Miha, 272, 278
Marinkovich, Voyislav (Vojislav Marinković), 82, 83, 86, 87
Markos, General, *see* Vafiades, Markos
Markovich (Marković), Dragoslav, 350
Marseilles, assassination of King Alexander in, 87, 89
Marshall Plan, 192, 206
Mauritius, 103
Mediterranean, 25, 98, 138, 145, 155, 168, 206, 207, 225, 245, 294, 323–5, 331, 332, 365
Memoirs of Pera Bogalja, 350
Meshtrovich (Meštrović), Ivan, 74
Methodius, Saint, 26
Metohiya, 38, 56
Michael Obrenovich, reigning prince of Serbia, 41–4, 47
Michael of Montenegro, Prince, 121
Mihailovich, General, 115–27 *passim*, 130–5 *passim*, 138–65 *passim*, 168–70, 172, 180–3, 270, 310
Mihaylov, Mihaylo (Mihajlo Mihajlov), 313, 314
Milan, king of Serbia, 44, 45
Military Frontier, 34, 35, 37, 43, 111, 129, 130

Milosh Obrenovich, reigning prince of Serbia, 40–2
Mitrovich (Mitrović), Mme Mitra, 251
Miyatovich, Tsviyetin (Cvijetin Mijatović), 345
Mohacs, battle of, 31
Molotov, Vyacheslav, 248, 259
Montenegrins, 38, 61, 122, 162, 163, 185, 186, 301, 302, 335, 358, 391, 393
Montenegro, 27, 28, 30, 32, 33, 36, 38, 40, 41, 44, 45, 49, 50, 53, 56, 61, 108, 110, 120–2, 125, 127, 129, 130, 135, 141–4, 147, 149–53, 156, 168, 186, 218, 255, 278, 302, 310, 318, 337, 338, 350, 355, 358, 384, 394
Montgomery, Field-Marshal, 126
Morava, 25, 125, 151, 163; see also Greater Morava; Western Morava
Morava-Vardar corridor, 25, 26, 29, 38, 56, 74, 162, 300
Moscow: declarations, 249, 257, 262; Radich's visit to, 68, 69, 73; Yugoslav legation sent away from, 123
Moslem irregulars during Second World War, 122, 128, 141
Moslems in Yugoslavia, 33, 38, 46, 55, 60, 67, 73, 98, 100, 109, 111, 112, 121, 127, 128, 131, 134, 136, 141, 142, 145, 150, 185, 186, 200, 239, 301, 302, 316, 354, 355, 377, 393–5
Munich agreement, 94
Murphy, Robert, 162
Mussolini, Benito, 75, 80, 82, 84, 86, 88, 92–5, 98, 100–2, 111, 112, 140, 143

Nagy, Imre, 256, 258
Napoleon I, emperor of the French, 39–41
Napoleon III, emperor of the French, 42
Nasser, President, 266, 324, 360, 361, 364
National Committee for the Liberation of Yugoslavia, 152, 164, 166
National Council in Zagreb, 51, 52, 58
National Defence Corps, 180, 236
National Party of Croatia, 41–4, 46
Nationalists in Italian zone during Second World War, 127, 128, 140, 141, 149, 163
N.D.H., see Croatia, Independent State of
Nedich (Nedić), General, 115, 116, 125, 126, 134, 144, 157, 161, 163, 168, 169, 181
Nektariye (Nektarije), Metropolitan, 239
Nemanjich (Nemanjić) dynasty, 28, 30, 32; see also Dushan; Sava; Stephen the First-Crowned
Neretva, 140–2, 172
Neshkovich, Blagoye (Blagoje Nešković), 212, 213, 242, 272, 345
Netherlands, 37, 100, 308, 364
Nettuno conventions, 75
Neubacher, Hermann, 163
New Class, The, 269, 351
New Leader, 314
Nicholas Tavelich (Tavelić), Saint, 354
Nicholas, king of Montenegro, 43, 45, 121
Nish, 327; University, 327
Nixon, President, 335, 364
North Atlantic Treaty Organization (NATO), 221, 225, 227, 294, 333, 334, 363
North Sea, 54
Norway, 364
Nova misao, 251
Nove, Alec, 386
Novi Pazar, 27; see also Sandjak
Novi Sad University, 268
Novotný, Antonín, 331

Obradovich, Dimitriye (Dimitrije Obradović), 38
Obrenovich (Obrenović) dynasty, 42, 45, 47; see also Alexander; Michael; Milan; Milosh
Office of Strategic Services (O.S.S.), 163
Ohrid, Archbishopric of, 29, 33, 36, 38
Organization for European Economic Co-operation (O.E.E.C.) *and* Organization for Economic Co-operation and Development (O.E.C.D.), 283
Orthodox in Yugoslavia, 33, 35, 36, 43, 46, 49, 55, 63, 95, 98, 111, 113, 114, 127–9, 131, 134, 136, 150, 183, 239, 316, 355, 377, 392
Orthodox Church, 18, 26, 28, 29, 31–3, 35, 36, 38, 95, 112, 184, 238, 267, 273, 315, 316, 319, 345, 350, 353, 354, 391, 392
Ottoman Empire, see Turkey, Ottoman
O.Z.N., see State Security Service

Palestinian Arabs, 395
Pannonian region, 25, 26, 77

Paris: Marshall Plan conference, 192; First World War Peace Conference, 54; Second World War Peace Conference, 196, 201
Partisans, 118, 119, 126, 127, 129, 130, 133–42 passim, 144, 145, 147, 149–52, 154, 156–72 passim, 175–177, 181, 187, 190, 194, 195, 197, 212–14, 272, 309, 333, 346; *see also* People's Liberation Army
Pashich (Pašić), Nikola, 21, 61–4, 66–71 passim, 75
Passarowitz, *see* Pozharevats
Paul VI, Pope, 316, 354
Paul of Yugoslavia, Prince, 88–91, 97, 102, 103
Paulus, Field-Marshal, 140
Pavelich (Pavelić), Ante, 18, 80, 87–99 passim, 110–13, 128, 155, 171
Pavlovich (Pavlović), Aleksandar, 270, 273
Peasant-Democratic Coalition, 71–3
Pech (Peć), Patriarchate of, 29, 33, 35, 36, 38
Pechuylich (Pečujlić), Miroslav, 345
Peloponnese, 26
People's Front *and* Socialist Alliance, 176–9, 182, 193, 212, 236, 237, 241, 242, 296, 298, 312, 320, 327, 343, 344, 346, 350
People's Liberation Army, 137, 139, 150, 160, 164, 171; *see also* Partisans
People's Liberation Movement, 17, 135–8, 155, 158, 160, 175, 391
Perovich (Perovič), Ivo, 88
Perspektive, 296
Peter I, king of the Serbs, Croats, and Slovenes, 45, 47, 50, 65
Peter II, king of Yugoslavia, 87, 98, 103, 108, 123, 144, 146, 152, 159–61, 164, 166, 167, 170, 180
Peter II Petrovich-Njegosh, prince-bishop of Montenegro, 45, 358
Petrovich-Njegosh (Petrović-Njegoš) dynasty, 38, 45, 61, 121, 338; *see also* Danilo; Helen; Michael; Nicholas; Peter II
Philippines, 385
Philosophical Society of Croatia, 296
Philosophical Society of Serbia, 351
Pichler, Bishop, 316
Piedmont, 42
Pius XII, Pope, 238, 273
Piyade, Mosha (Moša Pijade), 212, 213, 272, 345
Poland, 188, 205, 207, 256, 258, 260–2, 272, 292

Popovich, Kocha (Koča Popović), 290, 291
Popovich, Milentiye (Milentije), 345
Portugal, 288
Potsdam conference, 180
Pozharevats (Požarevac, Passarowitz), treaty of, 36
Poznań, 256
Prague: Communist *coup d'état* of, 197; Tito's 1968 visit to, 332
Pravda, 362
Praxis, 296, 313, 351
Pribichevich, Stoyan (Stojan Pribićević), 63, 64, 66, 67, 69, 71, 73, 81
Prishtina (Priština): demonstrations in, 336; University, 358
Protestants in Yugoslavia, 111
Protich, Stoyan (Stojan Protić), 64
Pure Party of the Right of Croatia, 46, 59, 72, 80
Purich, Bozhidar (Božidar Purić), 146, 159
Putsar (Pucar), Djuro, 242

Radical Party of Serbia, 44, 45, 47, 60–7 passim, 69–73, 82, 83, 87, 89–91, 97, 103, 176, 181, 182
Radich, Styepan (Stjepan Radić), 59, 61, 63, 64, 66–73 passim, 75, 80
Ragusa, *see* Dubrovnik
Rajk, Laszlo, 219, 220
Rákosi, Matyas, 249, 256
Rankovich (Ranković), Aleksandar, 179, 180, 210–14, 236, 237, 242, 250, 259, 261, 271, 272, 290, 295, 296, 299, 309–12, 314, 319, 325, 327, 345, 347, 348
Rapallo, treaty of, 54, 75
Rashka, 27, 28
Ravna Gora, 116, 119
Republican Party, 63, 64
Rhineland, reoccupation of, 92
Ribar, Ivan, 137, 178, 179
Ribbentrop, Joachim von, 139, 140
Ribichich, Mitya (Mitja Ribičič), 346–8, 350, 362, 364, 371
Rightists, *see* Croatian Party of the Right
Riyeka (Rijeka, Fiume), 54, 227; Free State of, 75; 1969 strike in, 366
Rogers, William, 361
Roman Empire, 26, 41
Roman Church, *see* Catholic Church; Rome
Romania, 55, 75, 85, 100, 101, 107, 108, 120, 163, 164, 166, 196, 204,

205, 207, 209, 214, 218, 247, 249, 257, 260, 273, 292, 308, 321, 324, 325, 331, 332, 344, 362
Romanian minority in Yugoslavia, 55, 108, 218, 393
Rome, Papacy of, 27, 31, 38, 95, 113, 170, 181, 184, 185, 238, 273, 315, 316, 325, 354, 355, 363
Rommel, Field-Marshal, 124–6
Roosevelt, President, 155, 166
Rozhman (Rožman), Bishop, 170
Rupnik, General, 149, 170
Rusk, Dean, 293, 333
Russia, Imperial, 40–2, 44, 48, 51, 96
Russia, Soviet, 19, 60, 89, 98, 100–102, 104, 109, 111, 114–23 passim, 126, 131, 135–7, 141, 145–8, 154, 156–8, 160, 162, 166, 180, 188, 192, 193, 194–8, 200, 204–21, 225, 235, 245–51 passim, 253, 256–68 passim, 271–3, 290–4, 299, 308, 313, 318, 322, 324, 326, 331–5, 343, 344, 348, 360, 361, 377, 379, 381, 383, 386, 388, 396
Ruthenian minority in Yugoslavia, 357, 393

Salay (Salaj), Djuro, 242, 277, 299
Salonika, 101, 126, 162; Allied offensive (1918), 51; Gulf of, 25; railway line, 124, 162; Yugoslav free zone in, 74, 85
Sandjak, 120, 122, 125, 127, 128, 130, 134, 141, 142, 150, 151, 153, 168
San Stefano, treaty of, 336, 337
Saragat, President, 363
Sarayevo (Sarajevo), 140, 151; assassination of Francis Ferdinand in, 50; congress of intellectuals, 66; University, 239
Sava, Saint, 28, 29
Sava, river, 29, 130, 165, 168, 300
Scotland, 395
Scutari (Shkodër), 27, 107
S.D.B., see State Security Service
Selenich (Selenić), Slobodan, 350
Selim III, Sultan, 38, 40
Serbia, 25, 28–57 passim, 61–4, 70, 79, 82, 93, 95, 100, 109, 110, 112, 114–25 passim, 128, 130, 132, 134, 138, 142–4, 150–7 passim, 160–5 passim, 168–70, 181, 186, 212, 301, 310, 318, 319, 327, 333, 336, 337, 339, 344–6, 354–7, 367, 369, 374, 391, 394
Serbia, principality and kingdom of, 40, 43–5, 53, 57, 59, 63, 64, 373–375

Serbian Agrarian Party, 60, 62–4, 67–9, 89, 98, 104, 182
Serbian language, 47, 186, 202, 318
Serbian monarchy in the Middle Ages, 28–33 passim, 46, 372
Serbian Orthodox Church, 28, 29, 33–9 passim, 44, 95, 183, 184, 238, 267, 315, 318, 337, 354–6, 358, 372, 392
Serbian State Guard, 115, 125, 126, 144, 157, 161, 163, 164
Serbian Volunteer Corps, see Zbor
Serbo-Croatian language, 40, 269, 300, 313, 357
Serbs, 26, 27, 29, 31–3, 35–40, 42–52 passim, 54–61 passim, 63, 64, 66, 70, 74, 78–81, 86–92 passim, 95, 97, 99–101, 103, 104, 108, 110–17 passim, 122–5, 128–136 passim, 142–5, 147, 150, 152, 153, 156, 167, 172, 181–3, 185–7, 197–200, 202, 203, 218, 255, 256, 269, 300–2, 310, 311, 316, 318, 319, 335–9, 354, 355, 357, 358, 373–8 passim, 389–94 passim, 396
Sharich (Šarić), Archbishop, 113
Sheper (Šeper), Cardinal, 315, 316
Shkodër, see Scutari
Shoshkich (Šoškić), Budislav, 345
Shpiljak (Špiljak), Mika, 327
Shubashich (Šubašić), Ivan, 159–61, 166, 167, 176, 177, 180
Shumadiya, 25, 32, 36, 38, 40, 77, 120, 163, 348
Shumonja (Šumonja), General, 348
Shutey, Yuray (Juraj Šutej), 176
Sicily, 143, 146
Silesia, 37
Simovich (Simović), General, 104, 108, 110, 111, 123, 124
Sisak, battle of, 34
Skopye (Skopje) University, 239, 269
Slavonia, 27, 30, 41, 52, 98
Slovakia, 98
Slovaks, 373, 393
Slovenes, 26–8, 31, 34, 35, 37, 44, 46, 50–2, 54–6, 64, 67, 68, 73, 95, 97, 100, 102, 103, 108, 109, 117, 132, 145, 152, 153, 167, 169, 170, 172, 185, 300–2, 317, 338, 346, 355, 356, 389, 392, 303, 396
Slovenia, 29, 31, 33, 34, 35, 39, 43, 49, 53, 55, 57, 58, 61, 107–9, 127, 132, 144, 152, 153, 167–70. 172, 184, 192, 203, 251, 270, 278, 288, 302, 310, 317, 328, 337, 338, 345, 354–7, 384, 396
Slovenian Alliance, 132, 133, 144, 145, 149, 169–71

Slovenian clericals, *see* Slovenian People's Party
Slovenian Home Guard, 149, 169, 170
Slovenian language, 44
Slovenian Liberal Party, 59, 60
Slovenian People's Party, 46, 59, 62–4, 67, 69, 71–3, 83, 89, 90, 96–8, 103, 132, 149, 182
Slovenian Populists, *see* Slovenian People's Party
Slovenian village guards during Second World War, 133, 149
Snowdon, Lord, 364
Socha, *see* Isonzo
Social Democrats, 59–61, 270
Socialist Alliance, *see* People's Front
Socialist Party of Yugoslavia, 60, 63, 64, 67, 69, 96, 152, 183, 270
Socialist Workers' Party of Yugoslavia (Communist), 59, 60, 70
Sokol societies, 78
Soviet armed forces during Second World War, 160–6 passim, 168, 170, 171, 177
Spaho, Mehmed, 90, 97, 111
Spain, 17, 360, 365, 385
Special Operations Executive (S.O.E.), 119, 138, 146, 147, 155, 157
Split, 108, 109, 129, 143
Srshkich (Srškić), Milan, 83, 87
Stalin, Iosif, 20, 155, 158, 164, 165, 178, 192, 199, 200, 204, 205, 207–209, 211, 212, 214, 215, 220, 222, 235, 241, 245–8, 252, 253, 257, 261, 263, 272, 283, 294, 384
Stalingrad, battle of, 140
Stambolich (Stambolić), Petar, 272, 327
Stankovich (Stanković), Radenko, 88
Starchevich (Starčević), Ante, 43, 44
State Security Service (S.D.B.), 177, 179, 201, 236, 310, 311, 319, 323, 346–8, 350, 359, 360, 365
Stefanovich (Stefanović), Svetislav, 310
Stephen the First-Crowned, King, 28
Stepinats (Stepinac), Cardinal, 113, 181, 182, 184, 185, 238, 273
Stoyadinovich (Stojadinović), Milan, 90–8 passim, 100, 103, 175
Stranjakovich (Stranjaković), Dragoslav, 270, 273
Strossmayer, Bishop, 43, 44, 46, 47
Student, 352
Styria, 28–30
Sudan, 266
Sutyeska (Sutjeska), 142, 147, 172
Sweden, 294, 360, 364

Switchboard Operator, 350
Switzerland, 28, 30, 135, 294, 363, 382
Syria, 325

Taipeh, 385
Tanzania, 360
Taylor, A. J. P., 390
Teheran conference, 155
Tetovo, demonstrations in, 336
Thailand, 288
Thrace, 202
Tito, Marshal, 17, 19, 20, 96, 117–120, 122, 126, 127, 133–41 passim, 143–8 passim, 150–77 passim, 180, 184, 190, 192, 194–6, 199–201, 203–17 passim, 220–9 passim, 236, 238, 241, 242, 244–73 passim, 286, 290–5 passim, 298, 303, 309, 310, 313, 314, 319, 321, 323–7, 331, 332, 334, 335, 341, 342, 344–8, 350–2, 356, 358–68 passim, 380, 384–6, 390, 395, 396
Tito-Shubashich agreements, 160, 163, 166, 169, 175, 180
Titograd, 384
Todorovich, Miyalko (Mijalko Todorović), 345
Togliatti, Palmiro, 196
Tolbukhin, Marshal, 164, 166
Tomislav, King, 27
Topalovich, Zhivko (Živko Topalović), 152, 163
Trade Union Organization, 193, 242, 277, 286, 329
Trieste, 29, 54, 149, 167, 196, 228, 245; Free Territory of, 196, 197, 227, 228; Yugoslav claims on, 195, 196, 207, 208; Yugoslav partisans in, 171
Trifunovich, Milosh (Miloš Trifunović), 176, 177
Tripalo, Mika, 356
Truman, President, 126, 225; doctrine, 206
Trumbich (Trumbić), Ante, 64
Tsrvenkovski (Crvenkovski), Krste, 345
Tsvetkovich, Draghisha (Dragiša Cvetković), 97, 98, 100, 111
Tsvetkovich-Machek agreement, 98, 99, 123, 124
Turkey, Ottoman, 29–44 passim, 47–9, 53, 57, 111, 117, 128, 203, 212, 302, 372, 374, 375, 377, 395, 396
Turkey, Republican, 56, 85, 183, 202, 206, 225, 226
Turkish minority in Yugoslavia, 335, 337, 393

INDEX 415

Tvrtko I, King, 30
U.D.B., *see* State Security Service
Una, 135
United Democratic Opposition, 176
United Nations Organization (UNO), 196, 260, 264, 266, 360
United Nations Relief and Rehabilitation Administration, 188, 189, 192, 193
United Opposition, 89, 96, 97, 103
United Principalities of Moldavia and Wallachia, 392
United States of America, 51, 53, 102, 126, 137, 166, 170, 171, 172, 180, 181, 183, 195, 196, 200, 204, 206, 208, 220, 221, 222, 223, 225, 226, 227, 228, 236, 248, 264, 265, 269, 283, 291, 293, 294, 308, 323, 324, 331, 333, 334, 339, 343, 346, 351, 364, 365, 377, 379
Unperfected Society, The, 351, 353
U.S. aid to Yugoslavia, 223–5, 227, 229, 236, 263, 265, 274, 283, 293, 303
U.S. armed forces during Second World War, 141, 143, 146, 148, 154, 162, 164, 165, 167–9, 171, 172
Ustashas, 18, 80, 83, 87, 88, 91, 99, 103, 108, 110–14, 118, 122, 123, 125, 129–36 passim, 142, 144, 145, 149–51, 155, 168–72, 177, 182, 184, 309, 317, 323, 349, 359, 377
Uychich (Ujčić), Archbishop, 273
Uzunovich (Uzunović), Nikola, 71, 87, 88

Vafiades, Markos, 209, 219
Vardar, 25; *see also* Morava-Vardar corridor
Vatican, *see* Rome
Vatican Council I, 43
Vatican Council II, 273, 315
Venice, republic of, 26–8, 31–3, 35, 36, 38, 39, 46, 50
Veselinov, Yovan (Jovan), 272
Vietnam, 365
Vikentiye (Vikentije), Patriarch, 238, 273
Vis, 157, 160, 162, 164
Vishegrad (Višegrad), operations around, 151, 156
Vitezovich (Vitezović), Pavle, 37
Vlachs in Yugoslavia, 393
Vlahovich (Vlahović), Veljko, 272, 299, 345
Voyvodina, 36, 37, 42–4, 46, 53–5, 93, 108, 110, 186, 190, 197, 302, 337, 344, 345, 357, 394

Vratusha (Vratuša), Antun, 21
Vukichevich (Vukićević), Velja, 71, 72, 82
Vukmanovich (Vukmanović), Svetozar, 210, 242, 265, 277

Wales, 395
Warsaw Pact, 247, 332
Welles, Orson, 346
West Germany, *see* German Federal Republic
Western Church, *see* Catholic Church
Western Morava, 116, 118
Western powers, 41, 100, 102, 131, 132, 138, 140, 146, 148, 150, 153, 157, 163, 164, 169–71, 175, 180, 181, 184, 195–7, 200, 201, 222–5, 236, 299, 383, 396
When the Pumpkins were in Bloom, 350
Wilson, General, 155, 158
Wilson, President, 51
Workers' and Peasants' Republican Alliance, 71

Yalta: conference, 175; Declaration, 180, 181, 204
Yaytse (Jajce), Anti-Fascist Council session in, 152, 153, 156, 175, 178
Yevtich (Jevtić), Bogoljub, 86, 88–91, 95, 97
Yosif (Josif), Metropolitan, 238, 273
Yovanovich (Jovanović), General, 214
Yovanovich, Blazho (Blažo), 272
Yovanovich, Dragoljub, 182
Yovanovich, Radivoye (Radivoje), 126, 327
Yovanovich, Slobodan, 70, 88, 124, 146
Yugoslav Academy in Zagreb, 43, 374
Yugoslav Central National Committee, 153, 163, 181, 270
Yugoslav Committee, 50, 51, 64
Yugoslav government in exile during Second War, 109, 110, 113, 117, 119, 123–6, 131–3, 137, 143, 144, 146, 148–53 passim, 158, 160, 166, 170, 181, 195
Yugoslav Home Army, 117, 124, 125, 131, 132, 138, 143, 144, 163, 172
Yugoslav language, 374
Yugoslav Moslem Organization, 60, 62, 64, 67–8, 72, 73, 89, 90, 96–8, 103, 111
Yugoslav National Party, 83, 104
Yugoslav Radical Union, 90, 91, 96–8

Zadar (Zara), 54, 83
Zagreb: congress of intellectuals, 66; Germans enter, 107; King Alexander's visit to, 70; local elections (1920) in, 60; 1932 manifesto, 83; partisans enter, 171; railway lines, 124, 130; University, 239, 269
Zara, see Zadar
Zbor, 89, 93, 97, 115, 120, 167, 181, 359; see also Ljotich

Zeta, see Montenegro
Zhanko, Milosh (Miloš Žanko), 356, 357
Zhivkovich (Živković), Bogosav, 239
Zhivkovich, General, 77, 82
Zhuyovich (Žujović), Milan, 270, 273
Zhuyovich, Sreten, 210, 211, 238
Zrinski, Petar, 35

Printed in Great Britain by
Western Printing Services Limited, Bristol